WHERE TO GO WHEN
THE AMERICAS

NORTH, CENTRAL, SOUTH AMERICA & THE CARIBBEAN

WHERE TO GO WHEN
THE AMERICAS

NORTH, CENTRAL, SOUTH AMERICA & THE CARIBBEAN

CRAIG DOYLE
CONSULTANT EDITOR

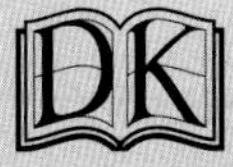

LONDON, NEW YORK, MELBOURNE, MUNICH AND DELHI

DK LONDON
LIST MANAGER Christine Stroyan
PROJECT EDITOR Ros Walford
EDITORS Sadie Smith, Fay Franklin,
Jacky Jackson, Alexandra Farrell & Hugh Thompson
DESIGN MANAGER Mabel Chan
ART EDITOR Shahid Mahmood
DESIGNERS Steve Bere, Paul Jackson
& Marisa Renzullo
DTP DESIGNERS Natasha Lu & Jamie McNeill
PICTURE RESEARCH Ellen Root & Sarah Smithies
CARTOGRAPHY Casper Morris
& Ed Merritt from Merrit Cartographic
PRODUCTION CONTROLLER Shane Higgins
PROOFREADER Stewart Wild
INDEXER Helen Peters

DK DELHI
EDITORIAL MANAGER Aruna Ghose
DESIGN MANAGER Sunita Gahir
PROJECT EDITOR Gouri Banerji
PROJECT DESIGNER Shruti Singhi
PICTURE RESEARCH Taiyaba Khatoon
EDITOR Shalini Krishan
DESIGNER Pooja Badola

SENIOR DTP COORDINATOR Shailesh Sharma
QUADRUM SOLUTIONS PVT. LTD.
www.quadrumltd.com

PUBLISHER Douglas Amrine

REPRODUCED BY Media Development Printing

PRINTED AND BOUND IN CHINA
First Published in Great Britain in 2008
by Dorling Kindersley Limited
80 Strand, London WC2R 0RL

16 17 18 19 10 9 8 7 6 5 4 3 2 1

Reprinted with revisions 2011, 2016

A CIP CATALOGUE RECORD IS AVAILABLE FROM THE BRITISH LIBRARY.

ISBN 978-0-2412-8517-6

www.traveldk.com

COVER IMAGE: Banff National Park, Canada
TITLE PAGE IMAGE: Iguazú Falls, Argentina
HALF TITLE IMAGE: Horse and rider in the Calgary Exhibition and Stampede, Canada
FOREWORD IMAGE: Manhattan, New York City

CONTENTS

FOREWORD 6

JANUARY 8
WHERE TO GO: JANUARY 10

Las Vegas USA 12
Mayan Riviera MEXICO 14
Cartagena COLOMBIA 16
Orlando USA 18
Grand Teton National Park USA 20
Vieques PUERTO RICO 22
Prince Edward Island CANADA 24
Maui USA 26
Palm Springs USA 28

FEBRUARY 30
WHERE TO GO: FEBRUARY 32

Ottawa CANADA 34
Baja California Sur MEXICO 36
Havana CUBA 38
Miami USA 40
Panama CENTRAL AMERICA 42
White Mountains Region USA 44
Inter-American Highway CENTRAL AMERICA 46
Trinidad CARIBBEAN 48
Salvador BRAZIL 50

MARCH 52
WHERE TO GO: MARCH 54

Whistler CANADA 56
Austin USA 58
Mexico City MEXICO 60
Boston USA 62
British Virgin Islands CARIBBEAN 64
Honduras CENTRAL AMERICA 66
Natchez Trace USA 68
Yucatán MEXICO 70
Patagonia CHILE/ARGENTINA 72

APRIL 74
WHERE TO GO: APRIL 76

Charleston USA 78
Branson USA 80
Iguazú Falls ARGENTINA AND BRAZIL 82
Turks & Caicos Islands CARIBBEAN 84
Galápagos Islands ECUADOR 86
Archipelago de San Blas PANAMA 88
Easter Island CHILE 90
Blue Ridge Parkway USA 92
Volcán Arenal COSTA RICA 94
Uruguay SOUTH AMERICA 96
Dominica CARIBBEAN 98

MAY 100
WHERE TO GO: MAY 102

Memphis USA 104
Ambergris Caye BELIZE 106
La Paz BOLIVIA 108
Inside Passage USA 110
Pacific Rim National Park CANADA 112
Amazon River BRAZIL 114
New York City USA 116
Toronto CANADA 118
Savannah USA 120
St. Lucia CARIBBEAN 122
Outer Banks USA 124

JUNE 126
WHERE TO GO: JUNE 128

Chicago USA 130
Niagara Falls CANADA/USA 132
Great River Road USA 134
Mesa Verde National Park USA 136
Stanley USA 138
Machu Picchu PERU 140
Montréal CANADA 142
Bermuda NORTH ATLANTIC 144
Finger Lakes USA 146
Chiquitos BOLIVIA 148

JULY 150
WHERE TO GO: JULY 152

Washington, D.C USA 154
Vancouver CANADA 156
Salar de Uyuni BOLIVIA 158
Gwaii Haanas National Park Reserve CANADA 160
Jasper National Park CANADA 162
Cordillera Blanca PERU 164
San Juan Islands USA 166
Calgary CANADA 168
Cape Cod USA 170
Avalon Peninsula CANADA 172
Newport USA 174
Dominican Republic CARIBBEAN 176

AUGUST 178
WHERE TO GO: AUGUST 180

Wisconsin State Fair USA 182
Santa Fe USA 184
Québec City CANADA 186
Yellowstone National Park USA 188
Salta and Jujuy ARGENTINA 190
The Viking Trail CANADA 192
The Hamptons USA 194
Mackinac Island USA 196
Mammoth Cave National Park USA 198
Manú National Park PERU 200
Barretos Rodeo Festival BRAZIL 202
Paraguay SOUTH AMERICA 204

SEPTEMBER 206
WHERE TO GO: SEPTEMBER 208

Fundy Isles CANADA 210
San Francisco USA 212
Utah's National Parklands USA 214
Mendoza ARGENTINA 216
Quito ECUADOR 218
Philadelphia USA 220
Portland USA 222
Ciudad Perdida COLOMBIA 224
Coast to Coast CANADA 226
Black Hills USA 228

OCTOBER 230
WHERE TO GO: OCTOBER 232

Cape Churchill CANADA 234
Mount Desert Island USA 236
Buenos Aires ARGENTINA 238
Grand Canyon National Park USA 240
Albuquerque USA 242
South Patagonian Fjords CHILE 244
Oregon Coast USA 246
Kaua'i USA 248
California Wine Country USA 250
Oaxaca MEXICO 252

NOVEMBER 254
WHERE TO GO: NOVEMBER 256

Tucson USA 258
Isla Margarita VENEZUELA 260
Guatemala CENTRAL AMERICA 262
Parque Nacional Torres del Paine CHILE 264
Panama City PANAMA 266
The Bahamas CARIBBEAN 268
Islas Ballestas PERU 270
Island Cruise CARIBBEAN 272
Martinique CARIBBEAN 274

DECEMBER 276
WHERE TO GO: DECEMBER 278

San Antonio USA 280
Jamaica CARIBBEAN 282
Hawai'i USA 284
St. Barts CARIBBEAN 286
Nicoya Peninsula COSTA RICA 288
The Cayo District BELIZE 290
Angel Falls VENEZUELA 292
Mexico's Colonial Heartland MEXICO 294
Cayman Islands CARIBBEAN 296
Falkland Islands SOUTH ATLANTIC 298
Pasadena USA 300
Rio de Janeiro BRAZIL 302

Festivals 304
Travel Information 308
Atlas of the Americas 311
Index & Acknowledgments 332

FOREWORD

Do you tend to think that because you have been to a country once, there's no need to go back? Well I disagree, and this book may help to change your mind. It will open up a part of the world that you may have thought was very familiar, as well as unfamiliar places that you may not have considered travelling to before.

Let's start with North America. The USA has fifty states on almost 4 million sq miles (6.5 million sq km) of land stretching from the Pacific to the Atlantic coast, with mountains, vast plains, deserts and some of the world's most exciting cities in between. It's one of the most undervalued holiday destinations I know, and you could spend a lifetime exploring it. Of course there are lots of things to fit into a lifetime, so this book picks out the very best of what's on offer – both well-known and less explored. The next time you travel to the Big Apple, stay on for a day or two and explore New York State – it has lakes, beaches and vineyards, and is the perfect antidote to the madness of the world's most exciting city. You have probably flown over Newfoundland on your way to the USA, but why not stop off in this stunning part of Canada? It's one of my favourite places in the world to visit.

Central and South America are less familiar to most people. In the past, they have often been seen as the preserve of the backpacker or more daring traveller. In fact, they are a land of riches for any would-be explorer. Argentina, for example, is a virtual "taster menu" for what South America has in store. With the world's widest waterfall at Iguazú, the vibrant capital Buenos Aires and the peace and utter beauty of Patagonia, this country is perfect for backpackers, pensioners and families alike. Names such as Cancún and Acapulco may be familiar to mass tourism, but they hardly provide a real taste of Mexico. We'll point you in the right direction, be it to the colonial towns, the stunning barrier reef or the historic Mayan ruins.

You'd be surprised who you might meet trekking through the wilds of Central America. OK, so this is just another opportunity for me to boast about kayaking with Cameron Diaz in Belize, but it just highlights how broad the region's appeal is. Sadly, she didn't join me on my bus trip through Guatemala and Honduras, but to be fair the locations would have stolen the show anyway. So the message is: delve into the book, pack your bags and think outside of the box as the unknown awaits.

CRAIG DOYLE

JANUARY

Where to Go: **January**

While January can offer nothing cheerier than a long hibernation in much of North America, the new year also offers crisp air, bright skies, and snowfall – perfect for skiing in the Rockies or for exploring the red-rock landscapes of the Southwest. Surf's up on the Hawaiian islands, which offer a balmy, sunny climate in January and, unlike many destinations in the Americas, don't suffer dramatic drops in temperature after dark. This is also a great time to venture out to the subtropical regions that get steamier as the year wears on. Florida is at its coolest and driest in January, while the levels of humidity in the stickier countries of South America are at their most comfortable. Below you will find all the destinations in this chapter as well as some extra suggestions to provide a little inspiration.

FESTIVALS AND CULTURE

CARTAGENA Young dancers at a street festival

VALPARAÍSO
CHILE

South America's most historic Pacific seaport

Head south for midsummer in Chile's prettiest city, with twisting cobbled streets of brightly painted houses tumbling down to the sea.

www.vinayvalpo.com

CARTAGENA
COLOMBIA

A celebration of literature from every continent

When you've finished sightseeing, mingle with poets, authors, and playwrights at Colombia's annual Hay Literary Festival.

See pp16–17

SAINT PAUL WINTER CARNIVAL
MINNESOTA, USA

USA's oldest winter carnival

First staged in 1886, this carnival hosts wintry activities including curling, skating, snow sculpting, and a spectacular ice palace.

www.wintercarnival.com

LAS VEGAS
NEVADA, USA

Prepare for one long party

Themed hotels, sizzling shows, all-night shopping, casinos, and cocktails are available 24/7 at this fast-growing desert city.

See pp12–13

SAN MIGUEL DE ALLENDE
MEXICO

Laid-back arty retreat

This pretty colonial town has a thriving artistic community thanks to its perfect climate and photogenic streets.

www.vivasanmiguel.com

UNFORGETTABLE JOURNEYS

MAUI Tour group at the summit of Haleakalā volcano

MAUI
HAWAI'I, USA

A stunning road trip with beaches and waterfalls

Drive the scenic road to Hana on Hawai'i's second-largest island, stopping to admire beaches, falls, and forests along the way.

See pp26–7

THE CALIFORNIA MISSIONS TRAIL
CALIFORNIA, USA

Delve into California's history

The Missions Trail stretches for 620 miles (1,000 km), linking historic missions and pueblos from San Diego to Sonoma.

www.parks.ca.gov

"Once past Ho'okipa, you feel as if you're leaving reality behind and entering some South Seas paradise."

MONUMENT VALLEY
UTAH, USA

Drive or hike through this iconic American landscape.

Instantly recognizable thanks to its sandstone towers, this surreal landscape is a great place to learn about Native American culture.

www.utah.com/monumentvalley

LAGO PATZCUARO
MEXICO

Traditional fishing, Mexican-style

On a boat trip across this lake, watch local fishermen working with their strange butterfly-shaped nets from tiny dugout canoes.

www.patzcuarovacations.com

PATAGONIAN CRUISE
ARGENTINA

Take a voyage of discovery at the "end of the world"

Follow legendary seafarers through the Magellan Straits and Beagle Channel to see whales, elephant seals, icebergs, and mighty glaciers.

www.patagonia-argentina.com

NATURAL WONDERS

PRINCE EDWARD ISLAND The red sand of Tignish Shore

'The island has managed to maintain a slow and pastoral quality that seems stuck in another era'

PRINCE EDWARD ISLAND
CANADA

Idyllic isle with literary roots

Follow in the footsteps of the red-haired heroine of Anne of Green Gables, and discover this island in the Gulf of St. Lawrence.

See pp24–5

EVERGLADES NATIONAL PARK
FLORIDA, USA

A vast subtropical wilderness

Hike or boat through the mysterious mangrove swamps and lagoons, home to rare species including crocodiles, panthers, and manatees.

www.nps.gov/ever

BIG BEND NATIONAL PARK
TEXAS, USA

Remote and majestic desert

One of the USA's wildest national parks, studded with cacti and pine-clad mountains, and bound by the majestic Rio Grande.

www.nps.gov/bibe

GLACIER PERITO MORENO
ARGENTINA

A magnificent glacier

This vast white mass ranks among Patagonia's prime tourist attractions, edging slowly forward then splintering into huge chunks of ice.

www.patagonia-argentina.com

COSTA RICA
CENTRAL AMERICA

An exquisite pocket of natural beauty and coastal rain forest

Manuel Antonio National Park combines palm-fringed beaches with mangrove swamps and a forest ecosystem full of wildlife.

www.visitcostarica.com

Previous page: Coconut palms on a tropical beach at sunset, Maui, Hawai'i

Weather Watch

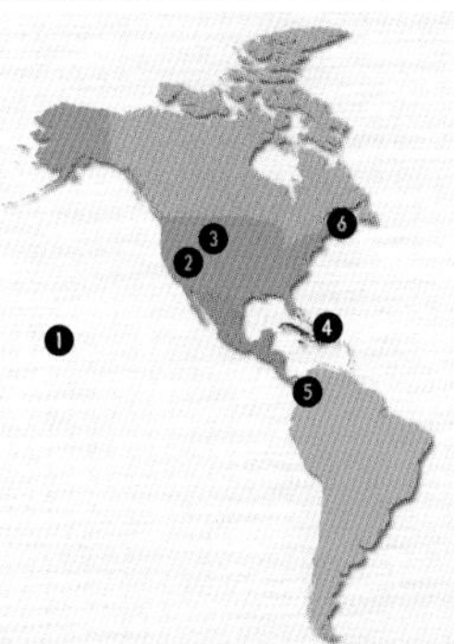

1 Hawai'i, USA In January, temperatures hover above 70°F (21°C) at sea level and the surf is far better than in summer. Rainfall varies significantly on each island.

2 Las Vegas, USA Though nights are cold – with potentially penetrating desert winds – the crisp, sunny days make this one of the most comfortable months to stroll along Vegas's world-famous Strip.

3 Wyoming, USA Dazzling blue skies and thick blankets of perfect white snow along the dramatic spine of the American Rockies create the ideal conditions for skiing and snowboarding.

4 Puerto Rico The sunshine, warm temperatures, low rainfall, and cloudless skies are a world away from the gloomy chill of much of the northern hemisphere. Swimming, snorkeling, and surfing are perfect at this time.

5 Colombia Humidity is at a comfortable level in January, one of the driest months. Snorkeling and swimming are pleasurable on the gorgeous islands, while in the capital, Cartagena, cool sea breezes temper the city's heat.

6 Prince Edward Island, Canada January's crisp, snowy weather transforms the islands into a hive of active, winter activities such as tubing and snowshoeing.

LUXURY AND ROMANCE

PALM SPRINGS Palm trees on a golf course

PALM SPRINGS
CALIFORNIA, USA

Glamorous desert playground

Celebrities flock to this sun-soaked city, surrounded by the Coachella Valley Desert, which is filled with luxurious hotels, shimmering swimming pools, and elegant spas.

See pp28–9

MERIDA
VENEZUELA

A wonderful city flanked by two vast mountain ranges

Stay in romantic *posadas* outside the city, explore the Sierra Nevada by day, and relax in a luxurious spa before dinner.

www.meridapreciosa.com

ATLANTA
GEORGIA, USA

Enjoy some Southern-style luxury and romance

Enjoy a break in one of the South's most dynamic cities, with a string of top hotels, cultural attractions, and cosmopolitan restaurants and bars.

www.atlanta.net

VIEQUES
PUERTO RICO, CARIBBEAN

Laid-back islands washed by warm tropical seas

The pace of life is slow here, so just relax. Be active if you want, but even the wildlife, turtles, and manatees move slowly.

See pp22–3

JAMAICA
CARIBBEAN

Savor the heady rum aromas and the hot rhythm of reggae

There's more to Jamaica than parties – try hiking in the Blue Mountains before soaking up the sun on a fabulous beach.

www.visitjamaica.com

ACTIVE ADVENTURES

GRAND TETON NATIONAL PARK Skiers take in the peaks

GRAND TETON NATIONAL PARK
WYOMING, USA

This is big-thrill territory for skilful skiers

Trek through vast wilderness, and then ski Jackson Hole, one of the premiere ski resorts in the country.

See pp20–21

"The valley is shrouded in fog but skiers above bask in blue skies, and the sensation is of skiing off the mountain and into the clouds."

VALLE DE LA LUNA
CHILE

The lunar landscapes of San Pedro de Atacama

Trek through one of the driest places on earth, a high-altitude desert with salt lakes and weirdly shaped outcrops of stone and sand.

www.visitchile.com

MOUNTAIN PINE FOREST PRESERVE
BELIZE

Jungle walks and waterfalls

Trek or bike through this verdant forest preserve, with jungle-clad mountains, plentiful wildlife, and the vertiginous Hidden Valley Falls.

www.travelbelize.org

MAMMOTH MOUNTAIN
CALIFORNIA, USA

Skiing and snowmobile drives

Get stuck into the white stuff at one of California's top winter sports destinations, based on the mighty slopes of Mammoth Mountain.

www.mammothmountain.com

WHALE-WATCHING IN SAMANÁ
DOMINICAN REPUBLIC

Ultimate marine spectacle

Thousands of majestic whales home in on Samaná Bay to mate and calve, and engage in elaborate courting displays.

www.whalesamana.com

FAMILY GETAWAYS

ORLANDO Disney cartoon characters come to life

SAN DIEGO
CALIFORNIA, USA

One of the west coast's top family destinations

Miles of beaches, plus plenty of child-friendly museums, parks, SeaWorld, the Birch Aquarium, and the world-famous San Diego zoo.

www.sandiego.org

ORLANDO
FLORIDA, USA

Every kid's dream vacation, but fun for all the family

Take the family to meet Mickey and his friends at Disney World, explore the other theme parks, and maybe even see a rocket launch.

See pp18–19

FLORIDA PANHANDLE
FLORIDA, USA

Drive off on an old-fashioned family vacation

A road trip down the Florida Panhandle takes you through time-warped towns, and past alligator-filled swamps and beaches galore.

www.floridapanhandlevacation.com

MAYAN RIVIERA
MEXICO

Bask in the sun and explore fascinating ruins

Fantastic beaches, coral reefs, and Mayan ruins, plus family resorts with quiet forested walks and water rides make this a great destination.

See pp14–15

KIAWAH ISLAND
SOUTH CAROLINA, USA

A delightful island resort that is relatively quiet in winter

The water is too cold to swim but the open spaces of the beach provide plenty of activities for kids and adults alike.

www.kiawahisland.org

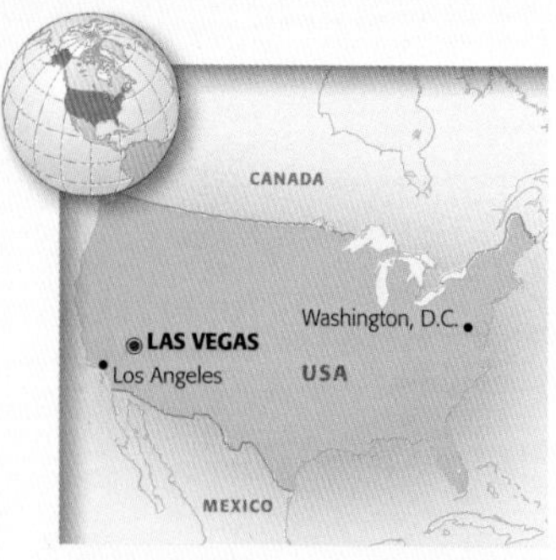

GETTING THERE See map p321, D4
Las Vegas is in southwest USA. International flights arrive into McCarran International Airport. Taxis run from the airport to the Strip.

GETTING AROUND
The best way to get around is by taxi, bus, or the Monorail that connects many of the major hotels along the Strip.

WEATHER
In January, daytime temperatures average around 60°F (16°C) but can dip to 30°F (-1°C) in the evening.

ACCOMMODATIONS
The centrally located Tropicana Resort & Casino is good value for families and the budget-conscious; doubles from US$79; www.troplv.com

Hard Rock Hotel and Casino, a mile east of the Strip, appeals to a younger crowd; doubles from US$69; www.hardrockhotel.com

Opulent Wynn Las Vegas is one of the most expensive resorts in the world; doubles from US$350; www.wynnlasvegas.com

EATING OUT
Casinos offer a dizzying choice. Buffets are good value, but vary in quality. For a view, head up to the Stratosphere's Top of the World (US$98).

FURTHER INFORMATION
www.visitlasvegas.com

Tying the Knot?

The pitfalls of a big night out in Vegas are like nowhere else in the world, as countless couples have discovered. With no blood tests or waiting periods required, all that's needed is the license fee (around US$77) and two people who are at least 18 years of age. About 82,000 couples a year get hitched in the many 24-hour chapels that line the Strip, making it the wedding capital of the world. It's a popular choice to have an Elvis impersonator present. If you're already married, don't feel left out – you can always renew your vows in style here.

Above (left to right): Gambling machines at the Casino, Venetian Hotel; giant guitar sign of the Hard Rock Cafe; Ghostbar on the roof top of the Palms Casino Resort **Main:** Neon cowgirl at the Fremont Street Experience

LAS VEGAS

AMERICA'S FOREMOST PLAYGROUND OFFERS SOMETHING for everyone to spend money on, regardless of your tastes. But why visit Las Vegas in January, when temperatures hit annual lows? That's a good reason right there – the heat that plagues the city throughout much of the year has eased, yet it's still warm. A city truly unlike any other, Las Vegas long ago shed its reputation as a destination primarily geared toward gamblers and sinners. Now, it has morphed into one of America's most multi-faceted – and fastest-growing – non-stop cities. The Fremont Street Experience, for instance, is a seven-block, open-air promenade that features the largest big-screen in the world, live entertainment, historic hotels, and unique shopping. Serious, late-night shoppers will be thrilled – where else can you wander a four-floor M&M candy superstore at 11pm? If the shops here don't satisfy, you can always head back to the Strip, where casinos like Wynn Las Vegas and the Venetian offer a wide array of high-end boutiques.

Commonly thought of as a high-roller's destination – after all, $150 show tickets, $50 blackjack tables, and $15 drinks are the norm – Vegas offers several freebies that would warrant admission fees almost anywhere else. The Bellagio's fountain shows, held on an 8-acre (3-ha) lake, are a sight to behold, as are the vivid eruptions of the Mirage's 54-ft (16-m) volcano each night. The trapeze artists, unicyclists, acrobats, and silk performers at Circus Circus, and the Flamingo Hotel's wildlife habitat are just two of the free family-friendly attractions.

The city that never sleeps, Vegas bursts into action after dark when big-name performers fill the casino stages and bars, and lounges throb with revelers. Celebs hit hot spots like the Palms and the Hard Rock, bringing a touch of LA or NYC glamour to the desert. Hungry? You can dine at a spectrum of eateries, from ballroom-sized buffets to elite places with international big-name chefs.

The city that never sleeps, Vegas bursts into action after dark when big-name performers fill the casino stages.

Inset: Gondolas on the Grand Canal, Venetian Hotel and Casino
Below (left and right): Mirage Hotel's nightly eruption; aerial view of Las Vegas

HIGH-ROLLER'S DIARY

Always ablaze with colors and lights, this cocktail of luxury and lurid laughs makes Las Vegas one of the world's glam fests, with a vast choice of over-the-top experiences to try. Not a gambler? The theme hotels and casinos are still fun to explore. In January you can see the city's best at a cool, leisurely pace in three days.

Three Days in Vegas

DAY 1

Explore the Strip, working your way from ancient Egypt to New York, and from Polynesia to Venice as you take in the magnificence of the mega-hotels. Later, head downtown to the Fremont Street Experience, a haven of under-cover entertainment and shopping. Or you could catch a steamy burlesque performance geared toward men (Fantasy), women (Thunder from Down Under), or... everyone (Zumanity Cirque de Soleil). Finish the night, at any hour, by hitting Mr. Lucky's 24/7 Café, the Hard Rock's cool all-night coffee shop.

DAY 2

For a spot of morning-after self-indulgence, head to the Venetian's Canyon Ranch Spaclub, an offshoot of the famed Arizona spot of the same name, which sports a thermal suite and a rock wall. Move on to Caesars Palace, where you can almost believe you're in Italy, and grab a bite at one of the numerous dining options. Keep the party going by spotting a celeb at Omnia, where top DJs spin all night.

DAY 3

Up for some action? Take a Red Rock Canyon tour, or if this is just too real, slip into the Red Rock Casino Resort, located off the Strip, with its "adventure spa" where guests can try rock climbing or rafting trips. Cap your weekend with a picturesque toast to the city at the Palms' Ghostbar, where night owls enjoy breathtaking views from the club's "ghost deck," some 55 floors above the hotel pool.

Dos and Don'ts

- ✓ Try to secure show tickets well in advance. Many shows sell out, so check your desired show's website ahead of your trip to Vegas.
- ✗ Don't stray too far from the Strip late at night. With several popular casinos and resorts located well off the Strip, it's wise to take taxis whenever possible.
- ✓ Wear a watch. Clocks are hard to find in casinos, especially anywhere near the gaming floors.
- ✗ Don't bother bringing a car to the city. While most of the casinos offer plenty of free parking, traffic on and near the Strip can be troublesome at all hours.

Below: Diners grabbing a bite at dusk, Caesars Palace

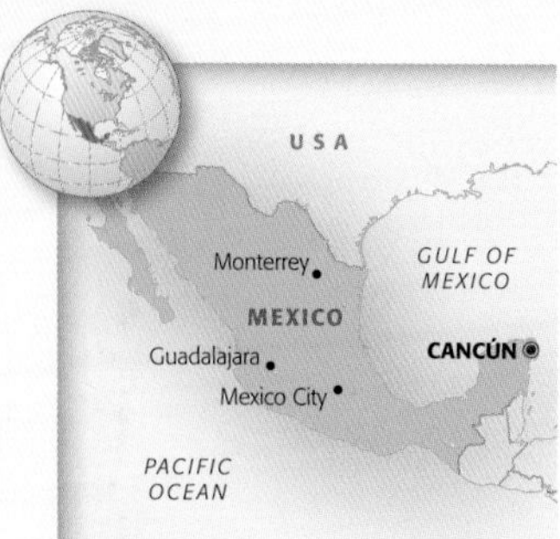

GETTING THERE See map p323, I5

The Mayan Riviera is a strip of coastline with offshore islands running 100 miles (161 km) south of Cancún on the Yucatán Peninsula. The international airport is at Cancún. Most resorts are within 2 hours' drive of Cancún.

GETTING AROUND

Regular fast buses link the major centers of the Mayan Riviera. Tours to the main sites are easy to arrange. Cars can be rented at the airport, in Cancún, and other major towns.

WEATHER

January is warm with average daytime temperatures of 82°F (28°C). It is frequently sunny, with only about 9 days' rain per month.

ACCOMMODATIONS

Nyx Hotel, Cancún, has simple rooms, two pools, and a kids' club; family rooms from US$180; www.nyxcancun.com

Crown Paradise Club, Cancún, is a large beach-front resort with pools and a water park; family rooms from US$385; www.crownparadise.com

La Tortuga Hotel & Spa, Playa del Carmen, offers lodgings, pools, a spa, and a restaurant in a nicely landscaped oasis setting; standard rooms from US$265; www.hotellatortugaspa.com

EATING OUT

Mexican staples – *quesadillas* and *burritos*, beans and rice – are everywhere, with or without seafood.

FURTHER INFORMATION

www.visitmexico.com

MAYAN RIVIERA

POWDER-SOFT BEACHES FRINGE THE EASTERN COAST of Mexico's Yucatán Peninsula, which is washed by an aquamarine Atlantic mellowed by a barrier reef and studded with little coral islands. Mayan temples built to worship the God of the Dawn sit sentinel on cliffs – poised to catch the rays of the rising sun. And at their backs lie vast stretches of rain forest, dotted with towering temples and broken by Mayan villages and little colonial towns.

Until the 1980s few tourists visited this area but then came Cancún – a purpose-built tourist city straddling a 10-mile (16-km) spit of gorgeous sand backed by a saltwater lagoon. As Cancún's popularity grew it spawned growth in little towns to the south such as Playa del Carmen, Akumal, and Tulúm. Resorts and adventure parks were built and the coast was promoted as the Mayan Riviera.

Main: Tulúm and its beaches

Calendar Stone

The end of the world has been given a date. At least that is according to the Mayan Calendar. Over 1,000 years ago Mayan astronomers invented a system of solar, lunar, and astral calendars which they used to mark agricultural seasons and ritual events. The most complex of these was the Long Count. It began with the mythological creation of the current universe on August 11, 3114 BC and was supposed to end with demonic disorder before a new one was created – on December 21, 2012.

Left: Indian dancer in full costume

Right (left to right): A boat trip on the lagoon; water sports for the kids at Cancún; underwater cross off Isla Mujeres; Playa del Carmen beach

Today, the Mayan Riviera's combination of exotic but gentle nature, large hotels, and theme parks makes it a winner for families. The ocean here doesn't crash, it laps – so swimming off the beaches and islands is usually good for children. Adventures are exciting but safe. In parks like Garrafón, Xel-Há or Nizuc, the forest has been trimmed back to make way for paths that even the smallest feet can tread. And there is a wide range of adrenaline-fuelled children's rides and water slides, snorkeling facilities, and tame tropical wildlife. With their lush Disney-style backdrops, the Mayan temples at rainforest-shrouded Cobá or the cliff-top ruins at Tulúm have a wide appeal. And there are plenty of animals – dolphins to swim with, sightings of wild parrots, monkeys, and macaws in the forests, and sleepy iguanas basking in the sun. The clubs and babysitting services at large hotels ensure that you can take the kids but occasionally be free of them too – to go diving off the coral reefs, or trek through vast caves, or simply to share a romantic meal with a partner.

RIVIERA DIARY

A week in pleasantly warm January will give you a taste of the Mayan Riviera's beaches, reefs, temples, and theme parks. Ten days would allow for further excursions such as a trip to Chichén Itza in the Yucatán, or for taking a boat ride out to the lovely Isla Cozumel. For more on the Yucatán, *see pp70–71*.

A Week of Beaches and Ruins

JAN

DAY 1 Once you've settled into your hotel in Cancún, head for the beach to unwind. In the afternoon take an adrenaline ride through the waves on a banana raft, or enjoy a more sedate trip in a glass-bottomed boat.

DAY 2 Make an early start for Isla Mujeres – a tiny island fringed with fine white sand and lapped by gentle waves. Spend the afternoon swimming, snorkeling, and ziplining in the Garrafón nature park.

DAY 3 Whiz down helter-skelter water slides with the kids and swim with dolphins in the Nizuc Water Park. In the late afternoon, if you're not too exhausted, hire a baby-sitter then head out for a night on the town.

DAY 4 Drive south to Playa del Carmen, check in to a hotel and spend the day at the Xel-Há theme park. This is set in original tropical forest and built around a series of glassy clear pools that offer great and safe coral reef snorkeling for kids.

DAY 5 Drive to the Mayan city of Tulúm, which looks out over the aquamarine Atlantic on a craggy honey-colored cliff-top above a series of coral coves. While away the afternoon on the beaches to the south of the ruins.

DAY 6 Take a tour into the wildlife reserve at Si'an Ka'an to see pristine rainforest and coastal wetlands; float down a crystal-clear river filled with fish and tiny baby crocs.

DAY 7 Drive to the ruins at Cobá and enjoy wandering the forest trails and climbing to the top of the vertiginous pyramids. Bring plenty of sunscreen and insect repellent. Return to Cancún for the flight home.

Dos and Don'ts

- ✓ Bring your own mask and snorkel from home. They'll fit better and you'll avoid the extortionate rental prices.
- ✗ Don't touch coral reefs. Many of the Mayan Riviera's reefs have been damaged by tourism and over-fishing.
- ✓ Learn some Spanish and win Mexican friends.
- ✗ Don't take photographs of Mayan people without asking.

Below: Xel-Há Natural Park, safe for kids to enjoy snorkeling

GETTING THERE See map p325, D6

Located in northwest Colombia, Cartagena is served by Rafael Núñez International Airport, which is 2 miles (3 km) from the center. Cruise ship passengers arrive at Terminal Maritimo, just a short distance from the hotel district.

GETTING AROUND

Unmetered yellow taxis are a good way to get around the city, but be sure to fix a price beforehand. Buses are slow going, but much of the city can be explored on foot.

WEATHER

Daytime temperatures average 86–90°F (30–32°C); humidity high all year round. The driest months are from December to April.

ACCOMMODATIONS

The relaxed Hotel Badillo Zen has cheerful, comfortable rooms, a pool, and friendly staff; doubles from US$130; badillozenhotel.com

The small but elegant Casa San Agustin has impeccable service; double rooms from US$400; www.hotelcasasanagustin.com

For the charm of an old colonial home, try El Marques Boutique Hotel; doubles from US$285; www.elmarqueshotelboutique.com

EATING OUT

A good three-course meal with wine will cost around US$25–30 per head. Try the seafood at El Kilo, vegan fare at Girasoles or indulge in a knock-out meal at Carmen.

FURTHER INFORMATION

www.ticartagena.com/en

Showbiz City

With its showbiz good looks and big-screen presence, Cartagena has enjoyed many film-star roles. It was the setting of the 2007 Hollywood adaptation of Gabriel García Marquez's powerful novel *Love in the Time of Cholera (above)*. The city's pretty plazas and bold, vivid colors formed the perfect backdrop to this allegorical love story. Other notable movies filmed here include the 1969 thriller *Burn*, starring Marlon Brando, *Romancing the Stone* (1984) and *Maria Full of Grace* (2004). City tours are always quick to point out any cinematic connections.

Above (left to right): Dancing at one of Cartagena's many celebrations; young dancers at a street festival; marching youth band
Main: Local women in brightly colored dress balancing baskets of fruit on their heads

CARTAGENA

SOARING TEMPERATURES ADD A STEAMY CARIBBEAN HAZE to Cartagena's streetscape, a picture-perfect labyrinth of balconied colonial buildings in a dazzling array of bubble-gum hues. Blossom-clad shutters look out on neat plazas hemmed by a riddle of cobblestone backstreets where vendors ply giant red papayas and juicy mangos in the shade. Sizzling curbside food stalls emit the heady aromas of Cartagena's buttery, deep-fried *arepas* (maize pancakes) and meat-filled *empanadas* (baked or fried corn-flour pastries), handicraft sellers and performers roam the streets, and strumming musicians serenade cappuccino-sipping tourists. This permanent state of festival is part of the city's unique historic character, which has experienced slavery, sainthood, and swashbuckling buccaneers.

Facing the Caribbean Sea to the northwest and with a sweeping bay to the south, this pretty seaport is a jewel-box of Spanish colonial ostentation, declared a UNESCO World Heritage Site in 1984. Its vibrant streets boast some fascinating monuments and stunning architectural sights, including the resplendent bronze Monumento a la India Catalina, which honors the region's pre-colonial indigenous people, the Los Zapatos Viejos (The Old Shoes Monument), which pays homage to a satirical poem by Luis Carlos Lopez (1883–1950), and the ancient, cannon-flanked fortifications that dominate the city's handsome, sea-facing ramparts.

A year-round cultural calendar runs from the Festival Internacional de Música (classical music festival), and Festival Internacional de Cine (film festival), to the star-studded Hay Festival – a magnificent celebration of literature from across the globe and a major A-list draw. The week-long Independence Day celebrations paralyze the city with high-tempo street parades and marching bands. A cluster of sandy offshore islands offer respite from the melee, with lobster cooked on open fires and hammocks slung from mud-and-thatch fishing huts – the perfect antidote to the non-stop revelry.

Blossom-clad shutters look out on neat plazas hemmed by a riddle of cobblestone backstreets where vendors ply juicy mangos in the shade.

Inset: Decorative panels on the side of a *chiva* (bus)
Below (left and right): Colorful colonial architecture; The Centro Histórico with skyscrapers in the distance

FESTIVAL DIARY

January plays host to a highlight in the world's literary calendar as Cartagena welcomes novelists, journalists, and screenwriters from all over Latin America – and beyond. The Hay Festival, a rich celebration of creative talent, runs to a hectic schedule, so be sure to make time to explore the city and take in the sights.

JAN

Three Days of Culture

DAY 1

Have breakfast on Plaza de Bolivar and pass by the grand Teatro Heredia. Sample some street food: *mango biche* (sour mango), *empanadas* (stuffed bread or pastry), and *carimañoles* (yucca stuffed with mince). Catch a taxi to visit the historic Convento de la Popa, perched atop a 450-ft (140-m) hill, then stroll along the cannon-topped crumbling stone ramparts, the oldest of which were built in the early 17th century.

DAY 2

Spend the day exploring the city's Centro. Visit the historic Ciudad Amurallada (Walled City) and the charming neighborhoods of San Diego and Santo Domingo. Take in the stylish elegance of the Hotel Santa Clara, located in the former Convent of Saint Clara of Assisi (c.1600), on Calle del Torno at lunchtime. Stick to the center for shopping, and find crafts and souvenirs in San Diego Square where Malanga presents incredible Cartagena-style ceviche. When the sun sets, soak up the buzz of energetic literati discussions in Cartagena's atmospheric bars and bistros.

DAY 3

Pack beachwear, sun hats, and snorkeling gear for a day out on the water. Cartagena's Rosario Islands, sit among the coral reefs and turquoise waters that make up the Parque Nacional Natural Corales del Rosario y San Bernardo. Most tour boats take in three or four islands, allowing you plenty of time on the beach. In the evening, take a taxi to the Getsemani neighborhood. Load up on traditional small plates at El Bar del Sur before hopping next door to Demente for the green mango cocktails. Absorb some local energy dancing to live salsa at Café Havana or champeta music (African-infused Reggaeton) at Bazurto Social Club.

Dos and Don'ts

- ✗ Don't be tempted to use *mototaxis* – these traffic-beating motorbikes may be fast and dirt-cheap, but they are also highly dangerous.
- ✓ Be sure to try the local *dedos de queso* (deep-fried cheese sticks). Street vendors sell them around the Plaza de Bolivar.
- ✗ Don't attempt to change any currency with black-market money-changers – any so-called "great deals" will almost certainly involve counterfeit notes and coins.
- ✓ Wear comfortable shoes for exploring the maze of streets.

Below: The clear azure waters of an offshore island

GETTING THERE **See map p317, G5**
The Walt Disney World® Resort is about a 30-minute drive southwest of Orlando International Airport.

GETTING AROUND
Car rental is widely available and inexpensive. In the resort a system of buses, monorails, and ferryboats connects the attractions.

WEATHER
January brings coolish, dryish weather, with daytime highs of around 72°F (22°C), dropping to around 50°F (10°C) at night.

ACCOMMODATIONS
Rosen Inn Pointe Orlando is a budget option, with a free shuttle to Universal Studios® and about 15 minutes from Walt Disney World®; doubles from US$130; www.roseninn9000.com

Disney's Fort Wilderness Campground has air-conditioned cabins or rustic tents; family cabins from US$300; tents from US$52; www.disneyworld.com

Best Western Lake Buena Vista Disney Springs is on Disney property, just steps from all the fun; family rooms from US$189; www.lakebuenavistaresorthotel.com

EATING OUT
There are hundreds of choices for all budgets and tastes, from fast food to gourmet dining. Most places welcome families and offer a children's menu.

FURTHER INFORMATION
www.visitorlando.com

One Man's Vision

Film producer, entrepreneur, and philanthropist Walt Disney (1901–66) said he wanted to enable people to "leave today and enter the world of yesterday, tomorrow, and fantasy." Walt Disney World®, his project to make this vision a reality, opened five years after his death. Walt would perhaps be most proud of EPCOT® (the Experimental Prototype Community of Tomorrow), which brings to life the "brighter tomorrow" of which he often spoke.

ORLANDO

A MODERN-DAY AMERICAN RITE OF PASSAGE, a family trip to Orlando has long been an ideal option for parents looking to get away with the kids in tow. Orlando's attractions present young and old with an assault on the senses, and a steady stream of opportunities to get up-close and personal with beloved cartoon characters, fairy-tale figures, and movie icons. A life-size Goofy or Spider-Man is always available for a photo opportunity, and million-dollar amusement rides put visitors right into the heart of the action. The Orlando area is a can't-miss reward for children of all ages, a place where one is as likely to hear "It's a Small World" as any contemporary radio hit. Such is the pull of Mickey Mouse and his pals that grown-ups turn into big kids and even jaded teenagers turn off their cell phones to reconnect with the favorites of their youth. The Magic Kingdom® continues to be the focal point of the whole

Main: Evening falls on Main Street USA, at Walt Disney World®

Above (top and bottom): Taumata Racer® at Aquatica™; family fun at Splash Mountain in the Magic Kingdom®

Bottom (left to right): Fireworks over Cinderella Castle in the Magic Kingdom®; Spaceship Earth geodisic sphere at Epcot®; Disney cartoon characters come to life; moonrise over the vast Vehicle Assembly Building and Titan rocket at the Kennedy Space Center

region, with most visitors starting at Orlando's original Disney property. But today, tourists have more options than ever before. Besides EPCOT®'s futuristic and international wonders, there are also Disney's Hollywood Studios® (formerly MGM Studios) and Disney's Animal Kingdom®, saving families trips to California and Africa, respectively. With numerous additional properties, such as the Typhoon Lagoon and Blizzard Beach water parks, "the mouse" – as some locals call the company – offers so much that most families don't bother leaving its friendly confines. That said, the Orlando area contains plenty more by way of great family-friendly experiences. Universal Orlando® Resort is a must for movie fans, and Aquatica™ offers the chance to get soaked on a variety of water rides. Kennedy Space Center is a magnet for youngsters curious about space exploration, and the nearby beaches are a surfers' paradise. Orlando's attractive Winter Park neighborhood is full of colorful galleries and cozy eateries. Ask any kid, though, and the focus of a trip to Orlando has to fall squarely on Walt Disney World®. It remains, to many, "the happiest place on earth."

THEME PARK DIARY

In a region with more than 60 million visitors a year, it's often impossible to escape the crowds. A winter visit, outside the main vacation periods, is ideal for families looking to enjoy multiple parks in a limited amount of time. Four days should be enough time to explore the area without getting park burnout.

Four Fun-Filled Days

DAY 1

Begin your trip at Magic Kingdom®, the original and still best-known of the parks. If it's a weekday, you may get to do the Pirates of the Caribbean ride more than once, a luxury most park visitors can't enjoy. Cap a full day at the park by snacking on mouse-ear-shaped treats while watching the nightly fireworks display.

DAY 2

Head to EPCOT®, splitting time between Future World and the World Showcase, where your family can tour the world in less than a square mile. Grab dinner and a well-deserved nightcap at Disney Springs, an outdoor complex of shops, restaurants, and nightclubs.

DAY 3

Take a break from all things Disney and visit the Kennedy Space Center for a fun, hands-on introduction to space exploration. If you're lucky you might see a rocket launch. Then take the kids to SeaWorld® Orlando, a marine theme park that features Kraken, a monster roller coaster. Or visit Harry Potter and pals at the Universal Orlando® Resort, which contains two theme parks and a large shopping district (Universal City Walk).

DAY 4

If your kids are Star Wars fans, the force is at work at Disney's Hollywood Studios®, where they can practice their light saber skills. Attractions range from sedate (lots of old-time Hollywood streets) to scary (the Rock 'n' Roller Coaster goes from 0 to 60mph/97kmph in 2.8 seconds). Younger kids may prefer Disney's Animal Kingdom®, which is a cross between a zoo and a theme park. There, you can take a jeep safari past lions, rhinos, and elephants; visit a mountain gorilla family; or take a raft ride through a tropical rainforest.

Dos and Don'ts

- ✓ Study maps of the larger parks in advance, plotting a course through the grounds to cut down on lengthy walks.
- ✓ If you hate crowds, or are traveling with small children, consider visiting the parks on weekdays, when lines, parking, and traffic are more manageable than on weekends.
- ✓ Bring sunscreen and bottled water, as both can be costly to purchase inside the parks.
- ✗ Don't overlook the Disney Parks' Fastpass options for popular rides. You can reserve a time to come back later in the day, skipping lengthy lines.

Below: *Liberty Belle* riverboat in the Magic Kingdom®

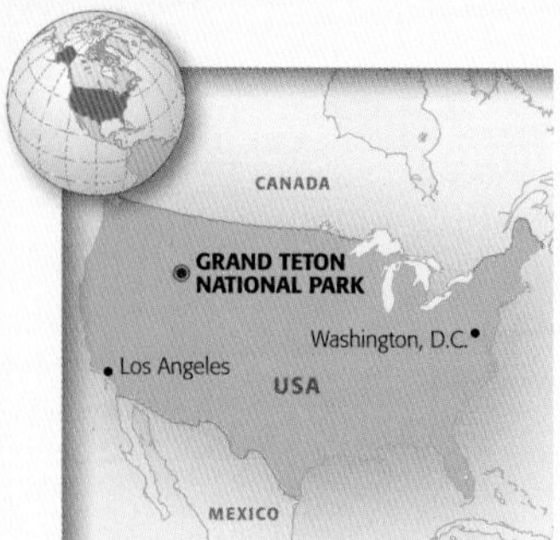

GETTING THERE See map p320, F5
Connecting flights from Chicago, Dallas, Salt Lake City, and Denver, among others. The airport is 10 minutes from the center, and about a half hour from Colter Bay.

GETTING AROUND
Hiking trails and viewpoints are well signed from the main roadways and there are regular shuttle buses between the town of Jackson and Jackson Hole Resort.

WEATHER
Springtime weather is brisk, usually around the 50s°F (10°C) to the 60s°F (15 °C), with occasional precipitation. Winter brings lots of snow, with below-freezing temperatures.

ACCOMMODATIONS
Relax at Snake River Lodge & Spa; doubles from US$350; www.snakeriverlodge.com

The upscale Four Seasons is at Jackson Hole Mountain Resort; doubles from US$375; www.fourseasons.com

There are campgrounds throughout the park (from US$22/site), including in Jenny Lake and Colter Bay.

EATING OUT
In Jackson and the Jackson Hole Mountain Resort, you'll find everything from traditional barbecue to sushi. A local favorite is Bubba's BBQ, from around US$16.

FURTHER INFORMATION
www.jacksonhole.com
www.nps.gov

Animal Kingdom

This is the land of America's emblematic wildlife: moose, elk, wolves, and bears. A wide array of birds fill the air, including bald eagles, cranes, the colorful double-crested cormorants and, in the alpine regions, ravens, rosy finches, and white-crowned sparrows. Near ponds and rivers, keep an eye out for trumpeter swans, the largest waterfowl in North America. The park is also home to pronghorns, which are indigenous to western and central North America. They may be hard to catch a glimpse of: pronghorns are among the fastest land mammals in the Western Hemisphere.

Above (left and right): Kayaking at Jackson Lake; Jackson Hole Valley
Main: Fly-fisherman casts his line in a lake in Grand Teton National Park

GRAND TETON NATIONAL PARK

THE UNITED STATES IS THE LAND OF GRAND NATIONAL PARKS, but few are as distinctly named as Grand Teton. French-Canadian trappers, upon seeing the park's three soaring peaks, called them Les Trois Tetons, or The Three Breasts, of which the Grand Teton is the tallest. The mountains preside over the surrounding 300,000-acre (120,000-ha) parkland, which is awash with bright-green valleys, reflective lakes, and the teeming Snake River, with wetlands extending from its banks. Snake River's Oxbow Bend is prime wildlife-viewing territory, with creatures ranging from elk to bald eagles. Another highlight of the park is Jackson Hole, a deep valley that extends between the Teton and Gros Ventre ranges. The term "hole" dates back to early trappers and explorers, who accessed the valley via its steep slopes, which felt, eerily, like descending into a giant hole. The real jewel of the valley is Jackson Hole Mountain Resort, made up of two distinct mountains – Rendezvous and Apres Vous. In winter, the resort is legendary among skiers for its challenging terrain, including Corbett's Couloir, a narrow plunge best suited to Olympians and described as "America's scariest ski slope." The resort claims 4,100 ft (1,250 m) of vertical skiing and Jackson Hole is also crisscrossed with miles of groomed pistes for effortless cruising, and deep-powder snowfields. The resort offers excellent novice programs, which introduce newbies to the joys of skiing and snowboarding. For a taste of daily mountain life, go to the town of Jackson. Cowboys clunk along wooden sidewalks to boisterous honky-tonk bars, which share the streets with a burgeoning number of classy galleries, boutiques, chef-driven restaurants and low-lit cocktail lounges.

Cowboys clunk along wooden sidewalks to boisterous honky-tonk bars, which share the streets with classy galleries and boutiques.

Inset: Beautiful sunset as seen from Oxbow Bend
Below (left and right): Boats near Colter Bay Village; Jackson Hole Aerial Tram

EXPLORER'S DIARY

January is peak season as snow falls in abundance, making this one of the premiere ski areas in the country. Five days is just right to explore the park and to fit in two days at Jackson Hole Mountain Resort. As you roam the park, always remember to look up: the best views are framed by the ever-present stunning Teton peaks.

Five Days in the Scenic Wilderness

DAY 1

Begin your adventure at Colter Bay, an information hub with a Visitor Center and the Indian Arts Museum, which offers an overview of American Indian history. Then hike to Jackson Lake and the northern reaches of the park, and check out Snake River's Oxbow Bend, filled with wildlife.

DAYS 2–3

Start the morning in Signal Mountain, a supply and accommodation center, with campsites and restaurants. For sweeping views, drive and trek to Jackson Point Overlook. Head to a series of lovely lakes, including Leigh Lake and Jenny Lake, where you can explore the lakeshore. Discover the east side of the park, which is criss-crossed with hiking trails and dotted with scenic viewpoints, including Glacier View Turnout.

DAYS 4–5

Spend the last two days in Jackson Hole Mountain Resort, one of the top ski resorts in the country, where you can slice down snowy peaks. Ride the Aerial Tram from the base of Teton Village to the top of Rendezvous Mountain, where you can take in splendid views of Snake River Valley, the Grand Teton National Park, and the Gros Ventre Range.

Dos and Don'ts

- ✓ Pack the outdoor gear: your daily uniform in the park will be durable shoes and clothing. Even in Jackson Hole Mountain Resort, the dress code is casual, from day to night.
- ✗ Don't miss a night out at Stagecoach Bar in Jackson – it's the perfect dive bar for a refreshing beer after a day of hiking and horseback riding.
- ✓ For winter, book ahead – very far ahead. The lodges and hotels fill up quickly.
- ✓ Look at the arches anchoring the four corners of Jackson town square, formed by thousands of intertwined elk antlers, all shed by the protected herd living just outside town.
- ✓ Consider returning in summertime to enjoy hikes through wildflowers and towering groves.

Below: Skiing at Jackson Hole

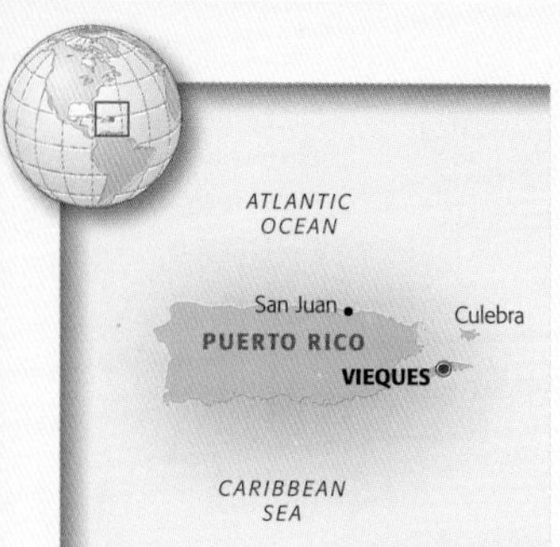

GETTING THERE See map p325, G4

Vieques has a small airstrip. Vieques Air Link and Cape Air connect San Juan to Vieques by air. Many people prefer to take the ferry from Fajardo for a 45-minute journey.

GETTING AROUND

Bus services are minimal, but taxis take you around for less than US$20. The island is small enough to bicycle around.

WEATHER

Though the weather is warm year-round, January is the best month to visit with temperatures averaging 76°F (24°C).

ACCOMMODATIONS

For budget accommodation, try Bananas Guesthouse, on Esperanza Bay; doubles from US$85; www.bananasvieques.com

Sublime elegance is the hallmark at Inn on the Blue Horizon; doubles from US$200; www.bluehorizonboutiqueresort.com

Try chic W Retreat & Spa on Martineau Bay; doubles from US$459; www.wvieques.com

EATING OUT

Local fare at simple restaurants should be about US$25 per day, but it costs more for a gourmet meal at Carambola, which has live jazz on Saturday nights.

FURTHER INFORMATION

www.vieques.com
www.seepuertorico.com

VIEQUES

AFFECTIONATELY KNOWN AS THE SPANISH VIRGINS, Vieques and nearby Culebra are the largest isles in a mini-archipelago off the east coast of Puerto Rico. These pearls in a sapphire sea are edged by silky sands dissolving into waters of lapis lazuli. Far from the mainland crowds, life moves at a languid pace on laid-back Vieques, the perfect place to get stranded. Used for US Navy gunnery practice since World War II, the island was eventually abandoned by the Navy in 2003 after a 50-year pounding, leaving Vieques' wild horses and leatherback turtles in peace.

Although the eastern half of the isle is still off-limits, this beach-lover's haven tempts with delightful guesthouses, and chic resort hotels, tucked into sandy coves fringed with coral reefs. Vieques may now be fashionable, but its tiny main town, Isabela Segunda, still clings to its

Main: The sun setting over a beach in Esperanza Bay

An Eerie Glow

The nocturnal glow in Phosphorescent Bay is produced by dinoflagellates – bioluminescent micro-organisms called *Pyrodinium bahamense*. Dinoflagellates live in water with just the right tidal flow, temperature, and composition to provide the creatures with nutrients which induce a chemical reaction that results in a flash when agitated by movement, such as from passing fish, swimmers, or waves. The glow is best seen on moonless nights.

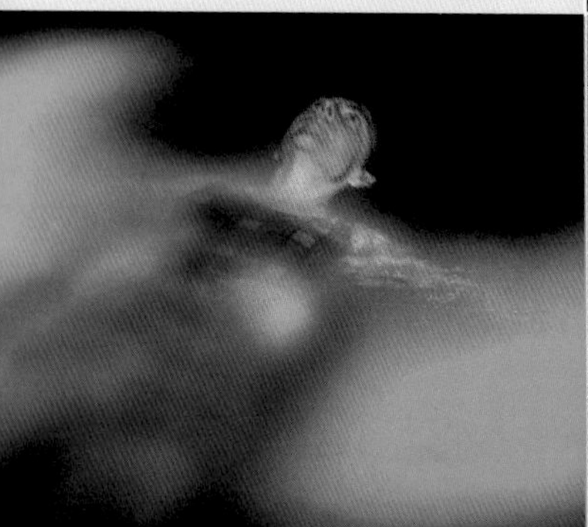

Left: A snorkeler holding aloft a starfish found in the waters off Vieques

Right (left and right): Faro Punta Mulas lighthouse in Isabela Segunda; fishing boats moored in the clear waters of Esperanza Bay

unpretentious ways – the main traffic comprises goats and locals on Paso Fino horses. The Faro Punta Mulas lighthouse and Fort Conde Mirasol, featuring historical artifacts and nature displays, are worth a visit. On the south shore, the sleepy hamlet of Esperanza tantalizes with its teal-blue bay setting, great for snorkeling or simply snoozing the day away on the beach while being caressed by the tropical breeze.

Ecotourism is a major draw. Green hawksbill and leatherback turtles crawl ashore to nest on the sands, while manatees paddle in mangrove-fringed Laguna Kiani, part of the Vieques National Wildlife Refuge. Laced with trails, it is perfect for hiking, mountain biking, or horseback excursions. Kayaking on Phosphorescent Bay is best done at night, when slipping out of your craft and into the waters triggers an explosion of bioluminescence, while if you glide on into the open ocean, you will discover a casket of gems such as a spectacular fringing reef. You may never want to leave.

Above: A cave at Vieques' Navio Beach

Below: Cheerful welcome sign greeting visitors to Vieques

ISLAND DIARY

January is the ideal time to visit Vieques as the weather is perfect – sunny and warm. The cloudless, dazzlingly deep blue skies make being outdoors a joy, and the isle's natural attributes beckon invitingly. Four days is adequate to take in the highlights at a leisurely pace, including a quick jaunt to nearby Culebra.

Four Days of Sun and Sand

DAY 1

After checking into your hotel in Vieques, go sightseeing to sleepy Isabela Segunda and visit the Faro Punta Mulas lighthouse and Fort Conde Mirasol, where you can pick up some cultural and island history. Opt for a picnic on nearby Bravos de Boston beach.

DAY 2

Head to Esperanza on the south shore to soak up the laid-back tropical charm of this village. Stroll through Calle Flamboyán and drop in at the Vieques Conservation and Historical Trust museum to learn about local sealife, then meet the fish eye-to-eye as you snorkel in the bay. Linger over dinner and rum cocktails at Bananas.

DAY 3

Rent a bicycle or sign on for a guided cycling excursion along off-road trails in the rugged Vieques Wildlife Refuge. Then take a well-deserved break for relaxation at Green Beach and explore the mangroves at Laguna Kiani. At night glide across Phosphorescent Bay in a kayak and slip into the ink-black waters to spark a ghostlike green silhouette as you swim amid billions of twinkling dinoflagellates.

DAY 4

Take the ferry to nearby Culebra for a day lazing on Playa Flamingo, the most sensational beach in Puerto Rico. Surfers can ride the big waves while snorkelers can hike over to Playa Carlos Rosario, which has a fabulous offshore reef teeming with chromatic fish.

Dos and Don'ts

- ✓ Take plenty of mosquito repellent for exploring the mangroves.
- ✓ Time your visit to Phosphorescent Bay for a new moon, as the light of a full moon makes seeing the phosphorescence difficult.
- ✗ Don't overdo the rum cocktails! And drink plenty of water to avoid dehydration.
- ✓ Learn some Spanish. Although a large percentage of the population is English-speaking, Vieques is part of Spanish-speaking Puerto Rico.

Below: Leatherback turtle nesting on the beach

GETTING THERE See map p314, G6
Air Canada flies to Charlottetown Airport year-round from Halifax, Montréal, Ottawa, and Toronto.

GETTING AROUND
If you'd like to fully explore the island, it's best to have a car. Buses travel regularly between the main towns.

WEATHER
Winter in PEI is crisp and cold, with ample snow throughout the season; spring warms up considerably, with temperatures ranging from 50°F (10°C) to 75°F (23°C).

ACCOMMODATIONS
The Great George is a fine boutique hotel; doubles from US$135; www.thegreatgeorge.com

The Fairholm National Historic Inn in Charlottetown has a variety of homey suites with fireplaces and wood-beam ceilings; doubles from US$169; www.fairholminn.com

The island is filled with campsites, from the woods to the coast; check with the tourist office in the main towns for more information.

EATING OUT
Sample the island's seafood, including its stellar oysters, at the friendly Claddagh Oyster House in Charlottetown. From end-January to early February, Charlottetown hosts the annual WinterDine, where local restaurants serve menus built around local PEI ingredients.

FURTHER INFORMATION
www.tourismpei.com

Confederation Bridge

Prince Edward Island may celebrate the simpler life, but it's also the site of one of Canada's greatest engineering triumphs, the Confederation Bridge. The curving 8 mile (12.9 km) multi-span bridge, which joins Prince Edward Island and New Brunswick, is the longest bridge in the world over ice-covered waters. Although the first proposals emerged in the 1870s, it wasn't until the mid-1980s that the development began in earnest. Since opening in 1997, the Confederation Bridge has become imperative for travel through the Maritime provinces.

Above (left and right): Winter sleigh ride; a mill on Hunter River
Main: Covehead lighthouse

PRINCE EDWARD ISLAND

ISN'T IT SPLENDID TO THINK OF ALL THE THINGS THERE ARE TO FIND OUT ABOUT? IT JUST MAKES ME FEEL GLAD TO BE ALIVE – IT'S SUCH AN INTERESTING WORLD." The wise words of Anne of Green Gables have echoed for more than a century, inspiring fans from around the world to visit this small, bucolic island in the Gulf of St. Lawrence, off Canada's east coast. The island's history is as diverse as its geography, with First Nations, French, English, Irish, and Scottish roots. The island's evolving name reflected the dominant culture at the time: Île Saint-Jean by the French; St. John's Island by the British, which was later changed to Prince Edward Island, named for Prince Edward Augustus, the fourth son of King George III.

Prince Edward Island (or PEI, as it's often called) is Canada's smallest province – and the only one to have no land boundary. Here on PEI, it's water all around and that, in many ways, is why the island has managed to maintain a slow and pastoral quality that seems stuck in another era. Lucy Maud Montgomery wrote *Anne of Green Gables* back in 1908 and yet even today, the beautiful story resonates and reflects what you'll see and experience here. The island is, not surprisingly, hugely popular with those wishing to follow in the footsteps of the fictional red-headed orphan Anne, particularly in the cute town of Cavendish, site of the Green Gables farmhouse.

Combine literary history with the the finest experiences nature has to offer on the 'Garden of the Gulf'

Other highlights include exploring PEI's rural splendor, from the wind-battered coast to driving routes that pass lush farmland and sand dunes punctuated by lighthouses piercing the blue sky. Peak season on the island is in the summer, but winter holds a very special appeal as well. Snowy outdoor activities include tubing, snowshoeing, skating, and skiing, as well as boisterous winter carnivals, and entertaining theater at the Confederation Centre of the Arts.

Inset: Actors in period costumes in Charlottetown
Below (left and right): North Cape Coastal Drive; Beaconsfield Historic House

THREE FAIRY TALE DAYS

Although summer draws the most visitors, winter highlights the old-world charm of the island. Three days is the perfect amount of time for exploring the island, giving you the chance to museum-hop and learn about the island's literary history, as well as engage in an abundance of outdoor activities.

Three Days Around the Lakes

JAN

DAY 1

Land in Charlottetown, the island's capital city, and spend a day walking the quaint streets – sip hot chocolate in a cozy café and pick up souvenirs at the *Anne of Green Gables*-inspired shops. Don't miss the town's historic houses, such as the beautiful Victorian Beaconsfield Historic House, and the Ardgowan National Historic Site of Canada, once the home of William Henry Pope, one of the Fathers of the Confederation. Also worth a look is the Romanesque Revival 1888 Charlottetown City Hall, the oldest municipal hall on the island.

DAY 2

Explore the outdoors with a day at the family-friendly Brookvale Provincial Ski Park, where you can frolic in the snow, take classes, and ski and snowboard. Plus, check the ski park calendar for fun events throughout the winter, from bonfire nights to alpine race weekends.

DAY 3

Calling all fans of Anne! En route to Cavendish – the *Anne of Green Gables* capital of the island – stop in to the lovely tiny town of New Glasgow. Visit the Prince Edward Island Preserve Company, where you can pick up local jams and teas. Then, continue on to Cavendish where all things Anne await: visit the Lucy Maud Montgomery Birthplace, a white cottage overlooking the harbor; Avonlea, a family-friendly recreation of Anne's fictional hometown, which includes an actual schoolhouse where L.M. Montgomery once taught; and Green Gables itself, a 19th-century farmhouse that inspired the one in the book.

Dos and Don'ts

- ✗ Don't miss out on the famous Prince Edward Island oysters, which are served at restaurants around the island.
- ✓ Bring the binoculars: the island is filled with more than 300 species of birds, including the provincial bird, the blue jay.
- ✓ Plan to return for the Charlottetown Festival (late May to mid-October), when *Anne of Green Gables – The Musical* is performed at the Confederation Centre of the Arts.

Below: Anne of Green Gables Museum

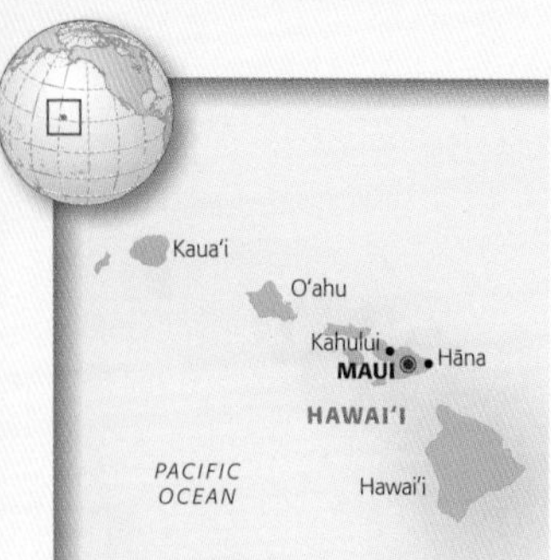

GETTING THERE **See map p322, H6**
Maui's main airport receives non-stop flights from all over the western USA, as well as shuttles from Honolulu on O'ahu. There's also a daily ferry to Kahului from O'ahu.

GETTING AROUND
By far the best way to get around Maui is in a rental car, though Akina Aloha (www.akinatours.com) and Valley Isle Excursions (www.tourmaui.com) run bus tours along the Road to Hāna.

WEATHER
Average daily temperatures in winter range from 78°F (26°C) down to 65°F (18°C).

ACCOMMODATIONS
The homely Mauian in west Maui offers seafront rooms at US$179; www.mauian.com

The Hyatt Regency Maui Resort & Spa at Kā'anapali has ocean-view rooms starting at US$430; www.maui.hyatt.com

Plantation-style cottages at Hāna's Travaasa Hana cost US$475–1,075 per night; travaasa.com/hana

EATING OUT
Maui's restaurants range from sophisticated "Pacific Rim" nightspots in the resorts, where a meal for two costs US$100, to simple diners where main dishes cost under US$10.

FURTHER INFORMATION
www.visitmaui.com

MAUI

THE LEGENDARY ROAD TO HĀNA WINDS FOR SOME 50 MILES (80 KM), threading its way through deep gorges, passing beneath towering waterfalls and above stunning black-sand beaches, and crossing more than 50 bridges. While it's not as perilous as the "I Survived the Road to Hāna" T-shirts might have you believe, it is essential to drive slowly and keep your eyes on the road. If you stay the night in Hāna you'll have more time to explore the area. However, the real point of the journey is not to see Hāna itself, but to enjoy the journey, which you can do as a long day trip from anywhere on Maui.

Almost all Hāna-bound drivers pass through the island capital, Kahului, but the road truly begins at the former plantation village of Pā'ia, now largely populated by surfers thanks to the proximity of the world's finest windsurfing beach at Ho'okipa. Once past that, you feel as if you're leaving reality

Main: An old bridge on the Road to Hāna

Land of Volcanoes

Maui is a "volcanic doublet," formed by two overlapping volcanoes. The larger is dormant Haleakalā in the east, which stands over 10,000 ft (3,050 m) tall – high enough to force rain-bearing clouds to shed their water, resulting in the deeply weathered gorges with cloaks of velvet vegetation as seen on the Road to Hāna. Daily at dawn, tour parties are kitted out not far below the summit with bicycles and protective gear, and set off on the exhilarating ride back down to the ocean.

Left: African tulip tree in full bloom

Right (left and right): Waves crashing onto lava rocks at the Ke'anae Peninsula; black-sand beach at Wai'ānapanapa, Wai'ānapanapa State Park

behind and entering some South Seas paradise. As the hillsides grow steeper, the road curves dramatically in and out of each successive gully. Rounding each cliff-top corner, you find yourself perched above the crashing waves; deep in the next recess, there's just time as you cross the slim valley bridge to glimpse another waterfall cascading down from the upper slopes of Haleakalā.

Among the many compelling sights along the way, be sure to stop and admire the white-spumed waves that crash unceasingly against rocky Ke'anae Peninsula; to marvel at the lava walls of the largest ancient temple in all Polynesia, in Kahanu Garden; to stroll on the black-sand beach at Wai'ānapanapa State Park; and to sample delicious fresh fruits or barbecued fish at a roadside stand. Many visitors barely pause at the sleepy village of Hāna, 50 miles (80 km) out from Kahului, but continue 10 miles (16 km) further on to 'Ohe'o Gulch, where you can bathe beneath breathtaking waterfalls or hike up into spellbinding rain forest.

Above: Rainbow Eucalyptus tree

Below: Part of the coastline seen from the picturesque Road to Hāna

MAUI DIARY

Most visitors come to Maui for breaks of a week or less, lured by its wonderful sandy beaches and turquoise waters. You should also make time to explore the island's spectacular tropical scenery. A road trip to Hāna – usually done as a day trip – is a great way to take in the many natural wonders of the island.

Five Days of Island Exploration

JAN

DAY 1

Fly into Kahului, and pick up a rental car or take a shuttle van to your hotel. Ideally you'll arrive in time to watch the sun set over the sea, and then enjoy a romantic dinner.

DAY 2

You'll want to spend your first full day on Maui on the beach, whether that's on the safe sandy strands near the main hotels, like Kā'anapali Beach in west Maui or Polo Beach in Wailea, or on some rougher and more remote spot like magnificent, wave-battered Big Beach near the island's southernmost point.

DAY 3

Now it's time to be a bit more active in the water, perhaps taking a snorkel cruise to the offshore islet of Molokini, or if you're an expert windsurfer, pitting yourself against the surf at fabled Ho'okipa Beach.

DAY 4

Set off early to drive the road to Hāna, pausing perhaps for breakfast in atmospheric little Pā'ia, and aiming for 'Ohe'o Gulch by early afternoon. Remember you can stop on the way back as well as on the way out.

DAY 5

Arrange to be picked up long before dawn, for a bus tour up to the 10,000-ft (3,050-m) summit of the volcano, Haleakalā. After enjoying stupendous views across the extraordinary moonscape, you're taken down to the lower limit of the national park, so you can freewheel back down again on a bicycle; you'll barely need to pedal on the 30-mile (50-km) ride to Pā'ia. There's still time for an afternoon on the beach before you catch the evening flight home.

Dos and Don'ts

- ✗ Don't take all your food and drink with you; it's more fun to stop at the fruit and snack stands along the way.
- ✓ Give way to oncoming traffic on narrow bridges; it's customary for several vehicles to cross at a time in each direction.
- ✗ Don't stop too long or too often in the first few miles; there's a long day's driving ahead, and you'll risk missing out on the major beauty spots further along.
- ✗ Don't end up driving back after dark, when you can't appreciate the scenery.
- ✓ Ask the rangers at 'Ohe'o Gulch about current hiking, swimming, and driving conditions.

Below: Waterfall cascading into the Blue Pool near Kahanu Garden

GETTING THERE See map p321, D5
Driving from L.A. takes around 2 hours. The nearest airport is the Palm Springs International Airport. Flights from Los Angeles International Airport to Palm Springs are 40–50 minutes.

GETTING AROUND
The heart of Palm Springs is pedestrian-friendly, with everything within easy walking distance. Beyond downtown, it's ideal to have a car to explore the surrounding desert.

WEATHER
From January to April temperatures range from the low 70s°F (21°C) to the high 80s°F (30°C). Summer is hot and dry, with temperatures soaring above 100°F (38°C).

ACCOMMODATIONS
Sprawl out poolside at the Rivera Palm Springs; doubles from US$116; www.rivierapalmsprings.com

The charming, historical Del Marcos Hotel has doubles from US$179; www.delmarcoshotel.com

The stylish Parker Palm Springs has doubles from US$349; www.theparkerpalmsprings.com

EATING OUT
Palm Springs is booming with creative cuisine, including the farm-focused Workshop Kitchen and Bar (from US$22 per dish).

FURTHER INFORMATION
www.visitpalmsprings.com
www.visitgreaterplampsrings.com

Hollywood Glamour

Since the 1920s, Hollywood stars have been frolicking in Palm Springs, thanks to the famous "two-hour rule," which stipulated that under-contract actors had to be within two hours of the studio, in case of last-minute filming. Among the Hollywood royalty who relaxed here were Frank Sinatra, Marilyn Monroe, Elizabeth Taylor, and Cary Grant. Many movies were also filmed here, from the 1937 *Lost Horizon* to the 1963 *Palm Springs Weekend*. These days, the Palm Springs International Film Festival in January still draws Hollywood A-listers.

Above (left and right): Indian Canyons; Palm Springs Aerial Tramway
Main: Palm Springs Golf Resort

PALM SPRINGS

Sun-soaked Palm Springs used to be the domain of retirees in shorts and sandals. But in recent times this lush pocket of golf courses, bingo parlors, and diners hawking senior specials has evolved into a retro playground of hipster hotels and elegant cocktail lounges, set against the shimmering backdrop of many, many swimming pools. In their heyday, Frank Sinatra and Marilyn Monroe escaped to Palm Springs for a weekend of indulgence and this desert oasis is once again a bastion of pamper palaces. The area's natural hot springs, discovered by Native Americans, form the basis of numerous resorts in the area.

Although Palm Springs places a premium on relaxation, it caters equally to adventure enthusiasts. The surrounding hot and dry Coachella Valley Desert lends itself to numerous outdoor pursuits, including hiking and horseback riding in nearby Indian Canyons, which is dotted with palm groves. Art-lovers will also enjoy the city's quirky art galleries, many of which feature desert-inspired crafts, as well as the lauded Palm Springs Art Museum. One of the most memorable ways to view the surrounding desert is to rise above it with a sunset balloon trip, offering a stunning bird's-eye vista of the desert as it changes color under the waning sun, from fiery red to pale yellow to cool gray.

Come evening, Palm Springs shows off its playful side at funky spots like Bar, on North Canyon Road, which serves old-fashioned cocktails, including Moscow Mules. Follow in the footsteps of famous bar regulars, and order a martini at the iconic Melvyn's – everyone from Marlon Brando to Liza Minnelli have warmed the seats here. Palm Springs is also a perennially popular destination for gay and lesbian visitors, and the streets are awash with gay-friendly bars, including the colorful Toucans Tiki Lounge.

Playground of the rich and famous, Palm Springs indulges every traveler's desire for sunshine, relaxation, culture, and activity.

Inset: Hot-air balloon trip high above the desert
Below (left and right): Elvis Honeymoon Hideaway; Palm Springs Art Museum

DESERT DIARY

While snow may be blanketing northern regions of the USA, this desert getaway is wonderfully warm in January: sun, spas, and swimming pools are abundant. Spend your days relaxing with hot-stone massages or basking poolside with a frosty cocktail, with some art gallery-hopping in between.

JAN

Three Days of Sun, Spas, and Shopping

DAY 1

Start your visit by combining culture and retail, with a visit to the Palm Springs Art Museum Architecture and Design Center. This sleek museum is filled with eye-catching sculptures, drawings, and photography, with a focus on the region's famous Desert Modern architecture. Afterward, browse the splashy Museum Design Store for unique gifts. For more shopping, head to downtown and the Uptown Design District. In the late afternoon, relax at Spa La Quinta at the La Quinta Resort & Club. If you're here during the esteemed Palm Springs International Film Festival (early January), carve out time to see at least a couple of movies.

DAY 2

Elevate yourself above the desert on the Palm Springs Aerial Tramway, the world's largest rotating aerial tramway. Soaring 8,500 ft (2,590 m) above the desert, the tramway offers sweeping views and access to the Mountain San Jacinto State Park, where you can hike the desert trails. After a day of working out your muscles, soak in the mineral springs at Two Bunch Palms Resort & Spa. Later, enjoy cocktails at one of the city's old-world tiki bars, like the colorful Bootlegger Tiki.

DAY 3

Splurge on a sunrise (or sunset) balloon trip over Palm Springs and the Coachella Valley. Back in Palm Springs, visit classic celebrity haunts, like the Elvis Honeymoon Hideaway – where Elvis and Priscilla honeymooned – and the Copey Restaurant, once part of Cary Grant's Estate. In the evening, dine at King's Highway at the trendy Ace Hotel & Swim Club. Sip on classic cocktails such as the Gold Rush, a potent mix of bourbon, lemon, and honey.

Dos and Don'ts

- ✗ Don't forget to carry plenty of water when venturing into the desert. The weather can vary widely from the desert floor to the mountains, so pack a jacket if visiting higher elevations.
- ✓ Take the time to explore the lesser-known local art galleries and craft centers, like the Backstreet Art District.
- ✓ Make hotel reservations at least four months in advance if you want to visit during the International Film Festival.
- ✓ If you're here in the summer, plan to relax under the shade during the day, and emerge at night – when temperatures are far lower, and the famous Palm Springs nightlife hits its stride.

Below: Melvyn's bar and restaurant

FEBRUARY

Where to Go: **February**

Conditions are still chilly in much of North America – though the snow makes a great winter wonderland of eastern Canada and New England. Balmier temperatures and warm seas greet you as you head south into Florida, where Miami is a sizzling destination. Mexico is temperate in February, while Central America is enjoying a dry season that allows you access to forested regions that are prohibitively drenched during the wetter months. The Caribbean, too, is delightfully dry, cooled by trade winds. The farther toward the Equator you venture, the steamier things get – perfect weather conditions for the sybaritic pre-Lenten carnival celebrated with style in Brazil. Below you will find all the destinations in this chapter as well as some extra suggestions to provide a little inspiration.

FESTIVALS AND CULTURE

TRINIDAD Colorful participant in the King and Queen of Carnival contest

TRINIDAD
CARIBBEAN

It's Carnival time – the West Indies' biggest party

Join in with the revelers for three days of outrageous costumes, music, and dance. And, stay on to discover more of Trinidad's rich culture.

See pp48–9

NEW ORLEANS MARDI GRAS
LOUISIANA, USA

Visit the birthplace of jazz

A riotous three-week festival with parades, parties, and street carousing accompanied by the city's best live musicians.

www.mardigrasneworleans.com

GUANAJUATO
MEXICO

See colonial-Spanish Mexico at its finest

One of the oldest cities in the Americas, Guanajuato preserves a vast array of colonial architecture, including almost 40 churches.

www.guanajuatocapital.com

HAVANA
CUBA, CARIBBEAN

Discover the culture capital of the Caribbean

While Cuba's vibrant arts scene pulses to an Afro-Latin beat, sip a mojito in Hemingway's favorite bar and enjoy *habanero* life.

See pp38–9

SALVADOR
BRAZIL

Salvador's "carnaval" is a joyous bacchanalian revel

This is a carnival where you take part in the parades instead of watching – and the music and partying is second to none.

See pp50–51

UNFORGETTABLE JOURNEYS

INTER-AMERICAN HIGHWAY Kayaking in the Sea of Cortez

INTER-AMERICAN HIGHWAY
CENTRAL AMERICA

A country-hopping adventure

This beautiful epic journey has something for everyone as it takes you past mountains, beaches, jungles, and volcanoes.

See pp46–7

"One minute you're winding through mile-high mountains, then the next you're plunging into lush valleys cloaked in subaqueous green."

DRIVING THE CARRETERA AUSTRAL
SOUTHERN CHILE

A road trip to remember

Traverse 1,000 km of unspoilt countryside, running between fjords, glaciers, rain forest, and snow-capped mountains.

www.experiencechile.org

LAGO DE NICARAGUA
NICARAGUA

A majestic lake crossing

Take a boat across the beautiful Lago de Nicaragua out to the dramatic Isla de Ometepe, topped by a pair of towering volcanoes.

www.world66.com/centralamericathecaribbean

RIDING THE ALTIPLANO TRAIN
PUNO–CUSCO BY RAIL, PERU

A "highly" scenic train ride

Travel across the spectacular altiplano in the Peruvian Andes on the highest railway line in the Americas.

www.perurail.com

GRAN SABANA
VENEZUELA

One of South America's best-kept secrets

Hike through the beautiful uplands of Venezuela's Gran Sabana, the inspiration for Conan Doyle's *The Lost World*.

www.lagransabana.com/english

NATURAL WONDERS

PANAMA A keel-billed toucan

"Panama is an emerald fantasia encompassing the Darién rain forests and the mist-shrouded cloud forests of Volcán Barú."

PANAMA
CENTRAL AMERICA

A fully feathered paradise for birders

Panama is now the top American destination for birding – look out for rainbow-colored toucans, macaws, and humming birds.

See pp42–43

PAINTED CANYON
NORTH DAKOTA, USA

An outlandish landscape

Hike through this bizarrely colored gorge in Theodore Roosevelt National Park, with its amazing hues of green, blue, red, and white.

www.nps.gov/thro/index.htm

HARP SEAL-SPOTTING
ILES DE LA MADELEINE, CANADA

New life on the archipelago

The remote archipelago in the middle of the Gulf of St. Lawrence offers a wonderful chance to see new-born harp seals.

www.tourismeilesdelamadeleine.com

RIO PLÁTANO BIOSPHERE RESERVE
LA MOSQUITIA, HONDURAS

Honduras's Mosquito Coast

One of the finest areas of undisturbed rain forest in the Americas, and home to myriad plant and animal species.

http://whc.unesco.org/en/list/196

SEA OF CORTEZ
MEXICO

Swim with sealions and manta rays

Go sea kayaking in the incredibly rich wildlife environment of this scenic gulf coast and islands – see whales, dolphins, and sea birds.

www.loreto.com

Previous page: Colorful Mayan textile, Guatemala

Weather Watch

1 Ottawa, Canada Snow is at its most luxuriant in Canada in February – great for skiers and skaters, and for the Winterlude festival. Watch out, though, in the east of the country, for icy winds coming in from the Great Lakes.

2 Mexico Mexico is pleasant in February, particularly along the coast, and the gray whales have the right idea, heading toward the warm waters off Baja California.

3 Panama Panama, with its micro-climates, can surprise when it comes to weather. February, however, is reliably dry throughout most of the country – though the tropical forests of the Darién can see heavy rain at any time of year.

4 Miami, Florida With its tropical climate, Florida is more than comfortable enough in February that hiking in the Everglades is as much of an option as basking on the trendy beaches.

5 Trinidad Trinidad's temperatures are higher than in its neighboring Caribbean Islands, and February sees less rain and lower humidity than in the wet season (May–Dec).

6 Brazil Steamy Salvador, on the country's northeastern coast, is about to enter its rainy season, but conditions are still hot, sunny, and dry enough to make visiting for carnival a bone-warming delight.

LUXURY AND ROMANCE

MIAMI An Art Deco-style lifeguard hut, South Beach

PORT ANTONIO
JAMAICA, CARIBBEAN

One of the Caribbean's most luxurious hideaways

Once described as "the most exquisite port on earth," Port Antonio has great beaches, lagoons, and jungle-shrouded mountains.

www.portantoniojamaica.com

MIAMI
FLORIDA, USA

Soak up the city's romantic Art Deco style

With a pulsating nightlife, laid-back beach lifestyle, and quirky architecture, Miami offers a plethora of hedonistic delights.

See pp40–41

EATING AT HOLETOWN
BARBADOS, CARIBBEAN

Romantic dining in the oldest town in Barbados

Enjoy a delicious meal in the atmospheric setting of Holetown, while watching the sun dip into the Caribbean.

www.barbados.org/htown.htm

"Sizzling, sultry Miami has it all: miles of sunny beach by day, pulsing nightlife, fine dining, and trendy shopping."

HOT SPRINGS NATIONAL PARK RESORT
ARKANSAS, USA

A time to unwind

Enjoy the friendly atmosphere of this appealing resort and relax in a bath of natural hot springs spa water.

www.hotsprings.org

US VIRGIN ISLANDS
CARIBBEAN

Beaches, forests, and Danish architecture

Ride the vertiginous Skyride in St. Thomas or check out the beaches and forests of St. John, or the old Danish settlements of St. Croix.

www.usvi.net

ACTIVE ADVENTURES

BAJA PENINSULA Diving among pork fish

BAJA CALIFORNIA SUR
MEXICO

Whale-watching in Los Cabos

Unwind on one of the many beaches or take part in an adventure sport in this beautiful Mexican destination.

See pp36–7

DOG SLEDDING
ALASKA, USA

Spectacular sub-Arctic tundra

Explore some of North America's most remote and beautiful wilderness, home to bald and golden eagles, wolves, caribou, moose, otters, lynx, and more.

www.alaska.org

CLIMBING BLUE MOUNTAIN PEAK
JAMAICA, CARIBBEAN

Conquer a Caribbean peak

Escape the coastal heat with a hike up the idyllic Blue Mountains.

www.visitjamaica.com/blue-mountain-peak

LAKES REGION
NEW HAMPSHIRE, USA

Scenic snow-based activities for adrenalin-junkies

Under clear skies amid snowy mountains, there are plenty of adventures and trails to try, and also quiet, quaint towns to explore.

See pp44–5

SPORTFISHING
COSTA RICA

Some of the world's best deep-sea sportfishing

Fishing expeditions off both the Pacific and Caribbean coasts, with marlin, dorado, wahoo, tuna, and snook aplenty all year around.

www.fishcostarica.com

FAMILY GETAWAYS

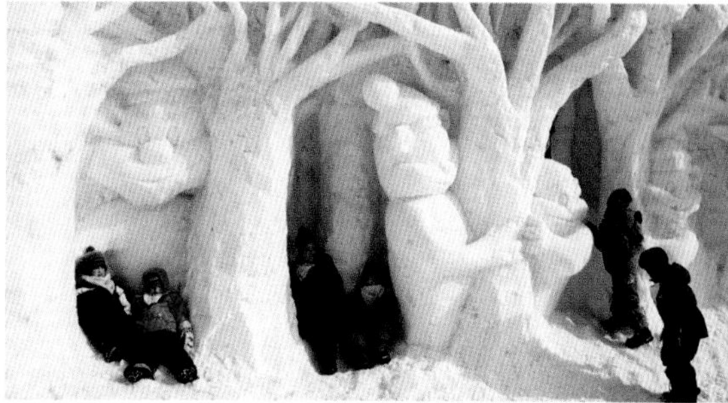

OTTAWA Children enjoying the snow during Winterlude

"A snow playground in Jacques Cartier Park rings with the joyful squeals of kids flinging themselves downhill on snow slides."

OTTAWA
ONTARIO, CANADA

Snowy family fun

Winterlude festival is on this month and the city comes alive with all sorts of activities. Skate, ski, toboggan, and then warm up with hearty food and hot toddies.

See pp34–5

DOMINICAN REPUBLIC
CARIBBEAN

Island fun and games

There are plenty of energetic activities to be had on this family- friendly island, including snorkeling and horseback riding.

www.godominicanrepublic.com

GULF SHORES
ALABAMA, USA

Popular Gulf of Mexico family hideaway

The white-sand beach is the main attraction, but there are also plenty of activities on offer too, including feeding alligators.

www.gulfshores.com

VANCOUVER
BRITISH COLUMBIA, CANADA

Something for all the family in the west coast capital

A plethora of city sights to take in, and a temperate climate, which means you can enjoy the beautiful countryside at any time.

www.tourismvancouver.com

FLORIDA KEYS
FLORIDA, USA

A beautiful and tropical getaway in the States

This strip of islands, improbably joined by the highway, allows for water sports galore, fine weather, and an interesting counter culture.

www.fla-keys.com

GETTING THERE See map p314, E6
Ottawa is situated in the Canadian province of Ontario, around 280 miles (450 km) northeast of Toronto. The international airport is 20 minutes from downtown by cab.

GETTING AROUND
Ottawa is a pedestrian-friendly city, and the downtown core is well served by city buses. In February, skating on the frozen Rideau Canal is a required activity for visitors and residents alike.

WEATHER
At 16°F (–9°C), Ottawa's average daytime temperatures in February are brisk, while the nights are usually colder.

ACCOMMODATIONS
The Lord Elgin Hotel is warm and comfortable, and situated in the center of Ottawa; doubles from US$160; www.lordelginhotel.ca

Hotel Indigo has one-room suites from US$175; www.ottawadowntownhotel.com

Westin Ottawa offers doubles from US$225; www.thewestinottawa.com

EATING OUT
In Ottawa, expect to pay about US$25 per head at most family restaurants. For elegant, dining, try Wilfrid's at the Fairmont Château Laurier (US$55 per head for three courses).

FURTHER INFORMATION
www.ottawatourism.ca
www.ontariotravel.net

The World's Longest Rink

Stretching 125 miles (202 km) from Ottawa to Kingston, the Rideau Canal – a UNESCO World Heritage Site – was built as a safe route for military ships sailing from Kingston to Montréal. After the War of 1812, the British feared that the St. Lawrence River, a natural supply route, was prone to American attack. Yet, the canal was not used for military purposes. In 1970, its 5-mile (8-km) section winding through downtown Ottawa was groomed for skating. In 2005, the *Guinness Book of World Records* named it the world's longest skating rink.

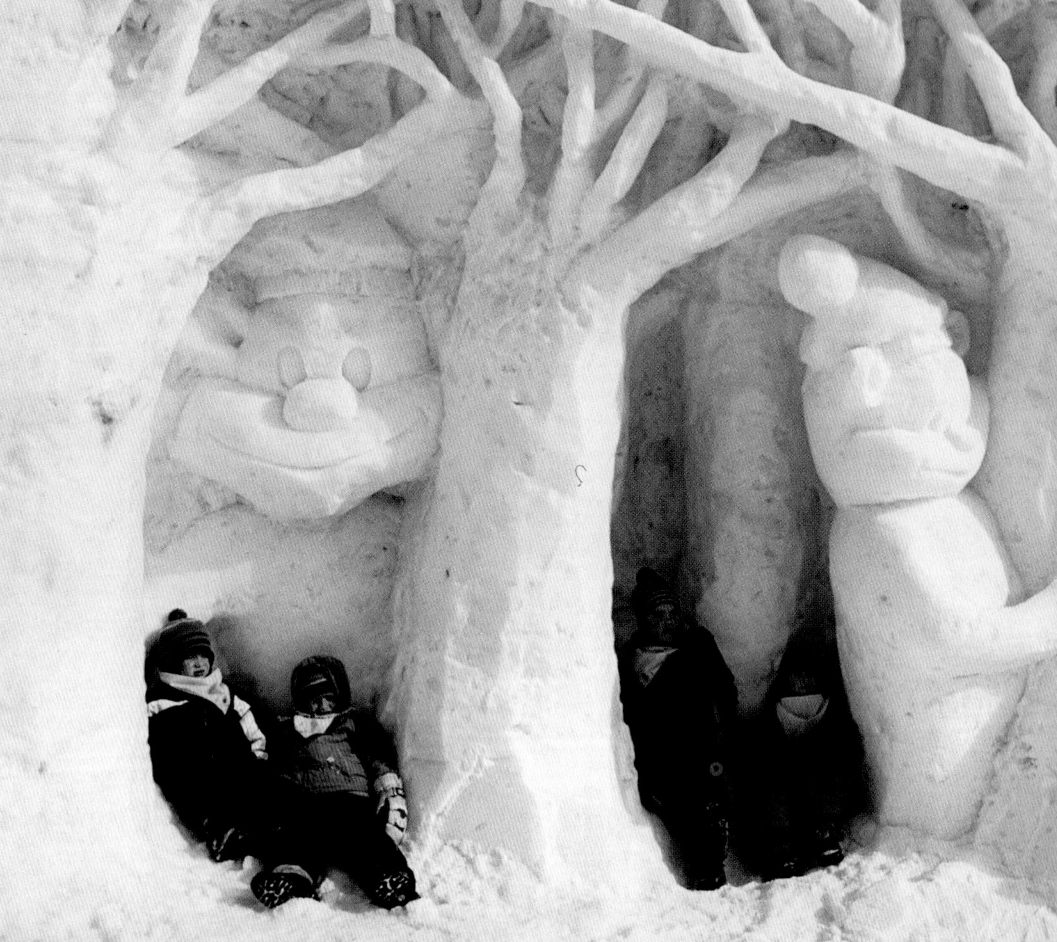

Inset: Facade of the Canadian Museum of History

Left (left and right): The cityscape at dusk; grand interior of the House of Commons

Right (left to right): One of the many snow sculptures made during Winterlude; an intricate ice sculpture at Confederation Park; visitors enjoying the ice slide at Jacques Cartier Park

Main: Children making the most of the snow in Ottawa during Winterlude

OTTAWA

SPACIOUS PARKS, EXCELLENT MUSEUMS, AND HISTORIC SITES GALORE – the culturally versatile and vibrant city of Ottawa has more than its fair share to entertain families at any time of year, but it's in February when Canada's capital city truly shines. The flavor of Ottawa stays festive, with the advent of Winterlude, featuring ice and snow sculptures, icy slides, and skating. The Rideau Canal springs to life with brightly clothed skaters, while the seasonal snow playground across the Ottawa River in Jacques Cartier Park rings from morning to dusk with the shouts and squeals of children flinging themselves downhill on snow slides. Keen hockey fans fill pubs across the city, cheering on the Senators in the hopes that this will be the year they bring home the coveted Stanley Cup.

February is also an excellent time to discover the city's museums and sights. If you have an airplane buff in your family, fly by the Canada Aviation and Space Museum, home to more than 130 vintage aircraft. Nearby, the

A snow playground in Jacques Cartier Park rings with the joyful squeals of kids flinging themselves downhill on snow slides.

RCMP Musical Ride Centre offers an inside peek at Canada's famous equine spectacle performed by the renowned Mounties – you can also see the stables and practice ring, discover how horses are named and raised, and pick up some Mountie memorabilia. Across the river, the Canadian Museum of History draws families with exhibitions focusing on Canadian and world history, and nature-themed movies on a huge IMAX screen. The building is also home to the Canadian Children's Museum, a hands-on place where kids can clamber aboard an elaborately decorated bus from Pakistan or try their hand at traditional crafts such as soapstone carving.

One of the great pleasures of winter in Ottawa is settling down to a leisurely restaurant meal. As snow drifts down outside, any eatery with a working fireplace will have it stoked with logs and glowing to ward off the chill. Menus offer rich, hearty fare from a wealth of culinary traditions, particularly French-Canadian. Adults and kids alike will enjoy thick slices of *tourtière* (meat pie), but *tarte au sucre* (sugar pie) might be a tad too sweet for calorie- and cavity-conscious grown-ups. Do make sure that your kids stick to a small serving, or you may be in for a long, sleepless night!

WINTERLUDE DIARY

Winter in Ottawa is all about enjoying the snow and ice. During Winterlude (the first three weekends of February) you'll need at least one long weekend to enjoy the city's attractions. The nation's capital is also home to over half-a-dozen national museums – great places to warm up between skiing and skating expeditions.

Four Frosty Days in Ottawa

DAY 1

Admire the glittering ice sculptures in Confederation Park, then tour the Neo-Gothic Parliament buildings. After lunch, take a cab to the Canadian Museum of Science and Technology, where vintage steam locomotives are family favorites. In the evening, catch an outdoor concert – be sure to dress warmly.

DAY 2

Mornings are the best time to rent skates and head to the Rideau Canal, just after the ice has had its overnight grooming. Skate to the Bank Street Bridge and then return your skates before you stop for shopping and a pub lunch either in Old Ottawa South or the Glebe. Walk along the Canal to Dows Lake, where you can take a jingling sleigh ride. Before heading back downtown, warm up with a cup of hot cider.

DAY 3

Walk or skate to the Canadian Museum of Nature, home to kid-pleasing dinosaurs.

Fuel up with a long and leisurely Sunday brunch before hitting the bustling Byward Market to browse for local crafts and maple syrup. Cap the day with a play or concert at the National Arts Centre.

DAY 4

Rent a car and head for the Gatineau Hills, across the river in Québec, for a day of gentle downhill skiing at Camp Fortune. In the evening, cheer on the National Hockey League's (NHL) Ottawa Senators in the Kanata, or West End.

Dos and Don'ts

- ✓ Ask your Parliament Hill guide to point out the faces lurking in the corners of elaborately carved ceilings. These carvings were done by the artists to immortalize themselves.
- ✗ When skating on the Rideau Canal, don't check your boots in at the kiosk. Carry them so you can change if you get tired.
- ✓ Buy hot packs for your boots and mittens from a local store.
- ✓ If you're skating with children, head to the Rideau Canal early to rent one of the popular sleds.
- ✗ Don't miss out on "beavertails," Ottawa's characteristic deep-fried pastries you can buy from huts along the Rideau Canal.

Below: Douglas DC-3 at the Canada Aviation and Space Museum

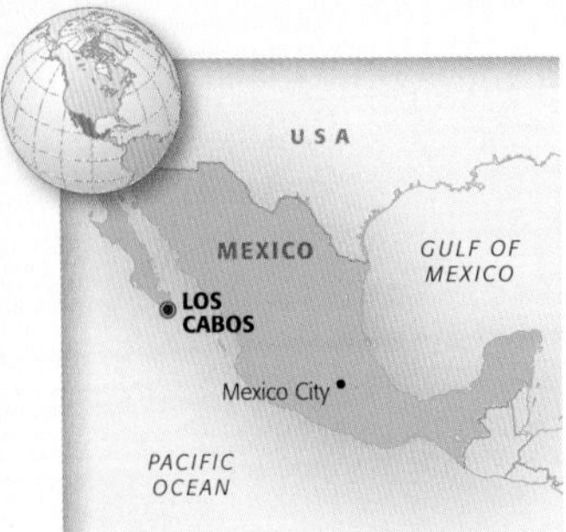

GETTING THERE See map p323, C4
Los Cabos International Airport is about 30 miles (48 km) from Cabo San Lucas and 8 miles (13 km) from San José del Cabo.

GETTING AROUND
It's easy to stroll around downtown Cabo San Lucas and San José del Cabo. Organized tours, taxis, public transportation, and rental cars and bikes are also available.

WEATHER
February temperatures average 80ºF (27ºC); but can drop to 60ºF (16ºC) in the evening. Sunscreen is recommended year-round.

ACCOMMODATIONS
Baja Bungalows in Cabo Pulmo Village offers solar-powered rooms with doubles from US$85; www.bajabungalows.com

Posada Real, San José del Cabo, includes a couple of restaurants and offers golf and fishing packages; doubles from US$215; www.posadareal-hotels.com

An all-inclusive golf and spa resort boasting a beachfront location, Grand Fiesta Americana has doubles from US$339; www.fiestaamericana.com

EATING OUT
Allow US$10–15 per person for breakfast and lunch, and US$15–25 per person for dinner at most Los Cabos restaurants.

FURTHER INFORMATION:
www.visitmexico.com
www.visitloscabos.travel

A Fragile Environment

The Sea of Cortez has one of the most pristine eco-systems on earth. Although development and economic exploitation pose threats to it, the Mexican government has initiated some safeguards. One such example is Cabo Pulmo National Marine Park, a 5-mile (8-km) stretch between southernmost Los Frailes and Pulmo Point on the East Cape. Home to three living reefs, including North America's only hard coral reef, this treasure of rich biodiversity contains hundreds of species of flora and fauna.

BAJA CALIFORNIA SUR

Poised at the tip of Mexico's Baja California Peninsula, which stretches nearly 1,061 miles (1,708 km) from the United States border and is almost physically separated from the Mexican mainland, stunningly scenic Los Cabos offers an abundance of activities on both land and sea. Postcard-perfect Finisterra (Land's End) is widely recognized for its eye-popping, naturally sculpted rock formations, including El Arco (The Arch) with its basking sealion colony, and Los Frailes (The Friars). Even more characteristic of the area is the contrast of rugged mountain ranges above startling cactus deserts that merge into white-sand beaches. Formerly a sleepy off-the-map fishing locale, much of the region has evolved into a celebrity haven and party zone. Collectively known as Los Cabos, the area comprises the tourist hub of Cabo San Lucas – a cruise port famed for its nightlife – on the Pacific side and the tranquil, traditional Mexican town of San José del Cabo, which nuzzles the Sea of Cortez (Gulf of California). In between these two sharply contrasting communities is the 20-mile (32-km) "corridor" with luxurious resorts and championship golf courses set atop rocky cliffs.

Humpback whales, dolphins, sealions, sea turtles, manta rays, and hundreds of marine-life species may be your companions at this teeming coral reef.

Although many tourists are content to hole up in their resorts, Los Cabos is also a magnet for adventurers seeking a wide range of experiences. World-class sportfishing for blue marlin is hugely popular, and during the gray whale migration season of mid-December through February, visitors flock to see these majestic mammals literally pop out of the sea. For closer viewing, you can join an excursion in a range of craft from high-speed inflatable Zodiacs to reach-out-and-touch-them small panga boats.

Along the shore near San José del Cabo, an estuary offers peaceful respite to approximately 200 native and migratory bird species, including egrets and brown pelicans. Protected and pristine, Cabo Pulmo National Marine Park on the Sea of Cortez offers superior scuba diving and snorkeling. Humpback whales, dolphins, sealions, turtles, manta rays, and hundreds of marine-life species may be your companions at this teeming coral reef.

Main: Gray whale breaching
Below (left and right): El Arco, Cabo San Lucas; horseback riding, Cabo San Lucas
Inset: Diver surrounded by a shoal of pork fish in the Sea of Cortez

WHALE DIARY

With warm temperatures and low humidity, February is a splendid month for a multitude of active adventures in this region, whether on land or in the water. Better still, it's prime time for viewing the gray whales which migrate each year from the cold waters of the Bering Sea to the bath-tub warm Pacific.

Four Days at Sea

DAY 1

Get your bearings on a sea-kayak ride in the blue Sea of Cortez, paddling to Finisterra where the calm sea meets the crashing surf of the Pacific Ocean with its much-photographed, nature-sculpted rock formations: El Arco and Los Frailes. Relax and soak up the sun at popular Playa del Amor (Lovers' Beach). Then explore or snorkel the Gulf's more secluded bays and coves, as well as the peaceful estuary near San José del Cabo, home to approximately 200 species of birds and other wildlife.

DAY 2

Sign up for an all-day snorkeling or scuba-diving excursion to the Cabo Pulmo Marine Park, about 60 miles (97 km) north of Los Cabos, on the Sea of Cortez. Surrounded by desert and mountains, the park features a living coral reef and is a haven to hundreds of varieties of marine life and passing manta rays, sea turtles, sealions, dolphins, and humpback whales.

DAYS 3–4

Pick and choose your favorite activities or try something new. Take a sportfishing excursion (the striped marlin and yellowfin tuna are usually biting this time of year), go parasailing above El Arco for an eagle-eye view, board a high-speed or easy-going vessel for a close-up visit to the gray and humpback whales, or pump adrenaline with an off-road safari through rural desert. If you are in need of something more relaxing after all the excitement this region has to offer, opt for a scenic horseback ride along one of Cabo San Lucas' beautiful beaches. Guided scenic rides are the best option, as the "cowboys" leading the tours point out local flora and fauna along the way.

Dos and Don'ts

- ✓ Although English is widely spoken in the area, learn a few pleasantries (hello, please, thank you, etc.) in Spanish.
- ✓ Taxi fares can be quite expensive in Los Cabos; negotiate with drivers before getting in the car.
- ✓ Check first before jumping into the waters of remote beaches; many have dangerous rip currents.
- ✓ Try to plan your trip outside the weekend, when you'll have fewer crowds to contend with.
- ✗ Don't drive after dark in Mexico, and don't drive at all without the requisite automobile insurance (non-Mexican policies are not valid).

Below: Inquisitive gray whale approaching a tour boat

GETTING THERE See map p325, B2
Several airlines serve Havana from Canada and Europe, and many fly from Central America. Charter flights link Havana to certain US cities for qualifying US travelers; regular flights are expected to become available by 2017 (see www.treasury.gov or havana.usembassy.gov).

GETTING AROUND
Old Havana is made for walking. Tourist taxis serve the city and are hailed outside hotels. Avoid buses and Cocotaxis. Chauffeur-driven classic autos cost around US$16 per hour from GranCar (www.cuba.cu/turismo/panatrans/grancar.htm).

WEATHER
February is usually dry, sunny, warm, and not too humid, with a daytime average of 75°F (24°C). Pack a jacket for evenings.

ACCOMMODATIONS
Many private room rentals are available; doubles from US$30; www.cubaparticular.com

Hotel Raquel is an Art Nouveau gem near the Old Town; doubles from US$250; www.hotelraquel-cuba.com

Hotel Nacional de Cuba is a 1930s classic with gardens overlooking the seafront; doubles from US$345; www.hotelnacionaldecuba.com

EATING OUT
Havana cuisine reflects a wide variety of African and South American influences and there are some very good restaurants to choose from. Try the fish soup at El Templete.

FURTHER INFORMATION
www.cubatravel.tur.cu/en

Cuban Cabaret

Sexy Las Vegas-style cabarets (*espectáculos*) have been a part of Cuban culture since the sizzling 1930s heyday of Havana. Even the Communist revolution didn't put a damper on these erotically charged shows featuring troupes of long-legged *mulattas* in skimpy, sensational outfits. Every town has at least one. The best of all is the Tropicana, which opened in Havana on New Year's Eve 1939, featured acts such as Carmen Miranda and Nat "King" Cole and his trio *(above)*, and still packs in the crowds for a night of "Paradise Under the Stars."

HAVANA

CUBA'S CAPITAL CITY, HAVANA, EXUDES EXOTICISM AND ECCENTRICITY. With its slightly surreal blend of colonialism and Communism, it is steeped, too, in an almost tangible 1950s, pre-revolutionary charm that is simply irresistible. Teeming with creativity and spontaneity, the city can rightly claim to be the cultural capital of the Caribbean. It's also a showcase of spectacular architecture. At its core, Habana Vieja (Old Havana) has been named a UNESCO World Heritage Site, with its 18th-century palaces, founded on the wealth brought by treasure fleets en route to Spain. Later, vast riches from sugar and slavery funded a new wave of lavish edifices, and cobbled plazas were enclosed by elegant confections in stone. In the 20th century, modern Havana was imbued with effusive Art Deco, Beaux Arts, and Modernist designs with a tropical twist. A restoration project, centered on four ancient

Main: The Tropicana's famous *Las Diosas de Carne* showgirls in action

Left: La Bodeguita del Medio bar

Right (left to right): Havana's colorful balconied buildings; locals passing the time with a game of dominoes; everyone seems to enjoy the huge Havana cigars

Right panel (top and bottom): Market stalls in front of the San Cristobál cathedral in Plaza de la Catedral; classic American autos of a bygone era

plazas, continues to transform historic buildings into hotels, restaurants, and eclectic museums that range from the grandiose Museo de la Revolución to the esoteric – such as the delightful Museo de Naipes (Museum of Playing Cards), on Plaza Vieja.

Havana's arts scene is the envy of Latin America. Cuba's fine literary tradition is written into the very soul of Plaza de Armas, where visitors and locals browse the outdoor used-book market, and bars such as El Floridita and La Bodeguita del Medio seem haunted by the spirit of Ernest Hemingway. The time-worn streets are lined with galleries. Music and dance, from sentimental *son* to sizzling salsa, are the pulsating undercurrents to Cuban life. High culture is epitomized by the world-class Ballet de Cuba but, for sheer entertainment, check out the sensational cabarets – a throwback to the days when Havana was something of a sin city. Many of the venues have hardly changed since the 1950s, offering a glimpse of a lost era, and drawing first-time visitors back for more.

HABANERO DIARY

February is an ideal month to visit Cuba, when humidity is at its lowest and walking Havana's streets in mild temperatures under cloudless skies is sheer bliss. In five days you'll have time to get a real flavor of *habanero* culture. And, even if you're not here at Mardi Gras time, you're likely to come across lively local festivals.

Five Days of Cuban Culture

DAY 1 Explore the heart of Habana Vieja, focusing on Plaza de la Catedral and Plaza de Armas. Break for a *mojito* (rum, lime, sugar, and mint) cocktail and lunch at the bustling, atmospheric La Bodeguita del Medio. Next, walk to Iglesia y Convento de San Francisco de Asis and Museo de Ron Havana Club (the sugar and rum museum). In the evening stroll the Malecón, the seafront promenade that teems with locals at sunset.

DAY 2 Today it's southern Habana Vieja, starting in and around Plaza Vieja. Take a look into the churches here and pause at the birthplace of Cuba's premier national hero, José Martí. In the evening, you could enjoy a choral concert at Iglesia y Convento de San Francisco.

DAY 3 From Parque Central, head for the Museo Nacional de Bellas Artes (Fine Arts Museum), the Museo de la Revolución, and the Capitolio Nacional. Visit the Partagás factory to see cigars being made, then stroll the Prado (Paseo de Martí). Dine at La Guarida before an evening dance performance at the spectacular Gran Teatro.

DAY 4 Hire a classic American auto and tour modern Havana, visiting the Hotel Nacional, Necropólis Cristobal Colón, and Plaza de la Revolución. Lunch at El Aljibe, then cross the harbor to El Morro and the Cabaña fortresses. Dine at a *paladar* (private restaurant), such as Hurón Azul.

DAY 5 Pay homage to Ernest Hemingway with a trip to Finca Vigía, his former home, and Cojímar, the setting for *The Old Man and the Sea*. Lunch at his favorite restaurant, La Terraza. Continue to Playas del Este to relax on the beach. Head back to the city center in time for a sensational finale at the Tropicana nightclub.

Dos and Don'ts

- ✓ Travel with perfect-condition cash notes to convert into Cuban pesos (CUCs). Be aware of the 11 percent tax added to all credit card payments
- ✗ Never buy cigars from a street vendor. Use government shops, and keep the receipt for customs.
- ✗ Don't carry any items of value when out in the streets. Take extra care of your camera, as snatch-and-grab is common.
- ✓ Consider a stay with a local family in a *casa particular* (private room rental), to get a feel for Cuban life.

Below: The view along the Malecón at sunset

GETTING THERE See map p317, G7
Located at the southern tip of Florida, Miami is served by most major airlines; rental cars are available at the airport.

GETTING AROUND
A car is essential to get to the various city neighborhoods, but once you arrive, each area is easy to explore on foot.

WEATHER
February average highs of 78°F (24°C) and lows of 60°F (16°C).

ACCOMMODATIONS
Mid-century modern rules at The Vagabond, a renovated hipster hangout, with a swanky bar and mermaid pool; doubles from US$139 per night; www.thevagabondhotel.com

For a truly romantic Miami Beach option, try The Hotel; doubles from US$225; www.thehotelofsouthbeach.com

In Coconut Grove, the Mayfair Hotel & Spa boutique hotel has doubles starting at US$359; www.mayfairhotelandspa.com

EATING OUT
Joe's Stone Crab is a South Beach institution, worth the wait in line. Cena by Mitchy on Biscayne Boulevard shows off the talents of top-rated chef Michelle Bernstein. In Little Havana, Versailles has been the spot for Cuban cuisine for nearly half a century, while Lulu in the Grove offers tasty tapas and outdoor seating.

FURTHER INFORMATION
www.miamiandbeaches.com

Sea of Waving Grass

Everglades National Park, a UNESCO World Heritage Site, is the largest subtropical wilderness in the USA. This sea of waving grass and wetlands is home to all manner of bird and animal life, including alligators, crocodiles, manatees, and egrets. A vast expanse of roughly 1.5 million acres (606,500 ha), the park offers solo hiking, or ranger-led tours, as well as air-boat tours and tram tours along a 15-mile (24-km) loop in the heart of the section known as the "River of Grass." Note that protection against biting insects is vital when visiting the Everglades.

Above (left to right): An Art Deco-style lifeguard hut, South Beach; Villa Vizcaya; sign for Calle Ocho, Little Havana
Main: The Colony Hotel in the heart of the Art Deco district

MIAMI

SULTRY, SIZZLING MIAMI HAS IT ALL: miles of sunny beach by day, pulsing nightlife, fine dining, trendy shopping, an exciting arts scene, and a vibrant cultural life. While there is a bustling commercial downtown, for many visitors Miami means Miami Beach. South Beach (the southernmost part of Miami Beach) is home to the city's unique interpretation of the Art Deco style, where hotels and other buildings constructed in the 1920s and 30s are decked out in funky pastels, bearing distinctively Floridian motifs such as flamingos and sunbursts. For many visitors, however, the Deco buildings are simply a backdrop for a hedonistic playground: days are for sleeping or relaxing on the beach; nights for serious partying. Fun-filled South Beach has a vibrant gay community, and for those who love to party, a legendary club scene offering myriad options for dancing the night away. Miami Beach is also an active arts conclave, home to the well-regarded Miami Ballet and to two museums, the Bass Museum of Art and the Wolfsonian. Beginning in the 1960s, an influx of Cubans fleeing Castro's regime swelled the city's population and gave Miami a unique Latin flavor and international air. A visit to vibrant Little Havana, with its authentic Cuban restaurants, is a must. It is enjoyable for its atmosphere and streetlife, with salsa beats pounding out from every other shop, as much as it is for its sights.

The scene shifts, however, in Coral Gables, a neighborhood of lush greenery and fine Mediterranean-style homes. Shoppers flock here for the boutiques and specialty stores along the "Miracle Mile" and the galleries, which showcase the best in Latin American art. Coconut Grove offers lots of off-beat vibrant shops to explore, but the more bohemian artists and stores have moved to Wynwood, an edgier neighborhood to the north of downtown. This used to be the Puerto Rican area of the city but has now become a hipster neighborhood.

For many visitors the Deco buildings are simply a backdrop for a hedonistic playground: days are for sleeping.

Inset: Art Deco building on Ocean Drive
Below (left and right): The pool at Biltmore hotel; Bayside Marketplace

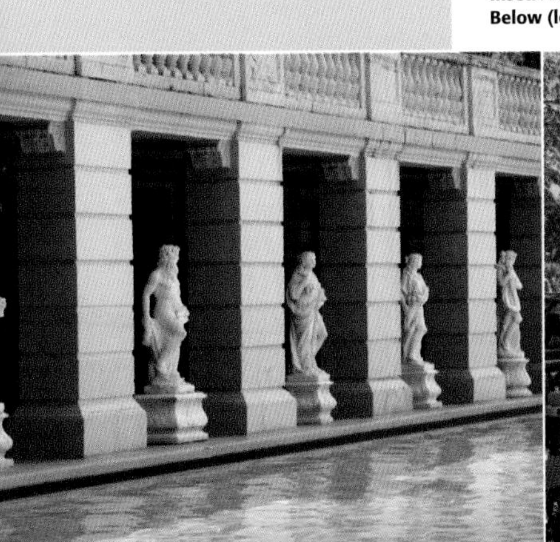

PLEASURE DIARY

Getting to know Miami means exploring its diverse neighborhoods and five days should allow time for a rich sampling of the city's offerings. February is perfect, with wonderful warm sunshine. Feel free to forget sightseeing when you prefer to spend time basking on the city's many glorious miles of beach.

Five Luxurious Days

DAY 1

Start with a morning walk in South Beach to admire the Art Deco architecture along Ocean Drive, followed by a long, romantic lunch and some shopping on Lincoln Road. Afterwards, visit the Bass Museum on Park Avenue. Take a nap in preparation for some late-night clubbing.

DAY 2

Admire the gleaming skyscrapers downtown and browse the shops at the Bayside Marketplace on Biscayne Bay. After a Cuban lunch on Calle Ocho in Little Havana, explore the open-air markets and cigar and music shops reflecting Cuban culture. Later in the afternoon, visit the museum and gardens of Miami's most famous mansion, Villa Vizcaya, on South Miami Avenue.

DAY 3

Today's the day for funky shops and avant-garde clothing stores amidst the tropical foliage of Coconut Grove. Have lunch in an outdoor café, then head north of downtown to the trendy arts and restaurant scene in Wynwood. The Walls of Wynwood offer a stunning mix of fine art and graffiti, and craft beers and innovative food abounds.

DAY 4

Coral Gables, developed in the 1920s, offers lush landscaping, vintage Spanish-style homes and romantic plazas with flowing fountains. Enjoy the exclusive shops and galleries and have lunch at the Biltmore, the luxurious 1920s classic hotel. Treat yourself to a blissful afternoon relaxing on the beach.

DAY 5

Take the hour drive to the Everglades and say hello to the alligators and egrets. Renting a canoe and following clearly marked, easy-to-navigate canoe trails is a great way for a close-up look at the wildlife.

Dos and Don'ts

- ✓ Visit Miami on Sunday to Thursday to get a better deal on hotels; weekend hotel rates are much higher.
- ✗ Don't bother going to a South Beach club early in the evening. The real action begins after midnight.
- ✓ Take a guided tour of the Art Deco district, offered by the Miami Design Preservation League on Wednesday, Saturday and Sunday at 10:30am. Self-guided tours are also available at the Art Deco Welcome Center at Ocean Front Auditorium, 1001 Ocean Drive.
- ✗ Don't forget a sun hat. That tropical sun is hot, hot, hot!

Below: Restaurants lining Lincoln Road

JAN FEB MAR APR MAY JUN JUL AUG SEP OCT NOV DEC

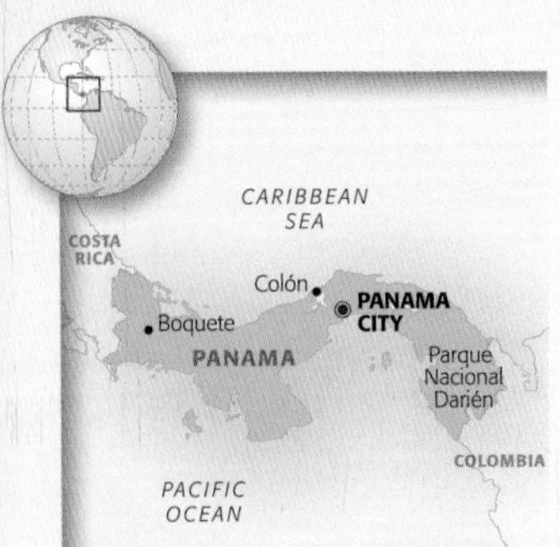

GETTING THERE **See map p324, H6**
Panama lies at the southern end of the Central American isthmus. Flights land at Tocumén International Airport outside Panama City. Boca del Toro and Boquete are served by flights from Costa Rica.

GETTING AROUND
Tocumén International Airport is a 20-minute taxi ride away from downtown; Air Panama offers domestic flights, while buses ply across the country. Guided birding tours are the best for maximizing your time.

WEATHER
The weather in February varies by region. Darién can get rain all year, and temperatures vary with elevation, from about 90ºF (32ºC) to 50ºF (10ºC) in the high mountains.

ACCOMMODATIONS
Canopy Tower Ecolodge in Parque Nacional Soberanía is dedicated to birding; doubles from US$129 for a minimum of two nights; www.canopytower.com

Boquete's Coffee Estate Inn has doubles from US$180 for a minimum of two nights; www.coffeeestateinn.com

Ancon Expeditions offers tours combining birding, hiking, ziplines, a coffee farm and cultural visits; from US$2,000 per person; www.anconexpeditions.com

EATING OUT
Panama has both cosmopolitan restaurants and eateries selling local fare. Boquete's Palo Alto Restaurante specializes in fresh trout.

FURTHER INFORMATION
www.fatbirder.com
www.anconexpeditions.com

Quetzal Country

Many bird-watchers visit Panama simply to spot the resplendent trogon, or quetzal – they're more numerous here than anywhere else in Central America. These denizens of the cloud forest were once worshiped by the ancient Maya for their iridescent green plumage. In springtime, the males woo their prospective mates by showing off their long tail plumes in swooping displays. Birders should listen for the quetzal's distinctive high-pitched, two-note whistle.

Main: A blue-and-gold macaw alongside a group of scarlet macaws

PANAMA

ENGULFED IN A THOUSAND SHADES OF GREEN, Panama is an emerald fantasia encompassing the Darién rain forests and the mist-shrouded cloud forests of Volcán Barú – home to the resplendent quetzal. An ecological crossroads between two continents and two oceans, this Lilliputian tropical land is Brobdingnagian when it comes to birds. Over 1,000 species inhabit ten distinct ecological zones, from coastal mangroves to dry deciduous forests.

A number of Panamanian tour companies specialize in birding, so there are plenty of competent guides with eagle eyes and an encyclopedic knowledge of bird habits and habitats. With such wild extremes of terrain and microclimates, the country never fails in its promise of phenomenal birding – over a quarter of the nation is protected as national parks, whose range and quantity of bird life is guaranteed to put a smile on any ornithologist's face. Coastal mudflats draw shorebirds in scores, their long bills jabbing at tasty morsels. Pick! Pick! Pick! The wetlands

Left (left to right): A keel-billed toucan; the rufous-crested coquette at the Canopy Lodge; the mist-shrouded Darién forest; tourists exploring the rain forest by aerial tram

Below: A hummingbird perching on a red heliconia

Inset: A watchful harpy eagle in Parque Nacional Soberanía

Massive harpy eagles sail overhead, talons at the ready, their hungry eyes scanning the forest canopy for sloths and monkeys.

are flush with fulvous whistling ducks and other waterfowl, many of them migrating between the Americas, and the cloud forests ring to the bell-like clang of the three-wattled bellbird. Pelicans, frigate birds, and boobies roost on the islands off the Azuero Peninsula and the thick rain forests reverberate with the squawks, whistles, and coos of their own unique avian fauna. Antbirds are easily seen as they scavenge for insects and lizards flushed out by columns of army ants, while chestnut-mandibled and keel-billed toucans are a dime a dozen. Parrots barrel past in jet-fighter formation: Panama boasts as many as 18 species, from the diminutive Panama Amazon to six species of giant macaw. Meanwhile, the massive harpy eagle – the national bird – sails overhead, talons at the ready, its hungry eyes scanning the forest canopy for sloths and monkeys.

Panama is the ultimate pilgrimage for birders keen to spot the Holy Grail of neotropical birds – the quetzal. This emerald jewel of the cloud forest is more abundant here than anywhere else in Central America. It's no wonder, then, that birders flock to this paradise like migrating macaws.

BIRDER'S DIARY

Blessed with varied terrain spanning from shoreline to high-altitude cloud forests, Panama boasts an astonishingly profuse bird population. February – the peak of dry season – is the best time to visit, when several migratory species are present. You'll need at least ten days to cover the best of the diverse ecosystems.

Ten Days in Avian Paradise

DAY 1

In the morning, drive to the Parque Nacional Soberanía, which is home to some 525 species of birds. At the Rainforest Discovery Center spot canopy bird species from the 100-ft (30-m) observation tower.

DAYS 2–4

The Fort San Lorenzo National Park is a good spot to search for diurnal raptors, the rufous-crested coquette, Montezuma oropendola and brown-hooded parrot. Catch a mid-morning flight to David and then transfer to the town of Volcan. After lunch spend your afternoon on the Janson Coffee Farm grounds. Visit La Amistad, a Biosphere Reserve and UNESCO World Heritage Site, and then drive to Baru Volcano National Park.

DAYS 5–7

Finca Ceriana houses 25 acres (10 ha) of protected land and one of the most beautiful views to Costa Rica's Golfo Dulce. After a picnic lunch, head to Boquete, which is surrounded by farms and coffee plantations. Explore Finca Lerida Cloud Forest, a privately owned preserve. At an elevation of 7,500 ft (2,286 m) above sea level, you have an opportunity to see the elusive resplendent quetzal and long-tailed silky flycatcher.

DAYS 8–10

Fly to Panama City, and enjoy a scenic 4–5 hour drive along the Pan-American Highway, to Puerto Quimba, Darién. Travel by motor boat along the Tuira River to the Punta Patiño Nature Reserve where naturalists lead wetland walks. On your final day embark on a motorized dugout canoe and head for the Mogue River. Search for the national bird, the harpy eagle. Return to the village in the afternoon to meet the Embera people and learn about their customs.

Dos and Don'ts

- ⊗ Don't forget to bring a strong insect repellent to keep away "chiggers" – parasitic mites that are plentiful in the tropics.
- ✓ Hire a professional guide. You'll see far more birds in their company.
- ⊗ Don't wear bright clothing. Birds are more relaxed and visible when humans blend into the landscape.
- ✓ Do carry a good pair of binoculars as well as a tripod for your camera.

Below: Sunlight pouring through the branches of trees in the rain forest

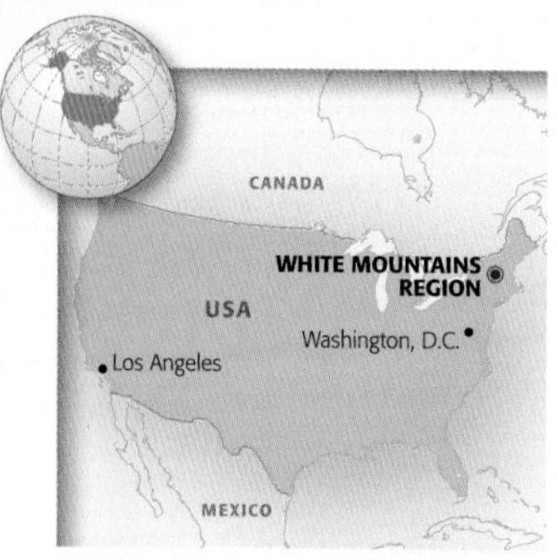

GETTING THERE **See map p316, H3**

The White Mountains are about 75 miles (120 km) north of the Manchester, New Hampshire regional airport and about 135 miles (217 km) north of Boston's Logan International Airport.

GETTING AROUND

Most scenic towns in the area are compact and walkable, but public transportation between towns is patchy; a car is essential.

WEATHER

With temperatures averaging around 35°F (1°C) and moderate snowfalls, February is a perfect time for winter sports fans.

ACCOMMODATIONS

Lincoln's Kancamagus Lodge, at the base of Loon Mountain, has an indoor pool and games room for relaxing; doubles from US$125; www.kancamaguslodge.com

Franconia Inn, a skiing base with breathtaking views of Franconia Notch; packages available from US$440; doubles from US$150; www.franconiainn.com

The photo-ready Omni Mt. Washington Resort has formal and informal dining options; doubles from US$259; www.omnihotels.com

EATING OUT

Apart from hotel restaurants, visitors face a surprising number of dining options in towns like Woodstock and North Conway.

FURTHER INFORMATION

www.skinh.com
www.visitwhitemountains.com

Dog Days of Winter

If visiting the region in early February, a trip to the Laconia World Championship Sled Dog Derby is a must. First held in 1929, the race's primary course, 18 miles (29 km) long, traverses the area's numerous lakes, and snakes through the woods. Competitors primarily come from the USA and Canada, with a few Europeans making their way over. Several secondary competitions are held as well, including a 6-mile (9-km), six-dog race and a junior-level three-dog race. The event is good for families, as kids can get close to the action.

Above (left to right): Lake Winnipesaukee at sunset; a climber; Mount Washington **Main:** Downhill thrills on Loon Mountain

WHITE MOUNTAINS REGION

PRISTINE MOUNTAIN TRAILS, FRESHWATER STREAMS, CRYSTAL-CLEAR SKIES: the White Mountains Region's abundant natural beauty is a wonder to behold any time of year. Some prefer it during the holidays, when festive sleigh rides provide thrills for the whole family. Others enjoy the autumn months for world-class leaf color amid breathtaking scenery. But for winter sports fanatics, from downhill speed skiers to cross-country walkers, February is the perfect time for a visit.

The region's numerous mountains hold top-notch downhill and cross-country trails for skiers of all levels. Nature-lovers can ditch the skis in favor of snowshoes and head out on lengthy walks, stopping to appreciate excellent bird-watching opportunities. Thrill-seekers can speed down luge runs, while the less adventurous can hop on inner tubes to glide down groomed hills. The list of available snow-based activities, including snowmobiling and ice fishing, just goes on and on. Located in northern New Hampshire, the White Mountains range covers nearly 25 percent of the state's land. At 6,288 ft (1,917 m), its highest peak, Mount Washington, is also the tallest summit in the northeastern USA and is famously inhospitable in winter. The weather observatory at the top (which is accessible in summer by road, hiking trail, and cog railway) has recorded some of the harshest weather in the country.

Quaint towns – the kind that New England is renowned for – line the lakes, and when it comes to town-to-town travel, personal pleasure boats are just as popular as cars. For decades, visitors of all kinds have appreciated the peace and quiet offered to them by towns such as Woodstock or Lincoln, virtues also recognized by thousands of Bostonians and New Yorkers who have second homes hereabouts. Old-fashioned general stores and inviting art galleries add to the area's attractions. Aspen it is not, but any drive through the White Mountains is truly a scenic one.

The list of available snow-based activities, including snowmobiling and ice fishing, just goes on and on.

Inset: Cannon Mountain cable car, Franconia
Below (left and right): The Swift River; a snowboarder takes off

WINTERTIME DIARY

The ideal depth of snow in the mountains in winter is never guaranteed. However, if timed right, February visitors can enjoy the year's best skiing conditions. And, if there's no snow on the ground, there are still plenty of outdoor activities to enjoy, and several quaint and historic towns waiting to be discovered.

Three Days of Outdoor Thrills

DAY 1

Start things off in the picturesque small town of North Woodstock, and the neighboring burg of Lincoln, where Alpine Adventures offers interesting snowshoe tours, or ziplining for the slightly more adventurous. Then head north to Loon Mountain for an afternoon of skiing or snowboarding. If the conditions aren't good, there's an indoor climbing wall. Stick around for the après-ski scene and share stories of near-misses with fellow snowbirds.

DAY 2

Drive to Franconia, where Cannon Mountain's 80-passenger cable car provides breathtaking views of the region (Fri–Mon in winter). Take an intense hike through the White Mountain National Forest, being sure not to deviate from the paths for fear of getting lost in the wild. If the weather's too much to handle, escape the elements by popping into the New England Ski Museum. Finish the day with a peek inside the grand red-roofed Omni Mount Washington Resort. Opened in 1902, it is the site of the conference that established the World Bank and gold standard in 1944. The hotel is also said to be the inspiration for Stephen King's thriller *The Shining* (1977).

DAY 3

Give your body a rest and sleep in before heading east to North Conway for mountain information and supplies, and then north to Jackson. The town is home to one of the country's top locations for cross-country skiing and the energetic should spend the rest of the day exploring this way under the imposing glare of Mount Washington.

Dos and Don'ts

- ✓ Carry a cell phone at all times, especially when driving or engaging in any activities off the beaten track or alone.
- ✗ Don't be too fashionable. To avoid frostbite or hypothermia, wear the right gear. Cover all body parts, especially the head, ears, toes, and fingers.
- ✓ When pursuing outdoor activities, get hold of a good map, as not all trails (hiking or cross-country skiing) are signposted.
- ✓ Bring comfortable footwear, as the compact town centers lend themselves to lots of on-foot exploration.

Below: Hikers enjoying the view, the White Mountains

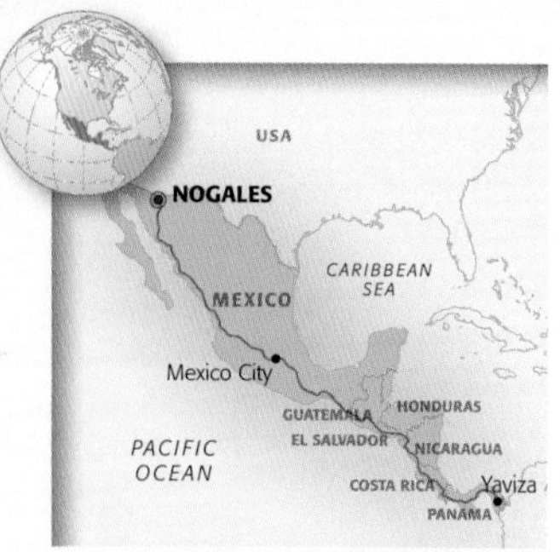

GETTING THERE **See map p323, C2, and p324**
Rental cars cannot cross national borders. Buying an inexpensive vehicle for the purpose of your journey is possible, but may come with complications. The entire journey amounts to 4,000 miles (6,500 km).

GETTING AROUND
The road can be bad so use a 4WD vehicle. There is public transport along the route, but it is not always reliable.

WEATHER
The highway passes through diverse climates and a variety of terrains. Go in February, the dry season, as sections may be impassible in other seasons.

ACCOMMODATIONS
The graciously modern Hotel Playa Mazatlán in Mazatlán, Mexico, offers doubles from US$129; www.playamazatlan.com

Hostal de la Noria, a restored colonial mansion in Oaxaca, Mexico, offers junior suites from US$85; www.hostaldelanoria.com

Hotel Posada de Don Rodrigo has old-world charm in Antigua, Guatemala; doubles from US$150; www.posadadedonrodrigo.com

Hostal Casa De Campo Country Inn is a cozy hostelry east of Panama City; doubles from US$120; www.panamacasadecampo.net

EATING OUT
Avoid street food, but try *gallo pinto* (rice, black beans, chicken or pork, and plantains).

FURTHER INFORMATION
www.drivetheamericas.com

End of the Road

The Inter-American Highway dead-ends at Yaviza, south of Panama City, near the largest tract of pristine rain forest in Central America. This "Darién Gap" is a notoriously inhospitable world of swamps and jungle within the 2,236 sq mile (5,791 sq km) Parque Nacional Darién. Panama is resisting calls to extend the highway, fearing ecological disaster: since the completion of the road to Yaviza, much of the rain forest in the region has disppeared.

Main: The Inter-American Highway stretching southwards past the New Millennium Panama Canal Bridge

INTER-AMERICAN HIGHWAY

A DRIVE FOR THE ADVENTUROUS, the Inter-American Highway offers one of the most extraordinary car trips in the world. Unfurling through Mexico, Guatemala, El Salvador, Honduras, Nicaragua, Costa Rica, and into Panama, the journey conjures up a whirligig of astonishing landscapes and colorful drama.

For the first leg of your drive, begin in Nogales, on the Arizona border, and take Highway 15 south along the palm-fringed beaches of Mexico's Pacific coast. Then, head into the highlands for Mexico City, where you pick up the "official" Inter-American Highway, and Oaxaca, known for its spring-like climate, colonial architecture, and chromatic fiestas. Crucible of ancient cultures, Guatemala astounds with its temple ruins and blazingly colored Mayan dress while neighboring El Salvador welcomes visitors with smiling faces and volcanic landscapes of surreal allure. Next up, Honduras is lent vibrancy by its celebrations, such as the February Feast of Our Lady of Suyapa, in

Left (left to right): Painted terra-cotta figurines in Nogales, Mexico; boats at harbor on Mexico's Pacific Coast; colonial-era doorway in Mazatlán, Mexico; Guatemalan women in traditional handwoven dresses

Below: Howler monkeys in Costa Rica's verdant rain forests

Inset: Kayaking in the Sea of Cortez

One minute you're winding through mile-high mountains, then the next you're plunging into lush valleys cloaked in subaqueous greens.

Tegucigalpa. Slow down through Nicaragua to soak in the yesteryear pace of Granada. And Costa Rica? This country delivers on its fame for wildlife, from howler monkeys to scarlet macaws.

One minute you're winding through mile-high mountains, then the next you're plunging into lush valleys cloaked in subaqueous greens. It's not a race, so take time for inviting detours: to the base of the Copper Canyon in Mexico, the Cobán ruins in Guatemala, Volcán Arenal in Costa Rica, perhaps even a boat ride on the Panama Canal. The highway is paved the entire way before withering down to a dirt track in the rain forests of Panama's Darién Gap – an impassable 55-mile (89 km) swathe of dense jungle separating Central and South America. Yaviza, a vaguely menacing frontier town, is worth the visit only to boast that you made it to the end.

Punctures and border delays are part of the equation. Localized flares-ups, bandito activity, landslides, or flooding may necessitate changes of route. Unpredictability is part of the adventure, but the lasting impressions are entirely positive on this journey to the center of the earth.

DRIVER'S DIARY

February guarantees you plenty of glorious sunshine, although you'll likely face rain at some stage. A month allows enough time to drive the highway's full length without rushing, as the span is well worth exploring, offering vibrant culture, serene beaches, enigmatic Mayan ruins, and rain forests teeming with life.

A Month in Central America

Leave Nogales for Guaymas, on the Sea of Cortéz. After a night by the shore, it's onward to Mazatlán via the Highway 15 toll road. Then over the mountains to Guadalajara, with time to savor this flavorful city. **DAYS 1–5**

Continue to Mexico City. Linger a day, and next day turn south for Oaxaca, a World Heritage Site steeped in colonial atmosphere. You'll probably want to spend a day sightseeing in this lovely city. **DAYS 6–9**

Descend the rugged Sierra Madre del Sur mountains and follow the Pacific Coast Highway via Tapachula to Guatemala City, with time to take in festivals and Mayan culture, before continuing to San Salvador. **DAYS 10–13**

Head east for Choluteca, in the extreme south of Honduras. Crossing into Nicaragua, you can bypass the capital city as you head on the mostly flat highway to the Costa Rican border at Peñas Blancas. **DAYS 14–17**

The ruler-straight Inter-American Highway slices through savannah country before climbing into the volcanic highlands, then snaking down to San Ysidro de General. Two days is a minimum for a side-journey to Volcán Arenal, and you may well choose to spend several more days exploring Nicoya *(see pp288–9)*. **DAYS 18–24**

Crossing into Panama, take the short diversion to picturesque Boquete, a bird-watcher's paradise *(see pp42–3)*. Then the fast-paced highway delivers you east via Panama City to the Darién region, where the tarmac turns to dirt well before the end of the road. **DAYS 25–30**

Dos and Don'ts

- ✓ Buy a set of accurate maps and do not drive at night.
- ✗ Don't rent a car for the journey as rental cars cannot cross national borders. You will have to own your vehicle.
- ✓ Carry plenty of essential spare parts, plus a spare can of gasoline, and an emergency kit in case of breakdown.
- ✗ Plan ahead, and check the conditions down the road during your journey. Get Temporary Vehicle Import Permits and visas for each country in advance (except US and Canadian citizens).
- ✓ Plan for the possibility of being turned back by the military in Darién as foreigners are not always allowed as far as Yaviza.

Below: Rivers of fire on the magnificent Volcán Arenal at night

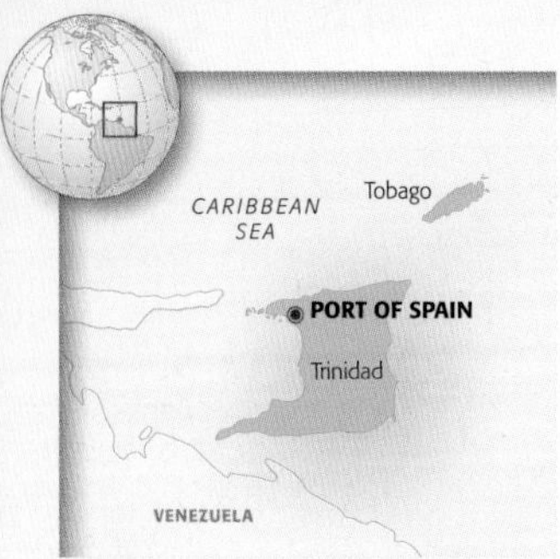

GETTING THERE See map p325, I6
Trinidad's Piarco International Airport is 20 miles (30 km) from Port of Spain. Authorized taxis have fixed fares to various island destinations (about US$30 to Port of Spain).

GETTING AROUND
Car rental is available at the airport or can be arranged by your hotel. Buses and route taxis follow scheduled routes and are cheap. Taxis can be used for short trips or day-long tours.

WEATHER
Trinidad is always sunny and warm, but now is the driest time of year. Temperatures are around 83°F (29°C) by day, 65°F (18°C) at night.

ACCOMMODATIONS
The intimate Maracas Bay Hotel is on the island's most beautiful beach; doubles from US$110; www.maracasbay.com

The luxurious Trinidad Hilton is built on a hill, with fantastic views; doubles from US$159; www.hiltoncaribbean.com

Kapok Hotel in St. Clair has rooftop dining and it's an easy walk to downtown Port of Spain; doubles from US$181; www.kapokhotel.com

EATING OUT
Dining options range from beach stall snacks at less than US$5 to fine international dining. The island's Indian heritage is evident in the food, with many vegetarian options.

FURTHER INFORMATION
www.gotrinidadandtobago.com

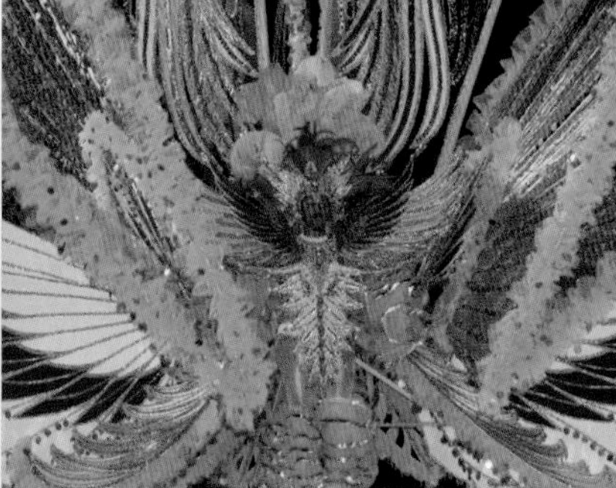

Above (left and right): Local reveler dancing to the Parade of the Bands; competitor in the King and Queen of Carnival contest

TRINIDAD

THE MELLIFLUOUS SOUNDS OF CALYPSO WERE BORN IN TRINIDAD. Lilting tunes, pulsating rhythms, and heartfelt lyrics form the soundtrack to life here, rising and falling on the warm island breeze every day of the year. This native beat is at its very best during Carnival week. This is the biggest party in the West Indies, when thousands of people descend on the island for five hedonistic days, transforming the dusty streets and picturesque beaches into a riot of color, sound, and motion.

Introduced by French settlers in the late 18th century, over the years Carnival has become an unashamedly exuberant celebration of freedom, and today's revelers swarm the capital city, Port of Spain, and party with unbridled energy. Thronged with fantastically costumed partygoers in ornate masks and gleaming jewels, who dance and drink long into the night, the streets of the historic Savannah district are lined with performers, arts and crafts stalls, and sizzling barbecues, while the tuneful, metallic sounds of steel bands playing calypso, soca, and limbo music fill the air. It is sensory overload. Keep your strength up with street food, such as *roti* (a flatbread rolled with curried chicken or pork); "doubles" (two fried flatbreads filled with curried beans); and *pholourie* (fried split-pea flour balls with sweet chutney sauce). "Shark and bake" stands offer highly seasoned, mouthwatering shark dishes.

J'Ouvert, one of Carnival's main parades, begins before dawn. Dominated by soca music it is attended by increasingly mud- and paint-slathered revelers, most of whom are still going from the night before. The highlight, however, is the Parade of the Bands, which takes place on the last day, when the bands, some with 200 or more pan drummers, parade through the streets accompanied by their splendidly costumed supporters. It's an unforgettable sight. To be named Calypso Monarch, or top steel band, is one of the island's greatest honors, and adds a competitive edge to the intoxicating atmosphere.

As well as the main attractions of Carnival, there are hundreds of other smaller events taking place, including fringe musical performances, competitions, and bustling markets. All you need is the stamina to keep on partying.

The Steel Drum

Steel drums, which are at the heart of the Carnival, originated in Port of Spain in the 1930s. They were originally carried on a neck-strap – hence the Pan Around the Neck Festival that precedes Carnival in early February. Plantation-owners banned African drums because they thought their slaves used them to send messages. The slaves improvized with gourds, stretched goatskins and whatever else was at hand. The steel pan is the latest example of this ingenuity.

Main: "Moko Jumbie" stilt-walkers in procession before the Parade of the Bands
Below (left and right): The beach at Maracas Bay; Queen's Royal College, in Port of Spain's historic Savannah district

CALYPSO DIARY

Port of Spain boasts the biggest, best, and brashest carnival in the Caribbean, held just before Lent. The official event lasts five days but the must-see parades are on the Monday and Tuesday. Spend the first day acclimatizing, then join in the party on days two and three. You'll be recovering for the last two days!

Five Sensational Days

SUN

Start *Dimanche Gras* (Fat Sunday) by relaxing on Maracas beach, then head for the center of Port of Spain to get caught up in the Carnival atmosphere. Relish great street snacks, cooked in front of you, and enjoy the loud, loud music. Then get an early night.

MON

Wake up early because the first J'Ouvert (pronounced "jou-vay") revelers are on the streets well before dawn wearing *ole mas* (old costumes) or rags and daubing themselves (and each other) with mud and paint. As the day progresses and the music gets louder everyone, including you, should be dancing, eating, and drinking.

TUE

Get up early again and head for Savannah, along with hundreds of thousands of other revelers. First, the fabulously costumed marchers make their way through the streets, accompanied by deafening, foot-tapping music. Then comes the Parade of the Bands itself, with tens of thousands of enthusiastic musicians and their supporters. Dance until the music stops.

WED

Have a lie-in, then visit the splendid National Museum and Art Gallery to learn more about the island's rich past. In the evening enjoy a moonlit dinner by the sea.

THU

Spend the day seeing the real Trinidad at the ASA Wright Nature Center on the Spring Hill Estate, a 90-minute drive from Port of Spain. While sipping a cold drink on the center's verandah, and without walking a step, you can see an amazing number of exotic birds including 18 types of hummingbird.

Dos and Don'ts

- ✓ Join in the celebrations. It may by noisy and tumultuous but it is all in fun and everyone is there to have a good time.
- ✗ Don't carry your passport, wear expensive jewelry, or flash large sums of money, and don't stray off the main thoroughfares.
- ✓ Take taxis or shuttle buses to and from the celebrations, especially late at night.
- ✓ Try the street snacks – they are safe and very tasty.
- ✗ Don't forget they drive on the left here – take extra care when crossing the street or if driving a rental car.

Below: White-necked Jacobin hummingbird at ASA Wright Nature Center

GETTING THERE See map p328, H7
Salvador lies on Brazil's northeastern coast. The international airport, Deputado Luis Eduardo Magalhães, is 21 miles (34 km) north of the city. Taxis from the airport to Pelourinho are around US$30, the bus is US$2.50.

GETTING AROUND
Taxis are recommended in the evening for safety, during the day visitors can get around on foot quite easily.

WEATHER
During Carnival expect hot, sunny days with a maximum temperature around 86°F (30°C).

ACCOMMODATIONS
For Carnival, you should reserve your hotel accommodation 3–6 months in advance, and there is usually a minimum stay of 5 nights.

F Design Hostel is a wacky design hostel; doubles from US$40; www.fdesignsalvador.com.br

Convento do Carmo is centrally located in an old convent; doubles from US$170; www.pestana.com/uk/hotel/pestana-convento-do-carmo

Villa Bahia is set in two magnificent colonial mansions; doubles from US$260; en.lavillabahia.com/pousada-bahia

EATING OUT
Local cuisine focuses on seafood, often served in *moqueca* stews, with coconut milk, spices and palm oil. A large meal will cost around US$18.

FURTHER INFORMATION
home.centraldocarnaval.com.br

The Room of Miracles

Salvador's symbolic church, Nosso Senhor do Bonfim, is famous for its power to perform miracles. Inside, in the *Sala dos Milagres (*Room of Miracles), grateful worshipers have hung replica heads, limbs, and organs to give thanks for miracles performed curing their afflicted body parts. The ostensibly Catholic church is also frequented by followers of the Afro-Brazilian religion *Candomblé*, which combines seemingly irreconcilable elements of Catholic worship with African spiritualist traditions.

Main: Celebrating Carnival in style, hundreds of thousands of partygoers dance in the streets
Above (top to bottom): Historic upper town of Pelourinho; woman in traditional Bahian dress; endless sandy coastline of Bahia

SALVADOR

FORGET THE FEATHERS AND FLOATS AND GIRLS IN TINY BIKINIS, and forget all notions of being a merely passive observer. The Salvador Carnival (Carnaval to the locals) is all about participation. Two million revelers flock to the Bahian capital to celebrate in an extravagant week-long street party. Hundreds of musicians, many of them Brazil's biggest names, perform musical marathons, singing and dancing for many hours, night after day after night.

Each band, or *bloco,* performs on a massive sound truck called a *trio elétrico*, a stage and multigigawatt monster sound system combined. Pied piper-like, the performers are followed by supporters, often dressed in specially co-ordinated outfits, and an excited crowd dancing in a musical frenzy as the truck slowly wends its way through narrow streets. Behind, in front and all around the *trios*, hundreds of thousands of people gather for the sheer fun of it – to drink, sing, and dance, to kiss a perfect stranger, make instant friends, and the next day do it all over again.

Above: Elaborate gilded interior of Igreja São Francisco Salvador da Bahia

Below: Costumed dancer representing the God of Medicine in a ritual *Candomblé* dance.

If you want, you can buy an *abadã* (a t-shirt-as-ticket) that allows access to a large roped-off area immediately behind the stage truck. Dozens of rope-carriers hold the rope ensuring that the cordon stays intact as the throng moves through the streets. Or you can opt to be a *pipoca* (a popcorn) and bop around in the slightly more unruly crowd on the fringes of the roped-off area.

As well as the big names of Brazilian music that perform regularly at Carnival, including Daniela Mercury, Gilberto Gil, and Carlinhos Brown, there are dozens more traditional, community-based *blocos*. The Afro-Brazilian *bloco* Ilê Ayê kicks off Carnival with a Candomblé ceremony the night before the parade. The Filhos de Gandhi (Sons of Gandhi) are a popular all-male *bloco*, who parade dressed in white Gandhi robes to the sound of African Afoxé drumming.

On Shrove Tuesday, the very last night of Carnival when most of the rest of Brazil is already sleeping, Carnival in Salvador comes to a dramatic close with the "Meeting of the Trios." In the early hours of Ash Wednesday morning, all the *blocos* that are still parading head to Praça Castro Alves and join together for a last joint concert, one that ends just as the sun rises over Salvador.

SALVADOR DIARY

Carnival is a last wild celebration before the 40 days of Lenten abstinence. The dates change every year due to the lunar cycle, but Carnival always takes place in February or early March. If you stay for the full five days you'll be able to join in the fun but relax and rest as well.

The Biggest Party in the World

FRI

Explore the historic Pelourinho quarter, the Afro-Brazilian museum, and the Convent of São Francisco.

Early in the evening, locals and musicians will start to gather for the more traditional *blocos* which parade through the narrow streets from about 7pm to 2am.

SAT

Save your energies for a full evening of Carnival and spend a leisurely day at one of the ocean beaches such as Stella Maris or Flamengo.

Enjoy a late lunch of *moqueca* to fuel up. In the evening, grab your *abadã* (the t-shirt that admits you to a *bloco*), and get dancing.

SUN

Enjoy some of the traditional sights around downtown. Start with the Bonfim church then stop in at the Mercado Modelo for some fine souvenir shopping.

Head over to the nearby Solar do Unhão. This restored 18th-century sugar mill and mansion now houses Salvador's Museum of Modern Art (Bahia MAM). Come sundown, you still have your *abadã*, so go and dance.

MON

Spend a day on the water by taking a schooner tour of the islands around the Baía de Todos os Santos.

Around 5pm head to the Barra Lighthouse to catch the sunset and secure yourself a good spot to watch the evening's *trios* as they parade past.

TUE

On the last night of Carnival don't miss the "Meeting of the Trios," a final musical get-together which takes place in the small hours of the morning of Ash Wednesday at the Praça Castro Alves.

Dos and Don'ts

- ✓ Wear comfortable shoes, shorts, or a skirt with a pocket and a light t-shirt. Leave your valuables at home and carry only enough cash for the day.
- ✗ Don't procrastinate. Those visiting Salvador for Carnival should book their flights and hotels at least three months ahead of time, if not more, as they fill up quickly.
- ✓ See as many different *blocos* as possible. Even if you buy an *abadã* for one *bloco* or *trio*, you can still mix and match to experience a number of others.
- ✗ Don't sleep in too late if you want to do some sightseeing. The easiest time to get around before the crowds gather is between 10am and 2pm.

Below: Pawpaws, pineapples, and bananas hanging from a street stall

MARCH

Where to Go: **March**

The third week in March brings the spring equinox to the northern hemisphere, and spring has certainly sprung in the United States. Historic Boston, beginning to warm up after a long winter, offers beer-soaked fun for St. Patrick's Day, while the southern states, and the deserts of the west, are coming into bloom. The bulk of Canada, on the other hand, has barely begun to thaw – indeed, the west of the country offers the best skiing at this time of year. Sun-seekers may want to head south to Central America, the Caribbean islands, or Mexico, to make the most of those countries' dry seasons before summer descends in all its sticky glory. Below you will find all the destinations in this chapter as well as some extra suggestions to provide a little inspiration.

FESTIVALS AND CULTURE

BOSTON Irish dancers in colorful costumes

BOSTON
MASSACHUSETTS, USA

Irish eyes are smiling at the St. Patrick's Day celebrations

This historic city turns shamrock green for the day, with parades, music, and dance to honor Ireland's patron saint. Even the beer is green!

See pp62–3

CALLE OCHO
MIAMI, FLORIDA, USA

The USA's biggest street party and Hispanic festival

Drawing over a million visitors every March, Miami's huge street party features plenty of Cuban rum, Caribbean food, and salsa galore.

www.carnavalmiami.com

ANTIGUA
GUATEMALA

A joyful celebration of Semana Santa in a pretty colonial city

Carpets of petals cover the streets for processions of religious statues carried by the joyful locals. Enjoy, too, the colonial architecture.

www.visitguatemala.com

AUSTIN
TEXAS, USA

The USA's favorite town of tunes

Music pours out of Austin's bars nightly, and especially during the legendary South by Southwest (SXSW) music festival.

See pp58–9

MEXICO CITY
MEXICO

Join the party in the city where the drumbeat never stops

From ancient ruins to world-class art, Mexico City has it all. Explore its cultural delights, then party at a fiesta in the Zócalo.

See pp60–61

SAN FRANCISCO
CALIFORNIA, USA

California's most cultured city

San Francisco has exceptional museums and performing arts venues, as well as an appealing café culture established by writers and artists in the 1950s.

www.onlyinsanfrancisco.com

UNFORGETTABLE JOURNEYS

NATCHEZ TRACE The formal gardens at Monmouth plantation

NATCHEZ TRACE
MISSISSIPPI, USA

Historic mansions and a warm Southern welcome

Take a leisurely drive up this ancient trail that features lush scenery, antebellum plantation houses, and Civil War memories.

See pp68–9

PICO DUARTE
DOMINICAN REPUBLIC

Climb the Caribbean's highest peak

Hike up Pico Duarte, the tallest mountain in the Caribbean, set amid the pine and cloud forests of the Cordillera Central.

www.godominicanrepublic.com

"To visit Natchez and the Trace is to be surrounded by Southern hospitality and a slower pace of life."

ISLAS BALLESTAS
PISCO, PERU

Explore the abundant marine life of the Peruvian Pacific

Take the boat out to this cluster of islands, the "Galápagos of Peru," which teems with sealions, penguins, and many birds.

internacional.peru.info/en/home

ISLA FERNANDO DE NORONHA
BRAZIL

Isolated tropical islands

Enjoy the small-scale tourism on these volcanic islands and go diving to explore the unique marine ecosystem.

www.noronha.com.br

ROUTE 66
USA

"Go west" may be a cliché but some clichés are worth doing

The urge to travel west is ingrained in the psyche of the USA – historically this has been a trip of promise and it still delivers on that.

www.historic66.com

NATURAL WONDERS

JOSHUA TREE NATIONAL PARK Joshua trees break up the desert

JOSHUA TREE NATIONAL PARK
CALIFORNIA, USA

Unearthly desert landscapes

One of the west coast's most memorable national parks, with a boulder-strewn desert dotted with weirdly shaped Joshua trees.

www.nps.gov/jotr

GREAT SMOKY MOUNTAINS NATIONAL PARK
TENNESSEE/N. CAROLINA, USA

Great for wildlife and hiking

This stretch of the Appalachian Mountains is lovely in March, when the hills are clothed in flowers.

www.nps.gov/grsm

PARQUE NACIONAL TORTUGUERO
COSTA RICA

A top turtle-watching spot

Watch magnificent hawksbill, green, and leatherback turtles haul themselves out of the sea to lay their eggs on this beautiful beach.

www.costarica-nationalparks.com

PEDRA AZUL
ESPÍRITO SANTO, BRAZIL

Brazil's remarkable, multi-colored mountain

A bare finger of rock almost half a mile high, Pedra Azul is famous for its surreal color changes at dawn and dusk.

www.pedraazul.com.br

Previous page: The pretty Château Whistler Resort, lit up at night, Canada

Weather Watch

❶ **Whistler, Canada** With the snow deep and powdery, and the temperatures higher than earlier in the ski season, March in Whistler is a Winter Wonderland – in springtime!

❷ **Mississippi, USA** The Deep South is idyllic in March – magnolias and camellias burst into flower, days are warm but not too hot and, though there may be showers, the sleepy, moisture-heavy summer seems a distant prospect.

❸ **Mexico** The comfortable temperatures make March the ideal time to visit the country. There are fewer rainy days in this month and the decreased humidity makes it the perfect weather for exploring.

❹ **Austin, USA** Although the Texan summer can be unbearable to incoming visitors, March offers agreeable temperatures. The South by Southwest (SXSW) festival attracts music-lovers to the city.

❺ **British Virgin Islands** With a tropical climate cooled by welcome trade winds, the British Virgin Islands hover at around 80°F (27°C) year-round. March is sunny and delightful, heralding the imminent end of the dry season.

❻ **Chile** Long skinny Chile's weather ranges from sub-tropical to sub-polar. Patagonia is reaching the end of its summer, with some rain and wind, but pleasantly high temperatures.

LUXURY AND ROMANCE

BRITISH VIRGIN ISLANDS Secluded bays, perfect for overnight mooring

BRITISH VIRGIN ISLANDS
CARIBBEAN

A tropical island cruise

The pace of life is slow, the water clear, and the sand soft. An island paradise, with calypso, cocktails, and spicy seafood in the evenings.

See pp64–5

XOCHIMILCO
MEXICO CITY, MEXICO

Latin America's answer to Venice

Take a ride around the romantic canals of Xochimilco in a colorful *trajinera* boat whilst being serenaded by roving mariachi bands.

www.visitmexico.com

"Eat, sail, snorkel, swim – in the British Virgin Islands, you'll spend much of your time in stress-free indulgence."

ECO-LODGES IN PANAMA
PANAMA

An emerging destination

Choose from rain forest lodges like The Canopy Tower to beach properties like Punta Caracol Acqua Lodge, suspended on stilts above a coral reef.

www.eco-tropicalresorts.com

PRIVATE ISLANDS
CARIBBEAN

Rent your very own tropical paradise

Indulge your wildest film-star fantasies and rent a private Caribbean island – for as little as US$500 a week.

www.privateislandsonline.com

CAYO DISTRICT
BELIZE

Caribbean luxury, eco-style

The largest and arguably the most beautiful district in Belize, with jungle-covered mountains, and a string of captivating eco-lodges.

www.belizex.com/cayo.htm

ACTIVE ADVENTURES

PATAGONIA Bringing in a lake fish at the end of the day

PATAGONIA
CHILE/ARGENTINA

Andean mountain lakes, leaping with salmon and trout

A fly-fisher's paradise – days spent by, on, or in crystal-clear water; evenings in a cozy lodge in the company of fellow anglers.

See pp72–3

CABARETE
DOMINICAN REPUBLIC

Perfect wind and waves on the island's north coast

One of the Americas' top water sports destinations, and self-proclaimed world kite-boarding capital. An excellent spot for surfing.

www.godominicanrepublic.com

WHISTLER
BRITISH COLUMBIA, CANADA

Heli-ski through perfect deep powder snow

Whistler's two huge and scenic mountains provide unforgettable skiing and snowboarding, and a lively and fun après-ski, too.

See pp56–7

NEW RIVER GORGE
WEST VIRGINIA

White-water rafting amid scenic mountains

Raft down the foaming waters of New River Gorge, a dramatic, thousand-feet deep fissure in the West Virginia Mountains.

www.nps.gov/neri

HONDURAS
CENTRAL AMERICA

Adventures and unspoiled natural beauty

Ride the white water in river canyons, dive the world's second-biggest reef, and explore untouched jungles in this amazing country.

See pp66–7

FAMILY GETAWAYS

YUCATÁN Snake head at the Warriors' Temple, Chichén Itza

"On the days of the vernal equinox, thousands gather at Chichén Itza to watch as the shadows form an undulating serpent of light and dark."

YUCATÁN
MEXICO

The Mayan snake-god makes his spectacular appearance

Explore the remains of two mighty empires – Mayan pyramids and pretty Spanish towns – whose legacy lives on in the local culture.

See pp70–71

PUERTO ESCONDIDO
MEXICO

Surf, sand, and sunsets on the Mexican Pacific

On the southern Pacific coast, this popular resort boasts excellent beaches, outstanding surf, and a laid-back ambience.

www.visitpuerto.com

THE AMAZON
ECUADOR

Wonderful rain forest adventures

Ecuador's Amazonian lowlands are relatively easy to reach and can be explored from a rain forest eco-lodge.

www.sachalodge.com

CLEARWATER BEACH
FLORIDA, USA

Beaches, boat trips, and dolphin-spotting

Dazzling white sands, a pleasantly small-town feel, and great water-based activities make this an ever-popular family holiday destination.

www.clearwaterbeach.com

FOSSIL RIM
TEXAS, USA

Overnight in this vast safari park near Fort Worth

This extraordinary park brings the sights, sounds, and smells of Africa to you. Plus, you're not far from lots of rodeo and sports action.

www.fossilrim.org

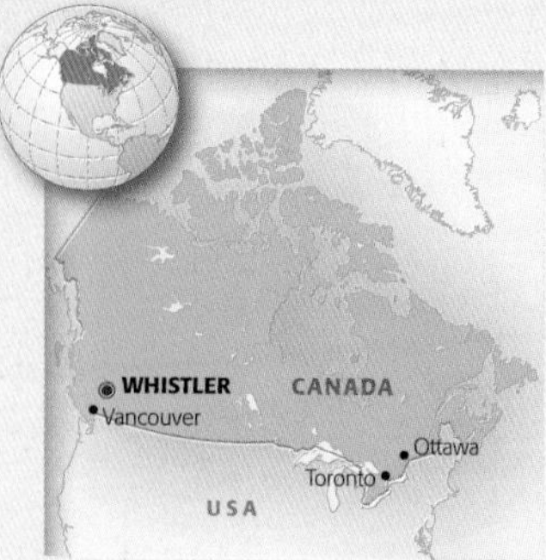

GETTING THERE See map p313, C6
Whistler is in western Canada, in British Columbia. International flights arrive into Vancouver airport, 75 miles (120 km) from the resort. A shuttle bus transports visitors from the airport and downtown Vancouver to Whistler. Car rental is also available.

GETTING AROUND
A free village shuttle provides transportation from hotels to the ski lifts, and runs every 10 to 12 minutes during the day.

WEATHER
Whistler's daytime temperatures average 36°F (2°C) in March, but it is colder on the mountain.

ACCOMMODATIONS
Executive Inn has chalet-style rooms; doubles from US$185; www.executiveinnwhistler.com

Glacier's Reach has a number of apartments with full kitchens; one-bedroom apartments from US$188; www.resortquestwhistler.com

Fairmont Château Whistler, with complete luxury and ski-in-ski-out facilities; doubles from US$439; www.fairmont.com/whistler

EATING OUT
A mid-range three-course meal in Whistler costs about US$50 per head. For a treat, try the seafood and other stylish west coast fare at Araxi, or the award-winning Bearfoot Bistro.

FURTHER INFORMATION
www.whistler.com

Olympic Whistler

Whistler's Olympic dream took over 40 years to happen. The resort was developed in the 1960s, with the hopes of landing the 1968 Winter Games. But the Rocky Mountain resort of Banff submitted Canada's bid for the 1968 and 1972 games, and Whistler's 1976 bid came to naught when the Summer Games were awarded to Montréal. In 2010, Whistler shared the honor with Vancouver, hosting the downhill and cross-country ski races, as well as ski-jumping, luge, and bobsleigh events.

Above (left to right): Skiers and snowboarders at top of a ridge; dogsledding through the Whistler woods; skier at speed going over a bump
Main: Snowboarder performing a cliff jump above the ski lift at Whistler

WHISTLER

IT'S ALL ABOUT THE GREAT OUTDOORS – winter in Whistler. If you can't climb up it, race down it, stride through it or suspend yourself from it, most visitors aren't interested. Everyone, from toddlers to octogenarians, clad head-to-toe in bright Gore-Tex®, carries ski poles or snowshoes.

This pretty resort village of around 10,000 permanent residents is cradled in one of the most scenic spots in western Canada. The Whistler and Blackcomb mountains – with a combined total of 38 lifts, more than 200 ski runs, 13 sq miles (34 sq km) of skiable terrain, and one of North America's longest lift-serviced vertical descents – dominate the landscape. Quiet trails through thick forests of fragrant pine and cedar beckon alluringly to cross-country skiers and snowshoers. The icy surface of the frozen Green Lake seems purpose-made for ice skating. And then there's the heli-skiing. Whistler is a prime center for this extreme activity with a superb choice of pristine deep-powder runs that are only accessible by helicopter. When you've been the first to ski an almost vertical slope of feet-thick unpacked powder, or carved smooth, floating turns through fresh snow as it sprays up around your ears, then you know you've really skied the mountain. And then you're hooked – normal skiing or snowboarding will never be the same again.

When you've been the first to ski an almost vertical slope of feet-thick unpacked powder...then you know you've really skied the mountain.

There are few winter sports that someone here hasn't tried, from ice climbing to snow tubing. And a bit of snow and wind doesn't deter daredevils from other year-round activities like ziplining or bungee jumping.

Whistler is a surprisingly cosmopolitan place, with a lot to offer even those with no interest in hurtling headfirst down mountains. With the award-winning Bearfoot Bistro restaurant cellar holding 2,100 labels, and shops selling Cuban cigars and French lingerie, the town has evolved far beyond its backcountry roots – but it remains at its most charming when under a blanket of snow.

Inset: A bit of Whistler nightlife at Dusty's Bar & BBQ
Below (left to right): Above the clouds – ski lift at Whistler; cross-country skiing through the delightful countryside; cabins set in the mountain forest

DEEP POWDER DIARY

Whistler has one of the longest snow seasons in North America, and March is a great time to visit because temperatures are mild but snow is still plentiful. Because of the excellent conditions, rooms sell out quickly, so book ahead. Ski fanatics could easily spend two weeks here, but others will probably find five days ideal.

Five Days on the Pistes

DAY 1 After arriving from Vancouver, grab lunch at a mountainside restaurant and unpack. Spend the afternoon soaring over the treetops on a zipline tour, or strap on your skis and hit the slopes. In the evening, enjoy illuminated nighttime snowboarding (early March, Thu–Sat only).

DAY 2 If you're a beginner or feeling a little rusty, brush up your skills with a lesson at the Whistler Blackcomb Ski and Snowboard School, then spend the rest of the day on the mountain. Afterwards, ease those aching muscles with a massage at one of the resort's spas and maybe a drink or two in one of the local bars.

DAY 3 Strap on some goggles and go snowmobiling along forested mountain trails, or spend a more leisurely day strolling through the village to shop for artwork, jewelry, and other luxury goods – there are more than 200 shops in the resort. In the evening, take a horse-drawn sleigh ride in the Blackcomb (about US$50), followed by an indulgent fondue dinner.

DAY 4 For a truly memorable experience, blaze your own track through the waist-deep, unmarked virgin powder of Whistler's spectacular backcountry on an exciting heli-skiing excursion. Finish the day with a dinner at one of Whistler's excellent restaurants.

DAY 5 Explore the beautiful Whistler countryside beyond the ski resort by trying your hand at cross-country skiing or learning to mush a team of Alaskan racing huskies along a snowy wilderness route.

Dos and Don'ts

- ✓ Buy a Fresh Tracks ticket, which will let you ski in pristine powder at sunrise, before the crowds arrive.
- ✓ Try skate-skiing, which combines elements of inline skating and cross-country skiing. Lessons are available at Lost Lake.
- ✓ Save money by booking self-catering accommodations – the village has a great selection of apartments.
- ✗ Don't think that you aren't good enough to heli-ski. If you can ski down a blue run you can do it – and you will never forget the experience (make sure to have a DVD made).

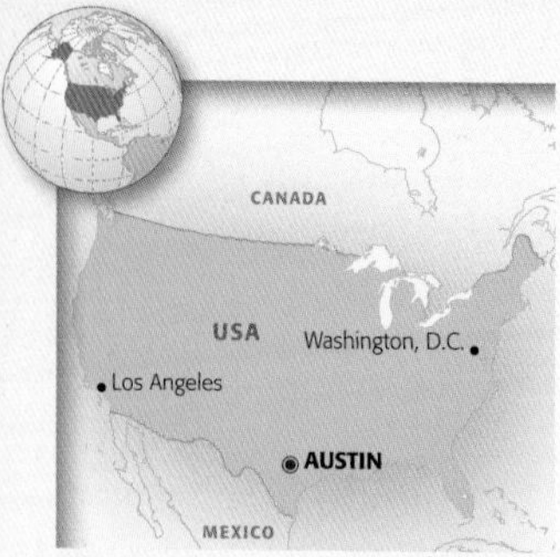

GETTING THERE See map p318, E5
The Austin-Bergstrom International Airport is 7.5 miles (12 km) from downtown Austin. Regular buses, shuttles, and taxis travel into town from the airport.

GETTING AROUND
Austin has a well-run network of buses and light rail, and it's easy to get around on foot.

WEATHER
Spring is a wonderfully pleasant time of year to visit, with temperatures in the 70s°F (21°C) and 80s°F (27°C). In the summer, temperatures climb up to the mid- to high 90s°F (35°C), often with an overpowering humidity.

ACCOMMODATIONS
On trendy South Congress Avenue stay at the quirky Hotel San José; from US$195; www.sanjosehotel.com

The stylish boutique Heywood Hotel in East Austin; from US$219; www.heywoodhotel.com

Splurge at the historic, opulent The Driskill; doubles from US$260; www.driskillhotel.com

EATING OUT
Austin has a diverse culinary scene, like the Texas-sized steaks at Perry's Steakhouse & Grille, to juicy barbecue at Franklin Barbecue and famous tacos at Torchy's Tacos.

FURTHER INFORMATION
www.austintexas.org
www.traveltexas.com

AUSTIN

Music isn't just a pastime in Austin, it's a way of life. Until you've tapped your toes to a live band at one of Austin's famous bars, you haven't truly experienced the city. After all, Austin markets itself (and rightfully so) as the Live Music Capital of the World. This is especially evident during the city's legendary music festivals, notably South by Southwest (SXSW), which takes over the city in March. Originally launched in 1987, this is one of the country's best-known annual events of music, film, and interactive media, showcasing talent from around world. Big names come for the spectacle – Iggy Pop, Katie Perry, Quentin Tarantino, and Michelle and Barack Obama have all attended. Also a huge draw is the Austin City Limits Music Festival in late September and early October, which celebrates music from Texas and beyond.

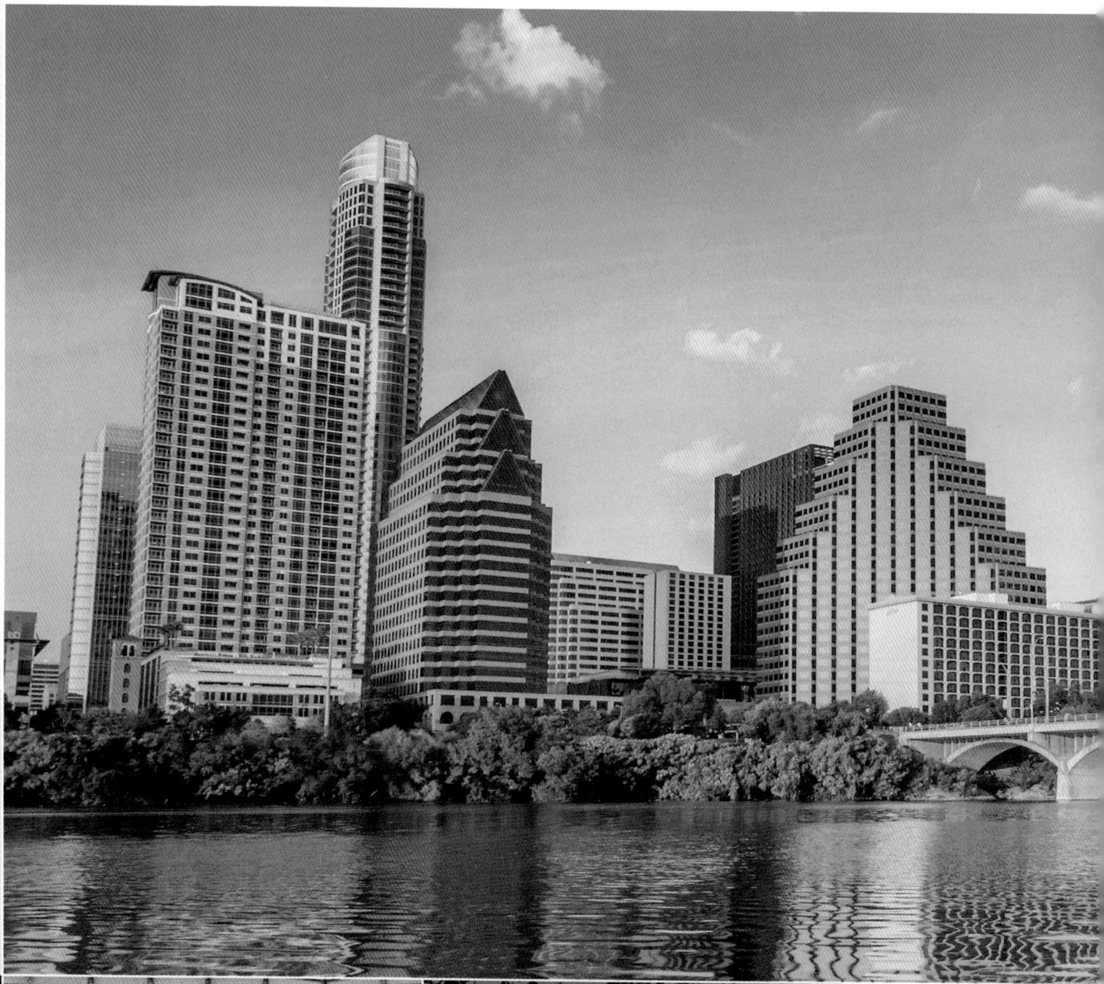

Main: The downtown Austin skyline

Comedy City

Austin made its name with music, but the city is also a thriving comedy hub. Comedians used to stop over in Austin before heading to bigger markets, like New York and Las Vegas. But now, Austin is the headliner town. Establishments like the Capitol City Comedy Club has hosted big names like Ellen DeGeneres and Jeff Foxworthy. Austin also hosts a variety of comedy festivals, including the annual Moontower Comedy and Oddity Festival.

Left (left and right): Fredericksburg; Sixth Street

Right: Bob Bullock State History Museum

But there's a lot more to Austin than music. It's also the capital of Texas and home to the massive University of Texas, which injects the city with a youthful, progressive energy. On campus, you'll find the terrific Blanton Museum of Art, one of the largest university art museums in the USA. Also, pay a visit to the colorful Mexic-Arte Museum, which celebrates traditional and contemporary Latin American art and culture.

The city's apt motto of "Keep Austin Weird" is embodied at one of its top sights: Congress Avenue Bridge, with its unusual residents – bats. The world's largest urban bat population lives here and every night you can watch the skies blacken as they soar into the air from the bridge.

Best of all, many spots combine Austin's beloved pastimes of music and barbecue. Here at the home of the classic barbecue, you can sink your teeth into sauce-slathered ribs and chicken (with a steaming side of grits). Stop by the legendary Stubb's Bar-B-Q Restaurant for a taste of both.

Above: Barton Springs Pool

Below: The Contemporary Jones Center

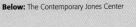

MUSICAL DIARY

Austin is a microcosm of the country's music scene. Check out diverse bands from around the USA every night of the week, from country to rock, jazz to soul. Plus, Austin is the cultural hub of Texas, with superb art and history museums and a thriving comedy scene.

JAN
FEB
MAR

Four Days of Music, Culture, and BBQ

DAY 1

The Contemporary Austin: Jones Center features contemporary art from emerging and established artists. Also worth a visit is the Bob Bullock State History Museum. Explore the lively streets of downtown, including the commercial main drag of Sixth Street. Cross the Colorado River at dusk to catch the urban bats emerging from their hideaway under the Congress Avenue Bridge. Later, celebrate the city's famous live music scene in the nearby South Congress neighborhood, lined with bars, clubs, and restaurants.

DAY 2

Stroll the student-thronged strip of Guadalupe Street, dotted with trendy cafes, galleries, and bookstores. Check out the Blanton Museum of Art. Come evening, you can find lots of shows on and around the campus, including those at Symphony Square and the University of Texas Performing Arts Center.

DAY 3

Roam the lush, 350-acre (142-ha) Zilker Park, taking a dip in the Barton Springs Pool. Then, head to the Umlauf Sculpture Garden. End the day with Southern comfort food and music at Threadgill's. Feast on chicken-fried steak and a frothy beer while listening to bluegrass.

DAY 4

Austin's best barbecue and outdoor activities are in nearby ranch-dotted Hill Country. Dig in to barbecue at the venerable Salt Lick, and then explore by hitting the open road, visiting Hill Country towns like Kerrville, surrounded by the region's signature hills and valleys, and the cozy German-influenced Fredericksburg.

Dos and Don'ts

- ✓ Book your hotel at least 5–6 months in advance if you plan to attend the annual South by Southwest (SXSW) festival in March – the coveted downtown hotels sell out quickly.
- ✗ Don't miss Austin's unique neighborhoods that are beyond downtown, like North Loop and East Austin, which are filled with creative restaurants and bars.
- ✗ Don't forget your comfortable shoes: one of the best ways to explore Austin is on foot.
- ✗ Don't overlook Austin's many lesser-known festivals, including the five-week FronteraFest (January–February), which celebrates fringe theater.

APR
MAY
JUN
JUL
AUG
SEP
OCT
NOV
DEC

Below: South by Southwest Festival

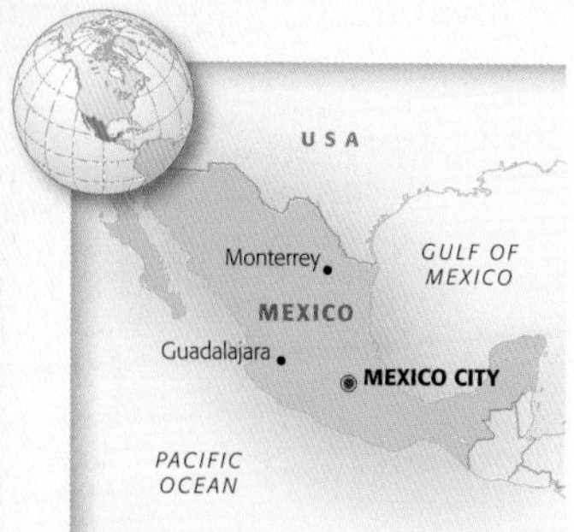

GETTING THERE See map p323, F5

International flights arrive in Mexico City at Aeropuerto Internacional Benito Juárez, which is about 20 minutes to an hour from the city center by taxi depending on traffic.

GETTING AROUND

Traffic is horrendous in Mexico City, with limited parking. The safest and most reliable mode of transportation is to use a taxi arranged for you by your hotel.

WEATHER

In March, Mexico City enjoys warm, sunny days with an average high of 75°F (24°C) and an average nighttime low of 46°F (8°C).

ACCOMMODATIONS

A great value guesthouse with a central location, Casa Comtesse has doubles from US$60; www.casacomtesse.com

Luxurious Las Alcobas Mexico DF offers state-of-the-art technology and personalized service; doubles from US$298; www.lasalcobas.com

Four Seasons has a serene courtyard; doubles from US$600; www.fourseasons.com/mexico

EATING OUT

In Mexico City, you will find cuisine from every region of the country, as well as dishes from South America and Europe. Be sure to try local entrées featuring *mole*, which is a rich, somewhat spicy, sauce made with a bit of chocolate. *Arrachera* (tender marinated beef) is also worth sampling.

FURTHER INFORMATION

www.visitmexico.com/en/mexico-city

Catedral Metropolitana

One of the largest and most important cathedrals in the western hemisphere presents an impressive display of architectural styles, with an ornate Spanish Baroque facade and Neo-Classical dome. Begun in 1525, Catedral Metropolitana was built with rubble from the adjacent ruins of the Aztec Templo Mayor, which was destroyed following the Spanish conquest of 1513. Designed and constructed in stages, it took 240 years to complete.

Above (left to right): Teotihuacán; Tlaloc (rain god) amphora at Templo Mayor; Coyoacán
Main: Street performer in the Zócalo

MEXICO CITY

ANCIENT YET MODERN, MEXICO CITY PULSATES WITH LIFE AND CULTURE, serving up a veritable feast of history, art, music, and cuisine. Once known as Tenochtitlán by the Aztecs who founded their city in a giant volcanic caldera in 1325, this is North America's oldest city and one of the world's largest. The city's stunning contrasts can both delight and assault the senses. Narrow streets bustle with traffic and pedestrians, the spicy aroma of cooking food mingles with exhaust fumes. Elegant towers of glass and steel rise above ornate Spanish colonial *palacios* and ancient Aztec ruins. A maze of colorful market stalls stands alongside elegant shops filled with high-end fashions and jewelry, and everywhere the harmonies of church bells and street musicians compete with the shrill whistles of police directing traffic.

The cobblestone streets in the historic area present an impressive variety of boutiques, restaurants, and galleries housed in elaborate colonial mansions, exceptional museums, Baroque churches, and lush urban parks. At the heart of the city, the vast open Zócalo is the gathering place for social and political events. On festival days, the plaza throngs with crowds that surround spectacularly dressed dancers as they stomp and chant to a rhythmic drumbeat. Overseeing the mayhem are some of the city's iconic structures: the magnificent Catedral Metropolitana, the Aztec ruins of the Templo Mayor, and the Palacio Nacional where Diego Rivera's mural *Epic of the Mexican People* tells the story of Mexico. Away from the Zócalo, organ-grinders play sweet, sad songs below the golden dome of the spectacular Palacio de Bellas Artes and in neighboring Alameda Central. The Paseo de la Reforma is lined with shimmering skyscrapers, embassies, galleries, hotels, and marble and gold monuments, while a few miles down the Paseo lies the green expanse of Chapultepec Park and the hilltop Castillo, which has commanding views of this splendid and constantly surprising city.

The plaza throngs with crowds that surround spectacularly dressed dancers as they stomp and chant to a rhythmic drumbeat.

Inset: Catedral Metropolitana in the Zócalo
Below (left and right): Mexico City skyline; colorful boats in Xochimilco

SPANISH CITY DIARY

The city is warm and sunny in late March and the delicate violet-colored blossoms of the jacaranda trees are beautiful. Five days is enough time to see the highlights in the central historic area, visit charming Coyoacán and San Ángel, see fabulous museums and ancient ruins, enjoy fine dining, and attend evening performances.

Five Days of Cultural Delights

TUE Explore the wonderful collection of Mexican and pre-Hispanic art and culture at the Museo Nacional de Antropologia. Visit the opulent Castillo de Chapultepec or Museo de Arte Moderno, with oils by the great Mexican muralists. Take a taxi along Paseo de la Reforma past the golden El Ángel (Winged Victory).

WED In Centro Histórico tour the sights surrounding the Zócalo, starting with Templo Mayor. Enter Palacio Nacional and admire Diego Rivera's brilliant murals. Explore Catedral Metropolitana's glittering altars and fabulous artworks. Have dinner overlooking the Zócalo and watch the honor guard lower the giant Mexican flag.

THU Tour the stunning white marble Palacio de Bellas Artes, then stroll through lovely Alameda Central, and visit the nearby museums. See Mexican masterpieces at Museo Nacional de Arte, decorative arts at Museo Franz Mayer, and Mexican folk art at Museo de Arte Popular.

FRI Hire a car and driver and head to Teotihuacán, the incredible ruins of Mesoamerica's cultural and commercial center. Climb the Pyramid of the Sun, and walk along the Avenue of the Dead to the Quetzalpapalotl Palace Complex. Ascend the Pyramid of the Moon for panoramic views of the complex.

SAT Take a taxi a few miles south of the center to lovely San Ángel and Coyoacán. Visit Bazar Sábado, a Saturday-only fine arts and crafts market, and the Museo Casa Estudio Diego Rivera y Frida Kahlo. Then head out to Xochimilco, 12 miles (20 km) southeast of the center, for a colorful canal trip on a flower-decked boat.

Dos and Don'ts

- ✓ For reasons of personal safety, behave and dress conservatively as you explore the city.
- ✗ Don't tempt pickpockets by wearing expensive jewelry or displaying wealth in public places.
- ✓ Visit Templo Mayor as early as you can in the morning, when it is easier to see the details of the carvings on the ruins and before the sun gets too hot.
- ✗ Don't hail a taxi from the street. It is a much better idea to ask your hotel to phone for a taxi for you.

Below: Monument El Ángel on the Paseo de la Reforma

GETTING THERE See map p316, H4
Boston's Logan International Airport is about 3 miles (5 km) from South Boston.

GETTING AROUND
Boston's extensive public transportation system (MBTA) means there's no need for a car. South Boston is on the red subway line.

WEATHER
March sees about 4 in (10 cm) of rain. Daytime highs average 45°F (7°C), and it may drop below freezing at night.

ACCOMMODATIONS
The Boston Park Plaza Hotel is an affordable hotel in the heart of the city; doubles from US$195; www.bostonparkplaza.com

Nine Zero is a cutting-edge boutique hotel, located on bustling Tremont Street; doubles from US$239; www.ninezero.com

The Seaport Hotel is on Boston Harbor (ask for a room with a view); doubles from US$359; www.seaportboston.com

EATING OUT
At Boston's countless Irish pubs, St. Patrick's Day visitors won't have to look too hard for staples like shepherd's pie, or corned beef and cabbage. Legal Sea Foods has locations throughout the city, and is a good place to try classic New England fish dishes such as Boston baked scrod and seafood chowder.

FURTHER INFORMATION
www.bostonusa.com

A Touch of the Irish

Among Boston's many Irish bars are a number of authentic ones whose fittings and staff hail from the Emerald Isle. To feel at home, non-Irish types should brush up on their Celtic folklore. Leprechauns are Ireland's national race of pixies, who guard the country's ancient treasure. If someone calls you Saint Brigit, that's a compliment, as she was renowned for her beauty and generosity. And Saint Patrick is the patron saint who drove the snakes out of Ireland.

Brogues as thick as Guinness can be heard in every pub, and the sounds of fiddles and penny whistles lilt through the streets.

Above: A shaggy parade leprechaun
Main: Crowds lining the streets to watch the parade pass by

BOSTON

ANYONE WITH IRISH BLOOD IN THEIR VEINS WILL ENJOY A TRIP TO BOSTON, regardless of the time of year. But in the days surrounding March 17, New England's largest city really rolls out the bright green welcome mat as a wide array of events, festivals, and parades are held in celebration of St. Patrick's Day, Ireland's national holiday. Around half a million visitors come each year just to join in the party. Brogues as thick as Irish Stout can be heard in every pub; the sounds of fiddles and penny whistles lilt through the streets; and tipsy revelers walk (or crawl) from one bar to the next. The Guiness flows freely, and there's nothing odd about seeing someone tip back a pint of lager colored green in honor of the holiday. The area's performing arts centers showcase Irish-themed shows, from traditional Celtic dance troupes to big-name touring acts such as the Chieftains and Ronan Tynan, while satellite towns host lively St. Patrick's celebrations of their own, most notably Scituate, Worcester, and Holyoke.

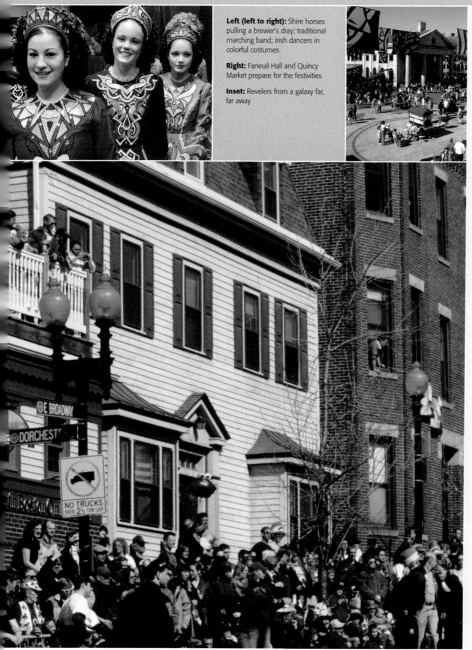

Left (left to right): Shire horses pulling a brewer's dray; traditional marching band; Irish dancers in colorful costumes

Right: Faneuil Hall and Quincy Market prepare for the festivities

Inset: Revelers from a galaxy far, far away

SHAMROCK DIARY

With its large Irish-American community, Boston stakes a claim as the best place in the USA to celebrate St. Patrick's Day. Much of the focus falls on South Boston, where Irish immigrants first settled, but everywhere gets into the Celtic spirit, with many non-Irish restaurants putting up decorations and serving green beer.

Three Days of Gaelic Revels

FRI

Dive straight in by donning a "Kiss me, I'm Irish" button and heading out on the town. The bars surrounding Faneuil Hall will be jammed – duck into the Black Rose for a pint or two. Since you are in Boston, stroll along a section of the nearby Freedom Trail for a spot of history, then tuck into Yankee pot roast, Indian pudding, or another Boston classic at Durgin Park, one of the city's oldest restaurants.

SAT

Start your day with a leisurely walk along Boston's Irish Heritage Trail, a 3-mile (5-km) self-guided walking tour that includes 16 different sites of Irish cultural, historical, and political significance (pick up a free trail map at one of Boston's Visitor Centers or visit www.irishheritagetrail.com). Learn about the city's most famous native son at the John F. Kennedy Presidential Library and Museum, including details of his connection to his ancestral homeland. Cap your night in Somerville with some authentic Irish fare and free live music at the Burren pub.

SUN

Rise early and head to South Boston to stake out a spot along the parade route. Buy some green carnations to hand out to your favorite parade participants, and stay warm with a coffee or whiskey from one of the many bars and pubs. After the parade, while the crowds disperse, enjoy a relaxed pint at Amrhein's, a cozy hangout with the oldest hand-carved bar in the USA.

Dos and Don'ts

- ✓ Be responsible when drinking. Use the excellent public transportation system and respect police officers, an extra contingent of whom work the holiday to keep the peace.
- ✗ Don't confuse South Boston with the South End, a different neighborhood known for its vibrant arts and dining scenes.
- ✓ The weather in March is notoriously fickle. Even if skies are clear, they could open up at any time, so dress for all eventualities, including comfortable, weatherproof shoes.
- ✗ Don't depend on credit cards, as many of the old-style pubs don't take plastic.

Everything culminates on the Sunday closest to the holiday, when South Boston ("Southie," as locals call it) hosts one of the world's largest St. Patrick's Day parades, and revelers in their hundreds of thousands descend upon this working-class neighborhood to celebrate all things Gaelic. Firemen, step-dancers, and pipe bands come from all over the country – and from Ireland as well – to march in the parade, and a spirit of celebration and goodwill fills the air. Family gatherings spill out of the neighborhood's numerous rowhouses, and the area's wide assortment of bars are packed to the gills. (In recent years the city has taken great pains to make it a family-friendly event, with public drinking strictly prohibited, keeping rowdy types off the streets and in the pubs.) But Southie's bars aren't the only ones that are packed, as the city's students, some 200,000-plus of them, use the weekend as an excuse to put on their green gear and let loose.

Anyone looking for a quiet, relaxed time, in which to discover one of America's greatest cities, won't stand a chance with all the excitement and commotion that the holiday brings, but everyone who loves a good time will be in heaven – an emerald one!

Below: Leprechauns performing an Irish reel

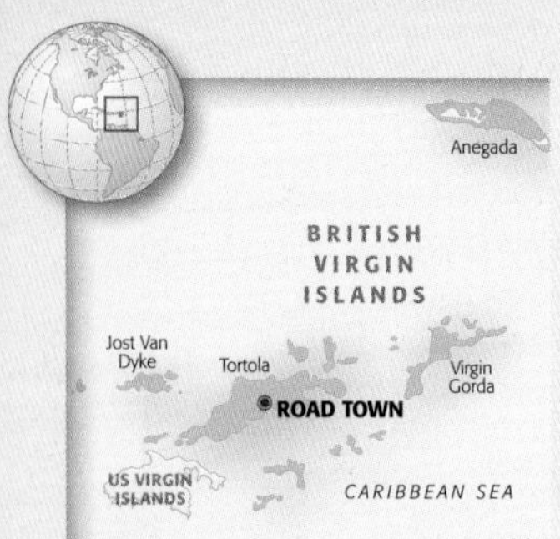

GETTING THERE **See map p325, G4**
The BVIs are a small group of isles lying east of Puerto Rico and the US Virgin Islands. The main airport is on Tortola. Flights from North America and Europe connect via Puerto Rico, St. Thomas, Antigua, St. Kitts, or St. Maarten.

GETTING AROUND
Sailing is the best way to see the islands. Ashore, you can walk, but explore farther afield by cab.

WEATHER
The climate is tempered by sea breezes ideal for sailing. Temperatures in spring average 82°F (28°C). Rainfall is seasonal, with February and March being the driest months.

ACCOMMODATIONS
Nanny Cay Marina and Hotel has a waterfront garden setting near the capital, Road Town; doubles from US$150; www.nannycay.com

On Tortola, Sugar Mill Hotel nestles into the hillside and offers fine dining; doubles from US$395; www.sugarmillhotel.com

A seven-day, live-aboard charter costs around US$1,100–2,500 per head, including meals.

EATING OUT
All yachts are stocked with food, but it's fun to eat at waterfront restaurants serving fresh seafood, conch gumbo, and grilled lobster.

FURTHER INFORMATION
www.bvitourism.com
www.moorings.com

Wreck of the *Rhone*

The BVIs' most celebrated dive site is the R.M.S. *Rhone*, which sank in a hurricane in 1867. One of the world's first iron-hulled ships, it split in two and came to rest at depths of up to 20–80 ft (6–24 m) just west of Salt Island. Protected in the BVIs' only marine national park, it is now emblazoned with corals. Marine turtles swim in and out, and moray eels and barracudas peer out at divers. The wreck starred in the 1977 film, *The Deep*.

Above (left and right): Secluded island bays, perfect for overnight mooring; setting off for an unforgettable experience

BRITISH VIRGIN ISLANDS

Caressed by constant warm breezes and turquoise water, and with an abundance of pristine secluded harbors, the British Virgin Islands (BVIs) are a sailor's paradise, promising both adventure and leisure. When it comes to sailing the Caribbean, there is no more appropriate a place than the BVIs and no better way than by yacht charter – the ideal choice for exploring these exquisite and exciting isles at your own pace.

Vacationing aboard a crewed yacht is like staying in an exclusive villa with well-trained staff to cater to your every whim. Eat, sail, snorkel, and swim – that's likely to be your daily pattern, and with a crew of two or more – from skipper to cook – you'll spend much of your time sipping cocktails and sunning in stress-free indulgence. You'll pass the days sailing indolently from isle to isle, but be sure to anchor in time for happy hours at the islands' many fun-filled beach bars.

The BVIs comprise the main islands of Tortola, Virgin Gorda, Anegada, and Jost Van Dyke, along with more than 50 smaller islands and cays – many of them tiny uninhabited islets. While your skipper can recommend the best itinerary, the best thing about a BVI yacht charter is that you're free to explore the destination as you choose – there's nothing quite like a sense of absolute freedom to go "gunkholing" (island hopping) between the prettiest harbors and secluded beaches. You should definitely not miss out on the Baths on Virgin Gorda; these sculpted boulders form grottoes and arches ideal for snorkeling in crystal-clear waters. Another must-see is Jost Van Dyke, a relaxed barefoot paradise of just 200 inhabitants clinging to traditional island culture. Here, for a break from the mariner's life, take to the forested hills before sipping a well-earned Carib beer or heady rum cocktail at Ali Baba's or Foxy's beach bar, while getting seriously mellow to calypso rhythms.

After a chillout session, it's time for some action – adventure loafing *is* the main raison d'etre of a Caribbean sailing vacation. Charter yachts always carry snorkeling and fishing gear, while bigger boats often feature a dinghy, scuba gear, and even jet skis. That said, you're likely to find contentment merely lazing on deck with a rum swizzle in hand and without a care in the world, as you race along with the warm, scented wind in your sails.

Main: Yachts anchored in the turquoise waters of an idyllic bay
Below (left and right): Foxy's Bar – the perfect place to chill out; inside the Baths on Virgin Gorda

YACHT CHARTER DIARY

While cruising in the British Virgin Islands is a year-round affair, March is the ideal time for sailing here, when the weather is at its finest. It's possible to cruise the main islands in five days, but most sailing charters are for seven or ten days, and you may want an additional day or two for exploring Tortola.

A Week of Sailing in the BVIs

DAY 1

Fly into Road Town, Tortola and take some time out to explore the islands' charming and somnolent capital city before boarding your yacht. Then set sail for Cooper Island to snorkel and dine.

DAYS 2–3

Sail to Virgin Gorda, stopping at the Baths for a swim around the rock formations. Later, anchor at the Dogs to snorkel. Continue to North Sound for water sports and an island tour.

DAYS 4–5

Cruise to Marina Cay or Trellis Bay on Beef Island, home to stunning coral reefs ideal for snorkeling and diving. Shop at Trellis Bay market and Aragon Studios, or try your hand at windsurfing or sea kayaking. Then, catch a dinghy to the long sandy beach along Cane Garden Bay back on Tortola. Take a dip or simply lounge under the sun before dining on the freshest seafood at a waterside restaurant. The rum distillery is another attraction you can visit.

DAY 6

Sail over to Jost Van Dyke, stopping en route at the white-rimmed Sandy Cay for a spot of beachcombing and a botanical tour. Next, anchor at Great Harbour and savor cool cocktails and a hearty meal at Foxy's, a quintessential island beach bar.

DAYS 7–8

Today, head over to Norman Island to explore the Caves, a popular snorkeling site. Anchor in the Bight – the largest anchorage on Norman Island – and dine aboard the Willie Thornton floating restaurant, fondly known as the Willie T.

Finally, return to Road Town for your flight back home.

Dos and Don'ts

- ⊗ Don't forget to book well in advance, as March is the most popular cruising season.
- ✓ Take the opportunity to learn sailing. Your skipper will be happy to teach you the basics.
- ✓ Study what's included in packages when comparing different charter companies.
- ⊗ Don't forget to budget a gratuity for the crew.
- ✓ Do a little background reading beforehand so you can select the places you'd like to visit.

Below: Mural painted on a wall along Ridge Road, Tortola

GETTING THERE **See map p324, D2/D3**
Arrive either at Villeda Morales International Airport, 7 miles (11 km) from San Pedro Sula, or at Golosón International Airport, 4 miles (6 km) from La Ceiba.

GETTING AROUND
You can reach Roatán by air from La Ceiba. Otherwise, rent a car to get around, as rates are reasonable, although taxis are also good value and mountain bikes readily available.

WEATHER
You can expect sunshine, with cool breezes to temper the humidity, and little rainfall. The average temperature is 81°F (27°C).

ACCOMMODATIONS
The Jungle River Lodge at Río Cangrejal has rooms from US$30; www.jungleriverlodge.com

Posada Arco Iris in Roatán offers simple but clean doubles with ocean views from US$48; www.roatanposada.com

The Lodge at Pico Bonito has great facilities; cabins are US$210; www.picobonito.com

D&D Brewery, Los Naranjos, has cabins from US$35; www.dd-brewery.com

EATING OUT
Try *sopa de caracol* (conch stew with vegetables, spices, and coconut milk). Inland, look out for *anafre* (a fondue-like dish, made with refried beans, cheese, and sausage).

FURTHER INFORMATION
www.honduras.travel/en

Unmissable photo-ops await in the transparent waters of the Blue Channel where fish play hide-and-seek in azure waters.

Main: Spine-tingling passage through the rapids of Río Cangrejal

HONDURAS

THE RAFT HEADS TOWARDS THE NEXT RAPID, a spine-tingling Class IV. Spray drifts across the front of the boat as it twists and turns in the current, buffeted by glistening boulders. You recall your training earlier in the day and row with all the strength you can muster. The boat gathers speed, hits the rapid with a sickening bump, tilts alarmingly, then hangs in the air before plunging into a torrent of swirling water. For sheer adrenaline rush, nothing beats white-water rafting, and Honduras' Río Cangrejal ranks among the top places in the world to enjoy this exhilarating sport. To appreciate the spectacular beauty of the Cangrejal Valley at a more leisurely pace, rent a mountain bike, or cross the river by zipline as a curtain-raiser to the canopy tour of the Pico Bonito rain forest.

From here the pristine, white-sand beaches of the Bay Islands are no more than a 30-minute flight away. Roatán, the largest and most popular island, offers a full range of water sports, from waterskiing and

Catarata de Pulhapanzak

This beautiful waterfall is 11 miles (18 km) from Lago de Yojoa, near San Buenaventura village. A guide will lead you down a path into chest-high water, then through the rolling 141-ft- (43-m-) high cascade to a cave under the falls. Bring goggles and a change of clothes, as you will end up throughly soaked. If you don't feel up to the challenge, admire the waterfall from the park through its veil of shimmering mist, often with rainbows forming in the sunlight. There are ponds for swimming and you can picnic or eat in the rustic restaurant.

WATER SPORTS DIARY

Honduras offers excellent opportunities for all sorts of water sports. Río Cangrejal is the ideal jumping-off point for an adventure holiday. You'll need three days to try out the activities on offer, before moving on to Roatán's reefs. Finally, peaceful Lago de Yojoa is a perfect antidote to the activity of the Bay Islands.

Ten Adrenaline-Fueled Days

DAYS 1–3

Test your nerves on the Class III–V white-water rapids of the Río Cangrejal. Later, explore the Pico Bonito Natural Park by walking the Zacate River trail. Cool off in swimming holes en route and look out for wildlife. Start your second day with a swim in the natural pools below Jungle River Lodge, before joining the Canopy Zip Line tour of Pico Bonito, the only one in Honduras. Spend a day exploring the stunning Río Cangrejal Valley and its scenic villages by mountain bike.

DAYS 4–7

Fly to Roatán from La Ceiba and spend the rest of the day swimming or snorkeling in Half Moon Bay. Diving conditions should be perfect, so take your pick from the huge variety of diving and snorkeling expeditions to the Barrier Reef over the next two days. On your last day in Roatán, explore the clear waters of the Caribbean by sea kayak, then swim with dolphins at Anthony's Key Resort.

DAYS 8–10

Take an early flight back to La Ceiba, then drive to Lago de Yojoa, arriving at Agua Azul restaurant where you can bird-watch while you eat. Drive to D&D micro-brewery for the night and ask for a tour of the Orchid Garden. Spend the next day hiking in Cerro Azul Meámbar National Park, enjoying the stunning scenery and cloud forest. Finally, hire a guide for the Taulubé caves where fruit bats lurk among 6-ft- (2-m-) high stalactites and stalagmites, and take in the fabulous Catarata de Pulhapanzak on your way back.

Dos and Don'ts

- ✓ Remember to bring your Open Water Diver Certification card to Roatán. Consult www.scuba.about.com for details.
- ✗ Don't forget to check the baggage restrictions for the internal flight to Roatán and pack accordingly.
- ✓ Take plenty of cash, as credit cards are not widely accepted.
- ✓ Bring baby oil as it is an effective deterrent against sandflies.
- ✗ Don't buy conch shells, black coral jewelry, dried seahorses, and other environmentally harmful products.
- ✓ Carry binoculars with you, as there are nearly 400 bird species around Lago de Yojoa alone.

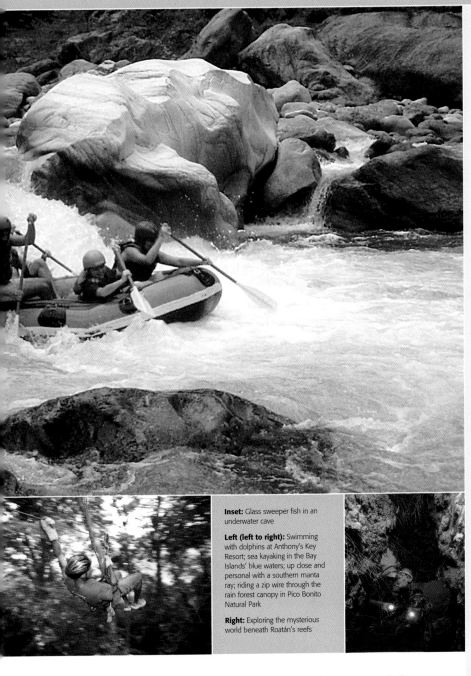

Inset: Glass sweeper fish in an underwater cave

Left (left to right): Swimming with dolphins at Anthony's Key Resort; sea kayaking in the Bay Islands' blue waters; up close and personal with a southern manta ray; riding a zip wire through the rain forest canopy in Pico Bonito Natural Park

Right: Exploring the mysterious world beneath Roatán's reefs

wakeboarding, to sea kayaking and deep-sea fishing. But it is Roatán's proximity to the longest barrier reef in the western hemisphere that attracts divers and snorkelers from around the world. There are nearly 40 sites to choose from, all within striking distance of the shore. Drift dive through mysterious underwater canyons and ravines in search of 6-ft- (2-m-) high barrel sponges, squat on the sea bed to watch reef sharks feeding, or visit the barnacled hulks of the *Odyssey* or *El Aguila*. Unmissable photo-ops await snorkelers in the transparent waters of Blue Channel, where tangs, damselfish, barracuda, and snapper play hide-and-seek in azure waters.

Return to the mainland and head south to the forested slopes of Cerro Azul Meámbar (6,700 ft/2,042 m) for jaw-dropping views of Lago de Yojoa, Honduras' largest inland lake. Fishing and bird-watching expeditions start from its reed-fringed shores, while those in search of more physically demanding challenges should look no further than the Taulubé caves or the spectacular Pulhapanzak waterfall, where the heart-in-mouth scramble across the cliff face could turn out to be the highlight of the trip.

Below: Rock formation on dolomite base in the Taulubé caves

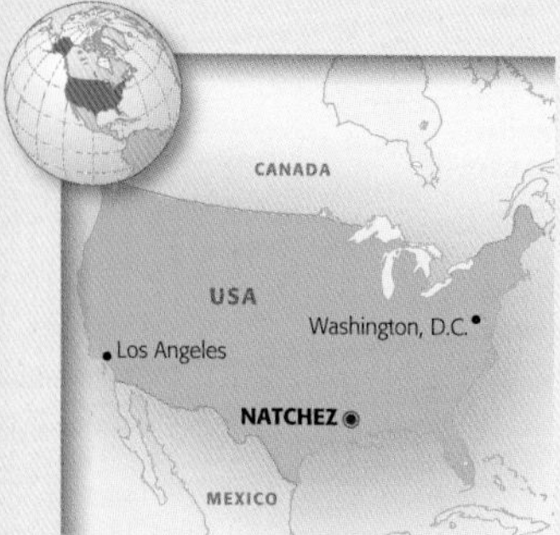

GETTING THERE See map p317, B4
Natchez is 90 miles (145 km) north of Baton Rouge's national airport, and 170 miles (275 km) from New Orleans' international airport. Car rental is available at both.

GETTING AROUND
Natchez is pleasant to explore on foot. The Trace is lovely for hiking, biking, and horseback riding, but a car is needed for longer trips.

WEATHER
Temperatures average a high of 70°F (21°C) and lows of 50°F (10°C) in March, with a high possibility of rain.

ACCOMMODATIONS
In Natchez or Clinton, try the reliable Hampton Inn and Suites; doubles from US$101; www.hamptoninn.com

The Natchez Eola Hotel marries Southern charm with modern amenities; doubles from US$106; www.natchezeola.com

The 1904 Bisland House Bed and Breakfast, with period antiques, is located a short walk from the historic district; doubles from US$125; www.bislandhouse.com

EATING OUT
You'll find plenty of traditional southern food such as fried chicken, turnip greens, and corn bread, as well as fine dining in grand style at mansions like Stanton Hall.

FURTHER INFORMATION
www.visitnatchez.com
www.scenictrace.com

Skirting the Issue

On the Natchez Trace, the sight of Southern Belles in sweeping hoop skirts soon becomes commonplace. In the 19th century, such skirts were de rigueur here, and now they're as much a symbol of the region as steamboats. Brutal to wear during the sweltering summer months, the multi-hooped petticoats are fitted over a bustle framework to keep their shape. Along with whalebone corsets, they are worn with pride by tour guides and re-enactors who take great pains, literally, to keep the South's rich history alive. Hoop skirts are part of the fabric of the region.

Above (left to right): Twilight over the Natchez Trace; paddle-steamer riverboat on the Mississippi; swampland forest walk on the Trace
Main: Magnificent Stanton Hall, a picture-book antebellum mansion

NATCHEZ TRACE

TO CAPTURE THE ESSENCE OF THE AMERICAN SOUTH IN A SINGLE JOURNEY is a romantic dream for many travelers. With its natural beauty and rich history, the Natchez Trace is a perfect introduction to one of America's most breathtaking regions. Springtime, when the sweet smell of magnolias fills the air, is the ideal time to visit, avoiding summer's humidity. The Natchez Trace is a 444-mile (715-km) scenic parkway that follows an old trail trekked by traders heading back to Nashville, Tennessee, from the port of Natchez, Mississippi. It links a series of towns and cities in Mississippi, Alabama, and Tennessee, each with its own charm. The region lends itself to leisurely drives, and traffic is never an issue, with strict speed limits and no trucks allowed on the Trace.

Natchez itself makes an ideal base from which to explore a stretch of the Trace. The town has more antebellum (pre-Civil War) houses than any other in the USA, but there is far more to Natchez than mansions and magnolias. The town is named for the native Natchez tribe, and their Grand Village offers a glimpse into the lives of the region's first settlers. Natchez-Under-the-Hill is today a genteel dock-side leisure district yet, in its 19th-century heyday, it was the most notorious landing on the Mississippi, teeming with gamblers and outlaws. The Natchez Museum of Afro-American History and Culture chronicles the experiences of Natchez's freed slaves in the wake of the Civil War.

Where ever you go, you will be greeted by friendly Southerners who strive to keep the history and culture of this region alive. To visit Natchez and the Trace is to be surrounded by Southern hospitality and a slower pace of life, as warm and easy as spring breezes off the Mississippi River. But it's those antebellum mansions – architectural wonders, regardless of their historical significance – that are the stars of Natchez, and you take a step back in time when you step through their magnificent portals.

To visit Natchez and the Trace is to be surrounded by Southern hospitality and a slower pace of life...

Inset: Spring Pilgrimage performance by a gospel choir
Below (left and right): Spectacular formal gardens of Monmouth; octagonal mansion of Longwood

ANTEBELLUM DIARY

The month-long Natchez Spring Pilgrimage is your best bet to visit some two dozen antebellum mansions. Guides wear period costume, and gospel choirs perform plantation songs. With Natchez as your base, five days allows you to discover the many facets of this historic region at a leisurely pace.

Five Days on the Trace

DAY 1

Take advantage of the year-round daily plantation tours of homes such as Melrose, the most intact antebellum estate in the USA; Monmouth, with its striking formal garden; quirky octagonal Longwood; Dunleith, whose colonnade encircles the house; and palatial Stanton Hall. End the day with dinner and music at Bowie's Tavern.

DAY 2

Stroll around town, then go for brunch at Biscuits & Blues, or Magnolia Grill in nearby Natchez-Under-the-Hill, which is well worth a visit for its shops, restaurants, and paddle-steamer riverboat trips. Call in at the Under-the-Hill Saloon for a lively happy hour, then enjoy an evening carriage ride around downtown.

DAY 3

Set off up the Trace. Worth a visit on your way are Emerald Bluff, a vast Natchez ceremonial mound; the Ruins of Windsor; and the Bullen Creek Trail forest walk. End the day in Port Gibson, the town Ulysses S. Grant found "too beautiful to burn."

DAY 4

Just outside Port Gibson is Sunken Trace, a moss-draped section of the original Trace. Mangum Mound is an ancient burial ground, and nearby Grindstone Ford marked the beginning of the Choctaw Nation territory. Visit antebellum Raymond, with its Confederate Cemetery and Civil War battle site, on your way to Clinton.

DAY 5

Explore the Clinton Nature Center, with trails through the lush native canopy and a butterfly garden bursting with color. Walk in the tracks of Andrew Jackson and John James Audubon at the Primitive Campsite exhibit. Allow a little time to see the beautiful brick streets of Clinton's Olde Towne before heading back to Natchez.

Dos and Don'ts

- ✓ Take advantage of guided tours; they really bring the history of the region to life.
- ✓ When driving the Trace, be aware of the many recreational cyclists and horseback riders who share the route with you.
- ✓ Make sure to allow enough time for plenty of stops along the Trace. You'll constantly see things that catch your eye.
- ✗ Don't forget comfortable footwear; Natchez is highly walkable and you'll want practical shoes for any trails you explore as well.

Below: Ruins of Windsor

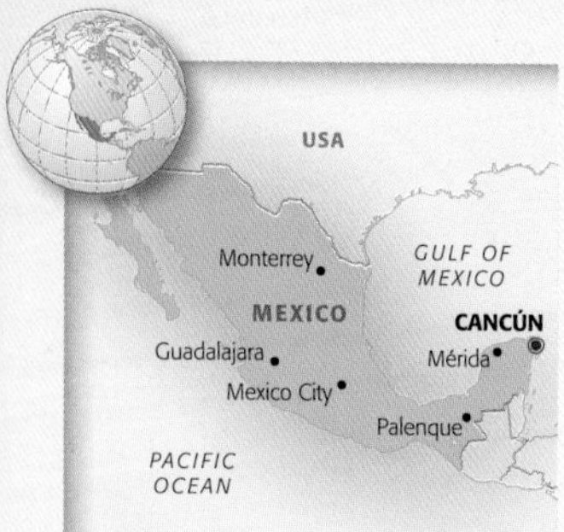

GETTING THERE See map p323, I5

The Yucatán is most easily reached via Cancún, which has flights from many parts of North America and Europe, or Mérida, which has air links with several North American cities.

GETTING AROUND

The best way to get around the peninsula is to drive. There is a choice of car rental agencies in Cancún and Mérida.

WEATHER

In March, daytime temperatures in Mérida range from 70°F to 90°F (21°C to 32°C). Days are hot and dry while nights are cooler.

ACCOMMODATIONS

Hacienda Chichén, Pisté, is a converted hacienda close to the ruins; family rooms from US$179; www.haciendachichen.com

Hotel Dolores Alba, Mérida, is a popular, friendly hotel; family rooms from US$50; www.doloresalba.com

Hacienda Uxmal is a luxurious hotel next to Uxmal ruins; doubles from US$99; www.mayaland.com/HaciendaUxmal.php

EATING OUT

Yucatecan cooking is a fusion of European techniques and Yucatec Mayan traditions and ingredients. Try refreshing lime soup and *pollo pibil* – chicken marinated in *achiote* (annatto), spices, and orange juice, then baked in banana leaves.

FURTHER INFORMATION

www.mayanruins.info

YUCATÁN

MEXICO'S YUCATÁN PENINSULA juts into the clear waters of the Caribbean just south of the Tropic of Cancer. It is most famous for the beaches that run like a sliver of mother-of-pearl near Cancún, but these are not the true jewels in its crown – the forest that swathes the peninsula is replete with ruined cities built by a civilization that began before the Romans and ended in the Renaissance. Many are still unexcavated, but others have been stripped of trees and vines to reveal the ornately carved temples, civic plazas, sports courts, and palaces that were the headquarters of the Mayan city states.

On the days of the vernal equinox, thousands gather at Chichén Itza to watch as the shadows cast down the great central pyramid form an undulating serpent of light and dark. This extends from the top of the temple, down the central stairway, to the gaping, fanged mouth of the snake-god Kukulcán. At

Main: Snake head detail from the Warriors' Temple in Chichén Itza

The Maize People

You will see corn or maize on sale all over the Yucatán as plain cobs, ground into flour and shaped into tortillas, even sweetened with sugar, turned into a thick cream, and put into donuts and cakes. Maize has been cultivated in the Mayan world for so many thousands of years that it has become an inseparable part of Mayan culture, and to many Maya, it is the very stuff of creation. Maize Gods appear in the temples, and according to the most sacred of Mayan books, the *Popul Vuh*, man was molded from maize by the Maize God Hun-Nal-Ye.

Uxmal and the nearby Puuc sites, pyramids and plazas are adorned with an elegant filigree of carved stone masks, geometric shapes, and sculpted animals. Wandering through the ancient Mayan cities gives a fascinating sense of a remote civilization, from its strange rituals to the details of everyday life.

These cities may be in ruins, but the Maya themselves are alive and well. From the sides of temples, they proffer woven hammocks and bright *huipil* shirts, and their friendliness and unhurried manner give a special tone and charm to Yucatecan life. Restored Spanish haciendas make wonderfully peaceful places to stay. The natural world is unique too: the limestone of the region is riddled with vast caverns, and underground rivers burst through into sapphire caves and waterholes called cenotes (sinkholes), which are unmissable places to swim. There is wilderness as well, from the flamingo-filled lagoons near the coastal village of Celestún to rain forests farther south. No matter how long you spend in the Yucatán, there is always more to see.

Above (top and bottom): A cenote, at Chichén Itza; the Temple of the Magician, allegedly built in a single night, in Uxmal

Bottom panel (left to right): Gracious portico of a traditional hacienda in Mérida; colorfully crowded vehicle in Mérida; jade burial mask from the Fuerte de San Miguel Museum in Campeche; view of the magnificent Five Floors Temple among the ruins at Edzná; bell tower at the Monastery of San Antonio de Padua in colonial Izamal

SPRING EQUINOX DIARY

The best way to see the Yucatán is to hire a car in Cancún and hop between the colonial towns that dot the peninsula. These towns can be used as bases for visits to the Mayan ruins and other sites. Ten days, starting on the vernal equinox (March 20–21), is enough time to experience the magic of this timeless world.

Ten Days in an Ancient World

Drive to Chichén Itza, stopping to swim in the Dzitnup cenote near Valladolid. Stay at a hotel close to the ruins.	**20th**
Reach the ruins around 8am, before the crowds, and stay all day, positioning yourself so that you can see the serpent shadow on the stairs in the afternoon.	**21st**
Head for Mérida, stopping at the charming colonial town and monastery at Izamal.	**22nd**
Wander around Plaza Mayor and the amazing market in Mérida, then on to the Anthropology Museum at Paseo de Montejo. Have dinner on a beautiful colonial patio.	**23rd**
Visit the flamingos at Celestún Biosphere Reserve, and then relax on the beach before returning to Mérida.	**24th**
Drive to Uxmal and visit the ruins there and at the small Mayan cities in the Puuc Hills – Kabah, Sayil, Labná, and the awesome caves at Loltún, a spellbinder for kids.	**25th**
Take the inland road south from Uxmal to Campeche, passing remote villages and stopping at the unusual Mayan ruins of Edzná on the way.	**26th**
In Campeche, explore the old town. Take a cab to Museo do la Arqueologia Maya at Fuerte de San Miguel to see Mayan jade funeral masks.	**27th**
Make an early start. Drive north past Mérida to the beach at Progreso and watch the sunset. Stay in Mérida.	**28th**
Return to Cancún. Stop for lunch at Valladolid and visit the small but superb Mayan ruin nearby at Ek-Balam.	**29th**

Dos and Don'ts

- ✓ Learn some Spanish since English is rarely spoken away from the coast.
- ✗ Don't drive at night.
- ✓ Book early to get a room near Chichén Itza around the equinox dates – they are in big demand.
- ✗ Don't take pictures of Mayan people without asking for their permission first.
- ✓ Carry plenty of water and wear a hat as the sun is fierce.

Below: Caribbean flamingos in a lagoon near Celestún

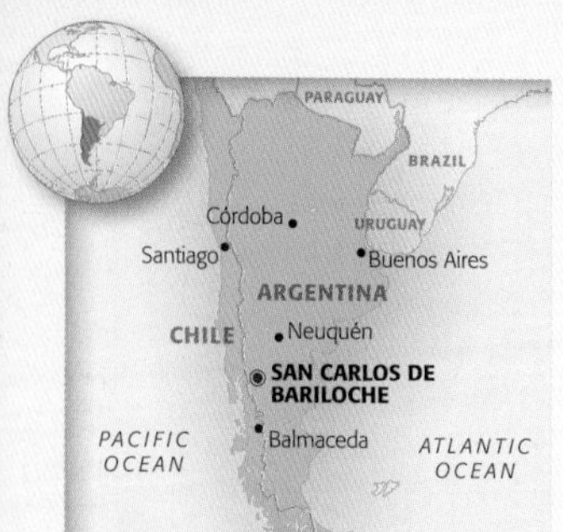

GETTING THERE See map p331, C4
From the international airport at the Chilean capital, Santiago, there are connecting flights to San Carlos de Bariloche, for the Alto Puelo area; Balmaceda for the Aisén region; and Neuquén. Your hosts will meet you and take you to your accommodation.

GETTING AROUND
Guides will accompany you on fishing trips.

WEATHER
March sees very little rainfall, with daytime temperatures of around 75–90°F (24–32°C).

ACCOMMODATIONS
Prices are per person, double occupancy, for 6 nights and 7 days' fishing, all inclusive.

Alto Puelo Lodge, in the Rio Puelo region, has three lodges in spectacular locations; from US$4,200; www.argentinachileflyfishing.com

The lodges at Cinco Rios and Estancia del Zorro offer packages from US$4,375, including meals and drinks; www.fishheadexpeditions.com

Jorge Trucco's Patagonia Outfitters, in the Neuquén area, has ten large, rustic lodges in beautiful settings on four watersheds; packages from US$6,430; www.patagonia-outfitters.com

EATING OUT
Fishing lodges serve three hearty meals a day plus snacks, using regional staples like Chilean sea bass, beef, lamb, and chicken. Excellent Chilean and Argentinian wine is included.

FURTHER INFORMATION
www.interpatagonia.com

One That Didn't Get Away

Every region has its fish story. This one tells of one of Argentina's original fly fishermen, José Evaristo Anchorena, "El Bebé", who popularized Patagonia in the USA through his friendship with noted American anglers. While he was happy for Yankees to fish his rivers, he didn't show them all the best spots. One he kept secret was a pool on the Rio Chimehuín where, in 1961, he hooked a huge brown trout that fought ferociously, speeding from one side of the river to the other for a full hour. The fish weighed in at 24 lb (11 kg), a record that stands to this day.

You might find yourself fishing a small spring creek, in waters so clear you can be up to your waist and still read the labels on your waders.

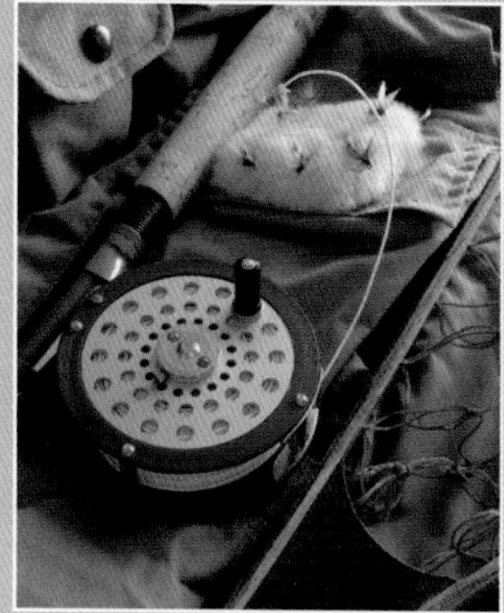

Main: Casting a line in a spectacular Patagonian lake setting

PATAGONIA

THOUGH THE VAST, BROAD PLAINS OF PATAGONIA ARE MOSTLY SEMI-ARID *pampas* rangeland, higher up in the foothills of the Andes the cool precipitation off the Pacific and the meltwater from glacial ice and snow give rise to hundreds of cold mountain lakes, and thousands of rivers, great and small, running down to the ocean. Fast-moving, clear, and cold, these rivers are much akin to those of Scotland or the American eastern seaboard, while the mountain landscape beyond owes more to Montana, or the high, cold slopes of the Himalayas.

It was in the early decades of the 20th century that American and European sports fishermen had the idea of introducing the fighting fish of the northern hemisphere into Patagonia's lakes and streams. With an assured food supply – and a lack of any natural predators – the brook, brown, and rainbow trout, steelhead, chinook, and Atlantic salmon all thrived in their new southern home, often reaching sizes never seen in their native northern waters.

ANGLER'S DIARY

Fly-fishing lodges straddle the border between Argentina and Chile, and usually prefer a mimimum one-week stay. In March the rivers are getting shallower, making the trout easier to hook, so it's an ideal month for the novice. This diary focuses on one region, but the overall experience is common to all three destinations.

A Week of Fly-Fishing Thrills

DAY 1

From San Carlos de Bariloche airport, it's a short car ride over the border into Chile, and then a transfer by jet boat across Alto Puelo Lake to your lodge. Take a deep breath of the mountain air and marvel at the stunning scenery. Chat with your fellow guests about the angling pleasures to come, over a delicious dinner and some excellent local wine (but don't forget, you'll want to make an early start in the morning!).

DAYS 2–3

Lake Puelo winds between fir-clad hills, and offers scores of fish-friendly nooks and crannies. Rainbow and brown trout are the prime species here, and your guide knows just where to set a fly to tease them out of hiding. You can easily spend two days fishing here.

DAYS 4–5

Puelo River offers rapids and whirlpools, small feeder streams, quiet green banks, rushing waterfalls and crystal-clear turquoise water. Try drift-fishing, or dry-land cast from the banks. The guide will point out the most promising places to try over a couple of days.

DAY 6

Chinook and Atlantic salmon were introduced into the Puelo system in the 1990s. For your last day on the water, re-tie those flies, take counsel with your guide and set out on the Puelo in search of salmon. Toast your success (or drown your sorrows) with fine Chilean wine accompanying a gourmet last supper.

DAY 7

Rise early, enjoy the dawn and a last hearty breakfast, then bid farewell to mountains, lake, and fish. Hop in the jet boat and zoom off across the still, turquoise surface of Lake Puelo on the way back to Bariloche.

Dos and Don'ts

- ✓ Practice catch-and-release, mandatory now in both Argentina and Chile. And remember – go barbless.
- ✓ Sample the superb local wines. Cool Chilean whites go well with a streamside lunch, while the richer Argentinian reds are perfect with dinner.
- ✗ Don't forget that most lodges offer fly-fishing lessons, plus a range of non-fishing activities such as nature treks and boat trips, for loved ones not devoted to the sport.

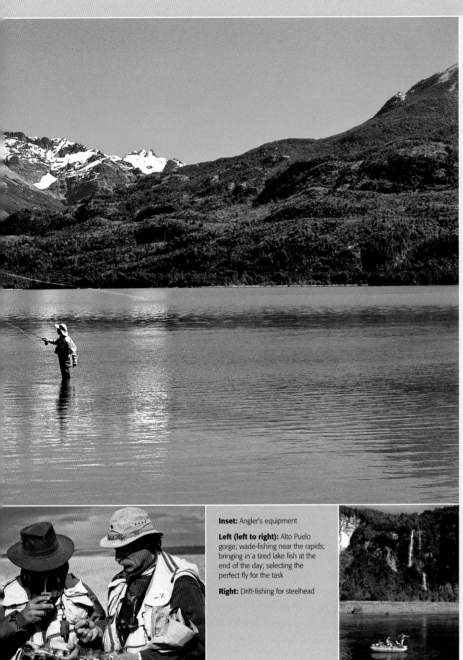

Inset: Angler's equipment

Left (left to right): Alto Puelo gorge; wade-fishing near the rapids; bringing in a tired lake fish at the end of the day; selecting the perfect fly for the task

Right: Drift-fishing for steelhead

Where the fish lead, the fishermen have followed. The varied terrain of the Andes provides a different type of water for every taste and skill level: small, shallow streams; riffled creeks; fast rivers with impressive rapids; and vast, long lakes that snake between the mountains, the water clear and cold, shimmering a lovely translucent blue when the sun shines, as it does most days in Patagonia. One day you might find yourself wade-fishing a small spring creek, in water so clear you can be up to your waist and still read the labels on your waders. On another you could be drifting through lush, impenetrable temperate rain forest, snow-capped mountains looming on the near horizon.

There are huge trout here, in abundance, but they don't give themselves up to just anyone. Professional guides will advise on choice of fly, and offer tips on where to cast your line. Once the bait is taken, the real contest begins. The fish here fight the line all the way, as much above the water as below it. They swirl, dance, leap, and tail-walk, trying everything to throw the hook. Only through true skill will you have the pleasure of easing the net below that tired fish, removing the barbless hook from its mouth and saying "thank you," as it swims away back to its lair.

Below: Typical wood-built Patagonian fishing lodge

APRIL

Where to Go: **April**

April is a beautiful month to be in the USA – the northern states are settling in to a sunny spring, while the South has yet to get hot and steamy. In Louisiana, visitors can comfortably enjoy outdoor food, music, and culture at the lively Festival International de Louisiane, while the old town of Charleston and the South Carolina Lowcountry are highly picturesque at this time. Central America is approaching the end of its dry season. Belize remains pretty sultry year-round; some countries, like Panama, show signs of getting very hot. In Brazil, summer is drawing to a close, which means temperatures are more comfortable and the heavy rains are easing. Below you will find all the destinations in this chapter as well as some extra suggestions to provide inspiration.

FESTIVALS AND CULTURE

EASTER ISLAND Ancient *moai* statue, carved from volcanic rock

UNFORGETTABLE JOURNEYS

BLUE RIDGE PARKWAY The winding Linn Cove Viaduct

NATURAL WONDERS

IGUAZÚ FALLS A footbridge overlooking the mighty cataract

EASTER ISLAND
CHILE

Remote home to one of the wonders of the world

This is one of the most isolated places on earth, with its huge, brooding, enigmatic sculptures, called *moai*.

See pp90–91

TOONIK TYME, IQALIT
NUNAVUT, CANADA

Week-long celebration of Inuit life

Marking the end of the long Arctic winter, this festival showcases Inuit skills and traditions – anything from throat singing to building an igloo.

www.tooniktyme.ca

LEXINGTON
VIRGINIA, USA

Historic 19th-century Virginian town

Set amid the undulating Shenandoah Valley, this appealing town has an old-world atmosphere and plenty of Civil War memorabilia

www.lexingtonvirginia.com

LOS ANGELES
CALIFORNIA, USA

More than just filmstars and freeways

The USA's mightiest metropolis is home to numerous attractions, from Art Deco landmarks to the superb collections of the Getty Center.

www.discoverlosangeles.com

BLUE RIDGE PARKWAY
NORTH CAROLINA, USA

A jaw-dropping scenic drive

This celebrated driveway winds through mist-shrouded hills and great National Parks, revealing American heritage along the way.

See pp92–3

HIKING THE APPALACHIAN TRAIL
EASTERN USA

A great walking challenge

Tackle this legendary long-distance wilderness trek, stretching for 2,000 miles (3,218 km) from Georgia to Maine.

www.appalachiantrail.org

"Built purely for the pleasure of driving, the road features gentle curves and frequent overlooks of sensually rounded, blue-misted hills."

BOAT TRIPS TO ISLA DE LA PLATA
ECUADOR

The alternative Galápagos

This island just off the coast of Ecuador is home to marine birds, sealions, dolphins, manta rays, and humpback whales.

www.ecuador.com

HELLS CANYON
IDAHO/OREGON, USA

Tackle some of the West's most challenging white water

Raft down the Snake River as it twists through Hells Canyon, the deepest river gorge in the USA.

www.fs.usda.gov/recarea/wallowa-whitman

ARCHIPELAGO DE SAN BLAS
PANAMA

Quintessential island adventure

Sail these stunning islands, which are ringed with palm-shaded white-sand beaches.

See pp88–9

CABOT TRAIL
NOVA SCOTIA, CANADA

This Cape Breton drive is wild, rugged, and beautiful

This route follows Cape Breton's northern shore before climbing to a high plateau. See fish eagles, moose, and pods of whales.

www.cabottrail.com

IGUAZÚ FALLS
ARGENTINA/BRAZIL

The largest waterfalls in the world

The thundering Iguazú Falls boil away on the border of Argentina and Brazil. Brace yourself and stare down the Devil's Throat.

See pp82–3

LOS GLACIARES NATIONAL PARK
ARGENTINA

Sub-Antarctic wilderness

Los Glaciares is home to almost 50 glaciers, fed by the giant Andean ice-cap, which slither into iceberg-dotted lakes.

www.losglaciares.com

VOLCÁN ARENAL
COSTA RICA

Spectacular volcano in the heart of Central America

Hike, bike, kayak and zipline through this lush and tangled national park that's watched over by the doormant Volcán Arenal.

See pp94–5

GALÁPAGOS ISLANDS
ECUADOR

A group of volcanic islands with unique flora and fauna

April is the best month to see the legendary giant tortoises, as well as sea turtles, baby sealions, and island flowers.

See pp86–7

DOMINICA
CARIBBEAN

The wild isle

Pretend to be Robinson Crusoe as you discover this untamed island of rain forests, geysers, towering palms, windswept coves, and Boling Lake.

See pp98–9

COLCA CANYON
PERU

The world's deepest canyon

Twice as deep as the Grand Canyon, the Colca Canyon boasts stunning natural scenery, along with condors and vicuñas, and beautiful old churches.

internacional.peru.info/en/home

Previous page: A shoal of razor surgeon fish, Galápagos Islands

Weather Watch

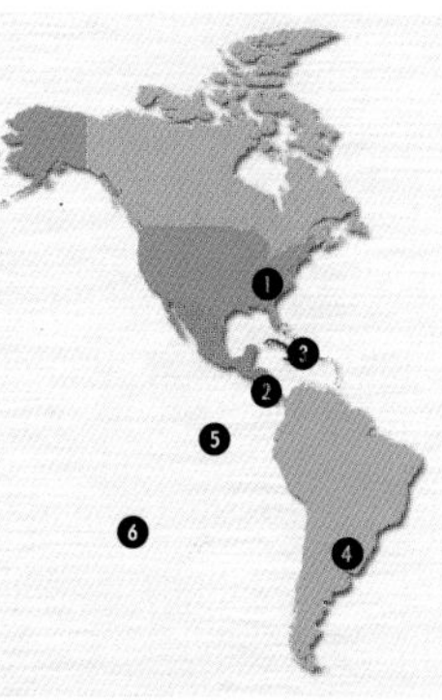

❶ North Carolina, USA April is a lovely time to drive the Blue Ridge Parkway. However, temperatures in North Carolina are cold at high altitudes and conditions can change at a moment's notice – you might even see snow.

❷ Panama Visiting the Archipelago de San Blas before the rainy season guarantees perfect weather for snorkeling, relaxing on the beautiful beaches, and sailing the islands.

❸ Dominica April ushers in the beginning of warm weather in Dominica and the island can be rather humid. This makes it the perfect location for beating the winter blues and ushering in the sun.

❹ Iguazú Falls, Argentina The falls are at their most impressive in April, as the water levels are high after the summer rains. Temperatures are cooling down.

❺ Galápagos Islands The rainy season is ending in the Galápagos Islands, off Ecuador, which means lower humidity, appealing temperatures of around 82°F (28°C), and brilliantly green, lush landscapes.

❻ Easter Island Though officially part of Chile, Easter Island is almost 2,500 miles (4,023 km) from the mainland and has its own climate. April is mild, if somewhat wet, with dazzling sunshine and cooling breezes.

LUXURY AND ROMANCE

TURKS AND CAICOS ISLANDS Snorkeling at Grace Bay, Providenciales

TURKS AND CAICOS ISLANDS
CARIBBEAN

Sun-bleached coral islands

Escape to these tiny islands for chilled-out days on the white-sand beaches, excellent diving among coral reefs, and luxurious pampering.

See pp84–5

"The isles and cays of the Turks and Caicos are fringed by snow-white sands and waters of startling electric blues."

CAPE MAY
NEW JERSEY, USA

The USA's most historic seaside resort

The historic town of Cape May has been famous for its invigorating sea breezes and genteel atmosphere since the 18th century.

www.capemay.com

PUERTO VALLARTA
MEXICO

Playground of legendary lovers Liz Taylor and Richard Burton

PV, as the locals call it, still retains an aura of Hollywood glitz but you can find delightful beaches away from the bright lights.

www.visitpuertovallarta.com

SCOTTSDALE
ARIZONA, USA

The place to live the Arizonan high-life

Nicknamed "The Beverly Hills of The Desert," Scottsdale is one of the liveliest and most affluent small cities in the West.

www.scottsdaleaz.gov

SANTA YNEZ VALLEY
CALIFORNIA, USA

Idyllic rural escape in the heart of Santa Barbara's wine country

Choose from over 70 world-class wineries, as well as a seductive array of romantic inns, top-notch restaurants, and tempting shops.,

www.visitsyv.com

ACTIVE ADVENTURES

URUGUAY A *gaucho* (cowboy) at work

URUGUAY
SOUTH AMERICA

Discover South America's hidden gem

From fun in the sun on Atlantic beaches to time in the saddle as a *gaucho*, this tiny country has many facets to discover.

See pp96–7

DIVING IN THE BOCAS DEL TORO
PANAMA

Remote archipelago

Plunge into the tropical waters surrounding these beautiful islands, home to abundant marine life and superb coral reefs.

www.bocas.com

BUCKSKIN GULCH
UTAH, USA

Hike through the world's longest slot canyon

A challenging trek through the dramatic Buckskin Gulch, navigating tiny gorges between towering sandstone walls.

www.americansouthwest.net

FAMILY GETAWAYS

BRANSON The terrifying "Wildfire" ride at Silver Dollar City

BRANSON
MISSOURI, USA

Amusement parks in a gorgeous setting

Rides, shows, music, festivals, and all-round fun – this scenic Ozarks resort is a vacation paradise that's as lively or as laid-back as you like.

See pp80–81

NATIONAL CHERRY BLOSSOM FESTIVAL
WASHINGTON, D.C., USA

Spring festivities

This festival started in celebration of the gift of 3,000 cherry trees from Tokyo in 1912.

www.nationalcherryblossomfestival.org

CHARLESTON
SOUTH CAROLINA, USA

More than springtime blooms and manners from heaven

There's a genteel air about these historic coastal towns, but beyond lie wild marshes and wide beaches that are perfect for exploring.

See pp78–9

ST. KITTS AND NEVIS
CARIBBEAN

Have some big family fun on these two small islands

Ride the sugar train, explore Brimstone Hill Fortress, walk through the rain forest, go snorkeling, or laze on the beach.

www.stkittstourism.kn

HILL COUNTRY
TEXAS, USA

Texas, German-style

This region boasts a distinctly German flavor, especially in historic Fredericksburg, and offers unspoilt scenery, lake swimming, hill views, and plentiful campsites.

www.hill-country-visitor.com

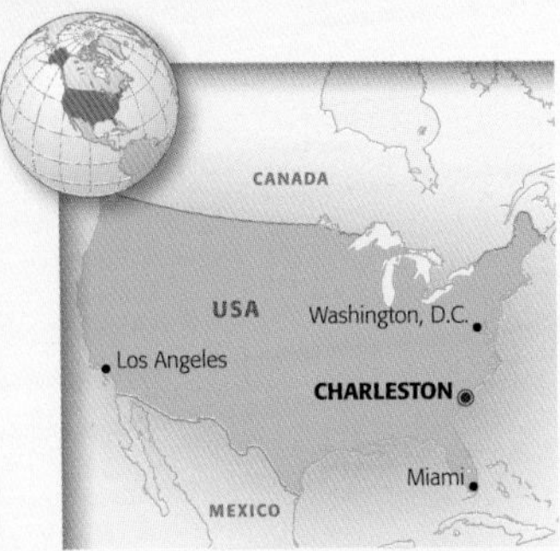

GETTING THERE See map p317, G3
Charleston and Beaufort are on South Carolina's coast, with Charleston International Airport 15 miles (24 km) west of the city.

GETTING AROUND
Travel beyond the Charleston Historic District requires a car. Within it, walk, take a taxi, or use the Downtown Area Shuttle trolley (DASH).

WEATHER
Spring in the Lowcountry has moderate humidity and mostly sunny weather. The daytime average is 76°F (24°C), with night temperatures dropping to 56°F (13°C).

ACCOMMODATIONS
King Charles Inn is a family favorite near the Historic District, Charleston; rooms from US$269; www.kingcharlesinn.com

Charleston Place offers an excellent location in Charleston and upscale family rooms from US$415; www.charlestonplace.com

Rhett House Inn is a gracious antebellum plantation home in Beaufort; family rooms from US$229; www.rhetthouseinn.com

EATING OUT
Many eateries offer family dining from US$10–20. Barbecue, fried chicken with grits (corn porridge) and hushpuppies (cornmeal fritters), and seafood are all local favorites.

FURTHER INFORMATION
www.charlestoncvb.com
www.beaufortsc.org

Gullah Culture

When the Civil War ended, the sea islands of this area became a haven for newly freed slaves who flocked here to live in peace, creating the unique Gullah culture. St. Helena Island, between Beaufort and Hunting Island State Park, is home to a large population of the self-sufficient Gullah people. Here too is Penn Center, which began in 1862 as the first school for freed slaves. Today, the Gullah are known for their farming, fishing, and fine crafts, including intricately woven sea-grass baskets.

CHARLESTON

Below (top and bottom): A cherub amid a bed of flowers at Magnolia Plantation; the grand spiral staircase at Nathaniel Russell House

Like the grand southern belle she is, the gracious seaside city of Charleston, South Carolina, is at her best in springtime, when her streets and historic gardens explode in a riot of blooming hues. The city's renowned house and garden tours open the doors to a hidden world of grandeur that set the stage for the lavish lifestyle of the antebellum South. Stroll along the cobblestone streets through one of the South's oldest and best-preserved historic districts, where graceful mansions and carefully tended homes stand close together along narrow streets. Flowering vines curve around doorways that lead to secluded gardens and courtyards – the soft sea air is rich with the scent of magnolia and jasmine blossoms, and azaleas, rhododendrons, hostas, and columbine add beauty to the already elegant buildings they adorn. Along the Ashley River, outside Charleston, stand the remains of great plantations that once produced unbelievable wealth from harvests of indigo and rice. Many plantations displayed their wealth through grand gardens, and one of the greatest was at

Magnolia Plantation, started in the 1830s as a gift for John Grimke Drayton's young bride. Each succeeding generation expanded the gardens in a natural style, and today visitors can explore the rambling paths through 50 acres (20 ha) of trees, shrubs, and flowers which gradually blend into the natural beauty of the Ashley River marshes. In contrast, the formal gardens of the nearby Middleton Plantation were carefully planned in the European style, incorporating geometric patterns, Greek-inspired statues, and terraced expanses of lawn leading down to the river.

Farther south along the coast, the town of Beaufort is a gem renowned for its elegant antebellum mansions and waterfront. If all this well-tended polite charm gets too much, just beyond the town lie the fertile tidal marshes of St. Helena Island, best explored by kayak – it's a teeming nursery of life where tall grasses shelter a rich abundance of shrimp, crab, and young fish, which in turn attract dolphins. A little farther on, Hunting Island State Park preserves a vast area of tidal marsh, lagoon, and maritime forest, and its expansive white-sand beaches are an invitation to run, cycle, and generally let off steam.

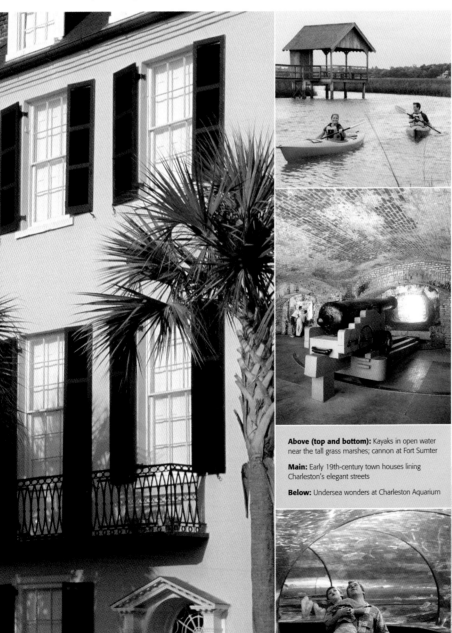

Above (top and bottom): Kayaks in open water near the tall grass marshes; cannon at Fort Sumter

Main: Early 19th-century town houses lining Charleston's elegant streets

Below: Undersea wonders at Charleston Aquarium

LOWCOUNTRY DIARY

Early April is the height of spring in Charleston. The area's rivers were once highways transporting cotton, rice, and indigo, and wealthy plantation owners had town homes, many of which are now open for tours. Allow six days to explore Charleston and Beaufort, the Atlantic beaches, and Lowcountry marshes.

Six Days of Heritage

DAY 1 Take a carriage ride down historic Charleston's cobblestone streets and hear local antebellum histories. Tour the 1808 Nathaniel Russell House and the antique-filled 1825 Edmondston-Alston House.

DAY 2 Gaze into the two-story-tall Great Ocean Tank at the South Carolina Aquarium to bond with a 220 lb (90 kg) loggerhead turtle, named Caretta, swimming with other marine life, including sharks and pufferfish. Take a 30-minute boat trip across Charleston Harbor to Fort Sumter National Monument, where the Civil War began on April 12, 1861.

DAY 3 Visit the legendary aircraft carrier, U.S.S. *Yorktown,* and other famous ships and aircraft at Patriots Point Naval and Maritime Museum. Then spend the afternoon building sand castles and sunning on Sullivan's Island.

DAY 4 Drive the Ashley River Road National Scenic Byway, canopied by moss-draped oaks, and explore the gardens at Magnolia and Middleton plantations. Stop at Charles Towne Landing, the Carolinas' first European settlement, and visit the zoo.

DAY 5 Explore the Lowcountry near Beaufort. Kayak through salt marshes and watch for bottlenose dolphins. Return to antebellum Beaufort, and browse the boutiques and galleries along Bay and Carteret streets.

DAY 6 Drive to Hunting Island State Park and walk through the maritime forest's sandy trails. Climb the lighthouse for sweeping views and then enjoy the beautiful beaches for the rest of the day.

Dos and Don'ts

- ✓ Wear comfortable shoes and explore the historic streets of Charleston and Beaufort on foot to glimpse private gardens, visit old churches, and admire the antebellum architecture.
- ✓ Stroll through Charleston's White Point Gardens beneath the huge live oak trees and let the kids climb on the cannons.
- ✗ Don't forget to spend time relaxing on a bench-swing in the Beaufort Waterfront Park for a magnificent view of the boats.
- ✓ Children of all ages love exploring the pathways that wind through Magnolia Plantation, discovering arched bridges over ponds and hidden nooks with garden statues.

Below: Carriage ride past antebellum mansions in Charleston's East Battery

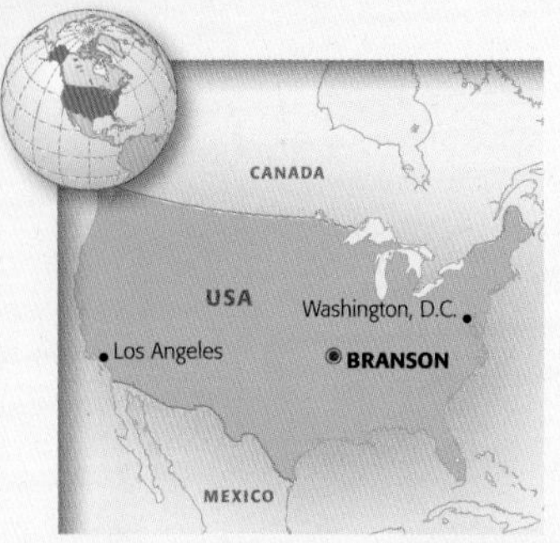

GETTING THERE See map p317, B1
Springfield-Branson National Airport is the arrival point for several domestic carriers that provide direct or connecting flights from most major US cities. Branson is 43 miles (70 km) south.

GETTING AROUND
Rental cars are the best option for getting to and around Branson. Because the Strip is relatively compact, many attractions are within walking distance of one another. Taxis are also available.

WEATHER
April highs can reach 68°F (20°C), with night-time lows around 45°F (7°C). Rain and an occasional thunderstorm are quite possible.

ACCOMMODATIONS
Grand Country Inn has its own free water park (indoor section open all year); family rooms from US$100; www.grandcountry.com

Baymont Inn & Suites has a pool and is close to the Strip; doubles from US$80; www.baymontinns.com

Still Waters Condominium Resort is on Table Rock Lake; one-bedroom condo from US$159; www.stillwatersresort.com

EATING OUT
Try Ozark specialties such as barbecue, cornbread, catfish, and handmade fudge. A restaurant dinner might cost US$15–25. Dinner theaters will be at least twice that.

FURTHER INFORMATION
www.explorebranson.com

Above (left and right): Branson country and western club; Table Rock Lake at sunset

BRANSON

For a fun-filled break, head for the hills of Branson. Nestled in the enchanting Ozark mountains, this family-friendly vacation paradise is surrounded by rolling green hills, tranquil lakes, and – come the warmth of springtime – blooming forsythia, dogwood, and wildflowers. The region is buzzing at this time of year, not just with the spectacle of nature returning to life, but also with festivals celebrating music, heritage, crafts, and food.

Once a sleepy little backwoods village, where the local folk took their young 'uns to favorite fishing holes, Branson has grown into a world-renowned mega-resort with lavish Las Vegas-style entertainment, thrilling amusement parks, abundant outdoor activities, and an impressive selection of accommodation and dining options. More than 50 live-performance theaters host everything from spectacular Broadway-type productions to toe-tapping, knee-slapping, twangy bluegrass and country music shows. Nearly all of this is on or around the 5-mile (8-km) stretch referred to as "the Strip" or "Country 78."

High on the list of family favorites is 1880s-mining-town-themed Silver Dollar City, with thrill rides, live shows, and demonstrations of pioneer handicrafts. Descending nearly 500 ft (152 m) beneath the theme park, Marvel Cave was a popular attraction before Branson's rise to fame. A National Natural Landmark, the cave is filled with glittering rock formations.

Dolly Parton's Dixie Stampede is another big hit, an action-packed extravaganza that includes stunt horseback riding, pyrotechnics, comedy, music, and other exuberant entertainment. The four-course dinner feast is especially enjoyable, with chowder, whole chickens, baked potatoes, and other goodies all to be slurped or eaten with your hands (silverware supplied upon request).

Plenty more activities await families: a scenic railway ride through the Ozark foothills; narrated sightseeing tours aboard World War II-inspired amphibious "duck" vehicles; and a lively lunch or dinner show on the elegant *Showboat Branson Belle*, an 1880s-style paddle-wheeler that plies the waters of Table Rock Lake. And, for a more peaceful interlude, you could always grab some poles and seek out a secluded fishing hole.

Marvelous Marvel Cave

Marvel Cave was discovered in the 1500s by Osage Indians, who dubbed it "The Devil's Den" and made it a forbidden place. In the 19th century, explorers renamed it Marble Cave (in fact the rock is limestone). It has been open as a tourist attraction since 1894, and deserves its current name. It's not for everyone, though – the descent is made by walking nearly 600 stairs, and some passages are low and narrow. A cable tram returns visitors to the surface.

Main: Silver Dollar City "Wildfire" ride
Below (left and right): "American Plunge" ride at Silver City; Dolly Parton's Dixie Stampede

DOWN HOME DIARY

Early spring is ideal for a fun-filled family adventure in the Missouri Ozarks. Some attractions may still be closed (water parks, for example), but you'll avoid the summer crowds, and two top music festivals are in full swing. Four days is just right to enjoy some lively shows, revel in amusements galore, and take a trip out of town.

Four Days of Rip-Roarin' Fun

DAY 1

Dive headlong into your adventure with a narrated sightseeing tour on an amphibious vehicle with Ride the Ducks. Choose from land or lake tours, or take one of each. Then get on over to Dolly Parton's Dixie Stampede for an evening of fabulous fun and a four-course dinner feast that kids of any age will love to eat with their hands.

DAY 2

Spend the entire day at Silver Dollar City, about 9 miles (14 km) from the Strip. Among 30 rides and attractions is the giant swing that blasts sky-high out of barn doors and will fit the whole family (minimum height 48 in/122 cm). View demonstrations of pioneer handicrafts including woodcarving, basket-weaving, blacksmithing, and candy-making, and try your hand at some. Take a tour of Marvel Cave and its beautiful "cathedral" cavern. Included in the price of admission are music and comedy shows and festivals. You'll be there during the month-long World-Fest, heralded as America's largest international cultural festival.

DAY 3

Relax strolling the boardwalk along the border of Taneycomo Lake at Branson Landing, a shopping and dining district with a water-fountain feature that fires at the top of the hour. In the evening, climb aboard the *Showboat Branson Belle* for the dinner-show cruise.

DAY 4

Chug through the lovely Ozarks on a narrated journey into local lore on the Branson Scenic Railway. End the day with one more family show – try "The Haygoods" music show, featuring eight siblings singing in harmony.

Dos and Don'ts

- ✓ Explore the local antique shops that offer traditional handmade quilts and other regional collectibles.
- ✗ Before casting your line, don't forget to check that you're in possession of any requisite fishing license.
- ✓ Be aware that there can be considerable traffic congestion along the Strip. Park and walk whenever possible, to save time and alleviate stress.
- ✓ Come prepared for changeable weather: bring rain gear, hats, sunglasses, and – no matter what the weather forecast predicts – sturdy footwear.

Below: Branson Scenic Railway in the Ozarks foothills

GETTING THERE See map p330, F6
Straddling the border of Argentina and Brazil, the Iguazú Falls stretch across a precipice for nearly 2 miles (3 km). Flights land at Puerto Iguazú, via Buenos Aires in Argentina and at Foz do Iguaçu via São Paulo in Brazil.

GETTING AROUND
The best way to discover the falls is on foot. Extensive networks of walkways edge the cataracts on both sides of the border.

WEATHER
In April, the average temperature range is 63–82°F (17–28°C). This is the rainy season, when humidity and water levels are high.

ACCOMMODATIONS
In Puerto Iguazú, Hotel Esturión offers suites with river and rain forest vistas; doubles from US$66; www.hotelesturion.com

The Sheraton Iguazú Resort and Spa is the only hotel within the Iguazú National Park on the Argentinian side of the falls; doubles from US$333; www.starwoodhotels.com

In Brazil, try Hotel Das Cataratas; doubles from US$375; www.hoteldascataratas.com

EATING OUT
Specialties in Argentina include tropical river fish such as *surubí*. In Brazil, fish, rice, beans, and fried bananas are tropical staples.

FURTHER INFORMATION
www.iguazuargentina.com/en
www.cataratasdoiguacu.com.br

Wildlife of the Paraná

Home to some 450 species of birds and 80 varieties of mammal, the Paraná rain forest around the Iguazú Falls is a treasure trove of exotic fauna. Most visible are the raccoon-like coatimundis *(above)* and vibrant butterflies. Capuchin monkeys chatter and scream, and iguanas and caiman lounge beside streams. Swifts nest on rock faces, darting in and out of the vapor kicked up by the falls. Predatory kites circle the sky and treetops come alive with colorful birds. However, feline forest dwellers, such as the puma and jaguar, keep a low profile.

This great wonder of the natural world is shared between Argentina and Brazil and derives its name from the native Guaraní word for "big waters."

Main: The mighty Iguazú Falls, drawing over a million spectators each year
Above: Iguacú River and the Devil's Throat – the crowning jewel of the Iguazú Falls

IGUAZÚ FALLS

Snaking westwards from southern Brazil for hundreds of miles, the Iguaçu River grows in size as it collects the water from over 30 rivers on its way to the Argentinian border. Here, the river, swollen to bursting point, widens and slows as if gathering itself for what is coming. Suddenly, the ground just falls away, forcing the river to plunge hundreds of feet in over 250 separate churning waterfalls, forming the planet's widest span of falling water.

This is the mighty Iguazú Falls, higher than Niagara and wider than the Victoria Falls. This great wonder of the world is shared between Argentina and Brazil and faces another country, Paraguay, and derives its name from the native Guaraní word for "big waters." Never was a name so apt.

The surrounding Iguazú National Park, a lush subtropical rain forest, forms a perfect green frame for the waterfalls, laced with trails of red earth – pathways into an enchanted kingdom of squalling toucans, screaming

Left (left to right): Thirsty butterfly atop a lantana floret; winding footbridge at the Iguazú Falls on the Argentinian side; the vast Itaipú – one of the biggest power plants on the planet; speedboats near the foot of the cascades

Inset: Characteristically colorful toucan at Parque das Aves in Foz do Iguaçu, Brazil

capuchin monkeys, and butterflies of kaleidoscopic colors. But it's the falls that are the star attraction, and visitors can walk far out across the churning surface of the river on a network of carefully constructed walkways, right up to the cataracts that tumble down like cascading veils into a frothing maelstrom of bubbling foam, spray, and water. Vapor clouds billow upwards from the crashing torrents, drenching skin and creating huge rainbows that arch across the falls. Up close this awesome spectacle almost overpowers the senses. Rich color abounds – the glistening falls, the emerald rain forest, and the soupy mud-brown river – while the thunderous roar of the water is deafening and a refreshing spray soaks you to the skin.

A sense of experiencing the planet at its most primordial and powerful heightens at the Garganta del Diablo (Devil's Throat). At 262 ft (80 m) it is the biggest of all Iguazú's cataracts. Standing above the Garganta, you see why it has been a source of legend for the Guaraní for millennia, as its torrents rage furiously over rocks and mist rises above the cataract's rim. Looking into the abyss that swirls at its core, the sensation is of peering into the very heart of the earth.

DEVIL'S THROAT DIARY

The falls are at their dramatic best during the April rains. For the full experience, take in the views from both sides of the border. With Argentina's Puerto Iguazú as your base, drink in the falls, explore the forest, and enjoy adventure activities. You could also take a city break to Rio *(see pp302–3)* or Buenos Aires *(see pp238–9)*.

Three Days at the Cataracts

DAY 1

Arrive early to the Argentinian side of the falls and begin your adventure with a jungle hike, spotting toucans and other tropical birds as you go.

Drink in the views from the Upper Circuit, as cascade upon cascade tumbles into the Lower Iguazú River.

After lunch, experience the falls from close quarters, along the Lower Circuit.

Later, hop on a boat to San Martín Island for stunning vistas of the San Martín cataract. Follow this with a powerboat ride to the foot of the towering waterfall.

DAY 2

Still on the Argentinian side, ride the eco-train through the forest before trekking to the lip of the legendary Garganta del Diablo waterfall – the mightiest of them all – and feel the jaw-dropping power of this cataract.

In the afternoon, take a gentle boat ride along the Upper Iguazú River drifting past gallery forests rich in bird life. Alternatively, to be more energetic, hike the quiet Macuco Trail to spot capuchin monkeys and tropical birds. At the trail's end, cool off beneath the beautiful Salto Arrechea waterfall.

DAY 3

Cross to the Brazilian side and head to the gigantic Itaipú hydroelectric dam – among the largest projects of its kind in the world.

Returning to nature, walk to the foot of the Garganta, which comprises 14 individual cataracts, and marvel at the panoramic vistas along the way.

Visit a tropical bird sanctuary before returning to Argentina for your flight home.

Dos and Don'ts

- ✓ Bring mosquito repellent, a plastic bag for your camera, and proper rain gear – you're going to get soaked.
- ✗ Don't forget that United States and Canadian citizens must obtain a Brazilian visa before traveling to Brazil.
- ✓ Check to see if your trip coincides with monthly full-moon walks to the Garganta del Diablo – the views are worth it.
- ✗ Don't start out on the lovely Macuco Trail too late into the afternoon – the return trek will take roughly 3 hours.
- ✓ Arrive early at the falls to avoid large crowds.

Below: Passengers on the unique eco-train ride to Devil's Throat

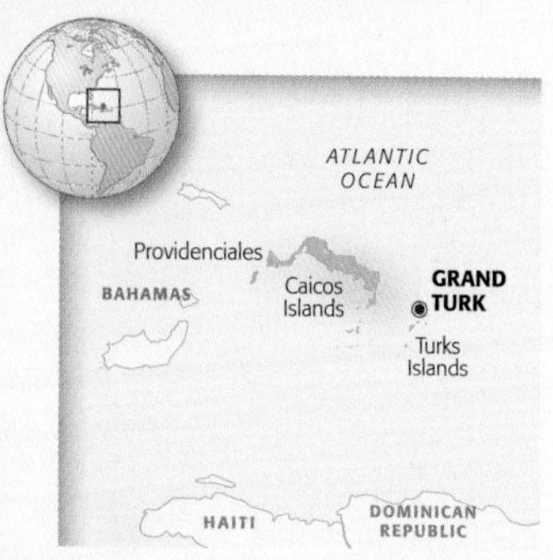

GETTING THERE See map p325, E3

There are daily international flights to Providenciales (Provo) and Grand Turk from Florida, New York, and Nassau; and weekly from London. Private charter planes link the isles.

GETTING AROUND

Provo has tourist charter buses and taxis; cars, scooters, and bicycles can be rented. Minivans act as communal taxis on Grand Turk and smaller isles, but Cockburn Town is walkable.

WEATHER

Temperatures are perfect in April, averaging 84°F (29°C) in the daytime. Rainfall is minimal.

ACCOMMODATIONS

Provo has dozens of fine hotels to choose from. Options on most other islands are limited.

Bermudan-style architecture and a pool at the Caribbean Paradise Inn; doubles from US$165; www.caribbeanparadiseinn.com

Historic colonial Grand Turk Inn, Grand Turk; doubles from US$300; www.grandturkinn.com

The Tuscany has a magnificent beachfront with doubles costing from US$775; www.thetuscanyresort.com

EATING OUT

There are local eateries in Provo town, and hotel restaurants serve international fare.

FURTHER INFORMATION

www.turksandcaicostourism.com

The National Dish

Local islanders love to eat the queen conch (pronounced "konk"), a giant marine snail that is easily identified by its gnarly, spiral shell with a lustrous pink inside. Feeding on seabed larvae, the conch grows to over 12 in (30 cm) long. The mollusk's sweet, slightly rubbery white meat is considered a delicacy and is eaten raw in conch salad, or made into fritters, chowders, gumbo, and it even makes a good burger. However, the conch has been over-exploited and is now endangered.

TURKS AND CAICOS ISLANDS

If you are looking for idyllic islands that are pristine, uncrowded, and made for a relaxing hedonistic escape, look no further. Part of the British West Indies, the Crown colony of Turks and Caicos (pronounced "kaykos") Islands are all this and more. Specks in the vast Atlantic Ocean southeast of the Bahamas and north of Hispaniola, they sit atop a marine plateau ringed by the third-largest coral reef system on earth. The Columbus Passage, the deep channel between Grand Turk and the rest of the islands, is a main route for migrating humpback whales, manta rays, turtles, and dolphins. Add exceptional cliff diving and excellent visibility, and it's understandable why divers are delirious about the opportunities here. Ashore, these quaintly named isles and cays are fringed by snow-white sands and startling electric blue waters.

Providenciales, or Provo as it is known locally, is the westernmost and most-developed isle. It has a plethora of ritzy resorts centered on Grace Bay Beach, a gentle 12-mile (19-km) scimitar of sand

Below (top to bottom): Sea anemone on the coral reef; a massage on the beach at Parrot Cay; Cockburn Town house, Grand Turk

that's ranked as one of the world's most beautiful beaches. Pure luxury and pleasure are on offer here. Choose your daily dose of fun from waterskiing, wakeboarding and parasailing or a relaxing pamper in a sumptuous spa. Or you can be whisked to sea on a sunset cruise after a round at the championship course at Provo Golf Club. At night, there's the eerie thrill of glowworms.

The lusher larger isles – Middle, North, and East Caicos – are a wildlife photographer's dream, boasting fantastic birds in wetlands easily accessed by a splendid trail system. South Caicos is where the turquoise flats of Belle Sound boil with bone fish and briny salt ponds draw flocks of rose-pink flamingos and local and migrating rare birds.

Grand Turk, the sleepy political and historical capital island, is all colonial wood-and-stone clapboard houses cloaked in crimson bougainvillea. Donkeys plod the dusty streets but you can saddle up on fine local steeds to splash through the waves. Old-world inns here prove picture-postcard-perfect places for romantic candlelit suppers. On neighboring Salt Cay, you'll see ospreys atop old wooden windmills, and in early April divers can swim out to commune with whales.

Main: One of the many inlets on Grand Turk

Above (top and bottom): Horseback riding on Grand Turk; sunset sailing trip on a catamaran

Below: Reggae band, Lovey and the Lively Stones, performing on Provo Island

BLISSED-OUT DIARY

Fringed by frost-white sands and waters of blue perfection, the Turks and Caicos Islands are ideal in April. Most of the best attractions are found on and around Providenciales and Grand Turk. You'll find six days is plenty of time to sample the best of these superb isles, with a trip to Salt Cay to see the humpback whales.

Six Days of Sun and Sea

DAY 1
Arriving in Provo, rest up at your hotel on Grace Bay or on a nearby cay. Head for the beach and take the occasional dip in the ocean. In the evening enjoy a romantic candlelit dinner alfresco, perhaps at the upscale Infiniti Restaurant & Raw Bar, at the Grace Bay Club.

DAY 2
Take a sightseeing jaunt around Provo, including the Caicos Conch Farm and lovely Sapodilla Bay. Later, enjoy a beach cruise, stopping off at Iguana Cay for a spot of snorkeling. End the day with a relaxing spa treatment and a cocktail as the sun goes down.

DAY 3
Hit the heights by parasailing at Grace Bay. Then either laze the day away on its long stretch of sensational sands or go out for a scuba dive or snorkel. Alternatively, you might like to spend the afternoon playing golf or take a sportfishing trip.

DAY 4
Fly to Grand Turk and pass the morning exploring Cockburn Town on foot, being sure to visit the Turks and Caicos National Museum. Savor a meal here and take in a rake 'n' scrape band at the Salt Raker Inn.

DAY 5
Jump onto a ferry or boat ride to Salt Cay for whale-watching (the entire herd of humpbacks passes through here), and to see sleepy Balfour Town. Visit the salt ponds to spot the local and migrating birds such as ospreys, pelicans, boobies, and flamingos.

DAY 6
Return to Provo by charter flight. Have one last swim before setting off for your return trip home.

Dos and Don'ts

- ✓ Be sure to shuffle your feet through the sand when wading in the shallows. Stingrays often hide beneath the surface and can lash out with their barbed tails if stepped on.
- ✗ Don't take home conch shells as souvenirs – they may be seized by Customs.
- ✓ Use plenty of sunscreen, as the sun is intense and can burn you even through a T-shirt.
- ✗ Don't be tempted to eat the local delicacy, conch, as it is now an endangered species.

Below: Snorkeling with sea stars along Grace Bay Beach, Providenciales

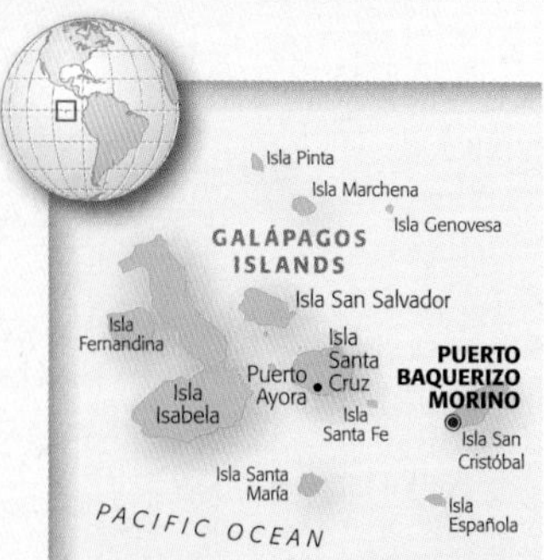

GETTING THERE **See map p327, A6**

The islands of the Galápagos archipelago straddle the Equator, 600 miles (1,000 km) off the coast of Ecuador, South America. International flights go to Quito and Guayaquil in Ecuador, then take a flight to a domestic airport in Santa Cruz.

GETTING AROUND

Small cruise ships and charter boats offer organized excursions around the islands.

WEATHER

Pleasantly warm with temperatures averaging 81°F (27°C). Feb–Apr are the rainiest months, when the islands are at their most verdant.

ACCOMMODATIONS

Finch Bay Eco Hotel, Puerto, Ayora has a great selection of tours; from US$1,923 per person for 4 days; www.finchbayhotel.com

The charming motor schooner *Beagle* holds 12 passengers in six cabins with private baths; from US$2,722 per person for 8 days; www.galapagostraveler.com

Nemo is a sleek catamaran for 12 passengers; from US$3,500 per person for 8 days; www.galapagosinformation.com

Galápagos Explorer II, a luxury cruise yacht, carries100 passengers; from $5,400 per person for 8 days; www.mvgalapagosexplorer.com

EATING OUT

Seafood is a specialty. Catered meals are included on boat charters.

FURTHER INFORMATION

www.galapagos.org

The Origin of Species

When naturalist Charles Darwin visited the Galápagos in 1835, he noted how each of the 13 islands had a unique species of finch. Darwin speculated that they were all descended from one mainland species and isolation had encouraged the development of individual species adapted to their unique environments. In 1859, using evidence he collected in the Galápagos, Darwin upset the established view of creation with the publication of his evolutionary theory in *The Origin of Species*.

Above (left to right): Galápagos tortoise resting; colorful Sally Lightfoot crab, San Cristobal Island; blue-footed booby displaying
Main: Brown pelican plunging to catch a mullet

GALÁPAGOS ISLANDS

NO ONE HAS EVER SUGGESTED THAT THE GALÁPAGOS ISLANDS ARE A TROPICAL PARADISE. One could hardly imagine a more forlorn piece of earth. Darwin called them "the gardens of Hell." In these volcanic islands, the youngest – those farthest west – are still rising from the sea, the product of a "hot spot" hundreds of miles below the ocean floor. The older isles – about five million years old – are softly worn down, in contrast to the newer, more rugged isles. Even the coconut palm, the supreme emblem of the Pacific, is missing. Yet people come back from these islands speaking of marvels and exotic encounters: the islands' namesake (*Galápagos* is Spanish for tortoise), the giant tortoise, heaving its 610-lb (275-kg) weight up the beach, sealions that let you lie down beside their newborn pups, and Galápagos hawks that land on your head.

The islands, which owe their unique quality to their isolation, were set aside as a national park in 1959. Visits are strictly regulated and a licensed naturalist guide accompanies each cruise boat to enforce the park rules and educate tourists on the unique ecology, geology, flora, and fauna of this fascinating and fragile archipelago.

Everywhere, lava lizards dart back and forth and iguanas lie torpid on shoreline lava floes like prehistoric flotsam washed ashore.

Huge manta rays glide shadow-like under the boat while bottlenose dolphins break the water's surface beside you. On Floreana and Jervis islands, go ashore to watch flamingos wading in pink-tinged, oozy mud. You can dive with hammerhead sharks off Bartolomé Island or snorkel with penguins off Fernandina. Everywhere, lava lizards dart back and forth, iguanas lie torpid on shoreline lava floes like prehistoric flotsam washed ashore, marine turtles' eggs are hatching, and female frigate birds wheel overhead as their mates proudly puff up their vermilion chests. You don't need to be interested in evolutionary theory to be thrilled by these islands, where 90 percent of the reptiles, 80 percent of the land birds, and 40 percent of the plants are unique.

Inset: Satellite image showing the craters on the islands of Isabela and Fernandina
Below (left to right): Isolated cove on Bartolomé island; diving among a school of striped salema; watchful marine iguana

NATURALIST'S DIARY

The Galápagos are unique in offering spectacular eye-to-eye encounters with wildlife: most of the animals and birds show no fear of humans. The islands are best explored on an organized cruise, departing from Puerto Ayora, Santa Cruz. It's worth adding a few days for exploring Quito and the Andean town of Otavalo.

Nine Days Exploring the Islands

DAY 1
Visit the Charles Darwin Research Station in Puerto Ayora to view the giant tortoise breeding program.

DAY 2
Explore the verdant Santa Cruz highlands, keeping a look-out for its giant tortoises.

DAYS 3–4
Depart by boat for Española (Hood). Commune with marine iguanas, sealions on sandy beaches, and colonies of albatrosses and blue-footed boobies.

On nearby Floreana, watch flamingos and snorkel with marina turtles and sharks at Devil's Crown. Leave your mail in the "Post Office Barrel."

DAYS 5–8
Hike through the misty highlands of Isabela and swim with sealions and Galápagos penguins at Tagus Cove.

Look for dolphins and whales in the Bolivar Channel. On Fernandina, photograph cormorants and hike to the summit of a spectacular crater.

After the long haul to Genovesa (Tower), anchor in spectacular Darwin Bay for fabulous birding plus a chance to snorkel with Galápagos fur seals.

Next stop – Bartolomé for a hike to the summit of Pinnacle Rock and panoramic views. Continue to South Plaza, to see the enormous sealion colony.

DAY 9
Go snorkeling at Santa Fe. Look out for its land iguanas and prickly pear cacti.

Return to Santa Cruz to begin your homeward journey.

Dos and Don'ts

- ✓ Stay on the trails. The ecosystem is delicate and wandering off the trails can do lasting damage.
- ✗ Don't touch the creatures – it is strictly forbidden.
- ✓ Travel by small boat (fewer than 20 passengers is ideal), which offers a more intimate experience.
- ✗ Don't overdo it on your first day if you fly in to Quito – you may need some time to adjust to the 9,350-ft (2,850-m) altitude.

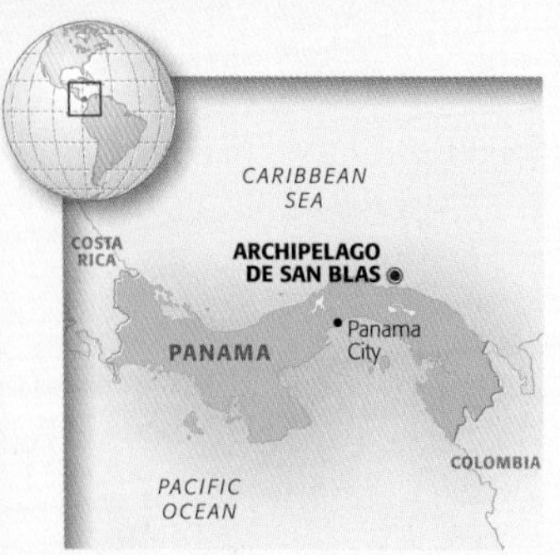

GETTING THERE See map p324, H6
Flights from Panama City to the San Blas Islands depart from Albrook (Marcos A. Gelabert) Airport.

GETTING AROUND
Sail charters offer trips around the islands, the ideal way to explore the archipelago.

WEATHER
The San Blas Islands are sunny and warm throughout the year; the perfect time to visit is in spring, just before the rainy season hits.

ACCOMMODATIONS
Most sail charters have sleeping quarters onboard. The islands have a number of casual hostels and hotels, including Cabanas Coco Blanco on Lemon Cays (from US$130 per night; no website or phone; ask your sail charter captain).

For budget lodging in Panama City, try the longrunning Mamallena (www.mamallena.com), which has dorm rooms (from US$12) and private rooms (from US$30). Mamallena can also arrange trips and accommodation on the islands.

EATING OUT
The Kuna Indians operate a number of small food stands throughout the islands, where you can feast on fresh lobster and other seafood.

FURTHER INFORMATION
www.visitpanama.com

The Kuna Language

The Kuna language, which forms part of the Chibchan language family, is spoken by the Kuna indigenous people of Panama and Colombia. In the Kuna language, *dule* or *tule* translates as "people," and the name of the language is dulegaya ("people mouth.") Though most of the Kuna speak Spanish, you'll still hear the Kuna language on the islands. A few words to learn: *mola* is shirt or clothing; *ogob* is coconut; *bede nued guddi* is "how are you?"

Sailing through the archipelago affords you the opportunity to island-hop, lolling on secluded beaches, and snorkeling amid colorful, darting fish and feathery corals.

Main: Diablo Island San Blas
Above (top and bottom): Close-up of a red-eyed tree frog on Kuna Yala; a Kuna fishing boat on Los Pelicanos island

ARCHIPELAGO DE SAN BLAS

Sailing the San Blas islands is the quintessential tropical adventure: the wide-open sky, glittering blue waters, palm-fringed white-sand beaches. The 365-plus San Blas islands, strewn across the waters off Panama's northern coast, are the picture of pristine island life. Sailing through the archipelago affords you the opportunity to island-hop, lolling on secluded beaches, snorkeling amid colorful, darting fish and feathery corals, and, after all this exploration, refueling over midday feasts of fresh lobster. The marine life is astonishingly diverse, and you will find stingrays, zebra fish, squid, and jellyfish on the reef. If you're lucky, you may even see dolphins leaping over the waves. The culture and history of the San Blas islands are as compelling as the scenery. The self-governing Kuna (or Guna) indigenous people, who inhabit about 49 of the islands, have impressively managed to maintain their language, economic structure, and traditions, including fishing from dugout canoes, subsistence agriculture with

Left (left to right): A bird-motif *mola* handicraft made by the Kuna; lobsters at Grullos Keys; yacht exploring San Blas

Inset: Seastar on seagrass

products such as coconuts, bananas, and sugar cane, and, most notably, creating their famed, colorful, handsewn mola (shirt or clothing). The Kuna people also throw festivals throughout the year, so it is worth asking your boat captain if one is taking place during your visit.

The islands, including El Porvenir, Achutupu, and Corazon de Jesus, are protected by a massive reef, making them ideal for leisurely exploring by sailboat. The Caribbean waters are calm with the optimal amount of breeze, so you can easily cruise between the islands, dropping anchor when you want to snorkel or disembark to explore dry land. Numerous boat charter companies offer trips, a common one sailing between Cartagena in Colombia, and Panama City, including a 2- to 4-day layover in the San Blas islands. Alternatively, many companies arrange air transfers from Panama City straight to the islands.

If the archipelago's allure is hard to resist, and you decide to spend some time on the islands themselves rather than on a sailboat, you'll find a range of rustic but comfortable lodges, many of which offer kayak and other tours.

ISLAND DIARY

Maximize your time in the sparkling Caribbean waters of the San Blas Islands by opting for a sail charter that includes a flight from Panama City to the islands, a 4 to 5-day sail around the archipelago, and then a return flight to Panama City.

Five Days of Sailing and Sun

DAY 1

From Panama City, fly to Corazon de Jesus, which has one of the longest airstrips on the islands. Spend the afternoon exploring the coastline, splashing in the waters, and then stretching out under the shade of palm trees.

DAY 2

Your sailing charter will stop into a variety of islands as you sail the archipelago. Highlights include Cayos Coco Bandero, a cluster of islands that include the famous "one-palm island," which is a tiny hump of sandy land, with one main palm shooting straight up into the sky. Snorkel and swim, snap photos of the palm tree-flanked horizon, and then buy chilled beer and lobster from a Kuna food shack and picnic on the beach.

DAYS 3–4

As you continue your sailing cruise, other popular spots include the Cayos Holandeses, uninhabited islands in the north of the archipelago, surrounded by a coral barrier. Also, many of the sailing tours stop into islands such as Anguja and Chichimei, which occasionally have small Kuna-run shops where you can pick up examples of the elaborately stitched *molas* and colorful, intricate beading.

DAY 5

Take a last dip in the Caribbean in the morning and then fly back to Panama City, from where you can catch domestic and international flights.

Dos and Don'ts

- ✗ Don't choose a boat charter company before doing your research. It's imperative that the captain and crew have lengthy experience in sailing the islands, and that you confirm this with the tourist office and/or your hotel. Also, note that the Kuna locals who manage the islands will sometime impose rules regarding which sailing charters can access the islands; make sure to inquire and confirm.
- ✓ Hydrate regularly while you're on the boat, slather your skin with sunscreen and wear a hat or other head protection. The sea breezes can be deceptive, making it seem cooler than it really is – the Caribbean sun is powerful, particularly around midday.
- ✓ Feel free to ask your captain about flexibility with the sailing itinerary; most crews are open to tailoring an itinerary to your needs, and this can often result in unique detours.

Below: The island of Achutupu

Above: *Moai* statue, carved out of volcanic rock

EASTER ISLAND

Ask your friends what they know about Easter Island, and they will almost certainly mention the huge, brooding statues known as *moai*. Almost 900 *moai* pepper this unlikely outpost of civilization, a small chunk of volcanic rock in the South Pacific some 1,250 miles (2,000 km) from Pitcairn Island, the nearest inhabited place. Why did the native inhabitants, the Rapanui, carve these *moai*? How did they move them from the quarry, high on the slopes of an extinct volcano, to locations miles away? And why were all the *moai* toppled? Definite answers are few, but a number of experts believe the statues represented the ancestors of the island's clans, and that clans pulled down each other's *moai* during a 17th-century war for control of the island's diminishing resources (all the *moai* now standing have been re-erected in modern times). There is less agreement about how the Rapanui moved these huge statues – the largest one that was transported weighs 82 tons – across the island. Sleds, log rollers, and other mechanisms have all been suggested, but no one knows for sure.

The mystery just adds to the allure of this utterly idiosyncratic place. Until its airport opened in 1967, Easter Island was extremely difficult to reach. Even now, it's a five-and-a-half-hour flight from Santiago, Chile. As a result, it's one of the few places on earth where you can almost completely escape the background noise of modern global culture. There are no chain stores or traffic lights; neither are there any malls, condos, cell phones, or billboards. Locals on horseback trot down dirt streets in Hanga Roa, the only town on the island. Shopkeepers and bartenders have time to chat, and no one cares about the latest Hollywood scandal. At night, the sky is spangled with impossibly bright stars – after all, Hanga Roa creates only the faintest amount of light pollution.

Many people dream of visiting Easter Island, but only about 40,000 arrive annually. Since April falls between high and low seasons, you may find yourself contemplating a *moai*, gazing across an ancient crater, or strolling along a beach without another human being in sight. As crying seabirds and the ceaseless wind create the only sounds, and salt-scented air fills your lungs, you may truly feel you've arrived at the end of the world.

Main: *Moai* on Anakena Beach, sporting red scoria topknots
Below (left and right): Traditional dancers showcasing Polynesian culture; horseback riders at Ahu Tahai near Hanga Roa

GETTING THERE See map p331, A8
Easter Island, one of the most isolated places on earth, lies 2,400 miles (3,800 km) west of the Chilean mainland. Cruise lines do call at the island, but Chilean airline LAN offers the only scheduled flights, via Santiago or Tahiti.

GETTING AROUND
Rent a 4WD car or mountain bike, get a taxi, or ride horses like the locals. Some walking is required to reach many *moai* sites.

WEATHER
Average temperatures vary from 65 to 76°F (18 to 24°C). April has about 15 rainy days.

ACCOMMODATIONS
Hotel O'tai is conveniently located on a main street in Hanga Roa, near shops and bars, with doubles from US$180; www.hotelotai.com

Hotel Taha Tai, a 10-minute walk from central Hanga Roa, has spacious if somewhat plain doubles from US$250; www.hoteltahatai.cl

Explora Rapa Nui offers chic oceanfront luxury, 4 miles (6 km) from Hanga Roa; doubles from US$2,266 for two nights; www.explora.com/hotels-and-travesias/rapa-nui-chile

EATING OUT
Jardin del Mau (US$20) serves decent seafood and pasta. La Taverne du Pêcheur (US$50) offers French-influenced fare, while Te Moana (US$15) has everything from burgers to curries.

FURTHER INFORMATION
www.chile.travel/en
www.easterisland.travel

Where is Everyone?

The indigenous Rapanui once lived all over Easter Island, but civil warfare and lack of resources had devasted the population by the 18th century. Another blow came in 1862, when slave raiders captured 1,000 Rapanui. Only 15 returned, bringing smallpox with them. By the 1870s, just over 100 Rapanui were left. Foreigners later forcibly moved them to Hanga Roa and ran the rest of the island as a sheep farm, until Chile ended the lease in 1953. Most lands outside town are now national parks, but some have been returned to the Rapanui.

ISLAND DIARY

April is a great time to visit Easter Island – the summer crowds of January and February are gone, but the winter chill hasn't set in yet. Surfers, hikers, and scuba divers might enjoy a longer stay, but for most visitors three days are sufficient to see the *moai* and get a taste of the island's unique Polynesian culture.

Three Days in Mid-Ocean

DAY 1

Visit the Father Sebastián Englert Anthropological Museum to learn about the island's history. Explanatory panels are in Spanish, so buy an English guidebook in the museum boutique. Return to town for a casual seafood lunch, then spend the afternoon browsing through small souvenir shops, the colorful artisans' market, and the outdoor municipal market. As dusk approaches, head to Ahu Tahai, near the museum. Bring your camera and tripod to capture the seven *moai* silhouetted against the spectacular sunset.

DAY 2

Since the island's archeological sites can be hard to find and few have interpretive panels, sign up for an all-day guided tour (English-speaking guides are plentiful and lunch is usually included). Make sure the tour features the Rano Raraku quarry, where *moai* in various states of completion stud the hillsides like lost soldiers from a different planet. Other popular stops include Rano Kau (a volcanic crater lake), the Orongo village archeological site, and the 15 *moai* at Ahu Tongariki. Finish the day with the touristy, yet immensely enjoyable, Polynesian dance and music show at the Hanga Roa Hotel.

DAY 3

Sporty types can book a horseback tour, indulge in some heart-thumping mountain biking along the hilly south coast, tackle the hiking trail from the museum to Orongo village, surf challenging waves, or scuba dive in the crystal-clear (if somewhat fish-free) waters. If all that sounds exhausting, simply pack a picnic and head to Anakena Beach for a relaxing afternoon.

Dos and Don'ts

- ✓ Bring lots of cash, in Chilean *pesos* or US dollars. Many businesses don't accept credit cards, or charge a premium if they do.
- ✗ Don't step on *ahus*, the stone bases supporting the *moai*. The Rapanui consider it sacrilegious to walk on or near them.
- ✓ Wear lots of sunblock since constant breezes make it easy to forget how powerful the sun is.
- ✗ Don't forget to bring an umbrella and jacket, in case of rain.
- ✓ Book rooms well in advance, as hotels often sell out.

Below: View from Orongo village along the eastern rim of Rano Kau

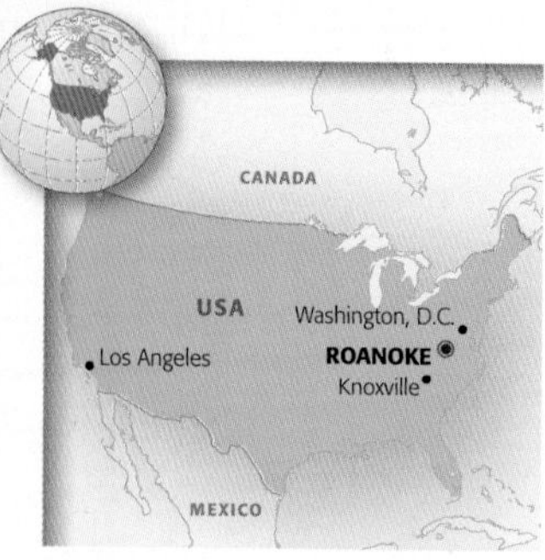

GETTING THERE See map p317, G1
Fly into Roanoke Regional Airport in Virginia and fly out from McGhee Tyson International Airport in Knoxville, Tennessee.

GETTING AROUND
Rent a car that is comfortable to drive for long stretches and on mountain curves. The parkway speed limit is 45 mph (72 kph).

WEATHER
Late April is warm in the lower slopes, but can sometimes reach near freezing at high altitudes. Be ready for all kinds of weather.

ACCOMMODATIONS
The Inn at Ragged Gardens in Blowing Rock has rooms with baths and fireplaces from US$145; www.ragged-gardens.com

The luxurious Inn on Biltmore Estate is near the Biltmore Estate Winery; doubles start at US$319 and two-night packages include admission to the Estate; www.biltmore.com

The rustic Fryemont Inn overlooking Bryson City and Great Smoky Mountains National Park offers double rooms from US$155 including breakfast and dinner; www.fryemontinn.com

EATING OUT
Try eclectic Metro! in downtown Roanoke (US$25) or Blowing Rock's Speckled Trout Café & Oyster Bar serves fresh local trout and seafood (US$20).

FURTHER INFORMATION
www.blueridgeparkway.org
www.nps.gov/blri

The Missing Link

All but 7 miles (11 km) of the 469-mile- (755-km)-long Blue Ridge Parkway were built between 1935 and 1967, but the remaining section took another 20 years. The engineering challenge of building an environmentally sensitive road at an elevation of 4,100 ft (1,250 m) around one of the region's oldest mountains resulted in the graceful sweep of the Linn Cove Viaduct. Assembled on site, the 1,243-ft- (379-m-) long viaduct was built in 153 segments, each weighing 50 tons.

BLUE RIDGE PARKWAY

TRACING A SERPENTINE PATH FOR 469 miles (755 km), the Blue Ridge Parkway is one of America's most celebrated scenic highways. Built purely for the pleasure of driving, the road features gentle curves and frequent overlooks presenting views of sensually rounded, blue-misted hills. Hawks glide above, while historic farmlands lie nestled in forested valleys below. In April, the mountains explode in a palette of pinks, reds, and violets as wild rhododendron and mountain laurel bloom, lining the parkway with brilliant hues for miles. The woodlands wear a thousand shades of newborn green, while the delicate blooms of dogwood, redbud, iris, and trillium color the landscape.

A National Park itself, the parkway connects two others, beginning in Virginia's Shenandoah National Park and ending at the Great Smoky Mountains National Park. There are numerous

Main: Scenic vista of misty hills from the Blue Ridge Parkway

Left (left and right): Peaceful Mabry Watermill; bright azaleas lining the parkway in spring

Right (left and right): Great Smoky Mountain Railroad; south facade of the magnificent Biltmore mansion

attractions along the way, such as Mabry Watermill, with its lovely millpond, or the elegant mansion of 19th-century denim millionaire, Moses H. Cone, which he willed to the Park Service for all to enjoy. Groomed carriage roads offer amazing views as they wind past mountain lakes and meadows.

Nestled in the mountains along the parkway, the artistic town of Asheville, renowned for its colorful residents, creative lifestyle, and galleries, deserves a longer stay. You'll want to explore the famed Folk Art Center, which showcases fine quilts, pottery, carvings, and crafts from the distinguished artisans of the Southern Highland Craft Guild. George Washington Vanderbilt built his famed Biltmore Estate here in 1895, with grounds by noted landscape architect Frederick Law Olmsted. Today it is one of the most visited historic sites in the USA.

The parkway ends at the Great Smoky Mountains National Park, 45 miles (72 km) from Knoxville, famed for its misty mountain vistas and for Cades Cove, with its hand-hewn farms.

OPEN-ROAD DIARY

The Blue Ridge Parkway is lightly traveled at this time of year and, while some of the smaller visitor facilities may be closed, the long stretches of open road without traffic are fun to drive on, as well as offering stunning scenic views and outstanding roadside beauty.

Seven Days on the Road

Enter the parkway at Roanoke and head south, stopping at Mabry Mill. Exit at Blowing Rock, where winds blow from the river gorge 3,000 ft (915 m) below. Explore the town, dine, and stay the night. **DAY 1**

Visit the Moses H. Cone Memorial Park. Marvel at Linn Cove Viaduct, and walk to pretty Linville Falls. Lunch at Little Switzerland before exploring the wild area near Craggy Gardens. Do stop at the Folk Art Center for locally produced crafts before exiting at Asheville. **DAY 2**

Take a break from driving and spend the day exploring Asheville. Visit the Biltmore Estate and tour the mansion, gardens, and winery, and enjoy the shops and restaurants in Historic Biltmore Village. Downtown offers the Thomas Wolfe Memorial State Historic Site, Grove Arcade, walking tours, and galleries. **DAY 3**

Back on the parkway, continue to the Pisgah Inn and, for a great view, hike to the ridge top where the Vanderbilt Hunting Lodge once stood. The Devil's Courthouse Trail also leads to grand vistas or you can take the self-guided nature trail at the parkway's highest point of 6,047 ft (1,843 m). **DAYS 4–5**

When the parkway ends, head into Cherokee to see the Museum of the Cherokee Indian and the native Qualla Arts and Crafts Shop. Then drive to Bryson City for the Great Smoky Mountain Railroad Depot.

Spend a day or two in the Great Smoky Mountains National Park, and take an auto tour, or explore the great outdoors on horseback. Highlights include Cades Cove Loop, with its fascinating pioneer history. **DAYS 6–7**

Dos and Don'ts

- ✓ Consider extending the trip, starting at the north end of Shenandoah National Park.
- ✗ Don't exceed the speed limit (45mph/72 kph) and adjust your speed to suit the conditions on the parkway.
- ✗ Don't hesitate to stop and explore whenever you spot something interesting along the way.
- ✓ Travel on the US 52 highway to Andy Griffiths' hometown, Mount Airy, the inspiration for his classic 1960s comedy.

Below: Carefully preserved mansion in the Moses H. Cone Memorial Park

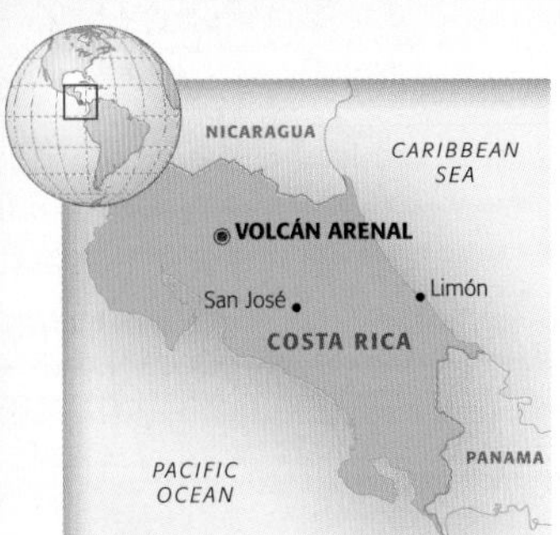

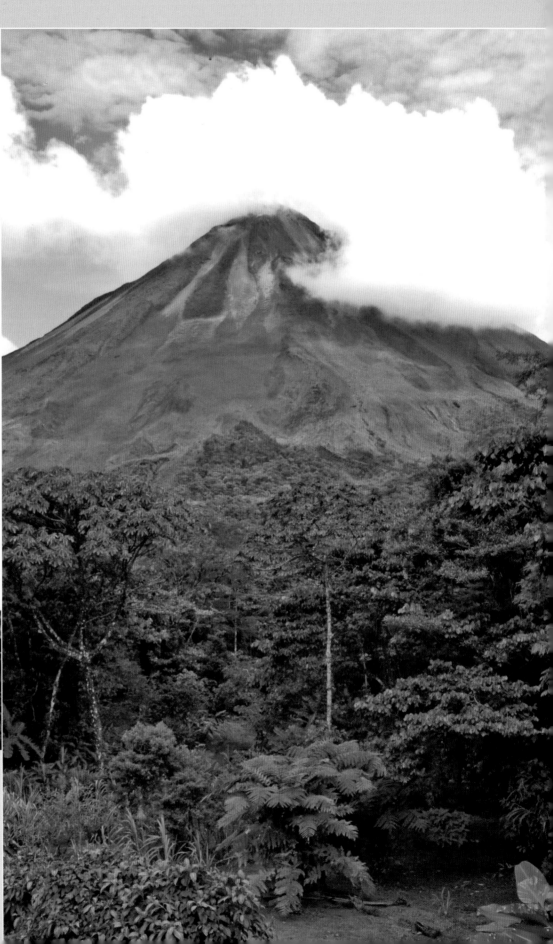

GETTING THERE See map p94, A6

A variety of transport options are available from Juan Santamaría International Airport in San José. You can drive (via taxi or bus; 3 to 4 hours), or fly on a local airline to a private airport near La Fortuna (30 minutes to 1 hour).

GETTING AROUND

The easiest way to explore the region is via a combination of taking tours (which generally include all transport), as well as taxis and local buses.

WEATHER

The spring season, just before the rainy season, is an ideal time to visit, with balmy average temperatures around 70–75°F (21–24°C).

ACCOMMODATIONS

Enjoy volcano views at the Arenal Observatory Lodge; from US$133; www.arenalobservatorylodge.com

Near El Castillo, unwind at the breezy Rancho Margot; from US$139; www.ranchomargot.com

Eco-friendly Nayara Hotel, Spa & Gardens has a spa perched on a cliff; doubles from US$320; www.arenalnayara.com

EATING OUT

La Fortuna is dotted with casual restaurants serving Mexican and Tico cuisine, like Las Brasitas, with a menu of tacos and ceviche.

FURTHER INFORMATION

www.visitcostarica.com
www.ticotimes.net

Ziplining in Costa Rica

Ziplining may have originated in China and the Himalayas, but modern jungle canopy ziplining was perfected in Costa Rica in the 1970s by a pair of US graduate students, who wanted to gain a new perspective on the teeming rain forest. Since then, ziplining has become synonymous with Costa Rica, which offers soaring tours across the country. Local outfitters run tours throughout the dense jungles around Arenal, including over La Fortuna waterfall. Best of all, ziplining is as much about spying wildlife and tropical vegetation as it is about just plain fun.

Above (left and right): Fortuna Waterfall; Lake Arenal
Main: Volcano Arenal surrounded by lush jungle landscape

VOLCÁN ARENAL

Volcán Arenal may be in a "resting" phase, but it still exudes a dramatic dominance that extends across the surrounding national park after which it's named. After hundreds of years of dormancy, Arenal erupted in July 1968, decimating a nearby village. Since then, the volcano was continually active until 2010, when it entered its current sleeping mode. No matter when your eyes alight on the volcano – at sunrise, at the height of the noonday sun, or at sunset – its cone piercing the sky is a majestic sight.

The natural park that unfolds around the volcano is equally remarkable, with tangled forests, meandering rivers, waterfalls, and quiet swimming holes. The shimmering highlight is Lake Arenal, which extends for a vast 33 sq miles (85 sq km), earning it the distinction of Costa Rica's largest landlocked body of water. Numerous outdoor companies offer tours, including hiking, horseback riding, mountain biking, white-water rafting, kayaking and, of course, ziplining, which has become Costa Rica's signature activity. Also popular are the Mistico Hanging Bridges, where you can explore the rain forest by walking across suspended bridges.

The town of La Fortuna, near the volcano's base, was thrust into the spotlight after the 1968 eruption, evolving from a tiny dusty settlement to one of Costa Rica's most popular tourist hubs. Though small in size, La Fortuna is crammed with all sorts of amenities such as hostels, guesthouses, eateries, tour companies, and more. La Fortuna is also a great base for exploring other natural sights in the region, including the Caño Negro National Wildlife Refuge, which is aflutter with a huge array of bird life, including egrets, roseate spoonbills, jabiru storks, and herons. Other visitor hubs in the area are the agricultural town of San Carlos and the village of El Castillo.

No matter when your eyes alight on the volcano – at sunrise, at the height of the noonday sun, or at sunset – its cone piercing the sky is a majestic sight.

Inset: Black-crested Coquette
Below (left to right): Church in La Fortuna; Mistico Hanging Bridges

ADVENTURER'S DIARY

April, which is the tail end of the dry season, is the ideal time to visit with the clearest views of the volcano. Five days will give you plenty of time to explore the area: trek the volcano, zipline over rain forest, and mountain bike the rocky terrain, with the reward of cooling off in the spray of waterfalls.

Five Days of Outdoor Adventure

DAY 1 Make your base in La Fortuna, and spend your first day exploring the volcano itself. Take a guided trek which includes clomping through humid rain forest and wide-open fields and climbing lava rocks. Later, soothe your muscles at the popular Balneario Tabacón.

DAY 2 Hike or horseback ride to La Catarata de La Fortuna, a lovely waterfall, flanked by rain forest, that spills into a pool far below. In the afternoon, visit the Venado Caves, an eerie network of labyrinthine subterranean caves with bats, stalactites, and damp sheer rock walls.

DAY 3 The vast Lake Arenal is ideal for water-based fun, like windsurfing and kitesurfing, stand-up paddling, kayaking, and fishing. The lake and its banks are also home to a rich array of wildlife and flourishing tropical plants – keep your eyes peeled for the vibrantly colored quetzal and the tapir.

DAY 4 Wind down in the tiny, less-crowded El Castillo, 14 miles (23 km) southwest of La Fortuna. Get the adrenalin pumping by embarking on one of the region's exciting ziplining tours, where you'll fly over the rain forest canopy. Or, if you're feeling brave, go bungee-jumping on 130- to 165-ft (40- to 50-meter) plunges.

DAY 5 Head on a bird watching tour at the Mistico Hanging Bridges Park. Suspended high above the forest, you'll spot a colorful array of birds, including toucans, hummingbirds, and the Tucanito Esmeralda. Top off your visit with a dip in the steamy Eco Termales Hot Springs.

Dos and Don'ts

- ✓ Bring sturdy hiking boots – the jungle and mountain trails, often dotted with jagged rocks, can be tough on footwear.
- ✗ Don't overlook the small family-run streetside food vendors (called "sodas") – these are among the cheapest and tastiest ways to refuel between outdoor activities.
- ✓ Consider staying outside of La Fortuna for reasonably-priced accommodations. The nearby village of El Castillo has an excellent batch of economical hotels.
- ✗ Don't forget your binoculars if you're going bird watching or wildlife-spotting.

Below: Village at the base of Volcán Arenal

GETTING THERE **See map p330, E9**

Carrasco International Airport is 9 miles (14 km) east of Montevideo center. From Buenos Aires, a ferry service operates across the River Plate to the Montevideo docks (US$100).

GETTING AROUND

Reliable bus services run in Montevideo and throughout Uruguay. Taxis are plentiful and affordable. Car rental is available at the airport and in town (from US$50 per day).

WEATHER

Temperatures range from a nighttime low of 52°F (11°C) to 75°F (24°C) during the day.

ACCOMMODATIONS

In the heart of Montevideo's old center is the Edwardian-style Hotel Plaza Fuerte; doubles from US$65; www.plazafuerte.com.uy

In Punta del Este, Hotel Remanso is near the beach but has a rooftop pool too; doubles from US$99; www.hotelremanso.com.uy

Estancia La Sirena Marinas del Rio Negro at Mercedes is a charming, historic working ranch; doubles from US$79 per person inclusive of full board and activities; www.lasirena.com.uy

EATING OUT

People eat late and eat meat – lots of it – usually in *parrilladas* (grill rooms). *Asado* (barbecue) is a favorite. Non-meat options include *tortilla española* (Spanish omelet). You can eat well for under US$15.

FURTHER INFORMATION

www.welcomeuruguay.com

Home on the Range

Uruguay has beautiful beaches and a cosmopolitan capital, but it also has a booming "*estancia* tourism" market. There's nothing to compare with riding herd on a range that's the size of a small state. The *gauchos* here are all but born in the saddle, and are considered among the finest horsemen in the world. Several of these working ranches date from the early 19th century and are magnificent inside and out. Many welcome visitors, whether or not you're handy with a lasso.

Take the less-traveled route and ride horseback along isolated beaches, across sand dunes and through palm groves.

Inset: Landmark Palcio Sa building in Montevideo's historic central plaza

Left (left to right): Colo del Sacramento lighthouse dramatic "fingers" sculptu on Punta del Este beach; sunset over Punta del Este

Right (left and right): *Gauchos* rounding up wil horses; ruined mission of Calera de las Huérfanas

Main: Uruguay's beautiful native *criollo* horses

URUGUAY

URUGUAY, AT ROUGHLY THE SIZE OF WASHINGTON, may be small by South American standards, but its manageable size is what endears it to so many travelers. You can do it all here. Where else can you wake up on a sprawling *estancia* (ranch) straight out of a Western movie set and still make it to the glittering sands of some of the world's most popular beaches that same afternoon? Or have breakfast near the silent ruins of a former Jesuit mission and dinner in the cosmopolitan whirl of the capital? Take the less-traveled route and ride horseback along isolated beaches, across sand dunes, and through palm groves. Drive the coast roads, stopping to revel in the sun and surf, and sign on at a working ranch where you'll be able to ride with the *gauchos* (cowboys) and even help with cattle drives. The country's beautiful *playas* (beaches) hardly need an introduction: names like Piriápolis, La Barra, La Paloma, and, above all, Punta del Este are famous for their heady combination of beautiful views, weather, and people.

If you're more inclined to watch the waves than the people, there are also dozens of lesser-known places towards the frontier with Brazil, ideally suited to a get-away-from-it-all vacation. You'll find plenty of empty sands, and a piece of seaside paradise to claim as your own.

When you're ready to trade in your beach sandals and sunscreen for boots and a cowboy hat, the famous *estancias* to the west will be happy to take you in – and to put you to work riding herd, if you're willing. Along the way are abandoned Jesuit missions such as Calera de las Huérfanas, and Portuguese fortresses like the delightful Colonia del Sacramento, a UNESCO World Heritage Site. Conchillas is a former British mining town while Nueva Helvecia was a Swiss settlement that is now best-known for its cheese. Half-hidden in the hazy distance of the green *pampas* are the great ranches, some the size of small countries.

As well as basking on the beach and taking to the trail, be prepared to succumb to the charms of the capital itself, lovely Montevideo, a little gem of a city nestled between the two contrasting sides of one of South America's most fascinating destinations.

GAUCHO DIARY

April is fall in Uruguay, but you won't need more than a light jacket for the evenings. It can be humid inland, but ocean breezes keep things very pleasant on the coast. This is the perfect time to visit: the high season has ended and even the beaches are less busy. Five days will give you time to appreciate Uruguay's many facets.

Five Days of Discoveries

DAY 1 Check into your hotel in Montevideo and spend some time in the fascinating Old City. The portside market, pedestrianized Calle Sarandí, and the grand Teatro Solís are must-sees within easy reach of each other.

DAY 2 Head out early to Punta del Este, 83 miles (130 km) east along the scenic coastal road. It's quieter at this time of year, but there's still plenty to do, from hang gliding and horseback riding to tennis and golf, all with ocean views. Take a tour on the *Muriel*, a century-old yacht. Later on, you can explore the town's museums and shops and, later still, its many nightclubs and cafés.

DAY 3 Continue east to La Barra and La Paloma to revel in the seaside solitude, or head back towards Montevideo and then west to your *estancia*. Pause at Nueva Helvecia, Colonia del Sacramento, Conchillas, and Calera de las Huérfanas, arriving at Mercedes before nightfall.

DAY 4 Spend the day with the *gauchos*, or you could bird-watch, fish, swim, or waterski. It's worth a visit to Mercedes, "the city of flowers," and the nearby historic settlements of Fray Bentos (where you can cross into Argentina) and Soriano. A meal cooked *parrillada*-style, under the stars back at the ranch, is the perfect end to your day.

DAY 5 Take the inland route back to Montevideo. Stop along the way in the picturesque towns of Palmitas and Cardona. You'll be back in time for an evening stroll along the riverside *ramblas* (boulevards) and a show at the planetarium before dinner in the Pocitos district.

Dos and Don'ts

- ✓ Rent a car for trips out of Montevideo. In the city, buses or taxis are fine, but you'll need your own transport for travel along the coast and to the *estancia*.
- ✗ Don't be surprised if you are charged for bread in restaurants. It's the norm here, as is having at least one beef dish at every meal.
- ✓ Remember that three currencies circulate freely: the *peso uruguayo*, *peso argentino*, and the US dollar. Brazilian *reais* are not widely accepted.
- ✗ Don't expect to cross freely into Argentina. You need to show your passport before you can purchase a ferry ticket.

Below: Fishing boats on Montevideo's waterfront

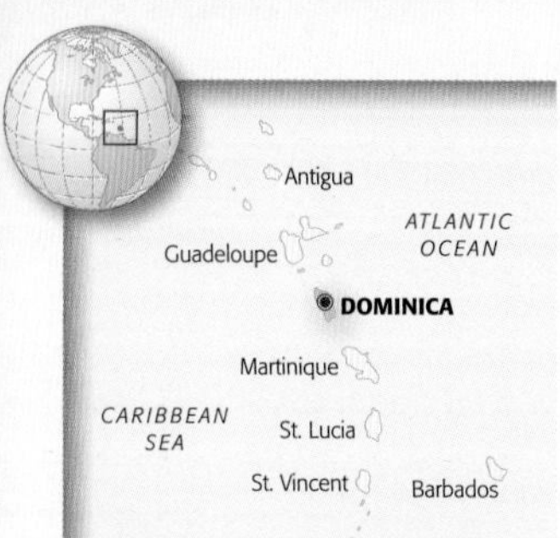

GETTING THERE See map p325, I5
International flights are connected to the island via hubs in Antigua, Barbados, St. Maarten, Puerto Rico, and Guadeloupe. Most visitors arrive in Douglas-Charles Airport in northeastern Dominica. The secondary airport is Canefield Airport, near the capital.

GETTING AROUND
The easiest way to get around is by taxi or rental car. The island has a number of small car rental companies, mostly in or near Roseau.

WEATHER
April is warm and humid, with an average daytime temperature of 80°F (27°C).

ACCOMMODATIONS
Castle Comfort Dive Lodge has doubles from $95; www.castlecomfortdiveldoge.com

Fort Young Hotel is set in former colonial military ramparts; doubles from US$120; www.fortyounghotel.com

Indulge at the clifftop Secret Bay, near Portsmouth, on the northwest coast; doubles from $390; www.secretbay.dm

EATING OUT
Traditional dishes have Creole roots, with ingredients like plantains. Roseau is dotted with an array of restaurants that serve everything from grilled chicken to French fare.

FURTHER INFORMATION
www.dominica.dm

Main: Scott's Head fishing village
Above (top to bottom): Emerald Park in Morne Trois Pitons National Park; Boiling Lake; Caribbean coral reef

The Carib Indians

It's not just the island's lush nature that has managed to survive the centuries. So has a small community, numbering some 3,000 and now called Kalinago, of the last few remaining Carib people in the Caribbean. The Kalinago now reside on a reserve in northeast Dominica which encompasses a series of small villages. You can learn more about Carib history at the Kalinago Barana Autê museum and center (www.kalinagobaranaaute.com), which covers Carib traditions, such as creating dugout canoes from tree trunks.

DOMINICA

On some Caribbean islands, it can be hard to see the sand and sea for all the crowds. Dominica offers an entirely different experience. This is a land of wild and flourishing nature, much of which you can have all to yourself. Morne Trois Pitons National Park, unfolding for 17,000 acres (6,880 ha) across the island's interior, is presided over by the mighty Morne Trois Pitons, a "mountain of three peaks." The park's verdant rain forest is punctuated by ponds, geysers, and, most notably, Boiling Lake, the second-largest hot lake in the world (after Frying Pan Lake in New Zealand).

Dominica may have fewer beaches than its Caribbean counterparts, but it makes up for it with unique water adventures like Champagne Beach and Reef. Volcanic gas bubbles float up from the sea floor, adding a fizz to the water, so it feels like you're frolicking in champagne. Why not strap on a snorkel and discover the multitudes of

Above (top and bottom): A Sisserou parrot, native to Dominica; a boat tour on the Indian River

Below: Downtown Roseau

underwater marine life, from darting tropical fish to swaying coral. Just north of Champagne Beach is Roseau, Dominica's compact, colorful capital, with narrow streets, lively markets, and the historic French Quarter.

Dominica's secluded, untamed side is especially evident along its northeastern coast. Embark on a drive from the town of Portsmouth, and you'll roll past the Indian River, towering palms, and windswept coves – this is the part of Dominica where key scenes from Pirates of the Caribbean: Dead Man's Chest were filmed. Dominica's early history is traced back to the Caribs who settled on the island in the 14th century. In 1493, Christopher Columbus arrived, bestowing the island with the name Dominica, after the day he landed here – a Sunday ("Domenica" in Italian). After several centuries of French and British colonization, the island was officially granted independence from the United Kingdom in 1978. The island faced many challenges in the subsequent decades, from economic struggles to deadly hurricanes, but Dominica is bouncing back and, most importantly, it has managed to protect many of its natural riches along the way.

ISLAND DIARY

Pretend to be Daniel Defoe's Robinson Crusoe as you explore this lush, verdant Caribbean island in April. Five days is just the right amount of time to trek to the mountain peaks, splash in the bubbling waters, and boat down the mighty rivers of this laid-back country.

Five Days Discovering Dominica

DAY 1

Start in the small but crammed capital of Roseau, which has a variety of historical buildings and squares, including the Old Market Plaza and the lush Dominica Botanic Gardens. Later take a dip at the popular Champagne Beach and Reef.

DAY 2

Explore the Morne Trois Pitons National Park, filled with wild orchids, lush valleys, and waterfalls. Trek through the rain forest to Trafalgar Falls and then splash in the pools at their base. For a memorable adventure, hire a guide to lead you to the park's famous Boiling Lake, a fumarole flooded with hot, bubbling water that emits clouds of vapor.

DAY 3

Visit Soufrière Bay, known for its steaming Soufrière Sulfur Springs in stone pools. Later, go diving, snorkeling, or kayaking in the Soufrière-Scotts Head Marine Reserve, which features a wealth of underwater wildlife in an extinct volcano crater.

DAY 4

Head north to the Morne Diablotin National Park, which is presided over by the 4,747-ft- (1446-m-) high Morne Diablotin, the tallest mountain on the island. Embark on nature trails through the park, which afford the best bird watching on the island.

DAY 5

Embarking from Portsmouth, cruise on a hand-oared boat down the mangrove-flanked Indian River. The slow-moving tour offers ample time to spy wildlife, from barracudas and iguanas to hummingbirds flitting through the air. Trek through the surrounding swampland, and top off the journey with drinks at a local riverfront bar.

Dos and Don'ts

- ✓ Slow down and give yourself ample time to travel between destinations. Dominica's roads are sometimes in varying states of disrepair, and bus breakdowns aren't infrequent.
- ✓ Find a qualified guide if you're planning on exploring the more secluded parts of the island, like the northeastern coast.
- ✗ Don't forget the insect repellent and long-sleeved shirts: in some parts, the mosquitoes and bugs – which can spread diseases – are out in force, so make sure to protect yourself.

Below: Old market square in Roseau

MAY

Where to Go: **May**

Summer is just around the corner in North America – even chilly Canadians and Americans from Alaska can get out and enjoy the sunshine. Mountain regions are less snowy and more accessible for non-skiiers, though things get dramatically colder at higher elevations. The Southern states are abundant with magnolia, but sunshine and bright skies are tempered by the odd rainstorm. It's not quite hot enough to swim in the Atlantic, but beach holidays are possible. Central America is heading into its wet season and the Caribbean islands are facing a thunderstorm or two. May is a good time to head for the Amazon which is a little less wet than earlier in the year. Below, you will find all the destinations in this chapter, and some extra suggestions to provide a little inspiration.

FESTIVALS AND CULTURE

MEMPHIS Rock 'n' Soul Museum sign

MEMPHIS
TENNESSEE, USA

Sing the blues at the Memphis in May festival

This sleepy Southern city comes alive in May, with a month-long festival of blues, soul, roots, and jazz music, and a sizzling barbeque-cooking contest.

See pp104–5

ST. LOUIS
MISSOURI, USA

One of the Midwest's most cultured cities

St. Louis has many cultural attractions, including the superb St. Louis Art Museum, and the historic towns of Ste. Genevieve and St. Charles are nearby.

www.explorestlouis.com

TORONTO
ONTARIO, CANADA

This lakeside culture capital has something for everyone

From blockbuster musicals to Shakespeare, from modern buildings to Victorian Gothic, and from wine to baseball – Toronto has it all.

See pp118–19

> "It's easy to while away a vacation in Toronto, feasting on paella, dancing to Peruvian folk music, and watching a festival parade."

DENVER
COLORADO, USA

Urbane city in the shadow of the Rockies

The region's most cosmopolitan city, Denver has cultural diversions and a surfeit of museums, including the stunning Denver Art Museum.

www.denver.org

ST. LUCIA
CARIBBEAN

The island gets hot and steamy – it's not just the weather

St. Lucia hosts one of the world's best jazz festivals – and when the music is over, there's stunning scenery and fascinating history to discover.

See pp122–3

UNFORGETTABLE JOURNEYS

AMAZON RIVER Canoeists paddling upriver

AMAZON RIVER
BRAZIL

The water teems with life in South America's longest river

Take a slow cruise within Brazil's interior, floating lazily on the Amazon, see pink river dolphins, and listen to opera in the jungle.

See pp114–15

TREKKING IN THE SIERRA MAESTRA
CUBA, CARIBBEAN

Cuba's loftiest mountain range

Trek through cloud forests to Pico Turquino, the island's highest mountain at the heart of the rugged Sierra Maestra.

www.dtcuba.com

WHITE-WATER RAFTING IN COSTA RICA
CENTRAL AMERICA

White water and rare wildlife

Costa Rica boasts some of the best rafting in Central America; there's a good chance of spotting crocs, too.

www.visitcostarica.com

CRUISING DOWN THE COLUMBIA RIVER
OREGON, USA

An unforgettable river journey

Take a sternwheeler ride through the spectacular Columbia River Gorge in the footsteps of legendary explorers Lewis and Clark.

www.portlandspirit.com

INSIDE PASSAGE
ALASKA, USA

Take a bracing sea voyage to this remote US state

Cruise the network of fjords that line Alaska's southeastern shore that harbor ice cliffs, misty mountains, and hardy sea mammals.

See pp110–11

NATURAL WONDERS

AMBERGRIS CAYE Blue-crowned motmots eating their prey

> "Stretching as far as the eye can see is a scattering of tree-shrouded islands enclosing sapphire lagoons."

AMBERGRIS CAYE
BELIZE

Quiet island paradise with diving sites galore

Belize is still relatively undeveloped, beautiful, and friendly, and the sea life is extraordinary on the world's second-largest coral reef system.

See pp106–7

CRATERS OF THE MOON NATIONAL MONUMENT
IDAHO, USA

Surreal petrified lava

This eerie landscape has vast expanses of solidified lava dotted with cinder cones and craters.

www.nps.gov/crmo

ANDROMEDA BOTANICAL GARDENS
BARBADOS, CARIBBEAN

The Caribbean's finest gardens

These coastal gardens feature arboreal curiosities, such as a Panama hat tree, a shaving brush tree, and a majestic old bearded fig.

www.barbados.org/androm.htm

MOUNT ST. HELENS
WASHINGTON STATE, USA

Scene of a devastating volcanic eruption in 1980

Its top blown off by the force of the explosion, this volcano is a monument to the natural power of the earth at its most destructive.

www.fs.usda.gov/mountsthelens

YOSEMITE NATIONAL PARK
CALIFORNIA, USA

Mountain spectacle

One of America's most celebrated national parks, enclosing the Yosemite Valley, walled by mile-high cliffs of sheer bare granite.

www.nps.gov/yose

Previous page: Manhattan Bridge at dusk, New York City

Weather Watch

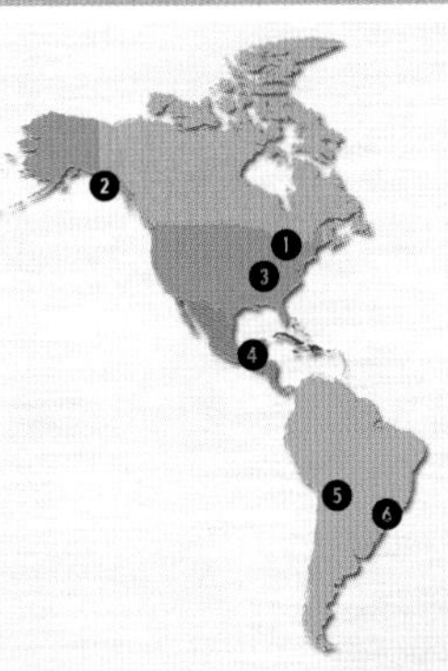

1 Toronto, Canada May might start off cool, but the snowfall that characterizes the winter months drops dramatically, and by the end of the month it's warm enough to spend a lot of time outside.

2 Alaska, USA This is the ideal time to get out on the water in this remote state. Long hours of sunlight, warm to hot daytime temperatures, and less rain than later in the year. Nights are very cold, however.

3 Tennessee, USA The steamy Southern summer is just around the corner. Temperatures hover around 75–78°F (24–26°C) with sunshine and the odd storm.

4 Belize May in Belize is hot and gets rainier as the month progresses. It is always steamy but is cooled by delicious sea breezes on the coast, and sea visibility is excellent.

5 Bolivia Winter is approaching in Bolivia. La Paz, the world's highest capital, is dry and warm, with cool evenings. Temperatures are higher at lower altitudes, while the lush rain forest is entering its dry season.

6 Brazil The Amazon Basin stays hot and chokingly humid year-round, but May is one of the less rainy months. Brazil's east coast is wet, while in the northeast, a very hot, dry period is beginning.

LUXURY AND ROMANCE

NEW YORK CITY View of Manhattan

NEW YORK CITY
NEW YORK STATE, USA

The perfect long-weekend break for city-lovers

Where better for a romantic holiday than the city that's played backdrop to some of the greatest movie love stories?

See pp116–17

VANCOUVER ISLAND
BRITISH COLUMBIA, CANADA

Wine tasting and whale-watching

Explore historic Victoria city, then enjoy a heady blend of wine and fine food, and myriad outdoor activities amid imposing scenery.

www.vancouverisland.travel

SAVANNAH
GEORGIA, USA

Sandy beaches, flower gardens, grand mansions, and mystery

This pretty city presents a picture-postcard facade while in the background simmers seductive jazz, spicy food, and steamy stories.

See pp120–21

THE BEACHES, TORONTO
ONTARIO, CANADA

Chic downtown Toronto

A stylish district on the banks of Lake Ontario, awash with beautiful houses, cool bars, trendy shops, and a string of appealing beaches.

www.thetorontobeaches.com

OUTER BANKS
NORTH CAROLINA, USA

Unspoiled barrier islands with wildlife and fabulous beaches

Explore these superb shores and dunes, historic sites, and romantic inns during the early summer before the heat and crowds arrive.

See pp124–5

ACTIVE ADVENTURES

LA PAZ Cyclists navigating the hair-raising "road of death"

LA PAZ
BOLIVIA

A high-altitude holiday that will take your breath away

The world's highest capital is a gateway to action adventures, vibrant cultures, and spectacular Lake Titicaca.

See pp108–9

SURFING AT BATHSHEBA
BARBADOS, CARIBBEAN

Top surfing destination

Known as the "soup bowl," Bathsheba receives a steady supply of big Atlantic rollers year-round.

www.barbados.org/bathsheb

BIRDING IN COSTA RICA
CENTRAL AMERICA

Your chance to spot a quetzal

One of the world's top ornithological destinations, Costa Rica is visited by almost 900 species.

www.birdwatchingcostarica.com

BAFFIN ISLAND
NUNAVUT, CANADA

Arctic adventures in Canada's far north

Hike and kayak through one of the Americas' final frontiers: a wintry wonderland of ice floes, northern lights, and polar bears.

www.baffinisland.ca

CHESAPEAKE BAY
MARYLAND, USA

The largest estuary in the USA

The peaceful waters of Chesapeake Bay make for superb marine adventures, including sailing, fishing, and crabbing.

www.baydreaming.com

FAMILY GETAWAYS

PACIFIC RIM NATIONAL PARK Kayakers in the Broken Group Islands

"In one day, you can dip your toes in the sand, trek through tangled rain forest, and slice through the waters on a kayak."

PACIFIC RIM NATIONAL PARK
BRITISH COLUMBIA, CANADA

From crashing waves to rugged trails

This family-friendly park is home to Native American cultural sites, sandy beaches, and rain forest.

See pp112–13

LAKESHORE
MINNESOTA, USA

Take time out at an old-fashioned lake-side camp

There's plenty for adults to do including fishing and golf – or just resting. And kids will love being the in the great outdoors.

www.lostlake.com

BELIZE
CENTRAL AMERICA

Affordable tropical destination for kids and adults

A great place for adventurous families interested in the Mayan culture, marine parks, jungle adventures, and shady hammocks.

www.belizenet.com

BUSCH GARDENS, TAMPA
FLORIDA, USA

Fun rides for all the family

This popular USA theme park offers roller coasters, encounters with gorillas, cheetahs and giraffes, plus special rides for little ones.

www.buschgardens.com

SANIBEL AND THE CAPTIVA ISLANDS
FLORIDA, USA

Seashell-rich Florida islands

These small islands boast miles of sandy beaches and outdoor activities, from fishing and birding to boating and snorkeling.

www.sanibel-captiva.org

GETTING THERE See map p317, C2
Flights land at Memphis International Airport, 11 miles (18 km) south of downtown by car. Greyhound buses and trains stop in downtown. Drivers can approach the city on the I-40 (east–west) or I-55 (north–south).

GETTING AROUND
Downtown Memphis is a pleasure to walk around, with a useful trolley route along the Mississippi. You will need a car or taxi to reach outlying attractions including Graceland.

WEATHER
The steamy Southern summer is approaching, but May is more appealing with an average daily temperature of 75–79°F (24–26°C).

ACCOMMODATIONS
Sleep Inn at Court Square is a good downtown option; doubles from US$135; www.choicehotels.com

Elvis Presley's Heartbreak Hotel, next to Graceland, is the top choice for Elvis fans; doubles from US$120; www.graceland.com/lodging/heartbreakhotel

The Peabody is elegant and historic; doubles from US$305; www.peabodymemphis.com

EATING OUT
The Arcade, open since 1919, offers homecooking from US$5 in an iconic diner building, while the Four Way near the Stax Museum serves hearty soul food. Try the Corky's chain for dry ribs and BBQ.

FURTHER INFORMATION
www.memphisinmay.org

MEMPHIS

MEMPHIS IS A MAGICAL CITY; UNIQUELY AMERICAN and unlike anywhere else in the world. Set in an evocative spot on the mighty Mississippi River, this is the place that brought us blues, soul, and rock'n'roll, the place that homeboy Elvis Presley could never quite leave, and the place tormented by the memory of Martin Luther King's assassination in 1968. A fairly poor Southern city, built on cotton and relatively untouched by the sanitizing effects of modernization, Memphis has a dreamy appeal. Sitting in faded, red-boothed diners where Elvis once ate, chatting to the chef who served Isaac Hayes his specials, or being measured for a suit at Lansky Brothers, the tailor that kitted out The King himself, you could imagine yourself in a timewarp. But it's not a city preserved in aspic. The Reverend Al Green may still sing sweet soul music at his gospel church, but he's likely to be clutching a skinny cappuccino. Old blues men

Graceland

In 1957, 22-year-old Memphis boy Elvis Presley, fresh from recording *Heartbreak Hotel*, spent just over $100,000 on a stone-clad mansion where he lived for the rest of his life. Graceland is surprisingly small and, despite the shag carpet lining the walls of the Jungle Room, not as tacky as you might expect. Audio tours provide snippets from Elvis's daughter, Lisa Marie, and snatches of his songs. In the garden are the graves of "the King" and his family, along with his airplanes and cars, witty movie montages, and boutiques selling Elvis coffee beans.

Main: The Blues City Café on Beale Street after dark

Left: The Memphis skyline and boats on the Mississippi River

Right (left to right): Dishing up at the World Championship BBQ cooking contest; Rock'n'Soul Museum sign; performer at the Beale Street Music Festival

Right panel (top and bottom): Elvis snow globes at Graceland; the Stax Museum of American Soul Music

still play urban juke joints unchanged for 50 years, but their audience is joined today by hipsters selecting Carl Perkins and Otis Redding on the jukebox.

The city's seductive mix of retro charm, edgy hip, and sleepy Southern eccentricity is rolled into one during the Memphis in May festival, which is held over the course of the month. The festivities kick off with the Beale Street Music Festival on the riverfront, with stages hosting acts as different as Blind Mississippi Morris and Gov't Mule. Lovers of blues, soul, and southern roots music rub shoulders, clink beer cans, and dance until their feet are sore. Mid-month, the World Championship Barbecue Cooking Contest begins and foodies descend on the city. Memphians are passionate about their BBQ, and this paean to the pleasures of pork is the place to join them. The Great American River Run rounds off the festival at the end of the month, a half marathon with a route lining the Mississippi River, live entertainment along the way and ending with music, food, and drinks on the river bluff.

MAY FESTIVAL DIARY

On a visit to Memphis in May, you should spend at least a few days in the city, focusing your trip around the music festival (held over a weekend early in the month) or the cooking contest in mid-May. Both events are spread over three days. The following diary has you in the city during the music festival.

Six Days of Musical Magic

DAY 1 Wander the streets of downtown, checking out Beale Street, where blues was born, and watching the river traffic on the Mississippi. The glossy Rock'n'Soul Museum gives a fascinating overview of the city's musical heritage, while tiny Sun Studio, where young Elvis recorded his first disc in 1953, offers evocative tours.

DAY 2 Rise early and head out to Graceland, which warrants a whole day. In the evening, stroll along Beale Street, where the music bars will be hopping with everything from blues to bluegrass.

DAY 3 The lively Stax Museum of American Soul Music, housed in the eponymous (now defunct) recording studio, tells the story of the only place in the 1960s Deep South where blacks and whites could make music together. In the afternoon, head to Tom Lee Park by the river for the first afternoon of the music festival.

DAY 4 The funky coffee bars and thrift stores of the Cooper-Young district, Midtown, are buzzing on weekend mornings – hang out here for a while before heading back to the music festival in the afternoon.

DAY 5 Sunday is church day: soul singer Al Green's Full Gospel Tabernacle holds services open to all, where the man himself makes regular appearances. Spiritually edified, head back to the festival for the final line-up.

DAY 6 Built around the old Lorraine Motel, where Dr Martin Luther King was assassinated in 1968, the National Civil Rights Museum tells the painful story of the struggle for desegregation in the South. It's an unmissable stop on any Memphis itinerary.

Dos and Don'ts

- ✓ Take a Mississippi sternwheeler tour. There's no better way to experience the river at close hand.
- ✗ Don't wander too far away from the main streets of downtown at night. Memphis is becoming safer, but it still has its problems and tourists can be seen as fair game.
- ✓ Forget about diets. This is a city that adores its food fattening and rib-sticking. Hunker down and join in.
- ✗ Don't go thinking you won't come home besotted by Elvis.

Below: A steamboat drifting along the lazy Mississippi River

GETTING THERE See map p324, C1
International flights arrive at Phillip Goldson International Airport, 11 miles (17 km) northwest of Belize City. From there, Tropic Air and Maya Island Air fly on to San Pedro, the only town on Ambergris Caye.

GETTING AROUND
San Pedro is easily negotiable on foot but golf carts and bicycles can be hired. Water taxis are used to get around Ambergris Caye.

WEATHER
May is hot and sunny, with late afternoon showers, but breezes temper the humidity. The average temperature is 81°F (27°C).

ACCOMMODATIONS
Ruby's basic doubles have a fan and a balcony with a sea view for US$45; doubles with air-conditioning for US$65; book in advance; rubyshotel.yolasite.com

Sun Breeze Hotel offers doubles with views of the pool for US$175; www.sunbreeze.net

Ramon's Village Resort has thatched cabanas with access to a sandy beach for US$250; www.ramons.com

EATING OUT
A wide variety of fresh seafood is available, but other local specialties include chicken stew cooked in coconut milk, with pepper sauce. Meals are usually served with beans, rice, plantains, and potato salad.

FURTHER INFORMATION
www.ambergriscaye.com

AMBERGRIS CAYE

The view is breathtaking as the light aircraft wings across the green hinterland of Belize City and crosses the coast towards the glittering expanses of the Caribbean. Stretching as far as the eye can see is a scattering of tree-shrouded islands enclosing sapphire lagoons fringed with dazzling white sand. These are the cayes, formed over thousands of years as salt-tolerant mangroves took root in the unusually shallow waters, trapping fragments of coral and river silt. The topography constantly changes as new islands form and others are eroded by storms, hurricanes, and human intervention.

The largest and most northerly caye, Ambergris, is a magnet for divers, snorkelers, and water sports enthusiasts. The major draw is the Belize Barrier Reef, the longest in the western hemisphere and undeniably a natural wonder. It appears as an uninterrupted line of breaking surf, dividing the

Above: Lighthouse Reef Atoll basking in the bright sunshine of the Caribbean

Below (top and bottom): Juvenile Morelet's crocodile, with its characteristic yellow color; *Pomacanthus paru,* the French angelfish, commonly found in shallow reefs

The Blue Hole

Located 40 miles (64 km) southeast of Ambergris Caye at the center of Lighthouse Reef Atoll, the Blue Hole did not even appear on Admiralty navigation charts when legendary diver Jacques Cousteau measured its dimensions in 1972. Now, UNESCO has added the Hole to its World Heritage List and the site draws more than 20,000 divers a year. While the Blue Hole, at 1,000 ft (305 m) across and 450 ft (137 m) deep, is not for the inexperienced, the perimeter teems with coral, fish, sea urchins, and giant green anemones. It is great for snorkeling.

Main: Elegant pair of foureye butterflyfish – they mate for life – looking for food on a coral reef near Ambergris Caye

Right (left to right): Brightly colored windsurfers; scuba divers silhouetted against the crystal-blue water; diver admiring colorful sponges

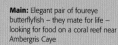

turquoise coastal waters from the lapis lazuli of the deepening sea. The best introduction to the reef is the Hol Chan Marine Reserve – prepare to be amazed at the shoals of iridescent fish darting among coral canyons, spurs, and ridges. This section of the reef is home to an astonishing variety of marine life from nurse sharks, stingrays, and moray eels to mollusks, tunicates, and sea anemones. Another jaw-dropping attraction is the Blue Hole, a seemingly bottomless limestone karst sinkhole. A third of the way down are stalactites and stalagmites, reminders of the Hole's cavernous origins. They protrude from the walls at a 12-degree angle, the result of a gigantic earthquake millions of years ago which set Lighthouse Reef Atoll at a tilt.

While diving and snorkeling top the activities list, Ambergris also offers fishing, parasailing, sailboarding, and bird-watching. Afterwards, relax at one of San Pedro's oceanside restaurants, with barbecued fish so fresh you might have seen them swimming in the sea just a little earlier.

DIVING DIARY

There are more than 35 diving and snorkeling sites off Ambergris Caye and the coastal islands are a short flight away. Underwater visibility is excellent around the Barrier Reef (about 100 ft/30 m), the sea is warm, and the skies are sunny. Visiting in May means missing the expensive seasonal peaks.

Five Days of Marine Life

DAY 1 Join a half-day excursion to Hol Chan Marine Reserve, which includes a swim in Shark Ray Alley, where you can touch nurse sharks and stingrays. After lunch, snorkel off the beach at Ramon's Village Resort, then take a romantic sunset cruise on the "No Rush" catamaran.

DAY 2 Spend the day diving and snorkeling off Lighthouse Reef Atoll, around the famous Blue Hole. In the evening, travel by water taxi to the north end of the island for dinner at Mambo, one of Belize's finest and most exclusive restaurants.

DAY 3 Take a boat to Swallow Caye Wildlife Sanctuary, east of Belize City, where you will see the endangered West Indian manatee in its natural habitat. Enjoy the snorkeling stops on the way and have a tasty barbecue lunch on the beach.

DAY 4 Try a new sport – kitesurfing or windsurfing off the shores of San Pedro. After lunch, visit the Marco Gonzalez Maya Site, the ruins of an ancient Mayan village in the heart of the jungle.

DAY 5 Take binoculars for the full-day excursion by boat and minivan to Lamanai. While traveling down the New River, your guide will point out herons, jabiru storks, ospreys, and even a crocodile or two. Later, hike from Lamanai Outpost Lodge into the rain forest to see Mayan ruins in a fabulous natural setting.

Dos and Don'ts

- ✓ Bring plenty of mosquito repellent. While breezes usually keep these pests at bay, they can be a nuisance when the wind drops. Check that your hotel rooms have netting.
- ✗ Don't forget to check the current baggage allowance with Tropic Air/Maya Island Air before departure.
- ✓ Remember to bring an underwater camera for diving and snorkeling expeditions.
- ✓ Before setting out for Hol Chan Marine Reserve, call in at the excellent interactive Visitor Center (open 9am–5pm daily) for information and brochures about Belize's marine habitats.

Below: Blue-crowned motmots with a catch of tropical butterflies

JAN FEB MAR APR MAY JUN JUL AUG SEP OCT NOV DEC

LA PAZ

FOR EVEN THE MOST SEASONED TRAVELER, a visit to La Paz is not one that will be forgotten. For a start, you arrive at one of the world's highest airports, more than 2.5 miles (4 km) above sea level. And the view is staggering, with phenomenal vistas of the encircling mountains and, above all, the sight of triple-peaked Illimani, with its snow-capped summit ignited a blazing orange by the sun.

La Paz is an adventure in itself. The city is a vast, colorful open-air market. Every square inch of street space is taken up by *cholas* (indigenous women of Aymara or Quechua descent) selling an endless array of unique handicrafts, clothing, food, and drink – everything you could ever need and much more. But it's the nearby Yungas and Lago Titicaca regions that really lure the adventure traveler. The Andes offer innumerable hikes along millennia-old Inca trails to beautiful hamlets such as Sorata and Takesi.

GETTING THERE **See map p330, B3**
El Alto International Airport is 6 miles (10 km) from La Paz city center.

GETTING AROUND
In La Paz, taxis and *trufis* (collective taxis) show their destination in the front window. *Micros* (buses) run from La Paz to all destinations.

WEATHER
In May, La Paz is usually dry, with a daytime average of 60°F (16°C); 38°F (3°C) at night. In the Yungas, conditions are more tropical.

ACCOMMODATIONS
In La Paz, Hotel Rosario is a charming, colonial-style guesthouse; doubles from US$80; www.grupororosario.com

La Cúpula in Copacabana, built in Moorish style, overlooks Lago Titicaca; doubles from US$30; www.hotelcupula.com

Sol y Luna, in Corioco, is an ecolodge; doubles from US$40 (discounts for stays of more than two nights, payment in *bolivianos* cash only); www.solyluna-bolivia.com

Hostal Las Piedras in Sorata is a clean and modern family-owned place, with excellent home-cooked breakfasts; doubles from US$22; (591) 7191 6341

EATING OUT
La Paz's best eateries are in the Sopocachi district and the Zona Sur. In villages, hotels double as restaurants.

FURTHER INFORMATION
www.boliviatravelweb.com

High Fashion, Andes-Style

A bowler hat, layers of petticoats, and multicolored *aguayos* (woolen wraps) are sartorial trademarks of every *chola*. The climate may explain the petticoats, and an *aguayo* is ideal for carrying everything from babies to produce – but bowler hats? The stories vary of their adoption by (or imposition on) the women of La Paz in colonial times, but today *cholas* wear a bowler as a sign of pride in their heritage. Most come from the last European bowler-maker, in Italy.

Main: View over bustling La Paz, the highest capital city in the world

Left (left and right): Coroico's colonial church and main square; cycling the hair-raising El Camino de la Muerte ("the Road of Death"), winding its way through the Yungas from La Paz to Coroico

Right: Totora-reed boat moored at Copacabana on Lago Titicaca

Tiwanaku, capital of a lost empire which predated even the Incas, is just two hours away toward beautiful Lago Titicaca. Colonial Copacabana is a gateway to the lake's many treasures, such as the mysterious Isla del Sol (Island of the Sun), believed by the Incas to be the home of the sun god. The lost-in-time Yungas villages of Coroico, Chulumani, and Yanacachi are reached through pristine rain forest, and hiking or canoeing is a delight in the heady, flower-scented lowland air.

You could happily spend your entire trip exploring at a snail's pace, but this part of Bolivia is home to the country's best, most adrenaline-filled experiences, and many of the region's larger towns offer exhilarating outings. Some folks might choose to hurtle down the world's highest ski run or one of the planet's most dangerous roads. For the more upwardly mobile there's the chance to tackle some of the tallest and most challenging peaks in the western hemisphere. Or why not take to the air and paraglide above virgin rain forest? On an Andean adventure, the sky's the limit.

Above: Stone carving on the entrance facade of Iglesia de San Francisco, La Paz

Below: Mountain hut on Chacaltaya, site of the world's highest ski run

ANDEAN DIARY

May is an ideal time to visit La Paz and the surrounding region, as the weather is pleasant and mild. At 2 miles (3,200 m) above the ocean, any strenuous activity will leave you a bit out of sorts initially, but a day of rest is generally all you'll need before you embark on a full week of unforgettable high-altitude adventures.

Eight Days Above the Clouds

DAYS 1–2

Spend the first day acclimatizing with the help of *yerbe mate* tea, prized by the locals for its restorative powers.

The next day, take the bus to Lago Titicaca, stopping on route for a tour of the ceremonial center of Tiwanaku. Continue to the tradition-steeped lakeside town of Copacabana. In the evening, try local trout for dinner.

DAY 3

Take a day tour to Isla del Sol and spend the day exploring the Inca ruins. The waters of the Fuente del Inca spring are said to be rejuvenating. Isla de la Luna (Island of the Moon) is a short boat ride away.

DAYS 4–5

Head for Sorata, the starting point for many awesome treks, from short jaunts to Cerro Istipata or San Pedro Caves, to the outrageously hard, Inca-era Mapiri Trail. Go east for the world's most dramatic and dangerous mountain bike descent, the Yungas road, to Coroico. Cool off in its waterfalls and pools before climbing sacred Cerro Uchumachi or exploring on horseback.

DAY 6

The pretty villages of Chulumani, Ocabaya, Chicaloma, and Yanakachi are in prime hiking and bird-watching country. Chicaloma is famous for *saya* music and dance. In Yanakachi you could volunteer a few hours' help at the Fundación Pueblo orphanage.

DAYS 7–8

Return to La Paz via Calaco to to see the eerie landscape of Valle de la Luna (Moon Valley). Back in La Paz, take in a *peña* – a Bolivian folk music club. The next day, stroll the main thoroughfare, the Prado; explore the old city, the museums, and churches; and don't miss the unique *mercado de hechicería* (witches' market).

Dos and Don'ts

- ✗ Don't over-exert yourself in the first few days. A debilitating case of *soroche* (mountain sickness) could ruin your trip.
- ✓ Ask politely before photographing local people, especially *cholas*, who are often vehemently camera-shy.
- ✗ Don't frequent money changers *(cambistas)* on street corners. If you must use their services (such as on a Sunday, when everything is closed), bring a calculator and have your bills handed to you one by one.
- ✓ Don't eat fruit or vegetables bought from an open-air vendor without washing them first.

Below: The stunning peaks of Illimani mountain

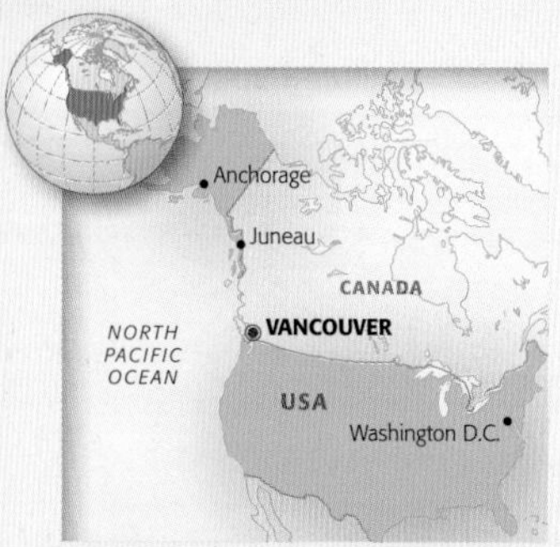

GETTING THERE See map p313, C6

Large cruise ships depart from Vancouver (British Columbia), Canada, and many cruise companies will provide a transfer from Vancouver International Airport to your ship. You can also fly to Juneau, Alaska, and join a small cruise ship.

GETTING AROUND

Vancouver International Airport is a 20-minute taxi ride from the city center. The Canada Line rapid transit rail link connects with downtown in 26 minutes.

WEATHER

The cruising season runs from mid-April to September. May is the driest month. Days are very long and generally warm at 62–80ºF (17–27ºC), but bring a sweater as nights are cool at 59–66ºF (15–19ºC).

ACCOMMODATIONS

Celebrity Cruises offers inside doubles from US$805 per person for 7 days; www.celebritycruises.com

Carnival Cruise Lines has ocean-view doubles from US$1,125 per person; www.carnival.com

Luxury can be found on the Holland America Line; ocean-view doubles from US$1,400 per person for 7 days; www.hollandamerica.com

EATING OUT

Meals are included on all the Inside Passage ships. On shore excursions, try an open-fire salmon bake for about US$50 per person.

FURTHER INFORMATION

www.travelalaska.com

Klondike Gold Rush

The now tiny hamlet of Skagway reached its peak in 1898, at the height of the Klondike gold rush. Skagway was the gateway town where miners assembled their gear and supplies before trekking up over the Chilkoot pass into Canada. The Canadian authorities didn't try to prevent the countless foreigners from entering, but the Mounties did insist that each miner bring one full ton of supplies, enough to keep himself alive for a year. Every pound of that ton was carried by the miners on their backs up the icy steps of the Chilkoot pass.

Above (left to right): Sockeye salmon swimming upriver to spawn; bear catching migrating sockeye salmon; tail of a humpback whale
Main: Sunset in Stephens Passage, just outside Juneau

INSIDE PASSAGE

In the 1770s, British seafarer Captain James Cook became the first to explore and map the rugged coast between Vancouver and the Bering Strait – Cook Inlet was later named after him. Spanish and Russian explorers – notably Vitus Bering in the 1740s – had led expeditions to Alaska, but none had managed to chart the coastline as thoroughly as Cook. Yet the network of channels that fringe Alaska's southeast shores remained untraversed, even by Cook.

It was not until a generation later that Cook's protégé George Vancouver charted a navigable course through this fractal coastline. He did not think much of the landscape, declaring it "useless." His senior lieutenants thought otherwise – they were younger men whose souls had been touched by the Romantic movement then sweeping Europe, whose spirits yearned for wild, untamed places where God and nature could commune, places they considered to be sublime. Sublime this coastline undoubtedly is. The product of a slow collision between tectonic plates, followed by four successive epochs of glaciation, the geography of the Inside Passage coastline has been sculpted on a scale to impress. Mountains rise steeply out of deep icy waters and soar 3,300 ft (1,000 m) above sea level, with headwaters lost in a crown of cloud and mist.

Mountains rise out of deep icy waters, and soar above sea level with headwaters lost in a crown of cloud and mist.

The region's channels, fjords, estuaries, and sea currents support an assortment of animal species. The cool currents give rise to an array of sealife including herring, salmon, porpoise, sealions, and sea otters, along with orca, humpback, and grey whales. Along the shore, the rocks are thick with sea stars, geoducks, and abalone, while grizzly and black bears feast at the river mouths in spring.

Although the Inside Passage has a vulnerable ecosystem, with some wildlife under threat of extinction, man's tread here has been relatively light – the fjords, forests, and salmon remain for visitors to experience, in all their sublime beauty.

Inset: *Radiance of the Seas* and *Rhapsody of the Seas* cruise ships in Skagway
Below (left and right): A ski plane; Creek Street, Ketchikan

NATURE-LOVER'S DIARY

May offers gloriously long days for cruising Alaska's Inside Passage. Large cruise ships sail from Vancouver to Juneau and Skagway, then back down past Ketchikan and Misty Fjords in a period of seven days. For those with more time, Vancouver merits an extra night's stay (*see pp156–7*).

JAN FEB MAR APR **MAY**

Seven Days in the Fjords

DAY 1 Departing Vancouver, find your sea legs the first full day at sea. Today's highlight is a visit to Tracy Arm, an L-shaped fjord with the dual ice cliffs of the Sawyer glacier lying hidden at the end.

DAY 2 From Juneau, Alaska's state capital, set out in search of humpbacks on Stephens Passage, or take a helicopter or ski plane up to the Mendenhall glacier and explore by dogsled. End the day with an Alaska salmon bake – freshly caught wild salmon grilled over an alderwood fire.

DAY 3 Sample the colorful history of Skagway by strolling the boardwalks and poking your nose into the saloons preserved as part of the Klondike Gold Rush National Historic Park. Take the fast ferry to Haines and explore the Chilkat Bald Eagle Preserve, an estuary habitat rich with wildlife, including moose and American bald eagles.

DAY 4 On day four, the ship noses into the Glacier Bay National Park. This 62-mile- (100-km-) long fjord has a dozen tidewater glaciers whose tall blue cliffs of ice regularly calve off icebergs, which crash into the ocean sending spray hundreds of feet into the air.

DAY 5 The cruise proceeds to Ketchikan, the gateway to the extraordinary Misty Fjords National Monument, which can be visited by fast boat or floatplane.

DAYS 6–7 The last full day of the voyage is spent entirely at sea. As the ship approaches Johnstone Strait near the north end of Vancouver Island, look out for orca whales feeding on salmon and rubbing their bodies along the shoreline in a small bay called Robson Bight.

Dos and Don'ts

- ✓ Keep your eyes peeled for wildlife. There are good chances of spotting an amazing array of land and sea mammals.
- ✗ Don't forget to bring a light waterproof jacket, as rain is never more than a day away. A Gore-Tex® jacket comes in handy after sunset, when the temperature drops a good 50ºF (28ºC).
- ✓ Feast on salmon. There are four different species on the west coast: chinook (or king), spring, chum, and sockeye.

JUN JUL AUG SEP OCT NOV DEC

Below: Sheets of ice crashing into the water, Glacier Bay National Park

GETTING THERE See map p313, C6

From Victoria International Airport on Vancouver Island, the drive to Tofino is about 5 hours. Local airlines fly from Vancouver or Victoria airports to Tofino-Long Beach Airport, which takes about 50 minutes.

GETTING AROUND

Numerous operators offer tours around the park. If you'd like to explore the park independently, you'll need your own car; rental car offices in Tofino and Ucluelet.

WEATHER

Late spring is cool and dry but sunny, with temperatures ranging from 49°F (9°C) to 58°F (14°C).

ACCOMMODATIONS

Camping options include Green Point campground, near Long Beach, and backcountry camping on the Broken Group Islands.

Water's Edge Shoreside Suites surround Ucluelet's quite harbor; doubles from US$189; www.watersedgesuites.com

For upscale comfort stay at the oceanfront Long Beach Lodge Resort; doubles from US$230; www.longbeachlodge.com

EATING OUT

Tofino has a wide selection of restaurants. At the cozy Shelter Restaurant, try Vancouver Island oysters and pan-roasted rockfish.

FURTHER INFORMATION

www.hellobc.com
www.tourismtofino.com

PACIFIC RIM NATIONAL PARK

Considering that in one day, you can dip your toes in the sand, trek through tangled rain forest, and slice through the waters on a kayak, Pacific Rim National Park really does have something for everyone. The park is perennially popular with active families, thanks to a wealth of adventures that appeal to all ages. Unfolding on Vancouver Island, it encompasses three geographically distinct parts: Long Beach, named after the stellar 10-mile (16-km) beach on Wickannish Bay; the Broken Group Islands archipelago; and the West Coast Trail, a trekking route that meanders in and out of rain forest, past waterfalls, sea cliffs, quiet coves, and gaping caves. Perhaps one of the greatest appeals of the surrounding coastline is the diversity – Wickannish Bay includes a sandy beach; a jagged, rocky shore of basalt and granite; a cobblestone beach, with small rocks and gravel; and mudflats in the protected

The Nuu-chah-nulth

The Pacific Rim National Park may be famous for its natural diversity, but it also thrives with cultural diversity. The park is set in the uuli (traditional territories) of the Nuu-chah-nulth people, whose name means "along the mountains and sea." The Nuu-chah-nulth have lived off the land for generations, and today they are composed of 14 individual nations, each with an elected Chief and Council. Stop into the Kwistis Visitor Center, at the south end of Wickaninnish Beach, for more information and to arrange tours to Nuu-chah-nulth settlements.

Brice Bay. The park's waters are also a boon for whale-watchers, with the longest migration in the world passing through in March and April; and you can also spy these majestic mammals all year around the Broken Group Islands on whale-watching tours.

The Pacific Rim National Park has several key hubs, including Tofino, just north of Long Beach. This friendly town offers easy access to coast and forest, and exudes a quirky charm, with comfy hotels and casual restaurants. This is also the place to book tours, from birding to stand-up paddleboarding. Tofino is also Canada's surf capital, with over 21 miles (35 km) of prime surfing coastline. Another popular base is Ucluelet, on the west coast of Vancouver Island, whose name means "safe harbor" in the language of the Aboriginal Nuu-chah-nulth. The grand outdoors extends around the town, and from here you can embark on adventures such as bear-watching and ziplining, as well as a variety of fishing excursions.

Main: Exploring the West Coast Trail

Left (left to right): A Humpback whale near Vancouver; a black bear near Ucluelet; paddle kayaks in the Broken Group Islands

Above (top and bottom): Surfing near Tofino; walkers on Long Beach

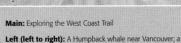

EXPLORER'S DIARY

With its bright sun and clear skies, May is a wonderful time to discover Pacific Rim National Park. In five days, you can engage in a range of outdoor activities and family fun, from hiking to kayaking, with plenty of time left over for a daily unwinding session at one of the park's lodges.

Five Canadian Wilderness Days

DAYS 1–2

There's no better introduction to Pacific Rim National Park than Tofino, a spirited former frontier town – current population 2,000 – that sits in the Clayoquot Sound UNESCO Biosphere Reserve. From here, you can explore the surrounding waters via boating and kayaking, and head into the verdant inland to hike and bird-watch. Also, embark on a tour to Hot Springs Cove, north of Tofino, in Maquinna Provincial Park. Trek through old-growth forest to a waterfall and inviting hot springs. Tofino is also a great base for day visits to the famous 7-mile (12-km) Long Beach. In the evening, cozy up at Wolf in the Fog for a hearty meal of locally sourced dishes, from roasted root vegetables with wild rice to smoked duck breast.

DAYS 3–4

Ucluelet makes the perfect base for fishing expeditions – the town used to be a top player in the area's fishing industry – and for exploring the Broken Group Islands. Go on a diving tour, which will take you to shipwrecks and reefs teeming with underwater wildlife including wolf eels and rockfish.

DAY 5

From Ucluelet, spend the day hiking the stunning Wild Pacific Trail, which meanders along the Pacific Ocean, rewarding you with sweeping views of the Amphitrite Point lighthouse rising above the crashing waves.

Dos and Don'ts

- ✓ Before kayaking in Broken Group Islands, always check the forecast and surf conditions. Also, wear a wetsuit – the waters are cold and can get rough in certain areas.
- ✗ Don't forget the binoculars: the park is filled with more than 300 species of birds. The end of April and early May are top times to catch glimpses of northward shorebird migrations.
- ✓ If you spot a black bear, alert park staff, and remember never to allow wildlife access to food, garbage, or toiletries.

Below: Boats docked near Tofino

AMAZON RIVER

DOWNSTREAM OF MANAUS, TWO TRIBUTARIES come together to form the mighty Amazon River. The Rio Negro is dark, with the color and acidity of cold black tea, while the Rio Solimões, in contrast, is a light milky brown, like warm *café com leite*. Curiously, their waters meet but do not mix. Instead, they travel on side by side for miles, hardly interacting. The two broad currents stream along together, with little swirls and eddies developing where they join. Differences in velocity and alkalinity, and the weight of suspended matter between the two rivers, prevent their blending. If you were to enter this water, you could float with your feet in the milky Solimões and your head in the cool dark Rio Negro. A few miles farther on, the differences dissolve and finally the two rivers merge. The Portuguese name for this bizarre and beautiful phenomenon is *encontro das aguas* – the meeting

GETTING THERE See map p328, A4
River cruises depart Manaus, the capital of Brazil's Amazonas state. Eduardo Gomes International Airport is 10 miles (17 km) from the downtown river terminal.

GETTING AROUND
Downtown Manaus is a pedestrian zone, easily covered on foot. For longer distances or after dark, take a taxi. Rainforest Cruises (www.rainforestcruises.com) arranges Amazon cruises on large ships, while Viverde (www.viverde.com.br) runs riverboat trips.

WEATHER
It is hot year-round in the Amazon, normally 86–96°F (30–36°C), with almost 100 percent humidity. By May, the wet season has ended.

ACCOMMODATIONS
Basic but comfy lodging is found at Local Hotel Manaus; doubles from US$37; www.localhostel.com.br

Luxurious Tropical Manaus has colonial-style decor and three vast pools; doubles from US$110; www.tropicalhotel.com.br

A short boat ride up the Rio Negro from Manaus is the Tariri Amazon Lodge, in the heart of the rain forest; 3-day packages for doubles from US$310 per person; www.tariri amazonlodge.com.br

EATING OUT
Try Amazonian fruits, such as nutritious *açaí* served crushed and frozen, and *cupuaçu* ice cream. Sample local dishes at Choupana from around US$25; tel. (92) 3635 3878.

FURTHER INFORMATION
www.visitamazonastour.com

Opera in the Jungle

The striking dome-topped Teatro Amazonas is the centerpiece of the restored historic central square in Manaus. This opera house was erected over a century ago in 1896, at the height of a rubber boom that had made the entire Amazon region rich. A guided tour of the theater reveals a lobby of Italian marble and parquet floors of rich tropical hardwood, plus a mural in the ballroom depicting scenes from the first Brazilian opera performed here – the tale of an Indian princess and her doomed love for a Portuguese explorer.

Main: The meeting of the waters at the confluence of the Rio Negro and Rio Solimões

Left: Freshwater fish for sale at the Mercado Adolpho Lisboa

Right (left and right): Colorful riverboats moored at the jetty on the Manaus waterfront; canoe paddling through a flooded forest on the Rio Negro

of the waters. River cruises usually save it for the journey's end, by which time visitors have developed some of the expertise and vocabulary required for exploring a region where the river can rise or fall over 39 ft (12 m) in a single season and where vast forest lands flood and become lakes, then swamps, then dry land again. As part of a cruise, you may find yourself paddling through forests where the water reaches the highest branches, called either *varzea,* if they border the Solimões and its tributaries, or *igapó,* if they border the Rio Negro. You will paddle past *igarapés,* countless tiny channels that lead in through the trees, and meet *caboclos* – the river people who spend their days in canoes, who eat piranha fish and *jacaré* (caiman), and who make their homes on high stilts to stay above the floodwaters. When you leave the Amazon, you will almost certainly feel a sense of *saudade* – nostalgic longing for a magical place that is unlike anywhere else in the world.

Above: A pair of gold-and-blue macaws

Below (top and bottom): Squirrel monkey; pink Amazon river dolphin

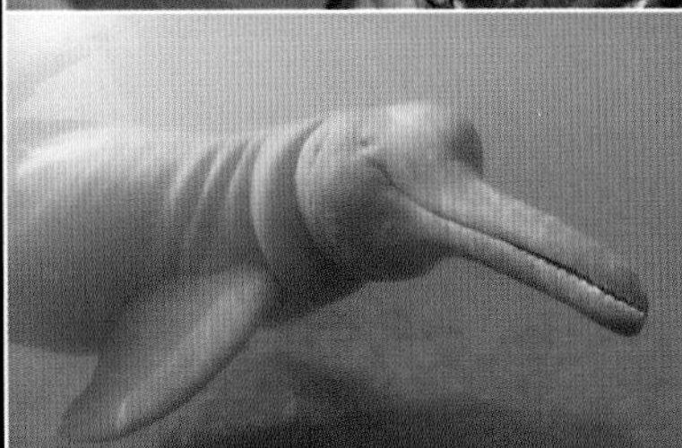

RIVER CRUISE DIARY

The rainy season is over by May, but the Negro and Solimões rivers are still near their highest, which makes this the best time to explore the flooded areas. Cruises depart weekly and provide an introduction to some of the astonishing sights and sounds along the world's largest river.

Five Days on the Amazon

DAY 1 Visit the Teatro Amazonas in Manaus, the luxurious opera house and concert hall built over a century ago in the heart of the jungle. Then head down to the river port to board your ship and set sail for your first night out on the water.

DAY 2 Trek through the *igarapés* to Novo Airão, where with luck you can see small bright-pink Amazon river dolphins. You might also spot alligators submerged in the water. While away the afternoon fishing with a hook and line for piranha at Lago Araçari, but watch out for their razor-sharp teeth.

DAY 3 Rise early to catch the sun coming up over a small side tributary called the Rio Padaurí, known for its bird life. Black cormorants, tiger herons, and tall white egrets are common sightings. Travel through the flooded forest around Igarapé Aturiá on a photo safari. Look out for squirrel monkeys, toucans, and gold-and-blue macaws along the way. Back on the boat, watch the sun go down to a soundtrack of soothing classical music or just the noises of the jungle.

DAY 4 Travel up Rio Cuieiras to visit the *caboclo* stilt-house community at Cambebas and learn how they process the poisonous mandioc root into staple carbohydrates. This is also a good place to pick up local handicrafts. Relax in the afternoon and just enjoy being here.

DAY 5 Rise early to experience the meeting of the waters. Afterwards sip champagne over breakfast, then sail back upstream to Manaus.

Dos and Don'ts

- ✓ Bring mosquito repellent and cover up in the evenings – mosquitoes are most likely to bite in the hour after sunset.
- ✗ Don't pass up a chance to visit the Mercado Adolpho Lisboa, the old wrought-iron market hall in the center of town.
- ✓ Pick up a cotton hammock in one of the chandlery shops near the riverboat terminal. It will make a fine souvenir.
- ✗ Don't skip the natural history lectures aboard the cruise ships. They are usually fun and extremely informative.

Below: A row of wooden *caboclo* stilt-houses

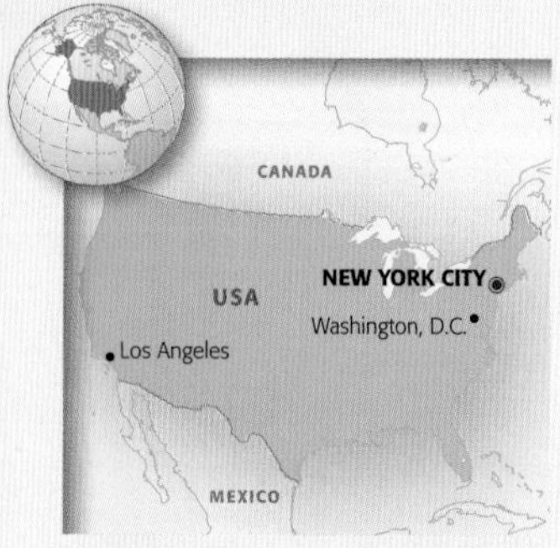

GETTING THERE See map p316, G5
LaGuardia domestic airport is 20 minutes from Midtown by taxi. Newark and JFK international airports are linked to the city by rail and bus (allow an hour by road).

GETTING AROUND
Walking is the best way to explore Manhattan but subways, buses, and taxis are plentiful.

WEATHER
May is very pleasant and fairly dry, with highs of around 75°F (24°C) and lows of 55°F (13°C).

ACCOMMODATIONS
The Comfort Inn Midtown West is conveniently located close to Times Square; doubles from US$289; www.choicehotels.com

The Library is among the most charming of the city's many small luxury hotels; doubles from US$250; www.libraryhotel.com

Classic elegance reigns at the Waldorf-Astoria, the ultimate "grand hotel"; doubles from US$250; www.waldorfnewyork.com

EATING OUT
Expect to pay US$20–25 for a sandwich and drink at Katz's and other classic New York delis, at least US$50 a person at a hip eatery like Spice Market in the Meatpacking District, and upwards of US$175 each at Le Bernardin and other temples of gastronomy.

FURTHER INFORMATION
www.nycgo.com

Hit the Heights

The Empire State Building, perhaps the world's favorite skyscraper, took shape above the skyline in just a little more than a year, with some 3,400 laborers constructing on average four floors a day. Inaugurated on May 1, 1931, it remained the tallest building in the world for the next 40 years. Its spire was originally intended as a mooring mast for airships. More than 114 million visitors have admired the spectacular views from the 86th-floor observation deck, the scene of romantic rendezvous in such films as *An Affair to Remember* and *Sleepless in Seattle*.

Above (left to right): Leafy Central Park; Metropolitan Museum of Art facade; Rockefeller Center at dusk
Main: Manhattan's fashionable bar scene

NEW YORK CITY

THE BIGGEST AND MOST BUZZING CITY IN AMERICA, one of the world's great hubs of commerce and culture, also happens to be one of the most appealing, even romantic, places on earth. It's partly the physical charms of the city, which are considerable. The soaring skyscrapers of stone and glass are majestic, the lawns and trees of Central Park are all the more welcoming, surrounded as they are by concrete, and the style for which the city sets the standard is in evidence in chic shops and on the streets. More than physical appeal, though, New York generates a jittery joy – the energy of the city is palpable. Part of the thrill of being in New York is feeling that something exciting, important, incredible seems to be happening all around you. Strolling though neon-lit Times Square or past Carnegie Hall, you can't help but sense that you are surrounded by legends, and walking down the narrow canyons of Wall Street you are aware that momentous decisions are being made in the eyrie-like offices above you. Adding to the city's charms is a sense of familiarity. The streets and landmarks appear in so many films and photographs, clubs and restaurants are mentioned so often in gossip columns and celebrity interviews, that first-time visitors will come upon sights they've seen and heard of time and time again. Even New Yorkers can be taken aback at just how much there is to see and do in their city, and the scene is ever changing. Downtown is flourishing, with new hotels, shops, and restaurants. Slaughterhouses in the Meatpacking District have been transformed into vibrant night spots. Beautifully landscaped walkways, in full bloom at this time of year, now line the banks of the Hudson River. So come and enjoy this intoxicating city for a few days. Go to the theater, dine well, dance into the wee hours, stroll the leafy streets of the West Village or Upper West Side. To paraphrase the song, be a part of it – the energy that makes the "city that never sleeps" eternally enticing.

Something exciting, important, incredible seems to be happening all around you.

Inset: Iconic New York yellow cab at night
Below (left and right): Manhattan from the air; A street in SoHo

BIG APPLE DIARY

A long springtime weekend in New York is the perfect time to indulge yourself and your loved one. Savor urbane delights like a Broadway show, sip on a Manhattan cocktail at twilight, stroll hand-in-hand through Central Park, and fall under the spell of a hard-edged city that can be the most romantic place on earth.

Four Perfect Days

THU

Arrive on Thursday in time for a show, with pre-theater cocktails at the King Cole Bar, the Algonquin, or any other one of the city's classic watering holes. Have a late-night supper at Joe Allen's or another Broadway haunt, where the star you just saw on stage may be sitting at the next table.

FRI

Fifth Avenue is the epicenter of New York luxury: treat yourselves at Saks', Cartier's or Tiffany's. Take the time to admire the lofty spires of St. Patrick's Cathedral and the Art Deco towers of Rockefeller Center. Sample some classic New York street food, such as hot dogs or pretzels, for lunch. Later, ascend to the observation platform of the Empire State Building. In the early evening, hail a horse-drawn carriage for a ride through Central Park to the Metropolitan Museum of Art. The strains of a string quartet float through the galleries and the views of the park and city from the Roof Garden are sumptuous.

SAT

Enjoy a leisurely Saturday: walk through Greenwich Village, gallery hop in Chelsea, shop in SoHo, lunch in Paris – that is, the city's ultra-Parisian bistro, Balthazar. Later, head to the Meatpacking District for a star-studded dinner and the cool club scene.

SUN

Brunch on the lakeside terrace of the Loeb Central Park Boathouse in Central Park, then slip into a gondola for a glide across the waters. If you have time, visit the Museum of Modern Art before a matinee or afternoon concert. To end your visit in style, enjoy a pre-departure cocktail at the Loopy Doopy Rooftop Bar atop the Conrad, Battery Park City, with its stunning harbor views.

Dos and Don'ts

- ✓ Make reservations for hot shows and cool restaurants well in advance to avoid disappointments.
- ✗ Don't be afraid to join New Yorkers underground on the excellent subway system.
- ✓ Buy inexpensive one-day travel passes for unlimited rides on buses or the subway.
- ✗ Don't confine your visit to Midtown; there's so much more to discover in the city's many neighborhoods.
- ✓ Bring a comfortable pair of shoes for walking.

Below: View across the Meatpacking District and Chelsea into Midtown

TORONTO

STEP INTO TORONTO'S ST. LAWRENCE MARKET and it's hard to figure out what to do first. Sample New Zealand manuka honey or Pakistani sea salt? Pick up some Chinese "forbidden" rice or Argentinean chorizo? Or simply wander the busy aisles of this Victorian market building in a happy daze, inhaling the mouthwatering aromas of fresh bagels and apple fritters? The dilemmas presented by a visit to the St. Lawrence Market mirror the bewildering range of choices available to you when visiting Toronto itself. What was once a restrained, WASP-y bastion is today one of the world's most cosmopolitan cities – more than half of Toronto's adult population was born outside of Canada. As a result, it's easy to while away your vacation feasting on paella and dim sum, dancing to Peruvian folk musicians and bhangra dance beats, and watching the latest festive parade wind its way through the city streets.

Main: The Michael Lee-Chin Crystal, the bold, futuristic extension to the Royal Ontario Museum

GETTING THERE See map p316, E4
Lester B. Pearson International Airport is 16 miles (26 km) from downtown Toronto. Outside of rush hour, it's 25 minutes by taxi or the UP Express rail link.

GETTING AROUND
Walk, use public transportation, or hail a taxi downtown, and cycle along the lakefront. A car is only needed for trips out of town (but Stratford can also be reached direct by rail).

WEATHER
May is generally mild and almost summery. Temperatures are 45–63°F (7°–17°C). The lakeside is usually cooler than downtown.

ACCOMMODATIONS
The basic Super 8 Downtown Toronto is great value for a downtown location; doubles from US$80; www.super8downtowntoronto.com

The Hyatt Regency is within walking distance of theaters, concert halls, and sports stadia; doubles from US$310; www.torontoregency.hyatt.com

The Hazelton Hotel in posh Yorkville offers celebrity style, with matching prices; doubles from US$380; www.thehazeltonhotel.com

EATING OUT
Meals from just about every world cuisine are available for US$15–20 per person. Expect to pay at least US$70–100 per person at gourmet hotspots.

FURTHER INFORMATION
www.seetorontonow.com

Impressive Impresario

When the late Ed Mirvish saved Toronto's Beaux Arts Royal Alexandra Theatre from the wrecker's ball in 1962, locals were skeptical. The theater and the stretch of King Street on which it stood were derelict, and Toronto's theater scene was moribund. But the man who'd made his fortune with a kitsch discount store called Honest Ed's revived the Royal Alex and built the 2,000-seat Broadway showcase Princess of Wales Theatre nearby. Today, King Street is known as the Entertainment District, and Toronto is the third-largest live theater center in the English-speaking world.

Above left (top to bottom): Francesco Pirelli's *Monument t[o] Multiculturalism* (1985) on Fr[ont] Street; quirky shops and stalls of the Kensington Market; a pa[ir] of Cabbagetown's ornate Victorian villas

Left: Ward Island, viewed from the top of the CN Tower

Right (left and right): Blue Ja[ys] pitcher Marcus Stroman; Toron[to] skyline, with the CN Tower and the Rogers Centre clearly visibl[e]

Enticing as Toronto's multicultural vibe is, it's just one reason culture buffs love the place. Toronto offers a huge range of exhibitions, concerts, and cultural festivals. Travelers with a classical bent head to the Canadian Opera Company or the Toronto Symphony Orchestra. Fans of cutting-edge drama buy tickets to the Soulpepper or Tarragon theatres, while more traditional theatergoers make the trip out to delightful Stratford for Shakespearian and modern classics.

The city also has many distinctive, pedestrian-friendly neighborhoods to discover. Cabbagetown is known for its many well-preserved Victorian houses; Queen Street West is where Goth kids mix with fashionistas; the restored Distillery District is a former industrial complex that's now a cultural and leisure hub; and clotheshorses spend their time prowling the quirky boutiques surrounding the Kensington Market. Even the Business District yields treats. Hop on a "Red Rocket" – the city's iconic streetcar – to "New" City Hall. It won raves for its futuristic design when it opened in 1965, of the sort now lavished on Daniel Libeskind's Crystal extension to the Royal Ontario Museum.

COSMOPOLITAN DIARY

Winter weather in Toronto features far too many damp, gray, cold days. So when May rolls around, the locals can't wait to get outside. Sidewalks sprout café tables, street theater abounds, and just about every weekend offers an outdoor festival or two. Five days lets you sample the city's buzzing scene and head out of town as well.

Five Days in a Culture Capital

DAY 1 View the city from the observation deck of the CN Tower, until 2007 the world's tallest freestanding structure at 1,815 ft (553 m) tall. Then take in a Blue Jays baseball game at the Rogers Centre (formerly called the Skydome for its fully retracting roof). If it's early May, end the day with a performance at Canadian Music Week.

DAY 2 Spend the morning – or the day – perusing everything from Egyptian mummies to modern art at the Royal Ontario Museum (ROM). To clear your head and empty your wallet, browse the luxury boutiques on nearby Bloor Street. Dine beneath the indoor vertical garden at Sassafraz, a stylish Yorkville restaurant.

DAY 3 Take the 15-minute ferry ride from Harbourfront to Ward's Island, the farthest east of the three Toronto Islands. It's worth renting a bike and cycling the trails that link the islands, stopping for lunch on the secluded, shady patio of the Rectory Café. Back at Harbourfront, a waterfront arts and retail complex, you might come across a literary reading or art exhibition.

DAY 4 Head out to Stratford, a picturesque small city 2 hours' drive southwest of Toronto, to enjoy a performance at the renowned Stratford Shakespeare Festival.

DAY 5 For your last day, explore one of Toronto's vibrant ethnic neighborhoods. You could fuel up with moussaka in Greektown or cannoli in Little Italy; or shop for silks in the Gerrard India Bazaar. Later, visit Casa Loma, the faux-medieval 1914 "castle" whose construction bankrupted its millionaire owner. End your visit with a blockbuster musical at the Royal Alex or Princess of Wales Theatre.

Dos and Don'ts

- ✓ Explore the PATH system, a strange but useful web of underground corridors linking many downtown buildings.
- ✗ Don't be afraid to walk across a lane of traffic to reach a waiting streetcar. Look carefully, but most locals are used to this somewhat hair-raising system and will stop.
- ✓ Go for afternoon tea at the Fairmont Royal York or the Omni King Edward Hotel, where it feels like the sun hasn't completely set on the British Empire.
- ✗ Don't forget to pronounce the city's name "Traw-na" if you want to sound like a local.

Below: A Toronto "Bombardier" streetcar

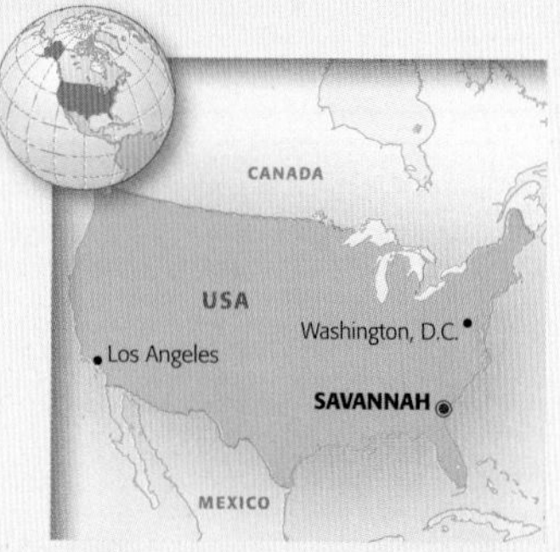

GETTING THERE See map p317, G4
Fly into Savannah International Airport, 11 miles (18 km) from the Historic District. The Golden Isles are 80 miles (129 km) south of Savannah, along the Atlantic Coast.

GETTING AROUND
Plan on walking, taking a tour, or using the hop-on trolley to explore Old Savannah. Rent a car for trips beyond the Historic District.

WEATHER
May has average daytime highs of 84°F (29°C) and nighttime lows of 61°F (16°C). Expect occasional showers, high humidity, and mostly sunny skies.

ACCOMMODATIONS
Catherine Ward House Inn, an elegant hotel with nearly 130 years of history, has rooms from US$180; www.catherinewardhouseinn.com

Romantic Gastonian, near Forsyth Park, has rooms from US$240; www.gastonian.com

Jekyll Island Club Hotel is a classic historic resort hotel, with rooms from US$210; www.jekyllclub.com

EATING OUT
From home-style restaurants to fine dining, there is a lot to choose from in Savannah. Try the stylish A.lure for contemporary low-country cuisine, or enjoy an elaborate meal in a fine mansion, at Elizabeth on 37th.

FURTHER INFORMATION
www.visitsavannah.com

SAVANNAH

ROMANTIC AS A SULTRY SOUTHERN BELLE and as eccentric as a Southern grande dame, Old Savannah is at her seductive best in spring when the perfume of magnolias fills the air and the gardens are awash with color. The city's cobblestone streets, shaded by moss-draped oak trees, are laid out in a grid with 22 beautiful green squares, each decorated with ornate fountains and statues.

A stroll along the charming streets, accompanied by the clip-clop of horse-drawn carriages, leads past elegant antebellum mansions displaying regal white columns, and restored late 19th-century town homes, trimmed with scrolled ironwork balconies. Here, too, are hidden gardens where azaleas bloom, elaborate Gothic churches, and fine Federal- and Regency-style mansions, decorated with handsome antiques. The sweet sounds of jazz, the alluring scent of roasting pecans, and the *Waving Girl* statue

Main: Forsyth Park Fountain, shaded by live oak trees

Garden of Good and Evil

John Berendt mingled in Savannah's high society for eight years, as well as among drag queens, voodoo witches, and various eccentrics. In 1994, he wrote *Midnight in the Garden of Good and Evil*, about a scandalous murder and a mysterious ritual in Bonaventure Cemetery. Detested by many locals for sensationalizing their gracious city, the book is a fictionalized exposé of Savannah's wealthy. A tour points out major locations, such as the cemetery.

Left (left and right): Horseback riding along the beach on Cumberland Island; historic stern-wheeler berthed on the Savannah River

Right: Balconies with elegant wrought-iron scrollwork at Marshall House, Savannah's oldest hotel

welcome visitors to promenade along the Savannah River. Shops in the historic brick-built warehouses display gifts and clothing, while galleries offer regional art and finely crafted jewelry, and the mouthwatering aromas of seafood and Southern fried chicken lure in hungry diners.

South of Savannah, the Golden Isles have warm sand beaches bordered by dunes and salt marshes filled with majestic herons and white-plumed egrets. These barrier islands along Georgia's Atlantic Coast were once the exclusive resorts of the vacationing wealthy. Today, most of Cumberland Island is protected as a National Seashore, where only 300 visitors each day can savor the fresh salt air and enjoy the pristine beaches. Here, vistas include grazing wild horses, sea turtle tracks on sandy beaches, and hundreds of bird species soaring on the sea breezes. On nearby Jekyll Island, wander past grand old mansions in the historic Millionaires Village and then head over to Driftwood Beach to walk hand-in-hand down the beach as the sun slowly sets into the sea.

Above: *Waving Girl* statue, of Savannah native Florence Martus (1869–1943), who greeted every ship entering and leaving harbor for 44 years

Below: Inviting verandah retreat at the Jekyll Island Club Hotel

OLD SAVANNAH DIARY

May is a wonderful time to visit Savannah and the Golden Isles. The weather is warm, flowers are in bloom, and the streets and island beaches are not yet inundated with summer visitors. Two days in gracious Savannah, followed by three days in the islands to enjoy the solitude, are the perfect getaway.

Five Days in the Old South

DAY 1

Take a horse-drawn carriage tour through Old Savannah and then stroll along the shady streets to explore Forsyth Park and the beautiful squares on your own. Tour some of the historic homes, notably Davenport House, Owens-Thomas House, and the Green-Meldrim House. Visit the Cathedral of St. John the Baptist and the First African Baptist Church. After dinner, walk along the riverfront and indulge yourself at a chocolate shop or a tavern.

DAY 2

Take a riverboat cruise aboard a 19th-century stern-wheeler for views of the bustling harbor, historic cotton warehouses, and the *Waving Girl* statue. Head over to the City Market for lunch and shopping, and then explore the Isle of Hope's antebellum community, Old Fort Jackson, or visit Bonaventure Cemetery. Take an early-evening ghost tour of haunted Savannah, and then dine at a fine restaurant.

DAY 3

Drive to Jekyll Island and rent bicycles to explore the historic town and cottages there, before heading to the beach for an afternoon of sun and sand. End the day with dinner at the famous Jekyll Island Club Hotel.

DAY 4

Take the morning boat out to Cumberland Island National Seashore to explore the white-sand beaches and shady woodlands of magnolia, oak, and pine, where herds of wild horses roam.

DAY 5

Drive to St. Simons Island to visit the lighthouse and Fort Frederica National Monument. Have lunch there before heading to the airport for your flight back home.

Dos and Don'ts

- ✓ Wear comfortable walking shoes and explore the tree-lined streets and squares of Old Savannah by foot.
- ✗ Don't forget to pack for the beach, as well as for fine dining in Savannah, where it is traditional to dress for dinner.
- ✓ Read or watch *Midnight in the Garden of Good and Evil;* it conveys Savannah's air of mystery and romance.
- ✗ Don't forget to reserve rooms and car rentals in advance.
- ✓ Check for city-sponsored concerts, and take a blanket to sit on the lawn of Forsyth Park, for an evening of music.

Below: Languid street-corner café on a summer's day

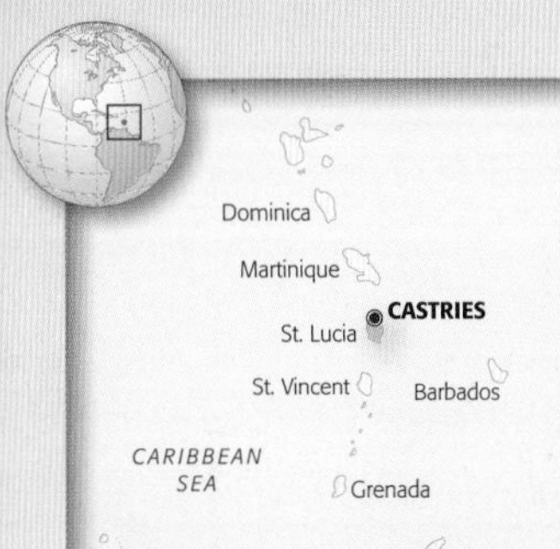

GETTING THERE See map p325, I5
Hewanorra, the main international airport, is in the south of the island, 35 miles (56 km) from the capital, Castries. Flights come in from major hubs in Europe, the USA, and Toronto and Montréal in Canada. The smaller George Charles Airport at Vigie Beach is just 1 mile (2 km) north of Castries.

GETTING AROUND
Taxis and minibuses are expensive, so rent a car to explore the island. If using taxis, fix the price and currency before setting off.

WEATHER
St. Lucia has great weather year-round: in May, daytime temperatures are about 85°F (29°C). Warm rains fall mainly between May and October.

ACCOMMODATIONS
The budget Blu St Lucia at Rodney Bay offers total relaxation; doubles from US$120 a night; www.harlequinblu.com

The chic Capella Marigot Bay is beside the island's prettiest bay; doubles from US$415; www.capellahotels.com

Sandals Grande St. Lucian Spa and Beach Resort is luxurious; doubles from US$690; www.sandals.com/main/grande/gl-home

EATING OUT
Enjoy seafood at Jacques in Rodney Bay Village, or savor local dishes at JJ's Paradise at Marigot Bay from US$40 per head.

FURTHER INFORMATION
www.stlucia.org

St. Lucia's "Pyramids"

The 2,619-ft (798-m) Gros Piton and the 2,461-ft (750-m) Petit Piton, St. Lucia's "pyramids," are the island's most spectacular landmarks. These volcanic pinnacles rising out of the sea dominate the southwestern landscape. From a distance, they appear to be side by side but on a closer look, you can see just how far apart they are. The Pitons, their summits covered by tropical rain forests, stand on either side of Soufrière Bay. Hire a guide to explore them – it is worth the visit and makes for an unforgettable day trip.

Main: Crowds enjoying the Jazz Festival on Pigeon Island

ST. LUCIA

St. Lucia in May means one thing – jazz. The long, balmy evenings are filled with the sweet scent of rum and the sensual sounds of jazz wafting on the breeze through open doorways. Up-and-coming stars entertain picnicking families, talented locals perform impromptu skits on side streets, and world-class musicians give sell-out concerts in dramatic settings. For 10 days each year this island paradise in the Lesser Antilles, known for its beaches and rain forest, comes alive with blues and ragtime at one of the world's greatest jazz festivals.

Initially held in the capital city of Castries, the main event moved to Pigeon Island, a handsome outcrop of land to the north of St. Lucia, accessed by a white-sand causeway. Fringe performances and scores of other live events take place day and night in the island's towns and villages. Soak up the atmosphere at sunset performances on the pier at Pointe Seraphine, on the Vigie Peninsula, or while having lunch at Derek Walcott Square in central

Left (left to right): Colorful heliconias in the Diamond Botanical Gardens in Soufrière; the bustle of Castries market; a man climbing a palm tree on Soufrière beach against a backdrop of the Pitons; boats moored at Marigot Bay

Below: Tessanne Chin performing at the Sant Lucia Jazz & Arts Festival in 2014

Inset: George Benson and Al Jarreau

The long, balmy evenings are filled with the sweet scent of rum and the sensual sounds of jazz wafting on the breeze through open doorways.

Castries. Relax to the soothing sounds of soul at afternoon gigs in the Fond d'Or Heritage Park on the east coast, or at midnight in the southern towns of Laborie, Soufrière, and Vieux Fort. A carnival-like atmosphere descends on the island – children dress up, dance, and sing at open-air concerts and fans cheer as their musical heroes roll out their favorite tunes. There are also arts and crafts displays, fashion shows, culinary events, and street theater, all allowing visitors to experience the island's cultural life. It is noisy and crowded but, above all, it is friendly.

This musical extravaganza might be the main draw, but there is a lot more to see. Attractions include historic colonial buildings in Castries, Soufrière, and on Pigeon Island, working cocoa and sugar plantations, a volcanic area with bubbling pools, fabulous beaches, and world-class scuba diving among other water sports. And of course the unforgettable Pitons, enormous peaks dominating the island's west coast. Together with the St. Lucia Jazz & Arts Festival, these magnificent sights will call you back to the island year after year.

JAZZ DIARY

Beautiful St. Lucia in the eastern Caribbean is renowned for its stunning beaches, towering Pitons, and tropical vegetation. In May, the silence of its long, warm days is broken by the strains of world-class jazz. A six-day trip gives you enough time to hear great live music and explore the island's other treasures.

Six Days on a Music Trail

DAY 1 Relax and get your bearings. Then stroll around Castries. Visit the Pointe Seraphine shopping center by the cruise terminal and buy some great duty-free gifts. Make your way back to the city center and enjoy some free jazz in Derek Walcott Square.

DAY 2 Head over to Pigeon Island for the world-renowned Jazz Festival. Make sure you have tickets – these grant admission only and do not guarantee seating. Take a blanket to sit on and a small cooler for drinks. You can also buy food and drink from numerous vendors.

DAY 3 In between listening to talented performers, take the time to explore Pigeon Island's National Park. Check out the old buildings, some of which used to be part of the largest British forts in the Caribbean.

DAY 4 Spend a day exploring Castries. Visit the bustling and colorful market and enjoy more jazz – there are scores of free events staged in the capital during the festival.

DAY 5 Head down the west coast to Soufrière, the place where the French first settled on St. Lucia (there used to be a guillotine in the town square). Visit the Soufrière Sulphur Springs, but stick to the paths. Then explore the nearby Diamond Botanical Gardens and take a dip in the mineral springs.

DAY 6 Enjoy your last day relaxing at the Reduit Beach, one of the most beautiful beaches in the Caribbean – the perfect way to end your stay.

Dos and Don'ts

- ✓ Enjoy as many jazz events as you can pack into your schedule, especially the free ones.
- ✓ Wear a sun hat if sitting outside during the day; the sun can be blistering.
- ✓ Relish the local food specialties such as conch (often called *lambi*), roti, and coconut fritters.
- ✗ Don't drink too much alcohol in the hot sun, you'll miss all that great jazz – and could get badly burnt.

Below: Ruined fortifications in Pigeon Island National Park

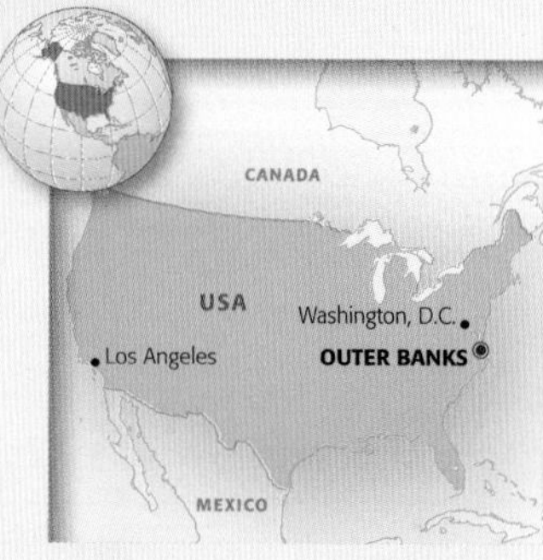

GETTING THERE See map p317, I2
Located in North Carolina, the closest airport is at Norfolk, 90 miles (145 km) to the north.

GETTING AROUND
Local ferries and a car are the only ways to get around on the Outer Banks.

WEATHER
The average May daytime temperature is 76°F (23°C) and nights are 60°F (15°C).

ACCOMMODATIONS
The 88-room Sanderling Resort, on the beach in Duck, is the most luxurious Outer Banks lodging; doubles from US$250; www.sanderling-resort.com

Near the glorious National Seashore beaches of Hatteras Island, the cozy 12-room Inn on Pamlico Sound in Buxton promises breakfast in bed or on your private deck; doubles from US$190; www.innonpamlicosound.com

The Captain's Landing hotel on Ocracoke Island has private suites with a balcony overlooking the charming harbor; doubles from US$200; www.thecaptainslanding.com

EATING OUT
Try elegant Blue Point, Duck, for fine country dining (US$30). In Kitty Hawk, High Cotton serves up chicken 'n' ribs (US$15); and Owen's Restaurant, Nags Head, features Carolina Shrimp and aged prime beef.

FURTHER INFORMATION
www.outerbanks.org

OUTER BANKS

THE OUTER BANKS IS A BEACH-LOVER'S DELIGHT comprising 100 miles (160 km) of unspoiled coastline across a chain of barrier islands. It is full of fascinating discoveries too: with hideaways where wildlife and birds abound, prize fishing grounds, and colorful historic sites such as Roanoke Island.

The developed communities of Nags Head, Kill Devil Hills, and Kitty Hawk in the center of Bodie Island are known for their mammoth sand dunes, formed by shifting winds. One of them was used by the Wright Brothers for their historic flight. The Wright Brothers National Memorial and Jockey Ridge State Park are two popular stops here. To the north is Duck, the most upscale island community. Beyond are the 7,000-acre (2,832-ha) Audubon Pine Island Sanctuary and the red-brick Currituck Beach Lighthouse, which is one of a series of lighthouses along the Outer Banks dating from the 1870s.

The Lost Settlers

Roanoke Island, between the mainland and the Outer Banks, has a fascinating history. Fort Raleigh National Historic Site marks the place where English settlers sponsored by Sir Walter Raleigh established a colony over 400 years ago. It was the birthplace of Virginia Dare, the first English child born in the New World. But the 116 men, women, and children of the settlement disappeared without explanation. Their story is recreated in the outdoor pageant "The Lost Colony" presented each summer in Manteo. Lovely Elizabethan Gardens have been planted here in memory of the lost settlers.

Main: The famous Cape Hatteras Lighthouse

Left (left and right): Ocracoke Island rum cocktails; Chicamacomico Lifesaving Station

Right (left and right): Sanderling Resort; Currituck wild horses

Right panel (top and bottom): Hang gliders and kite-flyers at Jockeys Ridge State Park, Nags Head; sailboats in Ocracoke harbor

The Outer Banks proper begins to the south, past Bodie Island Lighthouse and the busy marina and sportfishing center at Oregon Inlet. Across the inlet is Hatteras Island, with its protected National Seashore since 1953, which stretches for 72 miles (115 km), and is home to the Pea Island National Wildlife Refuge. Built in 1870, the much-photographed Cape Hatteras Lighthouse warns ships away from the perils of Diamond Shoals, known as the "Graveyard of the Atlantic." A few surviving early US lifesaving stations serve to remind visitors that more than 600 ships sank here.

A 40-minute ferry ride takes you to Ocracoke Island, the most romantic outpost of the Outer Banks. Its deep inlet made it suitable early on as a port for ocean-going vessels and it has been a town since 1735. The secluded location also made it a favorite haunt of the infamous pirate Blackbeard, who was killed somewhere nearby and whose treasure, some believe, remains buried on the island. Return ferries are frequent but you may never want to leave.

BEACHCOMBER'S DIARY

These unspoiled islands tucked between the Atlantic Ocean and Pamlico Sound boast 120-mile (193-km) strands of golden sand. Stay in a romantic inn in May, an ideal time before the summer crowds and heat arrive. While the ocean may be too chilly for swimming, days are warm enough for beachcombing.

Five Days at the Seashore

DAY 1 Your first day is probably best spent relaxing and savoring the wonderful sand and sea. Whether you choose a single base with day trips or plan to tour, there is a lot to see and do here on the Outer Banks.

DAY 2 Head for Kill Devil Hills and the Wright Brothers National Memorial to see a replica of Orville and Wilbur Wright's flying machine. At Jockey Ridge State Park in neighboring Nags Head, check out the hang gliders soaring from the highest natural sand dune in the eastern USA, one of several in the area that can reach 140 ft (43 m). Join kids of all ages who love climbing and sliding down these huge sand piles. Then drive across Roanoke Sound to Manteo and explore Fort Raleigh National Historic Site, which is the site of Sir Walter Raleigh's lost colony of Roanoke.

DAY 3 Follow N.C. Route 12 north to the town of Duck for the area's most upscale shops. Farther on, past the Audubon preserve, is the red-brick Currituck Beach Lighthouse in Corolla, built in 1875.

DAY 4 Cross the inlet south to Hatteras, and you're in the heart of the National Seashore with 70 miles (112 km) of pristine beach. For many, this is what the Outer Banks are all about. View the birds, wildlife, and wildflowers at Pea Island National Wildlife refuge. Join the photographers snapping the 208-ft (63-m) Cape Hatteras Lighthouse, the country's tallest.

DAY 5 Board the car ferry to picturesque, unspoiled Ocracoke Island, and spend your last day exploring the historic village and savoring the white sands that are a beach-lover's dream.

Dos and Don'ts

- ⊗ Don't miss a visit to Ocracoke's British Cemetery, the burial ground of four British sailors, casualties of a German submarine attack in 1942.
- ✓ Look for the herd of wild horses roaming freely on the northernmost Currituck Outerbanks, descendants of mustangs brought by the first Spanish explorers in the 16th century.
- ✓ Roanoke Island Festival Park is an interactive family attraction that celebrates the first English settlement in America.
- ✓ From mid-April you can climb up Cape Hatteras Lighthouse.

Below: Natural shoreline at Cape Hatteras National Seashore

JUNE

Where to Go: **June**

Summer has arrived in the northern hemisphere. Canada is warming up nicely, although showers are likely in the south. Throughout North America the tourist season is gearing up, but the summer hordes have yet to descend. In the USA, the Southwestern deserts are glorious, with manageable temperatures at higher elevations, while the Rocky Mountains are resplendent with colorful wildflowers. Even Chicago, famously cold in winter, is mild enough to allow some outdoor living. While much of Central America is drenched in daily downpours, June brings the winter solstice to the southern hemisphere, celebrated in Cusco, Peru with a spectacular Inca festival. Below you will find all the destinations in this chapter as well as some extra suggestions to provide a little inspiration.

FESTIVALS AND CULTURE

CHICAGO Band playing at Buddy Guy's Legends blues club

CHICAGO
ILLINOIS, USA

Try the three-day Chicago Blues Festival for a musical celebration

Tune into this amazing event, but when you need a break, explore this huge and interesting city, and enjoy shopping, museums, and visual arts.

See pp130–31

CUENCA
ECUADOR

Colonial gem in Ecuador's southern sierra

Explore this atmospheric city of Spanish churches, whitewashed houses, cobblestone streets, and spacious squares.

www.cuenca.com.ec

INTI RAYMI
CUSCO, PERU

Traditional Andean winter solstice festival

Traditional celebrations in honor of the Sun God, Wiracocha, held in the stunning Inca ruins at Sacsayhuamán, just outside Cusco.

www.aboutcusco.com

GETTYSBURG NATIONAL MILITARY PARK
PENNSYLVANIA, USA

Historic battlefield and cemetery

Explore the site of the Civil War's most devastating battle, with sobering mementos of the encounter which cost 51,000 lives.

www.nps.gov/gett

CHIQUITOS
BOLIVIA

A beautiful untouched region with historic churches

Follow the trail to the Jesuit mission towns and find a forgotten world in their glorious 17th-century churches and musical people.

See pp148–9

UNFORGETTABLE JOURNEYS

GREAT RIVER ROAD The lazy Mississippi

GREAT RIVER ROAD
MIDWEST, USA

Follow the Mississippi River on this Midwestern drive

Take this scenic drive along the Upper Mississippi River past boats, ancient Native American burial mounds, and pioneer log cabins.

See pp134–5

JEFFERSON NATIONAL FOREST
VIRGINIA, USA

On the Appalachian Trail

The west-central Virginia section of the trail passes through some outstanding displays of azaleas and rhododendrons in this month.

www.appalachiantrail.org

"The small fortress city sits majestically in a saddle between two mountain peaks, surrounded by dense vegetation and often shrouded in mist."

BLUEGRASS COUNTRY
KENTUCKY, USA

Horseback riding, wine tasting and old-time bluegrass music

Saddle up for a ride through classic equestrian country, then kick back in the local wineries and music venues.

www.bluegrasskentucky.com

MACHU PICCHU
PERU

A fantastic feat of construction on the side of a mountain

It's a strenuous high-altitude hike through the mountains, but the glorious views of this ancient city make the effort worthwhile.

See pp140–41

AVENUE OF THE VOLCANOES
ECUADOR

Fire and smoke in the Andes

Lining the highway south of Quito, this majestic line of snowcapped volcanic peaks is one of Ecuador's most unforgettable sights.

www.ecuador.us/volcano.htm

NATURAL WONDERS

NIAGARA FALLS Horseshoe Falls lit up at night

NIAGARA FALLS
CANADA/USA

A thundering wonder of the natural world

The Falls cast a magic spell over honeymooners and daredevils alike. Embrace adventure and sail right up to this awesome cataract.

See pp132–3

PANTANAL
BRAZIL

The world's largest freshwater wetlands

The animals here are far more visible than in the rain forest – see giant otters, tapirs, caiman, herds of capybara, and many birds.

www.turismo.ms.gov.br

KODIAK ISLAND
ALASKA, USA

As the salmon run they attract famously large grizzly bears

As well as huge bears you'll see moose with their calves, foxes, seals, and maybe orcas – and an astonishing amount of bird life.

www.kodiak.org

FINGER LAKES
NEW YORK STATE, USA

Shimmering lakes and wine tours

Tour the vineyards set along the shores of eleven slender ice-blue lakes, fed by waterfalls that cut through dramatic gorges.

See pp146–7

YUKON
CANADA

Midsummer in Canada's wild north

June is a memorable time to visit the pristine Yukon region, its great stretches of sub-Arctic wilderness bathed in the midnight sun.

www.travelyukon.com

Previous page: The magnificent Niagara Falls, Canada/USA

Weather Watch

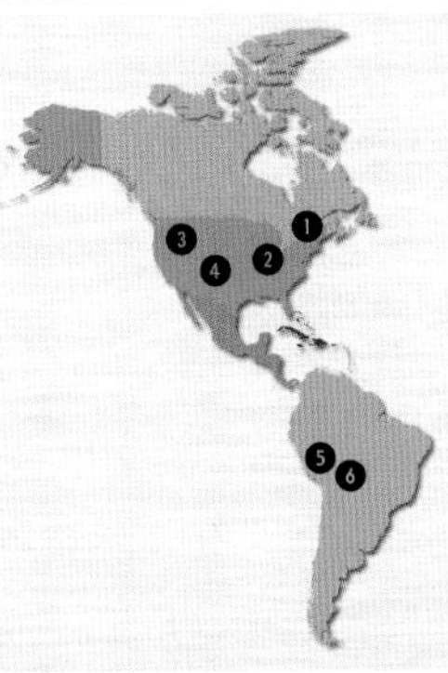

1 Montréal, Canada Montréal is mild and sunny in June, and humidity is not too much of a problem. You are likely to need an umbrella, but not for long.

2 Chicago, USA The Midwest's so-called "windy city" is delightful this month, with warm temperatures and pleasant breezes wafting off Lake Michigan. It will no doubt rain, but you should plan on packing your summer gear.

3 Idaho, USA With daytime highs around 60°F (16°C), the Rocky Mountain state of Idaho is an outdoor paradise in June, offering perfect conditions for fishing, swimming, rafting, and hiking.

4 Colorado, USA The cool 7,000-ft (2,133-m) plateau of Mesa Verde can provide welcome relief from the hotter desert plains below. Days are warm and sunny.

5 Peru June is a good time to visit Peru, and perfect for walking. Cusco, starting point for the four-day Inca Trail, is dry and sunny and relatively cool. Temperatures, and humidity, increase as you approach the ruins of Machu Picchu.

6 Bolivia June is mid-winter in Bolivia. The Amazon lowlands are enjoying a dry season, although humidity is high. Weather in the altiplano, on the other hand, is cool and crisp.

LUXURY AND ROMANCE

BERMUDA Turquoise sea and soft white sand at Elbow Beach

BERMUDA
NORTH ATLANTIC

The perfect tropical island getaway for two

Laze on coral sands, swim in turquoise waters, watch a spectacular sunset, and dine by candlelight under the stars – who could ask for more?

See pp144–5

"Enjoy romantic picnics in the warm island breeze, and sip rum punch while watching the vermilion beauty of a Bermudan sunset."

CUSCO
PERU

Be charmed by Peru's most romantic city

Ancient Inca monuments and magnificent scenery, best appreciated during a stay at the Monasterio, voted the best hotel in South America.

www.cuscoperu.com

WAIKĪKĪ
HAWAI'I, USA

Hawai'i at its brashest, glitziest, and most hedonistic

Pose on the beach, shop till you drop then chill out in one of Waikīkī's string of mouthwatering restaurants and bars.

www.waikiki.com

CHARLEVOIX
QUÉBEC, CANADA

Luxury and romance in rural Québec

This beautiful region combines superb scenery and outdoor attractions, and offers great boutique shopping and fine dining.

www.tourisme-charlevoix.com

CHARLESTON
SOUTH CAROLINA, USA

One of North America's most alluring cities

The most quintessentially southern city in the USA has a tropical ambience and rambling old streets of historic villas.

www.charleston.com

ACTIVE ADVENTURES

STANLEY Casting a line for trout in a waterfall

STANLEY
IDAHO, USA

Fantastic fly-fishing in clear mountain lakes

Outdoors activities abound in Idaho, from fly-fishing to white-water rafting, in a heavenly, snow-capped mountain setting.

See pp138–9

DAYTONA BEACH
FLORIDA, USA

Learn to surf at a summer camp on Daytona Beach

Florida is underrated as a surf destination, and while there aren't awesome waves in summer, they should be perfect for learners.

www.daytonabeach.com

"Fly-fishers can hike into the wilderness or just find a stretch of crystal-clear water into which to cast a line."

VOYAGEURS NATIONAL PARK
MINNESOTA, USA

A watery wilderness

Hop in a boat and lose yourself in Voyageurs' maze of unspoilt lakes and islands, home to eagles, moose, and bear.

www.nps.gov/voya

GLACIER NATIONAL PARK
MONTANA, USA

Superb alpine hiking

Over 700 miles (1,125 km) of trails wind through pristine forests and alpine meadows, and between small glaciers and rugged peaks.

www.nps.gov/glac

TRANS-APOLOBAMBA TREK
BOLIVIA

Challenging five-day trek

Bolivia's finest hike takes you deep into the Cordillera Apolobamba, surrounded by dramatic mountain scenery.

www.bolivianmountains.com

FAMILY GETAWAYS

MESA VERDE NATIONAL PARK Guided tour at Balcony House

MESA VERDE NATIONAL PARK
COLORADO, USA

Ancient cliff dwellings

Take a trip to the land of the Puebloan people preserved in Mesa Verde National Park, with 4,000 known archeological sites.

See pp136–7

CUSTER COUNTRY
MONTANA, USA

Follow in the footsteps of the controversial colonel

Scout out some of the historic sites associated with Custer, or enjoy the popular annual Battle of Little Big Horn re-enactment.

www.custer.visitmt.com

MYRTLE BEACH
SOUTH CAROLINA, USA

Seaside family fun in South Carolina

The cheerful Atlantic resort of Myrtle Beach offers something for all the family, from diving to paintballing, plus miles of sandy beach.

www.myrtlebeach.com

MONTRÉAL
QUÉBEC, CANADA

French-speaking city where the Old World meets the New

Tour the city from a horse-drawn carriage, see Cathédrale Notre-Dame, practice your French, and don't miss the fireworks.

See pp142–3

BOSTON
MASSACHUSETTS, USA

Relaxed family fun in a historic city

Glide across a lagoon on a Swan Boat in Boston Public Garden and come face to face with sharks at the New England Aquarium.

www.bostonusa.com

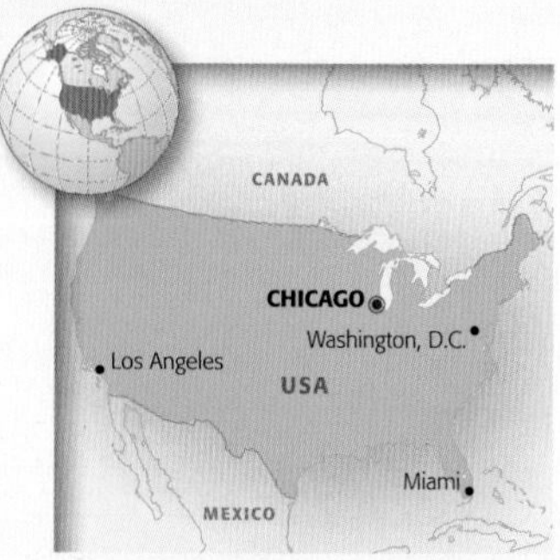

GETTING THERE **See map p314, B7**
Chicago sits at the edge of Lake Michigan. Most international traffic arrives at O'Hare Airport, 20 miles (32 km) northwest of the city center.

GETTING AROUND
Chicago's elevated railroad ("The El") is an easy way to get around. Rail and bus stops are within walking distance of the Blues Festival, as are public parking garages.

WEATHER
June brings pleasant temperatures, with an average daytime high of 81°F (27°C), dropping to 60°F (15°C) at night.

ACCOMMODATIONS
The Tremont Chicago, north of Michigan Ave (The Magnificent Mile), is a good base; doubles from US$270; www.tremontchicago.com

Dating from 1920, Drake Hotel is a Chicago classic; doubles from US$290; www.thedrakehotel.com

The Palmer House Hilton, in the heart of the Chicago Loop, a walk from Grant Park; family rooms from US$325; www.hilton.com

EATING OUT
From cheap fast-food favorites to stylish, high-end cuisine – Chicago has it. For a colorful intro to Chicago-style deep dish pizza, head to Gino's East (US$20).

FURTHER INFORMATION
www.choosechicago.com

CHICAGO

If you're a serious fan of the blues, there's no better place to be than at the Chicago Blues Festival. You'll think you're in heaven watching dozens of big-name performers, including a living legend or two. If new to the Blues scene, it's the perfect opportunity to immerse yourself in the sights and sounds that comprise its rich history. Considered by some to be the country's largest free music festival, Chicago Blues is held in the sprawling Grant Park, the city's so-called "front yard." Since its inception in 1984, the event has evolved into a three-day, five-stage monster. Each year, the festival hosts both top-tier acts and up-and-comers, and past performers have included B.B. King, Buddy Guy, and Stevie Ray Vaughan. It is also the nation's largest celebration of past Blues greats, with many big names recognized each year. Highlights have included the centennials of Louis Jordan and Tommy McClennan.

Main: One of the six stages at the Chicago Blues Festival

Talkin' 'Bout the Blues

An offshoot of the Mississippi Delta Blues of the 1920s, Chicago Blues evolved after the "Great Migration" of poor African-American workers from the south to northern industrial cities such as Chicago. While the Delta Blues leaned heavily on guitar and harmonica, Chicago Blues used drums, piano, and bass. Chicago Blues musicians have included Buddy Guy, Earl Hooker, and Muddy Waters *(below)*.

Hardcore fans arrive early to stake out their spots in front of the larger stages, while casual types hang in the back and munch on signature Chicago treats such as Italian beef sandwiches, spicy sausages, and loaded hot dogs; it's the reason why the Festival is also fun for all ages with its concession stands and music-themed attractions. Even after the festival closes, the action continues into the night, as revelers fill the city's numerous music clubs from the cavernous House of Blues to hole-in-the-wall dive bars and the city resounds to impromptu jam sessions.

Chicago's climate can be an unforgiving one, but June offers one of the surest bets – neither bitterly cold nor horribly humid – and its citizens find time to relax as kids are finishing school, sidewalk cafés are opening up, and they begin to spill out onto Lake Michigan's many beaches. Truly an international and populist gathering, attendees come from all over the globe and artists flock from as far as Australia and Japan.

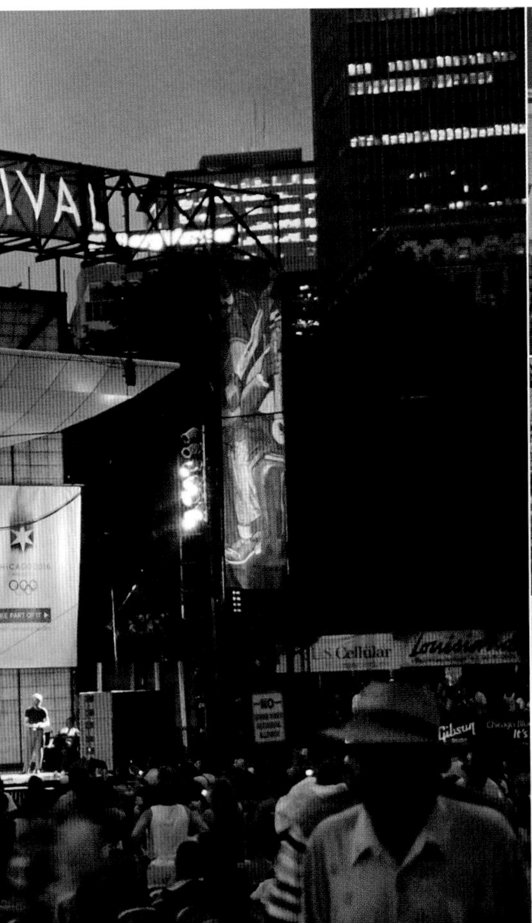

Above (top and bottom): Field Museum, Museum Campus; the entrance to Navy Pier

Below: Jay Pritzker Pavilion in Millennium Park

Left (left and right): Buddy Guy live at the Chicago Blues Festival 2013; Buddy Guy's Legends blues club

Right: Georges Seurat's *A Sunday Afternoon on the Island of La Grande Jatte* at the Art Institute of Chicago

FESTIVAL DIARY

One of the world's best music events, the Chicago Blues Festival runs from Friday through Sunday, with key acts throughout, but only true fans attend all three days. The grounds open at 11am daily, with performances running until 9:30pm. Consider alternating days at the festival with days spent exploring the city.

Five Days in the Windy City

DAY 1 Visit the festival site, walking the grounds and checking out vantage points from which to enjoy the sounds. Take a break and visit the nearby Art Institute of Chicago, known for having one of the country's foremost collections of Impressionist and American art.

DAY 2 Spend the day strolling along the Magnificent Mile, one of the world's great shopping streets. Stop to enjoy famous Chicago-style deep dish pizza at one of the originators – Pizzeria Due or Pizzeria Uno. Then, walk off the calories by exploring Water Tower Place, the city's premier upscale shopping mall.

DAY 3 Just before entering the festival, stop by Buckingham Fountain – to some, the symbol of the city – and snap postcard-worthy photos. Post-festival, immerse yourself even further in the Blues by catching a late-night set at a top venue like Buddy Guy's (where the owner makes frequent appearances) or at B.L.U.E.S.

DAY 4 Start the day with a filling brunch at a down-home eatery like Stanley's or Sweet Maple Café, before heading on to the Museum Campus, where you'll find three of the city's most popular museums – the Shedd Aquarium, the Field Museum of Natural History, and the Adler Planetarium. Walk through Millennium Park's architectural wonders before tuning into the festival one last time.

DAY 5 Enjoy Navy Pier's many attractions, without the weekend crowds, before raising a parting glass to the Windy City at the Signature Room, on the 95th floor of the Hancock Tower, while drinking in the fabulous views.

Dos and Don'ts

- ✓ Bring a camera to Millennium Park's *Cloudgate*, Anish Kapoor's reflective, bean-shaped sculpture. Below, be inspired by the optical vortex with dozens of reflections.
- ✗ Don't ask for ketchup on your hot dog. Many locals consider it a taboo, and some stands, despite offering many toppings (from banana peppers to dill pickle spears), will refuse.
- ✓ Try to catch a game at Wrigley Field. Dating back to 1914, it's the country's second-oldest ballpark still in use. Even if you can't get tickets, head to the surrounding neighborhood (Wrigleyville) and soak up the atmosphere.

Below: Buckingham Fountain

GETTING THERE See map p314, D7
Part of the border between Ontario, Canada, and New York State, USA, the Niagara Falls are 80 miles (129 km) by road from Toronto and 21 miles (34 km) from Buffalo. The nearest airports are in Toronto and Buffalo, with a small one in Hamilton, Ontario.

GETTING AROUND
You can reach Niagara by train or bus, but public transport in the area is limited. A bus plies between central attractions in summer, but you'll need a car to reach most wineries.

WEATHER
June is mild, with an average temperature range of 57–76°F (14–25°C). Rain is possible, so carry a jacket and umbrella.

ACCOMMODATIONS
Marriott Fallsview Hotel & Spa in Ontario has superb views; doubles from US$130; www.niagarafallsmarriott.com

Red Coach Inn in New York State has doubles from US$209; www.redcoach.com

Queen's Landing in Niagara-on-the-Lake overlooks Lake Ontario; doubles from US$230; www.vintage-hotels.com

EATING OUT
The towns around Niagara have inexpensive chain eateries and upscale bistros. Wherever you eat, don't miss the local strawberries.

FURTHER INFORMATION
www.tourismniagara.com (Canadian side)
www.niagara-usa.com (American side)

Roll Out the Barrel

The Niagara Falls have exerted a hypnotic power over generations of daredevils. In 1859, the Great Charles Blondin strolled over the gorge *(above)* on a tightrope, inspiring his rival, The Great Farini. The two eventually carted across a stove, a washing machine, and a washerwoman in a bizarre contest of one-upmanship. Some 40 years later, Annie Taylor became the first to go over Horseshoe Falls in a barrel. Later, others made the trip in everything from a rubber ball to a diving bell. Police now levy fines on those who try to repeat Annie's feat.

Main: The mighty Niagara Falls thundering in full force as the *Maid of the Mist* heads closer

NIAGARA FALLS

BACK IN 1842, CHARLES DICKENS WROTE OF THE NIAGARA FALLS, "When I felt how near to my Creator I was standing, the first effect, and the enduring one – instant and lasting – of the tremendous spectacle, was peace." Peace may not be your first impression when you visit the Niagara Falls today, as you try to drown out the tourist hubbub that roils around like a human whirlpool, particularly on the Canadian side. Instead, the entire experience can be either lively or overwhelming, depending on your fondness for the sugary scent of cotton candy and the clanging of slot machines. But just take a moment to tune out the background noise and focus on the inimitable thunder of 150,000 gallons (568,000 liters) of water hurtling over the Niagara Escarpment every second – that's not something you experience every day. It's a primal noise that rarely fails to stun visitors, no matter how jaded, cynical, or cosmopolitan they may be – the thrill never seems to die out.

Left (left to right): Swallowtail butterfly on a colorful flower at the Butterfly Conservatory Gardens; Horseshoe Falls lit up at night; tourists at the Niagara Falls

Right: A sidewalk in Niagara-on-the-Lake, a quaint, 19th-century small town in Ontario

WILD WATER DIARY

It began with the falls: the torrent that missionary Louis Hennepin called "a vast and prodigious cadence of water" when he first saw it in 1678. Today, there's so much more to see in the area. June – when attractions open, the weather is lovely, and the holiday crowds have yet to descend – is the perfect time to enjoy it.

Four Days at the Falls

DAY 1

After arriving in Niagara Falls, Ontario, head straight for the falls – the best views are from the Canadian side. Next, hop aboard the *Maid of the Mist*, a tour boat that cruises so near the falls you'll come away soaked. Then see the falls from the inside out on the cliff-hugging walkway known as Journey Behind the Falls. At dusk, see the cataract illuminated with multicolored lights.

DAY 2

Cross over to the American side on the Peace Bridge to enjoy a challenging hike along some 15 miles (23 km) of trails bordering the falls and river. For a simpler walk with stunning views, try the rim path in Niagara Falls State Park. After dinner, drive to Earl W. Brydges Artpark for an outdoor concert before crossing back to Canada.

DAY 3

Cycle or take a 10-minute drive along the Niagara Parkway to the Butterfly Conservatory, an enclosed tropical jungle home to more than 2,000 butterflies. Then visit Niagara-on-the-Lake, a town so picturesque it seems like a stage set. Browse for gifts in the myriad shops and take in a play at the Shaw Festival.

DAY 4

Tour the vineyards west of Niagara Falls, home to more than 60 wineries. Take the self-guided tour at Inniskillin, one of the largest vineyard companies, and get a taste of a family-run establishment at Marynissen. Indulge in a leisurely tasting dinner at On the Twenty, one of Canada's most renowned restaurants. Remember – don't drink and drive.

Dos and Don'ts

- ✓ Try Niagara ice wine: a rich, honey-sweet way to end a meal.
- ✗ Don't drive on the busy streets near the falls. Hop on the WeGo shuttle bus instead.
- ✓ Be patient if you're crossing the Canada–US border, as security is stringent and delays are common. Bring a passport or other authorized travel document *(see also p308)*.
- ✓ Bring a raincoat, even if it's sunny. The mist can drench you.
- ✗ Don't hesitate to check out at least one spectacularly tacky wax museum on Clifton Hill. It's part of the experience.

Of course, there's more to Niagara Falls than just the falls. There's the indefatigable honeymoon industry – check into a room with a heart-shaped whirlpool bath, if you must. Then there's the quaint elegance of Niagara-on-the-Lake, where genteel day-trippers from Toronto and Buffalo enjoy witty plays by George Bernard Shaw and his contemporaries at the Shaw Festival. There are flowerbeds banked with thousands of roses at the Niagara Parks Botanical Gardens, classical music concerts in winery vineyards, hiking and cycling trails, and a somewhat strange yet enjoyable sideshow of wax museums and souvenir shops lining Clifton Hill.

That being said, it all comes back to three cataracts – the immense Horseshoe Falls, the curtain-like American Falls, and the comparatively narrow Bridal Veil Falls. Other sights come and go, eventually yielding their place to the next trendy destination, but the falls maintain a constant hold on the traveler's psyche. Every self-respecting traveler should see the Niagara Falls at least once, despite – or perhaps because of – the cotton candy, the casinos, and the cacophony.

Below: The American and Horseshoe falls as seen from New York State

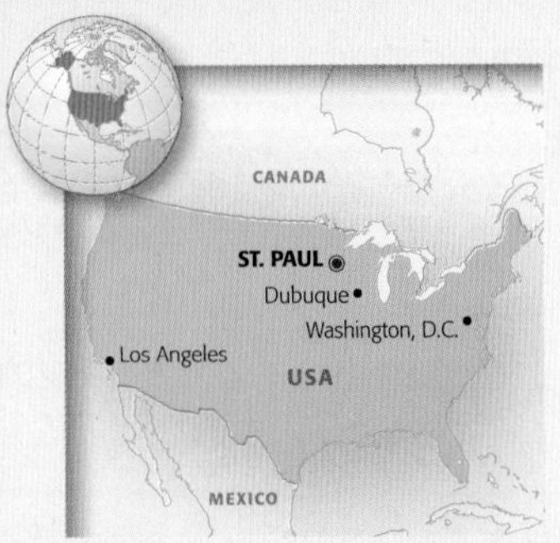

GETTING THERE See map p319, E3–F4
Arrive by car or fly to the International airport at Minneapolis-St. Paul, Minnesota. There's a regional airport at Dubuque, Iowa.

GETTING AROUND
A car is the only way to travel the Great River Road, marked by green Pilot's Wheel signs.

WEATHER
June is one of the best times to travel with daytime temperatures of 55–80°F (13–27°C).

ACCOMMODATIONS
St. Paul's sleek InterContinental Saint Paul Riverfront sits on a bluff overlooking the Mississippi; doubles from US$180; www.ihg.com

The Historic Trempealeau Hotel faces the river; modest rooms from US$60; suites US$110–130; www.trempealeauhotel.com

Charming 19th-century homes-turned-bed-and-breakfast inns in Galena are US$100–250; www.bedandbreakfast.com

In Dubuque, stay overnight in the elegant and historic boutique Hotel Julien; US$160 for two people; hoteljuliendubuque.com

EATING OUT
The Historic Trempealeau Hotel is a classic, with a river view. In Galena, The Generals' Restaurant has historic charm, and Fried Green Tomatoes serves Italian food in an 1838 store that belonged to Ulysses S. Grant's father.

FURTHER INFORMATION
www.experiencemississippiriver.com

Frontier Trading

Trappers, explorers, and Native Americans once gathered to barter goods in Prairie du Chien, where the Wisconsin and Mississippi rivers meet. Now, for three days in mid-June each year, a sea of white tents serves as home for over 600 latter-day traders at the Prairie Villa Rendezvous. Dressed like mountain men, pioneer women, or buckskin-clad Indian braves, they cook over open fires and compete in events. The selling or swapping of frontier-era wares such as furs, pipes, powder horns, pouches, moccasins, carvings, and Native American jewelry is all part of the fun.

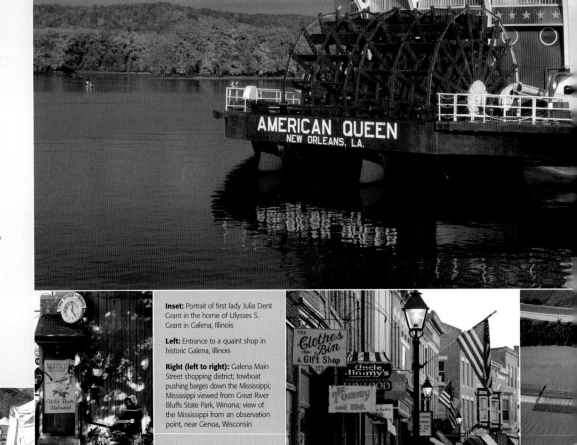

Inset: Portrait of first lady Julia Dent Grant in the home of Ulysses S. Grant in Galena, Illinois

Left: Entrance to a quaint shop in historic Galena, Illinois

Right (left to right): Galena Main Street shopping district; towboat pushing barges down the Mississippi; Mississippi viewed from Great River Bluffs State Park, Winona; view of the Mississippi from an observation point, near Genoa, Wisconsin

Main: Old-style paddle-steamer moored on the river in Wisconsin

GREAT RIVER ROAD

THE GREAT RIVER ROAD WAS ESTABLISHED IN 1938 AS A NATIONAL PARKWAY along the Mississippi. For 270 scenic miles (435 km) the Upper Mississippi River section of the Great River Road parallels the river through four Midwestern states, beginning in St. Paul, Minnesota, and ending in Dubuque, Iowa. There is a great deal to discover in this section of the river road: riverboats, ancient Native American burial mounds, frontier-style events, and pioneer log cabins are among the highlights. Quaint villages with fine examples of the ornate architectural style born in the heyday of river travel reveal the region's history. Small river towns also have a nostalgic story to share. One such is Galena, Illinois, which, with its spired churches and brick mansions on terraces up a steep hillside, still looks much as it did when Ulysses S. Grant was a clerk in his father's leather shop here before the Civil War. The Mississippi River undoubtedly played a crucial role in 19th-century America; it has been called the

Riverboats, ancient Native American burial mounds, frontier-style events, and pioneer log cabins are among the highlights.

country's first Interstate, a great transportation artery for commerce through ten states on the western frontier. It still provides drinking water for millions, is a playground, a shipping lane, and a boundary between states. The river scenery is also dramatic in places. The glaciers that drifted and flattened most of the Midwest missed this area, leaving intact the steep banks cut by the river so that limestone bluffs rise more than 500 ft (152 m) above the river.

This National Scenic Byway also gives you a good view of the river's system of locks and dams. Some 29 have been built between Minneapolis and Granite City, Illinois, alone, turning the river into a virtual stairway. The great and colorful steamboat era, roughly 1830 to 1870, has today given way to faster modern practices – enormous barges are pushed by towboats. One little towboat can push as many as 15 barges full of heavy grain, gravel, or chemicals – a load equivalent to a 3-mile- (4-km-) long train or a line of semi-trailer trucks 34 miles (54 km) long.

Dubuque, the final stop of this trip, offers fascinating river lore at the National Mississippi River Museum and Aquarium, and the chance to try your luck at a riverboat-turned-casino.

RIVERBANK DIARY

Five days is just long enough to do justice to one of the most scenic drives in the USA. The Great River Road along the Upper Mississippi River winds over hills, along towering bluffs, and through old river towns. June is one of the best times to travel in the Midwest, as the summer heat has yet to set in.

Five Days by the Mississippi

DAY 1

Visit the Mississippi River Visitor Center in St. Paul, then proceed on the east bank of the river into Pepin, Wisconsin, to see a replica of the pioneer log cabin birthplace of Laura Ingalls Wilder, author of *Little House on the Prairie*. Lake Pepin, formed by dams on the river, is a paradise for boaters and wildlife watchers. Drive on to spend the night in Trempealeau.

DAY 2

In Trempealeau there's a well-preserved 1890s Main Street and Perrot State Park, with 500-ft (152-m) river bluff panoramas. The observation platform here is the first opportunity for a good look at the Mississippi's amazing lock system. On to La Crosse, a thriving small city with plenty of history, plus the world's largest six-pack, standing near the visitable Heileman Brewery.

DAY 3

Next stop, Prairie du Chien, for the Prairie Villa Rendezvous *(see box)* and the Villa Louis Historic Site, a celebrated restored Victorian mansion. Prime river views and hiking trails can be found at Wyalusing State Park, 10 miles (16 km) to the south. Enjoy more views and a picturesque main street at Pikes Peak State Park in McGregor, Iowa. Turn north for Iowa's Effigy Mounds National Monument, with its 191 Native American burial mounds estimated to be 2,500 years old.

DAYS 4–5

Drive east across the river and south to Galena, Illinois, where many of the buildings are on the National Register of Historic Places. It makes for a wonderful stop with Victorian architecture, shopping for antiques, and the family home of President Ulysses S. Grant to enjoy. Finally, cross the river to Dubuque, the oldest city in Iowa, and visit the National Mississippi Riverboat Museum.

Dos and Don'ts

- ✓ Read Mark Twain's *Life on the Mississippi* to relive the colorful past when the Mississippi River was noted for the number of bandits that raided its islands and shores.
- ✓ Bring your bike. The Great River Bicycle Trail out of Trempealeau travels for 24 miles (38 km) through the prairies and backwaters of the upper Mississippi River valley.
- ✗ Don't forget your binoculars. An impressive array of North American bird life can be seen along the river. The Audubon Society's Great River Birding Trail parallels both sides of the Mississippi River. See www.audubon.org

Below: The modest log-cabin home of Laura Ingalls Wilder

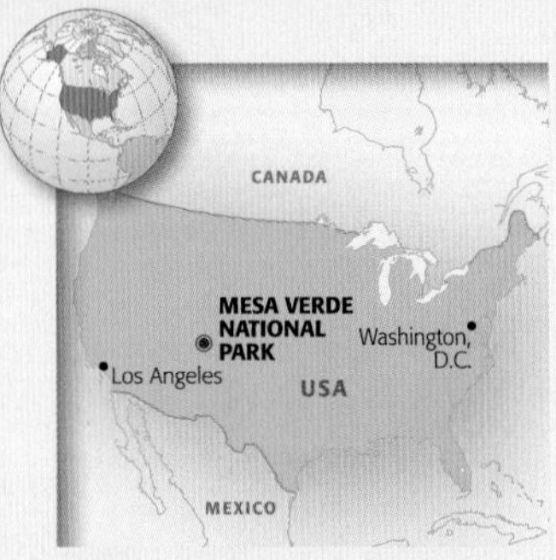

GETTING THERE See map p321, G4
Mesa Verde National Park, on US Highway 160 in southwestern Colorado, is a 1-hour drive east from Cortez or a 90-minute drive west from Durango. Rent a car at either airport.

GETTING AROUND
A car is essential to get to Mesa Verde. Half-day bus tours are available but a car is still needed afterwards to get around the park.

WEATHER
At an altitude of 7,000-ft (2,133-m), expect warm days – 75–85°F (24–29°C) – and cool nights – average 55°F (12°C).

ACCOMMODATIONS
Reserve ahead for the Far View Lodge, the only hotel in the park. Rooms with private bath, balcony, US$140–192; www.visitmesaverde.com

Tent and RV sites are found at the Morefield campground south of the park entrance, from US$30 per night. Equipment provided.

Outside the park, Durango is a colorful Old-West town. Rates at Best Western Durango Inn and Suites, a pleasant motel, begin at US$160; www.bestwestern.com

EATING OUT
The Metate Room Restaurant in Far View Lodge serves gourmet local cuisine; its Terrace Restaurant has a casual buffet.

FURTHER INFORMATION
www.nps.gov/meve

The Cliff Palace

Great skill was needed to create the cliff dwellings, some of which have survived by being protected by the overhanging cliff and need little supportive maintenance. Discovered in 1888 by two local ranchers, the largest site, the Cliff Palace, is a veritable apartment block with 150 rooms, housing anywhere from 100 to 150 people and includes 21 *kivas*, rooms used for religious rituals. A subterranean room remained at 50°F (10°C) all year round, making it comfortable in the summer, with only a small fire needed in the winter.

Main: The Cliff Palace, an astonishing architectural feat

MESA VERDE NATIONAL PARK

THE 700-YEAR-OLD PUEBLO HOMES OF MESA VERDE, stacked into alcoves in the canyon walls, never fail to amaze. Constructed during the Great Pueblo period around AD 1200, the cliff dwellings were beautifully designed communal houses that blended with the environment, displaying highly sophisticated architectural know-how. The builders were the Anasazi, the earliest inhabitants of the American Southwest, who evolved from nomadic hunters to an agricultural people and constructed these complex villages in multi-level pueblo style. They lived at Mesa Verde, which means "green table" in Spanish, from AD 500 to 1300.

Mesa Verde National Park preserves this spectacular ancient site, and also offers many opportunities for families to explore the ruins. The park contains over 4,000 known archeological sites including cliff dwellings, *kivas* (pit houses used for worship), masonry towers, and farming structures. The best-preserved site, Spruce Tree House, had

Left (left to right): Guided tour with a park ranger at Balcony House; doorway in Far View House; a thistle flower; mesa (table) tops at Mesa Verde National Park

Right: Interior of a room accessed by ladder in Spruce Tree House

Inset: Petroglyphs carved by ancient inhabitants, found at Petroglyph Point

Those who love to climb and explore ancient ruins – both adults and children alike – will find this an exciting visit.

130 rooms and was home to 60 to 80 people. There are several ways to explore Mesa Verde: the National Park Service offers a half-day ranger-guided bus tour to the best sites, with short hikes and many vantage points for photos. Or you can drive the 6-mile (9-km) loop road, with short paved trails, that covers 12 sites and gives an overview of the park. You can only enter the alcove cliff-dwelling sites on guided tours but many other sites and trails are open. Those who love to climb and explore ancient ruins – both adults and children alike – will find this an exciting visit.

Mesa Verde grew to an estimated population of 2,500, but the Anasazi lived in their cliff dwellings for less than a century. Why they abandoned these homes is not known. Theories range from drought that dried up the food supply to enemy attack. But contrary to popular belief, the Ancestral Pueblo people of Mesa Verde did not die out. They migrated south and today's Pueblo people in settlements such as Taos and Santo Domingo in New Mexico, and at the Hopi reservation in Arizona, are their descendants.

MESA VERDE DIARY

Exploring America's best-preserved pueblo ruins, the cliff dwellings of the ancient Anasazi people, is a learning adventure for all ages, whether you're on ranger-led tours or on your own. It takes two to three days to fully appreciate Mesa Verde, and sunny days in June, before the summer heat and crowds arrive, are ideal.

Three Days Exploring Ruins

DAY 1

First stop is the Visitor Center for information, for an orientation to the park and to reserve tours. Sign on for the half-day afternoon tour. If time allows, take a drive along the Mesa Top loop road to get an overview of the park. The evening campfire talks at 9pm at the Morefield Amphitheater are free, interesting, and fun. Don't forget to bring a flashlight.

DAY 2

While you are fresh in the morning, begin at the Chapin Mesa Museum for more in-depth information about the Anasazi. Then take the Cliff Palace loop road drive, ending with the guided tour of the Cliff Palace, a highlight of Mesa Verde. Come back at 5pm for the free, easy 1-mile (2-km) Far View Sites Walk with a ranger who describes life on the mesa top.

DAY 3

Take your pick: tour the self-guided Mesa Top Loop Road, a 6-mile (10-km) driving tour with short, paved trails, or drive out to the Wetherill Mesa to see mesa-top sites and views of cliff dwellings. A guided tour of the Long House here is available.

Another option is to take a hike on the nearly 3-mile (5-km) loop trail to Petroglyph Point along the edge of the plateau. Here, there's a panel where you can see petroglyphs, the delightful picture drawings and symbols carved into rock by ancient dwellers. The trail also provides awesome canyon views.

Dos and Don'ts

- ✗ Don't underestimate the drive from the entrance to the park headquarters. This narrow twisting 15-mile (25-km) mountain road can take an hour.
- ✓ Read descriptions of the various sites carefully before attempting them. Some require extensive climbing and hiking that may be too much for young children – not to mention their parents.
- ✗ Mesa Verde is very dry and can be deceptively hot in summer so keep drinking water: dehydration is a common cause of illness here.
- ✓ Sign up the kids for the free Junior Ranger program. Pick up activity sheets for ages 4–12 at the Visitor Center.

Below: Morefield Amphitheater

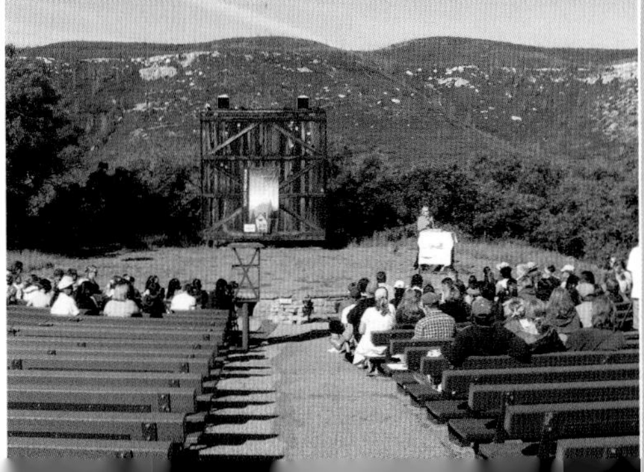

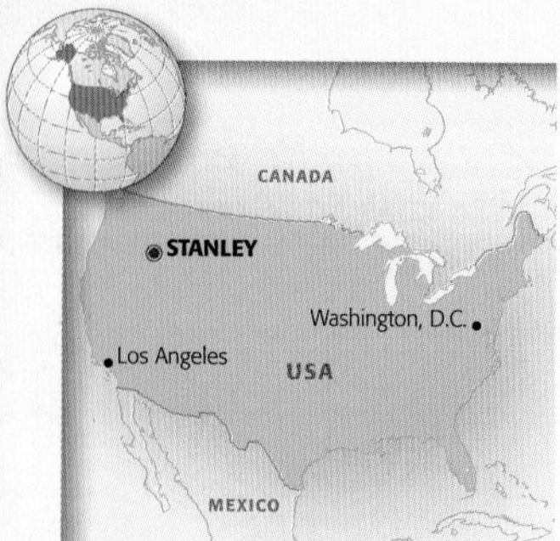

GETTING THERE See map p320, E4
The closest major airport is Boise, 130 miles (210 km) southwest of Stanley. Some regional airlines also fly to Hailey's Friedman Memorial Airport, about 80 miles (128 km) south of Stanley.

GETTING AROUND
A car is needed; 4WD is best for unpaved wilderness roads. Rental is available at both airports.

WEATHER
Expect daytime highs of around 65°F (18°C) dropping to around 35°F (2°C) at night.

ACCOMMODATIONS
Salmon River Lodge Resort has rustic but pleasant rooms on the banks of the Salmon River; doubles from US$165 (US$280 with a kitchen); salmonriverlodgeresort.com

Redfish Lake Lodge has lakeside cabins and motel-style units; doubles from US$75, cabins from US$150; www.redfishlake.com

Mountain Village Resort has hot springs on site; doubles from US$100; www.mountainvillage.com

EATING OUT
Stanley offers plenty of burgers and sandwiches at places like the Bridge Street Grill. For fancier fare, the rustic dining room at Redfish Lake Lodge serves Idaho trout, prime rib, and other local fare. Sun Valley has some fine restaurants.

FURTHER INFORMATION
www.stanleycc.org

The Stanley Gold Rush

In the 1820s, fur trappers discovered huge colonies of beavers on the banks of the Salmon River and the surrounding streams and lakes. Pelts were highly prized but gold, discovered in the 1860s, was even more valuable. Prospectors poured in by the thousand, among them John Stanley, a Civil War veteran. He stayed just long enough to give the town and the Stanley Basin their names. By the 1890s most of the others had also moved on to the Yukon's Klondike and other gold fields. All that now remains of the Gold Rush days are a few abandoned shacks.

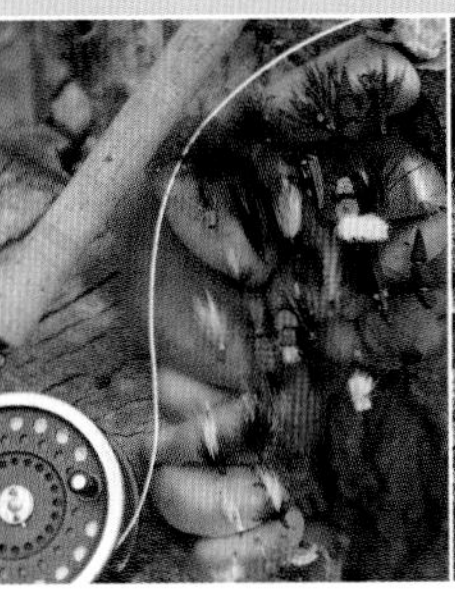

Above (left to right): Jagged Sawtooth mountain peaks; angler's equipment; fishing for trout in a waterfall
Main: Fly-fishing the clear waters of the Salmon River

STANLEY

YOU CAN'T MISS THEM. MOUNTAIN PEAKS, DOZENS OF THEM, many rising more than 10,000 ft (3,000 m) and forming a great wall of snow and granite. There's not much else here, just bracingly fresh air, a cobalt-blue sky and all those soaring peaks and craggy spires, capped with a blanket of white long into the summer. Fishing fans who are lucky enough to find themselves in Stanley, in the midst of the Sawtooth National Recreation Area in central Idaho, would have every right to think they'd died and gone to heaven. More than 300 alpine lakes, brimming with trout, are nestled in these mountains, and the Salmon River, one of the finest trout and steelhead (ocean-going trout) streams in the country, darts through the wide valley known as the Stanley Basin.

Native Americans have lived off the bounty of the Sawtooth waters for thousands of years, and some of the first white men to fish the Salmon were none other than Lewis and Clark. The explorers came upon the river in 1805. They thought it might be a passage to the Pacific Ocean but, finding it impossible to navigate, nonetheless delighted in the fish they plucked out of the rushing waters. Most modern-day explorers get no farther than the popular resort of Sun Valley. Stanley itself is an old frontier town of fewer than 100 residents, 70 miles (112 km) farther north. Blessedly off the beaten path, it's accessible only through vertigo-inducing mountain passes and scenic river-valley trails. Stanley records Idaho's coldest winter temperatures, but with the summer thaw come fishers, hikers, white-water rafters, and other outdoors enthusiasts to enjoy the largest tract of wilderness in the United States.

Fly-fishers in pursuit of steelhead can hike into the wilderness on well-maintained trails, float down the Salmon River on guided trips, or just find a stretch of crystal-clear water into which to cast a line. Wherever you choose to do so in this high mountain heaven, you won't be able to keep your eyes off the glorious peaks that surround you.

Fly-fishers can hike into the wilderness, float down the Salmon River, or just find a stretch of crystal-clear water into which to cast a line.

Inset: Trophy brown trout
Below (left and right): Riding a lakeside trail; sundown over Red Fish Lake

ANGLER'S DIARY

By June, wildflowers are blooming in the mountain meadows where elk herds feed, and the steelhead are running. Most trails and roads have been cleared of snow but the high peaks are still picturesquely white-capped. You can get a good taste of this ruggedly beautiful region in a week, and fish a range of excellent waters.

A Week of Fly-Fishing

DAYS 1–2 Grab your gear and familiarize yourself with Valley Creek, Stanley Lake, and other excellent fishing spots around Stanley. During your explorations, step into the Stanley Museum, housed in a ranger's cabin from the 1930s.

DAY 3 Experience the Salmon River on a float trip with a fishing guide, or on a white-water rafting trip – especially exciting during the high waters of the June runoff.

DAY 4 Pack a lunch and hike into the wilderness to fish in Sawtooth Lake, where Mount Regan is reflected in the clear waters (the round trip is about 10 miles/16 km). Or hike along any of the creeks flowing into Redfish Lake.

DAY 5 Drive over 8,700-ft (2,650-m) Galena Summit for sweeping views of the Sawtooth peaks. Galena Lodge is a great place for lunch, and the nearby Lake Trails provide relatively easy access to the angling waters of Baker Lake and Norton Lakes. For a dose of civilization, continue into bustling Sun Valley for dinner, but make the return trip before nightfall or stay over.

DAY 6 Sign on for another day with a fishing guide, either on the Salmon River or in the high mountain lakes. Alternatively, arrange a horseback trip deep into the wilderness.

DAY 7 Follow Route 75 along the Salmon River, stopping to cast a line every now and then, and to soak in the riverside hot springs. If you make it as far as Sunbeam, you could explore the nearby ghost town of Custer.

Dos and Don'ts

- ✓ Bring swimwear. You'll need it in some hot springs but you may also be tempted to brave a plunge into the icy waters of a mountain lake.
- ✓ Stop in at Stanley's Rod-N-Gun Whitewater Saloon for a drink.
- ✓ If you're in Sun Valley on Saturday night, catch the Sun Valley on Ice Show.
- ✗ Don't leave trash behind on your wilderness treks.
- ✓ Bring a sweater and jacket for cold nights.

Below: White-water rafting on the Salmon River

GETTING THERE See map p327, D5
Machu Picchu is located around 50 miles (80 km) northwest of Cusco. The flight from Lima International Airport to Cusco takes 2 hours.

GETTING AROUND
It takes around 4 hours to get to Aguas Calientes from Cusco by train; the price varies according to the standard of train. The Inca Trail is a 3- to 4-day hike from just outside Cusco.

WEATHER
June in Cusco is dry and sunny. The altitude keeps temperatures cool at around 55°F (13°C), dropping at night. Machu Picchu and Aguas Calientes have a wet and humid climate with average temperatures of 64°F (18°C).

ACCOMMODATIONS
El Monasterio is a sumptuous converted monastery in Cusco; doubles from US$385; www.belmond.com/hotel-monasterio-cusco

La Cabaña Hotel in Aguas Calientes is at the foot of the Inca ruins; doubles from US$120; lacabanamachupicchu.com

The Sanctuary Lodge is at the ruins; doubles from US$1400 (full board); www.belmond.com/SanctuaryLodge

EATING OUT
Typical Peruvian cuisine usually consists of rice and beans served with a meat. Guinea pig, or *cui*, is a specialty as is the local grain, quinoa.

FURTHER INFORMATION
www.machupicchu.org

Inti Raymi

On the day of the winter solstice, the ancient Incas honored their Sun God. They sacrificed a llama to ensure a plentiful harvest in the coming year. The festival was suppressed by the invading Spaniards as a pagan ritual but today it has been revived and is one of the most spectacular of its kind in South America. On June 24, thousands descend on Cusco for the week-long celebrations to mark the Festival of the Sun. There are street parties, live music and shows, and a procession to the Inca fortress of Sacsayhuamán, above the town.

Arrive at daybreak to be greeted by one of the world's most iconic sights – Machu Picchu.

Main: Ruins at Machu Picchu rising majestically out of the clouds

MACHU PICCHU

SET ON A RIDGE ABOVE THE ROARING URUBAMBA RIVER, this ancient Inca citadel is one of the most evocative sights in South America. The small fortress city sits majestically in a saddle between two mountain peaks in the subtropical Andean foothills, surrounded by dense vegetation and often shrouded in mist. The extraordinary stonework is a testament to the incredible skills of Inca stonemasons more than 600 years ago – vast gray granite blocks fitted together so exactly that a knife blade cannot be slipped between their joints. Invisible from below, and entirely self-contained, Machu Picchu was not found by the Spanish Conquistadors who were wreaking havoc throughout the continent in the 16th century. The ruins were forgotten, and it was an American archeologist, Hiram Bingham, who stumbled upon them in 1911. Short hikes from the site give some sense of its extraordinary position. A perilous ascent up Wayna Picchu, the small peak beyond the city, offers dizzying views.

Inset: Llama with traditional tasseled decoration

Left (left to right): People at a colorful Pisac market; detail of the incredible stonemasonry skills of the Incas at Sacsayhuamán; Cusco at night; train winding its way through the fertile Sacred Valley

Right: Steep steps on the Inca Trail

Machu Picchu is four hours by train from Cusco, a bustling and atmospheric colonial city, bursting with color. Cobbled streets, busy markets filled with rainbow-hued textiles, museums, and cafés make it a wonderful place to spend a few days relaxing and acclimatizing to the effects of the altitude and people-watching the ebb and flow of the visiting crowds. However, if you are keen to explore further, there are plenty of day trips to explore the small market towns nearby.

Later, a spectacular rail journey will wind its way through the fertile Sacred Valley, the breadbasket of the Inca civilization where corn, fruit, and vegetables grow in abundance, with sheer mountain walls on either side, taking you to Aguas Calientes, a small, ramshackle town that is a base for travelers exploring the site. Aside from the train, the ruins are accessible only by foot, and the Inca Trail is a spectacular three-to-four-day trek to the ancient site. Hikers pass through the regimented Inca terracing, a huge diversity of lush vegetation, and breathtaking views of the mountain draped in a shroud of morning mist, and eventually arrive at daybreak to be greeted by one of the world's most iconic sights – Machu Picchu.

PERUVIAN DIARY

Peru is incredibly diverse, with a long coastal stretch, dense Amazon jungle, colonial cities, and Andean splendor. To make the most of Machu Picchu and the Cusco region, a week is the bare minimum, as you'll need some time to acclimatize to Cusco's rarefied air and to explore the ruins at your own pace.

A Week on the Inca Trail

Most flights into Lima arrive in the evening so rest and prepare yourself for your onward journey. **DAY 1**

Try to get a window seat for some fabulous views of the Andes on the Lima to Cusco flight. Take it easy on your first day at altitude, by wandering around the cobbled streets of Cusco, enjoying its lively markets. **DAY 2**

Make a visit to Pisac in the Sacred Valley which has some extensive ruins as well as a wonderful textile market on Tuesdays, Thursdays, and Sundays. **DAY 3**

Take the Vistadome train to Aguas Calientes. The glass roofs of the Vistadome carriage allow you to enjoy the views of mountains and waterfalls. From Aguas Calientes it's a short bus trip to Machu Picchu. Stay over on-site or stay in Aguas Calientes and get the first bus up next day. **DAY 4**

The ruins look magical in the sunrise and skies are often clearer in the morning than in the afternoon. Take some time to wander by yourself, before the tour groups arrive. Take the afternoon train back to Cusco. **DAY 5**

Spend the day in Cusco, relaxing in one of its many cafés and watching the world go by. There are also numerous active excursions available from the town, such as rafting on the Urubamba River, and some excellent downhill cycling. **DAY 6**

Fly back to Lima and do a last bit of souvenir shopping before heading homewards. **DAY 7**

Dos and Don'ts

- ✓ Request a window seat on your flight to Cusco for a good view of the spectacular Andean scenery.
- ✗ Don't overdo it on your first day at altitude in Cusco. Avoid fatty foods, alcohol, and any strenuous activity. Keep hydrated and drink coca tea, a local remedy for sickness.
- ✓ Book early if you intend to walk the Inca Trail. Laws introduced in 2003 have restricted the number of people allowed on the trail to 500 at one time, and in peak season it can be booked up many months in advance.
- ✗ Don't miss out on the local textiles. Beautiful handwoven shawls are available in the markets at Pisac and in Cusco.

Below: Traditional Andean fabric found in local markets

GETTING THERE See map p314, E6
Montréal, on the shore of the St. Lawrence River in the province of Québec, is around 314 miles (505 km) from Toronto. Trudeau International Airport is around 30 minutes from downtown by cab.

GETTING AROUND
Don't bother with a car unless you're doing a day trip out of town, as the city's subway (Métro) and bus services are excellent.

WEATHER
Montréal is sunny and warm in June, with an average daytime temperature of 68°F (20°C). Showers are common but short.

ACCOMMODATIONS
Candlewood Suites has well-priced rooms a few blocks east of downtown; doubles from US$130; www.cwsmontreal.com

Check into the historic Auberge Bonaparte lodge in Old Town; doubles from US$175; www.bonaparte.ca

Le Saint-Sulpice is a sleek boutique hotel in Old Montréal; one-bedroom suites with sofa bed start at US$220; www.lesaintsulpice.com

EATING OUT
Montréalers love to eat, which makes the city a haven for foodies. You can dine well for US$50 per head, while family-style fare is easy to find at US$20 per person. Be sure to try Montréal's special smoked meat.

FURTHER INFORMATION
www.tourisme-montreal.org

A History of Fun

With its Ferris wheel, tot-friendly carousel, and gravity-defying roller coasters, La Ronde may look like any other fun park. Yet, it holds a unique place in Canadian history. Opened in 1967 – Canada's centennial year – as the amusement section of Canada's first World's Fair, La Ronde attracted millions and remained open until 2:30am every day. Ask most Canadian baby boomers if they went to La Ronde in 1967 – or if they just dreamed of it – and you're likely to get a misty-eyed smile.

Main: Stunning interior of the 19th-century Notre-Dame Basilica
Above (top to bottom): Inside Berri-UQAM Métro station; puffins at the Biodôme; Montréal Museum of Archaeology and History by night

MONTRÉAL

According to an old Canadian joke, you only *exist* in Toronto, while you truly *live* in Montréal. Although just a good-humored quip, it definitely captures something of the essence of the largest French-speaking city outside France. With its hugely popular jazz and comedy festivals, wide-ranging array of restaurants, thriving arts scene, and lively bars, Montréal crackles with an energy that's quite electrifying.

With a versatility to be proud of, Montréal is a city that suits every sensibility. Besides being a haven for grown-up pleasures, the city excels at entertaining families. The Montréal Biodôme, inside the velodrome originally built for the 1976 Summer Olympics, recreates four distinct ecosystems from North, Central, and South America, and houses macaws, penguins, lynx, and other creatures in their "natural" habitats, all year round. Affiliated institutions include a botanical garden, planetarium, and "insectarium" – the latter being a hit with bug-loving kids.

QUÉBÉCOIS DIARY

June is the perfect time to visit Montréal, before the heat gets too sultry and the crowds too large. If you dislike crowds, avoid the end of the month, when the city practically shuts down for the International Jazz Festival. Picnic on Mont Royal, stroll the streets of Old Montréal, and soak up the city's laid-back vibe.

Four Days of *Joie de Vivre*

DAY 1 Explore atmospheric Old Montréal (Vieux-Montréal) on foot. Coax the kids into visiting the Notre-Dame Basilica, definitely the city's most stunning church. Then head to the huge family restaurant at the Centre des Sciences de Montréal for lunch with a river view, before visiting the center's interactive exhibits and IMAX theater.

DAY 2 Spend the day getting dizzy on the rides at La Ronde, the amusement park. Stick around for an evening display of "pyromusical arts"– fireworks synchronized to music – at the Montréal Fireworks Festival, an annual spectacle that kicks off in mid-June.

DAY 3 Rent bikes in Old Port and cycle along Canal Lachine to Atwater Market to buy baguettes, cheese, fruits, and other treats. Ride back to the Old Port to return the bikes. Then take a cab to Mont Royal, the "mountain" (more of a big hill) that dominates the city and is topped with a landmark cross. Enjoy a picnic in the park on the slopes, while away the afternoon shopping in the nearby Plateau Mont-Royal, or try one of the neighborhood's chic restaurants for dinner.

DAY 4 Today, it's all about animals. Visit the Biodôme to see creatures from the Americas, and the Montréal Insectarium for your fill of creepy critters. If you still feel up to a carnivorous dinner, head to a deli for smoked meat sandwiches on rye (vegetarians can opt for cream cheese on a famously chewy bagel).

Dos and Don'ts

- ⊗ Don't refer to the city's airport as Trudeau. It was renamed in 2004 but most locals still call it Dorval.
- ✓ Dine fashionably late. Unless you have small children in tow, showing up for dinner at a restaurant before 7pm confirms that you're a tourist.
- ⊗ Don't be alarmed if store clerks address you in French. Say "*Je suis désolé, je ne parle pas français*" ("I'm sorry, I don't speak French"), and locals will usually do their best to help you out, as many of them are bilingual.
- ✓ Broach politics if you must, but be prepared for a long, and possibly testy, conversation.

Above (top and bottom): Vibrant display of color at the Montréal Fireworks Festival; shoppers on St. Paul Street

Below: Mouthwatering Montréal-style bagels at St-Viateur Café

For many families, the cobblestone streets and 18th-century buildings of Old Montréal are like a living history museum. Linger over *moules frites* (mussels and fries) in one of the pretty cafés lining Place Jacques Cartier. Poke your nose into any shop or hotel in the area and you'll likely discover intriguing evidence of times past: a pressed tin ceiling, an enormous stone fireplace, or some 300-year-old chinaware dug up during a renovation. To visit an actual historical museum, stop by the Pointe-à-Callière, the Montréal Museum of Archaeology and History, in the same neighborhood, or the McCord Museum of Canadian History on Rue Sherbrooke.

Even below street level, Montréal has an unmistakable verve. Underground City, a 19-mile (30-km) network of subterranean corridors, was created around the Métro system and is home to shops, restaurants, hotels, and entertainment venues. It also contains some of North America's most distinctive subway stations, designed by leading architects. And because the carriages roll on rubber wheels, stations don't vibrate with ear-splitting screeches each time a train pulls in. Sophisticated, practical, and just a bit unusual – Montréal's stations *are* the city in a nutshell.

Below: Cafés lining a sidewalk in Old Montréal

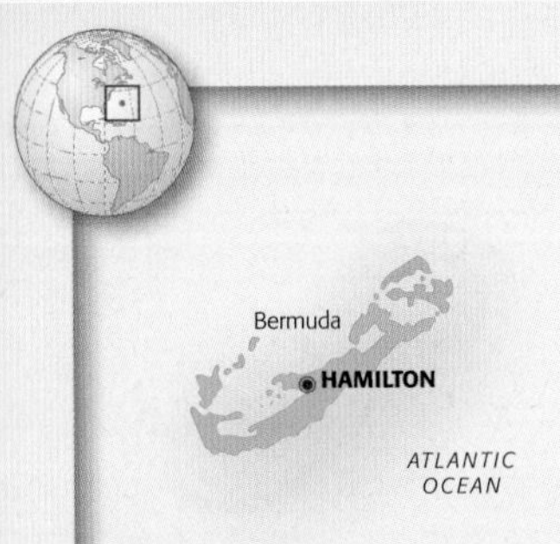

GETTING THERE See map p325, F1
Bermuda's international airport is 10 miles (16 km) east of Hamilton. Taxi or minibus are the only ways to reach your hotel.

GETTING AROUND
There is no car rental available on the island. Public transport is by taxi, bus, and ferry. Scooter and bicycle rental is widely available.

WEATHER
June is humid, with an average high of 81°F (27°C), dropping only to 71°F (22°C) at night. Short tropical downpours are common.

ACCOMMODATIONS
Bermuda's most casual beach option is Grape Bay Cottages in centrally located Paget. Both cottages lie on a private beach with full kitchens; cottages from US$355; www.gbcbermuda.com

The Fairmont Hamilton Princess is a luxury resort combining classic European chic with Bermudan style and atmosphere; doubles from US$599; www.fairmont.com/hamilton-bermuda

The Reefs is an elegant resort overlooking Christian Bay, with its own private beach; doubles from US$630; www.thereefs.com

EATING OUT
Bermuda's food is similar to Caribbean, with tropical fruits and vegetables, seafood, and spicy seasonings. Traditional dishes and top-range international cuisine are both available.

FURTHER INFORMATION
www.gotobermuda.com

Enjoy romantic picnics in the warm island breeze, and sip rum punch while watching the vermilion beauty of a Bermudan sunset.

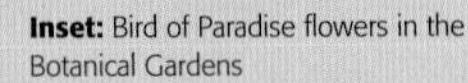

Inset: Bird of Paradise flowers in the Botanical Gardens

Left (top and bottom): Cruise ship docking in Hamilton at sunset; Commonwealth War Memorial in King Square, St. George

Left: Anglican Cathedral of the Most Holy Trinity, built in 1897, in Hamilton

Right (left and right): Spectacular views from the Port Royal golf course; beautiful Elbow Beach

Main: Typically colorful, white-roofed Bermudan houses in Hamilton

Precious Rainwater

Rainfall has for centuries been the island's main source of drinking water. From the stepped roofs of buildings it is funneled to underground storage tanks. The roof tiles are arranged so that the water is channeled along a series of hairpin-bend gullies to the downpipes. Bermudan roofs are painted white and kept spotlessly clean in order not to contaminate the water. Large hotels and other facilities have increasingly installed their own desalination plants and, in times of drought, it is no longer necessary to ship in water, as used to be the case.

BERMUDA

IT'S LITTLE WONDER THAT BERMUDA IS SUCH A DRAW FOR SWEETHEARTS and honeymooners from around the world. Not only does this charming archipelago have some of the most stylish and elegant island resorts, year-round sunshine, and abundant natural charms, but it is also surrounded by thousands of miles of clear, swirling Atlantic waters, lending it the intoxicating air of some mystical land perched at the edge of the world.

Bermuda is made up of seven main islands and hundreds of smaller ones, some not much more than large rocks. They are home to ultra-modern sophistication – exclusive spa hotels, world-class golf, and fine dining – as well as historic buildings that have remained untouched for centuries, and unspoilt beaches. Horseshoe Bay, a crescent-shaped expanse of glorious pink sand lapped by sapphire waters, is considered by many to be the most beautiful of all. Anywhere on the islands you will always be able to find a secluded spot in which to while away long, lazy days

BERMUDA DIARY

Bermuda is a near-perfect destination for a romantic getaway. There are beautiful beaches and turquoise seas, and intimate waterside restaurants for dining under the stars. June is an ideal month because it is not too hot, and four days is long enough to unwind, spend quality time together and still have time to explore the island.

Four Days of Tropical Romance

DAY 1

Relax and spend the day sunning on the beach and swimming in the warm, clear waters. Sit at the water's edge and let a stingray nibble at your toes. Then enjoy a side-by-side massage in the resort spa. A daily ritual should be watching the sunset together with a cocktail on your balcony, before dressing up for a romantic dinner at one of the many waterside restaurants.

DAY 2

Hire a two-seater scooter and set off to explore the eastern side of the main island. Take the South Shore Road to the Botanical Gardens with its splendid display of more than 1,000 different plants and trees. Continue east to St. George, a UNESCO World Heritage Site with strong British links, for a tour and a late lunch, then return along the northern coast, stopping off at the amazing Crystal and Fantasy Caves.

DAY 3

Get those scooters out again and head west along the south coast. Take your swimming gear as there are many fabulous beaches along this coast, including lovely Elbow Beach and Horseshoe Bay, both with spectacular pink sands. If you can tear yourself away, you could visit the historic mansions in Paget or continue to the northern tip of the island for a tour of the historic Royal Naval Dockyard.

DAY 4

Shop for gifts and souvenirs in historic Hamilton, but get your shopping out of the way by lunchtime. Spend the afternoon back on the beach, swimming and soaking up the sun before enjoying the the last spectacular sunset and alfresco dinner of your stay.

Dos and Don'ts

- ✓ The sun is fierce here. Be sure to use a high-factor sun cream, and wear a hat and sunglasses.
- ✗ Don't forget that they drive on the left here. Take especial care if you hire a scooter, and when you cross the road.
- ✓ Remember the rules of safe scootering – never speed, brake early, and take corners slowly. And, however tempting it might be to feel the wind in your hair, a crash helmet is obligatory and could be a lifesaver.
- ✗ Don't leave items unattended on the beach when you go for a swim.

basking on coral sands or in the dappled shade of a palm tree, enjoy romantic picnics in the warm island breeze, and sip rum punch while watching the vermilion beauty of a Bermudan sunset.

For an exhilarating change, you could take to the water for world-class scuba diving, kayaking, and sailing. Back on dry land, a gentle horseback ride along secluded, mangrove-lined shores is an unforgettable experience. A speedier option is to hop on a scooter and take a spin around the islands. Hamilton is one of the world's smallest, but busiest, ports. There is excellent shopping here, with top-name designer boutiques and art galleries lining the streets. Old-fashioned horse-drawn carriages are a romantic way to see the sights, such as the Royal Naval Dockyard in Sandys Parish, which was established in 1809 to defend Britain's interests in the region against Napoleon. The late-17th-century Verdmont Museum on Collector's Hill contains fine antiques made from island cedar and mahogany, and Waterville is a splendid Georgian home located in the parish of Paget. At either, you'll be transported back 200 years. But wherever you go and whatever you do, these jeweled islands, the ultimate in romantic getaways, won't fail to dazzle and delight.

Below: Spectacular rock formations in the Crystal Caves

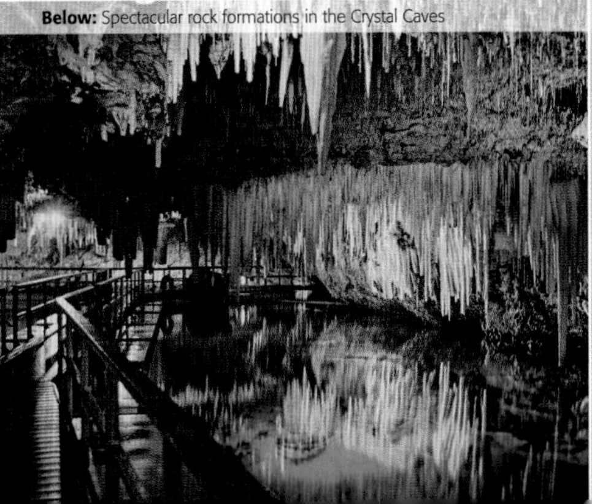

GETTING THERE See map p316, F4
The Finger Lakes lie just south of Lake Ontario. The closest airport is Rochester, 30 miles (48 km) northwest of Canandaigua.

GETTING AROUND
A car is needed for touring the lakes.

WEATHER
June days are mostly sunny, with an average temperature of 68°F (20°C).

ACCOMMODATIONS
The Acorn Inn is an elegant bed and breakfast in Canandaigua; doubles from US$195; www.acorninnbb.com

The Inn at Glenora Wine Cellars, near Watkins Glen, is on winery grounds; doubles from US$169; www.glenora.com

The 1850s Greek-Revival Rosewood Inn is a good choice in Corning; doubles from US$169; www.rosewoodinn.com

Taughannock Farms Inn overlooks Cayuga Lake, near Ithaca; doubles from US$149; www.t-farms.com

EATING OUT
The Upstairs Bistro at Canandaigua's Wine & Culinary Center is excellent. Ithaca's Moosewood is internationally famous for creative vegetarian fare and for its cookbooks.

FURTHER INFORMATION
www.fingerlakes.org

Rochester

Situated on Lake Ontario, Rochester is where the Finger Lakes meet the Great Lakes. It boasts one of the few major urban waterfalls, tumbling 96 ft (29 m) into the Genesee River, in the High Falls Historic District. Rochester gained fame as the home of George Eastman, the father of popular photography, and of the Eastman Kodak Company. Eastman House *(above)* is the oldest museum of photography in the world. Different but no less appealing is The Strong National Museum of Play, with the world's largest toy collection as well as lots of hands-on exhibits.

Above (left to right): Corning Museum of Glass; bison sculpture, Rockwell Museum of Art; historic boathouses on Canandaigua Lake
Main: Rainbow Falls in Watkins Glen State Park

FINGER LAKES

THE LONG, NARROW, GLACIER-CARVED, ICE-BLUE Finger Lakes are natural wonders surrounded by gorges brimming over with more than 1,000 waterfalls. The 11 lakes range from 3 to 40 miles (5 to 65 km) in length, yet some are as little as 600 yards (550 m) wide. Native American tradition has it that they were made by the fingers of Great Spirit as he blessed the land. They are beautifully framed by gentle hills of vineyards and farmland. Watkins Glen is a jewel, with its stunning gorge and a series of 19 waterfalls. Rainbow Falls was called a "poem of nature" by Mark Twain in 1871, and remains so today, with its rippling swirls of rock, shimmering waters, and the misty greens of ferns and moss. Walking trails wind through the glen, including one that leads behind the roaring 60-ft (18-m) drop of Central Cascade. An even more spectacular one, with a drop of some 215 ft (65.5 m) – making it the highest cascade in the eastern USA – is in Taughannock State Park, north of Ithaca. Even the Cornell University campus in Ithaca boasts gorges, as well as striking Triphammer Falls.

Called a "poem of nature" by Mark Twain in 1871, it remains so today, with its rippling swirls of rock and shimmering waters.

The lakes temper the climate, resulting in perfect conditions for the cultivation of wine grapes. This accounts for one of the largest areas of vineyards in the USA, with over 100 wineries, most offering tasting opportunities. Many run tours for visitors, and some have restaurants with splendid lake views. With conditions similar to northern Europe, the region is best known for Rieslings and other German-style wines, but in recent years the varieties of wine being made have expanded. Five wine trails, named for the lakes they border, make for delightful touring.

There are other delights tucked into these rural hills. The Corning Museum of Glass contains one of the most comprehensive collections of historic and art glass in the world, and the Rockwell Museum, also in Corning, has the best collection of western American art in the eastern USA. The region also offers hiking and biking trails, fishing, water sports, golf, and other outdoor pleasures galore.

Inset: 1940s postcard from the Finger Lakes
Below (left and right): Triphammer Falls; Taughannock Cascade

CASCADE DIARY

June is a sparkling month, when waterfalls fed with melted winter snow are at their splashiest, and vineyards are beginning to thrive. Spend a week touring the lakes, sampling the wines, tasting the local cuisine, and exploring the spectacular gorges, delightful trails, and inviting towns of this region.

A Week of Lakeland Trails

DAY 1

On arrival at Canandaigua, visit the New York Wine & Culinary Center for their 2-hour introduction to the region's wines, and lunch. Take a paddle-wheeler cruise on the lake, go hiking or biking on Ontario Pathway trails, or spend the afternoon browsing the many galleries and antiques shops on Main Street.

DAYS 2–3

Drive east to Geneva and south to Watkins Glen, visiting some of the 21 vineyards on the Seneca Lake Wine Trail on the way – Hermann Wiener and Glenora in Dundee are recommended stops. The next day, follow the gorge path winding over and under the waterfalls at Watkins Glen State Park. The park also offers swimming and fishing. Drive to Hammondsport.

DAY 4

At Hammondsport, visit Pleasant Valley, the region's oldest winery, as well as that of Dr Konstantin Frank, who pioneered quality German-style wines. Have lunch at Bully Hill, known for its colorful wine labels and its fascinating wine museum.

DAY 5

Drive to Corning. Watch glassblowers in action at the world-class Museum of Glass. The Rockwell Museum of Western Art is also well worth a visit.

DAYS 6–7

End the week in Ithaca, home to Cornell University. This cosmopolitan small town on the south shore of Cayuga Lake, between two stunning gorges, gives easy access to beautiful hiking and biking trails, as well as some 15 wineries lining the Cayuga Wine Trail. Spend your last afternoon enjoying a leisurely drive back to Canandaigua or Rochester.

Dos and Don'ts

- ✓ Consider taking one of the many guided winery tours if you want to do any serious wine tasting. Leave the car behind.
- ✓ Think about a detour to Seneca Falls, at the top of Cayuga Lake, if you have an interest in Women's Rights. The Women's Rights National Historic Park tells the story of the first ever Women's Rights Convention, held here in 1848.
- ✗ Don't forget that you need a license if you wish to fish, except for on Free Fishing Days during the last full weekend in June.

Below: Keuka Lake at twilight, viewed from vineyards near Hammondsport

GETTING THERE See map p327, G7
The gateway to the Jesuit mission churches of Chiquitos is Bolivia's modern city Santa Cruz. The international airport is a 10-mile (16-km) taxi ride from the center.

GETTING AROUND
The Jesuit missions circuit is a semicircular, 615-mile (990-km) journey from Santa Cruz to San José and back. Roads are variable in quality, so you'll need to rent a Jeep or similar.

WEATHER
In Bolivia's eastern lowlands, June is the midwinter dry season, with temperatures around 81–91°F (27–33°C), high humidity, and occasional thunderstorms.

ACCOMMODATIONS
Santa Cruz: Los Tabijos Hotel is a large, full-service hotel with gardens and pool; doubles from US$250; www.lostajiboshotel.com

Concepción: Gran Hotel Concepción is an old-style hacienda hotel with a garden and pool, located opposite the church; doubles from US$30; www.granhotelconcepcion.com.bo

San José: Hotel La Casona is a rustic, Old World-style hotel close to the main square; doubles US$45; www.lacasonachiquitana.com

EATING OUT
Lowland Bolivian cooking is simple, hearty fare of beans and rice dishes augmented by chicken or barbecued beef.

FURTHER INFORMATION
www.bolivia.travel

Dedicated Restorer

The fact that the Jesuit missions of Chiquitos continue to exist is thanks largely to the efforts of one man, the Swiss-born Jesuit architect Hans Roth. Roth arrived in San Rafael in 1972 at the age of 38 with a return air ticket and a six-month mandate to save that one church from collapse. He never returned home, choosing instead to dedicate the next 27 years of his life to restoring Chiquitos' churches. Roth's efforts were recognized in 1990, when UNESCO declared six of these churches World Heritage Sites.

Main: Elaborate decoration on the facade of the mission church of San Miguel de Velasco

CHIQUITOS

THE MASSIVE *TEMPLOS* (JESUIT CHURCHES) OF CHIQUITOS AREN'T RUINS, NOR MUSEUMS, but rather offer a glimpse into a vanished way of life; living monuments to a brief but glorious moment in history when peoples of the Old World and the New lived together in peace and harmony, sharing worldly goods, celebrating the works of a single god. Though this early utopia disappeared in less than a century, some of its unworldly aura still clings to the impressive buildings. In 1576 the Spanish colonial authorities permitted the Jesuits to set up missions throughout the Viceroyalty of Peru; 11 years later the Order reached Santa Cruz. It was largely a way of establishing Spanish sovereignty in the face of constant encroachment by slave-raiding expeditions from Portuguese Brazil. The Jesuits' first mission was built at San Javier, followed in quick succession by San Rafael, San José de Chiquitos, Concepción, San Miguel de Velasco, and Santa Ana. Each settlement, governed by a *cabildo* (council of chiefs) and a pair of

Left (left to right): Bolivian children playing music at the mission church at Santa Ana; Mass in progress at San Rafael de Velasco; baptistry of San Miguel de Velasco; exterior of the mission church at San José de Chiquitos; a Bolivian instrument-maker constructing a violin

Below: Decorated baptistry of the Jesuit mission at San Javier

Inset: Angel decoration on the facade of the Jesuit mission at Concepción

Living monuments to a brief but glorious moment in history.

Jesuit priests, was designed to be self-sufficient, with property held in common and communal activity – whether music, craft, or art – dedicated to the worship of God. At the center of each community they built a church. These are extraordinary structures, reflecting the Jesuits' ideals in their simple but massive shape and magnificent decoration. The wooden frame of tropical hardwood beams and columns supported a sloping roof large enough to shelter all 2,800 souls of a typical mission at once. Between the columns, mud and straw adobe was used to make walls, which were then covered with gesso and decorated with the intricate filigree of Iberian Baroque.

In 1767, the dream ended abruptly when the Jesuits were expelled by the Spanish and many churches destroyed. In Chiquitos, after nearly 150 years of control by the local church, in 1931 the Franciscan order took over the mission churches and they were left in peace. Six of the original churches survived in quiet decay until the last quarter of the 20th century, when they were rediscovered and restored to their former glory by Hans Roth, a former Jesuit himself.

BOLIVIAN DIARY

It takes at least five days to comfortably make the road trip through some of Bolivia's fascinating Chiquitos Jesuit mission towns. June is the start of the region's winter dry season and is the perfect time to travel, as the roads are usually dry and during the day the temperature is pleasant.

Five Days on the Mission Trail

DAY 1

Rent a 4WD in Santa Cruz and take Highway 10 north some 140 miles (225 km) on good paved roads to San Javier. Enter and marvel at the extraordinary church, begun in 1749. In the complex of mission buildings nearby, don't miss the Museo Misiones de Chiquitos (Museum of the Chiquitos Missions), which covers the history of the church and the region.

DAY 2

The second stop, Concepción, is an easy 50 miles (80 km) or so on paved roads, with beautiful scenery on the way. The cathedral complex here is arguably the most impressive in the region, so take your time exploring it. Concepción is also a good place to shop for art and crafts – the craftsmen who work restoring the cathedral sell their pieces in workshops nearby.

DAY 3

San Miguel de Velasco lies another 120 miles (200 km) or so along hard-packed dirt roads from Concepción. It was once a mining center, and over 1 ton of gold was said to have gone into decorating the rich Baroque interior and altar. After admiring the extravagance, stroll the streets of this isolated and authentic old colonial town.

DAY 4

San José is just over 120 miles (200 km) farther on. Unlike the other churches, the edifice in San José is built of stone and adobe, which gives it a look and ambience like no other.

DAY 5

Retrace your steps to Santa Cruz. Try to get back to Santa Cruz in time for an elegant dinner.

Dos and Don'ts

- ✓ Enjoy the scenery on the drive. In addition to the mission churches, the region has some of the loveliest verdant scenery in Bolivia.
- ✗ Don't forget to top up your gas tank in Concepción, as gas stations become rare from that point onwards.
- ✗ Don't drive at night. There are no lights on the roads, service stations close generally by 9pm, and cattle and livestock may be by or on the roadside.
- ✓ Roads are quiet but watch out for logging trucks on the back roads. These monsters move fast and their drivers often think they own the road. Give them a very wide berth.

Below: The Museo Misiones de Chiquitos (Mission Museum) at San Javier

JULY

Where to Go: **July**

The tourist season is in full swing in North America, and while you're spoilt for choice for places to enjoy summer fun, inland destinations can be hot and humid so it's wise to head for the coast. However, this is also the time to take a leisurely tour of the vacation retreats of New England or to get active among the natural wonders of the Pacific Northwest. Canada, bathed in long hours of daylight, reveals its natural splendors at this time of year. The remotest islands are accessible, offering endless scope for outdoor adventure. In the Dominican Republic, meanwhile, even the tropical Caribbean heat can't stop the city of Santo Domingo from dancing till it drops. Below you will find all the destinations in this chapter as well as some extra suggestions to provide a little inspiration.

FESTIVALS AND CULTURE

VANCOUVER Shakespeare play performed at Bard on the Beach festival

VANCOUVER
BRITISH COLUMBIA, CANADA

A month of summer festivals in a spectacular setting

While away the long summer days in Vancouver, where outdoor festivals offer folk, pop, and classical music, theater, and a huge firework display.

See pp156–7

NEW HAVEN
CONNECTICUT, USA

Historic home of Yale University

The USA's prettiest university town, centered on the delicate spires and cobbled courtyards of Yale's neo-Gothic collegiate buildings.

www.visitnewhaven.com

NEWPORT
RHODE ISLAND, USA

A charming coastal resort town with culture and outdoor fun

Sailing enthusiasts love this part of New England for the regattas in Newport, which was once home to the America's Cup.

See pp174–5

MONTRÉAL COMEDY FESTIVAL
QUÉBEC, CANADA

Massive comedy event

Montréal's long-running "Just For Laughs" festival showcases established and emerging comedy acts in both English and French.

www.hahaha.com

DOMINICAN REPUBLIC
CARIBBEAN

Tropical Fiesta de Merengue

Join the hip-swaying locals dancing in the streets to a Caribbean beat, but save time to enjoy beaches, rain forests, and historical treasures too.

See pp176–7

UNFORGETTABLE JOURNEYS

SALAR DE UYUNI Cacti and the other-worldly salt plains

SALAR DE UYUNI
BOLIVIA

Traverse the world's highest and largest salt lake

The incredible 4WD tour across this salty plateau includes amazing sunsets, mountain vistas, clear blue skies, and deep red sunsets.

See pp158–9

THE ALCAN HIGHWAY
ALASKA, USA–CANADA

Drive the remarkable Alaska–Canada Highway

Almost 1,400 miles (2,250 km) long, this highway is a spectacular engineering feat and a truly challenging roadtrip.

www.alcan-highway.com

DRIVING THE CASCADE LOOP
WASHINGTON STATE, USA

Forests and volcanic peaks

This 400-mile (644-km) round trip through the Cascade Mountains shows the pine-clad wilderness of northwestern USA at its finest.

www.cascadeloop.com

QUTTINIRPAAQ NATIONAL PARK
NUNAVUT, CANADA

A glaciated polar desert

Go hiking, skiing, or dogsledding across the icy tundra of Nunavut, located inside the Arctic Circle at the northernmost tip of Canada.

www.pc.gc.ca

AVALON PENINSULA
NEWFOUNDLAND, CANADA

Drive the most easterly corner of north America

Tour this isolated peninsula where small villages share the rocky cliffs with seabirds, the boggy tundra with caribou, and the sea with whales.

See pp172–3

"Thousands of golden-headed gannets cover the sea stack, rising and filling the blue sky with a whirlwind motion."

NATURAL WONDERS

SAN JUAN ISLANDS Orca breaching far out of the water

SAN JUAN ISLANDS
WASHINGTON STATE, USA

A nature-lover's paradise, teeming with wildlife

Over 100 sparsely inhabited islands washed by the nutrient-rich Pacific waters are perfect for seabirds, fish, and orca whales.

See pp166–7

JASPER NATIONAL PARK
ALBERTA, CANADA

Mountain wilderness

The largest park in the Canadian Rockies is home to the awesome Columbia Icefields, as well as grizzly bears, wolves, moose, and caribou.

See pp162–3

KLUANE NATIONAL PARK
YUKON, CANADA

Glaciers and lofty peaks

Home to Mount Logan, Canada's highest mountain, and a wild landscape of immense icefields and the mighty Kaskawulsh Glacier.

www.pc.gc.ca

LAKE TAHOE
CALIFORNIA/NEVADA, USA

One of America's highest, longest, and deepest lakes

This sprawling, pine-fringed lake on the California–Nevada borders offers excellent hiking, plus beaches in summer and skiing in winter.

www.tahoe.com

BOUNDARY WATERS
MINNESOTA, USA

The ideal place to find your own wild wonderland

A vast area of pristine forest with hundreds of canoe routes through island-studded, crystal-clear, fish-filled water.

www.canoecountry.com

Previous page: The dramatic Salar de Uyuni salt flat in the rainy season, Bolivia

Weather Watch

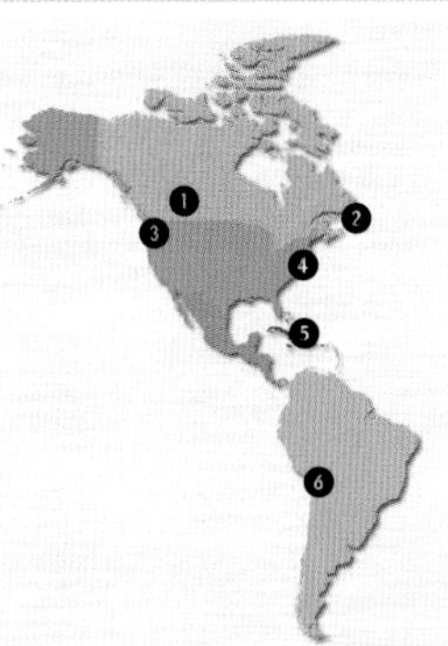

❶ **Calgary, Canada** Lying between the foothills of the Canadian Rockies and the prairies, Calgary is sunny and warm for most of the month. It's less stormy than earlier in the summer, but showers and cool nights should be expected.

❷ **Newfoundland, Canada** Sub-Arctic Newfoundland, the weather-beaten, easternmost part of North America, is at its best in summer. Though rain is still likely, this is a wonderful month to explore the island.

❸ **Washington State, USA** Washington's enchanting San Juan Islands are popular in July, when sunshine and warm temperatures offer perfect conditions for outdoor activities.

❹ **Washington, D.C., USA** Where better to celebrate July 4 – Independence Day – than in Washington, D.C.? The nation's capital gets hot and humid in summer, but there are many excellent air-conditioned museums to cool off in.

❺ **Dominican Republic** The Caribbean wet season isn't too dramatic here, with rain every few days. It is sunny and hot, of course, with temperatures of 70–95°F (21–35°C).

❻ **Bolivia** Though Andean Bolivia is in the midst of winter, and can get very cold at night, the volcanoes, lakes, and hot springs of the southern highlands amply reward exploration with bright sunshine, blue skies, and crystal-clear air.

LUXURY AND ROMANCE

CAPE COD Rose-covered cottage on Nantucket Island

CAPE COD
MASSACHUSETTS, USA

Golden beaches, quiet islands, and charming villages

Quaint clapboard cottages, historic inns, fabulous seafood to eat on the beach at sunset – this is a perfect romantic escape.

See pp170–71

"Shingled houses and cottages surround old churches, and fishing fleets return with oysters, mussels, and lobsters."

CARMEL VALLEY
CALIFORNIA, USA

A sun-soaked sylvan land of plenty

Close to the Monterey Peninsula, this valley offers a blend of award-winning wineries, world-class golf links, hotels, and fine dining.

www.carmelvalleychamber.com

TALL PINE LODGES
MANITOBA, CANADA

Hide away in this wonderful forested sanctuary

Choose an activity – from hiking, cycling, or riding to tennis, fishing, canoeing – then wind down in your own private Jacuzzi.

www.tallpinelodges.com

POCONO MOUNTAINS
PENNSYLVANIA, USA

Rural playground

Idyllic mountain scenery makes this a year-round retreat, with quaint country inns, restaurants, shops, and a host of outdoor activities.

www.poconomountains.com

VIEUX-MONTRÉAL
QUÉBEC, CANADA

A haven of Gallic charm in Canada's second-largest city

The biggest French-speaking city in the Americas, Montréal offers some of Canada's finest dining and an array of places to drink, shop, and sleep.

www.tourisme-montreal.org

ACTIVE ADVENTURES

CORDILLERA BLANCA Stunning high-mountain landscape

CORDILLERA BLANCA
PERU

One of the world's most spectacular mountain ranges

The terrain is so high you'll need to acclimatize before you can even think about trekking among the glacial lakes and snowy peaks.

See pp164–5

SKIING IN THE CHILEAN ANDES
SANTIAGO, CHILE

South America's best pistes

Tear down the slopes in one of the resorts around Santiago, enjoying the region's famed "champagne snow."

www.chileanski.com

GWAII HAANAS NATIONAL PARK
BRITISH COLUMBIA, CANADA

Adventures at sea

Kayak through the fertile waters of Gwaii Haanas in the Queen Charlotte Islands, and you may even spot bears and sealions.

See pp160–61

CERRO RICO MINES, POTOSÍ
BOLIVIA

Colonial-era silver mine

Plunge deep into the earth where vast seams of silver once made Potosí the most valuable city in the entire Spanish empire.

www.bolivia.travel

BIRDING IN WITLESS BAY
NEWFOUNDLAND, CANADA

Seabird wonderland

The four islands of Witless Bay Ecological Reserve are home to North America's largest Atlantic puffin colony.

www.env.gov.nl.ca/parks

FAMILY GETAWAYS

WASHINGTON, DC The Smithsonian Folklife Festival

"Washington's National Mall is filled with a colorful array of musicians, performers, artists, storytellers, cooks, and craftsmen."

WASHINGTON, D.C.
USA

Celebrate the July 4th in style in the nation's capital

This elegantly laid out city is filled with world-class museums and historical monuments – all lit up by fireworks on Independence Day.

See pp154–5

OKLAHOMA
USA

Take a break in the Sooner State

Explore Oklahoma City's National Cowboy Museum, sample the local steaks, and learn about the state's Native American culture.

www.travelok.com

WASKESIU LAKE
SASKATCHEWAN, CANADA

Versatile family destination

In the heart of the Prince Albert National Park, Waskesiu Lake offers the chance to hang out on sunny lakeside beaches or plunge into the wilderness to hike and spot wildlife.

www.waskesiulake.ca

CALGARY
ALBERTA, CANADA

Action-packed rodeo and the flavor of the Wild West

The drama and skills on display at the Calgary Stampede are best appreciated live and up-close – fun and excitement for the family.

See pp168–9

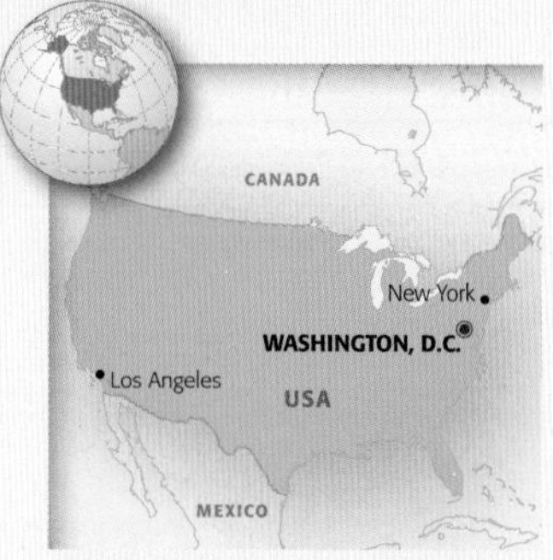

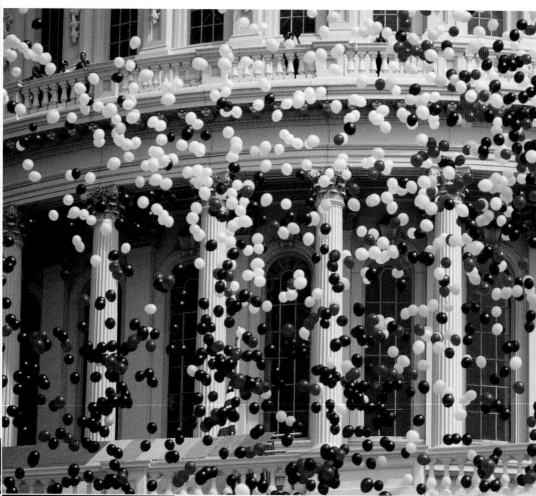

GETTING THERE See map p316, F6
Washington, D.C., is served by two international airports: Dulles and Baltimore-Washington. Taxis, metrorail, and buses connect to the city center.

GETTING AROUND
The metro is a great way to get around, with five lines serving downtown D.C. Metrobuses are another quick and cheap mode of transport.

WEATHER
Washington can be hot and humid in summer, with average temperatures of 88°F (31°C).

ACCOMMODATIONS
Hotel Palomar is a stylish boutique hotel; family rooms from US$230; www.hotelpalomar-dc.com

Holiday Inn Capitol Hill is great for families, with a pool and free children's meals; family rooms from US$260; www.hicapitoldc.com

Embassy Suites is a spacious hotel between the White House and the Capitol; family rooms from US$340; www.embassysuites.com

EATING OUT
The dining scene is eclectic, from traditional restaurants serving classic American and international dishes to a vast number of ethnic restaurants. Children will be happy with the wide range of diners, burger and chili joints, and pizza parlors. Maryland seafood and superior steaks will suit the grown-ups.

FURTHER INFORMATION
www.washington.org

WASHINGTON, D.C.

A HANDSOME CITY BUILT TO HUMAN SCALE, Washington, D.C. never fails to delight visitors. The highest points of the skyline will always be the gleaming Capitol dome and the slim shaft of the Washington Memorial, a profile that has been carefully protected by law. Standing at either end of the long lawns of the National Mall, they are part of the brilliant city plan of Frenchman Pierre-Charles L'Enfant. Inspired by Paris, L'Enfant envisioned the city's wide avenues radiating from scenic squares and circles, adorned by sculptures and fountains, a design unique in America.

The only difficulty in Washington is deciding what to do first. The city's world-class museums alone could fill days on end, and then there are the stately buildings of government – the US Capitol and the Supreme Court – which can be explored by guided visit.

Main: Red, white, and blue balloons float in front of the Capitol

Smithsonian Institution

Despite never visiting the USA, James Smithson, a British scientist, left his entire fortune to found the Smithsonian Institution in Washington, upon his death in 1829. He would surely be amazed to see that his bequest has grown into the world's largest museum organization and a highlight for every visitor to Washington. The Smithsonian oversees 16 D.C. museums, including the very popular Air and Space Museum, plus the National Zoo and six research centers. All are free and open daily, and the holdings include art, history, and natural science.

Left: Jazz at Blues Alley

Right (left to right): Studying the Vietnam Veterans' Memorial; elegant buildings in Georgetown; crowds at the Smithsonian Folklife Festival; colonial military demonstration at the Independence Day celebrations

Right panel (top and bottom): Interior of the National Archives; fireworks celebrating Independence Day with the Capitol in the foreground

July sees the city at its vibrant best, with two of its most important events taking place in close succession. The first, the Smithsonian Folklife Festival, celebrates cultural heritage and is an entirely free, open-air event. During the two weeks of the festival, the National Mall is filled with a colorful array of musicians, performers, artists, storytellers, cooks, and craftspeople, creating an energetic celebration. This coincides with Independence Day on July 4th, when a real electricity descends on the city, as fireworks explode over the striking Washington Monument.

Even when the heady excitement of these festival days has died down, there is still much to be enchanted by, from a ride on a mule-drawn barge on the Chesapeake and Ohio Canal (C&O) and watching elephant training in the National Zoo, to the exciting hands-on National Museum of Natural History and puppet shows in the Discovery Theater. There is nothing stuffy about this well-ordered, historic city – beneath its austere surface you will find a very modern heart.

Above: International Spy Museum in the Penn Quarter

BIRTHDAY DIARY

The Smithsonian Folklife Festival takes place during the last week of June and first week of July. Over a million visitors flock to the National Mall, which is filled with music, crafts, food, and entertainment. The Independence Day festivities of July 4th always fall during this festival, bringing a real vibrancy to the city.

Four Days in America's Capital

Head straight to the National Mall to enjoy the festival – watch the artisans at work, sample the wares in the food tent, dance to the lively music, and browse the craft stalls. When you've had your fill, stroll down to the Tidal Basin to see the moving memorials to America's famous presidents – Thomas Jefferson, Abraham Lincoln, and Franklin D. Roosevelt, and have a look at the abstract Vietnam Veterans' Memorial. **2nd**

Spend a day visiting some of the city's excellent museums. Start in the National Museum of Natural History for dinosaurs, an insect zoo, and a living coral reef. Afterwards, choose from the National Gallery of Art, one of America's most important museums, or the popular National Air and Space Museum. In the evening, head to Georgetown for jazz at Blues Alley. **3rd**

If you can face more museums, head for the Penn Quarter, home to the International Spy Museum, the Shakespeare Theater, the Smithsonian American Art Museum, and National Portrait Gallery. Otherwise, head to the Chesapeake and Ohio Canal (C&O) for a ride in a mule-drawn canal clipper, or to the Discovery Theater for a puppet show. End the day watching the spectacular fireworks over the city as it celebrates Independence Day. **4th**

See the pandas at the National Zoo, the fish at the National Aquarium, or the famous bonsai at the National Arboretum. Take a cruise on the Potomac or a tour across the river to Mount Vernon Estate, the home and gardens of George Washington. **5th**

Dos and Don'ts

✓ Get an insider's view of D.C. on a walking tour through Embassy Row, Georgetown, and other interesting neighborhoods (www.washingtonwalks.com), or consider a guided cycling tour of the sites (www.bikethesites.com).

✗ Don't overlook the city's sporting heroes – Washington Redskins' merchandise makes great souvenirs of the town.

✓ Be aware of the 14.5 percent tax levied on hotels in the city, which will be added to the bill at the end of your stay, on top of the room rate.

GETTING THERE See map p313, C6
The third-largest city in Canada, Vancouver is served by international and domestic flights. Vancouver International Airport is about 9 miles (14 km) from the city center.

GETTING AROUND
Downtown Vancouver is walkable and has a vast network of cycle paths. Ferries cross to North Vancouver and to the southern suburbs. An east–west rapid transit line takes you from downtown to the suburbs.

WEATHER
Vancouver in July gets 295 hours of sunshine and only 40mm of rain. Average daytime temperatures are around 75°F (24°C).

ACCOMMODATIONS
West End Guest House has doubles from US$265; www.westendguesthouse.com

A waterfront hotel near theaters and galleries, Granville Island Hotel has doubles from US$340; www.granvilleislandhotel.com

Pan Pacific Hotel Vancouver in the Canada Place cruise ship terminal has doubles from US$390; www.panpacific.com

EATING OUT
Raincity Grill serves delicious local cuisine and British Columbia wine by the glass for about US$60 per person. For top-quality seafood, try C restaurant (US$90 per person).

FURTHER INFORMATION
www.tourismvancouver.com

Local Wineries

Culinary culture has advanced in Vancouver over the past few decades, and nothing shows this better than the development of high-quality British Columbia wines. There are now over 250 wineries in the province. Sumac Ridge and Mission Hill are two of the better-known quality vineyards. Look for B.C. whites – especially Gewürztraminer, and the local specialty, ice wine. Many of Vancouver's restaurants have local vintages available by the glass.

Above (left to right): Planetarium; totem pole; *inuksuk*, an Inuit directional marker, overlooking English Bay at sunset
Main: Stilt-walker at Jericho Park Folk Festival

Above: View of the North Shore

VANCOUVER

VANCOUVER IS ONE OF THE MOST NATURALLY SPECTACULAR CITIES in the world, and at barely 100 years old it is also one of the youngest. Today the city has a booming center of imposing skyscrapers and world-class galleries, with a sophisticated arts and cultural scene - it is also a magnet for lovers of the outdoors. During the high summer month of July, the city hums with a series of festivals that simultaneously celebrate Vancouver's history as a meeting point of East and West, and its wealth of culture, both outdoor and in.

The first such festival is Bard on the Beach, a summer-long celebration of Shakespeare, with a pair of the Bard's plays performed every night in July in an enormous open tent set on the waterfront overlooking English Bay. As the evening's performance wears on, the sun sinks slowly behind the mountains of the North Shore, until the last red rays have vanished. On the third weekend in July, some 30,000 music-lovers head to the sandy beaches of Spanish Banks for a three-day festival of folk, acoustic, Indian classical, Hong Kong pop, and hip hop known as the Vancouver Folk Music Festival. Performances take place on two stages set at opposite ends of a green swath of land overlooking the beach, ocean, and mountains beyond.

Finally, over the last two weeks of July, Vancouver hosts perhaps the perfect combination of popular culture and art – the Honda Celebration of Light. Every third evening hundreds of thousands of spectators flock to the city's long undulating waterfront to watch a stunning fireworks display that explodes over the waters of English Bay, set off in time to the simultaneous stereo broadcast of classical symphony music. This annual fireworks festival is an ongoing work of art that is a perfect match for the breathtaking beauty of Vancouver's dramatic surroundings.

Hundreds of thousands of spectators flock to the city's waterfront to watch a stunning firework display.

Inset: Fireworks exploding over English Bay
Below (left and right): A band playing outdoors at Vancouver Folk Music Festival; actors performing in *Love's Labour's Lost* at the Bard on the Beach festival

SUMMER DIARY

Vancouver's stunning outdoor setting is at its best in July, when there is barely a drop of rain and the sunset and glimmering twilight last until well past 10pm. Three days is ample opportunity to sample the city's natural delights, culinary and cultural offerings, and festival entertainment.

Three Days of Festivities

DAY 1

Rent a bicycle and set out along the Stanley Park seawall, the thin black ribbon that loops around the tract of rain forest at the city's heart. The cycle ride offers glimpses of totem poles, towering Douglas fir, and bald eagles circling over the bay. On a July evening, you can watch Shakespeare played out beneath a large tent overlooking English Bay.

DAY 2

Walk to the hip high-rise community of Yaletown – a good place for a latte and a biscotti – and take a little blue ferry across False Creek to Granville Island, a vast covered market packed with regional delicacies, such as smoked salmon and ice wine. In the afternoon, head out to the beachfront at Spanish Banks for the Vancouver Folk Music Festival.

DAY 3

Cross the Lion's Gate Bridge to North Vancouver and take the tram 3,300 ft (1,000 m) up to the lookout atop Grouse Mountain. From your perch on the eyrie, you can gaze out over the whole of British Columbia's Lower Mainland – the long blue arm of Burrard Inlet, the slow proud Fraser River, teeming with homecoming sockeye salmon, and the rounded white volcanic dome of Mount Baker in the south. Come sundown, on three magical evenings in July, walk down to the waterline to see the sky explode with fireworks, to the sound of a classical symphony.

Dos and Don'ts

- ✓ Head for the beach at Sunset Beach, Kitsilano Point, Spanish Banks, just before sunset and watch the sun going down behind the mountains at English Bay.
- ✗ Don't forget a sweater or light coat to wear after sunset. Vancouver evenings are always cool, even in summer.
- ✓ Sample Vancouver's restaurants, which rival larger culinary centers, such as San Francisco, in the quality of their ingredients and preparation.
- ✗ Don't forget to stock up on that local staple, wild salmon, either fresh or smoked.

GETTING THERE See map p330, C4
Access to the Salar de Uyuni is via the town of Uyuni. Uyuni is a 5-hour bus journey away from Potosí, which can be reached via a 12-hour bus journey from La Paz. Alternatively, air-hop from La Paz to Sucre and take a bus from Sucre to Uyuni.

GETTING AROUND
The only way to explore the salt flats is by 4WD. Several agencies in Uyuni offer expeditions to the flats.

WEATHER
Winter is chilly. Daytime temperatures reach 54°F (12°C), but drop to 14°F (–10°C) at night. The skies are a clear crystalline blue.

ACCOMMODATIONS
Basic lodge-style accommodations are included in all guided tours into the Salar.

Hotel Toñito in Uyuni is clean and simple; doubles from US$65; www.tonitouyuni.com

Uyuni's Los Girasoles Hotel offers clean accommodation; doubles from US$90; Tel (591) 2693 2101

EATING OUT
Basic meals are included on all tours. In Uyuni, the Minuteman restaurant offers pizzas and espresso.

FURTHER INFORMATION
www.uyuni.com.bo

SALAR DE UYUNI

IT'S A TRIP FOR THOSE NOT AFRAID TO ROUGH it, for those on the lookout for something extraordinary and otherworldly. A horizon-to-horizon expanse of pure, blinding white, the vast high plain known as the Salar de Uyuni is the world's largest salt pan, 25 times greater in size than its more famous cousin in Bonneville, Utah. It is so out of the ordinary, it fully justifies the sobriquet of surreal. Not for nothing is one small corner of the Salar nicknamed the Salvador Dali desert.

Located in the highlands of southern Bolivia, the Salar is all that's left of a vast prehistoric lake that once lapped at the flanks of the High Andes. When Lake Minchin dried, it left behind a salt flat 4,650 sq miles (12,000 sq km) in area, containing some 10 billion tonnes of salt. Periodically, when the rains fall or the snow melts on the Andes, the Salar fills with a thin film of water, turning into a

Salt of the Earth

Salt forms the literal bedrock of the economy in the tiny pueblo of Colchani, a 12-mile (20-km) drive from Uyuni. The villagers, all members of the Colchani salt cooperative, extract blocks of nearly pure salt from the Colchani reserve, processing them for sale and export. Salt cutters live on the salt pan five days at time, sleep in tiny salt igloo domes, and rise each morning to hack out vast hunks of rock-hard salt and shape them into transportable blocks. Chewing coca to ward off fatigue, each man cuts, shapes, and stacks some 500 blocks a day.

Main: A jeep drives along a stretch of the flooded salt pan, Salar de Uyuni

Left: Red algae on Laguna Colorada

Right (left and right): Andean Altiplano flamingos; a steam train graveyard at Uyuni

Right panel (top to bottom): Luna Salada Lodge Hotel built with salt; the Arbol de Piedra ("Tree of Stone") in the Uyuni highlands; a kiln on Laguna Colorada; Sol de Mañana geysers

vast mirror that appears to dissolve into the blue sky. And in the midst of this salt sea stands Incahuasi Island, a tiny outcrop of rock and productive soil, where cacti grow up to 33 ft (10 m) high and rabbits nibble on the brown grass. The now-extinct volcanic cone of Mount Licancabur rises high at the southern margins of the Salar. Close to its lower slopes are the near-scalding hot springs of Laguna Challviri which, coupled with the cold snowmelt, provide a sublime outdoor soak. From here, a short rattling trip over stony ground leads to Laguna Colorada, the "Colored Lake," where an infestation of red algae has resulted in a rich assortment of bird life including three species of South American flamingos: the Chilean, the Andean, and the James flamingo.

Your last stop on this spectacular tour is the Sol de Mañana, or Morning Sun, where geysers spew forth in the morning air, hot mud bubbles up from the earth, and where every morning the sun rises in a glorious fantasia of reds over the salty white plain.

Above: Cacti in Salar de Uyuni

JAN FEB MAR APR MAY JUN **JUL**

SALT PAN DIARY

The high-altitude Salar de Uyuni is at its driest and clearest in the midwinter month of July. Four days is enough time to explore the salt flats, geysers and hot springs, high volcanoes, and the colorful lakes full of flamingos. The itinerary below is typical of the tours offered by agencies in the region.

Four Days in Empty Space

DAY 1

The journey, in a 4WD, starts with a stopover at the train cemetery, where dozens of abandoned engines and carriages rust beneath a deep blue sky. The tour then skirts the edge of the Salar to Colchani, where villagers dig out salt with pick and shovel and leave it in piles to dry in the sun. From here, the expedition heads due west into the unrelieved blinding whiteness of the salt plain. The first stop is the Luna Salada Lodge Hotel, which has walls, chairs, and beds made entirely of salt. Then it's off to Isla Incahuasi, a surreal outpost of cacti, grassy hills, and small brown viscacha rabbits, surrounded by a sea of salt.

DAY 2

On day two, the expedition heads for the Siloli desert, with its extraordinary stone formations including the Arbol de Piedra ("Tree of Stone"), and the tiny lakes Hedionda, Chiar Kota, and Ramaditas, colored cobalt blue, royal purple, and emerald. Day's end finds the tour at a simple lodge by the Laguna Colorada, a vast lake colored red with algae, rich food for the thousands of bright-hued flamingos.

DAY 3

An early morning departure brings the tour to Sol de Mañana, where bubbling springs and geysers fill the morning air with hot steam. From this otherworldly locale, the expedition moves to the Laguna Challviri hot springs for a refreshing soak. The expedition then climbs the wind-swept slopes of Licancabur volcano.

DAY 4

The 4WD re-enters the Salar for a leisurely day's exploration on the way back to the town of Uyuni.

Dos and Don'ts

- ✓ Remember to carry lots of water. The high altitude and strong sun dries you out quickly.
- ✗ Don't forget a sleeping bag and bring lots of warm clothes. There's little heat out on the salt flats, and the winter temperature at night is chilly.
- ✓ Take a couple of days to acclimatize to the altitude. Tours into the Salar de Uyuni start at 11,480 ft (3,500 m) and rise to 14,760 ft (4,500 m).
- ✓ Take your bathing suit for a soak in the hot springs.

AUG SEP OCT NOV DEC

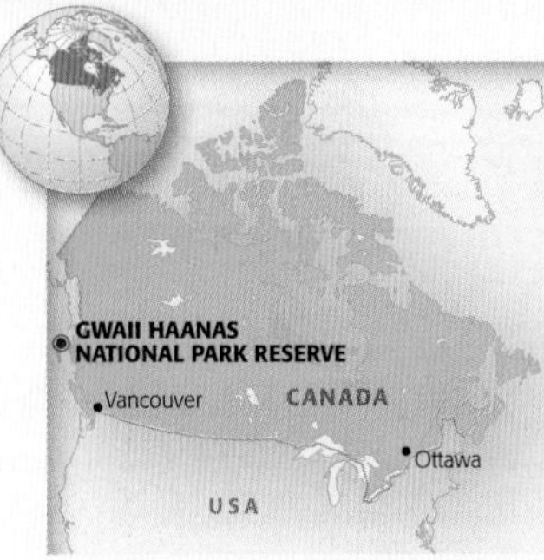

GETTING THERE See map p313, B5
Air Canada offers flights from Vancouver to the Haida Gwaii (Queen Charlotte Islands), from where you must take local transport. Daily ferries ply between Prince Rupert, on the Canadian mainland, and the islands. Access to Gwaii Haanas National Park Reserve is via floatplane, boat, or kayak.

GETTING AROUND
While on tour, you'll paddle a fair distance in your kayak, but the mothership – your base – will help. To get around the islands, hop on a taxi, seaplane, or ferry.

WEATHER
Haida Gwaii is at its best in July, with over 16 hours of sunlight and a temperature range of 57–63°F (14–17°C).

ACCOMMODATIONS
Kayak tours where you spend nights aboard a mothership offer adventure, activity, and comfort. For most tours, arrive the day before and stay overnight.

Archipelago Ventures offers six-day tours from US$2,020; www.tourhaidagwaii.com

Sea Raven Motel Queen Charlotte City has doubles from US$70 per night; www.searaven.com

EATING OUT
You don't come to Haida Gwaii for the food. Mothership tours usually include hearty fare.

FURTHER INFORMATION
www.gohaidagwaii.ca
kitgorokayaking.com

The Spirit of Haida Gwaii

Taking pride of place at Vancouver International Airport's departure lounge, *The Spirit of Haida Gwaii* is a gigantic jade sculpture by Haida artist, Bill Reid. The 18-ft- (6-m-) long canoe is filled with creatures from Haida mythology. Raven, the trickster, holds the steering oar while Grizzly Bear sits in the bow, his back shielding the others from the waves. Bear Mother looks ahead – she has cubs to care for. In the center is Kilstlaai, a shaman dressed in a Haida cloak and holding a staff carved with the Seabear, Raven, and Killer Whale.

Above (left and right): Ancient Haida mortuary poles at the UNESCO World Heritage Site in Sgang Gwaay; kayakers next to the mothership
Main: Starfish and sea urchins beneath a tide pool

Above: Soaking in a natural hot-spring pool at the preserve

GWAII HAANAS NATIONAL PARK RESERVE

MAGIC ABOUNDS IN GWAII HAANAS, the "Place of Wonders" in the Haida tongue, and no other name suits this enchanting forested archipelago more aptly. Amazing adventures and incredible sights greet you when you visit this hidden jewel. As you paddle your tiny kayak through the calm waters or simply dawdle along a rocky shore, you'll suddenly spot a black bear loping along or a sealion popping his head out of the water to give you a curious stare. Drifting in the shallows on a slackening tide, you'll glance into the clear water below and find a multihued garden of marine life – orange anemones, purple sea stars, and multicolored nudibranchs – carpeting the seabed.

Along the way, you'll find yourself spellbound by Gwaii Haanas: hot springs, spruce-clad mountains, whales, nesting puffins and auklets, black bears, and bald eagles. The works of man, too, are here. In now-abandoned settlements such as Nan Sdins and Sgang Gwaay, small groves of tall, intricately carved cedar poles display totems that declare a clan's lineage or tell the story of a prominent chief or family. Such is the power and artistry of these totems that UNESCO declared them a World Heritage Site as far back as 1981.

There are, of course, disadvantages to a kayak – they're slow, precarious, and lack shower facilities. But there's a simple solution – a mothership and kayak combo, blending the grace of a kayak with the comforts of a larger ship. At lunch or at day's end, when you tire, the mothership picks you up so you can refuel with a meal and shower. It then motors along in search of yet another spot for the next day, where you can discover more of the magic that lies in store in the Place of Wonders.

Glance into the clear water and find a multihued garden of marine life – anemones, sea stars, and nudibranchs – carpeting the seabed.

Inset: Starfish of every color in Gwaii Haanas
Below (left and right): A family of Steller sealions; painted paddles at Skidegate

KAYAKER'S DIARY

Often referred to as the Galápagos of Canada, Gwaii Haanas National Park Reserve – on the southern tip of Haida-Gwaii, formerly known as the Queen Charlotte Islands – is a species-rich archipelago of some 130 islands teeming with wildlife. July offers warm temperatures and sunshine-filled evenings.

Six Days in the Wilds

DAY 1 Be up early to make your way to the seaplane dock in Queen Charlotte by 7am. A half-hour flight over remarkable territory brings you to the northern limit of Gwaii Haanas National Park Reserve, where you'll board the mothership. The first stop is a hike and a visit to Taanoo, a Haida winter village.

DAY 2 A short paddle takes you to Hot Springs Island and a chance for a morning snack. A midday journey aboard the mothership traverses Juan Perez Sound, leaving enough time for a paddle in North Burnaby Strait.

DAY 3 At the bottom end of Burnaby Strait, Burnaby Narrows boasts one of the richest concentrations of marine life anywhere on the Pacific Coast. Drift and paddle your way over anemones, sea stars, and other intertidal creatures. When the tide rises, the kayaks, along with the ship, sneak through the narrows into Skincuttle, the inlet where the mothership spends the night.

DAY 4 Skincuttle is rich in wildlife and you're likely to spot tufted puffins, rhinoceros auklets, storm petrels, sooty shearwaters, and humpback, orca, and minke whales.

DAY 5 Paddle the tidal pools of the Gordon Islands, explore the natural caves, or walk on a black-sand beach.

DAY 6 Marvel at the houses and totem poles at Sgaang Gwaay and Nan Sdins. Stay overnight at Rose Harbour, an old whaling station near the southern tip of Gwaii Haanas. Early next morning, take the incredible 45-minute flight across the length of Gwaii Haanas back to Queen Charlotte City.

Dos and Don'ts

- ✓ Pack your things in a flexible bag you can cram into awkward spaces on a boat. Pack light, but bring clothes to cover every eventuality – fleece pants, a warm hat, shorts and T-shirts, shoes that like water, and a swimsuit for Hot Springs Cove.
- ✓ Bring your own alcoholic drinks if you're fond of a nip in the evening.
- ✗ Don't forget your saltwater-fishing license if you're keen on trying your luck with a line.
- ✓ Carry a dry bag to store your camera in while you paddle.

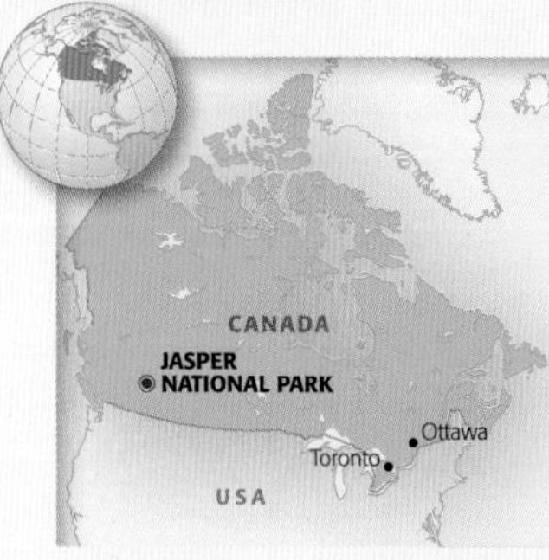

GETTING THERE See map p316, D5
Jasper is well-connected to the rest of Canada via train, bus, and highway. The nearest major airports are Edmonton International (4-hour drive) and Calgary International (5 hours).

GETTING AROUND
To explore the region, it's best to rent a car. Alternatively, you can make your base in Jasper, and then take day tours.

WEATHER
A prime time to take advantage of the great outdoors is from late June to mid-September, when the temperatures are pleasantly warm. Note, though, that even in summer, it can rain and, at the higher altitudes, snow.

ACCOMMODATIONS
Relax at the upscale and scenic Fairmont Jasper Park Lodge; doubles from US$170; www.fairmont.com

Alpine Village Cabin Resort offers comfort and seclusion; doubles from US$200; www.alpinevillagejasper.com

For the full backcountry experience, stay at one of the park's many campsites, including around Maligne Lake.

EATING OUT
Jasper has a variety of restaurants serving hearty mountain fare, like Raven Bistro, with dishes of venison and braised lamb.

FURTHER INFORMATION
www.jasper.travel

A place to discover miles upon miles of rugged trails flanked by thick forest and the glassy-blue shimmer of Maligne Lake, ringed by snow-brushed peaks

Main: Mountain peaks flank the clear-blue waters of Maligne Lake

JASPER NATIONAL PARK

Canada is the land of stunning national parks, so it says a lot that Jasper National Park is consistently the most-visited one in the country. And while the largest park in the Canadian Rockies sees many visitors, it's also undeniably and thrillingly wild. This is the Canadian outdoors at its finest. A place to discover miles upon miles of rugged trails flanked by thick forest; the glassy-blue shimmer of Maligne Lake, ringed by snow-brushed peaks; and the massive Columbia Icefield, which sprawls across both the southern end of Jasper National Park and the northern reaches of the neighboring Banff National Park. And the wildlife? It's equally fascinating, with wolves, moose, caribou, and grizzly bears all roaming around the mountainous terrain.

Make your base in the lively town of Jasper, which is dotted with an array of inviting accommodations, from mountain lodges to rustic cabins. The town is also the jumping-off point for tours that fan out across the park,

Bear Country

Jasper National Park is bear country, with both grizzly and black bears lumbering through the wilderness. A top spot to spy bears is around the Yellowhead Highway 16; dusk and dawn is when bears are most active. If you see one, be sure to stay in your car and keep your distance. Bears can be extremely dangerous and Parks Canada states that you should stay at least 330 ft (100 m) from them. Use binoculars to catch a closer glimpse, and if you want to get a close-range photo, bring a camera with a telephoto lens.

Above The scenic Icefields Parkway

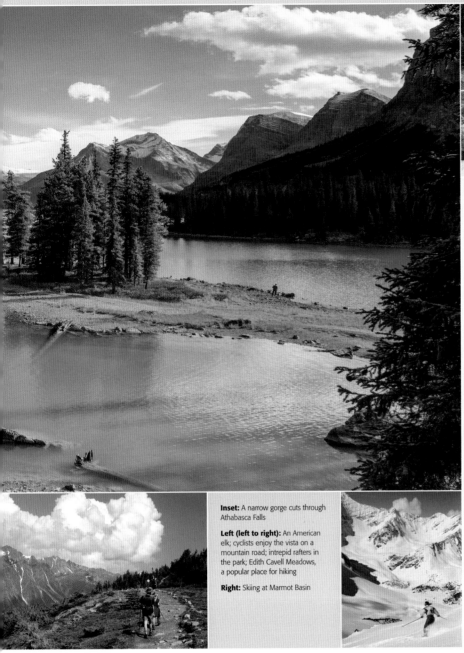

Inset: A narrow gorge cuts through Athabasca Falls

Left (left to right): An American elk; cyclists enjoy the vista on a mountain road; intrepid rafters in the park; Edith Cavell Meadows, a popular place for hiking

Right: Skiing at Marmot Basin

from mountain treks to horseback riding. Prepare to get wet: Jasper National Park is laced with rivers, and numerous outfitters offer white-water trips, including on the churning Athabasca, Fraser, and Sunwapta rivers. The park also abounds with less white-knuckle pursuits, like golf. The Fairmont Jasper Park Lodge has an 18-hole course that's one of the premiere places to play golf in the Rockies, with fairways that carve through thick forest amid majestic mountain vistas.

As for when to visit? Jasper National Park is an all-season stunner. In the summer, you can hike and bike amid greenery, and in winter, you can strap on the skis and head to Marmot Basin, an alpine area perfect for slicing through the deep, snowy valleys. Among the other popular activities are snowshoeing through Maligne Canyon, and skating at Mildred Lake.

Whether you're a thrill-seeker or a wildlife-watcher, you're bound to find the perfect itinerary of outdoor adventuring at Jasper National Park. And after enjoying the park by day, be sure to look to the skies to take in the galaxy of stars above. During the colder months, it's also a prime location to marvel at the otherworldly green glow of the Northern Lights.

ALPINE DIARY

Bring the binoculars and a bathing suit, as July is a prime month to explore the natural beauty of Jasper National Park. Trek mountain trails, spy colorful bird life through binoculars, and cool off under the spray of a waterfall. Top it off with a deep soak in the hot springs.

Five Days of Peaks and Valleys

DAY 1–2

Make your base in the friendly mountain town of Jasper. En route, drive through the Icefields Parkway, one of the grandest nature drives in Canada. The road unfolds parallel to the Continental Divide, and passes thundering waterfalls and thickly forested slopes. In Jasper, check in at the tourist office for a map of hiking and biking trails. For a relatively easy day trip from Jasper, drive to the shimmering lake at the base of Pyramid Mountain. An array of hiking trails meander through this area.

DAY 3

For a bird's-eye view of the park, hop on the Jasper SkyTram, which takes you up to sweeping views of glaciers and rivers framed by the Rockies. Head to the mighty Maligne Valley, and hike around Medicine Lake. Continue on to Maligne Lake, the park's largest, where you can take boat tours to Spirit Island.

DAY 4

Today, aim high – very high. Explore Mount Robson Provincial Park, which borders Jasper National Park's western flank. This large area of wilderness is watched over by Mount Robson, the highest peak in the Rockies. As you're trekking the trails, keep a lookout for the wildlife: the park is populated by an astonishing number of animals, including black bears, elks, whitetailed deers, and mountain goats.

DAY 5

Today is for relaxing. Soothe your muscles at the Miette Hot Springs, where you can soak in therapeutic waters, while taking in views of Fiddle Valley. In the evening, toast your visit with a hearty alpine meal and wine at one of Jasper's many restaurants.

Dos and Don'ts

- ✓ Check the conditions of hiking trails before you set out: the tourist office in Jasper, as well as the Parks Canada website (www.pc.gc.ca), has up-to-date information on trails.
- ✗ Don't forget your waterproof gear. This is mountain terrain, where even in the middle of summer, rain can fall without much warning.
- ✓ Check out Parks Canada Xplorers, a program geared to kids, with suggested itineraries and activities. Pick up Xplorers booklets at the park information offices.

GETTING THERE See map p327, B4
Treks into the Cordillera Blanca depart from Huaraz, 261 miles (420 km) north of Lima, a 7-hour drive away.

GETTING AROUND
Tour operators organize transport for treks and guides are compulsory. Huaraz is manageable on foot but taxis are ubiquitous.

WEATHER
In July, average daytime temperatures in Huaraz are around 70°F (20°C). On a trek, temperatures vary from 47°F (8°C) to 70°F (20°C), but can be freezing in the passes.

ACCOMMODATIONS
Cordillera Blanca Hiking offers alpine ascents and guided treks from US$120 per day, with equipment or US$1275 per person for a 4-day trek (including accommodation); www.cordillerablancahiking.com

Pony's Expeditions has a similar range of camping tours, plus mountain biking, from US$120 per day; www.ponyexpeditions.com

Hotel Colomba, a converted hacienda set in gardens on the river opposite the Huaraz town center, has simple double rooms from US$75; www.huarazhotel.com

EATING OUT
Food on the treks will be plentiful but basic campfire fare. In Huaraz, restaurants include Creperie Patrick and Café Andino, a popular meeting place with good lunches and coffee.

FURTHER INFORMATION
www.peru.travel/en-us

Peru's First Empire

Between 1000 BC and 500 BC, the Chavín people created the first great urban culture in South America. Despite the long duration of their empire, little is known about them, as few remains have survived. What we do know comes mostly from the scant remaining Chavín art. This is unique and beautiful, comprising series of interlocking patterns that seem abstract, but on closer inspection reveal religious images – notably a shamanic jaguar god.

CORDILLERA BLANCA

THE CORDILLERA BLANCA IN TROPICAL PERU is a breathtaking mountain range – the Andes seem to jostle each other here, forming a dramatic series of folds whose jagged tips are cloaked in ermine-white snow, while lower down, the indigo-hued forests and golden alpine grasslands are studded with myriad jewel-like lakes. At its heart lies Huascarán National Park – a UNESCO World Biosphere Reserve whose 27 icy peaks over 16,400 ft (5,000 m) glisten brightly against the deep-blue sky.

Archeological sites litter the region, crumbling on the sides of windy mountains, and freeze-dried mummies have been found on some of the highest summits. At the 1,300-year-old temple fortress of Chavín de Huantar, stone heads watch over a filigree of intricately carved walls and tunnels – the only surviving architectural testament to an empire which covered nearly half of northern Peru. The

Main: Trekkers at Lake Cullicocha in the Cordillera Blanca

Left: Viscacha, an alpine rodent closely related to the chinchilla

Right (left to right): Spectacular scenery from the edge of a glacier-fed lake; tents pitched for the night; mountaineering ascent in the Huascarán National Park

descendants of the Chavín people still live here in villages accessible only by foot or hoof, where Quechua, the ancient native language, is more commonly heard than Spanish. This life of growing quinoa (an indigenous cereal) and tending livestock has changed little since the 16th century.

Wildlife is abundant too, as spectacled bears roam the cloud forests in search of food, while llama-like vicuñas and viscachas nibble on the high slopes. Pumas hunt white-tailed deer in the mountain grasslands, and the air is thick with hundreds of species of rare and endangered birds, from huge soaring condors to tiny, flitting, emerald and iridescent-blue humming birds.

The only way to get to the heart of the Cordillera Blanca is on foot and, as treks involve long, steep stretches and overnight camping, walkers need to be active and adventurous. But the Cordillera Blanca's gain far outweighs its pain – the pure mountain air, magnificent views, and spectacular beauty more than compensate for the occasionally strenuous ascents and descents.

Above (top and bottom): Icy peak of Alpamayo in sunset colors; hiking through alpine grasslands overlooked by snowy crags

Above: Rock climbing in the Cordillera Blanca

TREKKING DIARY

There are shorter treks available, but to get a feel for the majesty of the Cordillera and see some wildlife too, it's best to spend five or six days trekking. You will also need a few days in Huaraz to acclimatize, as rushing straight from sea level into a long walk at high altitudes is a recipe for mountain sickness.

Ten High-Altitude Days

DAYS 1–3

Acclimatize in Huaraz, a pretty mountain town beautifully set against the snowy peaks of the Cordillera. On the third day, take a day tour to the Chavín de Huantar ruins, 2 hours away by road.

DAY 4

A dawn bus ride leads to the trailhead at Cashapampa where bags are transferred to mules. The trail cuts through lowland forest and grassland before ascending to the camp at 12,467 ft (3,800 m).

DAY 5

After an early dip in the icy water at Ichiccocha, make the climb to Alpamayo for sweeping panoramas over a wrinkled landscape of snowy crags and steep valleys.

DAY 6

A hearty breakfast is followed by a steep ascent to the Punta Unión pass, at 16,400 ft (5,000 m). The views over snow fields to forest-swathed valleys dotted with aquamarine lakes are as breathtaking as the climb.

DAY 7

Begin the day with a descent to Colcabamba, where you can stock up on provisions. A climb out of town leads to another viewpoint and the overnight camp.

DAY 8

The final climb to the 15,911-ft (4,850-m) Punta Yanayacu pass offers more incredible mountain vistas and a chance of seeing condors.

DAYS 9–10

The last trekking day is leisurely, with a walk to another mountain lake at Yanayacu and then along the Ulta Valley for the transfer back to Huaraz. Recuperate there, and then travel to Lima for your flight home.

Dos and Don'ts

- ✓ Book with a local firm. Many of the large agencies in Peru pay the Quechua guides they use a miniscule fraction of what you pay for your holiday.
- ✗ Don't trek without a pair of worn-in, sturdy boots. Blisters can ruin a walk and there are no medical facilities available.
- ✗ Don't leave for a trek without adequate supplies – warm clothes, plenty of sun cream, rain gear, a water bottle, Kendal mint cake or energy bars, a plastic bag to carry out all your rubbish, a sense of humor, and lots of resilience.
- ✓ Expect to tip the porters about 18 percent of your total tour cost at the end of the trek.

GETTING THERE See map p320, B2
Anacortes is the mainland terminus for the Washington State Ferries service to the San Juan Islands. The Airporter shuttle connects it with Sea-Tac International Airport and Seattle.

GETTING AROUND
Ferries stop at San Juan, Lopez, Shaw, and Orcas islands, where cars, bikes, motor scooters, and taxis can be rented. Public buses run on San Juan and Orcas islands.

WEATHER
Expect sunny skies, with highs of around 75°F (24°C) and lows of about 55°F (13°C).

ACCOMMODATIONS
Lopez Farm Cottages, set in pastureland and orchards outside Lopez Village, are from US$190 per night; www.lopezfarmcottages.com

Rosario Resort is a cliff-top mansion with modern annexes on Orcas Island; from US$190 per night; www.rosarioresort.com

The Kirk House is a 1907 Craftsman-style bed and breakfast in Friday Harbor with rooms from US$170 per night; www.kirkhouse.net

EATING OUT
Fresh shellfish and salmon with locally grown vegetables are sure bets on any menu. Top dining rooms in Rosario Resort and Roche Harbor (San Juan Island) serve innovative Northwest cuisine, while simpler restaurants abound.

FURTHER INFORMATION
www.guidetosanjuans.com

Orca Country

Orca whales are the stars of the show in the San Juans. These 25-ft- (8-m-) long creatures live in the cool waters of the Puget Sound in groups, or pods, of five or more, headed by females. They feed on the fish, squid, porpoises, dolphins, and other animals that thrive in the area. Orcas can sometimes be seen breaching and even sliding on to the shore to scare seals into the water and into the jaws of the rest of the pod. Maneuvers like this earned the orca its traditional name "killer whale." They are a majestic sight to behold.

Main: Flock of Bonaparte's Gulls above the Puget Sound

SAN JUAN ISLANDS

A first-time visitor who boards a ferry in Anacortes and glides into the San Juan archipelago may well have the sensation of entering an enchanted land. Here, in a maze of inlets and channels, more than 170 islands and islets emerge from the blue waters of the northern Puget Sound. Hillsides forested in old-growth Douglas fir rise from the shores, and the soaring snow-capped peaks of the Olympic Peninsula tower in the distance. Porpoises scythe through the water, while sealions and seals sun themselves on the rocks, and ospreys and bald eagles glide overhead, scanning the water for fish.

The presence of so much natural beauty is spectacular enough, but then something utterly remarkable happens – the calm waters erupt in a spout, fins cut the surface, a huge, shiny, arched, black mass rises out of the water, flashing a white underside. For half a second it hangs above the water, and then with a splash, it's gone. Another

Above: Picturesque lighthouse at Lime Kiln Point

Above (top and bottom): Cyclists relishing the winding coastal roads of San Juan Island; branches of the indigenous Douglas fir tree found all over the region

Below (top and bottom): Obstruction Pass in the San Juan Islands with Mount Baker in the distance; crimson anemone in the clear waters of a tidal pool

leap, another splash... a pod of the resident orca whales is feeding. Seeing these magnificent creatures encapsulates the magic of these islands, where every experience is memorable – viewing the landscape of sea, forests, and mountains from the top of Mount Constitution on Orcas Island; scouting the tidal pools on the Lopez Island beaches for agates, seahorses, and anemones; or just enjoying a glass of wine on a terrace overlooking seaside villages that hug the forested coasts.

These settings are the backdrop for as many outdoor adventures as an enthusiast can squeeze into a day. Kayaking is the preferred way to cut through the calm waters and explore the scores of inlets that etch the islands. More than 30 miles (48 km) of hiking paths lace Moran State Park, and the rolling landscapes of Lopez Island are especially appealing to cyclists, while scuba divers investigate undersea kelp forests and caverns brimming with octopuses and other marine life. Even if you aspire to nothing more active than a whale-watching cruise, the orcas never fail to make an appearance. As common as these sightings are, seeing an orca is always a thrill and, in the same way, these lovely islands grow more enchanting the better a visitor gets to know them.

ARCHIPELAGO DIARY

July is a lively month in the islands. The weather is excellent, and all activities are in full swing. In five days, you can enjoy the sights on the three major islands. To get the most out of your time, do not bring a car – the wait to drive on to a ferry can be 3 hours or even longer, but foot passengers can just walk aboard.

Five Days of Island Hopping

DAY 1 Make the 45-minute crossing to Lopez Island, often called "Slopez" for its easygoing lifestyle. Rent a bike and cycle on roads that roll over gentle hills, stopping at Shark Reef Park to explore the many tidal pools.

DAY 2 Continue on to Orcas Island by ferry and rent a car or a moped at Orcas Village. One of your first stops should be the 2,400-ft- (732-m-) high summit of Mount Constitution in Moran State Park for spectacular views over the islands and the mountains of the nearby Olympic Peninsula. Hike the 3-mile- (5-km-) long trail around Cascade Lake, also in Moran State Park, and end the day with a sunset sail from Deer Harbor, keeping a lookout for wildlife and whales.

DAY 3 Have your hotel pack a lunch and climb into a kayak for a full-day tour of the island's inlets and other nearby islets. Enjoy a cocktail and dinner with live entertainment at historic Rosario Resort in the evening.

DAY 4 Move on to San Juan Island and explore the lively waterfront of Friday Harbor. Visit the Whale Museum to learn about the orca whales that live in the waters surrounding the island. You may sight some of them from the beach at Lime Kiln Point State Park. Board a fishing charter and try your hand at landing a salmon.

DAY 5 Hike through San Juan Island National Historical Park, which commemorates the presence of 19th-century American and British troops on the island, to the top of Mount Young. Take an afternoon whale-watching cruise from Friday Harbor before leaving the islands.

Dos and Don'ts

- ✓ Bring binoculars for close-up views of whales, eagles, seals, and other wildlife. Don't forget the video camera to capture the orcas in motion.
- ✗ Don't leave trash behind on your hikes and kayak excursions.
- ✓ Pack lightly and only bring as much as you can comfortably handle. You'll be moving around quite a bit.
- ✓ Bring a pair of rubber shoes with you for walking on pebbly beaches or wading through water.

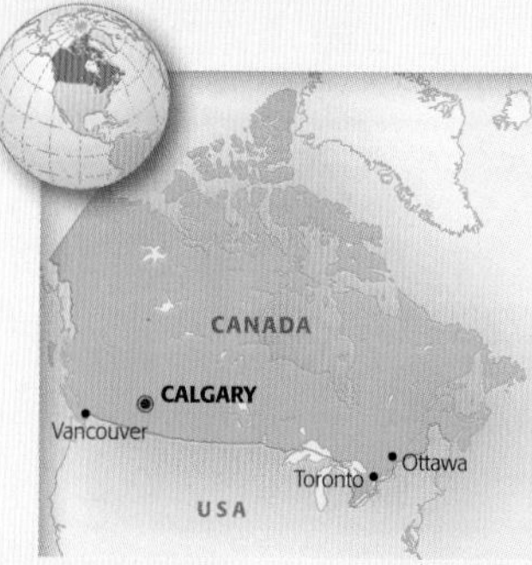

GETTING THERE See map p313, E6
Calgary's international airport is on the northeast edge of town, 20 minutes from the city center.

GETTING AROUND
Calgary's Light Rail Transit system, called the C-Train, has two stops at Stampede Park, and is a handy alternative to driving from your hotel.

WEATHER
Afternoon temperatures can hit 86°F (30°C) in July, but the average is closer to 75°F (24°C). Afternoon thunder showers are possible.

ACCOMMODATIONS
The Best Western Plus Suites Downtown has suites with kitchenettes or full kitchens; from US$160; www.bestwestern.com

The Kensington Riverside Inn is just minutes from downtown and offers free parking; junior suites from US$290; www.kensingtonriversideinn.com

The Fairmont Palliser Hotel is a historic hotel built in 1914 and restored to its original glory; family rooms from US$590; www.fairmont.com

EATING OUT
You'll find great meals available for around US$15–25 per person. Try the 1886 Buffalo Café in downtown's Eau Claire Market for hearty breakfasts and stroll downtown to Stephen Avenue for pubs, bistros, and fine restaurants.

FURTHER INFORMATION
www.visitcalgary.com

CALGARY

IT'S THE LONGEST EIGHT SECONDS IN THE WORLD—an eternity ticking by, as a cowboy grips with hand and knees and heart to the bull or the horse that's twisting and turning beneath him, doing everything in its power to buck him off. It's grit and it's gumption and it's the Calgary Stampede – ten action-packed days when every second counts, whether it is the eight-second qualifying bell in bull-, saddle bronc-, and bareback-busting; the race against the clock in tie-down roping, steer-wrestling, and barrel-racing; or the world-famous chuckwagon teams, emblazoned with colorful advertisements, thundering around the racetrack that's aptly known as the half-mile of hell.

They call the Stampede the greatest outdoor show on earth, and for good reason. It tempts the world's best cowboys and cowgirls to Calgary for the richest prize money in professional rodeo – and then it rolls out the red carpet for them, and for those who come to share in the action. In this most western of western Canadian cities, Stampede means that it's time to throw on hats and boots and

Main: Chuckwagon racing at the Calgary Stampede

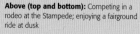

Above (top and bottom): Competing in a rodeo at the Stampede; enjoying a fairground ride at dusk

Below: Bar U Ranch National Historic Site

Head-Smashed-In Jump

A designated UNESCO World Heritage Site, Head-Smashed-In is the best preserved buffalo jump known. The native tribes, collectively known as the Blackfoot, were experts in the behavior of buffalo. By predicting the movement of the herds, they were able to hunt the beasts by running them over the precipice in great numbers. The animals were then carved up and the flesh dried for the coming months. There are still many buffalo skeletons and marked trails to be seen, and a superb interpretive center gives the site historical and cultural context.

offer a warm welcome. But it's more than that – it is a celebration of the pioneer spirit and ranching history that helped to found this part of the world, a living legacy of the days when herding on horseback was the only way to make a livelihood.

You can feel the energy as soon as you enter Stampede Park, on the edge of downtown and bordered by the Elbow River. A neon-trimmed fair lines the grounds, with gravity-defying rides for cowboys and non-cowboys alike. The Stampede Casino kicks into full gear, providing a high-end cousin to the bar-room poker of the old west. Cattle and horses vie for blue ribbons in agricultural competitions, while the Indian Village showcases the culture of the region's five First Nations peoples, including arts, crafts, and dancing. At the appropriately named Scotiabank Saddledome stadium, and throughout the grounds, top music artists boost the excitement.

You'll find the main events at the Grandstand where the itinerary goes almost as quickly as the wagons: rodeo in the afternoon and chuckwagon races in the early evening, followed by a high-energy musical show and topped off with fireworks. Prepare your best "yee-haw!" – you'll need it.

Above: Aerial view of the Calgary Stampede's grounds

RODEO DIARY

Prepare to spend two days fully immersing yourself in the excitement of the Stampede. Then take some time to explore the rest of this interesting city – its historic and elegant sandstone buildings, pioneering western heritage, thriving arts scene, and Olympic legacy. Calgary is also a gateway to four UNESCO World Heritage Sites.

A Week of Pioneer Spirit

Orient yourself with a trip up the Calgary Tower. Then hit the Stampede for the casino, midway, agricultural shows, Indian Village, and, of course, the rodeo and chuckwagon events, plus the Grandstand show. **DAYS 1–2**

Visit the Heritage Park Historical Village, on the edge of the sailboat-dotted Glenmore Reservoir, southwest of downtown. You'll find pioneer-era buildings, a steam locomotive, and even a paddlewheeler. **DAY 3**

There's plenty in town for the kids – Glenbow Museum is a must-see for its permanent exhibits dedicated to the Blackfoot and other First Nations peoples. For thrills, try Canada Olympic Park, with its zipline course, mountain-bike park, and Skyline Luge rides. **DAY 4**

Just east of downtown, Fort Calgary re-creates the late-1800s home of the North West Mounted Police, while nearby Calgary Zoo has wildlife from Canada to Africa. **DAY 5**

Visit Spruce Meadows in the city's southwest – consistently named the world's best outdoor show-jumping venue. From there, it's a quick trot down the Cowboy Trail to the Bar U Ranch National Historic Site. **DAY 6**

Leave the city behind to appreciate the dramatic Alberta scenery – head to the Rocky Mountains towns of Banff and Lake Louise, and then on to Jasper, past the ancient glaciers of the Columbia Icefield. Or day-trip 90 minutes northeast to the renowned Royal Tyrrell Museum and the land of the dinosaurs in Drumheller, or head two hours south to the ancient cliff-site hunting ground at Head-Smashed-In Buffalo Jump. **DAY 7**

Dos and Don'ts

- ✓ At night, Calgary becomes the city that doesn't sleep while the Stampede's in town – try Stampede Park.
- ✗ Don't delay in booking your accommodations – hotels in and around Calgary start to fill up as much as a year in advance for the 10 days of Stampede. The best rates and rooms go to those who make early reservations.
- ✓ Follow the cowboy example and wear a hat (and sunscreen) to protect yourself from the strong summer sun. Mountain breezes can fool you into thinking it's cooler than it really is.

JAN FEB MAR APR MAY JUN **JUL** AUG SEP OCT NOV DEC

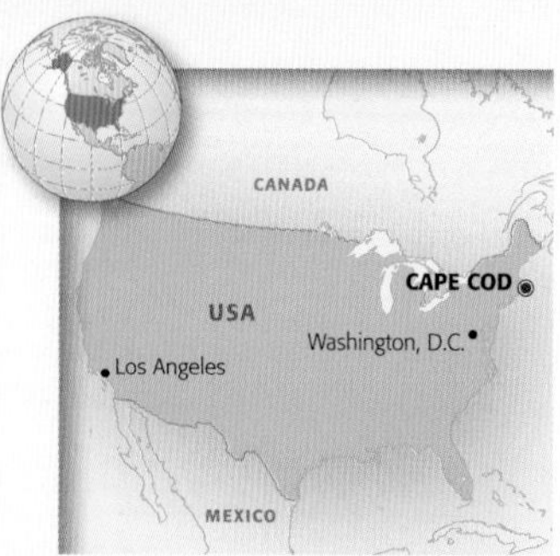

GETTING THERE **See map p316, H4–5**
Cape Air links Boston with Provincetown and Martha's Vineyard, while Nantucket Airlines links Hyannis (on Cape Cod) with Nantucket.. You can fly from Nantucket to Martha's Vineyard, but the boat trip is lovely.

GETTING AROUND
Explore Provincetown and its surroundings by bike. On Nantucket, rent a bike or hire taxis. A car is best for getting around Martha's Vineyard.

WEATHER
Expect plenty of sun, with highs reaching 80°F (27°C) and lows around 60°F (15°C).

ACCOMMODATIONS
The Jared Coffin House is one of Nantucket's finest mansions; doubles from US$295; www.jaredcoffinhouse.com

The Charlotte Inn is Edgartown's oldest and most elegant hostelry; doubles from US$395; www.thecharlotteinn.com

The charming Crowne Pointe Inn, Provincetown, is a former sea captain's home; doubles from US$400; www.crownepointe.com

EATING OUT
Seafood is everywhere, including local treats like clam chowder and lobster rolls. An order of fried clams at a clam shack is about US$15. A lobster dinner will cost around US$60.

FURTHER INFORMATION
provincetowntourismoffice.org
www.nantucket-ma.gov
www.mvol.com

Beacons of Hope

Over the past 300 years, some 3,000 shipwrecks have been recorded off Cape Cod, Nantucket, and Martha's Vineyard. Lighthouses were built to guide ships, and today these beacons, such as the one at Race Point near Provincetown, are a favorite of visitors. The Old Harbor Life-Saving Station in Provincetown is the last remnant of the Lifesavers, a corps of rescuers who patroled the beaches during storms to scour the rough seas for shipwrecks, and braved the surf to save as many souls as they could.

Above (left to right): Wharf at Menemsha; brightly colored buoys; striking red-clay cliffs at Aquinnah
Main: Cottage porch in Oak Bluffs

Above: Provincetown viewed from the top of Pilgrim Monument

CAPE COD

LIGHTHOUSES RISE ABOVE WIDE BEACHES, CLIFFS, AND SWEEPING DUNES, and stands of birches and pines grow to the edges of ponds and marshes. From some vantage points, a shoreline pounded by rugged surf stretches as far as the eye can see; from others, bays and inlets follow the curve of the land. In the many historic towns and villages, shingled houses and cottages surround proud old churches, and ports are home to fishing fleets that return from the wild sea with catches of oysters, mussels, lobsters, and swordfish. Some of America's easternmost, most beautiful, and most beloved shorelines are those that fringe Cape Cod and the islands of Nantucket and Martha's Vineyard. America's earliest history was forged on these shores: Norse explorers may have noted Cape Cod as early as the 10th century, and the Pilgrim Fathers made first landfall near Provincetown, at the end of the Cape, on November 20, 1620. The tiny island of Nantucket, 30 miles (48 km) south of Cape Cod, was the world's largest whaling port for much of the 19th century, and Martha's Vineyard, just off the southern coast of Cape Cod, was settled in 1642. Provincetown, Nantucket town, and Edgartown on Martha's Vineyard are especially historic and beautiful, and in all of them, many fine old houses have been converted to luxurious and romantic inns.

Cape Cod and the Islands have been summer resorts since the late 19th century. Natural wonders, especially the hundreds of miles of unspoiled beaches, are the major draw, and swimming, sailing, and other outdoor activities are popular. These are also places to enjoy spectacular sunsets, leisurely dinners overlooking moonlit bays, and exploring shops on quaint lanes. Nantucket is an exclusive retreat for the wealthy, and Martha's Vineyard counts many famous politicians and other celebrities among its summer visitors. As the song says, "if you're fond of sand dunes and salty air, quaint little villages here and there," this far-flung corner of the country will capture your heart.

Shingled houses and cottages surround proud old churches, and fishing fleets return with oysters, mussels, lobsters.

Inset: Rose-covered cottage on Nantucket Island
Below (left and right): Commercial Street, Provincetown; Nantucket beach

SEASHORE DIARY

You could certainly spend over a week on Cape Cod and the Islands, but seven days allows you time to savor the best of these historic and enchanting land- and sea-scapes. A short flight from Hyannis to Nantucket and a pleasant sea journey from Nantucket to Martha's Vineyard make it easy to get from place to place.

A Week on the Cape

DAY 1 Settle into your hotel in Provincetown and get into the swing of things with some people-watching and window-shopping along Commercial Street. Rent a bike for an evening ride to Herring Cove to watch the sunset, then dine at a waterside restaurant.

DAY 2 Climb the 116 steps of the Pilgrim Monument for a great view, before hitting the beach at Race Point. Take a sunset sail aboard the schooner *Bay Lady II*.

DAY 3 Bike along the Province Lands Trail or hike across the breakwater to Long Point. After lunch, take a whale-watching cruise to the waters of Stellwagen Bank. Maybe end your day with a clam bake on the beach.

DAY 4 Fly from Hyannis to Nantucket. After settling into one of Nantucket town's historic inns, stroll the cobblestone streets and do some shopping for antiques and folk art along Centre Street.

DAY 5 Make a morning visit to charming Siasconset village and its excellent beach. In the afternoon, take a Nantucket Historical Association Guided Walking Tour, then watch the sunset at Madaket Beach.

DAY 6 Board the boat for Martha's Vineyard. Explore Edgartown, where you can stay in one of the many old inns, and take the ferry to Chappaquiddick for a walk through Cape Pogue Wildlife Refuge to the adjoining beach.

DAY 7 Spend a day exploring the rest of the island: Oak Bluffs, with its gingerbread cottages; the fishing village of Menemsha; and Aquinnah, with its spectacular cliffs.

Dos and Don'ts

- ✓ If hiking, take precautions against deer ticks, which carry Lyme Disease – tuck trousers into socks, use insect repellent, and check your skin after being outdoors.
- ✗ Don't walk on dune grass and other fragile plantings. If an area is cordoned off, don't cross the rope.
- ✓ When swimming or surfing be mindful of the dangerous undertow. Only swim where it is safe to do so – take advice on that from locals.
- ✓ Be sure to try all the fabulous local seafood specialties.

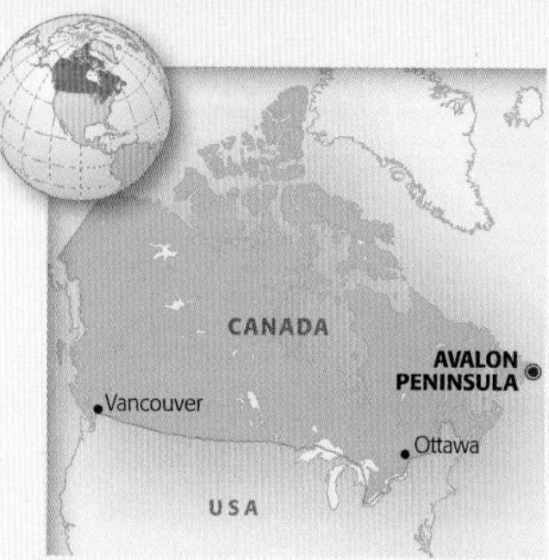

GETTING THERE See map p314, I5
Fly into St. John's International Airport, rent a car, and drive 4 miles (6.5 km) downtown.

GETTING AROUND
A car is needed for trips to seabird colonies, villages, and to venture beyond St. John's.

WEATHER
Average temperatures in July are 57°F (14°C) along the coast, with afternoon highs reaching 68°F (20°C) on sunny days. Expect periods of wet weather and chilly evenings.

ACCOMMODATIONS
The historic Murray Premises Hotel near the wharf in St. John's was a warehouse in the 1840s; rooms from US$160; www.murraypremiseshotel.com

The Sheraton Hotel Newfoundland in St. John's offers fine dining; rooms from US$200; www.sheratonhotelnewfoundland.com

Manning's Bird Island Resort near Cape St Mary's offers clean accommodation; rooms from US$90; www.birdislandresort.com

EATING OUT
Cod tongues, caribou stew, fish and chips, seal flipper pie, and Jigg's dinner (boiled vegetables and salted meat) are traditional Newfoundland fare, with baked apple pie or steamed pudding for dessert.

FURTHER INFORMATION
www.newfoundlandlabrador.com
www.stjohns.ca

The Rock

Newfoundland, an island fondly known as The Rock by those who call it home, is a world apart. Fiercely independent, locals are fun-loving, hard-working folk. Their ancestors arrived by sea from Britain, France and Ireland centuries ago to fish the icy Atlantic waters and, over the years, many chose to stay through the long winters rather than sail back to Europe. They speak a lilting form of English with traces of Elizabethan phrasing. Humor and toe-tapping music fill their evenings, helped along by the local brand of rum, Newfoundland Screech.

Thousands of golden-headed gannets cover the sea stack rising offshore, filling the blue sky with a whirlwind motion.

Inset: Gannets on Bird Rock in Cape St. Mary's Ecological Reserve

Left (left and right): The view from Cape Spear; caribou

Right (left to right): Cannon on Signal Hill, St. John's; an isolated house at Tors Cove; colorful facades of the houses in St. John's

Main: A brilliant summer sunrise over Cape Spear Lighthouse

AVALON PENINSULA

The cacophony of tens of thousands of nesting seabirds is heard long before Bird Rock in Cape St. Mary's Ecological Reserve comes into view. The foot-worn path across the coastal barrens is lined with fields of mosses, lichens, and wild iris trimmed by sheep grazing in the meadow high above the sea. The path rises to the rocky edge of the cliff, leading into clouds of birds. Thousands of golden-headed gannets cover the sea stack, rising and filling the blue sky with a whirlwind of motion. The mammoth rock is packed with nesting seabirds feeding chicks and preening mates jostling their neighbors. Periodically the gannets spread their wings to soar out to sea to fish. This then is the fantastic introduction to the winged wonders of Newfoundland's Avalon Peninsula.

The preserve is just one of the many natural delights along the narrow road that circles the Avalon Peninsula. The small villages that cling to the rocky shore are known as outports, with the earliest dating from the 1600s.

Above: Pouch Cove, an outport on the Avalon Peninsula

COASTAL ROAD DIARY

July is high season in St. John's and the Avalon Peninsula. Although there won't be huge crowds, rooms can still be hard to find, so book ahead. Four days is enough time to see the best of the area's natural wonders. If you have another day to explore, head over to Terra Nova National Park for a day of hiking.

Four Days on The Rock

DAY 1

Drive up Signal Hill in St. John's for the exceptional views. While you're up there, admire the stone Cabot Tower and explore the fascinating Johnson Geo Center. Then drive to Quidi Vidi Battery Historic Site. Head out next to Cape Spear Lighthouse, the most easterly point in North America. Return to St. John's and explore the boutique shops, churches, and waterfront. End your day with dinner and a pub visit for lively music and a bit of Screech.

DAY 2

Head south to Bay Bulls and take a boat trip to Witless Bay Ecological Reserve to watch the comical puffins, kittiwakes, mures, and graceful humpback whales in the icy waters. In the fishing village of Ferryland, visit the Colony of Avalon museum and watch archeologists search for artifacts from the 1620s.

DAY 3

Continue south through a remote plain of sub-Arctic tundra along the rocky coast. Explore the quaint fishing villages, watch for wild caribou near Trepassey, and stop at the observation platform in St. Vincent's to look for whales. Visit the Salmonier Nature Park to glimpse the animals and birds native to Newfoundland and Labrador. At Cape St. Mary's Ecological Reserve, walk along the footpath to see the seabird rookery.

DAY 4

Return to St. John's and visit the museum and art gallery at The Rooms. Then head to the Railway Coastal Museum to learn about the trains and boats that supported Newfoundland's fishing villages before highways were built. At Pippy Park, the Memorial University Botanical Garden features native flora and butterflies. Wind up with dinner in the Historic area.

Dos and Don'ts

- ✓ Be sure to plan ahead for accommodation; it can get booked up quickly.
- ✗ Don't look for fancy rooms or restaurants outside of St. John's, but do expect warm hospitality.
- ✓ Ask for help when you need it; the local people are amazingly friendly and helpful when asked.
- ✓ Take along a box lunch and warm clothes when traveling beyond St. John's, as local restaurants can be far apart and the weather can get chilly.

Most of the peninsula remains wild and remote, with vast open plains of sub-Arctic tundra where great herds of caribou graze. The cold blue waters of the Atlantic Ocean teem with capelin, providing a feast for whales and seabirds along the coast. Boats at Bay Bulls carry passengers into Witless Bay Ecological Reserve where they can watch humpback whales dive and resurface with a great whoosh, at times breaching far out of the depths with sheets of water streaming from their backs.

St. John's is one of the oldest settlements in North America, and the most easterly. From the top of Signal Hill the view stretches in all directions. The narrow rock-bounded entrance of St. John's Harbour has offered sanctuary to ships for four centuries, beginning with Basque fishermen who arrived in the 1500s to harvest cod for the European market. Surrounding the harbor, the characterful old town with its cobbled streets and colorful clapboard row houses buzzes with plenty of specialty shops and restaurants. At night the lilting strains of fiddles blend with the laughter drifting out of the pubs lined along historic Water Street that specialize in warming up cold travelers – just as they have for centuries.

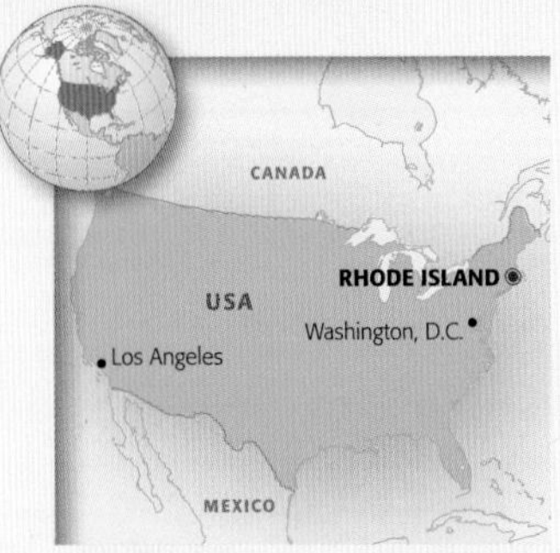

GETTING THERE See map p316, H5
Newport is 26 miles (42 km) from Providence's airport. Mystic is 49 miles (79 km) from Newport and 42 miles (68 km) from Providence. From Newport, ferries to Block Island take 2 hours.

GETTING AROUND
The towns are compact and walkable, but a car is essential for trips around the region.

WEATHER
July brings warm, humid conditions. Average temperatures hover around 80°F (26°C).

ACCOMMODATIONS
The Mystic Hilton is situated directly across from the Mystic Aquarium; doubles from US$170; www.hiltonmystic.com

The Newport Marriott is situated on Newport Harbor close to several attractions; doubles from US$370; www.marriott.com

Newport's secluded, upscale Castle Hill Inn & Resort is on a scenic, 40-acre (16-ha) peninsula; doubles from US$895; www.castlehillinn.com

EATING OUT
Try lobster at the summertime seafood shacks. Mystic Pizza, famous from the 1988 film, is popular for its cheap pies. In Newport, the Red Parrot and Brick Alley Pub are casual, lively eateries.

FURTHER INFORMATION
www.gonewport.com
www.blockislandinfo.com

NEWPORT

THE THOUGHT OF A FEW DAYS BY OR ON THE SPARKLING SEA in New England is pure heaven for many people. And when it comes to a seaside retreat, there's no better place than America's sailing capital: Newport, Rhode Island. Throw in a concert or two at one of the country's largest classical music festivals, and you have the ingredients for a perfect summer weekend on many levels.

Newport has attracted a legion of admirers and is proud of its rich history. More than a century ago, wealthy families from all over the country chose this remote port as the place to build their summer homes. And what fabulous homes they were, with the likes of the Vanderbilts and Astors sinking millions into mansions that still impress. While he was President, John F. Kennedy spent his summers here, and countless dignitaries have come to watch the world's premier sailing

Main: A racing yacht at a sailing regatta, Newport, Rhode Island

Above (top to bottom): Newport Bridge at dusk; the schooner *Adirondack* sailing past New York Yacht Club's Newport clubhouse; pianist Piotr Anderszewski performing at Marble House, Newport Music Festival

Bottom (left to right): Local lobster and clams at a clam bake; Sailboats race past Block Island North Lighthouse; Newport Harbor, Rhode Island; beluga whale, Mystic Aquarium

Architectural Opulence

Visitors to Rhode Island are often blown away by the splendor of its historic houses, most of which, built in the Gilded Age of the late 19th century, have been immaculately maintained and restored. Newport's famed Cliff Walk is an ideal starting point to admire the mansions, and take in the view of the rugged coastline. Don't miss The Breakers *(below)*, built for Cornelius Vanderbilt II in 1895 at a cost of $7 million (roughly $150 million today).

regatta, the America's Cup. Today, the city provides visitors with plenty of sightseeing and nautical attractions, not to mention shopping and dining opportunities.

In keeping with the sailing theme, no trip to the area would be complete without a stop in Mystic, Connecticut's loveliest summertime haven. A must for history buffs as well as serious sailors, the town's old seaport provides a glimpse into America's nautical past. But if skiffs and schooners aren't your thing, Mystic still has plenty to offer including a nationally acclaimed aquarium (most notable for its beluga whales) and a picturesque downtown that's chock full of inviting galleries, shops, and restaurants.

For a quieter but no less scenic outing, visitors should take the ferry to Block Island, a small parcel of land off the Rhode Island coast whose year-round population only numbers in the hundreds. The island possesses many attractive hiking trails and historic Victorian buildings, yet manages to maintain a nostalgic, small-town ambience that's hard to beat.

Above: The harbor in Mystic Seaport

ISLAND DIARY

July is warm and a perfect time to visit one of southern New England's most charming destinations. Places such as Newport and Mystic can be explored with just one night's stay in each, as both have compact centers. Don't miss Block Island, a scenic getaway that's just a quick ferry ride from Newport.

A Seaside Weekend

DAY 1

Spend the day at Mystic Seaport, the nation's largest maritime museum. Sailors of all stripes will have to be peeled away from the extensive collection of historic ships to explore the main draw, a recreation of a 19th-century seaport. Enjoy a lobster lunch at an old standby such as Abbott's Lobster in the Rough or S&P Oyster Co. Take a stroll through Mystic's quaint downtown before tipping back a nightcap at a cozy pub – the Harp and Hound is a good one.

DAY 2

Head for Newport and take a brisk walk along the 3.5-mile (5.6-km) Cliff Walk, popping into a couple of breathtaking mansions along the way. Classical music enthusiasts can attend the Newport Music Festival held at the mansions in July. Sport fans shouldn't miss the International Tennis Hall of Fame, which is housed in an ornate casino that dates back to 1880. Wander along Thames Street to pick up some souvenirs or freshly made fudge before heading off on a sunset cocktail cruise around the harbor. Cap off the day with a gourmet seafood dinner at an upscale waterfront restaurant such as The Mooring or One Bellevue.

DAY 3

Hop on the ferry for the 2-hour ride to tiny Block Island. A quiet place, the island boasts natural treasures that include 17 miles (27 km) of beaches and 32 miles (51 km) of trails. After a hike along one of these trails, make for commercial Water Street and chow down on a lobster roll or fried clam basket at the Harbor Grill.

Dos and Don'ts

- ✓ You won't find a market on every corner, so be sure to have supplies of sunscreen and water with you at all times.
- ✗ Don't forget to double-check the Block Island ferry schedule. With no other means of making it back to the mainland, you don't want to miss the last ferry back.
- ✓ If you have rented a car, allow time for finding parking when in Newport. Public parking is scarce in summer. Private lots are dotted throughout the city, though many are expensive.
- ✗ Don't forget comfortable footwear, as the compact town centers lend themselves to lots of walking, with most exploration possible only on foot.

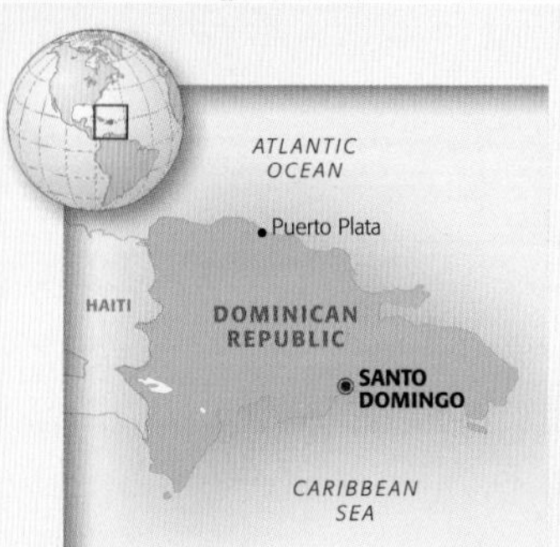

GETTING THERE See map p325, F4
Santo Domingo, Punta Cana, and Puerto Plata all have international airports. From the airport, many resorts will arrange transport, or you can easily catch a taxi.

GETTING AROUND
To explore, rent a car and get a good map. For day tours, take a taxi with a certified guide as a driver. Buses run between all major towns.

WEATHER
July temperatures can reach 86°F (30°C), only falling to 76°F (25°C) at night. Tropical rainstorms shower the island regularly.

ACCOMMODATIONS
The breezy Velero Beach Resort is fronted by a small reef; doubles from US$100; www.velerobeach.com

Enjoy a quiet stay at the Art Deco Hotel Villa Colonial; doubles from US$85; www.villacolonial.net

Relax at the charming Casa Colonial Beach and Spa Resort in Puerto Plata; doubles from US$290; www.casacolonialhotel.com

EATING OUT
Restaurants serve a wide range of fresh seafood and traditional dishes, like sancocho, a hearty soup with grilled meats and tubers. Los Tres Cocos, in Puerto Plata, and Miro, in Cabarete, serve tasty menus.

FURTHER INFORMATION
www.godominicanrepublic.com

Take a dip in the sparkling sea and then ease into the night against the backdrop of the hip-swaying tunes of merengue.

Main: Traditional dancing in Santo Domingo

Merengue: The Soul of the DR

Originating in the Dominican Republic in the mid-19th century, merengue resonates at the very soul of the DR. Merengue bands generally consist of a five-person lineup of the sax, accordion, tambora, güira, and bass guitar. The DR has exported its merengue music around the world, and top stars include classic performers like Wilfrido Vargas to contemporary musicians such as Juan Luis Guerra and Eddy Herrera. And, when you fly back home, you don't need to leave the music behind: stores around the island sell merengue CDs.

DOMINICAN REPUBLIC

Come for the coast – stay for the culture. The island of Hispaniola – the second-largest in the Caribbean, and the tenth-most populous in the world – encompasses Haiti in the west, and the Dominican Republic (or the DR, as it's often called) in the east. The island's size translates into a remarkable geographical diversity, from soaring peaks to deserts of cacti as well as unspoilt, sun-splashed beaches around every bend. For a broad sampling of the DR's natural bounty, center your trip on the island's north coast, traveling from Puerto Plata to the Samaná Peninsula. Puerto Plata is the oldest city on the north coast, exuding an air of history, commerce, but also that unmistakable relaxed looseness of Caribbean life. Whilst in the city, saunter the Malecón, take a dip in the sparkling sea and then ease into the night with a rum-spiked cocktail against the backdrop of the hip-swaying tunes of merengue.

Above: El Limon Waterfall, Eastern Peninsula De Samana

Inset: Local artist painting

Left (left to right): Windsurfer in Cabarete; Levantado Island; Fortaleza San Felipe

Right: Gazebo and Statue of General Luperon, Puerto Plata

The island is also the perfect location to feed your sense of adventure. Cabarete, east of Puerto Plata, is one of the watersports capitals of the Caribbean. Thanks to powerful winds and waves, surfers flock to this former fishing enclave. The good news is that all levels are welcome, from first-time body-surfers to pro kitesurfers. Top off your exploration of the island's north coast by venturing to the welcoming Samaná Peninsula, which is a blend of rugged nature and relaxed sands, with a number of luxurious all-inclusive resorts in the area.

Throughout your explorations of the DR, make sure to leave time to join in the country's many famous fiestas. In many countries festivals are a special occasion, but in the Dominican Republic, they're a way of life. Among the top festivals are the Cabarete Sand Castle Festival in February, when the beaches turn into an open-air museum of sand sculptures; Semana Santa (Holy Week) festivals in April, including at Cabral, where the locals don ferocious demon masks and pretend to punish passers-by with whips; and the Festival de Merengue (July–August) in Santo Domingo, when the streets and plazas explode with the sound of lively merengue bands.

DOMINICAN DIARY

The north coast of the Dominican Republic offers a rich overview of the island: verdant jungle, palm-shaded beaches, small fishing villages – and the best water sports in the country, if not the Caribbean. Plus, you'll also find a host of luxury resorts, with seafront suites, spas and al fresco restaurants.

Five Days of Coastal Treasures

DAYS 1–2

Fly into the Puerto Plata International Airport, and head to your resort. If the sun's shining, which is more than likely, plan to spend your first day simply lolling about on the gorgeous beaches, like the popular Playa Dorada and Playa Cofresi. Once you've had your fill, explore the island's history at Fortaleza San Felipe, a Spanish fortress that was completed in 1577. Hop on a cable car to take in a view of the coastline from the Isabel de Torres observation tower. The sea around Puerto Plata is called the Amber Coast, because of the sizeable deposits found here and you can pick up quality amber from the shops in town. Also worth a visit is the Parque Nacional La Isabela, which includes the ruins of La Isabela, Christopher Coumbus's settlement on the island. After the sun sets, head to one of the clubs on the Malecón, like Big Lee's Beach Bar, to dance to merengue.

DAY 3

Follow the winds to Cabarete, which is the surfing capital of the Dominican Republic. A huge array of outfitters offer classes and tours for all levels, including kitesurfing and windsurfing. After the sun sets, hang out at one of Cabarete's many casual beach bars, where you can tap your toes to live salsa while sipping cocktails.

DAYS 4–5

Spend your last few days at the Samaná Peninsula, which has some of the loveliest beaches in the Dominican Republic. Head to Playa Bonita for a day of snorkeling and sunning on the sands. On your second day, explore Las Galeras and Playa Rincón, which unfolds against a backdrop of looming cliffs.

Dos and Don'ts

- ✓ Make time to leave your all-inclusive resort: it's well worth venturing out to stroll the Malecón (boardwalk) and enjoy a drink at a local bar.
- ✗ Don't pick a tour operator without first shopping around. The island is filled with outfitters, so it's important to do research on pricing and what's offered before signing up.
- ✓ Plan a return visit to the Samaná Peninsula from mid-January to mid-March, when humpback whales migrate through the area.

AUGUST

Where to Go: **August**

Summer is in full swing in the northern hemisphere, with much of North America getting very hot. Ocean breezes keep things cooler along the coasts, while inland lakes and mountains offer their own refreshing respite. In the Rocky Mountains temperatures can plummet below freezing at night, though days will be gloriously sunny; Santa Fe is kept pleasant by its higher elevation. Even famously forbidding Newfoundland is a joy to explore at this time of year, when it is at its warmest. In the southern hemisphere, many of the South American countries offer good conditions, with rainfall and humidity at a manageable level, and daytime temperatures not prohibitively hot. Below you will find all the destinations in this chapter and some extra suggestions to provide further inspiration.

FESTIVALS AND CULTURE

BARRETOS A lively display by flag-waving cowboys

BARRETOS RODEO FESTIVAL
BRAZIL

Enjoy rodeo, Brazilian-style

Don your stetson for Wild West action like bucking broncos and bull-riding, followed by evenings of sizzling steaks and samba.

See pp202–3

POTOSÍ
BOLIVIA

Marvel at the world's highest city

With an altitude of over 13,125 ft (4,000 m), Potosí is an atmospheric colonial city.

www.potosy.com.bo

WISCONSIN STATE FAIR
WISCONSIN, USA

All the fun of the fair

Feast on cream puffs, relax to live music, or jump on thrilling fairground rides at this annual extravaganza.

See pp182–3

LEADVILLE
COLORADO, USA

Historic city with stunning natural scenery

Leadville boasts a historic center of old red-brick Victorian-era streets and breathtaking views of the surrounding mountain peaks.

www.leadville.com

UNFORGETTABLE JOURNEYS

THE VIKING TRAIL The beautiful Tablelands, Gros Morne National Park

THE VIKING TRAIL
NEWFOUNDLAND, CANADA

Follow in the footsteps of the Vikings

If exploring wild tundra landscapes with few people and roaming caribou appeals, take the Viking Trail across Newfoundland.

See pp192–3

DEVIL'S TOWER NATIONAL MONUMENT
WYOMING, USA

Surreal geological landmark

Hike around this soaring volcanic outcrop, whose rock walls tower above the Belle Fourche River.

www.nps.gov/deto

DRIVE THE ICEFIELDS PARKWAY
ALBERTA, CANADA

Spectacular highway

Stretching 143 miles (230 km) between Jasper and Lake Louise, the Icefields Parkway traverses an unforgettably rugged landscape.

www.icefieldsparkway.ca

HIKING THE GREAT DIVIDE TRAIL
BRITISH COLUMBIA, CANADA

An amazing trekking challenge

Tackle this epic trail, which snakes for around 750 miles (1,200 km) along the Continental Divide, traversing six national parks.

www.greatdividetrail.com

LA PAZ TO COROICO BY ROAD
BOLIVIA

Heart-stopping highway

Travel the highway that descends 3,500 m (1,067 ft) in just 40 miles (64 km) through mountain scenery.

www.trekker.co.il/english/la_paz

NATURAL WONDERS

YELLOWSTONE NATIONAL PARK Plains buffalo grazing in the park

YELLOWSTONE NATIONAL PARK
WYOMING, USA

An American wilderness

Yellowstone National Park is a great place to see bears, wolves, eagles, elk, steamy geysers, and herds of great thundering bison.

See pp188–9

GLACIER BAY NATIONAL PARK
ALASKA, USA

Dramatic coastal wilderness

Cruise through the fjords of Glacier Bay, home to no fewer than 15 glaciers, including the spectacular Grand Pacific Glacier.

www.nps.gov/glba/

MANÚ NATIONAL PARK
PERU

Wildlife in abundance

Visit one of the most important national parks in the world and see giant otters, caymans, and flocks of macaws.

See pp200–1

"The park is so isolated in parts that several indigenous groups rarely have contact with outsiders."

Previous page: Butterflies sipping minerals from a riverbank, Manú National Park, Peru

Weather Watch

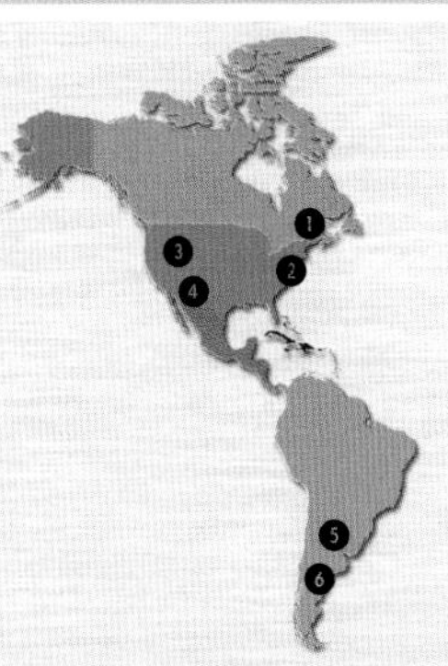

❶ Québec, Canada Summer has hit southeastern Canada. As ever, though, you should expect the unexpected, and be prepared for afternoon thunderstorms.

❷ The Hamptons, USA August is peak season in the swanky Hamptons and for very good reason – the beaches are by far at their best at this time of year, with warm waters and balmy ocean breezes.

❸ Yellowstone National Park, USA Long, warm days offer delightful conditions for exploring the surreal landscape of Yellowstone. Temperatures plummet at night, however, and there may be the odd afternoon storm.

❹ Santa Fe, USA At a higher elevation than the deserts to the south, New Mexico's loveliest city offers dazzling sunshine in August, along with crisp, starlit nights.

❺ Paraguay August is dry and pleasant in Paraguay; the summer heat has yet to kick in and humidity is low, making this cooler spring period the best time to explore the land-locked country.

❻ Argentina Much of Argentina is enjoying a warm winter. The northern regions are cooler and drier than during the rest of the year. Salta, at the foothills of the Andes, boasts sunny days, low humidity, and cold nights.

LUXURY AND ROMANCE

THE HAMPTONS The lighthouse in the hamlet of Montauk

MENDOCINO
CALIFORNIA, USA

A beautiful, tranquil slice of old America

This wonderfully preserved little town on the California coast has hotels full of charm, fine food, a laid-back feel, and fabulous sunsets.

www.mendocino.com

THE HAMPTONS
NEW YORK STATE, USA

Manhattan society's favorite seaside escape

Here you can rub shoulders with the rich and famous or chill out in a charming colonial oceanside hideaway – the choice is yours.

See pp194–5

QUÉBEC CITY
QUÉBEC, CANADA

A sliver of old France in the New World

Old Québec combines the best of both worlds – the romance of the Old World, with the excitement, comfort, and luxury of the new.

See pp186–7

SALTA & JUJUY
ARGENTINA

Colonial charm and colorful canyons

Enjoy the amazing colors of the Quebrada de las Conchas by day, and snuggle up by the fire at night with the local red wine.

See pp190–1

MACKINAC ISLAND
MICHIGAN, USA

Idyllic and old-fashioned island charm

It's small, it's quiet, it's romantic and only horses and carriages and bikes are allowed on the island.

See pp196–7

ACTIVE ADVENTURES

PARAGUAY Horseback riding in the forest in Gran Chaco

PARAGUAY
PARAGUAY

Go off the beaten track in Paraguay

Escape the crowds in Paraguay, which is filled with history and nature, including colonial buildings, Jesuit ruins and savannah grasslands

See pp204–5

APOSTLE ISLANDS
WISCONSIN, USA

Island retreat on lovely Lake Superior

These 22 wonderfully windswept lakeshore islands offer outdoor enthusiasts a wide ride of excellent water sports.

www.nps.gov/apis

"Roam the flourishing countryside, and you may be the only visitor that anyone has seen in days, if not weeks."

KAIETEUR FALLS
GUYANA

One of the world's most spectacular waterfalls

Hike around these majestic falls, which tumble for almost 755 ft (230 m) amid a pristine landscape of tropical rain forest.

exploreguyana.org/kaieteur-falls

COLUMBIA RIVER
OREGON, USA

A gorgeous inland utopia for windsurfers

The gorge of the Columbia in Oregon creates unique conditions for windsurfing enthusiasts.

www.el.com/to/hoodriver

MOUNT COTOPAXI
ECUADOR

A breathtaking test for the adventurous cyclist

Explore the stunning region around Mount Cotopaxi by mountain bike.

www.ecuadorexplorer.com

FAMILY GETAWAYS

SANTA FE Hispanic dancers at El Rancho de las Golondrinas

"Nestled in the Sangre de Cristo Mountains, the beautiful city of Santa Fe proudly calls itself 'The City Different'.

SANTA FE
NEW MEXICO, USA

Colorful desert city

The unique blend of Native Pueblo, Spanish, and cowboy cultures are displayed throughout this city in its many museums and ancient monuments.

See pp184–5

PAWLEYS ISLAND
SOUTH CAROLINA, USA

One of the east coast's best kept secrets

Laid-back family getaway with pristine beaches, excellent surf, and plenty of family activities ranging from biking to crabbing.

www.townofpawleysisland.com

PRINCE EDWARD ISLAND
CANADA

Anne of Green Gables country

Cycle or drive through the pastoral countryside and visit Green Gables House, the inspiration for L.M. Montgomery's classic novel.

www.tourismpei.com

LOS ANGELES
CALIFORNIA, USA

One of the USA's premier family destinations

Home to an unrivaled array of blockbuster attractions, including the world-famous Disneyland® and the popular Universal Studios.

www.losangeles.com/attractions

MAMMOTH CAVE NATIONAL PARK
KENTUCKY, USA

World's longest cave system

An enormous subterranean wonderland full of majestic caverns and perplexing limestone labyrinths.

See pp198–9

BRYCE CANYON
UTAH, USA

Weird and wonderful scenery that never fails to fascinate

Famed for its bizarre stone pillars known as "hoodoos," this Utah canyon can be toured by car and then further explored on paths.

www.nps.gov/brca

GETTING THERE **See map p316, B4**
The Wisconsin State Fair is held at the State Fair Park in West Allis, Milwaukee. Mitchell International Airport, 6 miles (10 km) from the city center, is linked to the city by Amtrak trains and shuttle and bus services.

GETTING AROUND
Milwaukee's bus system (Milwaukee County Transit System) is a good way to get to the fair. Park-and-ride shuttles also operate.

WEATHER
August temperatures average highs of 79°F (26°C) and lows of 62°F (17°C). It is the wettest month, but showers are short-lived.

ACCOMMODATIONS
For old-world charm try Knickerbocker on the Lake; doubles from US$150; www.knickerbockeronthelake.com

Hotel Metro is a luxurious boutique hotel; doubles from US$220; www.hotelmetro.com

The upscale Ambassador Hotel is in the heart of downtown; doubles from US$230; www.ambassadormilwaukee.com

EATING OUT
The fair has a vast range of food options, from traditional bratwurst to buffalo burritos. Outside the fair, go for a butter burger at Solley's Grille or check out the French-inspired Lake Park Bistro in leafy Lake Park.

FURTHER INFORMATION
www.wistatefair.com

Cream Puff Crazy

Appearing only during the 11 days of the fair, the legendary cream puff – a fluffy, calorie-laden delight – has been produced by a team of bakers and dairy farmers for more than 80 years. And what a team it is – more than 200 employees work all hours to produce the 50,000 cream puffs sold daily. Thousands of people line up, phone in, or drive through for the pastries, piled high with cream from Wisconsin's best dairy cows. An even sweeter treat is the Celebrity Cream Puff Eating Contest, featuring a slew of local celebrities eating giant puffs without using their hands.

Above (left and right): Biomes at Mitchell Park Conservatory; the ultra-modern Milwaukee Art Museum
Main: Exciting funfair ride illuminated against the night sky, Wisconsin State Fair

Above: Boats docked on the Milwaukee River

WISCONSIN STATE FAIR

STRAINS OF LIVE MUSIC DRIFT ACROSS THE FAIRGROUND, mingling with the squeals of delighted children on Ferris wheels, the lively chatter of picnicking families, and the din of noisy farmyard animals. This cheerful, chaotic atmosphere fills the warm summer air at the annual Wisconsin State Fair – an 11-day extravaganza showcasing the very best of the state, from livestock events and horticultural displays to food stalls, homebrewery exhibitions, and open-air concerts.

A beloved summer ritual since 1851, the fair has grown to host more than one million visitors annually. Today the range of events is breathtaking, but the focus is still Wisconsin's agricultural heritage. Watching a goat being milked or a calf being born is a favorite spectacle with kids and an eye-opener for anyone who wasn't brought up on a farm. Youngsters of all ages will also enjoy the interactive events. Sign up for the wacky "Moo-la-palooza" – a mooing contest – and you could walk off with US$1,000. From cup-stacking to Hula-Hooping, the spirit of honest competition is palpable.

Strains of live music drift across the fairground, mingling with the squeals of delighted children on Ferris wheels.

The fair is also famed for the quality and variety of its food. Where else can you enjoy so much good-natured gluttony in one place? On average, more than 40 different "foods on a stick" are offered, 60,000 baked potatoes sold, and 350,000 cream puffs gobbled up. You could attend every day of the fair, eat three meals and countless snacks, and still not come close to trying even half the delicacies. Cream puffs, meat pies, root-beer flavored milk, and roasted corn-on-the-cob dripping with dairy-fresh butter – the choice is dizzying.

Besides eating your weight in cheese and watching livestock watch people, there are plenty of other diversions. Magicians and rock legends give sell-out shows; shoppers revel in an endless array of stalls, selling everything from model cars to jewelry; and dozens of rides keep thrill-seekers happy. The definitive populist event, this vibrant fair offers something for everyone, a fact to which generations of Wisconsinites and legions of out-of-towners can attest.

Inset: Sign atop a live reptile booth, Wisconsin State Fair
Below (left to right): Fair entertainer; prize cow competition; Miller Brewery

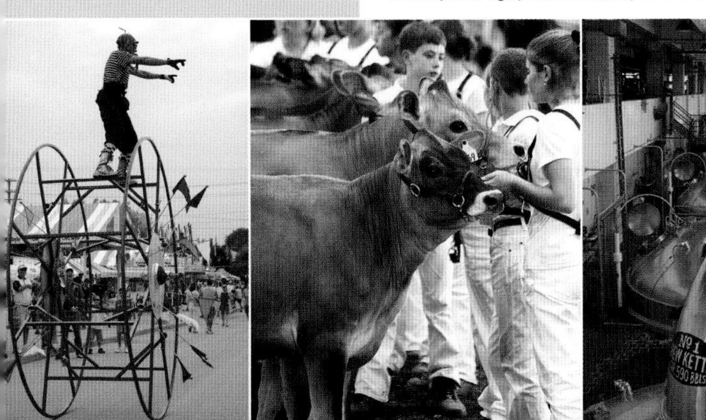

STATE FAIR DIARY

The fair runs for 11 days and nights, from 8am until midnight on weekends and 8am until 11pm on weekdays. Although exploring the fair could easily fill several days, be sure to make time to see the sights in historic Milwaukee, with its wealth of museums, vibrant arts scene, and old-world brewing traditions.

Three Days of Midwestern Fun

DAY 1

Head straight to the fair and hit the ground running. Check out Spin City for thrilling rides, then watch one of the free family-friendly shows of comedians, jugglers, or musicians. Stop by the horticulture building to see an amazing array of flowers and plants on display, or get a birds-eye view of the site on the SkyGlider. If you have young kids in tow, check out the Activity Zone. Be sure to snack along the way, then dance it all off at one of the evening shows.

DAY 2

Use this day to explore the sights in Milwaukee. Have a cooked breakfast such as "hoffel poffel" (scrambled eggs with potatoes, onions, salami, and cheese) at Jo's Café, or go for a healthy vegetarian option at the popular Beans & Barley. Walk off a few calories exploring the Milwaukee Art Museum, if you're feeling cultured, or the Harley-Davidson Museum, if you're feeling tough, or visit Mitchell Park Conservatory, which boasts a spectacular diversity of plant life, from shrubs and cacti to tropical flora. Milwaukee is all about beer, so be sure to go on a tour of the Miller Brewery. Browse eclectic boutiques on Brady Street or in the hip, arty neighborhood of Riverwest before sampling the trendy nightlife in each.

DAY 3

Spend a day with the animals. The fair showcases the best of Wisconsin's animals – cows, pigs, sheep, horses, chickens, and more. Witness a live animal birth in the Birthing Barn, get up close and personal with the Budweiser Clydesdales, and cheer on a swine or two at one of five daily pig races. See champion animals and the petting zoo in the Ag Village, and then stand in line for a famous State Fair cream puff.

Dos and Don'ts

- ⊗ Don't bother dieting. Foods at the fair run the gamut with the freshest of Wisconsin ingredients, none of which should be missed. Taste it all and walk off the calories later.
- ✓ Do be hands-on. The fair offers plenty of opportunities for you to participate.
- ⊗ Don't forget your rain gear. Wisconsin's weather is notoriously temperamental, so it's best to be prepared.

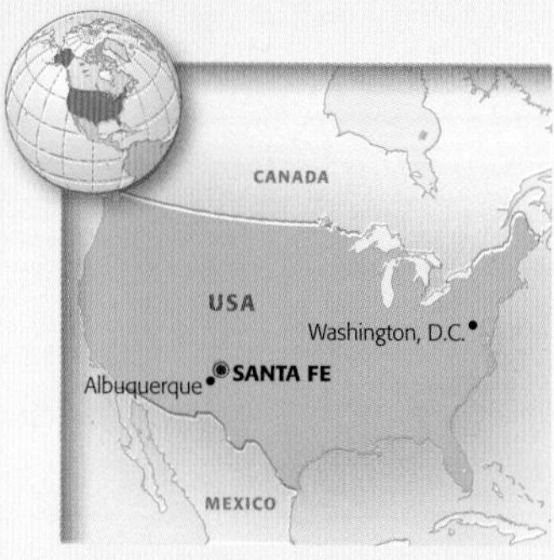

GETTING THERE See map p318, B2
Santa Fe is in northern New Mexico, 65 miles (105 km) northeast of Albuquerque's international airport, where you can rent cars.

GETTING AROUND
Santa Fe is best enjoyed on foot, but a car is needed to explore beyond downtown.

WEATHER
In August, daytime temperatures average 83°F (28°C) and the weather is generally dry and sunny, although it can change rapidly to heavy rain. Nights and mornings are cooler, with a nighttime average of 54°F (12°C).

ACCOMMODATIONS
The Santa Fe Motel is close to the Plaza; rooms from US$150; www.santafemotel.com

Fort Marcy Hotel Suites are conveniently located modern condominiums; from US$190; www.allseasonsresortlodging.com

The Rosewood Inn of the Anasazi, near the Plaza, offers rich decor with a blend of Native American, Latino, and Anglo styling; rooms from US$335; www.rosewoodhotels.com

EATING OUT
Creative, spicy Southwestern cuisine combines flavors found in Mexican and Native American dishes with unusual spices. Café Pasqual's (from US$17) has a festive atmosphere, while The Shed offers hearty cuisine with spicy chili sauces from US$10.

FURTHER INFORMATION
www.santafe.org

Georgia O'Keeffe

Innovative and provocative, noted modernist master Georgia O'Keeffe was already renowned for her canvases depicting intricately detailed flowers in softly graded colors when she first visited Taos, New Mexico, in 1929. She fell in love with the blue skies and landscape and began painting the stark white animal skulls she found while exploring, often including a delicate flower. The Georgia O'Keeffe Museum in Santa Fe houses 1,100 of her works, the world's largest permanent collection of her art.

Main: Terra-cotta pottery display outside a typical Southwestern adobe building
Above (top to bottom): Ladder to Alcove House at Bandelier National Monument; colorful local artwork; desert-bleached skulls for sale

SANTA FE

BATHED IN CLEAR HIGH-DESERT SUNLIGHT and nestled in the Sangre de Cristo Mountains, the beautiful city of Santa Fe proudly calls itself "The City Different." Here, traditions that go back hundreds of years honor the unique blend of Native Pueblo, Spanish, and Anglo cultures that are the foundation of this vibrantly creative city. Lining the streets are desert-hued adobe buildings with lovely walled garden courtyards, vivid blue-green doors, and styles derived from the traditional dwellings built by the Ancestral Puebloans long before the Spanish arrived.

Today, the fusion of these diverse cultures is expressed in the city's captivating collection of museums, art galleries, and restaurants. The Plaza is the heart of the city, and families will want to explore the Palace of the Governors, where Pueblo artisans offer exquisite natural turquoise and engraved silver jewelry under the portico, as they have for generations. Inside, the Wild West comes alive in a wealth of exhibits including authentic firearms,

Above (top and bottom): Canyon Road gallery, showcasing vibrant art; sculptures outside the boutique shops of Canyon Road

Below: Sculpture of a Native American warrior at the entrance of the Museum of Indian Arts and Culture on Museum Hill

Above: Colorful Hispanic dances at El Rancho de las Golondrinas

a working printing press, and even a clock shot by Pancho Villa, the Mexican revolutionary general. Guided tours relate the dramatic story of how the Spanish built this adobe building in 1610, as a fortress in the wilderness, and how the Ancestral Puebloans battled them and drove them away from Santa Fe for 12 years. Children especially like the Bland Mud Wagon, a real stagecoach that looks like it just rolled out of a John Wayne movie.

The boutique shops and galleries surrounding the Plaza offer a dazzling array of brightly colored ceramics, handwoven woolens, intricately tooled leather belts, and cowboy boots. Sparkling silver jewelry, earth-toned Southwest landscape paintings, and large whimsical sculptures are just a few of the offerings found in the hundreds of art galleries. Kids will be awed and enthralled by the exceptionally creative exhibits and hands-on play opportunities at the nearby Santa Fe Children's Museum. Parents with older children will want to visit the area's most popular museum, where the legendary paintings of Georgia O'Keeffe capture the unique beauty and ethereal light of New Mexico's sun-drenched desert landscape.

SOUTHWESTERN DIARY

The pleasantly warm days and cool nights of August are perfect for discovering the attractions of Santa Fe and for driving the scenic mountain roads to Bandelier National Monument. Four days allow enough time to see the highlights, visit the shops and art galleries, and enjoy the area's savory fusion cuisine.

Four Days of Fun and Culture

DAY 1

Explore the art galleries, museums, and churches near the Plaza. Learn Santa Fe's fascinating history at the Palace of the Governors, where displays depict cowboys, Native Americans, and life in the Wild West. Visit the famous Georgia O'Keeffe Museum, and admire the "Miraculous Staircase" in the Loretto Chapel.

DAY 2

Drive to Museum Hill to enjoy the colorful folk-art toys and miniature villages at the Museum of International Folk Art. The Museum of Indian Arts and Culture's multimedia exhibit "Here, Now, and Always" is a fun way to learn about Native American culture, while younger children will love the innovative displays and activities at the nearby Santa Fe Children's Museum.

Drive to El Rancho de las Golondrinas and explore this outdoor living history museum, where children can experience colonial life on a Spanish hacienda.

DAY 3

Stroll the length of Canyon Road and visit the sculpture courtyards, art galleries, and the intimate garden at El Zaguán. Then, head to the Santa Fe Southern Railway for a scenic trip through the desert in vintage rail cars.

DAY 4

Drive to Bandelier National Monument and walk through the canyon to explore Ancestral Puebloan cliff dwellings and village ruins. In the afternoon, visit Los Alamos for the Bradbury Science Museum, where interactive exhibits explain atomic power and tell the story of the Manhattan Project and the first atomic bombs.

Dos and Don'ts

- ✓ Remember to drink plenty of water, as it's very hot and dry in the summer.
- ✗ Don't forget to make reservations far ahead and to check the Santa Fe Southern Railway schedule.
- ✓ Purchase the New Mexico CulturePass for entry to the state's 15 museums and historic sites for 1 year. At US$25, it's well worth it.
- ✗ If staying in Santa Fe over the weekend, don't miss the traditional Native American folktales and Wild West yarns at the Wheelwright Museum of the American Indian.

GETTING THERE See map p314, E6

The Jean Lesage International Airport is 10 miles (16 km) from Québec City. A taxi costs about US$35. There is only one infrequent bus (#74) that links the airport with the bus terminal on the edge of the city (Mon–Fri only).

GETTING AROUND

Major sites are easy to reach by foot or a taxi. To visit outlying sites, rent a car.

WEATHER

Average August temperatures are 55–73°F (13–23°C). Warmer days aren't unusual, particularly early in the month. Late afternoon thunderstorms are common.

ACCOMMODATIONS

With a great Upper Town location Auberge Saint-Louis offers small, basic rooms; doubles from US$61; www.aubergestlouis.ca

Down the street, try the romantic Hotel Le Clos Saint-Louis; doubles from US$155; www.clossaintlouis.com

The Upper Town's castle-like Fairmont Le Château Frontenac is a city landmark; doubles from US$378; www.fairmont.com

EATING OUT

Restaurants serve Québécois or French food as well as world cuisines. A meal for two costs about US$40 in a casual eatery and US$120 or more in an upscale restaurant.

FURTHER INFORMATION

www.quebecregion.com

The Fall of New France

In 1759, at the height of the Seven Years' War, British forces commanded by Major-General James Wolfe scaled the cliffs below the Plains of Abraham outside the heavily defended Québec City walls. Lieutenant-General Louis-Joseph Montcalm, Marquis de Montcalm, made a call that changed the course of North American history: he met the attackers with a poorly trained militia. Both Wolfe *(above)* and Montcalm died, but the British captured the city, triggering a series of victories that led to New France passing under British control.

Above (left and right): A horse-drawn carriage saunters through an Old Québec street; colorful, flower-lined facades surround Place Royale
Main: A striking nighttime view of Fairmont Le Château Frontenac towering over Québec City

Above: A gift from France, Fontaine de Tourny lights up Parliament Hill

QUÉBEC CITY

CROSSING THROUGH THE PORTE SAINT-LOUIS (St. Louis Gate) past the stone walls encircling Vieux-Québec (Old Québec) is like stepping into another world, one that is familiar and contemporary but also rooted in a colorful and extraordinary past. Bustling rue Saint-Louis is abloom with flower baskets and alive with the buzzing of animated conversations that drift from sidewalk cafés. Galleries sell Inuit soapstone sculptures and bold abstract prints. Some of the stores could be those of any busy street in any North American downtown... but then you notice the steep mansard roofs of the 18th-century homes, the silver spires spearing the sky, and a Victorian-era cannonball lodged in the roots of a tree.

The past, present, and future shift effortlessly in this magical city like layers of sheer, colorful scarves laid one atop the other. Sleek young professionals chatter on cell phones outside Grande Allée nightclubs as horse-drawn carriages clop by. Guests snuggle under cotton sheets to watch Hollywood movies on plasma televisions in hotel rooms forged from Victorian warehouses. Like the settlers who carved this city from the vast woods of New France, food-lovers can dine on the region's famed duck, but these days, they can complement their meal with vintage wines from California and Australia, as well as from France.

The past, present, and future shift effortlessly in this magical city like layers of sheer, colorful scarves laid one atop the other.

The city is a magnet for history buffs, who can easily spend a whole vacation touring restored mansions, visiting historic military sights, and exploring museums. But even for those who would do almost anything other than look at exhibits about long-ago battles, Québec City's four centuries of history give the place an alluring glow. Every crooked street seems to lead to a garlic-scented restaurant with a chalkboard menu; every ancient staircase seems to offer a different view of the wide St. Lawrence River; and with every new day, the city unravels a new layer of itself for the curious visitor.

Inset: The Royal 22e Regiment at attention outside the Citadelle
Below (left and right): A cruise liner lies in port in Lower Town; diners enjoy the fare served at a sidewalk café along Grande Allée

QUÉBÉCOIS DIARY

Few North American cities rival Québec for sheer historical charm. August is a perfect time to leave behind the modern world and allow the relaxed pace of this timeless city to envelop you. Four days will allow you to see the city's main sights, and also fit in a little shopping, as well as time to sample the local cuisine.

Four Days Steeped in History

DAY 1
Start where the city itself began in 1608, Place Royale, a cobblestone square in Basse-Ville (Lower Town). Browse through boutiques on rue du Petit-Champlain. After lunch, visit the Musée de la Civilisation (Museum of Civilization) and hunt for antiques in the shops along rue Saint-Paul. Dine at renowned Laurie Raphaël, then enjoy a nightcap at Café du Monde, overlooking the river.

DAY 2
Stroll along the Terrasse Dufferin, a boardwalk along the cliffs in Haute-Ville (Upper Town). Visit the city's fortified walls and the Citadelle. Refresh yourself with a café au lait at Chez Temporel, then pose for a caricature at one of the artists' stalls on rue du Trésor. After dinner, tour the city by *calèche* (horse-drawn carriage) before visiting the Jazz Bar, the laid-back haunt at the Hotel Clarendon.

DAY 3
Venture outside the city walls to Parc des Champs-de-Bataille (Battlefields Park). Learn about Québec's art history at the nearby Musée National des Beaux-Arts du Québec before heading to Grande Allée, a lively boulevard lined with shops and restaurants. In the evening, take a cruise with Croisières AML on the St. Lawrence from Basse-Ville to the Île d'Orléans.

DAY 4
Sample the bountiful breakfast at the Fairmont Le Château Frontenac, then head to the west end of town for half a day of indulgent treatments at the Amerispa at Château Bonne Entente. Return to Haute-Ville for outstanding cuisine in the romantic solarium at Le Saint-Amour.

Dos and Don'ts

- ✓ If you have good knees, take the Escalier Casse-Cou (Break Neck Stairs) between Haute-Ville and Basse-Ville. But take the funicular back up – it's a steep trip.
- ✗ Don't drive within the city walls, unless your idea of a romantic getaway involves spending the whole weekend searching for a parking space.
- ✓ Dust off that high school French. While many tourism industry workers speak English, a well-timed *s'il vous plaît* (please) or *merci* (thank you) will often earn you a smile.
- ✓ Don't rush. Québec City is best savored at a relaxed pace.

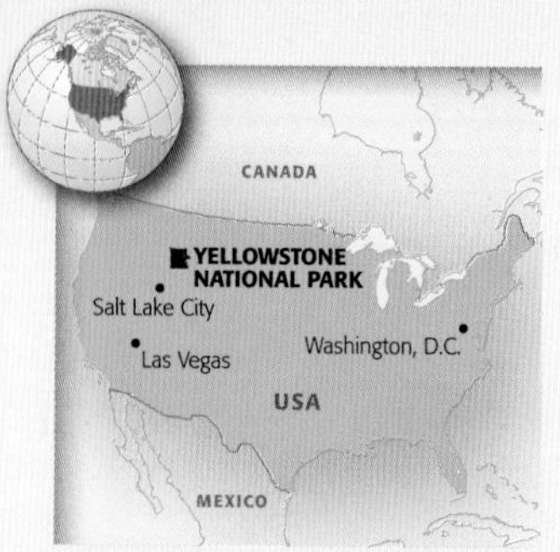

GETTING THERE See map p320, F4
Yellowstone National Park is in the Rocky Mountain Range. It is mainly located in the state of Wyoming. The closest major international airport is in Salt Lake City, Utah.

GETTING AROUND
Cars can be rented at the airport for the 320-mile (515-km) drive to Yellowstone. There are small airports closer to the park, within a 1–2 hour drive. Regional airports are in Cody and Jackson, WY; Bozeman and Billings, MT; and Idaho Falls, ID. The West Yellowstone, MT, airport is only open from June to September.

WEATHER
August has daytime temperatures of up to 86°F (30°C) but it can drop below freezing at night. Thunderstorms are frequent.

ACCOMMODATIONS
All of the accommodations in the park are managed by Xanterra Parks and Resorts, with rooms in historic lodges, motels, and cottages. Old Faithful Inn, Mammoth Hot Springs Hotel, and Yellowstone Lake Hotel are popular choices; doubles from US$150; www.xanterra.com

Budget accommodations, from US$88 a night, may require sharing a bathroom.

EATING OUT
Restaurants range from elegant lodge dining to an Old West Cookout. There are many cafeterias and grills that also offer packed lunches.

FURTHER INFORMATION
www.nps.gov/yell

Wonders of Yellowstone

Known as "Mi tsi a da zi," or "Rock Yellow River" to the Hidatsa tribe of Native Americans, the region's name was simplified by early fur trappers to Yellowstone. It took a major exploration by a forerunner of the U.S. Geological Survey in 1871 to introduce the world to the wonders of the park. Accompanying that expedition were photographer William H. Jackson and artist Thomas Moran. Their images helped convince President Grant to set aside the land as the world's first National Park in 1872.

Main: Aerial view of the Grand Prismatic Spring in Yellowstone – the spring is around 380 ft (120 m) in diameter

YELLOWSTONE NATIONAL PARK

THE DUST RISES AS HEAVY HOOVES FALL, the older males stand guard, young calves stay close to their mother's side. Time comes to a standstill to witness a primeval scene that once had all but vanished from the planet, but is now slowly returning – North American buffalo or bison on the move. You wait till the herd disappears into the valley below, then continue on your way, forever changed by the sheer magnitude of the wild beauty of Yellowstone National Park.

More than half a million years ago, a gargantuan volcanic explosion blanketed western North America in ash and scooped out a vast caldera 50 miles by 30 miles wide (80 km by 50 km wide). Today that caldera, located just north of the spectacular Grand Teton Mountains, is green and lush with landscapes and ecosystems unique in the world. Stunning tableaus of green mountain meadows, wild rivers, azure lakes, and snow-capped peaks set the

Left (left to right): Majestic bull elk; plains buffalo grazing in the park; stripey Least chipmunk on a tree stump; signpost for the Continental Divide – the ridge of mountains that runs from Alaska in the north to Mexico in the south

Left panel (top and bottom): Visitors on a horseback tour through the park; Old Faithful geyser

Above: Canary Spring, named after the yellow algae growing at its edge

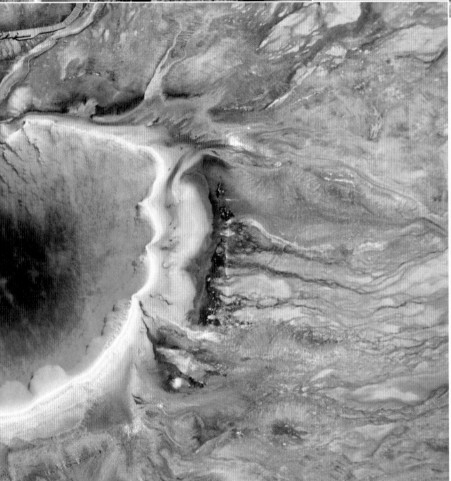

WILDERNESS DIARY

August days are long and warm, with the chance to participate in ranger-led tours and activities. It is possible to see the park's highlights in four days. Try to escape the crowds and explore the spectacular wilderness. Guided fishing and boating trips, naturalist-led outings, photo-safaris, and overnight hikes are all available.

Four Days in the Parkland

DAY 1

Watch the spectacular eruption of Old Faithful, Yellowstone's most popular geyser, early in the morning when crowds are thin.

Stroll along the walkways at Upper Geyser Basin to see spouting geysers, steaming pools, and bubbling springs. Be sure to see the colorful Morning Glory Pool.

DAY 2

Drive, or if you are feeling energetic walk, along the 20-mile (32-km) Grand Canyon of the Yellowstone, stopping frequently for breathtaking views of the waterfalls and magnificent, coppery-orange canyon.

DAY 3

Visit lovely, marshy Hayden Valley in the early morning and watch for herds of bison. Elk, grizzly bears, wolves, bald eagles, and geese may also be seen from the road.

In the afternoon, join in one of the ranger-led daytime programs offering guided nature and history walks. There are also evening slide-shows and talks offered at a variety of locations throughout the park.

DAY 4

Drive the length of Lamar Valley, starting as the sun comes up, stopping frequently to look for bison, pronghorn antelope, bear, and wolves in the valley and along the gently rolling hills.

Dos and Don'ts

- ✓ Stop in Visitor Centers for park maps and brochures, get the latest information on wildlife viewing, and peruse the exhibits on this incredible wilderness park.
- ✗ Don't try to see too much in one go – limit your exploration to one section of the park each day and take along a packed lunch or have meals close-by.
- ✓ Try to be outdoors at dawn when there are no crowds, getting out of the car often to walk, hike, take tours, and attend the ranger programs available at the park.
- ✗ Don't be caught out by the changeable weather; dress in layers as it may be below freezing at dawn and over 86°F (30°C) by mid-afternoon with a late-afternoon thunderstorm.
- ✓ Drive slowly, be patient, and watch closely everywhere you go. Sometimes animals can be seen very close to the road.

backdrop for an otherworldly landscape of 10,000 steaming fumaroles, geysers, bubbling mud pots, and psychedelically colored thermal springs (the color is caused by pigmented bacterial growth in the cooler water at the edge of the pool).

This huge park preserves one of the most intact ecosystems in the United States. August is an ideal time to visit because although tourists are present in large numbers, they tend to congregate in the popular areas, so discovering the real wilderness beauty of Yellowstone is as simple as getting off the beaten path anywhere in the park. A walk along the South Rim Trail east from busy Artist Point leads you up a brief, steep ascent that takes you far from the crowds and plunges you into a pristine world leaving civilization far behind. Following the gentle terrain of the canyon rim, the trail offers stunning views of the canyon, the Yellowstone River, and the cascading cataract of lower falls. A turn on the short Lily Pad Lake Trail takes you farther into the outback to the unspoiled splendor of the lily-covered lake where moose, bear, and elk roam freely and the vistas here are as wild and visually captivating as they were when the park was first discovered.

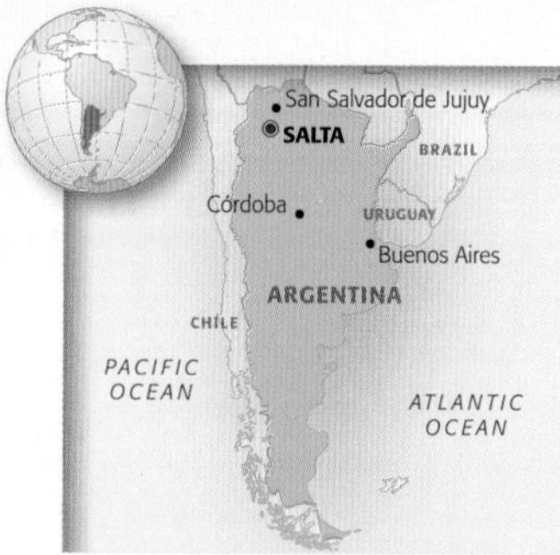

SALTA AND JUJUY

THERE'S SOMETHING SPECIAL ABOUT THE LIGHT here in Salta. A physicist might try to explain it by the altitude of nearly 4,000 ft (1,200 m), or by the latitude, just south of the Tropic of Capricorn, or perhaps by the almost total absence of humidity in the air. An artist would simply note its qualities, how the rich, golden hue of the light gives a special glow to everything it illuminates. It may be for this alone that Argentines refer to this city as Salta La Linda – Salta the Beautiful. Needless to say, it's the perfect setting for a romantic break. At least a day in Salta could be spent just enjoying the sunshine, idly strolling the ancient cobbles, hand-in-hand beneath the orange trees on Plaza 9 de Julio, admiring the delightful colonial architecture, browsing for treasures in the myriad handicraft stores, and sampling local delicacies, such as the tasty little meat-and-cheese pastries known as *empanadas salteñas*.

GETTING THERE **See map p330, C6**
Salta airport is a 2-hour flight from Buenos Aires. Taxis and shuttle buses run to the city center, 5 miles (8 km) away. San Salvador de Jujuy is 55 miles (88 km) north of Salta.

GETTING AROUND
Car hire is available at the airport and in town, with rates from about US$75 per day.

WEATHER
Days are clear and sunny with highs of 70°F (21°C), but evenings are chilly (42°F/5°C).

ACCOMMODATIONS
Hotel del Virrey is an old colonial mansion located in the historic part of Salta; doubles from US$80; www.hoteldelvirrey.com.ar

El Balcón de la Plaza is a romantic colonial-style property in the center; doubles from US$100; www.balcondelaplaza.com.ar

Hotel Solar de la Plaza is a converted mansion near Salta city center; doubles from US$170; www.solardelaplaza.com.ar

EATING OUT
El Solar del Convento, a former Jesuit convent in Salta, serves *parilla* (charcoal grills) and *tamales*.

Manos Jujeñas in Jujuy is great for regional specialties.

FURTHER INFORMATION
www.turismosalta.gov.ar
www.turismo.jujuy.gov.ar

The Ice Maiden

La Doncella (The Maiden) was found in an icy pit at 23,000 ft (7,000 m), near the peak of the Andean volcano Llullaillaco. The 15-year-old and two younger children found with her were preserved by the sub-zero temperatures and low humidity. They are believed to have been sacrificed over 500 years ago in an Inca ritual to thank the gods for the corn harvest. She is now on display in a chilled chamber in Salta's Museo de Arqueología de Alta Montaña. This angered some indigenous people, but had the blessing of Salta's own Quechua people.

Main: Spectacular colors of the Humahuaca Gorge

Left: Interior of the Basilica de Salta

Right (left to right): Church in Tilcara; seats in the shade at Cachi; young *gaucho* on horseback

Right panel (top and bottom): Sunset over the salt flats of Salinas Grandes; canyon road near Cafayate

Nature-lovers will revel in the afternoon drive south to Cafayate, where the Salta sun shines on lush green valley-floor vineyards, sere desert foothills and highland plateaus, and soaring rock formations sculpted into natural works of art. In the Quebrada de las Conchas, the striated cliffs and water-slashed gulleys come in every conceivable color: terra-cotta and rust, slate green, chalky yellows, lemon, orange, and bonfire red. Some of these striking formations have evocative names, such as Garganta del Diablo (the Devil's Throat). Others are simply nameless things of beauty.

Back in the city, come nightfall, the temperature drops steeply and swiftly. Those looking for the warmth of human company can stroll the lively cafés, clubs and *bodegas* of bustling, bright Balcarce. For others, the nip in the air makes the Salta evening a time for snuggling by a fire, a time in which to warm your insides with a glass or two of local rich, strong red wine, while enjoying the glow from the *parilla*'s bed of coals, and the sparkle in your companion's eyes.

Above: Salta's leafy Plaza 9 de Julio

HIGH-COUNTRY DIARY

Six days is an ideal length of time to explore Salta and nearby Jujuy and take some drives through the high country around them. If you are here in the third week of August you can enjoy the events of Jujuy Week, but all month you are likely to come across events marking the festival of Pachamama, the Earth Mother.

Six Days in the Sunshine

Stroll Salta's colonial center, basking in the warm winter sunshine. Admire the terra-cotta facade of the Iglesia San Francisco and the ornate interior of the Basilica. Take the cable car almost 1,000 ft (300 m) up to the top of San Bernardo Hill, and enjoy the panoramic view of the Lerma Valley. At night, feast on traditional Argentinean barbecue, *parilla*.	**DAY 1**
Have breakfast in bed, enjoying the colonial ambience of your hotel. Later on, take a walk and perhaps stop to view the tapestries and colonial art in the Museo de Bellas Artes. Visit the Museo de Arqueología de Alta Montaña. In the evening, visit a *peña folclórica*, a folk tavern, and watch dancers perform the *zamba*.	**DAY 2**
Hire a car and take the scenic route south through the Calchaquíes Valley. Wander the square in the tiny traditional pueblo of Cachi. Scramble up the edges of the eroded red hills at Quebrada de las Flechas (Ravine of the Arrows) near Angastaco. Peer into the Devil's Throat gorge near the Quebrada del Río de las Conchas (Canyon of the River of Shells). Stop in at a winery such as San Pedro de Yacochuya, near Cafayate.	**DAY 3**
Make the short drive north to San Salvador de Jujuy. Spend the day exploring its compact colonial heart.	**DAY 4**
Drive the striking road north through the Humahuaca Gorge, up into the high, arid desert country, to the artists' colony of Tilcara and the spectacular salt flats of Salinas Grandes. Enjoy a last romantic night in Jujuy, before driving back down the valley to Salta.	**DAYS 5–6**

Dos and Don'ts

- ✓ Try the wines. Argentinean vintages are inexpensive and of very high quality – the perfect accompaniment to a romantic fireside dinner. *(See pp216–7)*
- ✗ Don't overlook the Museo de Arqueología de Alta Montaña, even if you're not normally a museum person. The wind-dried sacrificial mummies are astonishing.
- ✓ Bring plenty of cash for local art and crafts. Metalware, textiles, pottery, and other handicrafts are all very tempting.
- ✗ Don't forget to bring a warm sweater or fleece. The temperature drops dramatically when the sun goes down. But also bring sunscreen and a hat for the daytime.

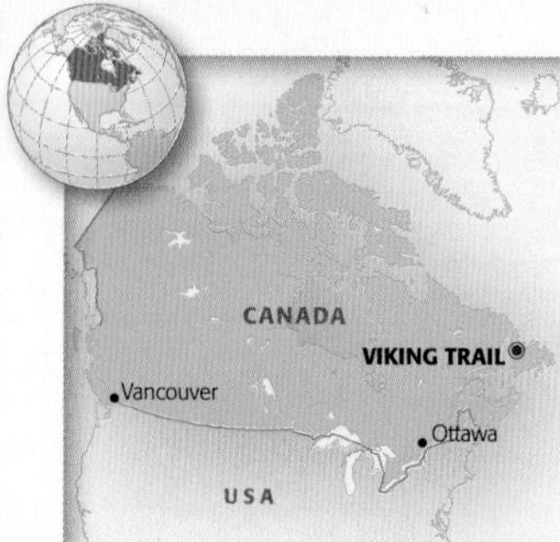

GETTING THERE **See map p314, H5**
Newfoundland has one primary international airport at St. John's, and smaller airports at Gander, Deer Lake, Stephenville, and St. Anthony. Rent a car from Deer Lake to get to Gros Morne National Park, which is 20 miles (32 km) away. A car ferry from North Sydney, Nova Scotia, docks at Port aux Basques, 186 miles (300 km) from the park entrance.

GETTING AROUND
A car is required for the Viking Trail.

WEATHER
August is one of the warmest and driest times to visit, with average daytime temperatures of 61–77°F (16–25°C).

ACCOMMODATIONS
Bonne Bay Inn, Woody Point, offers sensational views across the bay; rooms from US$130; www.woodypointmagic.com

Neddies Harbour Inn, Norris Point, is a modern waterfront inn in the heart of the park, with rooms from US$170; www.theinn.ca

Tuckamore Lodge, Main Brook, offers luxury accommodation with breakfast, from US$120; dinner available; www.tuckamorelodge.com

EATING OUT
The best restaurants are in or near the Gros Morne National Park. Smaller places have reasonably priced simple fare, such as chowders, cod tongues, and seal flipper pie.

FURTHER INFORMATION
www.newfoundlandlabrador.com

Viking Village

In 1960, explorer Helge Ingstad was combing the northeast coast of America for evidence of the existence of the fabled Viking settlement recorded in the saga of Leif Erikson, a Norse explorer (AD 970–1020) who may have been the first European to land in north America. After much searching, locals told Ingstad of earth mounds near L'Anse aux Meadows. In 1961, he returned with his archeologist wife and uncovered an ember pit like one found in Greenland at the house of Eric the Red. A full excavation revealed a whole Viking village.

Above (left to right): Boat trip in Gros Morne National Park; large bull moose; kayaking fun
Main: Hiking in Gros Morne National Park

Above: Lobster Cove Lighthouse, Lobster Cove

THE VIKING TRAIL

THIS IS A STUNNING TRIP ALONG A NARROW SLIVER of highway carved through the spectacular tundra landscape. Known as the Viking Trail, the route follows the Great Northern Peninsula that stretches into the Atlantic Ocean toward Greenland. It takes you from the dramatic coastal mountains and fjords of Corner Brook north along an unforgettably wild coastline to the remote northern tip of the island of Newfoundland, where a handful of Viking explorers – possibly led by Leif Erikson – made a base, over a thousand years ago.

At the southern end of the Trail is Gros Morne National Park, treasured by geologists who come to study some of the world's oldest rocks, part of the earth's mantle that rose through the ocean floor as tectonic plates collided. Abandon the car and follow hiking trails that lead through arctic-alpine barrens in which caribou roam, past volcanic cliffs and sea stacks along a coast where minke whales can be seen feeding offshore. A boardwalk leads through coastal bog, where moose often graze, to Western Brook Pond, and boat tours take passengers into this vast glacier-carved fjord where streams turn to misty cascades as they tumble down sheer rock walls 2,000 ft (609 m) above the water. Heading north, the Long Range Mountains shelter beautiful sapphire-blue fjords while timeless fishing villages cling to tiny harbors along the boulder-strewn shoreline. L'Anse-aux-Meadows, at the northern end of the Viking Trail, is the oldest known European settlement in the western hemisphere. The landscape today is much as it must have been when the Vikings arrived, with coastal bogs and tuckamore forests of stunted white spruce and balsam fir twisted by the constant force of onshore winds. Reconstructions of the Viking longhouses built of sod stand on a grassy headland by the sea, and costumed re-enactors portray the self-reliant lifestyle of the mighty Viking seafarers who built their outpost here.

Follow hiking trails that lead through arctic-alpine barrens in which caribou roam, past volcanic cliffs along the coast.

Inset: Viking re-enactors in the recreated village, L'Anse-aux-Meadows
Below (left and right): Exposed sedimentary rock; Tablelands, Gros Morne

NEWFOUNDLAND DIARY

August is the warmest and driest month of the year in Newfoundland, and although it is also the busiest, you will still find beaches and mountain vistas where you are the only ones enjoying them. August is also the best time to see wildlife in the National Park. Five days is all you need to enjoy the wild scenery.

JAN FEB MAR APR MAY JUN JUL **AUG**

Five Days on the Viking Trail

Explore Gros Morne National Park, stopping at the Visitor Center and the Discovery Center to learn about the park's geology. Hike with a park geologist to the Tablelands – barren mountains formed when tectonic plates collided millions of years ago – and walk on the earth's mantle. Kayak on the blue waters of Trout River Pond for fascinating views of the Tablelands. There are fabulous sunsets from the Lobster Point Lighthouse.	**DAY 1**
Visit Bonne Bay Marine Station and watch marine life as seen by a real-time underwater camera. Drive to Western Brook Pond, walk through the wetlands on the boardwalk, and take the boat trip down the fjord beneath towering mountains. For an evening of comedy and drama, attend the Gros Morne Theatre Festival.	**DAY 2**
Head north along the coast and stop at the Arches to watch the waves crashing onshore. Stop at Port au Choix National Historic Site and learn about the area's earliest inhabitants, the Maritime Archaic people, who lived here 4,000 years ago.	**DAY 3**
Drive to L'Anse-aux-Meadows National Historic Site with its Viking re-enactors at the recreated village. The museum at this UNESCO World Heritage Site relates the discovery and excavation of the village. Visit nearby Norstead Village to see the recreation of the Viking ship that sailed from Greenland. In St. Anthony, the museum at Grenfell Historic Properties tells of the good Doctor Grenfell who tended those in remote outposts.	**DAY 4**
Return along the Viking Trail to Deer Lake Airport.	**DAY 5**

Dos and Don'ts

- ✓ Dress in layers and be prepared for cold, wet, and hot weather. Bring a camera and binoculars for watching wildlife.
- ✗ Don't forget to book accommodations well ahead of time as August is the busy season and there are a limited number of rooms available.
- ✗ Don't forget to check the schedule for Gros Morne Festival Theatre, Western Brook Pond boat trips and ranger-led activities as soon as you arrive. Make reservations at once.
- ✓ Look out for moose at dawn and dusk, drive slowly, and if you spot one, keep a safe distance.

SEP OCT NOV DEC

THE HAMPTONS

SPEND ANY TIME AT ALL IN NEW YORK IN AUGUST and you'll hear the mantra all around you: "The Hamptons, the Hamptons." What folks are talking about are a string of villages at the east end of Long Island, the oceanside antidote to summer in the city, a vacation playground only a couple of hours away. Manhattanites refer to a visit to Southampton, Bridgehampton, East Hampton, Amagansett, Sag Harbor, Montauk, and their neighboring villages as "making the scene in the Hamptons." The "scene" is a reference to the lifestyles of the rich and famous who have beachside mansions here, to cocktail receptions and lawn parties, trendy clubs, and stellar restaurants. Sometimes, in fact, the social scene can be so overwhelming that the real appeal of the Hamptons, the stretches of white sand (some of the finest beaches in the United States) and the landmarks of a colonial past, can get lost in the fray.

Main: Beach with dunes, Southampton

GETTING THERE **See map p316, G5**
From Manhattan, the Hampton Jitney, a bus service, operates frequently. The Long Island Railroad runs several times a day. Or rent a car at LaGuardia or JFK international airports, and drive there (100 miles/ 160 km), avoiding Manhattan traffic.

GETTING AROUND
You will need a car. There are rental agencies in and around East Hampton.

WEATHER
Ocean breezes keep temperatures around 80°F (27°C), with nighttime average lows of 68°F (20°C). The sea temperature is warm.

ACCOMMODATIONS
The Hedges Inn, an historic clapboard mansion, offers 13 period rooms; doubles from US$500; www.thehedgesinn.com

1770 House has just six rooms, some with fireplaces, or a private carriage house, and a choice of casual or fine dining; doubles from US$550; www.1770house.com

Mill House Inn is a luxury bed-and-breakfast in an 18th-century East Hampton cottage; doubles from US$995; www.millhouseinn.com

EATING OUT
Many restaurants in East Hampton set the same high standard as the best in Manhattan, with prices to match. Seafood is a specialty.

FURTHER INFORMATION
www.hamptons.com
www.discoverlongisland.com

A Pirate in the Hamptons

Of all the celebrities who have visited the Hamptons, Captain William Kidd is perhaps the most notorious. In 1792, he raided the *Queddagh Merchant*, one of the largest treasure ships on the high seas, off the coast of Madagascar. Rumor has it that he buried gold from his haul on the shores of Long Island, and he did indeed stash some booty at an estate on Shelter Island before sailing for Boston, where he was captured and sent to England for trial and execution.

Above (top and bottom): Mansion on Georgica Lane, East Hampton; Sag Harbor Whaling Museum

Left: East Hampton windmill

Right (left to right): Lighthouse at Montauk Point; Sag Harbour restaurant on Main Street; shops in central East Hampton

As the old story goes, a stranger asks someone on the street of East Hampton the way to the ocean, and the reply is, "What ocean?" The first people to discover the appeal of the Hamptons were Puritans, who sailed across Long Island Sound from settlements in Connecticut and Massachusetts to farm, fish, and hunt whales. Their houses and churches surround village greens and, at Montauk, the lighthouse commissioned by President George Washington in 1792 still stands atop a rocky promontory. Summertime visitors began to arrive in the 19th century, on the new Long Island Railroad, and the quaint villages soon became a playground for wealthy Northeasterners, whose lavish "cottages" still line the country lanes. These days, the Hamptons are among America's most charming seaside retreats. Colonial houses are now enticing inns, windmills and church steeples are scenic markers for countryside walks, and large tracts of woods and farmlands remain. Where ever you are in the Hamptons, you are never far from a beach. And, gazing out to sea from any of them, the scene hasn't changed for centuries.

Above: Fishing at sunset in East Hampton

OCEANSIDE DIARY

August is by far the busiest month in the Hamptons. On weekends, traffic is often at a standstill and reservations at hotels and restaurants are as prized and hard to come by as a big win on the lottery. Plan a midweek visit, when the scene is tamer, and in three days you can discover the towns and beaches at a leisurely pace.

Three Days in the Hamptons

DAY 1

Arrive in East Hampton in time for lunch and a walk around town to see such colonial landmarks as the Osborne-Jackson House and Hook Mill. Drive out to the Pollack-Krasner House to see the paint-splattered studio where abstract expressionist Jackson Pollock created many of his masterpieces, then follow Georgica Road, passing lavish mansions, on your way to the beach for a walk and a late-afternoon swim.

DAY 2

Begin the day with a morning swim at Egypt Beach then explore the surrounding villages. In Southampton, another colonial-era town built around a green and pond, the Parrish Museum of Art houses an important collection of works by Fairfield Potter and other American artists. In Bridgehampton, Duck Walk vineyards offer tastings and tours. The best way to explore Montauk, at the far east end of Long Island and surrounded by water on three sides, is on the trolley that stops at the lighthouse and other sights. End the afternoon with a sunset cruise from Montauk harbor.

DAY 3

After a leisurely morning at the beach, drive across the peninsula to Sag Harbor, a quaint village with a colonial-era customs house, a 19th-century whalers' church, and a museum of whaling. From here you can board a ferry to Shelter Island for a walk through the woodlands and along the beaches of Mashomack Preserve. Return to Sag Harbor in time for a drink and a play at the acclaimed Bay Street Theater, then return to East Hampton for a late-night supper.

Dos and Don'ts

- ✓ Base yourselves at East Hampton. With its good selection of inns and restaurants, it's the most convenient place to stay.
- ✗ Don't forget to obtain a beach-parking permit (ask at your hotel) and obey the rules to the letter as fines are stiff.
- ✓ Take a break from Manhattan-style haute cuisine to enjoy a lobster roll or fish and chips.
- ✓ Pay attention to warning flags when swimming: white means it's safe to swim; blue advises caution; red means danger. No flag – no swimming.

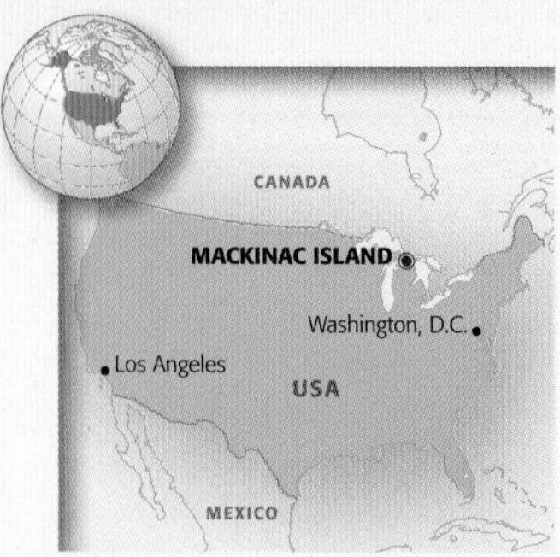

GETTING THERE See map p319, H2
Mackinac Island lies in Lake Huron, where Michigan's Upper and Lower peninsulas meet. Ferry services run from Mackinac City and St. Ignace. The closest regional airport is in Pellston, 35 miles (56 km) away. The closest major airport is at Detroit, 300 miles (480 km) away.

GETTING AROUND
Cars are forbidden but the island is compact enough for most visitors to explore on foot. Bicycles can be rented, and horse-drawn carriages are popular as well.

WEATHER
August brings warm, pleasant conditions, with temperatures reaching about 75°F (24°C). Occasional thunderstorms can produce 3 in (7 cm) of rain for the month.

ACCOMMODATIONS
The Mission Point Resort offers old-world hospitality and stunning sunset views; doubles from US$250; www.missionpoint.com

The Lake View Hotel, the island's oldest (1858), is charming, Victorian-style; doubles from US$250; www.lake-view-hotel.com

The luxurious Grand Hotel has hosted many presidents; doubles from US$785; www.grandhotel.com

EATING OUT
Most restaurants serve plenty of fresh fish and seafood.

FURTHER INFORMATION
www.mackinacisland.org

Fudging It

For well over a century, Mackinac Island has been acclaimed for its fudge, made the old-fashioned way using a marble slab (*above*). For true candy-lovers and chocoholics, there's no better time to indulge than during the official Fudge Festival, held every August. Events include bike tours, concerts and extreme kite-flying exhibitions. "Golden tickets" are randomly hidden in packages sold at fudge shops around the island, and those who discover one could win a vacation package for a future visit.

Main: The vast verandah of the Grand Hotel
Above (top to bottom): Marquette Park by the waterfront; a bike used as planter; a horse-drawn carriage with a uniformed driver

MACKINAC ISLAND

WHATEVER YOUR DEFINITION OF "REST AND RECUPERATION," from a luxury spa service or gourmet meal to a quiet ride along untouched coastline, Mackinac Island is likely to provide it – and more. A tiny speck of land in Lake Huron in the upper reaches of Michigan, Mackinac (pronounced "mack-in-awe") has, for more than a century, provided a romantic, luxurious getaway spot. Today it has an approximate year-round population of 500 but draws almost one million visitors throughout the summer, attracting international crowds for its natural beauty and relaxed atmosphere. For some, it's the island's old-fashioned charm and refreshing resistance to certain modern annoyances, including a ban on cars, that appeal. For others, it's the bike- and horse-friendly environment.

A walk down historic Main Street, lined with Victorian-style storefronts, the aromas of freshly made fudge wafting throughout the island from its many fudge shops (especially during the Fudge Festival) invokes a feeling of

Above: Red Coat re-enactors, Fort Mackinac
Below: Victorian-style storefront display

Above: Round Island Lighthouse, the Straits of Mackinac

stepping back in time. Most visitors approach the island by ferry, and arrive at the docks to be greeted by porters from all the major hotels and resorts with horse-drawn taxis. Not only are the carriages ubiquitous throughout the island, but you can hire one to drive yourself and those looking to hop on horseback have several riding stables to choose from. Visitors who would like a more energetic ride opt for a bike, Mackinac's main mode of personal transport. You'll find standard two-wheelers are available for rental, as well as tandems, kids' bikes and covered models.

The town's compact size of less than five square blocks lends an unhurried vibe to most activities but if the shops, eateries, and historic hotels produce a sensory overload, visitors can always lose themselves in the island's natural wonders. Hiking and biking trails lead to fields of summer wildflowers such as wood lilies, hawkweeds, and buttercups, and to dramatic limestone formations. A popular resting place for migrating birds, the island can boast a dizzying array of visitors including cormorants, great blue herons, Canada geese, and loons – a thrill for amateur ornithologists. You might catch otters frolicking in the waters, while bats help keep mosquitoes at bay.

MACKINAC DIARY

A weekend on Mackinac Island provides an idyllic escape – and August is the warmest month. The island has remained relatively unchanged over the years, with Victorian-style storefronts and buildings. You'll find a distinct Midwestern civility and, since no cars are allowed, the only traffic is on horseback, on foot, or by bike.

Three Days of Car-Free Charm

DAY 1

Rent a bike to explore the far reaches of the island, using Lake Shore Road, a mostly flat, 8-mile (12-km) ring around Mackinac. (When veering off-road, be careful to navigate the series of hills and bluffs that have stalled many a novice cyclist.) Peruse Main Street's many shops, galleries, and eateries, and then enjoy an evening tour through the town center on a horse-drawn carriage. Finish your first night at the Chippewa Hotel Waterfront with a drink at the Pink Pony, an old-fashioned bar that has been slinging drinks since the 1930s.

DAY 2

Take a free tour of the Michigan Governor's summer residence, which dates back to 1902 and offers fantastic harbor views. Buy some fudge before stepping back in time with a visit to historic Fort Mackinac (recreated to suggest an 1880s atmosphere). Swing by St. Anne's Church to watch locals partake in a weekly square dancing hoedown, then cap your night with a cocktail at the Mustang Lounge, a popular local watering hole housed in an 18th-century log cabin.

DAY 3

Go along to the historic Grand Hotel, where non-guests can dine at any of the six restaurants on site. Be sure to enjoy the view from the vast porch – at 660 ft (200 m) the longest in the world, according to the hotel. Finish your weekend with a romantic harbor cruise, passing by the Round Island and Old Mackinaw Point lighthouses while admiring a perfect sunset under the Mackinac Bridge.

Dos and Don'ts

- ✗ Don't ignore the general rules regarding the island's many horses. Don't touch a horse without its owner's permission, and don't ever approach a horse from behind.
- ✓ Consider renting a bike, the only means of transportation possible for those looking to explore all corners of the island.
- ✓ Bring comfortable footwear, as the island provides opportunities for lots of walking, with much exploration possible only on foot.
- ✗ Don't fail to sample the famous local fudge.

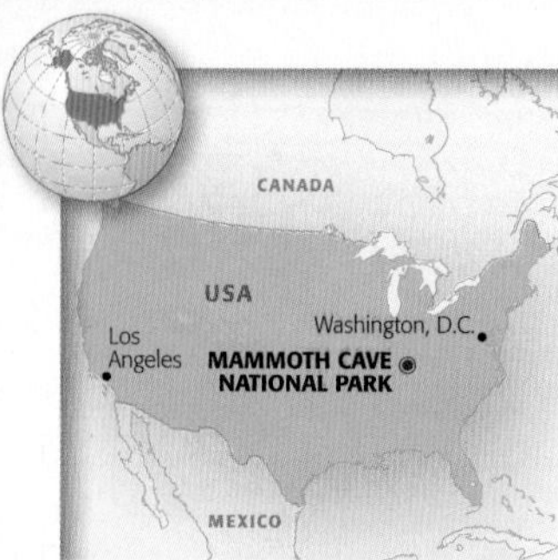

GETTING THERE See map p319, H6

The park is about 90 miles (144 km) southwest of the Louisville International Airport and well connected to Louisville and other cities around Kentucky by main roads and highways.

GETTING AROUND

The park is filled with trails, so you can access all areas via hiking and biking. The park tourist office also runs a wide variety of tours, from caving to canoeing.

WEATHER

August is warm and humid, with temperatures ranging from 67°F (19°C) to 88°F (31°C). The caves have lower temps, offering a refreshing respite from the heat.

ACCOMMODATIONS

In the forest Mammoth Cave Hotel; doubles from US$85; www.mammothcavehotel.com

Bowling Green (23 miles/37 km southwest), is home to a variety of hotels, including the Hotel Sync; doubles from US$129; www.thehotelsync.com

The park is dotted with campgrounds, including along the Green and Nolin rivers.

EATING OUT

The Mammoth Cave Hotel has a variety of restaurants, including the Travertine Restaurant, where you can refuel with hearty dishes.The park also has plenty of picnic tables.

FURTHER INFORMATION

www.nps.gov

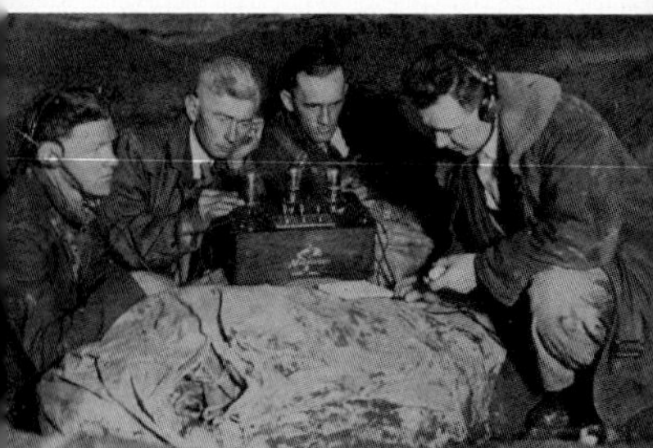

Floyd Collins: Caving Pioneer

In 1925, an enterprising explorer descended into Sand Cave in what is now Mammoth Cave National Park. He never came out. Collins, who had been managing a tourist cave in the area, was looking for a new one when he got stuck in a narrow crawlspace 55 ft (17 m) below the surface. The rescue efforts became one of the biggest news stories on the broadcast radio. He perished after 14 days – just three days before rescuers eventually reached him. Today, his story lives on in documentaries, books and, most improbably, in the musical Floyd Collins.

Above (left to right): Autumn in Mammoth Cave National Park; a ranger checking a cave ceiling; Mammoth Cave Railroad Bike and Hike Trail
Main: Mammoth Dome

Below: Canoeing on the Green River

MAMMOTH CAVE NATIONAL PARK

MOST NATIONAL PARKS HAVE FLOURISHING NATURE ABOVE GROUND. At Mammoth Cave National Park, the geological riches lie beneath the ground. Founded in 1941, the park is home to the longest system of caves in the world, and more than 400 miles (664 km) of gaping chambers and pitch-black tunnels have been discovered. The history of the area dates back to prehistoric times, with evidence pointing to human exploration of the caves some 4,000 years ago. The main entrance to the caves was discovered in the late 1700s by Robert Houchins, who was following a wounded bear while hunting.

Tours of the caves are creatively tailored to all skill levels and led by entertaining park rangers. Bring the family: popular tours include the Frozen Niagara Tour, with a meander past the soaring Rainbow and Moonlight domes and the Onlyx Colonnade; the family-friendly Historic Tour which winds past Mammoth landmarks that have been visited by celebrated writers and scientists; and the Violet City Lantern Tour which explores some of the cave system's oldest passageways, lit only by the flickering light of a lantern. The hugely popular Trog Tour is an off-road caving trek for kids only, led by experienced rangers.

When you're ready to emerge into the sunlight, you'll find acres upon acres of hardwood forest, crisscrossed by more than 84 miles (135 km) of trails. Embark from trailheads throughout the park, including Big Hollow and First Creek, and hike or horseback past trickling creeks, ancient trees, and sun-dappled clearings. After a sweaty day of trekking, canoe or kayak down the aptly named Green River with the breeze in your hair.

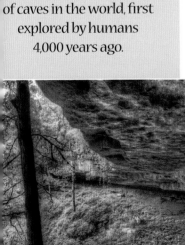

The geological riches of the park lie beneath the ground: the longest system of caves in the world, first explored by humans 4,000 years ago.

Inset: A cave crayfish
Below (left and right): Moss on overhanging rock; limestone caverns

MAMMOTH DIARY

August is the perfect month to visit the park. Thanks to daily sun and bright-blue skies, you can maximize your time by exploring both above and below the earth's surface. Three days will allow you to embark on several in-depth cave tours, as well as float down the park's breezy rivers and trek its nature trails.

JAN FEB MAR APR MAY JUN JUL **AUG** SEP OCT NOV DEC

Three Days of Underground Exploration

DAY 1

On the first day, go caving with the family. Embark on a kid-friendly tour, like the Domes and Driptsones Tour, which meanders through fascinating formations and dripstones. After a morning underground, spend the afternoon under the summer sun, canoeing the gentle Green River.

DAY 2

Celebrate the history of the caves on the Historic Tour, where you can follow a timeline of US history by learning about famous folks who have visited the caves. Continue your historic explorations on the Gothic Avenue Tour, which winds through the famous Rotunda and Church, and travels down Gothic Avenue, one of the oldest passageways in the cave. Here you'll see everything from unique rock formations to 19th-century candle-written signatures. Another history tour option is the lantern-lit Star Chamber Tour, where you'll view ancient rock monuments from hundreds of years ago and hear stories about tuberculosis patients who sought a cure inside the cave.

DAY 3

Time to pull on your sturdy hiking boots. Numerous trailheads, including at Maple Springs, Big Hollow, and Temple Hill, lead to verdant trails for hiking and biking. With the family, discover the kid-friendly trails around the Visitor Center, like the Cedar Sink Trail, the Sand Cave Trail, Turnhole Bend Nature Trail, and the Mammoth Cave Railroad Bike and Hike Trail.

Dos and Don'ts

- ✓ Leave the strollers and large backpacks at the hotel. Caving tours prohibit them, as well as tripods and flash photography.
- ✗ Don't forget to make reservations for cave tours, especially in the summer high season when tours fill up quickly. Note that you cannot make same-day reservations.
- ✓ Where there are caves, there are bats. Time your visit for the annual Bat Night in late August, which showcases and explains the latest bat research.

GETTING THERE See map p327, D5

The closest international airport is at Lima. From there, Cusco is a 2-hour flight. A further 40-minute flight aboard a small twin-engined plane will get you to Boca Manú. Then a motorized canoe takes you on the 90-minute trip down the Madre de Dios River to your accommodation.

GETTING AROUND

In Cusco you can explore on foot. In the Park all your trips, on land or water, will be with a guide.

WEATHER

This is the dry season, and Park temperatures can reach a humid 88°F (31°C), with lows of 64°F (18°C). In Cusco, daytime temperatures average 68°F (20°C) but drop sharply at night.

ACCOMMODATIONS

The Hotel Costa del Sol Ramada, in central Cusco, is in a charming colonial mansion; doubles from US$130; www.ramada.com

The Manú Wildlife Center has accommodation in rustic cabins, with en-suite facilities; 4-night, full-board packages, including transport from Cusco, from US$1,925 per person; www.manuexpeditions.com

EATING OUT

Peruvian dishes include *arroz con pollo* (a spicy chicken and rice dish) and *lomo salteado* (fried beef with tomatoes, onions, and potatoes). Food will be provided when staying in the park.

FURTHER INFORMATION

www.manuadventures.com
www.manuexpeditions.com

For sheer wilderness, it doesn't get much better than this.

Main: Group of red-and-green macaws taking off from a claylick in Manú National Park
Above: Overlooking the misty rain forest **Inset:** Tufted capuchin in an acrobatic pose
Top (left to right): Typical lodge accommodations; violet-fronted brilliant hummingbird; roots of palms in Manú National Park; steering through the Madre de Dios River

MANÚ NATIONAL PARK

THE VIEW OVER MANÚ NATIONAL PARK from the small, twin-engine plane that takes you to Boca Manú is humbling. Nearly 3,125 sq miles (8,095 sq km) of dense lowland tropical jungle and misty cloud forest, sloping up into the Andes, stretch out around you, crisscrossed by the sludgy brown waters of the Manú and Madre de Dios rivers. Manú National Park is the largest tropical park in South America, and home to an extraordinary diversity of plant and wildlife. Found in this verdant jungle are more than 1,000 species of bird including the flamboyant, strutting cock-of-the-rock, 200 species of mammal, such as the giant otter, tapir, and majestic jaguar, and more than 15,000 species of plant. All of this is remarkably preserved in pristine condition due to the inaccessibility of the area and careful controls and monitoring of the numbers now allowed to visit. The park is so isolated in parts that several indigenous groups within rarely have contact with outsiders.

Giant Otters

One of the world's most endangered species, the giant otters that are found in Manú National Park are actually quite ferocious animals – fending off jaguars and killing caymans that cross into their nesting territory. The park was made a UNESCO World Natural Heritage Site in 1987. This has helped in some ways to stave off the reduction in numbers of these otters over the years, maintaining the clean water and fish stocks that are essential for the survival of the species.

Above: Manú River meandering through Manú National Park

PERUVIAN PARK DIARY

You will need at least three nights in Manú in order to fully experience all that the jungle has to offer. August is also an excellent time of year to visit the Andean region, so it's worth exploring the pretty colonial streets of Cusco. You could extend your trip with a visit to the Inca citadel of Machu Picchu *(see pp140–41)*.

A Week in the Rain Forest

DAY 1 Flights tend to arrive into Lima in the evening; if there's time, explore some of the capital's excellent museums.

DAY 2 Fly over the Andes to Cusco and spend the day exploring its churches and colorful markets.

DAY 3 A short flight by light aircraft will take you to Boca Manú, a small frontier town on the banks of the Manú River. From here a motorized canoe ploughs deep into the forest along the Madre de Dios River, to the Manú Wildlife Center. Settle into your cabin then, in the afternoon, explore the jungle in search of monkeys.

DAY 4 A pre-dawn start for the 25-minute boat trip to the macaw lick to see Amazon parrots and large macaws feasting on the clay. Later, climb the 110-ft- (34-m-) high platform over the rain forest canopy to observe the frantic dusk activity of the jungle fauna. Take a night hike to a tapir lick to watch them feed.

DAY 5 Head out onto the nearby Blanco Oxbow Lake in search of the resident giant otter family, and take a nighttime boat trip on the Madre de Dios River, following the reclusive black caiman.

DAY 6 Emerging from the jungle by canoe at Boca Manú, take a flight back to Cusco and enjoy the dry air and laid-back atmosphere of this bustling town.

DAY 7 Fly back to Lima, or you could choose to extend your trip with a visit to the lost Inca city at Machu Picchu.

Dos and Don'ts

- ✓ Make sure you take a good insect repellent and long-sleeved clothing. Mosquitoes here are large and persistent.
- ✗ Don't expect luxury. Accommodations here are basic, but you'll feel like you are in the heart of the jungle.
- ✓ Bring a good pair of binoculars. You may not get close enough to see some of the more elusive birds and mammals.
- ✓ Bring several changes of clothes for your time in the jungle – nothing dries in the humidity!

No tourist or commercial activity is permitted inside the reserve, so your stay in Manú will be in a lodge, located just outside. These are rustic wooden structures surrounded by jungle, with screened cabins, limited or no electricity, and terraces equipped with hammocks that look out over the forest. The lodges provide the obligatory guides who are extremely well informed and an invaluable aid in helping visitors to spot the more evasive jungle-dwellers and spectacular flora.

Hiking along forested trails in search of tapir, and following the faint footprints of the elusive jaguar, brings out the adventurer in visitors. On the river, the boat becomes a silent viewing platform as everyone waits with bated breath for the slick head of a rare giant otter to emerge from the water, or for a black cayman to catch the light as it slides from the bank and into the mud. Ploughing deeper into the preserve aboard a long, slender motor-canoe, the foliage becomes thicker, the humidity more intense, and the chattering of monkeys and birds and the steady hum of insects almost deafening. The scale and density of the jungle is breathtaking here. For sheer wilderness, it doesn't get much better than this.

BARRETOS RODEO FESTIVAL

IT BEGAN IN A BAR IN THE RANCH COUNTRY OF NORTHERN SÃO PAULO, in 1956, when a dozen wealthy young ranchers had the idea of staging a weekend display of bull carts, leather violins, and other items of traditional Brazilian cowboy culture. It has since grown into a ten-day high-stakes rodeo, with its own purpose-built stadium and extensive fairgrounds, an annual celebration of cowboy traditions that attracts over half a million visitors. The Festa do Peão de Boiadeiro de Barretos is the premier rodeo event in Brazil, and one of the major stops on the international rodeo circuit. Rodeo fans from north of the Rio Grande will recognize most of the competitive events on offer in the 35,000-seat stadium: bronco-riding (known as *sela americana* or "American saddle" in Brazil), steer-wrestling, bareback-riding, barrel-racing for the female competitors, and the incredible and dangerous spectacle of bull-

GETTING THERE **See map p329, E3**
Barretos lies 260 miles (420 km) northwest of São Paulo. There is a local airport 3 miles (5 km) from the city, and a larger regional airport in Ribeirão Preto, 75 miles (120 km) south of Barretos.

GETTING AROUND
The Parque do Peão, or rodeo ground, is just over a mile (2 km) from the city center. Taxis are plentiful but, on rodeo days, the roads fill up and traffic may be reduced to a crawl.

WEATHER
Days are normally sunny and hot, reaching 85°F (30°C). Nights are pleasantly warm.

ACCOMMODATIONS
DAN Inn Barretos is basic, clean, and comfy, with gardens and pool; doubles from US$70; www.hoteldaninnbarretos.com.br

The Barretos Country Hotel is 2 miles (3 km) out of town, near the airport; doubles from US$200; www.barretoscountryhotel.com.br

Mabruk Apart Hotel is located in a small highrise in the city center; doubles from US$250; www.mabrukhotel.com.br

EATING OUT
At the rodeo you will find all-you-can-eat barbecue for US$25. Elsewhere an average meal for two will cost US$30–50.

FURTHER INFO
www.independentes.com.br

Rodeo Queen

The very first *Rainha da Festa,* or Rodeo Queen, was picked by the group of ranchers who originated the Festa. From then on, the title was awarded to the Barretos girl who had sold the most tickets for the rodeo's charity raffle. In 1970, good works gave way to beauty, as young women from the city and region paraded in (often skimpy) cowgirl costumes, a process that went nationwide in the 1990s. Since 2002, however, the competition has returned to its regional roots, as a contest in beauty and elocution among the young women of Barretos.

Main: *Cutiano* competitor struggles to remain on his mount

Left: High-speed action in a barrel-racing event

Right (left to right): "Bull dogging" or steer-wrestling; display by flag-waving cowboys; young competitor on sheepback

Right panel (top to bottom): A children's mini-stadium; rodeo clowns during the bull-riding competition; handcrafted saddle

riding. More unusual – unique to Brazil, in fact – is the riding style called *cutiano*. In this terrifying event, the rider has to stay on a bucking horse with the aid of only two straps secured around the animal's girth. A stroll through the fairgrounds outside the stadium only reinforces the exotic nature of the Festa do Peão, with its unique blend of American-style rodeo and Brazilian country culture. In the restaurants and on food stalls, *churrasco* – Brazilian barbecue – is everywhere but, unlike the American cookout, in Brazil the beef is held close to the coals and cooked quickly, the thin slices served up hot and juicy with more than a modicum of coarse barbecue salt. Given the superb quality of the meat, *churrasco* can't be anything but mouthwateringly delicious.

The evenings are purely Brazilian, with all-night parties on two stages, featuring Brazil's biggest artists playing everything from *sertaneja*, Brazilian-style country music, to *forró*, an upbeat country polka, as well as the ever-popular samba. Everyone dances, and everyone sports a cowboy hat.

Above: The spectacular horseshoe-shaped rodeo arena

FESTA DIARY

The Festa do Peão de Boiadeiro de Barretos lasts a full ten days, but much of the first week is taken up with qualifying rounds for the various rodeo events. The final three days see the breathtakingly thrilling finals of all the competitive events, capped off every night by a big-name music performance in the rodeo grounds.

Three Days of Thrills and Spills

DAY 1

Go straight to the big arena to see the action. The day features a full program of bronco-riding, calf-wrestling, barrel-riding and bucking bulls. Take time out to stroll the fairgrounds and sample Brazilian country cooking. Save some energy for the evening festivities on either of the fairground's two main stages.

DAY 2

Today offers more thrills in the main stadium. In between, stroll the craft and saddlery shops in the rodeo grounds. The leatherware in particular is of exceptional quality. If you are a rider you can buy a superb, handcrafted saddle at a fraction of the cost up north. Saturday's evening show is traditionally the biggest concert of the rodeo, with both main stages featuring top Brazilian artists playing pop, country, *forró* (like polka), and sometimes samba.

DAY 3

The last day of the rodeo is also the finals of the International Rodeo Competition. This is the day that the top riders from Brazil and around the world have been working towards since the Festa began. The rides are guaranteed to be wild, fast, and furious. In the evening, head for the town of Barretos and indulge in a blow-out meal of Brazilian *churrasco*, where the cuts of meat are grilled on skewers over a pit of glowing coals. Prime cuts include *picanha* (rump steak) and *maminha* (shoulder steak). If you're particularly hungry, look for a restaurant offering *rodizo* – all you can eat for a single, reasonable price.

Dos and Don'ts

- ✓ Book your accommodation early – hotels fill up months in advance of the rodeo dates.
- ✓ Try the traditional Brazilian cowboy food – dishes made with *carne seca* (jerk beef), fried manioc, and sweet corn meal cake for dessert.
- ✗ Don't forget your equine loved one's measurements. Brazilian saddles, bridles, and other riding gear offer top quality leather and workmanship.
- ✓ Buy and wear a big cowboy hat. Everyone else will be wearing one and, as long as you don't take photos, no one back home need ever know.

GETTING THERE See map p330, E6
Silvio Pettirossi International Airport is 9 miles (15 km) northwest of the center of the capital, Asunción.

GETTING AROUND
If you plan to visit the national parks and rural countryside, you'll need a car. Asunción and the airport have a number of car-rental offices. If you plan to stick to the cities, then you can generally get around by bus.

WEATHER
With a mix of tropical and subtropical climates, Paraguay can be hot and humid during summer. The optimal time to visit is during the spring, before the heat.

ACCOMMODATIONS
The Bella Vista Hotel in Encarnación has snug but well-maintained rooms; doubles from US$95; www.bellavistahotel.com.py

The Sabe Center Hotel in Asunción has comfortable rooms; doubles from US$99; www.sabecenterhotel.com.py

La Mision Hotel Boutique in Asunción boasts a rooftop pool; doubles from US$152; www.lamision.com.py

EATING OUT
Paraguayan cuisine is rooted in its Guaraní history, with plenty of root vegetables and maize. In the main cities, you'll also find grill houses and some seafood restaurants.

FURTHER INFO
www.senatur.gov.py

An Unlikely Hero

Although former US President Rutherford B. Hayes may be little known in American history, in Paraguay, he's a national hero. There's even a region, Presidente Hayes, named after him, and he is the namesake of its capital of Villa Hayes, on the banks of the Paraguay River. Why all these tributes? When Hayes was in office in 1878, he was called on to arbitrate a dispute between Paraguay and Argentina over who owned the vast Chaco grasslands. Hayes sided with Paraguay and the rest, as they say, is history.

PARAGUAY

Many destinations claim to be "off the tourist trail" but these days, few are. Paraguay is a different story. The superstar South American countries such as Argentina, Brazil, and Chile receive a massive influx of visitors every year, but Paraguay? Roam the flourishing countryside, and you may be the only visitor that anyone has seen in days, if not weeks. Also off the beaten path is the lively capital of Asunción. Here you'll encounter colonial buildings like the grand Panteón Nacional de los Héroes, the stately Palacio de López, and the attractive Catedral de Nuestra Señora de la Asunción. The city also offers easy access to a range of side trips, including to the scenic Ypacaraí Lake.

For a glimpse into Paraguay's religious evolution, visit the well preserved ruins of the Jesuit missions of La Santísima Trinidad de Paraná and Jesús de Tavarangue, near Encarnación, the capital

Main: Jesuit mission ruins near Encarnación

Left panel (top to bottom): Manicured gardens front Palacio de López; the city center of Asunción; the domed Panteón Nacional de los Héroes

Right (left to right): Waxy monkey tree frog in the Gran Chaco; the colonial edifice of Catedral de Nuestra Señora de la Asunción; diners in downtown Asunción

city of the Itapúa region. Nicknamed the Perla del Sur (Pearl of the South), Encarnación has become one of the country's prime visitor hubs, with inviting, sandy beaches and a breezy boardwalk. The city shows off its most vibrant side every weekend in February for the electric Carnaval, when the streets fill with music and dancing.

To see Paraguay's rich wildlife, venture into the massive plains of the Gran Chaco region. This is an area with few amenities and infrastructure, so it's best to hire a guide to explore; inquire at the tourist office in Asunción or Encarnación. Although Gran Chaco has large tracts of deforestation, it's nonetheless home to an incredible array of flora and fauna, reflecting the roots of its name, derived from the local Quechua peoples' word for "hunting land." The landscape encompasses savannah grasses, palm groves and thorn forests, and is home to jaguars, giant armadillos, capybaras, and rheas, which are large, flightless birds similar to ostriches.

Above: A relaxing spot to enjoy the waters of Ypacaraí Lake

EXPLORER'S DIARY

Roam Paraguay for a diverse array of sights, from historical villages to beautifully preserved Jesuit missions to vast savannah plains. August is a great time to visit the country, with pleasant temperatures before the heat and humidity of summer.

Five Days of Discovery

DAY 1–2

Explore Paraguay's capital, Asunción, which is dotted with historic buildings, such as the 1774 Casa de la Independencia, which doubles as a museum with colonial artifacts. The Manzana de la Rivera is a block of historic houses that includes the Art Nouveau Casa Clari; the interesting Museo de Bellas Artes (Fine Arts Museum); and the botanic gardens and zoo. You can also visit the scenic waters of Ypacaraí Lake, a short drive from the capital.

DAY 3–4

Travel to the south-central region of the country, and venture into the rural countryside, where you'll come across quiet, little-visited towns that are straight out of the past, like Caazapá, with a palm-tree lined main street, a plaza, and church. Continue farther south to the Itapúa region, to visit the well maintained ruins of the Jesuit missions. First built in 1609, they are said to be among the least-visited UNESCO sights in the world. Afterward, head to the regional capital of Encarnación, where you can settle in for the evening, dining out and enjoying a local beer.

DAY 5

Make this a day of wilderness and wildlife, and hire a guide to explore the Gran Chaco, a vast swath of wild parkland filled with local flora and fauna. Keep an eye out for everything from armadillos to capybara. The Low Chaco region is excellent for bird-watching, with storks, parakeets, ibises, and hawks all living here, while the drier High Chaco region is great for spotting tapirs, giant anteaters, and red brocket deer.

Dos and Don'ts

- ✓ Bring sturdy shoes and protective clothing. If you plan to hike outside of the main cities, you'll be trekking through remote terrain, so the more durable your shoes and gear, the better.
- ✗ Don't leave your skin exposed to mosquito and bug bites. Though the risk of malaria is low in Paraguay, it's imperative to take precautions, especially around swampland and in the more untamed parts of the country.
- ✓ Try *sopa Paraguay* (Paraguayan soup), which, in fact, is not soup at all. It's a local corn bread, generally made with flour, corn, cheese, and milk.

SEPTEMBER

Where to Go: **September**

Autumn is a glorious time to be in North America. The peak season crowds have thinned out, and most destinations take on a softer, more mellow complexion once the summer has faded. The east coast of the USA and Canada, and the higher elevations of the Southwestern states, are showing early signs of their rich fall colors. This is a fine time to enjoy the great outdoors, when the skies are still blue. The deserts of western USA are a little more forgiving this month than the rest of the year, and even San Francisco, famed for its climatic mood swings, is relatively settled in September. Meanwhile, in South America, spring is well on its way. Below you will find all the destinations in this chapter as well as some extra suggestions to provide a little inspiration.

FESTIVALS AND CULTURE

QUITO Tropical wildlife in the Mindo Nambillo cloud forest

QUITO
ECUADOR

Take a trip back in time to a 16th-century colonial capital

Splash in thermal baths, ascend volcanoes, admire giant butterflies in the cloud forest, and scare yourself silly on the Devil's Nose train.

See pp218–9

"A true Andean gem, Quito has two distinct but complementary facets, each with its own unforgettable sights and styles."

PENDLETON ROUND UP
OREGON, USA

Sharpen your spurs for rodeo

Steer-wrestling, Brahma bull-riding, and greased pig-catching are just some of the attractions on offer at this cowboy extravaganza.

www.pendletonroundup.com

ALOHA FESTIVALS
HAWAI'I, USA

A unique celebration of Hawaiian culture

Celebrated across the whole of Hawai'i, this is the islands' premier cultural event, with traditional music, dance, and history.

www.alohafestivals.com

TIWANAKU, LA PAZ
BOLIVIA

Bolivia's most important archeological site

The capital boasts significant monumental stone ruins from the pre-Colombian civilization.

en.wikipedia.org/wiki/Tiwanaku

BUMBERSHOOT, SEATTLE
WASHINGTON, USA

America's best pop-culture fest

Summer's over, but Seattle makes up for it with the USA's biggest new music and arts festival, hosting a range of international performers.

www.bumbershoot.com

PORTLAND
OREGON, USA

Oregon's largest city celebrates culture and nature

Rebellious yet relaxed, Portland has the best of all worlds: art galleries, cafés, cocktail lounges and Forest Park, a massive urban forest.

See pp222–3

UNFORGETTABLE JOURNEYS

BLACK HILLS Horseback riding on the Plains of South Dakota

BLACK HILLS
SOUTH DAKOTA, USA

Remote frontier territory with spectacular landscapes

Mt. Rushmore and the Crazy Horse Memorial are dramatic man-made additions to the natural wonders of canyons and mountains here.

See pp228–9

ALGONQUIN PROVINCIAL PARK
ONTARIO, CANADA

Unforgettable parklands

Paddle a canoe around the park's myriad waterways, with over 2,400 lakes and miles of streams and rivers to explore.

www.algonquinpark.on.ca

VERMONT
NEW ENGLAND, USA

Catch the fall on a tour of the northeast back roads

The prime place to see all the colors of the New England fall: maple, beech, and ash frame picture-perfect clapboard villages.

www.vermontvacation.com

COAST TO COAST
CANADA

A legendary train ride east to west over the mountains

Canada's interior is a land of wide vistas so there's a lot of scenery to enjoy, but the mountains are the true highlight of the journey.

See pp226–7

IQUITOS
PERU

Unforgettable Amazon river journeys in Peru

Take a boat from Iquitos through Peru's lush lowland rain forests, some of the best preserved and least explored in the Amazon

www.amazoncruise.net

NATURAL WONDERS

CIUDAD PERDIDA Overlooking La Ciudad Perdida

CIUDAD PERDIDA
COLOMBIA

Trek through the jungle to Colombia's Lost City

At first sight of the Lost City, you'll think you're in an adventure fantasy film: crumbling ruins are enveloped in swirling mists.

See pp224–5

ISLA DEL SOL
BOLIVIA

Mystical cradle of the Inca civilization on Lake Titicaca

Hauntingly beautiful Isla del Sol was revered by the Incas as the birthplace of the sun and moon.

www.andeantreks.com/trip/island-sun

"No picture can prepare you for the mystery of these vast designs, etched into the dry, rocky desert of western Peru."

SEQUOIA NATIONAL PARK
CALIFORNIA, USA

The forest giants

Wander amidst an array of giant Californian redwoods, including the General Sherman, the largest tree on the planet.

www.nps.gov/seki

OZARK MOUNTAINS
MISSOURI, USA

Sylvan uplands in the heart of the USA

The Ozarks present a beguiling landscape of rocky peaks surrounded by rolling forest and crystal-clear lakes.

www.ozarkmtns.com

Previous page: Mesa Arch and canyon walls, Canyonlands National Park, Utah

Weather Watch

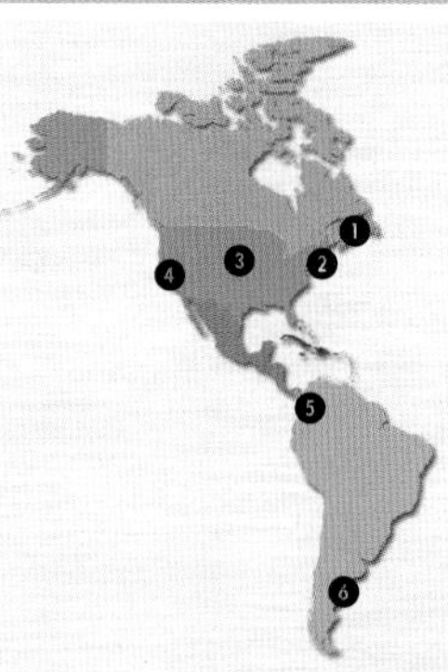

1 Fundy Isles, Canada This is as good as it gets, climate-wise, in New Brunswick, with bright blue skies and fall landscapes more than compensating for cold temperatures.

2 Philadelphia, USA The harsh heat of the summer should start to abate in September, though expect some still very warm days with bright and sunny skies, and high humidity in the city center itself.

3 South Dakota, USA The rugged Great Plains state enjoys pleasant conditions in September, with warm daytime highs and much cooler evenings. The sun can still be harsh during the day, however. Take sunscreen.

4 San Francisco, USA September is warm and sunny. Rain is unlikely, and although those summer fogs have abated, you should still bring warm clothing just in case.

5 Colombia On the coast, September is in the midst of the whale-watching season. Further in land, and around Ciudad Perdida, there are frequent rain showers but you will welcome these whilst hiking.

6 Argentina Spring is an appealing time to visit Buenos Aires and the Andean foothills. The highlands around Mendoza are bright and cool, with warm daytime temperatures, dropping dramatically after dark.

LUXURY AND ROMANCE

MENDOZA Sycamore-lined road between the vineyards

MENDOZA
ARGENTINA

Wine tasting and breathtaking natural beauty

Charming, leafy Mendoza; great mountain views and a colonial mansion, set amid the vines, are all part of this Argentinian wine tour.

See pp216–7

SEDONA
ARIZONA, USA

Crystals, cameras, and canyons

This popular New Age, film and cultural center boasts a string of top restaurants and hotels, such as the Enchantment Resort.

www.visitsedona.com

TAOS
NEW MEXICO, USA

A town with a special mix of cultures and atmospheres

Wander through the historic pueblo and its art galleries and New Age centers, or just chill out in the lovely hot springs.

www.taos.org

SAN FRANCISCO
CALIFORNIA, USA

America's favorite city with a beautiful bayside location

San Francisco combines iconic landmarks with vibrant ethnic communities, bohemian neighbor-hoods and world-class art.

See pp212–3

"This west coast capital of sophistication has something for everyone, from fine-art museums to casual dining."

COLONIA DE SACRAMENTO
URUGUAY

Take a step back in time

Explore the delightful winding streets and pretty Portuguese architecture of this riverside resort town.

whc.unesco.org/en/list/747

ACTIVE ADVENTURES

UTAH'S NATIONAL PARKLANDS A hiker in a narrow pass, Zion Canyon

UTAH'S NATIONAL PARKLANDS
UTAH, USA

Surreal landscapes

A spectacular desert with a vast collection of amazing geographic features that provide great, if occasionally challenging, hiking.

See pp214–5

THE JOHN MUIR TRAIL
CALIFORNIA, USA

Unforgettable wilderness trek

Enjoy miles of prime hiking through some stunning national parks, starting at Yosemite and finishing at Mount Whitney.

johnmuirtrail.org

OLYMPIC NATIONAL PARK
WASHINGTON STATE, USA

Prime west-coast wilderness

Take a hike through this varied national park, with landscapes ranging from Pacific Ocean beaches to glaciated peaks.

www.nps.gov/olym

BANFF NATIONAL PARK
ALBERTA, CANADA

Canada's oldest national park

Encompassing a spectacular section of the Canadian Rockies, see glaciers, icefields, coniferous forest, and mirror-blue lakes here.

www.pc.gc.ca/banff

COLORADO
USA

Discover your inner cowboy on a dude ranch

Try a real outdoor adventure, learning how to really ride on a western ranch – and hike, fish, and go climbing and rafting, too.

www.coloradoranch.com

FAMILY GETAWAYS

PHILADELPHIA Carousel ride at Giggleberry Fair

PHILADELPHIA
PENNSYLVANIA, USA

Take a walk through a living history book

A sophisticated city that has plenty to offer families – as well as historical sights, it has sports, museums, and rides for the kids.

See pp220–21

THE THOUSAND ISLANDS
NEW YORK STATE, USA

Upstate New York family fun

The Thousand Islands region provides plenty of entertainment, ranging from balloon rides to white-water rafting.

www.1000islands.com

FUNDY ISLES
NEW BRUNSWICK, CANADA

Island-hopping far from the usual tourist routes

Kids will marvel at a close encounter with a humpback whale, and you can't help but laugh as comical puffins take flight.

See pp210–11

CAPE BRETON ISLAND
NOVA SCOTIA, CANADA

A wild island hideaway

Here are misty waterfalls, forests of fall colors, whales rising majestically beyond the waves, and fabulous seafood.

www.cbisland.com

LAKE GEORGE
NEW YORK STATE, USA

An inland sea in upstate New York

In the heart of the Adirondacks, this giant forest lake is ringed by campsites, fine hotels, and places to swim, hike, sail, and more.

www.visitlakegeorge.com

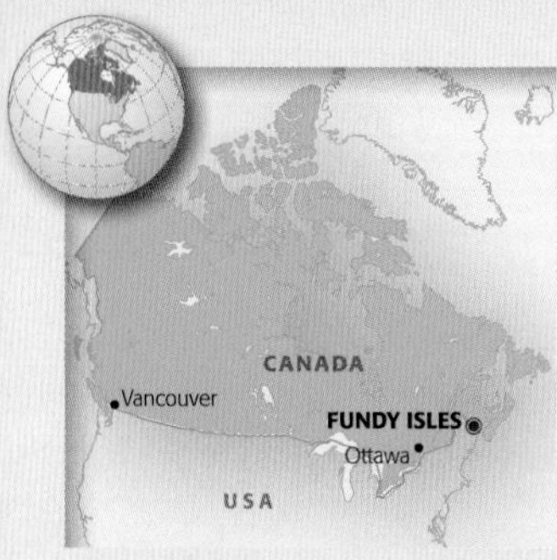

GETTING THERE See map p314, F6
The Bay of Fundy separates New Brunswick from Nova Scotia. St. John's airport is around 50 miles (80 km) northeast of the Isles, with flights from Montréal and Toronto. Deer Island is reached by ferry from Letete. Campobello Island is linked by seasonal ferry to Deer Island and Eastport, and by road from Lubec. Grand Manan ferries run from Blacks Harbour.

GETTING AROUND
Car rental is available at the airport, and the ferries take vehicles. Some lodgings rent bikes.

WEATHER
September daytime temperatures average 66°F (19°C), but nights are cooler.

ACCOMMODATIONS
Deer Island Inn offers restored Victorian rooms with private baths; doubles from US$100; www.diinn.com

In Saint Andrews, Seaside Beach Resort offers waterside apartments; two-bed suites from US$100; www.seaside.nb.ca

Beach Front Cottages, on Grand Manan, are self-contained sea-view chalets; family units from US$120; theradicle.ca/beachfront/

EATING OUT
Fresh, locally caught lobster, scallops, and salmon are abundant on all three islands. Try seafood chowder sprinkled with dried dulse.

FURTHER INFORMATION
www.tourismnewbrunswick.ca

A Seaweed Feast

For many people, seaweed may not be as appetizing a prospect as seafood, but it forms an important part of the islands' economy. Dulse, a red-hued variety, is collected by hand at low tide, then sun-dried on the distinctive racks that dot the shoreline. Islanders tend to eat it freshly dried, as a snack, but it may be served fried, or added to salads and soups. While dulse is an acquired taste, it is filled with minerals and vitamins, and is found in health-food stores worldwide. Nori, used for sushi and sashimi, is now also being cultivated for export to Japan.

Main: Colorful Atlantic puffins on Machias Seal Island, in the Bay of Fundy

FUNDY ISLES

Far off the beaten tourist track, and little-known outside of Atlantic Canada, the Fundy Isles draw outdoor-lovers searching for adventure beyond the ordinary. The three main populated islands – Deer, Campobello, and Grand Manan – each have their own personalities, but are linked by history and geology. The natural phenomenon of the world's highest tides dictates the pattern of life for residents and visitors alike, with ferry links to the outside world, islanders' working hours, and even simple pleasures like beachcombing totally dependent upon the tide.

Closest to the mainland is Deer Island. This is a peaceful fishing community, its shorelines dotted with herring weirs and lobster pounds. The most exciting thing going on here is Old Sow, the largest whirlpool in the western hemisphere at 250 ft (76 m) across. Campobello Island's road link to the USA has attracted many wealthy Americans to spend their summers here. The most famous was Franklin D. Roosevelt, whose family estate now forms the Roosevelt

Left (left to right): Harborside on Grand Manan; live lobster; grey seals; Franklin D. Roosevelt's summer cottage on Campobello Island; meadows of lupins edge the Bay of Fundy

Below: Swallowtail Lighthouse at North Head on Grand Manan

Inset: Herring weir on Deer Island

Above: Spectacular results on a whale-watching trip

Bike rides through waterside meadows of lupins and wild roses; beachcombing on the shoreline for agate and amethyst...

Campobello International Park. His charming Arts and Crafts summer cottage is open to visitors, and the park offers lovely vistas and perfect picnic spots. Herring Cove Provincial Park is another favorite, with a long sandy beach, walking trails, and a golf course to keep all the family happy.

Grand Manan is the largest of the Fundy Isles. While its setting is blissfully peaceful, the extreme tides stir up nutrients from the ocean floor, which attract an amazing variety of marine life. Humpback whales are the species most often spotted, but finback and minke are also present. Late August through mid-September is considered the best time of year to view these magnificent creatures. Bird-watchers will be captivated by the hundreds of varieties recorded on the Isles, and no one can fail to be entertained by the comic appeal of the local puffins. The best way to view them is on a boat tour to Machias Seal Island. But there's much more to enjoy as well – bike rides through waterside meadows of lupins and wild roses; beachcombing on the shoreline of Red Point for agate and amethyst; or simply immersing yourself in island life and doing nothing much at all.

ISLAND DIARY

September visitors to the Fundy Isles will encounter fewer crowds while still enjoying pleasant weather. This is also one of the best times of year for whale-watching. Four days is a good length of time to visit all three islands, even though, by virtue of the ferry routes, you must inevitably include a return to the mainland mid-trip.

Four Days on the Bay

DAY 1

Catch the ferry from Letete, New Brunswick, to Deer Island. Take a leisurely drive down the coast, through seaside villages dotted with art galleries and past impressive lobster pounds, to the island's southern extremity, Deer Island Point Park. With a bit of forward planning, you could time it right to view Old Sow. From the Point, it's a short ferry ride to Campobello Island.

DAY 2

Get up early to watch the sun rise over Herring Cove Provincial Park. Divide your day between here and Roosevelt Campobello International Park. Later, return to the mainland, by ferry or the road bridge, and spend the night in the mainland resort town of Saint Andrews.

DAY 3

Drive to Black's Harbour and set off aboard a morning ferry for Grand Manan Island. The crossing takes 90 minutes. Allow a couple of hours to explore the island by road. After lunch, join a whale-watching trip into the Bay of Fundy, from which you can expect to see magnificent humpbacks in close proximity. In the evening, try to get an ocean-view table at the Compass Rose Restaurant for dinner.

DAY 4

Take a morning bird-watching boat trip. Puffins will steal the show but you may also spot playful seals in calmer waters. In the afternoon, take the time to explore wildflower meadows along the west coast and seek out gemstones along the beach at Red Point, before heading back to the ferry for the mainland.

Dos and Don'ts

- ✓ Accommodations are limited, so make reservations before traveling to the islands.
- ✗ Don't forget to carry a tide timetable with you.
- ✓ Be at Deer Island Point Park 3 hours before high tide to get the best view of Old Sow whirlpool.
- ✓ Sample the local scallops, which are renowned for their size and sweetness. And do give dulse a try!
- ✓ Catch the sunset at the Long Eddy Point Lighthouse (the Whistle) on Grand Manan Island.

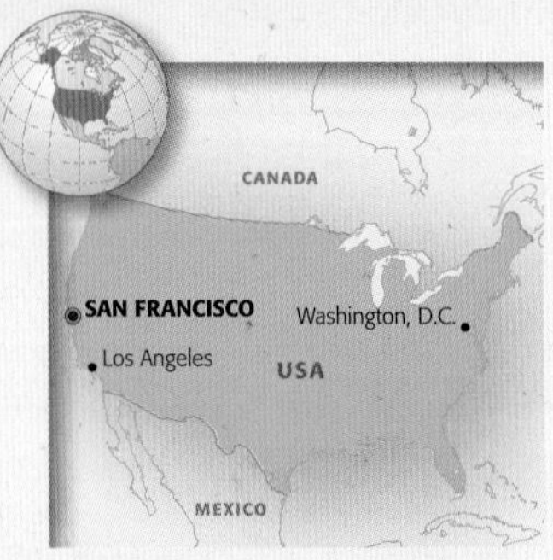

GETTING THERE See map p321, A3
San Francisco is a major transportation hub on the Pacific Coast. Most flights arrive at San Francisco International Airport, 13 miles (20 km) south of the city center.

GETTING AROUND
Cable cars are an easy way to get to many downtown sites, while Muni buses and the BART light rail connect other parts. The street grids make driving easy, but parking can be difficult.

WEATHER
September is one of the warmest months, with bright sunny days, little fog, and an average high of 72°F (22°C).

ACCOMMODATIONS
Experience the beat-generation atmosphere at the historic Hotel Boheme; doubles from US$225; www.hotelboheme.com

The sumptuous Westin St. Francis is at the heart of downtown Union Square; doubles from US$385; www.westinstfrancis.com

The Clift Hotel combines traditional luxury and contemporary styling; doubles from US$404; www.clifthotel.com

EATING OUT
Book ahead at award-winning Restaurant Gary Danko, near Fisherman's Wharf (US$100), or sample tantalizing French-Vietnamese fare at Le Colonial (US$60).

FURTHER INFORMATION
www.onlyinsanfrancisco.com

Golden Gate Bridge

An engineering marvel, the Golden Gate Bridge was the world's largest man-made structure when built in 1937. The vermilion bridge spanning the 2-mile-(3.2-km-) wide Golden Gate Straits was designed by Charles Ellis and Leon Moisseiff. Supported by two elegant 746-ft (227-m) tall piers, each suspension cable weighs 11,000 tons and contains 27,572 parallel wires that could circle the earth three times.

SAN FRANCISCO

With a spectacular waterfront setting made more dramatic by the iconic Golden Gate Bridge, cosmopolitan San Francisco is a stylishly chic and bohemian city. This West Coast capital of sophistication has something for everyone, from fine art museums to casual dining. In fact, "The City" (it's never referred to as 'Frisco) is a culinary trove, with more restaurants per capita than any other place in North America.

San Francisco is a city of neighborhoods, each as distinct as a thumbprint: peoples from all over the world have stitched their cultural enclaves on to the city's quilt. Chinatown whisks you to the Orient with its giddy whirligig of scents, sights, and sounds, while the nearby North Beach exudes laid-back Italian charm. Haight-Ashbury is a must-visit for its offbeat reminders of the Flower Power era. Pacific Heights boasts astounding Beaux Arts mansions and Victorian gingerbread houses. The glittering skyscrapers of the Financial District rub shoulders with the fashionable department stores of Union Square, while Golden Gate Park offers plenty of outdoor pursuits as well as one of North America's foremost museums: the splendid de Young. The SOMA district's Museum of Modern Art and Legion of Honor (replete with classics from Rembrandt to Rodin) are also guaranteed to satisfy culture vultures.

> This West Coast capital of sophistication has something for everyone, from fine art museums to casual dining.

Despite its large size, it's easy to get your bearings. San Francisco – at the tip of a peninsula – is laid out in a rough grid, with glittering boulevards running west from the waterfront to the Pacific Ocean. While local neighborhoods are best explored on foot, San Francisco's 42 hills will have you huffing and puffing. Fortunately, the legendary cable cars, comfortable BART subway, and Muni bus system make getting around a cinch. To really feel like a local, take in an opera or the comedy cabaret, *Beach Blanket Babylon*. Hop on a ferry at Pier 39 for a cruise on the bay, being sure to step ashore on Alcatraz for a thrilling tour. Join the early risers practicing *tai chi* in Washington Square and jog along the windswept Marina. It soon becomes apparent why San Francisco is consistently rated as America's favorite city.

Main: Golden Gate Bridge against the San Francisco skyline
Below (left and right): Sailing past the historic island prison of Alcatraz; cable cars on California Street
Inset: Telling time in an age-old manner at the de Young Museum

Above: Revelers at a masked ball at the San Francisco Opera

CITY LIGHTS DIARY

Fall in San Francisco is the best time of year weather-wise, as the famously cold summer fogs clear and rainfall is rare. Brilliant sunny weather makes for enjoyable days exploring on foot, while the lush parks draw families and picnickers. Five days are just enough to savor the main sights and attractions.

Five Days of Urban Culture

DAY 1

Admire the incredible modern art at the San Francisco Museum of Modern Art in the SOMA district, then stroll around Union Square, where the main attractions are the fine boutiques and upscale department stores. In the evening, dine at Gary Danko before enjoying cocktails and the spectacular view from the Starlight Room.

DAY 2

Enjoy the atmosphere of Chinatown, with time to savor some of the local specialties. Then invigorate yourself with a cappuccino in North Beach for the climb to Coit Tower. Be sure to visit City Light Bookstore and, in the evening, take in an opera or laugh tears at the longest-running music revue, *Beach Blanket Babylon*.

DAY 3

Ride the cable car to Nob Hill for great views. Visit Grace Cathedral and the Cable Car Museum, then continue to Ghiradelli Square. Walk the waterfront, visiting the U.S.S. *Pampanito* and Fisherman's Wharf. Then walk downhill to fun-filled Pier 39. Afterwards, board a ferry for a guided tour of Alcatraz.

DAY 4

Drive out to Golden Gate Park, which fills most of the day. Allow time for the spectacular de Young Museum and California Academy of Sciences. Then enjoy the serene beauty of the Japanese Tea Garden or admire the redwoods at the San Francisco Botanical Garden.

DAY 5

Dress warmly for a walk across the Golden Gate Bridge, not missing Fort Point National Historic Site. Spend the afternoon in awe of the art at the Palace of the Legion of Honor.

Dos and Don'ts

- ✓ Bring some cold-weather clothing so that you can easily add an extra layer. San Francisco can be bitterly cold if a rare late summer fog rolls in.
- ✓ Ride the famous cable cars and historic trams – a great way to get to know the city and enjoy a unique and integral aspect of San Francisco's heritage.
- ✗ Don't restrict yourself to one area. Explore the city's many neighborhoods, from North Beach and Chinatown to the Marina District.

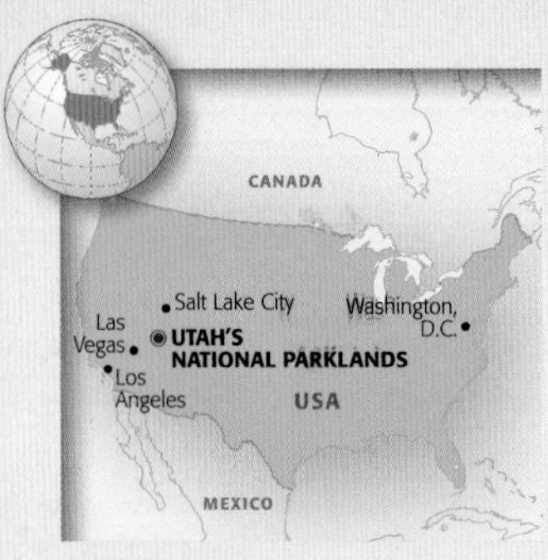

GETTING THERE See map p321, E3–4, F3–4
The largest airports near southern Utah are in Las Vegas, (southwest of Zion Canyon), and Salt Lake City (northeast of Zion). Small airports near the towns of Moab and St. George get some regional flights.

GETTING AROUND
The practical way to reach and explore the parklands of southern Utah is by car; rentals are available in Las Vegas and Salt Lake City.

WEATHER
September has hot days and cooler nights. The average daytime high in Moab reaches 87°F (31°C), while the nighttime low is 51°F (11°C). Springdale is warmer. Rain is rare.

ACCOMMODATIONS
Driftwood Lodge is a welcoming motel with a restaurant attached; doubles from US$159; www.driftwoodlodge.net

The riverside Desert Pearl Inn in Springdale offers great views; rooms from US$230; www.desertpearl.com

Upscale Red Cliffs Lodge, northeast of Moab, offers horseback riding and rafting; rooms from US$240; www.redcliffslodge.com

EATING OUT
Standard American fare comes cheap at US$12–15 for a full meal. For variety, try Springdale's Spotted Dog Café or the Desert Bistro in Moab (around US$25–30).

FURTHER INFORMATION
www.utah.com

Lake Powell

Perhaps southern Utah's most incongruous spectacle is the mighty body of water that lies at its heart. Created by the Glen Canyon Dam in 1963, Lake Powell took 17 years to fill. The price of its construction, apart from the US$300 million, was the drowning of idyllic Glen Canyon, hailed by the few river-runners who saw it as the finest of Utah's canyons. While none could mistake the lake as being natural, four million visitors descend here each year to cruise around its many buttes-turned-islands and explore its countless hidden recesses.

Main: A boat plying the waters of Lake Powell between unearthly rock formations
Above (top to bottom): The forests of Boulder Mountain putting on a display of color in the fall; Delicate Arch; a hiker crossing Zion River in Zion National Park; the gushing waters of Calf Creek Falls

UTAH'S NATIONAL PARKLANDS

If the word "desert" suggests a featureless expanse of windblown sand to you, the spectacular scenery of southern Utah will come as a revelation. From the surreal, incandescent hoodoos – bizarre rock formations – of Bryce Canyon to the awesome jigsaw-puzzle plateaus of Canyonlands stacked one atop the other toward the panoramic horizon, Utah's so-called "high country" is a wonderland of stunning beauty, where the bare bones of the earth lie eroded in a million peculiar formations perfect for exploration. While trails in the national parks provide immensely rewarding opportunities to hike into the wilderness, the whole place is on such a scale that to appreciate it in full will take many hours just driving through the prodigiously breathtaking landscape.

Zion Canyon makes for a deceptively gentle welcome, with lush meadows lining the valley floor beneath mighty walls of red sandstone. Head east from here to reach the fiery pinnacles of Bryce Canyon, then continue into Utah's largest park, Grand Staircase-Escalante National Monument. Much of this vast expanse is accessible only to the hardiest of backpackers, but a trail setting off from beside Highway 12 leads to rainbow-hued Calf Creek Falls. The high slopes of Boulder Mountain beyond are a prime location to enjoy fall colors. Once past Capitol Reef, a jagged anticline that formed a fearsome natural barrier to Mormon settlers, you discover Utah at its most desolate, with stark mounds of gray clay towering over the highway. It's amazing to think that prehistoric peoples painted the eerie pictographs of remote Horseshoe Canyon here over a thousand years ago.

The funky outpost of Moab in southeast Utah, a haven for lycra-clad devotees of extreme sports, makes a great base for exploring the final two parks, Arches and Canyonlands. Arches, small enough to explore in a day, holds over 2,000 natural rock arches. This includes Utah's state symbol, Delicate Arch, a free-standing stone crescent that frames the La Sal Mountains. Largest of all Utah's parks is the vast Canyonlands, offering the opportunity to take in fabulous desert vistas in its Island in the Sky District, and explore sublime hiking trails in the Needles District.

Above: A hiker negotiating a narrow passage in Zion Canyon

ROCKBOUND DIARY

September is ideal for touring southern Utah; the edge is off the summer heat, the sun sets late enough to allow for long days outdoors, and the fall colors are spreading downward from the higher elevations. Each of the desert parks can hold your interest for days, so allow for over a week to get a real sense of them.

Nine Days on the Canyon Trail

A drive of a few hours on the I-15 Interstate from Las Vegas or Salt Lake City will bring you to Zion Canyon; camp here or check into a motel in Springdale. **DAY 1**

For a memorable day's hiking in Zion Canyon, climb the West Rim Trail to perilous Angel's Landing, then stroll the Riverside Walk back on the canyon floor. **DAY 2**

Drive east to Bryce Canyon and hike down into its maze of multi-hued, top-heavy sandstone pillars. **DAY 3**

Continuing east through Grand Staircase-Escalante National Monument, hike to Calf Creek Falls, and be dazzled by the fall colors on Boulder Mountain. **DAY 4**

Having spent a day exploring Capitol Reef National Park, drive on to the town of Green River. **DAY 5**

Take a day trip from Green River: drive a dirt road south, then venture deep into the Horseshoe Canyon to see the ancient pictographs in the Great Gallery. **DAY 6**

Head southeast from Green River to Moab, detouring to swoon at the sweeping views from the Island in the Sky District of Canyonlands National Park. **DAY 7**

On a day trip into Arches National Park, hike up to Delicate Arch for excellent photo opportunities. **DAY 8**

Drive south from Moab to the Needles District of Canyonlands for another day-long hike, threading between rock pillars to reach the confluence of the Green and Colorado rivers. From Moab, drive north to the I-70 to return to Las Vegas or Salt Lake City. **DAY 9**

Dos and Don'ts

- ✓ Get up early; by the end of September, the sun sets at 7pm. For a full day on the road, you need to make an early start.
- ✗ Don't expect to spend your nights carousing; you can buy alcohol in Utah, but it's only served with restaurant meals.
- ✓ Make sure you have enough gas in your tank before you set off into the backcountry.
- ✓ Carry emergency supplies – especially enough water and a flashlight – when you're hiking or driving in the desert.

GETTING THERE **See map p330, B8**

There are daily flights to Mendoza from Buenos Aires and Santiago in Chile. The 5-mile (8-km) taxi trip from airport to city center takes around 15 minutes, and costs about US$8.

GETTING AROUND

Mendoza's city center is pleasant to explore on foot, but to reach the wineries you'll need a car. Automendoza (www.automendoza.com) rents a mid-size sedan with AC and unlimited mileage for about US$75 per day.

WEATHER

Mendoza's skies are usually clear and sunny. September's spring weather reaches highs of around 68°F (20°C), lows of 43°F (6°C).

ACCOMMODATIONS

Argentino Hotel offers luxury accommodation; doubles from US$95; www.argentino-hotel.com

Club Tapiz is a restored colonial villa with an elegant restaurant, on a working vineyard; doubles from US$150; www.club-tapiz.com

Park Hyatt Mendoza is the premier hotel in town, with stylish, modern rooms; doubles from US$250; www.mendoza.park.hyatt.com

EATING OUT

1884, with a romantic setting and huge list of local wines, has mains from US$20. Azafran serves delicious food, with mains from US$15, amid the barrels of an historic wine shop.

FURTHER INFORMATION

www.welcometomendoza.com

The Malbec Grape

Argentina's signature varietal is Malbec, a grape that may have originated in Hungary. It has long been cultivated in France, where it serves as one of the six grapes used in blending Bordeaux. A purple-black grape with a thin skin and plum-like taste, it needs sun and heat, as well as a wide swing between day- and nighttime temperatures. This has resulted in Malbec falling from favor in the Old World, but Argentinean wineries have perfected its use, making intense wines with plum and cherry flavors, and a nose heavy in vanilla, which improve with ageing.

Above (left and right): Sycamore-lined road between the vineyards; decorative tilework in Plaza Espagna, Mendoza
Main: Mount Tupungato, towering over the vines of the Catena Zapata winery

Above: Maipu's relaxing, leafy central plaza

MENDOZA

HAPPY IS THE MAN WITH A HOME IN MENDOZA, runs an old expression still heard at times in Argentina. Almost as happy are those who merely get to visit. It is a city of hot days and constant sunshine, kept cool at night by its high-altitude location. Mendoza breathes the crisp, dry air of the desert, yet is lush with greenery and flowing water, channeled into the city from the Andes snowmelt via ancient irrigation works and elegant canals. It is a city where one becomes accustomed to seeing beauty – not just in the people or the elegant monuments and plazas, but also in the glimpses of a snowy peak that one happens upon in the course of a Mendoza day.

These little droplets of loveliness become a torrent when you venture out into wine country, and yet still, somehow, they come as a surprise. You'll be cycling down a tree-lined lane near Maipu when the vista will open up to a view of snow-capped Mount Tupungato. Or, standing in a tasting room, trying to conjure the right wine-vocabulary word for the delicious red liquid swirling over your palate, you'll look up and be confronted by the looming snow-white ranks of the Andes. Or you'll be crossing the Uco valley, trying to fit in just one last winery, when you'll be dazzled by the sudden glow of sunset on the low golden hills that form the valley's walls.

The vineyards themselves are centuries old, but the opportunities to visit and taste – and indeed Argentinean wine as a thing of quality and beauty – are fairly new. Only in the last 15 years have the vintners of Mendoza begun to win awards, particularly for their Malbec reds, and Torrontés and Semillon whites. With the success of tasting visits, many wineries have started to establish small on-site inns, and even upscale spas. With its nearly 700 wineries, one could spend a lifetime exploring Mendoza's wine and landscapes. Unhappy is the man who, having once discovered Mendoza, finds he has to leave again.

You'll be cycling down a tree-lined lane when the vista will open up to a view of snow-capped Mount Tupungato.

Inset: Corks from one of Mendoza's fine estates
Below (left and right): Harvesting Malbec grapes; cellar at Catena Zapata winery

TASTING DIARY

The spectacular high plains around Mendoza are the center of Argentina's wine country, home to hundreds of wineries large and small. Six days in the spring gives time to visit a representative sample of historic, traditional *bodegas* and modern wineries, traveling both with a guide and on your own, by car, by bike, and even on foot.

Six Days Amid the Vines

DAY 1 Arrive in Mendoza and check into a luxurious hotel on the city's central square. Stroll the paths and pergolas of Plaza Independencia, then get into wine country mood with a long, leisurely lunch. Ask the sommelier for a light varietal like a Semillon or Torrontés. Save the hearty Malbec for dinner, to take off the evening chill.

DAY 2 Put yourself in the hands of the local experts and take a guided wine tour, such as the one offered by Trout and Wine (www.troutandwine.com).

DAY 3 Pick up a copy of *Caminos de las Bodegas*, a set of maps showing the location of most Mendoza wineries and available in most hotels. Rent a car and set out to explore on your own.

DAY 4 Move on from Mendoza to nearby Maipu, to the relaxed and charming setting of the hotel Club Tapiz. Dine that evening at its lovely Terruños Restaurant.

DAY 5 Set out to explore Maipu's local wineries by car or on foot. Maipu's roads are quiet, flat, and tree-lined, and several wineries offer a gourmet luncheon – with wine of course.

DAY 6 Drive back to Mendoza, have a final wander round the city's quintet of formal central squares, and a last leisurely outdoor lunch, sampling some of the vintages you've come to love in the surrounding countryside.

Dos and Don'ts

- ✓ Check your country's restrictions on wine imports. At any Mendoza winery you'll be tempted to pick up a bottle or a case, which could cost you dearly in import duty.
- ✓ Talk to your restaurant sommelier, who can match a local wine perfectly to your meal and budget.
- ✗ Don't drink and drive. Consider hiring a local driver and car, at a cost of about US$15 per hour.
- ✓ Study the wine maps available online before your trip, to help you get the best from your tour.

GETTING THERE See map p326, A6

Mariscal Sucre International Airport is 11 miles (18 km) east of Quito. Taxis from there are US$25–30.

GETTING AROUND

Use the excellent local bus system, although taxis are inexpensive and recommended at night. Children must ride in the back seat.

WEATHER

September is warm and sunny, ranging from a nighttime low of 53°F (12°C) to 75°F (24°C) in the afternoons.

ACCOMMODATIONS

Sol de Quito Museum Hotel is nearly that: a museum of Ecuadorian culture; rooms from US$61; www.soldequito.com

The tiny but beautiful Hotel de la Rábida is an elegant colonial-style hotel with doubles from US$75; www.hotelrabida.com

Hotel Relicario del Carmen, built in 1705, has locally handmade furniture. Rooms start at US$100 and extra rooms are discounted; www.hotelrelicariodelcarmen.com

EATING OUT

While traditional highland dishes reign, fish ceviche, and *fanesca* (fish stew) are also popular. Soups include *locro de papas* (potato and cheese) and *sancocho de yuca* (vegetables with manioc). Try *empanadas* or *humitas* (ground corn steamed in the husk).

FURTHER INFORMATION

www.quito.com.ec

The Old City

Quito's Centro Histórico is so faithful to its colonial heritage that the entire district was declared a World Heritage Site by UNESCO in 1978, the first city ever to be so named. A walking tour is a must: turn down a narrow cobblestone street and instantly you're back in the 16th century. There is pristine colonial architecture and ambience at every turn, from courtyards with quiet fountains and centuries-old tilework, to churches and convents that have remained unchanged for nearly five centuries. If you have only one day in Quito, spend it here!

Main: Night view of the splendid cathedral in the Plaza de la Independencia, Old City

QUITO

THE CONTINENT'S SECOND-HIGHEST CAPITAL CITY, QUITO is nestled in a narrow valley at the base of the Pichincha Volcano. A true Andean gem, the city has two distinct but complementary facets, each with its own unforgettable sights and style. To the north lie the modern suburbs of El Norte (New City), with their sleek avenues lined with impressive embassies and offices. Touted as Quito's main business and tourist area, you'll find most banks, businesses, hotels, upscale shops, and restaurants here. Farther south is the Centro Histórico (Old City), which forms the colonial center and has some of the finest views of the Andes. Many of the city's well-known festivals and cultural venues are located here and the area has a vibrant atmosphere. The district's narrow cobblestone streets are crammed with Baroque churches, pastel-colored houses, tranquil courtyards, and stunning architecture. It's easy to see why the Centro Histórico was named a World Heritage Site by UNESCO.

Above: The Nariz del Diablo (Devil's Nose) train curving around a mountain

Below (top and bottom): Colorful toy toucans in Otavalo's market; hikers in search of tropical wildlife in the Mindo Nambillo cloud forest

Above: The interior of the Basilica de Voto Nacional

Quito thrives on this diversity. By night and on weekends, the Latin zest for life takes over, and El Norte springs to life in a riot of color and celebration. On Sundays, Quiteños and travelers alike flock to the Centro Histórico to hang out in its many parks and bistros.

Ecuador is small – and affordable – so visitors can see more than just the capital in a few days, without breaking the bank. Guided day trips and extended excursions to the Andean villages that ring the city, as well as to the area's many nature preserves, are popular. In particular, Ecuador's best-known national park is home to Cotopaxi, one of the world's highest active volcanoes, and shelters some of the continent's last remaining herds of wild horses. At the thermal baths of Papallacta, visitors can splash or soak in naturally heated pools varying in temperature from comfortable to boiling, and the Mindo Nambillo cloud forest's lush depths offer activities from tubing along quiet rivers to challenging rock climbs. The handicraft center of Otavalo, and the spectacular Nariz del Diablo (Devil's Nose) train ride – with its series of steep switchbacks which put most roller coasters to shame – are perennial favorites.

ECUADOREAN DIARY

Whether you're walking through the cobblestone streets of Quito's Old Town, or the majestic cloud forests of Mindo, September in the Andes is ideal, with little precipitation and plenty of sun – perfect for all outdoor activities. You'll want at least six days to do justice to Ecuador's many cultural delights.

Six Days in the Highlands

DAY 1 Spend your first day relaxing. Stop at a café in El Norte and visit the Parque El Arbolito and the Casa de Cultura, or the nearby Museo del Banco Central.

DAY 2 Take a walking tour of the Centro Histórico, starting with the Plaza Grande, and visit the Basilica de Voto Nacional with its gargoyles and clock tower with a café at the top. Hire a taxi to the summit of El Panecillo and end the day with a meal at a quaint restaurant in La Ronda.

DAY 3 Take the *teleférico* (cable car) to the top of Guagua Pichincha, an active volcano that overlooks Quito. In nearby La Mariscal, the tourist epicenter of Quito, take in a free *rondador* (pan pipes) concert and then head north to the market town of Otavalo.

DAY 4 A riot of color, Otavalo is the most impressive market extravaganza in South America. You'll want all morning to take it in. After lunch, head south to Riobamba.

DAY 5 Take a ride on the Devil's Nose train – it leaves at 8am or 11am. The final descent, at an angle that seems physically impossible, offers great views (trenecuador.com/en/nariz-del-diablo-en). After returning to Quito, take a well-earned rest and admire the panoramic vistas of the Centro Histórico in the evening.

DAY 6 A trip to the Mitad del Mundo Equatorial Line Monument is in order. Nearby is the Bosque Protector Mindo-Nambillo. This cloud forest is an astonishing subtropical paradise with millions of butterflies, rare plants and flowers, tubing rivers, and well-maintained mountain biking trails.

Dos and Don'ts

- ✓ Rest easy for the first day. At more than 9,200 ft (2,805 m), you will need to acclimatize yourselves to the thinner air.
- ✗ Don't leave anything unaccompanied in a taxi or bus.
- ✓ Ask before photographing local people, even in Otavalo. While most will not object, some older merchants may.
- ✗ Don't forget that the US dollar is the legal currency in Ecuador. This applies not only to bills, but to coins as well.
- ✓ Carry your passports at all times and make a copy of it as well, just in case.

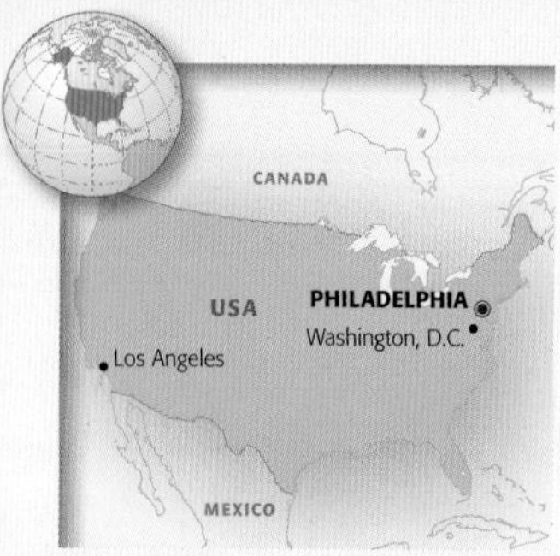

GETTING THERE See map p316, F5
Philadelphia is accessible by car, bus, train, and air. The international airport is 7 miles (11 km) from Center City.

GETTING AROUND
Center City, the downtown core, is easy to get around on foot or by train. To reach outlying sites, such as Gettysburg, you need a car.

WEATHER
September temperatures range from 58 to 78°F (14 to 26°C), and it's one of the sunniest and driest months of the year.

ACCOMMODATIONS
Family-friendly, the Holiday Inn Philadelphia is a short walk from historic sites and has a rooftop pool; doubles from US$170; www.ihg.com/holidayinnexpress/hotels/us/en/philadelphia

The Gables B&B in the University City area, has a wraparound porch; from US$210 for two doubles with shared bath; www.gablesbb.com

The elegant Ritz-Carlton Philadelphia has valet parking, a spa, and flat-screen TVs; from US$459 for a room with two double beds; www.ritzcarlton.com

EATING OUT
You can't visit Philly without trying a cheesesteak at Pat's or Jim's (US$10). Family-style eateries abound at US$20 per head; expect to pay US$60 a head at fancier spots.

FURTHER INFORMATION
www.visitphilly.com

Benjamin Franklin

It seems everywhere you go in downtown Philadelphia you encounter the city's most famous son, Benjamin Franklin, whether it's in bronze (*above*) or as real-life impersonators. Contrary to popular belief, Franklin was never president of the USA. He did, however, manage an impressive number of achievements. He helped found Philadelphia's first hospital, subscription library, and volunteer fire brigade, as well as the University of Pennsylvania. He was one of the five men who drafted the Declaration of Independence. And, as many schoolchildren know, he dabbled a bit in kites and electricity.

Above (left to right): Carousel ride at Giggleberry Fair, Peddler's Village; fast action at a Flyers hockey game; Philadelphia Museum of Art
Main: Shark-spotting at the Adventure Aquarium

Above: Food counters at Reading Terminal Market

PHILADELPHIA

If you tend to think that your kids don't like history, think again. Obviously, you haven't been to Philadelphia lately and seen youngsters shifting on their parents' shoulders to get a better glimpse of the Liberty Bell, or listening with rapt attention as a re-enactor in colonial costume explains some detail of 18th-century life – from the way early Americans cast their votes to the methods once used to make ice cream. You haven't heard kids begging their parents for a ride in one of Philly's horse-drawn carriages or to go on a lamp-lit ghost tour of Society Hill.

This compact city has more to offer than just a taste of American history, however. It provides endless scope for learning, but that's just the beginning. Philadelphia is also a sophisticated city that's awash with art and culture, sports, and fun attractions for all ages. Those who wouldn't be caught dead in an art gallery are happy to visit the steps at the Museum of Art, where Rocky ran in the movie, and can be captivated by the colorful murals that decorate walls across the city depicting everything from sports heroes to Noah's Ark. The Adventure Aquarium in Camden gives budding naturalists a fascinating close-up of sharks, penguins, and crocodiles. And children who aren't certain that science is their thing often wake up to the thrill of experimentation at the Franklin Institute Science Museum where, among other things, they can walk through a giant model of a human heart.

A sophisticated city that's awash with art and culture, sports, and fun attractions for all the family.

Hungry youngsters? Stop by the lively Reading Terminal Market for picnic food – local cheeses, soft pretzels, the works – for lunch, or bring your feast aboard a sunset cruise along the Delaware River. Need open spaces? Head out to visit the world of the Amish in Lancaster County. Or get a taste of farm life at Fox Chase Farm, a 112-acre (45-ha) farm in Fairmount Park. Don't forget to see historic Gettysburg – site of one of the most famous battles of the Civil War, and President Lincoln's address.

Inset: Impressive and historic, the Liberty Bell and Independence Hall
Below (left and right): Amish man driving a buggy; Benjamin Franklin Parkway

FAMILY FUN DIARY

September is the perfect time to visit this, the birthplace of the United States: the summer crowds have thinned and it is usually sunny and warm – with a bit of crispness late in the month. With its full program of arts, sports, and, as always, great food and shopping, you'll have a jam-packed four days.

Four days of Entertainment

DAY 1

Do the history bit first – take in Independence National Historical Park and visit Independence Hall (where the Declaration of Independence was adopted and the Constitution signed) and photograph the Liberty Bell. If you are hungry to know more, go to the nearby National Constitution Center. In the evening, loosen up by joining the cheering throngs at a Philadelphia Flyers pre-season hockey game.

DAY 2

If your children are seven or under, they'll love the interactive Please Touch Museum. If they're older and "been there, done that," go for the unusual – drop by the fascinating Eastern State Penitentiary, now a museum, to see gangster Al Capone's cell. For something quirky, visit Philadelphia's Magic Gardens, a unique house and courtyard covered in mosaics made from old plates, bottles, bicycle wheels, and more.

DAY 3

Get out of the city and explore some of the region's rolling countryside with a day trip to Peddler's Village in Bucks County. The attraction includes shops, restaurants, and a 10,000-sq ft (930-sq m) indoor entertainment complex with rides, called Giggleberry Fair.

DAY 4

Work off excess energy with a bike ride along Fairmount Park's network of scenic paths. After lunch, visit the Philadelphia Zoo – the nation's oldest – known for its success with animals that are reluctant to breed. Get a bird's-eye view from the Channel 6 Zooballoon, which ascends 400 ft (122 m) above the park. Then treat yourselves to rich sundaes and milkshakes at The Franklin Fountain, a re-creation of a Victorian shop.

Dos and Don'ts

- ✓ Catch some action at an exciting sports event while you're here – try a major league baseball, football or hockey game.
- ✓ Sample the local favorite snack – a Butterscotch Krimpet. Tastykake bakes up 3.5 million of these snack-sized cakes every week.
- ✗ Don't be too self-conscious to attempt Rocky Balboa's famous run up the front steps of the Philadelphia Museum of Art – few movie buffs can resist. For extra points, get your picture taken with the Rocky statue at the foot of the steps.
- ✓ Call the city "Philly" – even locals do.

GETTING THERE See map p320, B4
Portland International Airport is 9 miles (14 km) northeast of downtown Portland. A regular MAX light rail connects the airport to the city center for the 40-minute trip.

GETTING AROUND
The city has excellent public transportation, so you can easily get around via buses, light rail, and trams. For day trips it's best to have your own wheels.

WEATHER
The months of July to September bring glorious weather to Portland – pleasantly warm and sunny, with cool nights.

ACCOMMODATIONS
Relax at the lovely Victorian-style Lion and the Rose bed and breakfast; doubles from US$190; www.lionrose.com

The quintessential Portland hotel, Ace Hotel, is trendy, friendly, and filled with local flavor; doubles from US$205; www.acehotel.com

Celebrate Portland's quirky style at the inviting Kimpton Monaco; doubles from US$244; www.monaco-portland.com

EATING OUT
Portland has a wonderfully diverse array of restaurants, like the perennially popular Paley's Place, which serves French favorites with a Pacific Northwest spin – try the salmon with cauliflower couscous and the crispy sweetbreads with glazed carrots (dishes from US$19).

FURTHER INFORMATION
www.travelportland.com

Forest Park

Portland's love for the outdoors is most evident in Forest Park. Overlooking the Willamette River, on the west side of the city, this sprawling green getaway is filled with wildlife like the northern flying squirrel, black-tailed deer, and hairy woodpecker. Sprawl out on the grass and soak up the sun, or just spend a joyful day walking amid looming trees and chirping birds.

Main: Downtown Portland skyline along the Willamette River

PORTLAND

Rebellious yet relaxed, Portland is the embodiment of the Pacific Northwest. The largest city in Oregon unfolds on the banks of the Willamette River, surrounded by a stunning array of natural riches, from Mount Hood, Oregon's tallest peak, to the lush wine country. If that's not enough, the Pacific Ocean laps the coast to the west, reachable within an easy hour's drive. With this kind of backyard, it's not surprising that Portland has emerged as one of the country's leading eco-aware cities and here, preserving the great outdoors is as important as enjoying it.

Balancing out this healthy obsession for the outdoors is an equally fervent love of indoor, intellectual pursuits like readings, political discussions, and performance art, all of which find an enthusiastic audience in the city's myriad bookstores, coffeehouses, brew pubs, and funky art galleries. If all this sounds like the perfect setting for a quirky TV show, you're right. *Portlandia,* the popular comedy series, celebrates and gently satirizes the city, with

Left (left to right): A microbrewery in the city; Barista coffeeshop in the Pearl District; Pioneer Courthouse Square; Portland Art Museum

Above: Japanese Garden in Washington Park

episodes that cover everything from neo-feminist bookstores to the city's great fondness for flannel as a fashion statement.

Portland practically invented the term "farm to fork" and many visitors make a pilgrimage to the city for one sight: the year-round Portland Farmers' Market, whose flagship market is at Portland State University, where over 200 vendors sell everything from mushrooms just pulled from the earth, to pungent cheese from local cows, and warm apple or cherry pies.

Beyond its cozy neighborhoods, Portland's top sights are angled to the outdoors, including the serene Japanese Garden and Lan Su Chinese Garden, the International Rose Test Garden, and the massive Forest Park, the country's largest urban forest. Portland's lively center is marked by Pioneer Courthouse Square, which hosts everything from outdoor concerts to pop-up art displays and political rallies. Also here is the delightful Weather Machine, a sculpture that forecasts the day's weather – key information for the locals, who spend so much of their time outdoors.

PORTLAND DIARY

During harvest season in September the markets are bursting with fresh produce and the weather is ideal for partaking in Portland's outdoor and urban pleasures. Spend your mornings at cozy coffeehouses then trek through city forests and end the day sampling the city's famous homegrown beer.

Three Days of Urban and Outdoor Fun

DAY 1

Head downtown to kick off your visit at the heart and soul of Portland, the Pioneer Courthouse Square. Stop by the Portland Farmers' Market and then pay a visit to the Portlandia statue, the icon of Portland, and the second-largest hammered metal sculpture in the USA after the Statue of Liberty. Check out the Portland Art Museum, the oldest art museum on the West Coast, which is especially known for its Native American and Northwest art. In the evening, explore Portland's boisterous beer bars, like Bailey's Taproom, many of which pour Oregon brews.

DAY 2

Make it a day of exploring the city's green spaces. Stroll the Tom McCall Waterfront Park, on the Willamette River, and then head to Washington Park, to the fragrant Japanese and International Rose Test gardens. In the afternoon, explore Forest Park, which has more than 5,000 acres (2,000 ha) of verdant forest, and the nearby Portland Audubon Society.

DAY 3

Head to the cobblestoned, trendy Pearl District, spending the morning in the famous Powell's City of Books, which sprawls over an entire city block, and is one of the largest independent new and used bookstores in the world. Relax in Jamison Park, and then experience the city's culinary renaissance at one of Pearl District's many well-regarded restaurants, like Oven and Shaker, where local chef Cathy Whims and her team turn out wood-fired pizzas (try the Maple Pig pizza, with apple butter, bacon, and maple mascarpone), as well as creative cocktails.

Dos and Don'ts

- ✓ Build time into your itinerary for at least a couple of day trips from Portland. The surrounding area is prime for outdoor fun, from strolling sun-warmed vineyards to hiking mountains.
- ✓ Embark on a brewery tour (whether pedaling, walking, or via bus) to sip your way through Portland's 65-plus breweries.
- ✗ Don't forget to pack a light jacket for the evenings – though the summer days are warm, the evenings turn brisk, with the temperatures dipping considerably.

GETTING THERE **See map p327, C2**
Simón Bolívar International Airport is 10 miles (16 km) south of Santa Marta city center.

GETTING AROUND
All Ciudad Perdida tours arrange transport to and from the start of the hike. Within Santa Marta, you can walk or take public buses.

WEATHER
September has consistently high temperatures, with a daily average of around 88°F (31°C).

ACCOMMODATIONS
Colonial meets contemporary at the welcoming Hotel Boutique Casa Carolina in Santa Marta; doubles from US$84; www.hotelcasacarolina.com

Casa de Isabella has a leafy courtyard and a rooftop pool; doubles from US$86; www.kalihotels.com

Kick back at the Zuana Beach Resort, which has a spa, and a lively restaurant and bar; doubles from US$160; www.hotelzuana.com

EATING OUT
Local delicacies like empanadas and fried cornmeal pastries are often served at small roadside eateries, perfect for refueling stops. For a taste of the Caribbean, head to Lulo in Santa Marta, which serves fresh ceviche.

FURTHER INFORMATION
www.colombia.travel.en

Preserving Ciudad Perdida

For over a thousand years, Ciudad Perdida was hidden from public view, which ensured its preservation. These days the Global Heritage Fund has developed a site management plan for the area, documenting and conserving archeological features and artifacts, in partnership with the local community. The goal is simple: to ensure it lasts another thousand years, and beyond.

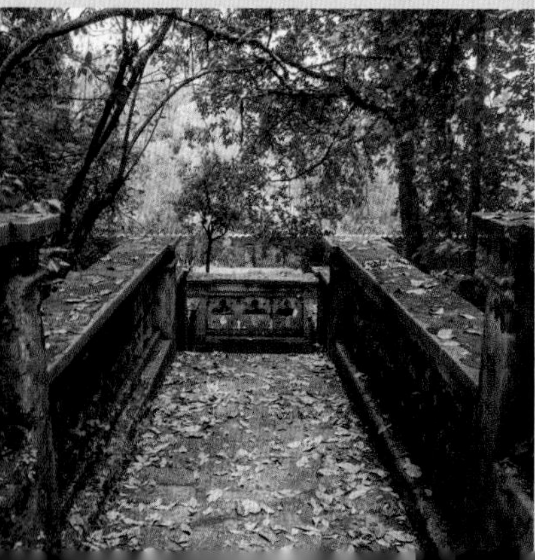

CIUDAD PERDIDA

"The Lost City" is a term that conjures up the location of an adventure fantasy film, of abandoned, crumbling ruins shrouded in mist, with the only sounds to be heard coming from the screech of a vulture overhead. The truth isn't so far off this image as you would expect. Colombia's Ciudad Perdida was built in AD 800, long before Peru's Machu Picchu. For more than a thousand years, this ancient city was hidden in the tangled Sierra Nevada jungle, existing as little more than a giant playground for slithering snakes and darting lizards. In the early 1970s, Ciudad Perdida was "discovered" by treasure-hunters, who ascended its grassy steps to emerge into a sprawling abandoned city of hundreds of terraces, plazas, pyramids and paths, all of which had managed to hold their own amid the hungry tropical jungle.

Left (left and right): River running through Sierra Nevada de Santa Marta; hikers on route

Right: Kogi village

Main: La Cuidad Perdida

Today, The Lost City has become one of Colombia's top travel experiences, and rightly so. Ciudad Perdida will take your breath away and so will the trek to the site, literally. The only way to access The Lost City is via a sweaty, scrambling 27-mile (44-km) hike through dense Colombian jungle. Be prepared for slippery, muddy paths, steep climbs, and river crossings. But, the trek is also punctuated by refreshing swims and gorgeous viewpoints, with nightly stops at campgrounds where you'll sway quietly into the night on comfortable hammocks.

En route to La Ciudad Perdida – which is also known by its indigenous name, Teyuna – you'll observe the daily life of the local Kogi people, descendants of the Tairona, who live in circular huts around the Sierra Nevada de Santa Marta. A Kogi file climbing up and down the bright-green mountains is a memorable sight. They wear all-white clothing, in honor of the purity of nature and Aluna (The Great Mother). Upon returning to Santa Marta from your trek, unwind at a breezy resort on the Caribbean coast – after a week in the jungle, you deserve it.

Above: The shoreline next to Santa Marta

JUNGLE DIARY

September is at the end of the rainy season, so while the trails will be muddier, the surrounding vegetation is at its greenest and lush. In seven days, you can easily fit in a five-day trek to Ciudad Perdida, with a prep day before, and a recuperation day after your hike.

Seven Days of Rain Forest and Rivers

DAY 1

Make your base in Santa Marta, the capital of the Magdalena department, which is the base for Ciudad de Perdida guided tours. Note that no independent hikers are allowed at The Lost City; you must book a guided trek. Once you've reserved your tour, explore Santa Marta, which is on the Caribbean Sea and the oldest surviving city in Colombia. Santa Marta is a major commercial port, so it has a gritty, urban energy, but the central old town is worth a wander, as is Quinta de San Pedro Alejandrino, just outside town, a hacienda-turned-museum where Simón Bolívar (El Gran Libertador) died. Go to sleep early, to be fully rested for your Ciudad Perdida hike.

DAYS 2–6

Numerous companies, including Expotur and G Adventures, run guided treks to Ciudad Perdida; most trips are between 4 and 6 days roundtrip. Tours usually depart from the small town of El Mamey, where you'll fill up on a local lunch before starting the hike, to reach the first camp before nightfall. Your daily hikes will take you through dense jungle, clambering up muddy hillsides and fording rivers. Along the way, cool off in natural pools and waterfalls. Nightly, you'll stop at camps to eat dinner and fall into a deep slumber in hammocks. At Ciudad Perdida, you'll have a half day to explore before beginning the trek back.

DAY 7

Splurge at one of Santa Marta's beachside resorts where you can indulge in some relaxation and recuperation beside the sparkling Caribbean.

Dos and Don'ts

- ✗ Don't forget the mosquito repellent. The trails and especially Ciudad Perdida can swarm with mosquitoes.
- ✓ Travel light – very light. On that first (and second, and third) steep climb, you'll be happy that you did.
- ✓ Bring a light-colored cotton hat to protect you from the sun; you can dip it into pools and rivers along the way to stay cool.
- ✓ Pack water purification tablets. The guides carry water, but it's key that you have your own supply as well.

GETTING THERE See map p312, H6
Halifax is a small waterfront city on Canada's east coast. The international airport is 22 miles (35 km) from the city center. There are also international flights to other major cities, including Vancouver, Toronto, Montréal, and Edmonton.

GETTING AROUND
You can travel across Canada both east- and westbound by train, beginning in Halifax or Vancouver, and between other towns and cities.

WEATHER
Daytime temperatures average 65°F (18°C) in Vancouver, 68°F (20°C) in Toronto.

ACCOMMODATIONS
The most economical way to travel is in Via Rail's Economy class, with a partially reclining seat and a shared bathroom; www.viarail.ca

On the *Rocky Mountaineer*, choose from SilverLeaf (luxury) and GoldLeaf (more luxurious). The difference is the meal service (SilverLeaf passengers are served at their seats) and the amount of free alcohol; both levels of service stay overnight in hotels en route; www.rockymountaineer.com

The *Royal Canadian Pacific* trains through the Rockies offer pure luxury in vintage rail cars, but is only available for private group bookings; www.cpr.ca

EATING OUT
Dining carriages serve meals featuring regional ingredients like salmon, beef, and local wines.

FURTHER INFORMATION
www.canada.travel

The Spiral Tunnels

In the late 1800s, near the mountain town of Field in British Columbia, the "Big Hill" and its dangerous 4.5 percent gradient caused many a heart to race – and several runaway train engines. To solve the problem, engineers began building the Spiral Tunnels in 1907. Still in use today by the *Rocky Mountaineer*, the tunnels corkscrew into Mount Ogden and Cathedral Mountain, essentially doubling back on themselves inside the mountains and allowing a much more gradual slope.

Main: *Rocky Mountaineer* travels alongside the Bow River through Alberta

COAST TO COAST

THE TWIN RIBBONS OF STEEL that stretch for thousands of miles across Canada have tales to tell of the travelers who have made history on this journey – Mounties and military men, royalty and roustabouts, pioneers and poets. More than a century ago, these rails united a nation still in its infancy, weaving together the threads of a landscape as varied as the people making their home within it. It's still an epic journey today, following the mighty St. Lawrence River to the granite outcroppings of the Canadian Shield; across the great prairie plains and through pine and spruce in the Rockies; emerging from west coast cedar rain forests to greet the Pacific Ocean.

Ride the rails from sea to sea and you'll glimpse the old stories, set against the rhythmic sway of the train. Lobster traps piled on eastern wharves, the train slowing to a stop at the Great Lakes to let a party of canoeists off, the grain harvest waiting in the fields as the sun silhouettes a first glimpse of the Rockies.

Above (left to right): Via Rail train traveling from Toronto to Vancouver; Peggy's Cove Lighthouse in Nova Scotia; dining carriage on Via Rail; Union Station in Toronto; observation dome car on a Via Rail train; *Rocky Mountaineer* crossing the dramatic Stoney Creek Bridge

Below: Entrance to one of the spiral tunnels in Yoho National Park, British Columbia

Above: Sunrise on Maligne Lake and Spirit Island in Jasper National Park

There, among the saw-toothed peaks and climb-me-if-you-dare mountains, the stories reach their climax. They tell of the explorers who found the first routes through treacherous mountain passes, the engineers who mapped the rail line, the thousands of workers who laid down the tracks (and sometimes their lives) to build high, heart-in-mouth bridges and long tunnels into unforgiving rock. Once through the mountains, the stories blow with the tumbleweed of British Columbia's semi-arid interior, where iron and copper deposits paint the cliffs rusty red or blue-green – and, finally, they drift in the mist across Vancouver's harbor, where cruise ships and seaplanes launch from the Pacific shoreline.

Many travelers choose a small portion of the cross-Canada route, focusing on the east coast, for example, or charting a grand circle through the Rockies. But the intrepid can cross the entire nation by rail between Halifax and Vancouver. So settle back in your seat, relax, and let the scenes unfold outside your picture window. This trip is all about the journey.

CROSS-COUNTRY DIARY

The train can transport you between Canada's east and west coasts in as little as five days, but this vast and varied country is worth a more in-depth experience – whether it's exploring the arts scene in Toronto, the dramatic Rocky Mountains, or the wave-washed shores of the Pacific and Atlantic coasts.

Two Weeks by Train

DAY 1

Fly into Halifax the day before the train departs to explore the historic wharves of the harbor, where tall ships often dock, and the rocky coast and dramatic lighthouse of Peggy's Cove, a nearby fishing village.

DAYS 2–4

Overnight on Via Rail's *Ocean* service between Halifax and Montréal, traveling alongside Canada's windswept Atlantic coastline to the St. Lawrence River. Spend a night in Montréal to enjoy the boutiques and bistros of this cosmopolitan French-speaking city.

DAYS 5–6

Take the train to Toronto. Stroll the waterfront, hit the museums, or head to the theater district to enjoy Broadway shows. Then board Via Rail's *The Canadian* for the journey north of Lake Superior, a landscape known as the Canadian Shield.

DAYS 7–9

The Canadian then sweeps across captivating prairie plains through the rural and dramatic landscapes of Manitoba and Saskatchewan and on to Alberta, revealing the snow-capped Rocky Mountains. Take a self-drive or tour option between Jasper and Banff on the Icefields Parkway, past spectacular glaciers and through expansive national parks.

DAYS 10–12

In Banff, join the *Rocky Mountaineer* for its two-day trip on the historic track through the Rockies into British Columbia's desert-like interior and on to lush Vancouver.

DAYS 13–14

Spend your last days in Vancouver on Stanley Park's waterfront, at the VanDusen Botanical Garden, or exploring in Gastown and Chinatown.

Dos and Don'ts

- ✓ Take advantage of the friendly on-board atmosphere to strike up conversations with fellow travelers.
- ✓ Keep your eyes open for wildlife – deer and moose are often seen across the country, while elk and bears might be spotted in the Rockies.
- ✗ Don't underestimate distances in Canada: 3,915 miles (6,300 km) of railroad tracks join Halifax, Nova Scotia, with Vancouver, British Columbia.

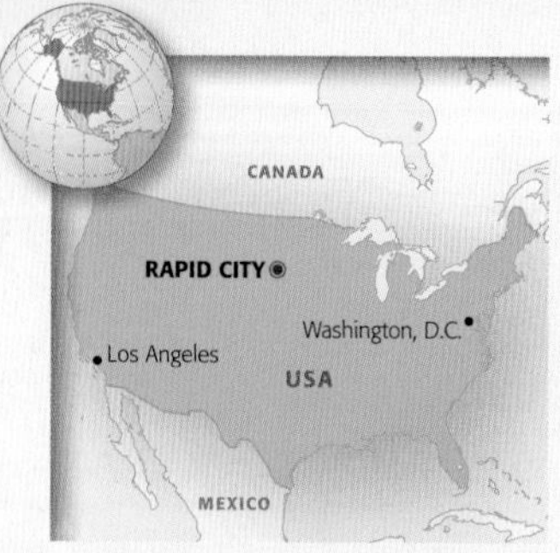

BLACK HILLS

HERE, IN A REMOTE CORNER OF SOUTH DAKOTA, is where the grandeur of the Great Plains meets the rugged, spruce-covered Black Hills; where the history and culture of the great Sioux tribe sit alongside those of the American people. Dramatic doesn't begin to describe the terrain, which has been scoured and scraped by glaciers into hills, canyons, and prairie. It's a place of man-made as well as natural splendor. Overlooking a sylvan landscape of pine, spruce, birch, and aspen is Mount Rushmore, the epic, inspiring sculpture of American presidents George Washington, Thomas Jefferson, Theodore Roosevelt and Abraham Lincoln. In counterpoint, not far away in Custer, the Crazy Horse Memorial will depict the great Native American warrior astride his horse. Begun in 1948, when completed it will be the world's largest sculpture. Some Native Americans are at odds with the statue because it is carved on sacred land.

Main: Native American of the Sioux tribe

GETTING THERE See map p319, B3
In the west of South Dakota, 400 miles (650 km) north of Denver and 600 miles (950 km) west of Minneapolis, Rapid City has a regional airport and is a fine hub from which to explore.

GETTING AROUND
Rent a car at the airport to access the area's many parks, monuments, and byways.

WEATHER
September is pleasant and dry, with average daytime highs of about 75°F (24°C) cooling down to about 45°F (7°C) at night.

ACCOMMODATIONS
Family-owned Sweetgrass Inn B&B is just outside Rapid City at the foot of the Black Hills; doubles from US$140; www.sweetgrassinn.com

Hotel Alex Johnson, in the heart of Rapid City, was built in 1928 and is on the National Register of Historic Places; doubles from US$189; www.alexjohnson.com

Within Custer State Park is historic Sylvan Lake Lodge; cabins with full kitchen from US$150; www.custerresorts.com

EATING OUT
This is carnivore country; you'll find steak from locally reared cattle or buffalo on almost every menu (try Rapid City's Delmonico's Grill). Other local specialties include pheasant, trout, walleye (pike-perch), and pasties (meat pies).

FURTHER INFORMATION
www.travelsd.com

Icons in Stone

Designed in 1925 by sculptor Gutzon Borglum, Mount Rushmore is one of the most revered patriotic sites in the United States. Carved into a granite peak in Harney National Forest, the monument commemorates four iconic American presidents. For its construction, around 400 workers labored from 1927 to 1941, removing an astonishing 450,000 tons of rock. Not one life was lost during the work – remarkable, given the amount of dynamite used. Mount Rushmore is considered the largest work of art on earth, and welcomes more than two million visitors each year.

Left (left and right): Ridin the range in Custer State pa Crazy Horse Memorial.

Right (left and right): Entrance to the Black Hills National Forest; rock formations in the Badlands National Park.

Right panel (top and bottom): Spires of Needles highway; Chinese red ring pheasant, the state bird

Driving is one of the great pleasures of visiting South Dakota, whether it's along the hypnotically beautiful Spearfish Canyon Byway, which roves through a picturesque narrow canyon, or the famous Needles Highway, a gorgeous stretch that winds sharply through forests of high trees and towering granite "needles" and plunges through tunnels blasted out of the living rock. In contrast to the lush vistas of the Black Hills, Badlands National Park is a surreal, Martian-esque landscape of towering red sun-baked rock formations that stretch over the arid landscape as far as the eye can see.

It's easy to believe that you've stepped back in time as you wander the lovingly restored streets of Deadwood, explore the trails of Custer State Park, and revel in the spectacle of the autumn Buffalo Roundup, a rollicking celebration where full-blooded Sioux mingle with cowboys and local merchants. In some ways you have – this is still wild, untamed territory, where the spirit of the frontier lives on, set against a backdrop of some of the nation's greatest natural wonders.

Above: Buffalo grazing the Dakota prairies

BLACK HILLS DIARY

Comfortable weather, manageable crowds, and the lively annual Buffalo Roundup at the end of the month make September an ideal time to visit the Black Hills region. In three days you can see all the major sights, from Mount Rushmore to Badlands National Park, and still have time to watch the roundup at Custer State Park.

Three Days on the Frontier

DAY 1

Wake up early to beat the crowds to Mount Rushmore, with its four 60-ft (18-m) faces carved into the rockface at a height of 500 ft (150 m). Have lunch back in Rapid City, then take the scenic drive skirting the Black Hills northwest to the Spearfish Canyon National Scenic Byway, which offers stunning views of the surrounding mountains. Be sure to stop for a stroll through Deadwood, a preserved Old West town famous as the site of the murder of Wild Bill Hickok.

DAY 2

Take Route 44 about 60 miles (96 km) southeast of Rapid City to the breathtaking rock formations of Badlands National Park. Get your bearings at Ben Reifel Visitor Center, then head out to explore the park on the picturesque 5-mile (8-km) Castle Trail, a great spot for spotting wildlife such as buffalo, coyote, prairie dogs, buzzards, and chickadees.

DAY 3

Drive to Custer State Park, about 45 miles (73 km) southwest of Rapid City, via the Crazy Horse Memorial which is on your route. Hike the trails, check out the wildlife, and take part in the festivities at the park's annual Buffalo Roundup, when the thundering herd of nearly 1,500 beasts are expertly corralled by skilled riders. After a chuckwagon lunch in the park, take in the astonishing spectacle of towering granite spires along the 14-mile (23 km) Needles Highway.

Dos and Don'ts

- ✓ Dress in layers – the weather in the Black Hills can be quite cool in the mornings and evenings, warm during the day.
- ✓ Check the dates of the Buffalo Roundup in advance – in some years it falls on the first weekend of October.
- ✓ Stay hydrated (be sure to bring your own water bottle when walking the trails in the various parks), and wear sunblock; though the weather may not be overly hot, the sun can still be intense.
- ✗ Don't feed wildlife in the parks, and don't approach buffalo as they may charge at speed if threatened.

OCTOBER

Where to Go: **October**

Fall is bedding down nicely in North America. The colors are at their resplendent peak along the east coast – quite simply, there is no prettier time to vacation in New England. California is warmer than the east, and the Pacific Northwest contrasts its golden fall foliage with wild beaches. Hiking conditions are perfect in the Southwest, while the big surf breaks have yet to arrive in Hawai'i, making it safer to swim. A lively festivals calendar takes advantage of fall's clemency; in Mexico, the days surrounding the Day of the Dead are unmissable. Canada's snowy northern wastes offer the chance to see polar bears, while in South America you can almost travel to the ends of the earth. Below you will find all the destinations in this chapter and some extra suggestions to provide inspiration.

FESTIVALS AND CULTURE

ALBUQUERQUE Preparations in Balloon Fiesta Park

ALBUQUERQUE
NEW MEXICO, USA

Blue skies filled with a graceful kaleidoscope of colors

Few sights can match the spectacle of 750 hot-air balloons all taking off at once in the desert at the Albuquerque Balloon Fiesta.

See pp242–3

FANTASY FEST
FLORIDA, USA

The world's biggest fancy-dress party in Key West

Locals and visitors take to the streets of Key West in costume, with parades, parties, and plenty of music and rum.

www.fantasyfest.net

CÍRIO DE NAZARÉ FESTIVAL
BRAZIL

A joyous religious celebration

The Círio de Nazaré honors the image of the Virgin Mary of Belém with parades and wild partying.

www.paraturismo.pa.gov.br/english/eng_cirio.asp

ANNAPOLIS
MARYLAND, USA

Historic state capital

Explore this time-warped little city on Chesapeake Bay, its captivating red-brick streets dotted with historic landmarks, including the venerable Maryland State House.

www.annapolis.com

BUENOS AIRES
ARGENTINA

European culture combined with Latin passion

Buenos Aires might be a great place to party, but it also has history, fabulous architecture, and the best steaks in the world.

See pp238–9

UNFORGETTABLE JOURNEYS

OREGON The lighthouse at Haceta Head

OREGON COAST
OREGON, USA

A scenic drive along a stunning coastline

Drive along Highway 101 and take in the timeless landscapes of the Oregon coastline, with scenes of surf, sand, and rain forest.

See pp246–7

HIGHWAY 61
USA

Scenic journey around Lake Superior

Drive the magnificent stretch of Highway 61 from Duluth to the Canadian border, immortalized in song by local boy Bob Dylan.

www.visitduluth.com

SOUTH PATAGONIAN FJORDS
CHILE

Explore a fantastical icy world on a cruise liner

Wonder at astonishing glaciers and imagine yourself as an Antarctic explorer.

See pp244–5

"In this magnificent natural theater, great vertical rock faces rise from the sea, and gushing waterfalls plunge into deep channels."

NEW ENGLAND FALL
NEW ENGLAND, USA

North America's woodlands at their most spectacular

Take a road trip through New England in fall, when the forests turn a thousand brilliant shades of red, yellow, purple, and gold.

www.visitnewengland.com

BIG SUR
CALIFORNIA, USA

Wild coastline drive between San Francisco and LA

Driving between these two great coastal cities you'll see some of America's finest wind- and wave-lashed coastlines and a lot more.

www.visitcalifornia.com

NATURAL WONDERS

GRAND CANYON The awe-inspiring landscape of the canyon

GRAND CANYON
ARIZONA, USA

Explore the Grand Canyon by car and on a mule

To truly appreciate this huge fissure sculpted by the Colarado River, take mule trips and enlist on canyon hikes.

See pp240–41

WHITESHELL PROVINCIAL PARK
MANITOBA, CANADA

Natural hideaway

Enjoy a spot of rejuvenation in this beautiful park, with its mix of unspoilt scenery and cozy inns, particularly beautiful during fall.

www.whiteshell.mb.ca

IWOKRAMA RAINFOREST
GUYANA

Rain forest hike

Hike or boat through this rain forest in central Guyana, one of the best places to spot Jaguars.

www.iwokramacanopywalkway.com

THE LAURENTIANS
QUÉBEC, CANADA

Wilderness retreat in Québec

Hike or kayak in the rugged Laurentian mountains, which are clothed in dense tracts of maple forest and dotted with pretty hidden lakes and waterfalls.

www.laurentides.com/en

"No other place in Hawai'i so perfectly fulfils dreams of a pristine Polynesian paradise as this island."

KAUA'I
HAWAI'I, USA

A volcanic island with spectacular landscapes

Hike though tropical bird-filled jungles, snorkel fish-filled waters, and enjoy views over a wild and rugged Polynesian paradise.

See pp248–9

Previous page: Heceta Head Lighthouse at dusk, Oregon coast

Weather Watch

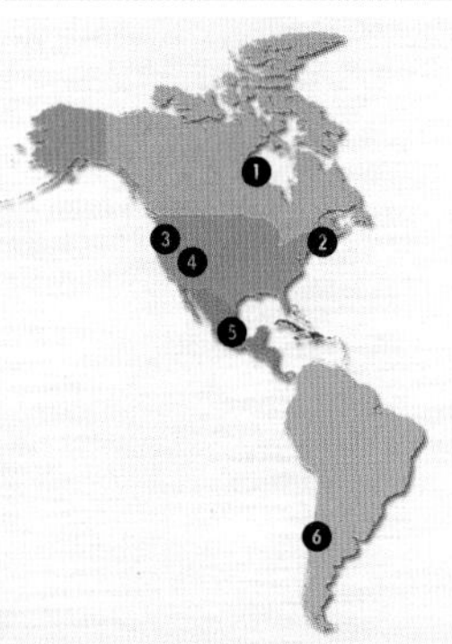

❶ Cape Churchill, Canada Mid-fall in Canada's icy wilderness, when the polar bears migrate, is bitterly cold, with temperatures consistently well below freezing. Wind, rain, and sun conditions can change at a moment's notice.

❷ Maine, USA October is sunny and crisply cold, with the constant possibility of rain and wind. The best of the fall colors will be fading by the middle of the month.

❸ Oregon, USA Though winter is approaching on the wild, ocean-pounded coast of the Pacific Northwest, there is still sunshine to be had; temperatures can get as high as 60°F (16°C), but rain showers are practically a given.

❹ Grand Canyon, USA Arizona's Grand Canyon sees sunshine and the odd shower in October; the rim has warm daytime highs and cooler nighttime lows, with more extreme contrasts in the inner gorge.

❺ Mexico October is a lovely month to be in Mexico; the heat and the rains of summer are over. In Oaxaca in the Yucatán daytime temperatures stay reasonably high.

❻ Chile October brings long, bright (and practically ozone-layer free) days in the south of this skinny country, with high temperatures. Howling winds add drama, as do sudden changes in conditions.

LUXURY AND ROMANCE

MOUNT DESERT ISLAND Wooden bridge over the pond in Somesville

MOUNT DESERT ISLAND
MAINE, USA

Fall colors by day and fine seafood at sunset

Explore winding forest and waterside trails on this unspoiled and far-from-desert island retreat.

See pp236–7

ILHABELA
BRAZIL

Exquisite island just off the Brazilian coast

This stunning volcanic island is swathed in dense tropical foliage and studded with waterfalls and beautiful beaches.

www.visitbrasil.com

CALIFORNIA WINE COUNTRY
CALIFORNIA, USA

A riot of fall colors

The rolling hills, quaint towns, and warm hospitality will make this a special holiday. As will, of course, the fine wines to be had here.

See pp250–51

BAHÍA CONCEPCIÓN
MEXICO

Beautiful beaches on the Sea of Cortez

This idyllic bay stretches for miles along the Bay of Cortez, with beautiful white-sand beaches and many adventure activities.

www.allaboutbaja.com

COPACABANA PALACE, RIO
BRAZIL

Sumptuous Art Deco palace

One of Latin America's most memorable places to stay is located right on the world-famous Copacabana beach.

www.copacabanapalace.com.br

ACTIVE ADVENTURES

CAPE CHURCHILL Young male polar bears sparring

CAPE CHURCHILL
MANITOBA, CANADA

The undisputed polar bear capital of the world

Polar bears aplenty gather here to await the coming of the sea ice. Buggies will take you out onto the tundra for a close, safe encounter.

See pp234–5

BIG BEND NATIONAL PARK
TEXAS, USA

Rafting, Rio Grande-style

Ride one of America's most famous rivers on a variety of rapids. Santa Elena canyon is the most common destination.

www.nps.gov/bibe

CLIMBING MOUNT WHITNEY
CALIFORNIA, USA

Conquer an amazing peak

Trek to the top of Mount Whitney, a challenging hike with superlative views from the summit.

www.nps.gov/seki/planyourvisit/whitney.htm

AQUÁRIO NATURAL
BRAZIL

Brazil's premier underwater wonderland in Bonito

Snorkel or dive amid teeming shoals of tropical fish in the waters of this marine sanctuary.

www.amazonadventures.com/bonito.htm

GAULEY RIVER
WEST VIRGINIA, USA

Top white-water rafting destination

Raft down the free-flowing Gauley River, through scenic gorges and valleys, with several challenging class V+ rapids en route.

www.nps.gov/gari

FAMILY GETAWAYS

OAXACA Colorful sand picture

"In the gorgeous colonial city of Oaxaca, the celebrations are at their most vivid."

OAXACA
MEXICO

Kids will enjoy the macabre but joyous Day of The Dead

Feast on skulls and other ghoulish delights – chocolate of course – as Mexican families honor their dead with parties and celebration.

See pp252–3

CURAÇAO
CARIBBEAN

Dutch-style diminutive Caribbean island

Curaçao boasts plenty of kids' attractions including the Curaçao Seaquarium, Dolphin Academy, and an Ostrich Farm.

www.curacao.com

NAPLES
FLORIDA, USA

Holiday in Florida with a local flavor

Rent your own holiday home in this genuine Floridian town on the Gulf of Mexico coast, with sun-drenched beaches and calm waters.

www.naples-florida.com

SCOTTS BLUFF
NEBRASKA, USA

Family recreation on the Oregon Trail

The area around this famous Nebraskan landmark has loads of family activities, as well as Oregon Trail attractions.

www.visitscottsbluff.com

HALLOWEEN
NEW YORK CITY, USA

America's biggest Halloween celebrations

Join the crowds for the Big Apple's riotous Halloween party, with bands, parades, and people in spooky costumes.

www.halloween-nyc.com

GETTING THERE See map p313, H3
Churchill is not accessible by road. Calm Air flies daily from Winnipeg's international airport (www.calmair.com). Return fares start from US$1,000. The VIA Winnipeg-Churchill train departs Winnipeg on Tuesday and Sunday. The journey time is about 48 hours, and return fares are around US$300.

GETTING AROUND
Everything in Churchill is within walking distance. Tundra vehicles take you to the bears.

WEATHER
Temperatures range from 40°F (5°C) to 5°F (-15°C), but a northerly windchill can make it feel much, much colder. Dress in layers.

ACCOMMODATIONS
To wake with the bears, Tundra Lodges are remote mobile bunkhouses, but are for tour groups only. There's a wide range of B&Bs.

Polar Inn is warm and welcoming; doubles from US$195; www.polarinn.com

Bear Country Inn is simple but cozy; doubles from US$220; www.bearcountryinn.com

The Tundra Inn offers either hotel or hostel lodging; doubles from US$265; www.tundrainn.com

EATING OUT
Gypsy Bakery is a Churchill landmark serving northern delicacies like arctic char and caribou.

FURTHER INFORMATION
www.polarbearalley.com

Confident and curious, bears walk right up to the vehicles, standing up and offering the chance to gaze deep into their eyes.

Main: Majestic adult polar bear taking his first steps of the winter out onto the frozen sea-ice of Hudson Bay

CAPE CHURCHILL

POLAR BEAR CAPITAL OF THE WORLD – Churchill's nickname pretty much says it all. It's around 30 years since a local mechanic invented the first Tundra Buggy™, basically a big metal can on over-sized tires, and bounced out across the tundra in search of polar bears. Churchill now attracts visitors from all over the world for the first six weeks of winter, known locally as "bear season." It begins with a trickle of polar bears – and bear tourists. The bears, forced ashore three months previously by melting sea-ice, are hungry to hunt again for seals on frozen Hudson Bay. Churchill is the first place on the Bay where the sea freezes so, as each passing day grows colder and more ice builds, the trickle of bears becomes a flood. As they gather on the Cape, the human visitors follow, piling aboard lumbering tundra transports, eager to get up-close and personal with a polar bear. Confident and curious, bears walk right up to the vehicles, sometimes standing up and offering the chance to gaze deep into their brown and bloodshot eyes.

Prince of Wales Fort

Churchill was founded on the fur trade. In 1717, the Hudson's Bay Company built a trading post on the Churchill River, establishing ties with a nomadic tribe known as the Dené. In 1732, to solidify their grip on the area, they began work on a giant stone fortress, across the river from present-day Churchill. Hampered by the sub-Arctic conditions, it was 40 years before Prince of Wales Fort was completed. Only ten years later, three French warships weighed anchor at the mouth of the Churchill River, and the under-manned post surrendered without firing a shot.

Inset: Polar bear cub cleverly sheltering from the elements

Left (left to right): Young adult male bears play-fighting; team of husky sled dogs; downtown Churchill; arctic fox, with its dense winter coat

Right: Arctic hare in white winter camouflage

Once the ice is stable they'll be gone but, at this time of year, bears are a constant presence around Churchill. "Polar Bear Alert" vehicles patrol the small town, and everyone has a bear-encounter story ready to tell, true or mostly true. You may even see a bear in the sky, as conservation officers perform a "bear lift," relocating a miscreant animal north along the coast by helicopter.

However, there is more to Churchill than polar bears. This northern outpost lies on the treeline, a transitional zone where the boreal forest gives way to barren tundra, and wildlife abounds. It's a place where a walk downtown may be accompanied by a red fox, and an arctic hare may hop past your restaurant window. It's a cultural meeting place too, in which three native cultures – the Cree, Dené, and Inuit – are linked by fur-trade history. Beaded mukluk boots sit alongside polar-bear T-shirts in gift stores. Roast caribou and poached arctic char vie with cheeseburgers on menus.

"Bear Season" can be crowded, chaotic, and cold. But there's something about Churchill, the place and the people, and something about being so incredibly close to wildlife in its natural habitat, that make this trip of a lifetime even more thrilling than you can possibly imagine.

Above: Bears and Buggy in a close encounter at sunset

POLAR BEAR DIARY

Polar bears can be spotted throughout October and early November, gathering along the coast and on Cape Churchill. By month's end, over 40 polar bears may be seen in one day. A trip to this far-flung outpost is bound to be costly but, after five days of wildlife encounters, you'll feel you've had a money-can't-buy experience.

Five Days in the Tundra

DAY 1

You're sure to want to get nose-to-nose with a polar bear as fast as possible! Head out on a tundra vehicle to the Churchill Wildlife Management Area in search of bears. This is by far the best way to see them in their natural environment.

DAY 2

A bus tour of the town and its environs explores the cultural and natural history of the "accessible Arctic." Learn about the fur trade and local history, and try to spot wildlife such as arctic foxes, arctic hares, and a partridge-like bird called a ptarmigan.

DAY 3

Every day is different on the tundra. A second trip by tundra vehicle will give you just the right amount of "bear time." With luck you'll see a mother with her cubs (called coys), or watch young males in their ritual play-fight sparring.

DAY 4

Visit a northern trapping camp for a ride on a husky dogsled (or a training cart if there's no snow yet). Try some bannock, a Native-American flatbread, and hot chocolate before heading back to town. Later you could join a helicopter tour for an aerial view of Wapusk National Park of Canada and the forming sea-ice.

DAY 5

Spend your last day in town. The Eskimo Museum, one of North America's oldest and most extensive collections of Inuit sculpture and artifacts, is a true northern treasure. Visit the Parks Canada Visitor Centre for a glimpse inside a replica of a polar bear maternity den, and to learn more about Prince of Wales Fort and other historic sites in the area.

Dos and Don'ts

- ✓ Bring extra memory cards and batteries. Polar bears eat up pictures and the cold eats up batteries.
- ✗ Don't expect the train to be on time! It often runs between 4 and 12 hours behind schedule.
- ✓ Be sure to get your passport stamped at the post office with Churchill's unique polar bear logo.
- ✓ Remember that group tours fill up a year in advance. Also, tour companies book almost all "bear season" hotel space at least a year ahead. Independent travelers can try checking for cancellations around midsummer.

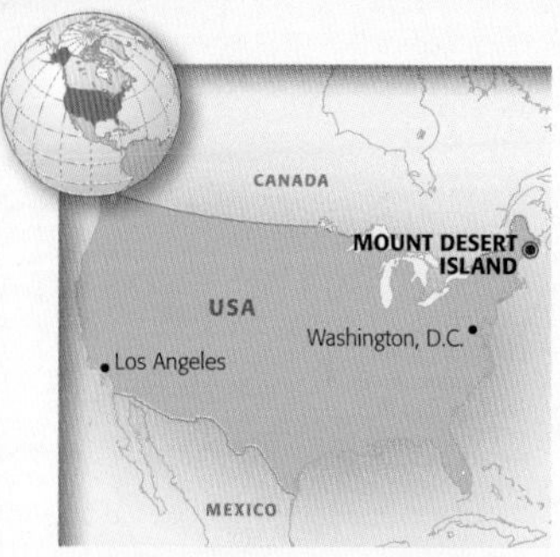

GETTING THERE See map p316, I3
Hancock County Airport is 12 miles (19 km) from Bar Harbor, with direct flights from Boston. Bangor International Airport is 50 miles (80 km) away, and has a shuttle service to Bar Harbor.

GETTING AROUND
Free Island Explorer Buses operate until mid-October, visiting major points of interest in the Park. A car offers more freedom to explore, and rental is available at both airports.

WEATHER
October is generally sunny and crisp, with highs around 58°F (14°C) and nighttime lows of 38°F (3°C). It is often breezy, with rain always possible.

ACCOMMODATIONS
Bar Harbor Inn & Spa has a waterfront location within walking distance of shops and restaurants; doubles from US$209; www.barharborinn.com

Ullikana offers French country charm in a Tudor-style house at Bar Harbor; doubles from US$255; www.ullikana.com

The Claremont Hotel at Southwest Harbor is a historic shoreline resort; doubles from US$170; www.theclaremonthotel.com

EATING OUT
Maine is known for its excellent lobster, crab, and other seafood, as well as wild blueberry pie and cobbler. On the island, there's everything from fine-dining options to ultra-casual eateries.

FURTHER INFORMATION
www.barharborinfo.com

The Carriage Roads

In the early 1900s John D. Rockefeller Jr., a summer resident, decided to create a way for visitors to enjoy the island by horse-drawn carriage. He personally supervised the construction of over 45 miles (73 km) of Carriage Roads – delightful, gently-graded, winding crushed-stone lanes that afford wonderful views of sparkling water and tree-covered mountain-sides. Today they are part of the Acadia National Park, a gift to the nation from Rockefeller.

MOUNT DESERT ISLAND

An island of misty mountains, surrounded by miles of rugged coastline, Mount Desert is home to charmingly weathered New England villages nestled along deep coastal coves and fjord-like inlets. Over two-thirds of the island is preserved for all time as spectacular Acadia National Park. In fall, the island's woodlands explode with the finest crimsons, reds, and brilliant golds. Miles of groomed Carriage Roads, speckled with brilliantly hued leaves, meander through the woods, gently curving up the mountainsides to expose vistas of cerulean blue ponds below. Reveling in crisp fall air filled with the fragrance of the north woods, walkers, horseback riders, and cyclists follow these graceful paths across elegant stone bridges that span sparkling mountain streams. All roads eventually lead to Jordan Pond House, where afternoon tea and popovers on the lawn by the pond are an Acadia tradition.

Main: The still, clear waters of Jordan Pond

Above (top to bottom): Road through the Park; view of Northeast Harbor from the observation hut at Asticou Terraces; wooden bridge over the pond in Somesville

Bottom (left to right): Colorful foliage in Asticou Gardens; Sand Beach; Bar Harbor restaurants; sunset over Bass Harbor Head Lighthouse

Bar Harbor is the island's main town. Quaint and romantic, its seaside streets are lined with colorful shops, fine restaurants, and upscale galleries. Laughter and conversation fill the air as browsers admire Maine handicrafts, whimsical moose carvings, and warm woolen sweaters. Tour operators offer adventures for tomorrow's pleasure: a kayak trip along the coast; a boat ride to see whales and seals or catch lobsters; bicycle rental for exploring the Carriage Roads.

There are two things that you must do. First, take a leisurely drive along the scenic Park Loop Road through vibrant woodlands and along the stunning coastline. At Otter Point, climb down to the water's edge and savor the salt-laden breeze, crashing waves, and seagulls soaring overhead. Second, join the evening throngs at the summit of Cadillac Mountain, with panoramic vistas of the fiery woodlands and the island-dotted bay beyond. At sundown, visitors sit in quiet reverence, broken only by gentle applause as the sun dips below the horizon. Afterwards, relax in a cozy inn by a crackling fire, then snuggle under a goose-down comforter to the sound of waves rolling ashore.

Above: Cadillac Mountain's pink granite at sundown

ISLANDER'S DIARY

The end of the first week of October is when fall foliage typically reaches its peak in Acadia National Park, but by mid-month many businesses will have closed for the season. Three days allows enough time to drive the scenic routes, discover the pretty villages, and also explore the Carriage Roads and hike or kayak for half a day.

Three Days in Acadia

DAY 1

Explore Acadia National Park by driving the Loop Road, stopping often for the views and to see Sand Beach, Thunder Hole, Otter Cliff, and Otter Cove. Head to Jordan Pond House and walk the Carriage Roads until mid-afternoon, and then enjoy popovers on the lawn at Jordan Pond House. Take a private horse-drawn carriage ride for two, and then drive to the top of Cadillac Mountain for the sunset. At Bar Harbor, have a romantic dinner at The Reading Room, which offers ocean-fresh seafood and continental cuisine.

DAY 2

Drive to Northeast Harbor and stroll the serene paths at the Asticou Azalea Garden, where autumn foliage forms a backdrop to the arched bridges, stone lanterns, and benches in the Japanese Garden. Continue into Northeast Harbor to visit the art galleries and shops, and have lunch. Follow the blue waters of Somes Sound into Somesville, a charming enclave of white clapboard buildings, where a lovely bridge arches across the pond. Continue on to Southwest Harbor and explore the shops and galleries before an early dinner at casually elegant Red Sky. Finally, drive out to Bass Harbor Head Light to watch the sun go down.

DAY 3

Take a hike in Acadia National Park, rent a bike in Bar Harbor and cycle round Eagle Lake, or join a kayak or boat trip run by one of the adventure shops in Bar Harbor. Later, head to Southwest Harbor for a relaxed lobster dinner on the deck at Beal's Lobster Pier, by the light of the setting sun.

Dos and Don'ts

- ✓ Reserve far in advance for the most luxurious rooms, as early October is one of the busiest times of the year.
- ✗ Don't bring fancy clothes, unless you like to dress up for dinner, as casual attire is standard everywhere.
- ✓ Walk or cycle along the Carriage Roads. Slow is best for appreciating the amazing stonework of the bridges, brilliant autumn foliage, and the many mountain and water views.
- ✗ Don't be surprised to hear the island's name pronounced "dessert" as well as "desert" – either is acceptable.
- ✓ Help reduce traffic congestion by riding the free Island Explorer buses to the Carriage Roads.

OCTOBER

GETTING THERE See map p331, G1
International flights to Buenos Aires land at Ministro Pistarini Airport (known locally as Ezeiza), 35 miles (22 km) from downtown. The city is 45 minutes away by bus or taxi.

GETTING AROUND
Both the city's subway system and taxis are reliable, but the best way to explore Buenos Aires is on foot: distances are short and streets follow an easily navigable grid system.

WEATHER
October is springtime in Buenos Aires and the weather is great, with an average temperature range of 59–73°F (15–23°C).

ACCOMMODATIONS
The chic Home Hotel is located in the heart of Palermo Viejo; doubles from US$130; www.homebuenosaires.com

In San Telmo, the tango-inspired Mansión Dandi Royal offers doubles at US$130; www.mansiondandiroyal.com

The Hotel Emperador combines a central location with traditional elegance; doubles from US$200; www.hotel-emperador.com.ar

EATING OUT
Steakhouses are ubiquitous in the city – try La Brigada for some juicy cuts. Palermo Viejo is the trendy dining zone, where restaurants serve modern Argentinian and fusion food.

FURTHER INFORMATION
www.turismo.buenosaires.gob.ar

City of the Dead

La Recoleta Cemetery has been the burial place of Argentina's elite since the 19th century. Presidents, generals, artists, and aristocracy lie interred here in mausoleums of granite and bronze adorned by marble sculptures of angels and crying mothers. Built tightly against each other, the tombs are visited via a labyrinth of streets and narrow passageways. The most famous resident here is Evita Perón, while the most beautiful tomb is said to be that of newspaper baron José C. Paz, crowned by allegorical sculptures of the immortal soul.

Above (left to right): Puerto Madero's modern waterfront; the glitzy facade of Galerios Pacifico; street performer in Dorrego Plaza, San Telmo
Main: Avenida 9 de Julio, one of the widest streets in the world

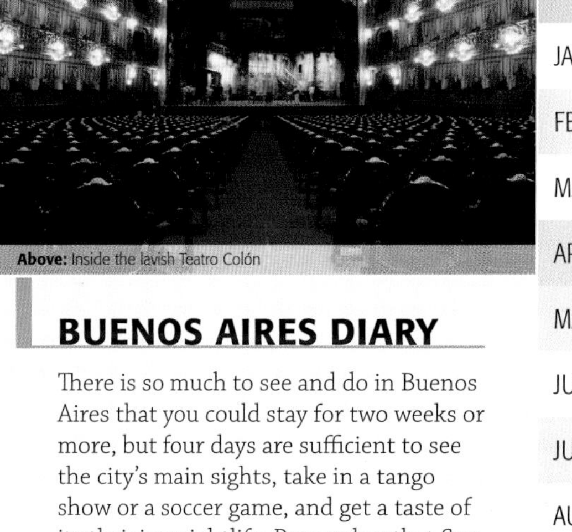

Above: Inside the lavish Teatro Colón

BUENOS AIRES

MARBLE STAIRS SNAKE UP TOWARDS A 19TH-CENTURY MANSION, and in its lavishly cool interior, crystal chandeliers drip from a grand ceiling, antique smoked mirrors adorn wine-red walls, and luxurious velvet chaise longues sprawl across a mosaic floor. You weave through a crowd of hip, gorgeously dressed twenty- and thirty-somethings before reaching the bar and ordering cocktails from flirtatious staff. Welcome to Buenos Aires, South America's most intoxicating city.

In Argentina's beautiful capital, highlights come dizzyingly fast – the colorful houses of La Boca, built by Italian immigrants a century ago; the extraordinary La Recoleta Cemetery; the magnificent Teatro Colón opera house; and the iconic Obelisco. Wander the city and you might be forgiven for thinking you're in Europe, as you soak in tree-lined boulevards lined with *belle époque* mansions or wide avenues of French-style palaces and Parisian cupolas. In the central Tribunales lie great squares such as Plaza de Mayo, where Evita Perón once wooed the masses, while San Telmo is all about cobblestone streets, colonial facades, and whitewashed Spanish churches.

In the central Tribunales lie great squares such as the Plaza de Mayo, where Evita Perón once wooed the masses.

But peek beneath the city's European veneer and you'll discover the vibrancy of South America. It's in the electrifying atmosphere of its soccer stadiums, in the eroticism of the tango – the passionate dance that so embodies the Argentine psyche – and in the *porteños* (locals), who love leisurely lunches and hedonistic nights.

Most strikingly, Buenos Aires now has a flair for the chic and modern, which stands brashly against the city's backdrop of old-world grandeur. Find it in Palermo, home to the groundbreaking Museum of Modern Latin American Art (MALBA); in Puerto Madero, the slick new docklands complex; and in ultra-cool Palermo Viejo, with its hip stores, boutique hotels, and stylish bars. Once known as the Paris of South America, this wonderfully complex city is today more seductive than ever before.

Inset: Bronze plaques of Evita and Juan Perón at San Telmo's famous street market
Below (left to right): Colorful Caminito Street; iconic figure in La Boca; Viva tango!

BUENOS AIRES DIARY

There is so much to see and do in Buenos Aires that you could stay for two weeks or more, but four days are sufficient to see the city's main sights, take in a tango show or a soccer game, and get a taste of its thriving nightlife. Remember that San Telmo is best visited on a Sunday, when its famous antiques fair takes place.

Four Days in the City of Tango

DAY 1

Spend the day in the downtown area, starting at Plaza de Mayo, and then walk along Avenida de Mayo to view the Plaza del Congreso and the Palacio del Congreso Nacional (National Congress) building.

After lunch, admire the monumental grandeur of Avenida 9 de Julio, and browse the shops on Florida, the main shopping street. In the evening, take a riverside stroll in Puerto Madero.

DAY 2

In La Recoleta, visit Evita Perón's tomb, view art at the National Museum of Fine Arts, and walk along Avenida Alvear, the city's most Parisian avenue. Later, stop for a glass of bubbly at the sumptuous Alvear Palace Hotel.

DAY 3

Discover the city's historical heart along the streets of San Telmo, with their crumbling mansions, Spanish churches, and antique shops. Stop at Plaza Dorrego for the antiques fair and join the tango dancers and buskers on Calle Dorrego.

In La Boca, browse Diego Maradona memorabilia on a stadium tour of La Bombonera, home to the Boca Juniors soccer team. Then it's back to San Telmo for dinner and a tango show.

DAY 4

Gorge on modern art at the MALBA and stroll the neighborhood's ornate parks and gardens. Wander the cobbled streets of Palermo Viejo, dipping in and out of designer shops. Stop for coffee at Plaza Serrano.

End your stay with a romantic dinner at one of Palermo Viejo's stylish restaurants.

Dos and Don'ts

- ⊗ Don't think about dining early. Restaurants start getting pretty busy around 10pm.
- ✓ Take in the frenzied atmosphere of a local soccer match.
- ⊗ Don't miss out on Malbec red wine – it's Argentina's best *(see p216)*.
- ✓ Check out Night of the Museums (Noche de los Museos) – when over 100 of the city's museums, and many impressive private buildings, remain open for free all night.

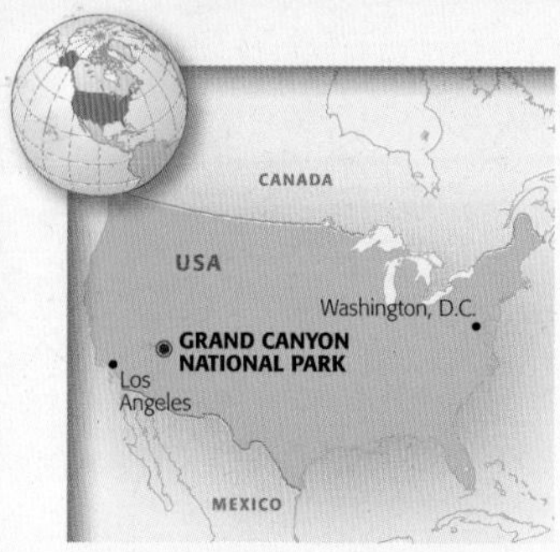

GETTING THERE See map p321, E4
Las Vegas McCarran International Airport is served by a number of airlines, has car-rental agencies on site, and is conveniently located for a drive to the Grand Canyon.

GETTING AROUND
Once at the National Park, it is best to park your rented car and walk, or use the shuttle service or a taxi.

WEATHER
Sunny days with a chance of showers are normal for October. Expect average highs of 65°F (18°C) and lows of 36°F (2°C) on the South Rim, while the inner gorge has a high of 86°F (30°C) and a low of 58°F (14°C).

ACCOMMODATIONS
Designed in the 1930s, Bright Angel Lodge is centrally located, with doubles from US$105; www.grandcanyonlodges.com

Historic adobe hotel Thunderbird Lodge has doubles from US$215; www.grandcanyonlodges.com

El Tovar on the canyon rim offers rooms from US$251; www.grandcanyonlodges.com

EATING OUT
Meals are readily available at major hotels, with fine dining at El Tovar and family-style dining at Bright Angel Lodge. Prices vary, but good meals are available at all budget levels.

FURTHER INFORMATION
www.nps.gov/grca
www.nps.gov/cach

Desert View Watchtower

Inspired by the Ancestral Puebloans' ancient towers that can still be seen at Hovenweep, Wupatki, and Mesa Verde, legendary architect Mary Ann Colter captured the essence of the past in the design of the Watchtower, which opened in 1933. On the edge of the canyon at Desert View, the four-story tower was designed to harmonize with the setting and provide exceptional views from the top floor. Inside, the walls are decorated with native paintings by Hopi artist, Fred Kabotie. Colter also designed five other Grand Canyon structures.

The inner world of the canyon is fascinating, with unexplored side canyons, waterfalls, and hidden grottos.

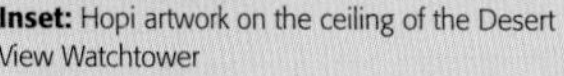

Inset: Hopi artwork on the ceiling of the Desert View Watchtower

Above: Spider Rock Overlook at Canyon de Chelly

Right (left to right): A California condor in flight; a desert cactus in bloom; The Lookout – gift shop and observation station on the South Rim; awe-inspiring landscape of the Grand Canyon; tourist mesmerized by the grand views

Main: The Grand Canyon from Toroweap Point

GRAND CANYON NATIONAL PARK

GRAND DOESN'T EVEN BEGIN TO DO THIS CANYON JUSTICE. Carved by the mighty Colorado River and shaped by millennia of wind and rain, the Grand Canyon is an awe-inspiring natural work of art. From the South Rim, overwhelming vistas open up in every direction, stretching 15 miles (24 km) to the North Rim. Down below, the multihued rock walls descend over 5,000 ft (1,524 m) to a green ribbon of river on the canyon floor. At sunset, a hush settles over the throngs of visitors gathered along the Rim, mesmerized by the majestic play of light and color across the craggy rock formations.

The inner world of the canyon is even more fascinating, with unexplored side canyons, waterfalls, and hidden grottos where a lush, emerald-green world of plants is fed by trickling ground water. The few trails into the canyon twist as they descend through the strata of the ages, leading past weathered, red rock walls and towering spires of

Above: Tourists exploring the canyon on mules

stone in hues of pink, buff, violet, and gray. The tapestry of life in the canyon is rich and conducive to hardy plant life; chipmunks scurry looking for food, gopher snakes glide across rocks, and overhead the great California condor soars on the rising thermals.

The heart of the canyon is the Colorado River, where raging rapids challenge those who venture into its powerful torrents by canoe, kayak, and raft. Hikers descend to camp beside the river and each year, thousands mount sturdy mules to ride deep into the canyon to spend the night at the celebrated Phantom Ranch. On the canyon floor, the voice of the river dominates, with the constant sound of rushing rapids echoing off the walls.

Beyond the canyon's grandeur, other natural wonders await. At Canyon de Chelly, natives take visitors into their spiritual home to see the multistoried cliff dwellings built by Ancestral Puebloans 2,000 years ago. A half-day away lie the rock formations of Monument Valley, where you can wrap up your visit by exploring less-frequented corners by horseback or 4WD.

CANYON DIARY

October is an excellent time to visit the Grand Canyon, as the summer crowds are gone and the weather is pleasant. Five days are enough to drive to the national park and explore the inner depths of the canyon by foot or mule. If you have eight days, include a side trip to Canyon de Chelly and Monument Valley.

Eight Awe-Inspiring Days

DAY 1

Arrive in Las Vegas, explore the casino fantasyland, and dine at one of the city's restaurants.

DAYS 2–4

On your first day of exploration around the canyon, get an early start and drive to the South Rim for the awesome view. Take a shuttle to the Information Plaza and arrive at Hopi Point in time for the sunset.

The next day, head to the corral for a two-day mule trip, or grab your backpack and go to the trailhead for an overnight hike.

Alternatively, take a short hike into the canyon and return to the village for lunch. After browsing the galleries and shops, take the shuttle to Hermit's Rest and walk the Rim Trail to Yaki Point.

Take a one-day mule trip into the canyon or drive to Desert View Watchtower for superb views, and explore the museum to learn about the canyon's Native Americans. Then, watch the sunset from Lipan Point.

DAYS 5–7

Head farther east to Canyon de Chelly and take the South Rim drive to Spider Rock Overlook. Then drive out to Massacre Cave Overlook.

Hire a guide to see the ancient ruins up close. Later, hike the steep trail for views of the Whitehouse Ruins.

Take the unpaved 17-mile (27-km) loop drive along the plateau above the valley. Later, hire a Navajo guide and ride horseback through Monument Valley.

DAY 8

On your last day, head south through Oak Creek Canyon into the red rock country surrounding Sedona.

Dos and Don'ts

- ✗ Don't forget to book at least a year ahead for mule trips into the canyon, raft trips down the Colorado River, and backcountry camping permits.
- ✓ Dress in layers, wear sturdy hiking boots, and carry plenty of water and food when hiking.
- ✓ Find a time and place where you can be alone to soak in the serene beauty of the canyon.
- ✗ Don't miss views of the sunset over the canyon.

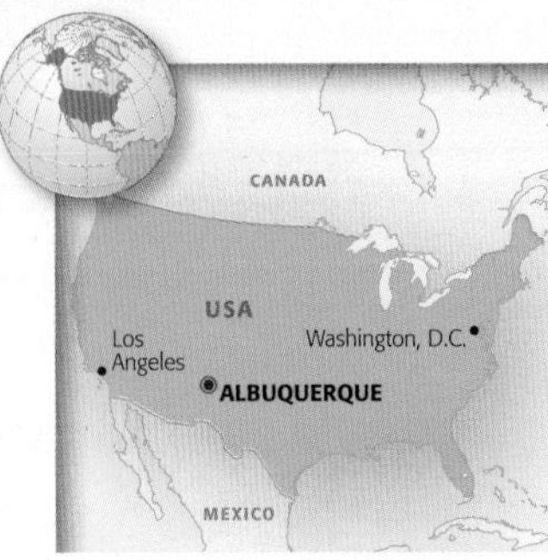

GETTING THERE **See map p318, B2**
Balloon Fiesta Park is located in North Albuquerque, west of I-25, approximately 12 miles (19 km) north of Albuquerque Sunport, the state's only major airport.

GETTING AROUND
Most visitors rely on rental cars but Albuquerque (at the junction of the I-40 and I-25 does have the ABQRide bus system. In addition, there are multiple ways to get to the fiesta from the city: park and ride, by bike, or the New Mexico Rail Runner which offers a rail pass with a shuttle to and from the park.

WEATHER
The Balloon Fiesta is held when the weather is cool and crisp. Temperatures in the morning are around 40°F (4°C), warming up to about 70°F (21°C) in the afternoon.

ACCOMMODATIONS
The Albuquerque Marriott Pyramid North is situated near Balloon Fiesta Park; doubles from US$239; www.marriott.com

Hotel Albuquerque in Old Town offers doubles from US$269; www.hhandr.com

The Hyatt Place Albuquerque/Uptown provides comfortable lodgings; doubles from US$249; albuquerqueuptown.place.hyatt.com

EATING OUT
You'll find food at Balloon Fiesta Park, but for a real taste of New Mexico cuisine at US$15 per head, try eateries such as Little Anita's, or Perea's and Sadie's, both famous for the use of fiery green chilis in their culinary creations.

FURTHER INFORMATION
www.balloonfiesta.com

Let the Ballooning Begin...

One of the most interesting aspects of the world's largest balloon event is its rather unimpressive start. In 1972, to celebrate the 50th birthday of local radio station KOB, its manager planned the world's biggest congregation of hot-air balloons. He received a go-ahead from 21 pilots, but bad weather limited the turnout to just 13 balloons. Nevertheless, on April 8, 1972, 20,000 people gathered at a parking lot for the very first Balloon Fiesta. The number of registered balloons touched 1,019 in 2000, but has since been capped to ease aerial congestion.

Above (left and right): The Old Town Cat House, one of the city's most charming stores; downtown Albuquerque aglow during late evening
Main: Preparing the balloon for the spectacular take-off known as Mass Ascension

Above: The Sandias, named for their watermelon colors at sunset

ALBUQUERQUE

IT'S A ROMANTIC PICTURE – a single hot-air balloon sailing gracefully and silently across the sky, floating with the clouds wherever the wind goes. There's something enchanting about ballooning, as the huge colorful orb just hangs in air as if by magic. If one balloon is magical, seeing hundreds of them dotting the sky in an endless canvas of abstract shapes and vivid colors is beyond words. But this is just what happens once every year at the thrilling Albuquerque International Balloon Fiesta, the largest convention of hot-air balloons in the world and also, according to many, the world's most photographed event.

Held across nine days in early October, well past the sweltering conditions of summer, the fiesta is also the perfect time to enjoy New Mexico's natural beauty. Albuquerque pulls out all the stops, welcoming both visitors and participants from all over the world. From building-sized liquor bottles to mythical creatures and cartoon characters, balloons in shapes previously unimagined fill the barren desert sky as the crowds gaze in amazement from below.

Those hoping to catch the best of the action rise at the crack of dawn, when more than 500 balloons lift off simultaneously. Roughly the size of 54 football fields, the Balloon Fiesta Park accommodates the huge crowds the festival draws with absolute ease. When you're not staring up at the spectacle, weave your way through countless docked balloons, chat with pilots, capture breathtaking photographs, and sample traditional New Mexican fare, such as warm, puffy Navajo fry bread and steaming tortilla soup. Enjoy a live musical performance as you eat. At night, stand in awe of the Balloon Glow, as hundreds of balloons on the ground light up all at once from the glow of their burners. Once the field clears, a lively fireworks display wraps up the evening with a bang.

If one balloon is magical, seeing hundreds of them dotting the sky in an endless canvas of shapes and colors is beyond words.

Inset: Balloons in the sky: dabs of color on a clear, blue canvas
Below (left and right): Balloon Fiesta Park in the thick of activity; Balloon Glow, a magical nocturnal event

NEW MEXICO DIARY

Easily the state's largest festival, the Balloon Fiesta is held every October, when tourists flood Albuquerque and surrounding regions, overbooking hotels and restaurants. If the crowds prove too much, you can always escape north to Santa Fe *(see pp184–5)*, a lovely city known for its history and beauty.

A Weekend in Albuquerque

FRI

Ease into the weekend by exploring Albuquerque's Old Town, stopping at shops selling Native American and southwestern wares. Chow down the city's most beloved burger at Bob's, known for its hot green-chili sauce. At sundown, head to the fiesta for Balloon Glow, as grounded balloons glow in the light of their propane burners. Finish off with a bite and a brew at Monte Vista Fire Station, a relaxed hangout housed in a converted Depression-era firehouse.

SAT

Rise early to watch the Dawn Patrol, which begins around 6am. About an hour later, the Mass Ascension begins. Munch on fresh Navajo fry bread. Around noon, explore the area around Albuquerque. Drive along the 52-mile (84-km) Turquoise Trail on Highway 14 on the east side of the picturesque Sandia Mountains. Later in the afternoon, take in the America's Challenge balloon race and cap off the evening with a firework show.

SUN

Kickstart your day with a balloon ride, offered by Rainbow Ryders. Then head outside the grounds and visit the Anderson-Abruzzo Albuquerque International Balloon Museum (free on Sunday mornings). Later, make your second ascension of the day via the Sandia Peak Aerial Tramway, and after, enjoy first-rate barbecue at County Line BBQ. Be sure to stop by the Bien Mur Indian Market Center.

Dos and Don'ts

- ✓ Before heading out for the day, check the television or the Internet for the "balloon report." Each year, at least one day of the fiesta is usually called off due to inclement weather.
- ✓ Brace yourself for the weekend crowds – waiting lines, parking, and traffic can be quite trying.
- ✗ Don't forget to charge up your camera – you'll likely end up snapping more photos than expected.
- ✓ If you're at the fiesta at night, carry a flashlight; traversing the grounds (and finding your car) may prove difficult.
- ✓ Dress warmly – pre-dawn conditions can be chilly.

GETTING THERE See map p331, C8
International flights land at Chile's capital Santiago. From there fly south to Punta Arenas, the departure point for your cruise aboard the *Mare Australis* cruise ship.

GETTING AROUND
Each day of the cruise features onshore excursions which include forest hikes, wildlife observation, and glacier visits. The Argentine city of Ushuaia is easily explored on foot.

WEATHER
In October expect temperatures of 41–59°F (5–15°C) with rain. Cabo de Hornos and Canal Beagle are prone to rough winds.

ACCOMMODATIONS
In Punta Arenas, Hotel Nogueira is a restored century-old mansion; doubles from US$190; www.hotelnogueira.com

The stylish Hotel Cabo de Hornos has rooms with views of the Magellan Strait; doubles from US$210; www.hoteles-australis.com

The *Mare Australis* cruise ship has three cabin categories with most cabins falling within the highest price band, so book well in advance for scarcer cheaper options.

EATING OUT
Seafood is the specialty in Punta Arenas and Ushuaia. Onboard, meals are lavish four-course affairs accompanied by Chilean wines.

FURTHER INFORMATION
www.australis.com

Domestic Bliss in the Wild

Mid-October is nesting season for Magellanic penguins, which migrate here. During a 40-day incubation period these monogamous birds are models of dual parenting. The male and female incubate eggs in shifts, each spending 15–20 days at sea to feed. Once the eggs hatch, the parents share duties. This cycle is repeated the next year. The male arrives first to reclaim the same burrow. Then the female follows, calling out to her mate. If one of the birds perishes while migrating, it takes the other up to two years to find a new partner.

In this magnificent natural theater, great vertical rock faces rise from the sea, and gushing waterfalls plunge into deep channels.

Main: A cruise ship glides past a wall of glaciers in southern Patagonia

SOUTH PATAGONIAN FJORDS

Sailing the South Patagonian Fjords, you glide slowly toward the bottom of the world, drifting past one stunning scene after another. In this magnificent natural theater, great vertical rock faces rise from the sea, gushing waterfalls plunge into deep channels, and winds howl off massive blue-white glaciers which spill majestically into crystalline blue bays. Elephant seals and Magellanic penguins converge noisily on rugged shorelines, under the watchful gaze of predatory marine birds that dive and soar in search of prey.

Weaving a labyrinthine course through a network of channels, islets, and inlets, and navigating fabled straits, the luxury liners that cruise the fjords of southern Patagonia take you up close to breathtaking scenery and marine wildlife. Cruises start at the city of Punta Arenas in southern Chile and voyage southward toward Cape Horn (Cabo de Hornos), the wind-lashed outcrop that marks the end of the Americas, beyond which lies only Antarctica.

Above: A full moon over the town of Punta Arenas

ICEBOUND DIARY

October is springtime in the southern hemisphere, which means longer daylight hours and magnificent light and scenery. A seven-night cruise of the southern Patagonian Fjords combines a four-night trip south and east and then a three-night sail back, starting and ending in Punta Arenas.

Eight Days in the Fjords

Walk the streets of Punta Arenas before you depart to cross the Estrecho de Magallanes (Strait of Magellan).	**DAY 1**
Cruise the Seno Almirantazgo to Bahía Ainsworth. In the shadow of the Glaciar Marinelli, disembark to see an elephant seal colony. Then take a Zodiac excursion to the Islote Tucker shores, a haven for colonies of Magellanic penguins, sealions, and cormorants.	**DAY 2**
Crossing the Seno Pía, the roar of breaking ice heralds your arrival at Glaciar Pía. Back on ship, sail Canal Beagle (Beagle Channel), passing "Glacier Avenue," and watch as glaciers fall from the Cordillera Darwin.	**DAY 3**
Drink in the view at the end of the world – Cabo de Hornos. Return northward and stroll the ruins of a native settlement at historic Bahía Wulaia.	**DAY 4**
Arrive at Ushuaia, the world's southernmost city and visit the Museo Marítimo, Argentina's Alcatraz.	**DAY 5**
The second leg of the cruise starts by revisiting Cabo de Hornos and Bahía Wulaia. At the Cape view a monument to fallen sailors. From the bay hike through virgin Magellanic forest.	**DAY 6**
Cruise through narrow channels with more glacial vistas. At night, enjoy the Captain's farewell dinner.	**DAY 7**
Before returning to Punta Arenas, sail Canal Gabriel to Isla Magdalena, home to a breeding colony of Magellanic penguins.	**DAY 8**

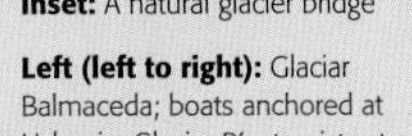

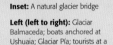

Inset: A natural glacier bridge

Left (left to right): Glaciar Balmaceda; boats anchored at Ushuaia; Glaciar Pía; tourists at a monument at Cabo de Hornos

Right: Cabo de Hornos lighthouse

As you sail, Zodiac excursions offer vistas of the fjords from water level. You can even venture onshore to observe the stunning flora and fauna. In the playful company of pods of dolphins, your boat skirts the shorelines of small islets and coves where colonies of elephant seals and sealions congregate in October to breed. Onshore hikes reveal lush forests and sheltered beaches with nesting colonies of cormorants and Magellanic penguins. Other excursions capture the thrilling drama of the Patagonian Fjords. Close to the great Glaciar Pía, in the shadow of jagged-white peaks, one huge chunk of ice after another breaks away from the glacier's towering front wall to tumble into the frigid waters of Bahía Pía in a concerto of thunderous cracks and booms.

After four days of navigating sheltered waters you reach the desolately beautiful Cape Horn. Here, looking out across the Cape to where the Atlantic and Pacific oceans collide, the sensation is one of utter remoteness. Tiny ice floes pepper the powerful sea and fierce, howling winds that once thwarted many an expedition lash against steep, ragged cliffs. Antarctica and the end of the Earth are just 500 miles (800 km) away.

Dos and Don'ts

- ✓ Head to top deck around midnight for dreamy views of peaks and glaciers illuminated by the moon and stars.
- ✗ Don't expect stuffy formality on this cruise. The onboard atmosphere is relaxed and dress code is informal. However, do bring smart clothes for the farewell dinner.
- ✓ Be prepared for seasickness; rounding Cape Horn, the going can be very rough.
- ✓ Try the *centolla* (king crab) in Ushuaia, a regional specialty.
- ✓ Bring high-factor sunblock. The ozone layer is paper-thin and disappears almost completely in October–March.

OCTOBER

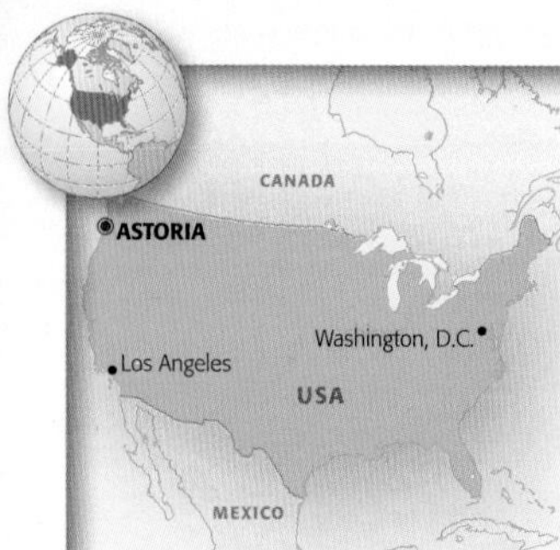

GETTING THERE **See map p320, A3**

The closest large airport is in Portland, served by most major airlines. Rent a car here and follow the Columbia River northwest to Astoria along scenic Route 30 (a 2-hour trip).

GETTING AROUND

Driving is the only option for the coastal route.

WEATHER

October highs range between 50 and 60°F (10 and 15°C) , with lows in the mid-40s (around 7°C). Rain is always a possibility.

ACCOMMODATIONS

Ecola Beach Lodge in Cannon Beach offers rooms and suites near the beach; doubles from US$89; www.cannonbeachlodge.com

The Ester Lee in Lincoln City rents basic but charming seaview cottages with fireplaces from US$89 per night; www.esterlee.com

Ireland's Rustic Lodge in Gold Beach has oceanfront suites from US$114 per night; www.irelandsrusticlodges.com

EATING OUT

Eat your fill of fresh seafood: razor clams, Dungeness crab, and Yaquina Bay oysters are local favorites. Mo's, in Cannon Beach, and elsewhere along the coast, is renowned for its clam chowder and oyster stew. Stephanie Inn in Cannon Beach serves the finest food on the coast, and offers a US$79 prix-fixe dinner.

FURTHER INFORMATION

www.visittheoregoncoast.com

The Haunted Lighthouse

Tall tales of buried pirate treasure and phantom galleons abound on the mist-shrouded Oregon coast, and a favorite is that of the ghost of Rue, the wife of a 19th-century lighthouse keeper at Heceta Head. One day (so the story goes) Rue sent her daughter out to play, and the child never returned, believed lost to the waves crashing against the cliffs far below the lighthouse. Silver-haired Rue, wearing a black dress, apparently still awaits her daughter's return, and is seen peering out of the lighthouse windows and heard opening and closing doors.

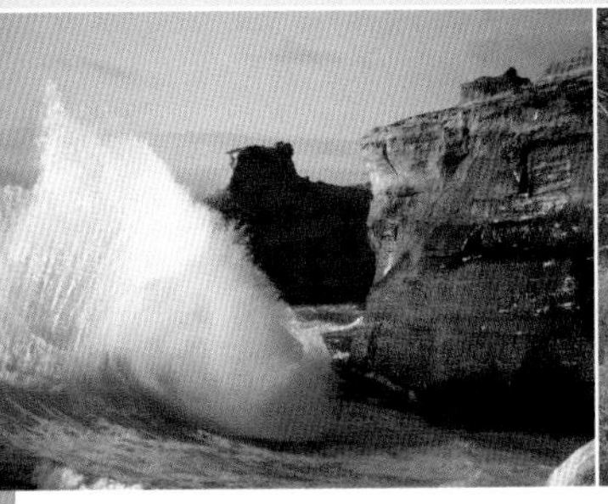

Above (left to right): Cape Kiwanda State Natural Area; fall colors on the coastal road; Haystack Rock, Cannon Beach
Main: Horseback riding on Bandon Beach

Above: Ecola State Park

OREGON COAST

"Ocean in view, oh the joy," the explorer William Clark enthused into his diary in 1805 upon first sighting the Pacific Ocean crashing into the Oregon coast. This is one of America's most scenic coastlines and evokes similar excitement in many a modern-day traveler. Every bend in the road along the 350-mile (563-km) length of Highway 101 seems to reveal yet another natural wonder – the waves breaking against the cliffs of Cape Kiwanda, the 40-mile- (65-km-) long expanse of sand dunes south of Florence, the heights of Cape Perpetua carpeted in old-growth rain forests, sea stacks rising from the sea off the coast at Bandon, to mention but a few. A drive along this stretch of coast involves pulling over at dozens of viewpoints and scenic lookouts simply to admire a view. It is equally tempting to stop and explore the beaches and forest trails along the way – a walk along the Umpqua Scenic Dunes Trail south of Florence and into the Pacific on a narrow spit of lava at Yaquina Head Outstanding Natural Area, where you'll get to keep company with sealions, are among the possibilities. In places, the coastline seems utterly remote, with nothing in sight but surf, sand, and forests growing right to the edge of the sea. It's easy to envisage the past, when the galleons of Sir Francis Drake and Juan de Fuca sailed past these headlands and Lewis and Clark built a fort at the end of their momentous transcontinental journey. The realization that these timeless landscapes have fascinated the great explorers adds all the more zest to your own discovery of this magical coastline.

A journey along the Oregon coastline is loaded with sensory experiences – the scent of evergreens in Ecola State Park mingling with the tang of sea brine, the roar of surf drowning out the screech of gulls at Cape Meares, and the spectacle of sealions sunning on the rocks beneath the lighthouse at Heceta Head. All make for one amazing and memorable road trip.

In places, the coastline seems utterly remote, with nothing in sight but surf, sand, and forests growing right to the edge of the sea.

Inset: Green anemones and starfish in a tidepool
Below (left and right): Fishing boats, Yaquina Bay; Highway 101 at Cape Sebastian

COASTAL DIARY

Many diversions await you along the Oregon coast, so allow four days for the 350-mile (563-km) drive. At this time of year, you can enjoy near-deserted beaches and hike in forests where vine maples and other deciduous trees are putting on a brilliant show of fall color.

Four Days on the Road

DAY 1

Arrive in Astoria, where the Columbia River Maritime Museum chronicles the region's seagoing past. Just south of town, in Fort Clatsop National Memorial, is an authentic recreation of the stockade where 19th-century American explorers Lewis and Clark passed the winter of 1805–6. Pull into Cannon Beach in time for a sunset walk along the beach to Haystack Rock.

DAY 2

Spend the morning hiking the trails that crisscross Ecola State Park, a 1,100-ft (335-m) headland that is often shrouded in mist. Continue south through Tillamook, famous for cheddar cheese, and along the Three Capes Scenic Route (Capes Kiwanda, Meares, and Lookout), where viewpoints are perched high above the crashing surf, to Lincoln City.

DAY 3

Begin the day with a climb through the rain forests and maritime prairies of Cascade Head Preserve. Then head south through the fishing port of Depoe Bay, where at Devil's Punchbowl the thundering sea blasts through rocky channels and erupts in geysers. Stop in Newport for visits to the Oregon Coast Aquarium and Yaquina Head, and plan to arrive in Yachats in time for sunset.

DAY 4

Round Cape Perpetua, the highest coastal viewpoint, to Heceta Head State Park, where trails overlook a lighthouse. From Florence, sand dunes stretch south for 40 miles (65 km), and at Bandon, craggy sea stacks rise out of the surf. The route rounds Cape Blanco, the westernmost point in the western United States, and passes through forests before coming to Gold Beach, where the Rogue River flows into the sea.

Dos and Don'ts

- ✓ Indulge in the coast's culinary delights. These include oysters, Dungeness crabs, and salmon, as well as rich cheddar cheese and saltwater taffy made up and down the coast.
- ✗ Don't disturb starfish and sea urchins found around tidal pools.
- ✓ Bring a sweater, because sea breezes can be brisk.
- ✓ Be careful of sneaker waves (which rush in unexpectedly).
- ✓ Bring binoculars to catch a glimpse of sealions and other creatures.
- ✓ Wear waterproof shoes on beach walks.

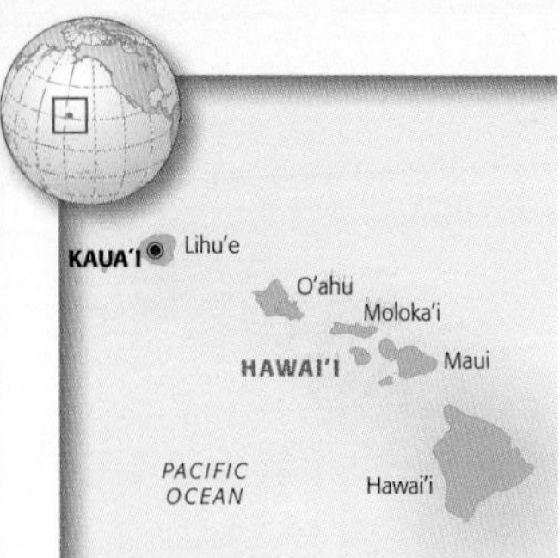

GETTING THERE **See map p322, F5**
Direct flights from the West Coast to Kaua'i, the northernmost of the major Hawaiian Islands, land at Līhu'e. There are also regular connections from other islands, and cabs to resorts range between US$15 and 40.

GETTING AROUND
Renting a car is the only practical way to explore Kaua'i as a whole, although its best wildernesses can only be penetrated on foot.

WEATHER
Mount Wai'ale'ale's peak receives the world's highest average rainfall, while Po'ipū gets less than 40 inches (102 cm) per year. Daytime highs at sea level in October are 82°F (28°C) and lows are 68°F (20°C).

ACCOMMODATIONS
The Waimea Plantation Cottages cost US$220 a night; www.coasthotels.com

Rates at the Grand Hyatt Kaua'i Resort in Po'ipū start at US$459; www.kauai.hyatt.com

With great views of the North Shore, Princeville Resort charges from US$600 per room; www.stregisprinceville.com

EATING OUT
Kaua'i's resort-area restaurants offer entrées ranging between US$12 and 30. For Pacific Rim cuisine using local ingredients, visit Roy's or the Beach House (US$35 per head).

FURTHER INFORMATION
www.kauaidiscovery.com

KAUA'I

FOR SUCH A TINY SPECK OF AN ISLAND, Kaua'i holds a breathtaking diversity of landscapes. No other place in Hawai'i so perfectly fulfils dreams of a pristine Polynesian paradise as this island, where Pacific surf rolls on to golden beaches fringed by palm trees and backed by densely forested valleys and spectacular, rugged mountains. Exploring Kaua'i is not so much about soaking in the views as immersing yourself in its ravishing wildernesses.

Kaua'i's finest hike, the tough 11-mile (18-km) Kalalau Trail, threads its way along the Nā Pali cliffs, on the northern coast. From the moment the trail climbs away from Kē'ē Beach, 7 miles (11 km) beyond Hanalei, you feel you're leaving civilization behind. Barefoot warriors once ran this path to bring news to chiefs, while the platforms of lava boulders below mark the spot where legend says hula was

Main: Waipoo Falls in Waimea Canyon

The Birds of Kaua'i

Having emerged from the ocean as barren lava thousands of miles from land, Hawai'i has evolved its own unique wildlife. Before human contact, new species evolved every 100,000 years. Most of Hawai'i's indigenous birds are now extinct, due to hunting and the arrival of new predators and diseases. Kaua'i's upland wildernesses, though, are still rich in native birds. Eagle-eyed hikers in Kōke'e State Park may spot such rare species as the *'i'iwi*, a scarlet honey-creeper, the red and black *'apapane (above)*, and the tiny, greenish-yellow *'anianiau*.

Left (left and right): Diver observing green sea turtles; beauty in bloom – another common sight in flora-rich Kaua'i

Right: Snorkelers at Lumaha'i Beach

danced for the first time. Each turn opens up new vistas of the precipitous, furrowed cliffs that lie ahead, pleated in gigantic folds and topped by eroded pinnacles so sheer that only velvet moss can cling to them. As you pick your way across waterfalls that cascade from the slopes, white tropicbirds soar overhead. The trail drops back to sea level after a point, where you wade a rapid stream to reach Hanakāpī'ai Beach. In its last few miles, the trail is nerve-wracking at times, consisting of a groove worn into the sloping cliff face. Most day-hikers turn back after exploring Hanakāpī'ai Valley, but if you have a permit – and a head for heights – proceed to camp in Kalalau Valley.

It's possible to drive to the highest peak above Kalalau Valley, but it's only accessible from the south side of the island. Follow the road to the top of Waimea Canyon – an awe-inspiring chasm that nearly splits Kaua'i in two – and you're in Kōke'e State Park, where two overlooks command stunning views over Kalalau Valley, a truly wild and rugged Garden of Eden.

Above: Giant roots of a fig tree at Allerton Garden

Below: A hiker on the verdant Kalalau Trail

Above: The Nā Pali cliffs on Kaua'i

ALOHA DIARY

If you stay less than a week in Kaua'i, you'll regret it – especially in October, when the crowds have gone. The Nā Pali cliffs are a must-see from every angle – on foot, along the Kalalau Trail, from Kōke'e State Park, and by boat. No one can resist the beaches, so keep a few days aside to simply stretch out on the sands.

Seven Days in Kaua'i

Fly in to Līhu'e airport, drive a rental car to your hotel, and enjoy a fine Pacific Rim dinner.	**DAY 1**
Take a leisurely drive along the North Shore, stopping at beaches like Secret Beach, Lumaha'i, and Kē'ē, with a break for lunch and shopping in funky Hanalei.	**DAY 2**
Park early at Kē'ē Beach for a full day's hike along the Kalalau Trail. With a permit from the State Parks Office in Līhu'e, you can go beyond the spectacular Hanakāpī'ai Beach, either inland to the waterfalls or farther along the cliff face.	**DAY 3**
Take a half-day boat trip on the coast of Nā Pali, ideally starting at Hanalei and including a long snorkel stop.	**DAY 4**
Drive round to the West Shore and up Waimea Canyon. At the top of Kōke'e State Park, swoon at the mile-high views of Kalalau Valley, before hiking the boardwalk of the Alaka'i Swamp Trail, deep into the island's interior.	**DAY 5**
Drive up Waimea Canyon once more, so you can hike through the rain forest along the Awa'awapuhi Trail, which leads to a staggering overlook of the sinuous Awa'awapuhi ("slippery eel") Valley.	**DAY 6**
Take an early-morning helicopter ride for spectacular views of the island. Then, spend the day on South Shore, combining a few hours on Po'ipū Beach with a tour of the lush, orchid-laden Allerton Garden in the lovely Lāwa'i Valley.	**DAY 7**

Dos and Don'ts

- ✗ Don't take a Nā Pali boat tour from the West Shore if boats are running from Hanalei.
- ✓ Bite the bullet and pay for a helicopter tour – it's the best way to see much of Kaua'i's most stupendous scenery.
- ✗ Don't leave too little time to hike in Kōke'e State Park; allow a full day for the expedition to the top of Waimea Canyon and back.
- ✓ Wear sturdy hiking boots on the Kalalau Trail; the going is muddy and rough.

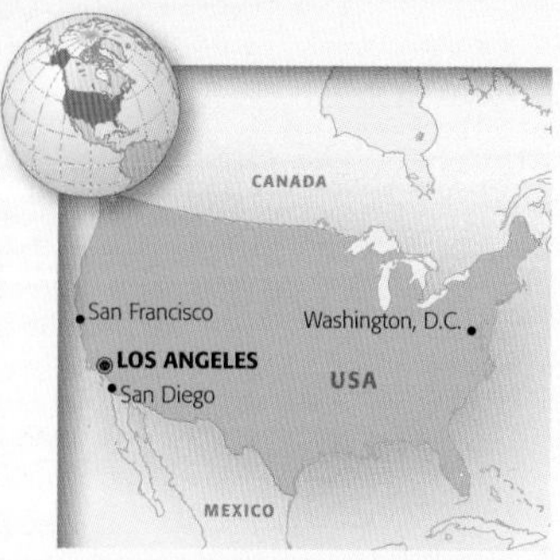

GETTING THERE **See map p321, B3–C5**
Los Angeles, San Diego, and San Francisco international airports are served by scores of domestic and international flights.

GETTING AROUND
Car rental is the only practical and affordable way to visit the various wineries, but whoever drives should drink as little as possible.

WEATHER
October is one of the sunniest times of the year, with temperatures above 82°F (28°C) in the wine valleys. The vines are turned out in their gold and crimson fall colors.

ACCOMMODATIONS
Southwestern decor and a golf course setting at Temecula Creek Inn, Temecula; doubles from US$159; www.temeculacreekinn.com

The Cozy Wine Valley Inn in Solvang is close to many wine-tasting rooms; doubles from US$206; www.winevalleyinn.com

Romantic Inn at Depot Hill, Capitola is close to the Santa Cruz wine district; doubles from US$319; www.innatdepothill.com

EATING OUT
California has a world-famous reputation for its food, including nouvelle cuisine. A great meal will cost about US$75 for two.

FURTHER INFORMATION
www.scmwa.com
www.sbcountywines.com

California is a wine-lover's haven – numerous wineries are sprinkled through the Golden State, like clusters of grapes on a rambling vine.

Main: The sun sets over a Napa Valley vineyard

CALIFORNIA WINE COUNTRY

As if California weren't blessed enough, the state's passion for viticulture is given a helping hand by nature; a range of microclimates and soil conditions result in wines that are renowned all over the world. With so many distinct regions to choose from, California is a wine-lover's heaven paralleled only, perhaps, by the famed traditional wine regions of France, Spain, and Italy. The number of wineries continues to bloom: over 750 wineries are sprinkled throughout the Golden State like clusters of grapes on a rambling vine.

Napa and Sonoma valleys are so popular with wine-lovers that weekends bring more traffic than stomping feet in a winery crush. The popularity has led to a Disney effect, with some wineries perhaps becoming a touch too glitzy. More reason, therefore, to escape the well-trodden path and venture into unsung wine districts specializing in grape varieties that make the most of the specific geography and climate of particular regions. The unusual

California Cuisine

The roots of sophisticated cuisine in California go back to the launch of *Sunset* magazine in 1898. The publication embraced the state's multi-ethnic traditions and popularized the use of fresh products from one's own kitchen garden. By the 1970s, these products fused with a search for pure flavors in cooking. Innovative and laboriously prepared according to French traditions. More recently, Mexican flavors have joined the menu, and chefs have focused on the freshest local organic ingredients from which to create inventive new dishes..

Above: Grapes in a vineyard in Napa Valley

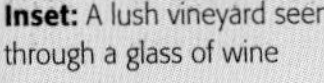

Inset: A lush vineyard seen through a glass of wine

Left (left to right): A hot-air balloon gliding over vineyards; colorful houses in Danish-influenced Solvang; wine barrels in the cellar at Opus One Winery, Napa Valley

Right (left and right): Grape vines clad in fall colors in Santa Barbara wine country; rolling hills of vines in Esparto county

east–west orientation of the coastal mountains around Santa Barbara permits the flow of ocean fog and cool breezes perfect for the cultivation of Pinot Noir. The mountain vineyards of the Sierra foothills are ideal for grape varieties such as Syrah, Zinfandel, and Sauvignon Blanc. For oenophiles, as for everybody else, the superb juxtaposition of valleys and mountains is a bonus.

A leisurely drive through the region allows you to enjoy the wine-making experience while appreciating distinct appellations and the dazzling colors during fall harvest. Most wineries have tasting rooms, some offer guided tours, while others are known as much for their spectacular art as for their labels. Smaller wineries may require an appointment, but the person pouring the wine may be the wine-maker himself. And almost all wineries host events, from tastings to dinners.

Plan on visiting four to five wineries each day, with overnight stays in country inns. For a comprehensive wine adventure, a recommended stretch is from the southernmost wineries of Temecula, south of the Los Angeles sprawl, to the ocean-cooled valleys of the Russian River and Mendocino north of Napa, with their world-class Rieslings.

WINE-LOVER'S DIARY

Fall is when California wine country is at its best. The vines explode with color and the weather is often at its warmest without a cloud in sight. And the wineries are busy crushing or bottling, making a visit engrossing. Eight days is a minimum for enjoying the state's best wine-growing regions, including upcoming areas.

Eight Days on a Tasting Tour

DAY 1

After a day or two enjoying LA, drive south to Temecula, an evolving wine district at 1,500 ft (460 m). Try the Bella Vista Winery, the region's first commercial vineyard.

DAYS 2–3

Journey up the coast to Santa Barbara, an elegant coastal town. Inland, the Santa Ynez Valley has more than 40 wineries, most scattered along US101. Be sure to visit the charming towns of Solvang and Los Olivos to browse antiques. Rise early next day for a scenic balloon ride over the valley before exploring some more wineries.

DAYS 4–5

Take in the stunning coastal scenery along Hwy 1. Arrive in Santa Cruz by mid-afternoon, allowing for time to savor the vineyards and wineries of Soquel. One place not to be missed is the family-run Bargetto Winery. Cross the Coast Range mountains the next day and drop by San Mateo to visit the Thomas Fogarty Winery, located on a mountaintop.

DAYS 6–7

The twin valleys of Napa and Sonoma await you. You're spoiled for choice, with scores of fine wineries to tempt your palate. High on your list in Napa include the Hess Collection Winery for its remarkable art, Francis Ford Coppola's Rubicon Estate, and the Tuscan castle in the hills called Castello di Amoroso. For a lovely picnic, stop at Sattui for cheeses and cold cuts. In Sonoma, between winery visits, see the historic sites, such as Sonoma Barracks.

DAY 8

Travel north to the Russian River region, where Korbel Champagne Cellars provides an insight into the art of making sparkling wines.

Dos and Don'ts

- ✓ Read up on the art and science of wine-tasting before you set out. A little education will help you gain far more from your experience.
- ✗ Don't restrict yourself to just one region. California's wines are amazingly diverse.
- ✓ Do be cautious about how much you drink. Pace yourself and drink plenty of water.
- ✓ Splurge on a great meal. Some of the best restaurants in California are in wine country.

OAXACA

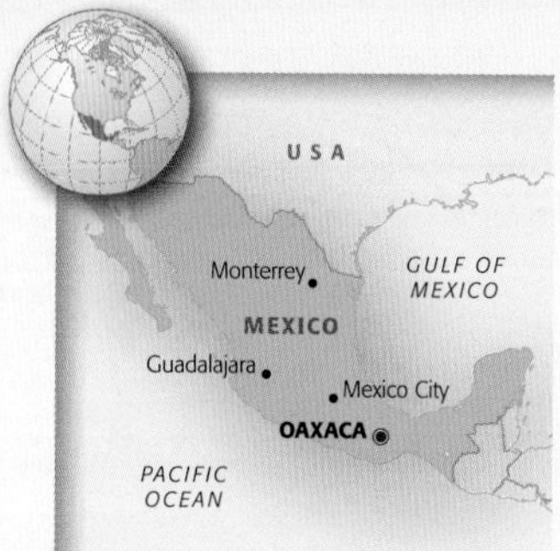

GETTING THERE **See map p323, F6**
Oaxaca is in Mexico, 250 miles (400 km) southeast of the capital, Mexico City. Oaxaca's airport has a few international flights from the US, but travelers usually arrive via a domestic flight from Mexico City. Taxis and minibuses cover the 4 miles (6.5 km) between airport and city.

GETTING AROUND
Taxis, *colectivos* (shared taxis), and crowded, stop-anywhere buses run out to the villages and archeological sites outside the city.

WEATHER
By late October, summer rains are more or less over. Temperatures reach a pleasant 77°F (25°C) by day, cooling to around 57°F (14°C) at night.

ACCOMMODATIONS
Hostal de la Noria, is a converted colonial mansion in the heart of Oaxaca; doubles from US$65; www.hostaldelanoria.com

Misión de los Angeles is a roomy hotel; family suites from US$70; www.hotelesmision.com.mx

Hotel Las Golondrinas has a simple charm; rooms from US$80; www.hotellasgolondrinas.com

EATING OUT
Specialties include the city's famed seven *moles* (sauces), grasshopper, and even the corn mold called *huitlacoche*. Try the Restaurante Los Danzantes, which offers innovative dishes from US$7 in an avant-garde setting.

FURTHER INFORMATION
www.visitmexico.com

THIS MOST MEXICAN OF FIESTAS IS A TRULY SUPERNATURAL EVENT where the dead return to earth to commune with their living relatives. In the colonial city of Oaxaca, full of beautiful churches and mansions built by the Spanish colonists, and surrounded by indigenous villages where even more ancient beliefs still thrive, the celebrations are at their most vivid.

Mexicans generally consider death to be a continuity, a transition into another realm, rather than an ending. And, happily, the dead come back to visit their nearest and dearest every year on All Souls' Day (November 2) – more commonly referred to as *Dia de los Muertos* (Day of the Dead). In Oaxaca the deceased are believed to arrive back at 3pm on November 1

> In the gorgeous colonial city of Oaxaca ... surrounded by indigenous villages where ancient beliefs still thrive, the celebrations are at their most vivid.

and they stay for 24 hours. The preceding 24 hours are for the return of those who died as children, known as *angelitos* (little angels).

The reunion between the living and the dead is at least as joyful as it is poignant, and the atmosphere in homes and cemeteries can be amazingly animated and happy. To welcome their dead, families create elaborate "altars of the dead" in their homes. A table is set under an arch of palm leaves, flowers, and fruits, and is adorned with photos of the dead, saints' images, candles, flowers, favorite foods, drinks, even cigarettes, for the deceased to enjoy. And just to help returnees know they've found the right house, there'll be chocolate or sugar skulls, often inscribed with their names, and miniature skeletons engaged in the kind of things the deceased used to do – dancing, playing soccer, riding a bicycle.

Families also decorate loved ones' graves – with more flowers, candles, photos, drinks, and miniature skulls and skeletons – and will spend hours in graveyards communing with the dead on the afternoon and evening of November 1, even staying for night-long vigils and sharing food and drink with friends and relatives. The magical sight of a cemetery glittering with hundreds of candles, the buzz of talk among the crowds of excited, often joyful people, and the music and dancing that accompany these reunions, lingers in the memory.

Main: Traditional papier-mâché skeleton colorfully decorated with animals and plants
Inset: Zapotec architecture at Monte Albán near Oaxaca
Below (left and right): Carpet of colored sand; costume parade in the Zócalo

Cults of the Dead

All of Mexico's many pre-Hispanic civilizations – the Aztecs, the Maya, the Zapotecs, the Mixtecs and others – believed in forms of afterlife and performed rituals in honour of the dead, often involving feasts and offerings to the departed. Spanish colonial missionaries were able to reinterpret these activities under the umbrella of All Souls' Day, when Catholics pray for departed souls – hence the November 2 date for the Day of the Dead. However, strong elements of the pre-Hispanic ritual beliefs still remain in the way the fiesta is celebrated.

Above: Child wrapped in local textiles at a market in Oaxaca

FIESTA DIARY

Oaxaca is the best place to see the Day of the Dead celebrations. Activities run from October 31 to November 2; if you give yourself six days you can experience the essence of this unique event and explore the city and its fascinating surroundings, or extend your trip by visiting Yucatán *(see pp70–71)*.

Six Days with the Spirits

OCT 29

Soak up the atmosphere in the Zócalo, the city's leafy central square. Stroll up Calle Alcalá to the lavish Santo Domingo church. See the Market of the Dead, where special flowers, foods, papier-mâché skeletons, and chocolate and candy skulls are sold.

OCT 30

For a different perspective on the Day of the Dead Markets, head out of Oaxaca to one of the local villages. The biggest markets include those at Zaachila, Ocotlán, and Tlacolula – but check what day they are held on as it does vary from place to place.

Back in town, the fascinating Museum of Oaxacan Cultures is worth a look, and take in any Day of the Dead dancing or theater in the evening.

OCT 31

See the altars of the dead in your hotel and in local restaurants. After dark, visit the nearby village cemeteries of Santa Cruz Xoxocotlán and Santa María Atzompa – aglow with candles and full of people.

NOV 1

Experience the city's main cemetery, Panteón General, as people gather to decorate graves and celebrate. Later, enjoy the vibrant costume parade at the Zócalo.

NOV 2

To explore the area's fascinating history, head to the spectacular ruins of Monte Albán, the ancient Zapotec capital dating from around 200 BC–AD 700, which has a superb hilltop site. If you want to visit another cemetery in the evening, try the one in San Felipe del Agua.

NOV 3

Oaxaca has a fantastically vibrant indigenous crafts scene, so spend your final day shopping for souvenirs or head out of town to see more of the area.

Dos and Don'ts

- ✓ Though the atmosphere in graveyards and around altars may be surprisingly happy and light-hearted, always be respectful.
- ✗ Don't take photos without asking, or unless you have been told it's okay by a guide or someone with authority.
- ✓ Join a class in altar-decoration or Day of the Dead cooking for a unique insight.
- ✓ Local agencies offer tours to cemeteries and markets, and a good guide will make everything more accessible.

NOVEMBER

Where to Go: **November**

November is a great month for winter sports fans. The Rocky Mountains are gearing up for ski season while the desert states bask in crisp sunshine. Central America's rainy season is drawing to a close and the crowds have yet to arrive, so it's a good time to visit the ancient sites and colonial cities. With the worst of the hurricane season over, winterphobes can head off to the Caribbean, either on a cruise or to bask on a paradise island. November is also the best month for wildlife-watching in Argentina's Península Valdés, while the extraordinary natural wonders of Parque Nacional Torres del Paine, Chile, are at their peak and spring brings long, sunny days. Below you will find all the destinations in this chapter and some extra suggestions to provide a little inspiration.

FESTIVALS AND CULTURE

PANAMA CITY Colorful colonial buildings in Casco Viejo

PANAMA CITY
PANAMA

A cosmopolitan colonial port and its famous canal

Wander the charming Old Quarter in this sultry city and take a boat excursion through the locks of the world's largest commercial waterway.

See pp266–7

BANFF
ALBERTA, CANADA

Join the fun at Winterstart to welcome the new ski season

Banff comes alive with a week-long celebration at the start of winter. Join in the winter sports and festivities, then bathe in hot springs.

www.banff.ca

PALENQUE
MEXICO

One of Mexico's finest Mayan sites

Atmospheric Palenque is home to some of the most beautiful Mayan architecture in existence, including a unique palace, and pyramid tomb.

www.visitmexico.com

OLD SALEM
NORTH CAROLINA, USA

Monument to North Carolina's Moravian pioneers

Historic Old Salem town comprises a living museum of beautifully preserved houses and gardens built by the earliest European settlers.

www.oldsalem.org

LA DIABLADA
PUNO, PERU

It's time to have some devilishly good fun

Held on the shores of Lake Titicaca, La Diablada features a spectacular parade of locals wearing demonic costumes and a week-long party.

www.visitperu.com

UNFORGETTABLE JOURNEYS

GUATEMALA Women in traditional woven blouses

GUATEMALA
CENTRAL AMERICA

Explore this land of temples, rain forests, and mountains

Marvel at Tikal, the Mayan city hidden in the forest, stroll around pretty colonial Antigua, and gaze upon the Pacaya volcano lava flow.

See pp262–3

"Leave behind Tikal's lush tropical forest for the exhilarating highland scenery of western Guatemala."

ISLAS BALLESTAS
PERU

Trace the timeline of South America's wildlife history

Keep your eyes peeled as you cruise the Ballestas Islands: sea lions bray atop rocks, penguins waddle and dolphins leap.

See pp270–271

THE TELEFÉRICO, SANTIAGO
CHILE

Fly – without a plane

Take to the air in a spectacular *teleférico* cable car, with the snow-capped peaks of the high Andes close to hand.

www.funicularsantiago.cl

LAGO DE COATEPEQUE
EL SALVADOR

Volcanic highland lake

Hike around the stunning crater lake of Lago de Coatepeque, which is ringed by a trio of volcanic peaks.

www.lagodecoatepeque.com

HIGH ROAD FROM SANTA FE TO TAOS
NEW MEXICO, USA

Historic mountain drive

Drive this scenic road through the pine-covered Sangre de Cristo Mountains past Native American pueblos and Spanish-style towns.

www.newmexico.org

MISSISSIPPI CRUISE
LOUISIANA, USA

Take a paddle-steamer up the great river to the US heartland

Travel in a genuine "floating palace" from New Orleans past stately antebellum houses, historic plantations, and Civil War sites.

www.steamboatnatchez.com

NATURAL WONDERS

ISLA MARGARITA Baby green turtles

ISLA MARGARITA
VENEZUELA

Perfect for snorkeling, water sports, and nature

Fine sandy beaches, a verdant and mountainous interior, and a fabulous mangrove national park teeming with wildlife.

See pp260–61

BOSQUE DEL APACHE
NEW MEXICO, USA

Ornithological winter wonderland

One of North America's best birding sites, attracting tens of thousands of birds during winter.

www.fws.gov/refuge/bosque_del_apache

REDWOOD NATIONAL PARK
CALIFORNIA, USA

Towering trees

This coastal park has some of the world's tallest trees, including a 367-ft- (112-m-) tall leviathan. Bear and elk are common sights.

www.nps.gov/redw

CENOTES, YUCATÁN
MEXICO

A unique underwater, subterranean world

The world's largest underwater caves, these cathedral-like caverns beneath the Yucatán are unforgettable places to dive.

www.visitmexico.com

LAGO DE ATITLÁN
GUATEMALA

Central America's deepest lake perched in the highlands

This breathtaking lake lies a mile (1.6 km) above sea level, surrounded by volcanic peaks and colorful Mayan villages.

www.lake-atitlan.com

Previous page: Lenticular clouds over Parque Nacional Torres del Paine, Chile

Weather Watch

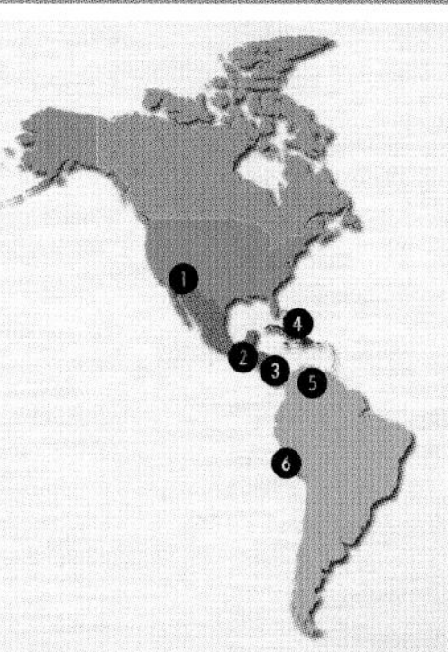

❶ **Tucson, USA** This is a glorious time to visit Southwestern states, with plenty of sunshine, dry, warm days, and cool, clear nights.

❷ **Guatemala** Though the wet season is over in Guatemala and the sun is shining, you'll be lucky to avoid the odd afternoon rainshower. The tropical forests are very humid, while the western highlands get chilly after dark.

❸ **Panama** November temperatures are constantly high in Panama City. Although it is the rainy season, this just makes the country even more verdant. On November 4, Panama celebrates its flag; a must-see celebration for visitors.

❹ **Bahamas** The Bahamas are just settling into winter – which means daytime temperatures of around 75°F (24°C), and a decrease in humidity. Tropical storms are a possibility.

❺ **Venezuela** At the northernmost reach of South America, Venezuela's coast is hot throughout the year, though cooled by pleasant sea breezes. The rainy season in the rest of the country is abating and summer is on its way.

❻ **Islas Ballestas, Peru** The islands in the south Pacific is warm and comfortable in summer, with long hours of daylight. Fewer people visit the country in November, making it an ideal time to visit.

LUXURY AND ROMANCE

TUCSON Pretty flower-filled courtyard at Tucson Botanical Gardens

BÚZIOS
BRAZIL

Chic Mediterranean-style coastal resort

Stylish Buzios near Rio de Janeiro was put on the map by Brigitte Bardot, and now its cool lifestyle attracts Rio's rich and famous.

www.buziosturismo.com

TUCSON
ARIZONA, USA

A desert retreat imbued with a Wild West atmosphere

Hide out in the arid hills outside this desert city and spend a few days pampering yourself in luxurious sports and health resorts.

See pp258–9

MAR DEL PLATA
ARGENTINA

Sample the scene in the chicest resort in the south

Argentina's vacation season starts here, in this stylish town with dynamic nightlife and long, beautiful beaches.

www.argentina.travel/en

BARBADOS
CARIBBEAN

Brilliant sunshine and a rather cozy charm

Cricket, golf, driving on the right – it's like a little piece of England with Caribbean beaches and a buzzing nightlife.

www.visitbarbados.org

ISLAND CRUISE
CARIBBEAN

Sail the trade winds on a sail-powered cruiser

Shiver me timbers! This feels like pirate territory. The pirates have left but the beautiful corals, beaches, and forests remain.

See pp272–3

ACTIVE ADVENTURES

PARQUE NACIONAL TORRES DEL PAINE A *gaucho* on his horse

PARQUE NACIONAL TORRES DEL PAINE
CHILE

Trek beside glaciers and lakes

In a beautiful but harsh landscape, shaped by the wind and the ice, trek this legendary landscape and see incredible sights you'll never forget.

See pp264–5

ECUADOR
SOUTH AMERICA

Bike, hike and raft in this paradise for fresh-air fiends

Ecuador is packed with options for active types, from hiking in the Amazon and biking in the Andes, to rafting the fast-flowing rivers.

www.ecuador.com

"Kayak in an iceberg-choked lagoon or gallop on horseback over wild moors in the shadow of the Paine massif."

ORINOCO DELTA
VENEZUELA

Explore the mouth of South America's third-largest river

Ride the waterways of this great wetland wilderness, with its tangled labyrinth of wildlife-rich rain forest and swamp.

www.orinocodelta.com

LAGUNA SAN RAFAEL
CHILE

Icebergs, glaciers, and penguins

Kayak in the iceberg-studded waters of this spectacular lagoon at the foot of the San Rafael Glacier, and spot penguins and sealions.

www.turismochile.com/guide/

HIKING IN THE FITZ ROY MASSIF
ARGENTINA

Spectacular Andean range

Hike amidst dozens of razor-sharp rock needles surrounding Monte Fitz Roy, one of the most dramatic peaks in South America.

www.ripioturismo.com.ar

FAMILY GETAWAYS

THE BAHAMAS Floating above the reef in this snorkelers' paradise

THE BAHAMAS
CARIBBEAN

Sun and fun are guaranteed at this island paradise

The Bahamas is like a vast natural theme park, with safe sandy beaches, warm waters, top-notch hotels, and pirate hide-outs.

See pp268–9

RIO GRANDE VALLEY
TEXAS, USA

Family holiday hotspot in the south

On the border between Texas and Mexico, this region offers fishing, birding, dolphin-spotting, and diving opportunities.

www.valleychamber.com

COSTA RICA
CENTRAL AMERICA

The most family-friendly destination in Central America

This enticing little country has activities to suit all: turtle-watching, wildlife-spotting, jungle treks, rafting, or lazing on the beach.

www.costarica.com

MARTINIQUE
CARIBBEAN

A slice of France in the Caribbean

Martinique's tropical pleasures rival its French-inspired boutiques and gastronomy: by day, frolic in the sea and shop; by night, toast the sunset.

See pp274–5

PLYMOUTH
MASSACHUSETTS, USA

First landing site of the Pilgrim Fathers

Mark Thanksgiving where it all began – watch the parade, eat at the Pilgrim Village, and visit the reproduction Mayflower.

www.plimoth.org

GETTING THERE **See map p321, F6**
The drive from Tucson International Airport to downtown takes 20 minutes. Taxis and airport shuttles are available, and some hotels and resorts provide transportation for their guests.

GETTING AROUND
Rental cars are the most convenient option for exploring Tucson, although downtown is fun to navigate on foot. The surrounding mountains provide numerous hiking, biking, and horse trails.

WEATHER
Autumn is delightful with sunny, mild, usually rain-free days, and highs of 74–86°F (23–29°C) and lows of 44–55°F (8–14°C).

ACCOMMODATIONS
Two golf courses, tennis, and a spa are offered at Loews Ventana Canyon Resort; doubles from US$199; www.loewshotels.com

Hacienda del Sol Guest Ranch Resort was a retreat for Katharine Hepburn and Spencer Tracy; doubles from US$200; www.haciendadelsol.com

JW Marriott Star Pass Resort and Spa has a 27-hole golf course; doubles from US$269; www.jwmarriottstarrpass.com

EATING OUT
Feast on mesquite-grilled meats, tasty salsas, and sizzling fajitas. Don't miss a meal at El Charro Café (311 N. Court Ave.), family-owned since 1922.

FURTHER INFORMATION
www.visittucson.org

Top: Courtyard at Tucson Botanical Gardens

Below (top and bottom): Mission San Xavier del Bac; rock art in Saguaro National Park

Right panel (top to bottom): The painted dome ceiling of Mission San Xavier del Bac; ornate door handle at Mission San Xavier del Bac; cowboy hats

Main: Saguaro cacti silhouetted in the sunset

A Thorny Masterpiece

Rising from the Sonoran Desert floor are the majestic saguaros. Pronounced "sah-wah-roh," these intriguingly shaped, tree-like cacti with multiple arms average 30 ft (9 m) tall and live for up to 200 years. A slow grower, the saguaro spurts less than 2 inches (51 mm) during its first eight years of life. Indeed, one side arm can take up to 50–75 years to develop. It is well worth the wait. The saguaro's white blossoms, which are Arizona's state flower, appear in spring and only open at night, remaining on display until the following day.

TUCSON

SHADES OF VIOLET, DUSTY SAGE, AND COBALT BLUE PAINT TUCSON'S SUNRISES AND SUNSETS, mountain vistas, and desert oases. Imbued with the spirits of Native Americans, Spanish missionaries, lawmen Wyatt Earp and Doc Holliday, black-hat banditos, and sultry saloon queens, Tucson segues between its bygone-days atmosphere and status as an ultra-luxurious playground. Surrounded by the rugged Santa Catalina Mountains and the hauntingly beautiful Sonoran Desert, the city is home to some of the world's most opulent sports and health resorts.

Tucson was founded in 1775 and is a thriving metropolis with a major university, yet it continues to embrace its early heritage. Oozing with colorful character, historic downtown (the "Old Pueblo") hosts a thriving contemporary arts district that features long-standing landmarks, such as the 1934 Hotel Congress where infamous bank robber John Dillinger lived, and El Charro Café, which as been owned by the same family since 1922. Wander the streets in

Above: Downtown Tucson

WESTERN DIARY

Autumn is the perfect season for a splurge in Tucson. Days are bathed in warm sun, evenings are basked in starlight, and you can choose from an extensive list of activities and attractions. Five days will allow you to enjoy your favorite sport, spend down time in a spa, visit historic sights, and tour the wine trail.

Five Indulgent Days

DAY 1

Rent a bike or a horse, or take a hike and explore the diverse beauty of the Santa Catalina Mountains or marvel at the prehistoric rock art in the Saguaro National Park. At the end of the day, savor the magical sunset with a margarita in hand.

DAY 2

Hit the golf course or the tennis courts at one of Tucson's luxury resorts, and then be soothed and pampered in one of its lavish spas. Try out desert-inspired treatments and rituals. Couples can arrange for simultaneous sessions in private treatment rooms.

DAY 3

Start the day floating above the mountains and desert on a champagne hot-air balloon ride. Explore downtown Tucson, dubbed the "Old Pueblo," and its ten surrounding historic districts. Among the highlights are the 1934 Hotel Congress, 1775 Presidio San Agustin de Tucson, and the thriving arts district. Stop for lunch or dinner at El Charro Café.

DAY 4

Take another day to enjoy your favorite activity, relax by the pool, or soak in a hot tub surrounded by spectacular mountain vistas. Celebrate another sunset and watch myriad stars emerge from the darkening sky, or view the skies through a telescope at the University of Arizona's Flandrau Science Center and Planetarium.

DAY 5

Visit the Arizona-Sonora Desert Museum, an all-in-one zoo, natural history museum, and botanical garden, or linger in the Tucson Botanical Gardens. Afterwards, head to dazzling white Mission San Xavier del Bac (1783–97) and marvel at its architectural styles and intricate paintings.

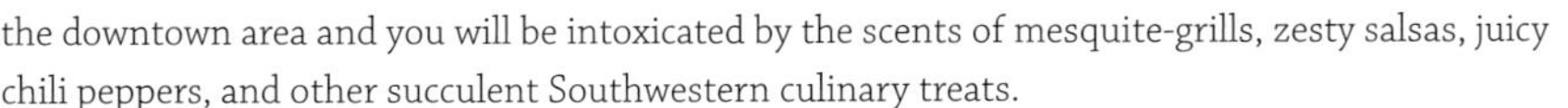

the downtown area and you will be intoxicated by the scents of mesquite-grills, zesty salsas, juicy chili peppers, and other succulent Southwestern culinary treats.

The hills around Tucson hide other treasures. Looming over the Santa Cruz Valley is the striking "White Dove of the Desert," Mission San Xavier del Bac, a welcoming beacon of elegant domes and arches in a blend of Moorish, Byzantine, and late-Mexican Renaissance architecture. Inside, gaze heavenward at the so-called "Sistine Chapel of North America" with its intricate paintings on the walls and ceiling. About an hour's drive south of Tucson, amid rolling grasslands and tree-covered hills, are a smattering of vineyards that produce Mediterranean and Spanish varietals and invite visitors to stop for tours and tasting. Early frontier life can be experienced by staying on an authentic dude ranch where you can rest up in a comfortable *casita* (guestroom) and soak in a hot tub after a day of horseback riding, hiking, birding, and cookouts. Alternatively, treat yourself to one of the pampering resorts featuring championship golf courses, tennis facilities, and lavish spas and be as active or relaxed as you wish in this picturesque paradise.

Dos and Don'ts

- ✓ Ask permission before taking photos of Native Americans, especially at ceremonies.
- ✗ When walking in the desert, watch your step lest you tread on a snake.
- ✓ Don't venture into the desert or mountains without maps and information about weather and road conditions.
- ✓ Bring a good pair of binoculars in order to view some of the 250 bird species that inhabit the local area.

GETTING THERE See map 325, H6
Isla Margarita is 14 miles (23 km) north of the Venezuelan coast. Direct flights arrive at the island's Del Caribe International Airport from cities around the world, or flights from Caracas, Venezuela's international airport, take around 45 minutes.

GETTING AROUND
Roads are good on the island and rental car is an excellent way to explore. Boat trips are available from most beaches and harbors to visit some of the offshore sights and islands.

WEATHER
Isla Margarita enjoys an average temperature of 81°F (27°C), with a gentle sea breeze.

ACCOMMODATIONS
The colonial-style Hotel Costa Linda Beach is near El Agua beach; doubles from US$55; www.hotelcostalinda.com

Luxurious Hesperia Playa El Agua is a modern complex on the beach; doubles from US$150; www.hesperiaislamargarita.com

The IKIN Margarita Hotel & Spa has a lovely large swimming pool; doubles from US$212; www.ikinmargarita.com/en

EATING OUT
Tuna, snapper, and lobster are typical local fare, as are tropical fruits. Look out for the national dish, *Pabellón Crollo* – shredded beef with black beans and fried plantains.

FURTHER INFORMATION
www.islamargarita.com

Historical Margarita

The island has been the setting for many notable events in South American history. Christopher Columbus himself happened upon the island paradise in 1498, and the inhabitants inevitably became slaves to the conquering Spaniards. In 1814 it became the first territory in Venezuela to rid itself of Spanish rule, and it was here that Simón Bolívar, famous liberator of the continent, was confirmed Commander-in-Chief of the new republic. Traces of Spanish influence can be seen throughout the island in the typical Spanish-style architecture in the towns.

ISLA MARGARITA

FLYING OVER THE CARIBBEAN FROM MAINLAND VENEZUELA, you will see a collar of islands, their lush, green interiors ringed by the whitish-yellow of their beaches and an outer circle of light turquoise where the sand is visible through the shallow waters of the sea. Isla Margarita is the largest of the Minor Antilles, although at its longest it stretches a mere 39 miles (62 km), and is a bustling, diverse, and beautiful place to spend an unforgettable vacation.

Mountainous and subtropical, the island is divided into two regions. Its eastern section is developed and populous; Porlamar is a thriving commercial city, and its status as a duty-free port draws in Venezuelan tourists who enjoy its nightlife, casinos, restaurants, and cheap shopping.

> You can explore the labyrinthine channels that meander through the tangled roots of the mangroves, a dense green canopy blocking out the sun from overhead.

The west of the island, in contrast, is relatively quiet and unspoiled. The Macanao is an expansive, arid peninsula, with shrubs and cacti peppering the landscape and wild hare darting across the path of your jeep. A string of verdant mountains makes up the interior, encircled by wide, deserted beaches and dunes, with crashing surf and picture-book palms. Often the only people you will see here are local fishermen, rigging their hooks and setting off in search of tuna and red snapper which you can sample, freshly grilled, in one of the small restaurants in town.

The narrow isthmus that connects these two regions is a sand spit that forms part of the Restinga National Park, an area of mangrove swamps filled with bountiful wildlife. Aboard a small wooden *peñero* – a traditional local fishing boat – you can explore the labyrinthine channels that meander through the tangled roots of the mangroves, a dense green canopy blocking out the sun from overhead. The crystal-clear waters are a window on to some spectacular marine life, including green and leatherback turtles and the enormous oysters that cling to the underwater mangrove roots. For visitors wishing to prolong their experience of totally unspoiled Venezuelan sea-life, trips can be made out to the coral reefs of Los Roques, an amazing National Park of sandy beaches and waters that teem with colorful fish, swimming amongst some of the best-preserved reefs in the world.

Main: Aerial view of the coral reefs at Los Roques, Venezuela
Inset: Parrotfish, a common sight in the waters around Isla Margarita
Below (left to right): Nueva Esparta; Playa el Agua; baby green turtles

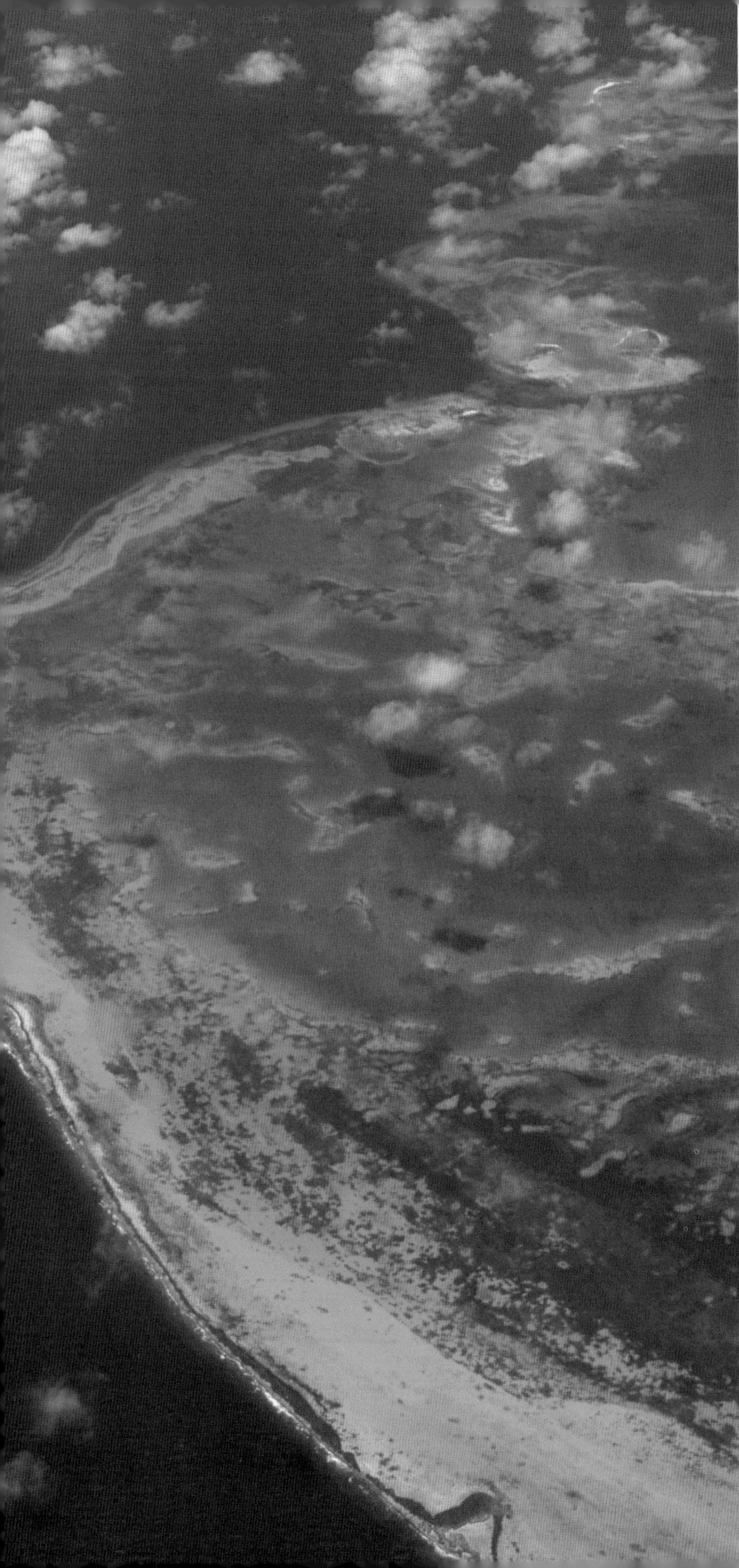

Above: A flock of scarlet ibis in a tree

ISLAND DIARY

November should bring clear skies, warm temperatures, and a refreshing offshore breeze. The island is a manageable size for a week's stay, with enough time to kick back and relax, view the wildlife, and enjoy the nightlife as well. Visitors can extend their trip by visiting the Angel Falls *(see pp292–3)* on the mainland.

A Week of Tropical Treasures

DAY 1

International flights arrive just outside Porlamar, so you can begin your trip visiting the duty-free port.

Spend the afternoon relaxing in the warm waters at El Agua beach and have a cocktail at a beachfront bar.

DAY 2

Take a day to explore Macanao, the unspoiled beaches of the eastern region, then drive to Manzanillo on the peninsula's northeastern tip and watch the local fishermen unload their catch.

DAY 3

Try your hand at some water sports: the beach at El Yaque has some excellent windsurfing, while the tides and swell at Parguito make it good for surfing.

DAY 4

Take one of the daily boat trips from Margarita Island to the islands of Coche and Cubagua. The former is a quiet fishing village with white-sand beaches, and Cubagua has some excellent diving.

DAY 5

Visit the archipelago of Los Roques, a group of 42 coral reefs and beautiful sandy beaches. Observe the amazing variety of wildlife and try your hand at bonefishing with the locals.

DAY 6

Board a *peñero* to explore the mangroves of the Restinga National Park. Colorful sea and bird life and beautiful natural scenery make this one of the undoubted highlights of a trip to Margarita Island.

DAY 7

Take the short flight back to Caracas to connect with your onward flight.

Dos and Don'ts

- ✓ Be careful of strong currents and tides. Some beaches are dangerous, even for strong swimmers; make sure you know the situation before you take the plunge.
- ✗ Don't underestimate the sun – a light sea breeze takes the edge off the heat, but the tropical sun is still very powerful.
- ✓ Get off the beaten track – the island still has many quiet corners and deserted beaches. Rent a car to explore, and you will be rewarded.
- ✗ Don't miss out on the tax-free bargains in Porlamar.

GETTING THERE See map p324, B2
International flights to Guatemala land at La Aurora Airport, 4 miles (6 km) south of the capital, Guatemala City. Transfer to the domestic terminal for the short flight to Flores. From here, Tikal is around an hour by taxi.

GETTING AROUND
Bus tours and shuttle buses are useful for getting to most major attractions, but you can take a taxi (US$30) from Guatemala City to Antigua, which can be explored on foot.

WEATHER
Tikal is humid, warm, and sunny, with an average high of 74°F (23°C) and maybe the odd shower.

ACCOMMODATIONS
Jungle Lodge Hotel provides bungalow accommodation in Tikal; doubles at US$153 per night; www.junglelodgetikal.com

Hotel Villa del Lago in Flores has doubles for US$40 per night; www.hotelvilladelago.com.gt

El Convento Boutique Hotel in Antigua offers well-furnished doubles from US$140; www.elconventoantigua.com

La Casa del Mundo on Lake Atitlán offers swimming, kayaking, hiking, and bicycle tours; US$66 per night; www.lacasadelmundo.com

EATING OUT
Specialties include *pollo en pepián* (chicken in a spicy sauce) and *tamales dulces* – corn cakes with fruit baked in plantain leaves.

FURTHER INFORMATION
www.inguat.gob.gt

The Grand Ceiba

With a straight, gray trunk and flat-topped canopy, Guatemala's national tree – the ceiba – can grow to over 100 ft (30 m) in height, while its branches span up to 150 ft (46 m) across. To the Mayans, the ceiba was the "World Tree," connecting the earth to the heavens and the underworld. From its limbs hang epiphytes – moss-like plants that nurture orchids, ferns, and bromeliads. It also shelters hummingbirds, iguanas, and anteaters; bats pollinate its flowers and rest beneath its buttressed roots, while harpy eagles roost in the leaf canopy.

Main: The magnificent ruins of Tikal's Great Plaza, now swathed in forest

GUATEMALA

IT'S BARELY FIVE IN THE MORNING and an eerie silence looms over the rain forest as you tread your path in pitch darkness, when all of a sudden, the air erupts with the raucous call of hordes of howler monkeys as they awaken. Soon after, as you climb the broken steps of the pyramid known to archeologists as Temple IV, day is all set to break and, as the mist clears, the towering ruins of a great civilization come into view.

Once the most powerful and prosperous of Mayan cities, Tikal is now emerging to reclaim its place in history as a national park rich in both natural and man-made beauty. As your guide leads you expertly through the stupendous remains of temples, palaces, and plazas, he describes the astonishing variety of flora and fauna found here – majestic ceiba and sapodilla trees as well as spider monkeys, silver foxes, tarantulas, keel-billed toucans, and oropendulas, as well as the elusive jaguar, held sacred by the Mayans.

Left (left to right): Antigua's Santa Catarina Arch aglow at dusk; black howler monkey in the rain forest; Pacayá Volcano spewing lava; Maximón, the "smoking deity"; the clear and calm waters of Lake Atitlán

Below: Chichicastenango Market's colorful array of fruits and vegetables

Inset: Tapestry work at a market in Antigua

Above: Women wearing traditional, woven blouses

Once the most powerful and prosperous of Mayan cities, Tikal is now emerging to reclaim its place in history.

Leave behind Tikal's lush tropical forest for the exhilarating highland scenery of western Guatemala; waiting to greet you is a magical lake, formed 85,000 years ago by a volcanic eruption 30 times greater than Pompeii – the stunningly radiant Atitlán Lake.

With its placid surface ruffled only by the afternoon breeze and motor launches that serve shoreline settlements, Atitlán Lake is over 5,000 ft (1,524 m) above sea level and surrounded by mountains and volcanoes. Most people here still speak the Mayan languages of their ancestors and wear traditional clothes, such as *huipiles* – colorful, hand-embroidered traditional blouses – which can be found in Chichicastenango, home to Central America's largest native market.

A short drive from Lake Atitlán is the sensitively restored colonial town of Antigua. The colonial capital of Guatemala, this architectural gem has earned a place on UNESCO's World Heritage list for its old-world charm, photogenic squares and cobbled streets, and picturesque ruins of churches and convents damaged by earthquakes in the 18th century.

GUATEMALAN DIARY

Six days are sufficient for you to become acquainted with this multifaceted country. At this time of year, unbroken sunshine is the norm, which is why locals refer to the dry season as "summer." You will also be arriving before peak tourist season, an important consideration when visiting Tikal, where crowds are common.

Six Days of Color and Culture

DAY 1

Be up before dawn in Tikal for the dramatic awakening of the rain forest. Spend the day exploring the ruins and following scenic nature trails. Later, head to Flores in time for a swim in Lake Petén Itzá as the sun sinks dramatically over the horizon. Dine at a terrace restaurant, on freshly caught fish from the lake.

DAY 2

Fly to Guatemala City and take a taxi to the charming colonial town of Antigua. Spend the morning at the Centro La Azotea, a museum devoted to Mayan culture, around 1 mile (2 km) north of Antigua. Return to the town center to explore its ruined churches.

DAYS 3–4

Join a tour to the active Pacayá Volcano. Climb to within 984 ft (300 m) of the summit to photograph the glowing lava that snakes down the mountainside. On your return trip, ride part of the way on horseback.

Ride a mini shuttle to Lake Atitlán. After lunch in Panajachel, jump on a motor launch to El Jaibalito and check in at La Casa del Mundo. Bathe in the lake and then take a pre-dinner stroll to the village. Return later to see the changing hues of the lake at sunset.

DAY 5

Go kayaking on the lake, followed by a motor-launch ride to the Mayan village of Santiago Atitlán. Ask a guide to show you the wooden statue of Maximón (San Simón), a Mayan deity who "smokes" a cigar.

DAY 6

Visit Chichicastenango and its market (Thursdays and Sundays). Wander the cobbled streets of this attractive town, home to the Kaqchikel people. Here, admire their weaving skills and colorful folk costumes.

Dos and Don'ts

- ✓ Stay the night at Tikal to compare the stunning views of the ruins at sunset and at sunrise, as the mist rises.
- ✓ Dress warmly when you visit the western highlands, where it will feel cooler. Do also pack a flashlight, a camera, mosquito repellent, sunscreen, and headwear.
- ✗ While in Guatemala, don't stray too far from established tourist routes without a guide or checking with your hotel.

GETTING THERE See map p331, C7

Take a flight from Santiago to Punta Arenas. From here, travel 249 miles (400 km) by road to Parque Nacional Torres del Paine.

GETTING AROUND

Explore trekking circuits independently or on guided hikes. The southern area's *hosterías* (small hotels) run shuttles between trail-heads; boats cross the Grey and Pehoé lakes.

WEATHER

In October, temperatures range from near-freezing to 64°F (18°C), but the windchill factor can make it seem colder. Conditions veer from high winds and rain to sunshine.

ACCOMMODATIONS

Spread along trails are privately-run *refugios* (huts with dorm beds) and camping grounds, which rent out tents and sleeping bags.

Hostería Lago Grey, on the shore of a lake, has doubles from US$368; www.lagogrey.cl

Hostería Las Torres offers great views; doubles from US$400; www.lastorres.com

Hotel Salto Chico overlooks Lago Pehoé; min 3 nights; doubles from US$2,000; www.explora.com

EATING OUT

Regional dishes include barbecued meats, freshwater salmon, and organically sourced salads. Wash it down with Pisco, the national drink, chilled with cubes of glacial ice.

FURTHER INFORMATION

www.torresdelpaine.com

What's in a Name?

The origin of the name Torres del Paine is open to debate. The word Paine means "pale blue" in the tongue of the Tehuelche natives, who are thought to have been inspired by the area's turquoise lakes. Yet, Patagonian names traditionally pay tribute to early explorers who made historic discoveries in the region, and any quick glance at a map of Torres will throw up the surnames of many European pioneers. According to this more prosaic theory, Paine derives from the name of an early Welsh climber. Romance or revisionism? You decide.

Above (left to right): Glacier climber traversing a frozen stream; a *gaucho* on his horse; hikers on Glaciar Grey
Main: Kayakers near icebergs on Lago Grey

Above: Camper at Lago Pehoé

PARQUE NACIONAL TORRES DEL PAINE

AFTER WALKING THROUGH LUSH FORESTS OF SOUTHERN BEECH running with tumbling glacial streams, you break the treeline. Suddenly you're exposed to the clear light and unhindered views of extraordinary glacial peaks. As you surge ahead, you unexpectedly find yourself beside a jade-colored lagoon. From the water's far shore three great granite towers, tinged pink in the dawn sun, soar magnificently, piercing the blood-orange skyline with jagged, snow-capped peaks. From the base of the towers, glaciers spill dramatically downwards to empty meltwater into the lagoon. This is Parque Nacional Torres del Paine; renowned trekking destination and natural wonderland.

The majestic Torres del Paine spires lend their name to the national park and form part of the greater Paine massif, whose ice-capped summits lord over lakes, glaciers, rivers, waterfalls, and forests. World-class trekking circuits traverse the park, venturing deep into the interior of the Paine massif and encircling the lakes and glaciers that mark its outer limits. Trails that hike the perimeter of the massif reveal the turquoise Lago Pehoé and wind westwards towards the immense ice mass of Glaciar Grey. Look east from here and the peaks of the Cuernos del Paine rise above you, draped with glaciers that calve huge chunks of ice into lagoons of brilliant blue-green. Turn to the west and the dizzyingly beautiful panorama of rock, ice, and water is completed by Cerro Paine Grande, the national park's highest summit.

On every side, you'll find not just breathtaking beauty, but also the potential for adrenaline-charged adventure. Kayak an iceberg-choked lagoon; gallop on horseback over wild moors or experience the heady rush of scaling Glaciar Grey's ice crevasses. Wherever you look, the possibility of adventure and thrills beckons.

Kayak an iceberg-choked lagoon or gallop on horseback over wild moors in the shadow of the Paine massif.

Inset: Icebergs afloat on a lake in Torres del Paine
Below (left and right): Patagonian puma; the three granite towers of Torres

BLUE LAKE DIARY

October is springtime in Patagonia, so you'll have longer days and lots of time to explore Torres del Paine. There are two main circuits: the W Circuit (4–5 days) and the Paine Circuit (8–10 days). "Do the W," followed by two days of kayaking and horseback riding. Factor in another two days for transfers.

Eight Days Among Glaciers

DAY 1

Fly to Punta Arenas and complete a 5-hour road transfer across open plains to the national park. Dine under the stars at a Torres del Paine *hostería*.

DAYS 2–5

"Do the W". Start by trekking to the mighty Torres. Then lunch at the base, on the shore of the lagoon.

Hike west along the north shore of Lago Nordenskjöld, splashing across forest streams and trekking through woodland to the base of the Cuernos del Paine.

Trek into Valle Francés and drink in the vistas of the Torres and the Cuernos, Lago Pehoé, and Cerro Paine Grande, whose eastern face is draped by Glaciar Francés. Watch as ice blocks tear themselves off the glacier and crash into the lagoon below.

Take the gentle hike from Valle Francés to Lago Grey. After lunch, take on an ice-climbing excursion.

DAY 6

Congratulations, you've done the W! Now hop on a boat to the scenic Ultima Esperanza Sound, located in the park's most southerly sector. Spend the afternoon riding horseback across the moors.

DAY 7

Round out your adventure by kayaking across one of the Sound's iceberg-peppered lagoons.

DAY 8

Return to Punta Arenas and visit the historical heart of this picturesque town before flying back to Santiago.

Dos and Don'ts

- ✓ Look out for stunning wildlife. More than 40 mammals inhabit the park, including *guanaco* (a type of llama), the Patagonian gray fox, and the extremely shy puma. Bird species include the condor, the ostrich-like *ñandú*, swans, flamingos, and torrent ducks. Colorful Magellanic woodpeckers are also easily spotted in the forests.
- ✓ Book accommodation in advance if you are not camping – especially for *refugios,* which fill up quickly.
- ✗ Don't light open fires in the park. The threat of bush blazes means they are prohibited.
- ✓ Stop at rivers or streams to stock up on chilled glacial water.

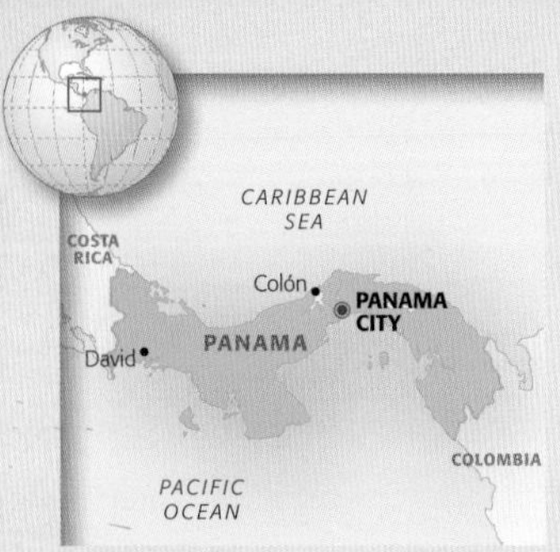

Left (left and right): Independence Square, Casco Viejo (Old City); Panama City's high-rise buildings

Right (left to right): Inside a lock; Miraflores Lock's viewing platform; aerial view of the canal, Miraflores Locks

Below: Wall decoration in Casco Viejo (Old City)

Inset: *Rojos diablos* buses at Chorrillo Bus Terminal, Panama City

GETTING THERE See map p324, H6
Panama City is on the Central American isthmus. Flights arrive at Tocumen International Airport, 15 miles (24 km) east of the city center.

GETTING AROUND
Diablos rojos ("red devils") – the formerly ubiquitous brightly painted buses – are disappearing in favor of the safer modern metrobuses. These new buses require a metro card. A tourist taxi from the airport costs about US$30.

WEATHER
By late fall, the rainy season is coming to a close, although humidity remains high. In November, the temperature has cooled to a daytime average of 79°F (26°C).

ACCOMMODATIONS
Escape the hubbub at the intimate B&B La Estancia; doubles from US$85; www.bedandbreakfastpanama.com/ancon.htm

The luxurious high-rise International Miramar has modern amenities; doubles from US$149; www.miramarpanama.com

The ritzy Hotel Bristol has deluxe rooms, stylish bar, and fine dining; doubles from US$279; www.thebristol.com

EATING OUT
Panama City offers cosmopolitan dining. Expect to pay US$25–35 per person at better restaurants. Try Eurasia for exquisite French-Asian dishes, and Azahar, which serves Mediterranean dishes in a bright, modern space.

FURTHER INFORMATION
www.visitpanama.com

Quaint colonial port and high-rise modernity are juxtaposed in dramatic counterpoint.

Main: A cruise ship heading into the waterway that leads to the Panama Canal locks

Engineering Feat

A genius of human triumph over nature, the Panama Canal was carved through the isthmus at its narrowest point to connect the Caribbean Sea and Pacific Ocean. Completed in 1914 after an eight-year endeavor that claimed 5,609 lives (20,000 died during an earlier French effort), the 50-mile (80-km) -long canal runs north to south and features three sets of locks that raise and lower vessels 85 ft (26 m). The lock chambers are paired to permit two-way traffic. Ships sail through the locks while tethered to *mulas* – electric locomotives.

PANAMA CITY

PANAMA CITY CAUSES A DOUBLE-TAKE; QUAINT COLONIAL PORT AND HIGH-RISE MODERNITY are juxtaposed in dramatic counterpoint. The ghosts of pirates past seem to walk beside you as you stroll the venerable plazas of Casco Viejo, the colonial core of this sultry port city at the southern mouth of the Panama Canal. And there's a special thrill if you take a small-boat excursion through the locks of the world's largest watery highway of commerce as massive cruise and cargo ships loom overhead.

Casco Viejo, founded in 1673, simmers with sentimental allure. Though a fire in 1878 destroyed much of the colonial quarter, this ancient district has arisen like a Phoenix that prizes its colorful past. The leafy plazas teem with historic museums and colonial churches and now, too, with trendy restaurants, jazz clubs, and boutique hotels. A 19th-century French effort to carve a canal lent Casco Viejo its Parisian airs: strolling its cobbled streets is

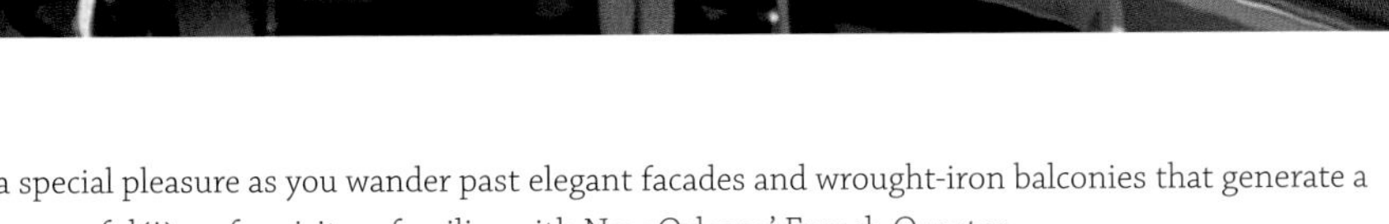

Above: Skyscrapers in Panama City

CANAL DIARY

November is a great month to explore Panama's capital city because the weather is usually temperate. There's lots to see and do: four days is enough to see the main sights before striking out to outlying regions, but you could easily spend another day or two immersing yourself in Casco Viejo.

Four Days in Panama City

DAY 1

Start with a walking tour of Casco Viejo, the colonial core of the city. From Plaza de Francia follow a clockwise route that takes in Plaza de la Independencia, the main square and site of the Catedral Metropolitana and Museo del Canal Interoceánico, telling the tale of the canal's construction. After lunch at Manolo Caracol, view the Baroque gold altar in Iglesia de San José, then stroll around Plaza Bolívar and finish with a tour of the Palacio Presidencial (you'll need to book in advance). Later, enjoy salsa music and live jazz at Platea.

DAY 2

Get a handle on Panama's past with a guided walking tour of Panama Viejo. Wander the ruins of the original city (destroyed by pirate Henry Morgan), and linger in the excellent Museo de Sitio de Panama Viejo, which displays pre-Columbian and colonial artifacts. You'll want to browse the Mercado Nacional de Artesanías, where Kuna Indians sell their crafts. Later, take in a classical concert at the Teatro Nacional.

DAY 3

Art-lovers will enjoy the fine pieces in the Museo de Arte Contemporáneo; nearby, Mi Pueblito recreates villages that replicate those of Panama's diverse cultures. Lunch at Niko's Café before exploring Balboa and Ancón, the old US canal administrative zone where the Administration Building features fantastic murals.

DAY 4

Take to the water on a boat excursion of the Panama Canal. This half-day tour puts you up close and personal inside the lock chambers. After, stop at the Miraflores Locks Visitor Center, with its superb museum, then head across the road to Fondo Peregrino Panama, where you can handle a tame harpy eagle.

Dos and Don'ts

- ✓ Do take a sightseeing boat excursion on the canal. It's the best way to gain a perspective of the immensity of the locks.
- ✓ Visit the real tailor of Panama at La Fortuna, on Vía España, and measure up for a *guayabera* – a traditional men's shirt – or even a suit.
- ✗ Don't go to the Chorrillo area west of Casco Viejo.
- ✓ Do be cautious crossing the road; Panama City's pell-mell traffic doesn't give way.

a special pleasure as you wander past elegant facades and wrought-iron balconies that generate a sense of déjà vu for visitors familiar with New Orleans' French Quarter.

The other side of the coin is the cosmopolitan, contemporary city – a center for international finance that thrums with modernity – where skyscrapers needle the skyline. Towering marble hotels replete with casinos sparkle in the El Cangrejo district. Adjacent middle-class Bella Vista and Marbella offer a parade of ritzy restaurants and swinging nightclubs. To chill a little, wander along Avenida Balboa, with its monument to the Spanish *conquistador* who first saw the Pacific.

Panama City was thrust into an important world position by the completion, in 1914, of the canal, and ships anchor offshore by the dozen. The leafy enclaves of Balboa and Ancón – former US administrative headquarters for the canal – offer delightful escapes. From the lush rain forests that surround the city and feed the canal with fresh water, comes a cacophony of wildlife. This can be seen in Parque Nacional Soberanía and in Parque Natural Metropolitano close to the city's heart.

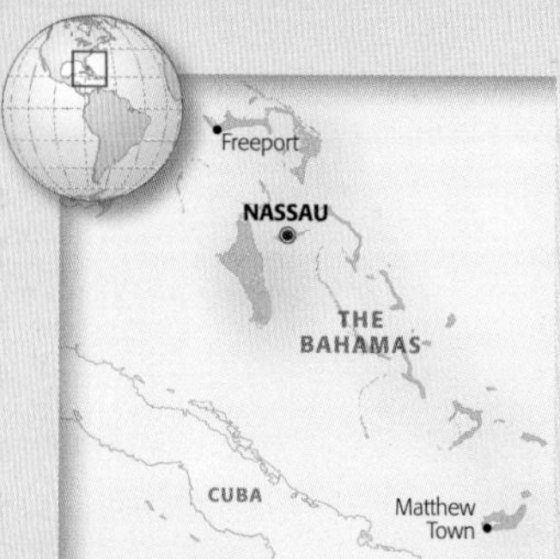

GETTING THERE See map p325, D2

The Bahamas is a chain of some 700 islands spread over 100,000 sq miles (259,000 sq km) in the western Atlantic, southeast of Florida. Nassau has the main airport, but flights from North America also serve Bimini, Eleuthera, and Grand Bahama.

GETTING AROUND

Taxis and minivans operate on most islands, and car rental is available on major islands. Water-taxis run between the cays of Abacos.

WEATHER

November is sunny, with cooling trade winds and temperatures of around 79°F (26°C).

ACCOMMODATIONS

Atlantis Paradise Island offers family-sized doubles from US$290; www.atlantis bahamas.com

Abaco Beach Resort has family-sized doubles from US$297; www.abacobeachresort.com

Nassau's Meliá Nassau Beach has children's programs; family-sized doubles start at US$360; www.melia.com

EATING OUT

Dining in the Bahamas is expensive. The conch is the local staple, often served marinated raw as a ceviche, but it is endangered so avoid ordering.

FURTHER INFORMATION

www.bahamas.com
www.seaworldtours.com
www.brendal.com

Pirates of the Caribbean

By the 1690s, Nassau's harbor had evolved as a center for pirates, including "privateers," licensed to prey on Spanish ships. In 1703, they proclaimed a "Privateers Republic" – and the notorious Edward "Blackbeard" Teach was the magistrate. Employing hit-and-run tactics, they preyed on merchant shipping that plied nearby trade routes. In 1718, the English Crown offered a "pardon or death," an ultimatum for the pirates to cease their activities. The hair-raising tales of pillage and plunder are revealed in the superb Pirates of Nassau Museum.

Above (left to right): Colorful sails on Treasure Island, Abacos; Queen's Staircase in Nassau; the Bahamas – a snorkeler's paradise
Main: Underwater plexiglass tunnel at Predators Lagoon on Paradise Island

Above: The Dig at Atlantis – the largest saltwater aquarium in the world

THE BAHAMAS

CLEAR WATERS, GORGEOUS BEACHES, and exciting encounters with wildlife – welcome to the Bahamas, the most-visited destination in the Caribbean, and for good reason. Every colorful island here boasts gorgeous beaches of cotton-white (or pink) sands and bathtub-warm shallow waters in electrifying shades of turquoise and blue.

But there's so much more to the Bahamas, too. The historic capital city of Nassau was once an infamous lair of pirates, but these days it buzzes with water sports and a sizzling nightlife. Head to the famous Cable Beach to lounge, explore the city's fortresses, and visit Junkanoo Expo so your kids can learn about the unique and colorful cultural heritage of the Bahamas. At Blue Lagoon Island near Nassau, you can even swim with trained dolphins or feed stingrays by hand.

Next to Nassau, Paradise Island is the setting for the renowned Atlantis Resort – a fantastical family-focused hotel resembling a set from *Indiana Jones and the Temple of Doom*. Its amazing fish-filled lagoons, waterslides, and Atlantis Kids Adventures keep both children and adults enthralled from dawn to dusk. The pillow-soft sands of the island also offer water sports, from aqua-biking to parasailing.

The farther you travel from Nassau, the more traditional and relaxed the islands become. The distant Out Islands are known as the Family Islands for their traditional sense of community and laid-back ease. In Abacos, the Loyalist Cays whisk you back in time, with their painted churches, artists' studios, and Victorian gingerbread homes. Green Turtle Cay, with its pastel-colored historic inns, is the perfect spot for a bit of snorkeling in gin-clear waters or paddling a kayak through mangroves and sheltered lagoons teeming with birds and marine life...a perfect prelude to days spent doing nothing but relaxing on talcum-soft sands and drying off under the Bahamian sun.

Every colorful island here boasts gorgeous beaches of cotton-white (or pink) sands and bathtub-warm shallow waters in many shades of blue.

Inset: Colorful umbrellas on Guana Cay in the Abacos Islands
Below (left and right): Typical Bahamian architecture; masks at Straw Market

BAHAMIAN DIARY

November is the ideal time to visit the Bahamas, when the weather is delightfully balmy, rainfall is low, the hurricane season is nearly over, and the teal-blue seas are bathtub warm. Five days are sufficient to enjoy the best of Nassau, with time for a foray to one of the peaceful yet fun-filled Family Islands.

Five Days of Fun in the Sun

DAY 1

Take a day out to enjoy the water park at Atlantis on Paradise Island. The waterslides here provide an adrenaline rush to remember, while the plexiglass tunnel and walls bring you closer to sharks and turtles than ever before. A video games center keeps kids amused, while teenagers get their own disco.

DAY 2

In the morning, go on a horse-drawn carriage ride through downtown Nassau and visit the Pirates of Nassau Museum, with its realistic enactments. After lunch, climb the spectacular Queen's Staircase to see the view at Bennett's Hill, then enjoy the exhibits at Junkanoo Expo before heading to the Straw Market for some shopping.

DAY 3

Experience an underwater voyage on the *Seaworld Explorer* submarine to view the coral reef. Later, head by boat to Blue Lagoon Island for lunch and to swim with dolphins, watch the sealion show, or hand-feed stingrays. Spend the rest of the day lazing on the soft sand while the kids wade in shallow waters.

DAY 4

Powerboat around Paradise Island before landing at Blackbeard's Cay for half a day on the beach. In the afternoon, fly to Marsh Harbor and transfer to Green Turtle Cay. Balance off the afternoon with a walk through the colonial village, including a visit to Vert Lowe's Model Ship Shoppe.

DAY 5

Join a full-day "Family Adventure" with Brendal's Dive Center – a chance to hand-feed stingrays, snorkel, ride in a glass-bottomed boat, or sail on the Sea of Abaco. Spend another night in an intimate historic hotel before returning to Nassau the next day.

Dos and Don'ts

- ✓ Watch the children while they're playing in the ocean and teach them to shuffle their feet to disturb any stingrays that may be hidden in the sands.
- ✗ Don't overdo the powerful Bahamian cocktails! In any event, be sure to drink plenty of water.
- ✓ Do plan on a spot of snorkeling or another activity that enables you to tour the stunning underwater world.

GETTING THERE See map p327, C6
Regular buses travel from Lima's Jorge Chávez International Airport to Pisco; the trip takes around 3 hours. From here you can travel on by bus to the town of Paracas, and the Ballestas Islands.

GETTING AROUND
The best way to explore the Ballestas Islands and the Paracas National Reserve is via guided tours, which provide all transportation.

WEATHER
November weather is warm and comfortable, ranging from 69°F (20°C) to 77°F (25°C).

ACCOMMODATIONS
Enjoy the sea breezes at Bamboo Paracas Eco Bungalows; doubles from US$75; www.bambooparacas.pe

Relax by the poolside at DoubleTree Resort by Hilton Hotel Paracas; doubles from US$159; www.doubletree3.hilton.com

The inviting La Hacienda Bahía Paracas has elegant rooms and a swimming pool; doubles from US$220; www.hoteleslahacienda.com

EATING OUT
Fresh seafood is on the menu throughout the region. Restaurant Chalana, in Paracas, is a great place to enjoy ceviche, a traditional Peruvian dish of raw fish in a spicy sauce. It is also one of the many great spots to sample Peru's famous cocktail, the pisco sour, a mix of pisco, tangy lime, egg white, and bitters.

FURTHER INFORMATION
www.peru.travel/en-us

Profitable Droppings

The Ballestas Islands have a white shimmer, due to the *guano* (bird droppings) that covers its cliffs and rocks. The term *guano* comes from the Quechua *"wanu"*, or manure. Seabird *guano* is powdery white, and rich in minerals such as nitrate and phosphorus – and over the decades, the droppings grew into multi-meter-high mounds. While the islands are now uninhabited, since pre-Inca times, *guano* was widely mined as a valuable fertilizer, and *"guaneros"* used to live on the islands making their living from harvesting the droppings.

Main: Brown pelicans and guanay cormorants on a rock in the Ballestas Islands near Paracas, Peru

ISLAS BALLESTAS

TAKE A BOAT TOUR AROUND THE BALLESTAS ISLANDS and you'll understand why it's often called the Peruvian Galápagos. Here off the west coast of Peru, you'll spy a fascinating array of wildlife. These rocky islands, which hunker down in the Pacific Ocean near the mainland towns of Pisco and Paracas, are teeming with wild critters on the ground, in the sea, and up above. As your boat rounds the islands, you'll see sealions relaxing in the sun; cormorants dive-bombing the waters; and seabirds eagerly watching over everything from rocky perches.
You can also spot flocks of black-and-white Humboldt penguins, waddling over the undulating terrain in their tuxedo-like plumage. Don't forget to turn your eyes away from the islands, and toward the vast ocean around you – if you're lucky, you may see dolphins leaping from the water. Although tours don't stop on the islands – only scientists and researchers are allowed on them – the boats take you up close to the islands' natural wonders.

Left (left to right): Humboldt penguins waddle down an incline; the sandy cliffs of the Paracas National Reserve; a Peruvian booby; the strikingly colored Inca tern; the mysterious Candelabra etchings

Below: Sealions relax on an outcrop

Inset: A Peruvian pelican takes flight

Above: A pisco vineyard backed by sand-covered hills

You can also spot flocks of black-and-white Humboldt penguins, waddling over the undulating terrain in their tuxedo-like plumage.

The port town of Paracas makes an ideal base for visiting the islands and surrounding Ica Region. The town is the gateway to the Paracas National Reserve, the oldest marine reserve in Peru, which encompasses vast desert landscapes and wave-battered coastline. A fascinating highlight is the Paracas Candelabra, on the Paracas Peninsula, a famous prehistoric geoglyph that stands at an astonishing 595 feet (180 meters) in height, etched on a rocky slope. Theories abound as to why this enormous three-pronged etching is here – some say it can be attributed to early sailors, who used it as a navigational tool, while others think it is a rendering of an ancient god, or connected to the Nazca Lines. The Lines are a series of ancient geoglyphs found on the mainland.

If you want to try pisco – Peru's national drink – this is the perfect region to do so. The distilled wine is named after the Port of Pisco, and can be sampled at beachfront bars along the coast and on tours of local wineries and distilleries. While some purists enjoy it as a standalone drink, many prefer to drink it in a pisco sour.

NATURE-TOUR DIARY

November is the shoulder season, between the dry and rainy months, which equates to pleasant weather, plenty of sun, fewer crowds, and lower prices. Three days in this region is the perfect amount of time to visit the Ballestas Islands, explore the nature around Paracas, and take a tour of a pisco distillery.

Three Days Around the Coast

DAY 1

Make your base in Paracas, and spend the first day exploring the surrounding coast and parkland of the UNESCO World Heritage Site of the Paracas National Reserve. The diverse reserve encompasses tropical desert, windswept beaches, and the sun-soaked Bahía de la Independencia. Along the coast, keep a lookout for the varied bird life, including Peruvian pelicans and Inca terns.

DAY 2

Continue your discovery of the region's wildlife by embarking on a guided boat trip to the Ballestas Islands. Although you won't disembark, the boats sail near to the coastline and cliffs, for a close-up view of the flora and fauna. Numerous companies offer trips, departing from the El Chaco wharf near Paracas; tours generally last from 2 to 4 hours. Be sure to wear waterproof clothing, and bring plenty of snacks.

DAY 3

Take a pisco tour to learn about – and, just as importantly, to sample – Peru's national drink, which is a clear, potent liquid distilled from a variety of grapes. Pisco, which means "bird" in the indigenous Quechua language, is named after the Port of Pisco, where pisco used to be exported from. Tour vineyards, such as the esteemed Hacienda La Caravedo, where you can observe the distillery process. At your tour's end, you can pick up a bottle to bring home.

Dos and Don'ts

- ✓ If possible, bring a camera with a telephoto lens for the boat tours. The vessels cruise around the perimeter of the Ballestas Islands, so it's key to have a strong camera lens if you want to snap close-up images of the seabirds.
- ✓ In Pisco, if you plan to travel beyond the tourist-friendly center, it's safest to take a mototaxi, particularly after dark.
- ✓ Shop around and inquire at your hotel for recommendations before selecting a boat tour to the Ballestas Islands; tour prices and amenities vary widely.
- ✗ Don't hesitate to opt for a more adventurous tour that includes a flight in a light aircraft to see the islands and their surrounds from above.

GETTING THERE See map p325, I5
The starting point of the Windstar and Star Clipper ships, Bridgetown, in Barbados, can be reached by air from the UK and North America.

GETTING AROUND
Grantley Adams Airport is 8 miles (13 km) from Bridgetown. Island excursions ashore are offered and dockside taxis await custom.

WEATHER
November is delightful, with sunshine, steady trade winds, and daytime temperatures averaging 81°F (27°C). Hurricane season is all but over, and rainfall is limited.

ACCOMMODATIONS
En suite cabins on the ships offer a choice of elegant staterooms or wood-paneled suites.

Bridgetown's secluded, all-suite Cobblers Cove offers country-house sophistication; doubles from US$490; www.cobblerscove.com

Sandy Lane in Bridgetown offers pampered luxury and a colonial ambience; doubles from US$1,300; www.sandylane.com

EATING OUT
Excellent meals are served on board, but do sample local fare. Try pepperpot stew and a pan-fried flying fish sandwich at Bridgetown's Waterfront Café. In Speightstown, Mango's by the Sea is famous for fresh seafood (US$10).

FURTHER INFORMATION
www.windstarcruises.com
www.starclippers.co.uk

Above (left and right): Unwinding in the hot tub on board; relaxing on deck

ISLAND CRUISE

IT'S DAWN IN THE CARIBBEAN and roseate sunlight glitters upon glassy waters silhouetting emerald isles rising sheer from seas of impossible blues and greens. Coral reefs edge up to frosted sands that coruscate like diamonds washed ashore from a Spanish treasure ship and the colors seem to pulsate in the Caribbean light.

A voyage aboard a modern tall-masted ship inspired by the grand age of sail is different from your typical cruise experience, offering an intimacy that mega-cruiseliners can't deliver. These ships operate Caribbean cruises from November through March, plying the isles of the eastern Caribbean, from the Virgin Islands to Barbados. Itineraries vary, as there are so many islands to choose from and most cruising is done at night to maximize the time you have ashore. Towering, computer-operated sails define the sleek modern vessels, with their casual yet elegant atmosphere.

Gliding from isle to isle and anchoring in pristine bays, cruising reveals the exquisite landscapes that make the Caribbean unique. The colorful Caribbean cultures, influenced by the French, Dutch and English, are as distinct as your thumbprint. Just the printed itinerary seems to conjure up the shrieking of parrots and pirates.

While on board, you can laze on deck to savor the beauty of the passing isles, while spas offer relaxing treatments. Donning snorkel mask and flippers, you'll discover a world more beautiful than a casket of gems. Cloaked in deepest verdure, magnificent mountains rise grandly behind quaint villages of gaily painted wooden houses edged with gingerbread trim. Steel bands welcome you ashore to explore markets piled high with tropical fruits. Well-planned excursions will take you on city tours, into the rain forests, kayaking, or even to the crater of a simmering volcano. Sun on palm-lined beaches, dive with dolphins, or possibly thrill to humpback whales cavorting in bathtub-warm waters. Mother Nature melds with history at colonial-era towns, fortresses, and plantations: Basseterre and Wingfield Plantation on St. Kitts, St. Lucia, and Marigot town and St. Louis fort on St-Martin/St. Maarten. Sailing before the wind to these pearls teeming with wildlife and colonial intrigue only adds to the romance of cruising.

Main: Sailing under blue skies
Below (left and right): St. Lucia and the Pitons; colorful sarongs billowing in the Barbados trade winds

Split Personality

Half French, half Dutch, the island of St-Martin/St Maarten (and nine more spelling variants) is as schizophrenic as its name suggests. Though they share gorgeous beaches and scrubby terrain, the two halves – there is no border post – are distinctly different. The Dutch capital, Philipsburg, is known for casinos and duty-free shopping, while Marigot, on the French side, is famous for its fort (*see below*), nude beaches, chic hotels, and fine dining.

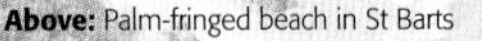

Above: Palm-fringed beach in St Barts

TRADE WINDS DIARY

The Windward and Leeward islands are perfect in balmy November weather. Cruising is the way to go, and nothing can quite compare to the romantic thrill of a voyage aboard a tall-masted sailing ship, each with its unique itinerary. Explore ashore, and in the evenings don your tux (or not) and enjoy the good life.

Eight Days Under Sail

Arrive in, and explore, quaint colonial Bridgetown before boarding your vessel for a midnight departure.	**DAY 1**
Shake off the workday routine on your first full day at sea and relax with a good book and spa treatment.	**DAY 2**
Put ashore at Basseterre, St. Kitts, where Georgian architecture nestles against lush foliage. Back on board, continue to neighboring Nevis – another gem with dramatic architecture and mountains.	**DAY 3**
Anchor at St-Martin/St. Maarten and take a shore excursion to compare chic Marigot – a kind of St. Tropez of the Caribbean – with Philipsburg, offering excellent duty-free shopping. Next morning, laze on any of the island's 37 white-sand beaches before departing for picture-perfect St. Bart's. Explore by open air Jeep or "mini-moke."	**DAYS 4–5**
Guadeloupe is home to the enchanting Deshaies Botanical Gardens, sugar estates, and rum plantations. Take the Planter's Experience excursion, and then it's on to quaint Îles des Saintes to explore on your own.	**DAY 6**
Admire the spectacular scenery as you approach St. Lucia. There, cruise by catamaran to Soufrière Volcano, or ride the cable car into the rain forest.	**DAY 7**
After berthing back in Bridgetown, either fly home or spend a day or two exploring this welcoming island.	**DAY 8**

Dos and Don'ts

- ✓ Pack sunscreen, a shade hat, and comfy walking shoes.
- ✗ Don't fail to spend time in Barbados before or after your cruise. It's a lovely island, with lots to see and do.
- ✓ Take advantage of the shore excursions offered on board. They make experiencing each island's highlights easy.
- ✓ Research prices for electronic goods, perfumes, and other duty-free items, as they aren't always bargains ashore.

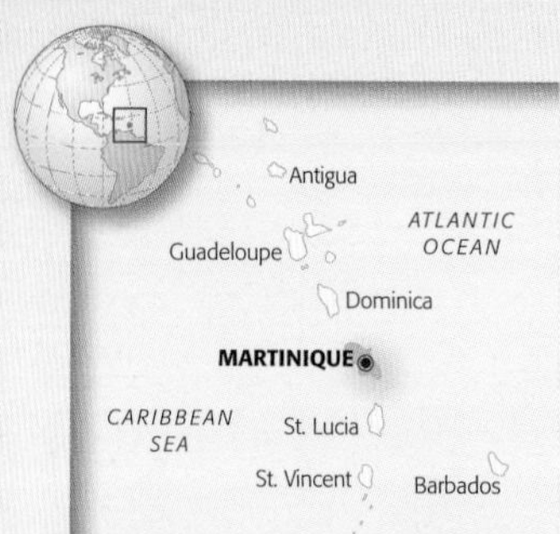

GETTING THERE See map p325, I5

Martinique Aimé Césaire International Airport is near the village of Lamentin, 5 miles (8.5 km) east of Fort-de-France.

GETTING AROUND

Martinique has limited public transport. The best way to explore is in a rental car or taxi.

WEATHER

Martinique enjoys balmy, sunny weather throughout the year, with temperatures ranging from 75 to 88°F (24 to 31°C).

ACCOMMODATIONS

L'Hôtel L'impératrice is a stylish hotel in the heart of Fort-de-France; doubles from US$95; www.limperatricehotel.fr

Splurge at the relaxing Cap Est Lagoon Resort & Spa, with elegant rooms overlooking a breezy lagoon; doubles from US$350; www.capest.com

Club Med Buccaneer's Creek offers a wonderful array of kid-friendly activities; doubles from US$390; www.clubmed.us

EATING OUT

Feast on French-Creole cuisine, as well as fresh seafood, which is served at restaurants around the island. Try traditional dishes like like *fricassée de chatrou*, a delicious stew of octopus, tomatoes, and spices.

FURTHER INFORMATION

www.tourismfdf.com
www.caribbeantravel.com

The Empress of France

When Marie-Josèphe-Rose Tascher de La Pagerie was born in Martinique in 1763, no one could have ever imagined that she would one day become the French Empress. Joséphine, as she was eventually called, moved to France and married. After the death of her first husband, she met the young Napoleon Bonaparte. They married in 1796. Learn more about their fascinating union at Musée de la Pagerie, in the birthplace of Joséphine, in Les Trois Illets.

MARTINIQUE

Main: The pristine waters of Fort-de-France Bay

Few destinations embody the phrase "the best of both worlds" like Martinique. This is a slice of France in the Caribbean. The tropical side is evident everywhere you turn: long silky beaches, towering palm trees, tangled rain forests, sweet-smelling flowers. But the island also exerts its Francophile side, with French-infused Creole cuisine – like fresh seafood with delectable sauces, with a side of yucca – followed by espressos at Parisian-style roadside cafés. Looming over everything is the mighty Mont Pelée, which means "bald" (or "peeled") mountain. This semi-active volcano ferociously erupted in 1902, decimating the largest city on the island, Saint-Pierre, and killing about 30,000 people, in one of world's largest volcanic tragedies of the 20th century. Today, Martinique's buzzing capital, Fort-de-France, is the island's commercial and business hub. It's also dotted with

historical sights that offer deep insight into Martinique's history, including Fort Saint-Louis, a grand stone fortress that has been watching over the city for centuries. The first strongholds were built on this site as early as the 1600s. Other highlights include Schoelcher Library, an ornate Romanesque library, and nearby La Savane, a central park with benches and fountains.

Martinique's south is quintessentially Caribbean, studded with palm-shaded, white-sand beaches and lovely resorts. This sun-splashed region is perfect for a family vacation, especially at beaches like the famed Grand Anse des Salines, near Sainte-Anne, with its beautifully calm waters. Many of the hotels and resorts here offer family amenities, including special menus for kids and fun water activities. Martinique's north is more rugged, presided over by Mont Pelée, near the village of Morne Rouge. Hire a guide to trek the volcano – or just explore the lush base, which is surrounded with rain forest and waterfalls.

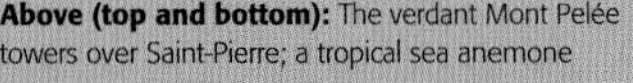

Above (top and bottom): The verdant Mont Pelée towers over Saint-Pierre; a tropical sea anemone

Left (left to right): The colorful Schoelcher Library; the picturesque seafront of Saint-Pierre; a pier in Sainte-Anne, Martinique

Above: Lush vegetation at Jardin de Balata

MARTINIQUE DIARY

While the chill may be setting in elsewhere in the Northern Hemisphere in November, Martinique is as gorgeous as the rest of the year. By day, relax on Martinique's beaches and splash in the clear waters. By night, enjoy the island's lively bars and French-style restaurants.

Five Days of Island Style

DAYS 1–2

Delve into Martinique's history in the lively capital Fort-de-France. Check out the city's imposing fort, as well as the eye-catching Schoelcher Library. The Romanesque library was originally built for the Paris Exposition in 1889, after which it was dismantled, shipped to Martinique, and rebuilt. Visit the small but informative Musée d'Histoire et d'Ethnographie, which reveals the island's past via paintings, period furnishings, and photographs. Take an afternoon trip to the lovely Jardin de Balata, about 6 miles (10 km) north of Fort-de-France, which has more than 3,000 varieties of tropical plants. In the evenings, dine out at one of Fort-de-France's many restaurants, which serve everything from French to Creole to Italian cuisine.

DAYS 3–4

Lush beaches await in the south, Martinique's sun-and-sand territory. The island's top resorts, many of which cater to families, are around Pointe de Bout, which also abounds with outdoor activities, from diving to snorkeling to windboarding. For more secluded sands, head to lovely Diamond Beach, in the town of Le Diamant. While here, visit the haunting Anse Cafard Slave Memorial – 20 white-stone effigies that memorialize those who lost their lives when a slave ship sank in 1830 in dangerously rocky waters.

DAY 5

After a few days of kicking back on the beach, head north to hike the wilderness. From Fort-de-France, embark on the scenic drive to Saint-Pierre. Hire a guide to trek the steep slopes of the Mont Pelée volcano. Also, explore Caravelle Nature Preserve, near the town of La Trinité, which unfolds on the verdant La Caravelle Peninsula that juts out into the Atlantic Ocean. The diverse vegetation includes mangroves and sheer cliffs, and is populated by a wonderful array of bird life, from orioles to hummingbirds.

Dos and Don'ts

- ✓ Brush up on a few French phrases before arriving: French is the official language, and is spoken throughout the island.
- ✗ Don't forget to bring suitable footwear and clothing if you plan to hike the island, particularly in the north, and binoculars for birding.
- ✓ Sample the island's delicious Ti Punch, a cocktail of cane juice rum, with sugar cane syrup and lime.

DECEMBER

Where to Go: **December**

From the beginning of the month, most of North America is consumed by Christmas fever. Chill temperatures are compensated for by the warmth of colonial-style decorations and steaming mulled wine. Hispanic San Antonio, Texas, drapes its pretty River Walk with lights and has carolers sing from boats. Hot on the heels of Christmas comes New Year – Pasadena, in southern California, offers a big parade and balmy temperatures. Canada, meanwhile, comes into its own in December, with vast swathes of pristine skiing territory. Tropical Hawai'i offers a tantalizingly warmer alternative, while much of Central America is dry and sunny, and South America enjoys a sultry summer. Below you will find all the destinations in this chapter and some extra suggestions to provide inspiration.

FESTIVALS AND CULTURE

RIO DE JANEIRO Colorful performers at a samba club

RIO DE JANEIRO
BRAZIL

This is a New Year's party like you've never seen before

New Year's celebrations on Copacabana Beach in Rio are an unbeatable mix of hedonism, music, fireworks, and potent cocktails.

See pp302–3

CHICHICASTENANGO
GUATEMALA

Crafts and curios in handicraft heaven

The pretty little town of Chichi hosts a spectacular market, with colorful clothes, crafts, and curios.

www.enjoyguatemala.com/chichicastenango.htm

BALTIMORE
MARYLAND, USA

One of the east coast's most engaging cities

Off-beat Baltimore musters an absorbing mix of attractions and an attractively restored waterfront.

www.baltimore.org

MEXICO'S COLONIAL HEARTLAND
MEXICO

Rich in history

Explore Mexico's rich legacy of art and architecture at its handsome, historical silver-mining cities – San Miguel de Allende and Guanajuato.

See pp294–5

PASADENA
CALIFORNIA, USA

See in the New Year at the Tournament of Roses Parade

This extravaganza featuring rose-adorned floats and marching bands is an all-American way to celebrate New Year's.

See pp300–1

JUNKANOO
BAHAMAS

The biggest party in the Bahamas

Nassau is taken over by competing "crews" and their spectacular floats amidst a riot of music, color, and dancers in fabulous costumes.

www.bahamas.com

UNFORGETTABLE JOURNEYS

DEATH VALLEY A 4WD drives through the Valley

DEATH VALLEY
CALIFORNIA, USA

One of the hottest places on Earth

Death Valley National Park is a place of legend, and this desert presents nature at its most extreme and unforgiving.

www.nps.gov/deva

CHILOÉ
CHILE

Beautiful islands off the Chilean coast

Ride the ferry from Puerto Montt to the windswept and unspoilt archipelago of Chiloé in the Pacific Ocean.

www.visitchile.com

OLD PATAGONIAN EXPRESS
ARGENTINA

Journey Esquel to Nahuel Pan

Hop on this traditional steam-drawn railway, made famous by Paul Theroux.

www.patagonia-argentina.com/i/andina/esquel/trochita.htm

FROZEN ALASKA
ALASKA, USA

Get to the heart of the Arctic winter

Drive a 4WD through frozen woods from Anchorage to Fairbanks and back, and, with luck, you'll see the aurora borealis.

www.alaskatours.com

NATURAL WONDERS

ANGEL FALLS A *tepuy* swathed in cloud

ANGEL FALLS
VENEZUELA

Explore a magical "lost world" and a waterfall

Visit a Permon Indian village and travel upriver in a dugout canoe to see the world's highest falls in their beautiful rain forest setting.

See pp292–3

NORTHERN LIGHTS
ALASKA/NORTHERN CANADA

Head north in search of the remarkable aurora borealis.

These unforgettable lighting effects are a common sight in Alaska and northern Canada from October through March.

www.travelalaska.com

"Isolated at the bottom of the world, the Falklands make for one of the Americas' most breathtaking stops."

FALKLAND ISLANDS
SOUTH ATLANTIC

Islands at the end of the world – a nature-lover's paradise

Set in splendid isolation, the wildlife here (including five types of penguin) has little fear of man, so you'll see it close-up.

See pp298–9

LAGUNA VERDE
CHILE

Surreal volcanic lake high in the Andes

The strangely colored waters of Laguna Verde ringed by towering volcanoes including the soaring Ojos de Salado.

www.visitchile.com

SAN BLAS ISLANDS
PANAMA

Explore the customs and landscape of Native America

Remote islands that are home to the Kuna Indians, who guide visitors to the abundant wildlife with intimate knowledge.

www.explorepanama.com

JAMAICA
CARIBBEAN

Reggae, relaxation, and rum

Jamaica is a microcosm of the Caribbean, serving up a sampling of what the region is known for: beaches, looming palms, luxurious resorts, and verdant rain forest.

See pp282–3

Previous page: Carnival time in Rio de Janeiro, Brazil

Weather Watch

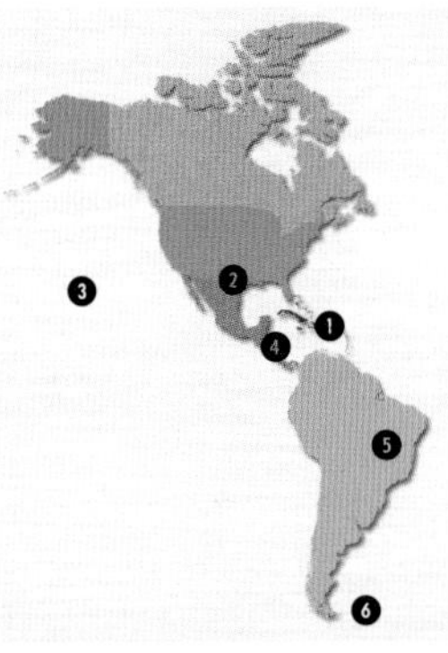

❶ St. Barts, Caribbean December is the peak season in St. Barts for a good reason. The weather is nearly perfect: warm and sunny with little rain. There is no better place than here to escape the winter chill.

❷ San Antonio, USA San Antonio tends to be warm, sunny, and dry, though temperatures can plummet from one day to the next, and nights are far cooler.

❸ Hawai'i, USA If you're beach-bound, you can expect some nice warm weather; up at the crater of the Kilauea volcano, temperatures can drop. Sunshine in the coastal resorts is pretty much guaranteed.

❹ Costa Rica The wet season is over in the Nicoya Peninsula, where hot, sunny days and balmy breezes are the norm and downpours are a distant memory.

❺ Brazil Summer is in full flight in Brazil; it's hot and humid in Rio. South of the city the humidity increases, tempered by rain showers. Rain is generally heaviest south of the Amazon.

❻ Falkland Islands Famously changeable, the Falkland Islands are well into their summer, which brings sunny days and pleasant temperatures. There is always the possibility of wind and rain, however, and it can get cool.

LUXURY AND ROMANCE

ST. BARTS Strolling on Flamands Beach

ST. BARTS
CARIBBEAN

The good life in the tropics

St Barts is a celebrity magnet, thanks to its quiet, impeccable beaches, preserved fishing villages, fine dining, and stunning resort, not to mention a plethora of yachts.

See pp286–7

MANZANILLO
MEXICO

Vibrant yet laid-back resort on the Pacific coast

The busy port of Manzanillo is surrounded by plush resorts and sandy beaches, with plenty of outdoor fun, too.

www.gomanzanillo.com

TORTOLA
BRITISH VIRGIN ISLANDS, CARIBBEAN

An island paradise

Simply enjoy the talcum-soft sand and crystal-clear waters for swimming, freshly caught seafood, and fruity cocktails.

www.bvitourism.com

NICOYA PENINSULA
COSTA RICA

Miles of sun-kissed coastline backed by thick forest

With Pacific coast surf, good weather, beautiful beaches, jungle adventures, and wildlife, the Nicoya Peninsula is the hot place to visit.

See pp288–9

"The mountainous interior forms a rugged backdrop to sensational beaches in every shade, from taupe to gold. "

TELLURIDE
COLORADO, USA

Winter sports with a very fashionable buzz

Every winter sport can be tried in the Rockies' most fashionable resort, or you can just enjoy the stunning view from a luxurious suite.

www.thepeaksresort.com

ACTIVE ADVENTURES

CAYMAN ISLANDS Diving around a wreck

CAYMAN ISLANDS
CARIBBEAN

A tropical paradise with some of the world's best dive sites

The crystal-clear waters of these magical islands are perfect for diving, snorkeling, or paddling with gentle stingrays.

See pp296–7

SIAN KA'AN BIOSPHERE RESERVE, YUCATÁN
MEXICO

Mangroves and history

Go walking or boating through this pristine coastal preserve, dotted with Mayan ruins.

www.cesiak.org

THE CAYO DISTRICT
BELIZE

West is best in beautiful Belize

Nature reigns supreme in western Belize, from thundering waterfalls to pine forests. Plus, don't miss Caracol for Maya culture.

See pp290–91

DOMINICA
CARIBBEAN

This pristine ocean rain forest is a great active destination

Go hiking, scuba diving, or horseback riding and fully experience this wonderful natural wilderness.

www.dominica.dm

THE EXUMAS
THE BAHAMAS, CARIBBEAN

Sea kayak through the Bahamas

The Exumas' 365 tiny islands and cays are perfect for paddling, with shallow waters and hundreds of deserted sandy beaches.

www.outislandexplorers.com

FAMILY GETAWAYS

SAN ANTONIO Decorated candle-holders

SAN ANTONIO
TEXAS, USA

Get in the Christmas spirit along the River Walk

Near the historic site of the Alamo, Paseo del Rio in San Antonio puts on a fabulous display of Christmas cheer.

See pp280–81

MOUNT TREMBLANT
QUÉBEC, CANADA

Family-friendly skiing near Montréal

At the highest point of the Laurentian Mountains, this purpose-built, family-friendly ski resort has facilities for all ages.

www.tremblant.ca

ACAPULCO
MEXICO

Playas aplenty and a family-fun atmosphere

Fringing one of the most beautiful bays on Mexico's Pacific coast, Acapulco is the country's most famous resort.

www.visitmexico.com

"Hawai'i is not just a smorgasbord of astounding geographical features, but is also home to friendly island communities."

HAWAI'I
HAWAI'I, USA

Also known as "Big Island," it packs a lot in for its size

Famous for its beaches, Hawai'i offers more besides. Explore volcanoes and rain forests and lap up the warm welcome.

See pp284–5

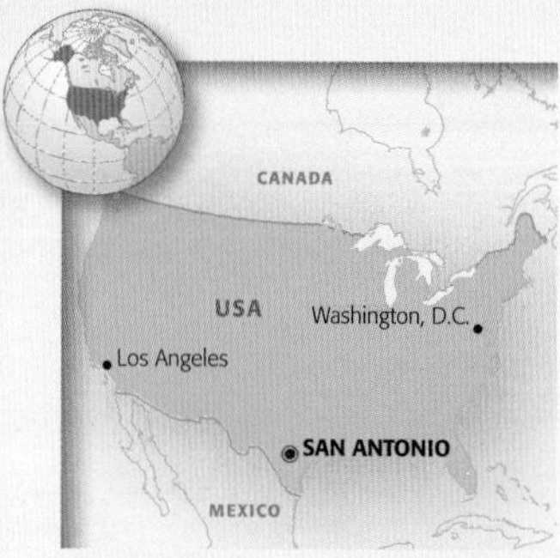

GETTING THERE **See map p318, E5**
San Antonio is in south Texas, served by the San Antonio International Airport, 8 miles (13 km) north of downtown. Cars can be rented at the airport. There is a shuttle service into the city.

GETTING AROUND
In the downtown area most attractions are within walking distance or on the VIA Streetcar route. However, there is also taxi and VIA Bus service. A car is the best way to explore farther.

WEATHER
December is generally sunny and pleasant, with low humidity. Temperatures range from 41 to 64°F (5 to 18°C) with cooler nights of 41°F (5°C).

ACCOMMODATIONS
Hyatt Place San Antonio Riverwalk offers River Walk location and rooms with kitchenettes from US$169; www.hyatt.com

Hyatt Regency San Antonio has a section of the River Walk running through it; rooms start at US$249; www.sanantonioregency.hyatt.com

Menger Hotel is a favorite choice; rooms from US$189; www.mengerhotel.com

EATING OUT
Local favorites include mildly spicy TexMex, barbecue, steak, and local wild game. Southwestern and International cuisines are usually available at upscale restaurants.

FURTHER INFORMATION
www.sanantoniocvb.com

"Remember the Alamo!"

This popular rallying cry for defenders of freedom derives from the battle in which 189 Texas/American defenders, and more than 600 Mexican soldiers fought called the Battle of the Alamo. Although the first of five Spanish Missions was built along the San Antonio River in the early 18th century, by the Texas Revolution in 1836 the old mission had been used as a military outpost for years. Today, the Alamo is seen as a symbol of bravery, and a shrine honors those who died.

Main: River Walk, a yearly festive celebration of song and good cheer

SAN ANTONIO

EVERY WEEKEND IN DECEMBER, THE PATHWAYS OF SAN ANTONIO'S historic Paseo del Rio attract thousands of families to enjoy its celebration of Christmas. San Antonio is a small, unpretentious city with a warm heart, especially at this time, when the focus is on genuine festive fun. Here the beautifully landscaped walkways are softly illuminated by thousands of glowing candles that line the river's edge. Overhead, myriad tiny glimmering lights hang in festoons from the branches of century-old trees. Strolling musicians play seasonal music as happy crowds fill the walkways, restaurants, and gaily lit bridges that arch gracefully over the river.

Along the River Walk, the joyful melodies of familiar Christmas carols fill the air as boats laden with singing carolers slowly float by, their songs echoed by diners joining in from riverside cafés. The marvelous scents of slow-roasted wild turkey, Mexican fajitas, and hot apple pie waft on the night air, emanating from dozens of riverside

Above (top and bottom): Boy hitting a festive *pinata* (lantern) to break out the candy; three wise kings in procession

Below (top and bottom): Religious candle-holders; Mexican dancer

Above: Store front in La Villita

SAN ANTONIO DIARY

Although the River Walk is festooned with glittering lights for all of December, the first half of the month is particularly enthralling. Three days allows enough time to explore the Alamo and major attractions, and still have time to shop at Market Square and the boutique shops while listening to caroling choirs.

Three Days of Christmas Magic

DAY 1

Head over to San Fernando Cathedral. During the Battle of the Alamo, this is where Mexican General Antonio López de Santa Anna flew the red flag of no mercy. Explore the Spanish Governor's Palace and then go to Market Square for lunch; afterwards, shop in the huge Mexican marketplace.

Drive to the McNay Art Museum where masterpieces by Gauguin, Picasso, O'Keeffe, Hopper, Renoir, and many more are presented in a stunning Spanish Colonial Mansion. Explore the nearby Lucile Halsell Conservatory at the San Antonio Botanical Garden and wander through lush indoor jungles. Or, visit San Antonio Zoo with its 3,500 animals from around the world. Have dinner along the vibrant River Walk.

DAY 2

Walk south along the River Walk to the end of the King Williams District for breakfast, or lunch at Guenther House and visit the museum there. Stroll past the mansions in the King Williams District, and check out La Villita's historic buildings, boutique shops, and galleries. Walk over to the Alamo and visit the shrine.

Wander back to the River Walk, take a boat cruise and have dinner in an outdoor café. Meander along the River Walk, admire the festoons of lights, sing along with the carolers, and stop into Barriba Cantina for live music.

DAY 3

Drive to nearby San Antonio Missions National Historic Park and tour the four 18th-century missions standing majestically along the Mission Trail. Head back to the major malls for some last-minute Christmas shopping.

Dos and Don'ts

- ✓ Make reservations early for accommodations along the River Walk – they become booked up far in advance.
- ✓ Before booking hotels, check the December schedule for the dates of Bazar Sábado (Saturday Bazaar), which features Mexican folk art, and San Fernando Cathedral's *La Gran Posada*, a re-enactment of the Christmas story.
- ✓ Splurge and attend a holiday performance at the Lila Cockrell Theatre or in the lavish Majestic Theatre, surrounded by ornate 1920s vaudeville-style decor under a simulated night sky.
- ✗ Don't miss the lobby in the famous Menger Hotel where Theodore Roosevelt stayed in 1898.

restaurants. The lobbies of historic buildings and gleaming hotels all along the river are decked out in appropriate garb, vying with each other to present the prettiest displays of fresh greenery, red poinsettias, and brightly decorated Christmas trees. Take a peek into the magnificent Victorian lobby of the elegant, famous Menger Hotel where Theodore Roosevelt stayed while recruiting Rough Riders during the Spanish-American War.

Around the river, the boutique shops, hotels, and gracious churches of old San Antonio are also decorated with numerous candles and colored lights. Along Alamo Street, the shop windows showcase animated displays of elves and crackling Christmas hearths, and Alamo Plaza has a huge festive tree with lights. Residents and visitors alike enter the Alamo shrine and remember those young men who fought bravely in 1836. A few blocks away, at San Fernando Cathedral in the heart of old San Antonio, the essence of Christmas is celebrated by the annual re-enactment of Joseph and Mary looking for shelter, and visitors and San Antonians join together to rejoice in this historic city's most joyful season.

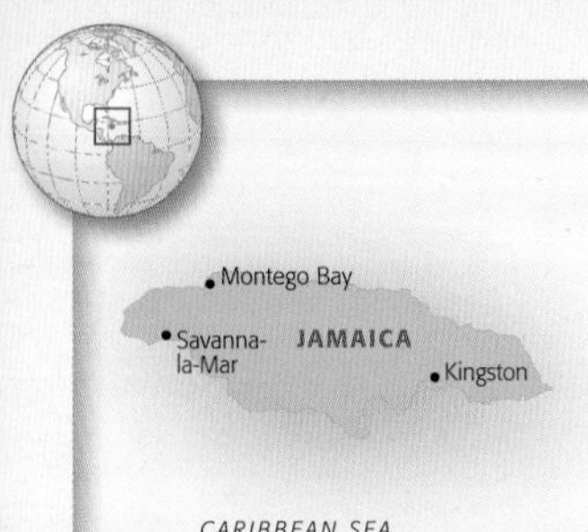

GETTING THERE See map p324, C5
Jamaica has two international airports in Montego Bay and Kingston. Jamaica is also a major cruise ship destination, and ships pull into ports like Montego Bay and Ocho Rios.

GETTING AROUND
Rental car agencies are readily available in all main towns and from the two airports. You can also discover Jamaica via tours along with the occasional taxi and shuttle.

WEATHER
Jamaica enjoys beautifully balmy weather all year, with sunny days and refreshing sea breezes. High season is December to March.

ACCOMMODATIONS
The iconic Sandals Montego Bay has airy rooms and a pool overlooking the ocean; doubles from US$450; www.sandals.com

Relax in a beachfront villa at Rondel Village in Negril; doubles from US$150; www.rondelvillage.com

EATING OUT
Jamaica's local delicacies are a tasty blend of Creole and international influences, including the justly famous jerk chicken, liberally spiced with island-grown seasonings like Scotch bonnet peppers; and rice and peas, which is rice and beans tossed in coconut milk. Plus, kick off the mornings with ackee and saltfish, the popular breakfast dish of codfish and ackee fruit.

FURTHER INFORMATION
www.visitjamaica.com

The Roots of Reggae

Jamaica's most famous musical export dates back to the 1960s. Reggae, named after the Jamaican term for "rags or ragged clothes," evolved from ska and rocksteady, and incorporated African-style musical beats. The king of reggae was Bob Marley, who first emerged in 1963 with the group The Wailers, and ultimately pursued a solo career, releasing the album Exodus in 1977, cementing his worldwide acclaim. Today, reggae continues to be the soundtrack of Jamaica, as ubiquitous as the island's sun and sand.

Above (left and right): Roadside fruit stall, St Mary Parish; Doctors Cove beach
Main: Negril island

Above: Cannons and tower in the courtyard of Fort Charles, Port Royal

JAMAICA

"ONE LOVE. ONE HEART. Let's get together and feel all right." For many, Jamaica is synonymous with reggae, best captured by the vocals of the country's most famous son, Bob Marley, but there's also a lot more to the third-largest island in the Caribbean. In many ways, Jamaica is a microcosm of the region, offering a taste of everything it is famous for: glorious beaches and sunshine, lush palm trees, rain forests, mist-shrouded mountains, grand golf courses, fruit cocktails sprouting tiny paper umbrellas and among the finest all-inclusive resorts in the Caribbean, if not the world. A bonus of course is the outstanding local coffee, grown on the verdant slopes of the Blue Mountains.

Jamaica's capital of Kingston, though packed with lovely historical buildings, boisterous street markets, and several top museums, has something of a rough reputation, particularly in the west side of the city. So it is best to plan your itinerary around the island's stunning natural wonders, and everything else will fall into place. The beach at Negril is the stuff of dreams, long and silky, giving way to warm, crystal waters. Montego Bay sparkles with a mix of historical architecture, superb local cuisine, and rocking nightclubs.

From here, you can take in lovely day trips on the coast, including the historic Falmouth in Trelawny, where fortunes were built on the sugar trade in the 1700s, earning it the nickname "the Paris of the Indies." Ocho Rios has upscale resorts and manicured golf courses. Also, carve out time to climb Dunn's River Falls and Park, where you can take a guided trek up the waterfall, snap the vacation's best selfies at the top, and then descend to stretch out on the beach at the base. In short, Jamaica pretty much has it all.

The island offers glorious beaches and sunshine, lush palm trees, rain forests, mist-shrouded mountains

Inset: Rainbow over the Blue Mountains. **Below (left and right):** Colonial theatre building in Kingston; Barrys Bar, Negril beach

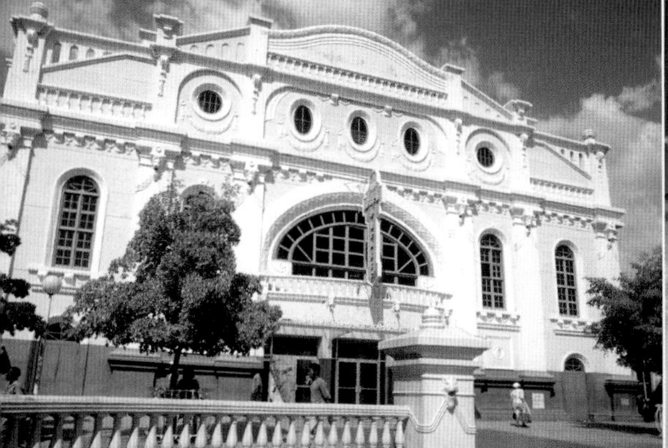

JAMAICAN DIARY

Whether you want to chill out or get adventurous (or both), six days in Jamaica is the perfect length of time to explore the island. Plan to spend a few days simply relaxing followed by water sports, museum-hopping, and touring a coffee plantation for a taste of the island's famous coffee.

Six Days of Island Life

DAYS 1–2

Ease into resort life in Montego Bay, thriving with resorts: families gravitate toward the luxurious Half Moon, which abounds with kid-friendly amenities; honeymooners get romantic at Sandals Montego Bay; and groups of friends opt for the spacious villas at Round Hill Hotel and Villas. Around the bay, enjoy the sun and sand of Walter Fletcher Beach, and then visit the nearby Rose Hall Great House, one of Jamaica's most famous historical structures. This Georgian mansion has been the subject of numerous Gothic ghost novels because of the former mistress of the house, the "White Witch of Rose Hall."

DAYS 3–4

Negril has some of the most beautiful coastline in Jamaica so plan to spend a couple of days taking full advantage, kicking back on the famous Seven Mile Beach and cooling off with cocktails and reggae at beachfront bars. For some of the best snorkeling, head to nearby Rockhouse Beach, with underwater corals and caves filled with tropical fish and snake eels. For an afternoon of greenery, check out the 300-acre (121-ha) Royal Palm Reserve.

DAYS 5–6

Fly to Kingston, and delve into the island's history at the National Gallery, which showcases Jamaica's top artists. Also, visit the classical 1881 Devon House, with a beautifully restored interior, as well as shops that sell Jamaican arts and crafts. Take a day-trip tour to a coffee plantation in the Blue Mountains, like the lovely Craighton Estate, which dates back to 1805.

Dos and Don'ts

- ✗ Don't forget that here they drive on the left side of the road. Also, keep in mind that some of Jamaica's roadways can be rough going, with minimal road signs and poor conditions.
- ✓ While Jamaica is generally safe for tourists, it does have a high crime rate, particularly around Kingston and New Kingston. Take all the usual precautions: keep an eagle eye on your belongings at all times, don't carry large amounts of cash and stay in well-lit areas at night.
- ✓ Book your hotel at least 3–5 months ahead if you're visiting in the high season: More than elsewhere in the Caribbean, Jamaica's resorts and hotels fill up very quickly.

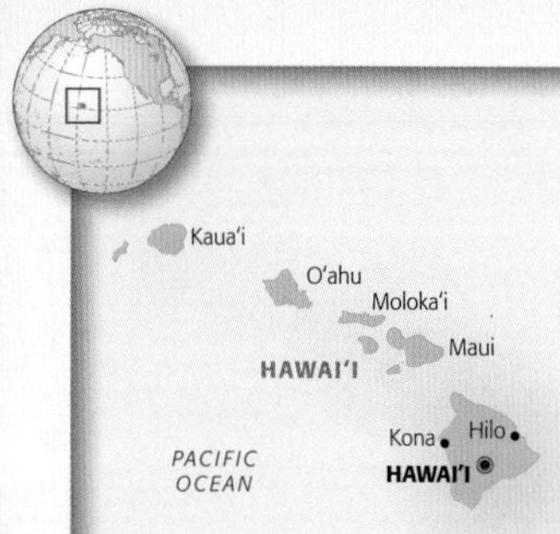

GETTING THERE See map p322, H7, I7
Flights from mainland USA and other Hawaiian islands land at Kona International Airport on the west side of the Big Island and at Hilo International Airport on the east.

GETTING AROUND
This island is best explored by car; rentals are available at the international airports.

WEATHER
December temperatures average 71–77°F (22–25°C) at sea level and around 57–63°F (14–17°C) at the 4,000-ft (1,219-m) Volcanoes National Park.

ACCOMMODATIONS
Most resorts and hotels are on the Kona and Kohala coasts on the west side.

Near Volcanoes National Park, Volcano Inn offers rustic accommodation; family rooms from US$95; www.volcanoinnhawaii.com

Casual Outrigger Kanaloa at Kona offers apartments with kitchens; two-bedroom units from US$160; www.outrigger.com

Further north, luxury resort Hilton Waikoloa Village has a dolphin pool; doubles from US$240; www.hiltonwaikoloavillage.com

EATING OUT
Most restaurants serve Pacific Rim and Hawaiian food. Café meals are under US$10; restaurant dinners cost US$35–50.

FURTHER INFORMATION
www.gohawaii.com

HAWAI'I

HAWAI'I, KNOWN TO HAWAIIANS JUST AS THE "BIG ISLAND," IS ONE BIG BLAST – literally. Comprising five volcanoes, the island presents startling climatic and dramatic diversity, from beneath its coral-fringed sea to the top of the snow-capped Mauna Kea and Mauna Loa peaks. The Big Island's attractions include black- and white-sand beaches, calm inlets and wild surf, humpback whales and basking sea turtles, thundering waterfalls and molten lava deserts, thousands of petroglyphs, and working cattle ranches. Mingling with these stunning images are rare native flora. The aromas of freshly roasted Kona coffee, crunchy macadamia nuts, chocolates, vanilla, and honey waft in the air.

Soaring overhead are flocks of kaleidoscopic birds, including Hawai'i's national bird, the endangered *nene* (Hawaiian goose). And towering over the island is the steep, hard-to-get-to Mauna

The Hawaiian Wild West

Big Island cowboy culture can be traced to 1798, when Captain George Vancouver gifted King Kamehameha some longhorn cattle. Later, horses were introduced, followed by the arrival of rancher John Palmer Parker, who hired Mexican *vaqueros*. Dubbed *paniolo* or Español, these men brought along a hard-working albeit flamboyant lifestyle. Hawaiian women also took to horses. Lei-wreathed and elaborately dressed, the Pau riders created a sort of "hula on horseback," which is still performed at festivals and international parades.

Main: Tourists photographing a humpback whale

Left: Thurston Lava Tube at Kīlauea Volcano

Right (left and right): Fourspot butterfly fish; a Hawaiian *luau*

Right panel (top to bottom): A crowd of people watching the lava spewing forth at the Volcanoes National Park; Hawai'i's national bird, the endangered *nene*; Mauna Kea Observatory; the black volcanic sands of Punalu'u Beach

Kea, which at 13,796 ft (4,200 m) is Hawai'i's highest point. In fact, Mauna Kea rises approximately 32,000 ft (9,754 m) from the ocean floor to its summit, making it reputedly the tallest mountain on the planet. Great for stargazing, this peak is home to world-renowned observatories. It is possible to drive to the Mauna Loa summit, but it can be treacherous and is best undertaken with a tour operator and 4WD vehicle.

The Volcanoes National Park, the volcanic wonderland to the southeast, is home to still-active volcanoes Mauna Loa and Kīlauea. Although there's no guarantee of an eruption (it all depends on the mood of the Volcano Goddess, Pele), there are superb drives and hikes through this landscape of lava tubes and rain forests. Hawai'i is also home to friendly island communities. These include resort towns, sleepy fishing villages, and the "old Hawai'i," Hilo Town. The Big Island encompasses a big *'ohana* (family) that welcomes all with a heartfelt *aloha*.

Above: Rainbow Falls

HAWAIIAN DIARY

December is an ideal time to visit the Big Island with your family and go on a *holoholo* (pleasure trip). The island offers a range of activities, from whale-watching to stargazing beneath snowy peaks or simply going on leisurely drives. Extend your stay by visiting Maui *(see pp26–7)* or Kaua'i *(see pp248–9)*.

A Week of 'Ohana

DAY 1
Settle into a relaxed first day and soak up some Hawaiian culture at a traditional *luau*.

DAY 2
From Kona, head to the beach. Family favorites include Spencer and Kahalu'u beach parks, good spots to view green sea turtles. In the evening, stroll in Kailua-Kona.

DAY 3
Drive north to the tip of the Kohala Coast. Along the way see the Kalāhuipua'a Fishponds, the Puakō Petroglyphs, and the birthplace of warrior-king Kamehameha the Great. Venture inland from arty Hawi, through *paniolo* (cowboy) country, to Waimea. Explore Parker Ranch on horseback or in an all-terrain vehicle.

DAY 4
From Kona aim south, stopping at the Captain Cook Monument and the black-sand beach of Punalu'u. Continue to the Hawai'i Volcanoes National Park and Kīlauea Visitor Center. Drive the Crater Rim Drive, which circuits rain forests, Thurston Lava Tube, and the Jaeger Museum. Spend the night at a local inn.

DAY 5
Rise early to catch a rainbow at misty Rainbow Falls and the ancient pools known as Boiling Pots. Enjoy the exhibits at Imiloa Astronomy Center in Hilo. Head north along the east coast, admiring the awe-inspiring Akaka Falls before driving back to Kona.

DAYS 6–7
Spend another day at the beach. Go snorkeling or take a submarine excursion. View migrating humpback whales and other marine life aboard a cruise. On your last day, wake up and smell the Kona coffee with a coffee-farm tour.

Dos and Don'ts

- ✓ At Volcanoes National Park, always check with park rangers regarding road and trail closures and stay on marked trails.
- ✗ Don't feed or otherwise tamper with the *nene* (Hawaiian goose) and be careful not to hit one on the road!
- ✗ Don't stock up on coffee, nuts, orchids, and other agricultural products without making sure whether they can be brought back into your home country.
- ✓ Make inquiries before diving into the water – even the loveliest of beaches may have dangerous rip currents.

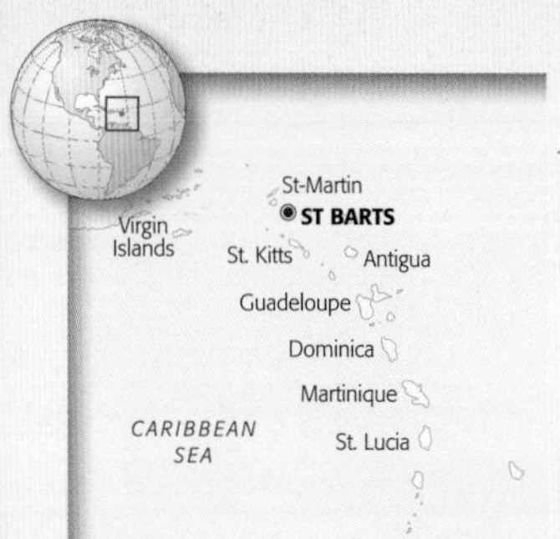

GETTING THERE See map p325, H4

There are no non-stop international flights to St. Barts. From the US, the most popular route is to fly into St. Martin, and then hop on a 10-minute flight from there.

GETTING AROUND

There are taxis at the airport to take you to destinations around St Barts. If you plan to explore the island during your trip, it's best to rent a car, as there is little public transportation. You can find rental car offices at the airport and in Gustavia.

WEATHER

St. Barts is bathed in sun year-round. The weather is optimal during high season, from December to March.

ACCOMMODATIONS

Near Lorient Beach, the elegant Normandie Hotel sports a nautical theme; doubles from US$225; www.normandiehotelstbarts.com

The deluxe Le Toiny, near Toiny Beach, has villa suites with views of the Caribbean Sea; doubles from US$650; www.letoiny.com

The spacious Villa Brume de Mer has a breezy gazebo and solar-heated pool; prices vary; www.stbartsblue.com

EATING OUT

St. Barts is a food-lover's paradise, with fresh seafood and a delicious range of French, Creole, and West Indies cuisine.

FURTHER INFORMATION

www.saintbarth-tourisme.com

St. Barts Bucket Regatta

St. Barts is home to numerous luxury yachts, and you can see them, stately and gleaming white, in ports around the island. For the ultimate in yacht-spotting, check out the St. Barts Bucket Regatta, an annual regatta in March, when some of the world's most impressive sailing yachts head en masse to the island. The event is marked by a series of races, award ceremonies, fundraising events, and the champagne-fueled Bucket Bash.

Main: Luxury boats populate the clear blue waters of Gustavia

ST. BARTS

When you see glossy magazine photos of celebrities frolicking in the Caribbean, there is a good chance that they were snapped in St. Barts. The embodiment of the good life in the tropics, St. Barthélemy (variously nicknamed St. Barths or Barts) is a French territory in the West Indies that boasts an enticingly chic and laid-back atmosphere. Here, amid the palm trees and sea breezes, you can dine on elaborate French cuisine, sip silky wines, and shop for Chanel and Cartier in perfume-scented boutiques. Of course, it's the beaches that, deservedly, have catapulted this island into being one of the Caribbean's top destinations. Lovely strips of sand ring the island, including on the secluded Anse de Colombier (Colombier Beach) which is flanked by outcrops offering stunning perspectives of the coastline. It is an ideal spot for snorkeling and swimming, and accessed by a several hiking trails. The sun-soaked Flamands Beach is also worth visiting as it is one of the largest and most pristine on the island.

Above (top and bottom): Windsurfing is a popular watersport at St Barts; the laid-back center of Gustavia

Below: A scenic outcrop above Anse de Colombier

Above: The picturesque Flamands Beach

St. Barts is also a boon for outdoor activities: You name it, and it's offered, including windsurfing, kayaking, sailing, body-surfing, and fishing. Plus, the snorkeling and diving are phenomenal, particularly if you head out on a catamaran day trip to favorite snorkeling sites. Surrounded by a coral reef, the island offers the chance to view a colorful array of marine life.

Once the sun sets, the nightlife of the island holds as much allure as its daytime activities. You can sip frosty cocktails at Nikki Beach in St. Jean as the sunset colors the sky in bright red-and-orange hues; groove to dance tunes at Modjo in St. Jean; or toast the night at the legendary Le Ti in Pointe Milou, which hosts full-moon parties, cabarets and much more.

St. Barts may be the Caribbean playground for the rich and ever richer, but there's still a very authentic side to the island, namely in its small fishing villages, such as Corossol. The charming little capital of Gustavia manages to balance out its posh shops and mega yachts with a rustic ambience. Narrow streets are lined with quaint houses, and around every bend you'll catch tantalizing glimpses of the bluest of blue sea glinting beyond.

COASTAL DIARY

St. Barts is all about decadence, from the fine dining to the luxury boutiques. Alongside its glitzy reputation and relaxed atmosphere, you'll find achingly beautiful beaches that give way to bright blue waters. Here's how to celebrate four days on this pearl of the French West Indies.

Four Days of Indulgence

DAY 1

Start your St. Barts vacation in Gustavia, the adorable French-infused capital, where you can pamper all the senses. Stroll along Shell Beach, so-called because it's covered with millions of, yes, sparkling shells. Then stroll Rue de la République, dotted with designer shops that sell everything from Bulgari to Hermès. St. Barts attracts a slew of celebrity chefs, and Gustavia is a prime spot to sample the latest in creative French-Caribbean cuisine.

DAY 2

A relatively small island, St Barts is perfect for beach-hopping. In the morning, sprawl out on the sun-soaked Gouveneur Beach and, in the afternoon, head to Baie de St. Jean on the island's northern coast. This bay is home to the island's first – and most famous – hotel, Eden Rock St. Barts, which has welcomed everyone from Mick Jagger to Greta Garbo. Enjoy a cocktail while gazing out at the Caribbean: life doesn't get much better than this.

DAY 3–4

Get your adrenaline pumping with a couple of days of water sports. With its year-round warm temperatures and consistent winds, St. Barts is ideal for kitesurfing, which is one of the island's most popular activities. The eastern part of the island provides the best kitesurfing territory, particularly on Grand Cul-de-Sac, and numerous outfitters offer tours. You can also slip on the fins and go snorkeling in the clear waters off Gouvernour Beach. The colourful reef teems with underwater riches. Top off the day with a sunset sail, taking in the brilliant hues of the setting sun, with a champagne in hand.

Dos and Don'ts

- ✓ On St. Barts' wide, sunny beaches, shade can be hard to find, so make sure to bring plenty of protection. Pack a hat, sunglasses, sunscreen and, for those who burn easily, a long-sleeved, breathable cotton shirt.
- ✗ While the island is filled with pricey restaurants, don't miss the budget beach shacks and other smaller restaurants, many of which serve very affordable daily specials.
- ✓ Splurge on a night out for cocktails amid the beautiful people at one of St. Barts' trendy nightspots, like the Yacht Club on Gustavia Harbor.

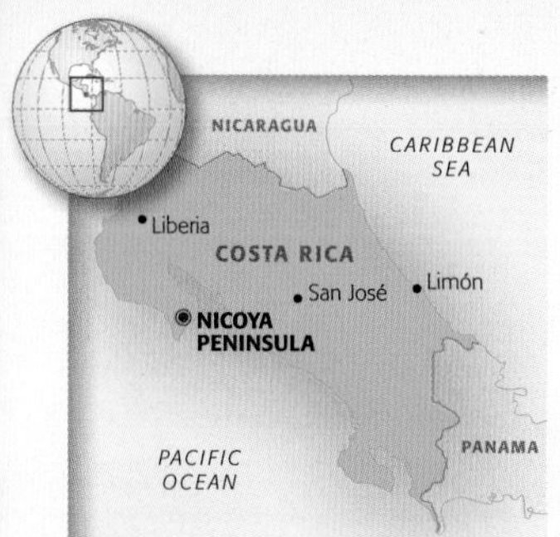

GETTING THERE See map p324, D6

Major North American airlines fly to Liberia's Daniel Oduber Quirós International Airport, near the beaches. Many people also prefer to fly to San José, the capital, and drive to Nicoya, with a cruise to Tortuga Island on the way.

GETTING AROUND

The numerous beaches are accessed via a network of roads, many unpaved. Rent a 4WD car for the potholed roads.

WEATHER

December is the perfect time to visit, as the rainy season has ended. The weather is clear, with temperatures averaging 82°F (28°C).

ACCOMMODATIONS

Hotel Puerta del Sol, at the Playas del Coco, has a delightful aesthetic and an Italian restaurant, with doubles from US$110; www.lapuertadelsolcostarica.com.

Intimate and colorful Hotel Bula Bula, at Playa Grande, offers fine dining with doubles from US$120; www.hotelbulabula.com

Enjoy luxury at the Four Seasons Papagayo, with its own golf course; doubles from US$540; www.fourseasons.com/costarica

EATING OUT

All types of cuisine are available, but local seafood is the way to go. Start with *ceviche*, followed by *corvina al ajillo* (garlic sea bass).

FURTHER INFORMATION

www.visitcostarica.com

Turtle Invasion

Ridleys are unique among the world's six species of marine turtles. Instead of nesting singly and at night, they come ashore en masse during the day. Tens of thousands of Ridleys storm select beaches together to dig nests and lay eggs in unison. *Arribadas* (arrivals) are timed to coincide with a waxing full moon and occur on only about a dozen beaches worldwide, two of which – Ostional and Playa Nancite – are in Costa Rica.

Above: Bathroom with a view at the Four Seasons Papagayo

Above (left and right): Peaceful bays near Nicoya; Playa Flamingo at sunset
Main: Boats setting off from the sandy beach at Tortuga Island

NICOYA PENINSULA

IF YOU'VE EVER IMAGINED YOURSELF AS AN INDIANA JONES, Nicoya is just the place to live out those dreams – glide through the forest on a canopy zipline, whiz around on an ATV, or rent a Jeep for an off-road adventure. Or, if dreaming is the only activity you had in mind, Nicoya is also a prime spot to laze in a hammock. Once a snoozy backwater beloved mostly by backpacking surfers, Nicoya has been thrust into the spotlight by the opening of Liberia airport in the late 1990s. Nearby Bahía Culebra, a vast bay, is now the center of Costa Rica's deluxe resort development and today the region boasts almost three-quarters of the country's hotels, with something for every budget and mood, no matter how sophisticated or adventurous.

Although no longer remote, Nicoya is still wild. This broad rectangular peninsula in northwest Costa Rica shows off the potential of the Central American tropics to full effect. Its mountainous interior forms a rugged backdrop to sensational beaches in every shade, from taupe to gold. Crafty capuchin monkeys scamper along the sands, where marine turtles can be seen at predictable times of year and, at Playa Ostional, in astounding profusion. Like a modern-day Garden of Eden, the wildlife is all around you. Howler monkeys hang by many a hotel pool, like paying guests. Toucans may land at your breakfast table to beg for fruit tidbits, while high overhead, frigate birds hang in the sky like kites on invisible strings. In the warm seas, scuba divers are in awe of pelagics – big fish – and you won't find a sportfisher who disagrees!

Tamarindo, a surf and sportfishing haven midway down the coast, is the main resort and makes a good base for exploring. The northerly beaches are backed by sun-scorched dry forests that explode in Monet colors with the rains. Southward, verdant rain forests spill down steep mountain slopes to meet the Pacific. Coastal resorts such as Malpaís and Santa Teresa may no longer be tiny, sleepy fishing hamlets, but the beaches just keep getting better as you keep heading south, and, for Indiana Jones types, the winding coastal drive and river crossings will supply plenty of thrills and excitement.

The mountainous interior forms a rugged backdrop to sensational beaches in every shade, from taupe to gold.

Inset: White-faced capuchin monkeys lazing on a tree branch
Below (left to right): Palm-fringed Playa Carrillo near Sámara; an inviting poolside, perfect for a siesta; colorful village church along the road to Sámara

PENINSULA DIARY

December is the ideal time for a trip down the coast. The sun blazes, but fresh breezes keep temperatures within reason. Despite Nicoya's compact size, the dirt roads can be a challenge, turning a seemingly short drive into an adventure the farther south you go. Allow a week to explore the west coast without rushing.

Seven Adventurous Days

Arrive in Liberia and drive the short distance to Playa del Coco if you're on a budget, or Bahia Culebra for the Four Seasons if you're feeling flush. In the afternoon, whiz through the treetops on a zipline during the Witch's Rock Canopy Tour. **DAY 1**

In the morning, laze on the beach as the prelude to an afternoon of sportfishing or scuba diving. Guests at the Four Seasons might enjoy the hotel's golf course. Indulge in a massage or spa treatment before dinner at Playa Hermosa. Next day, follow the "Monkey Trail" (with a river fording) to Playa Flamingo and continue via Huacas to Tamarindo. Walk on the beach, surf, or dine at a beachfront café. Register with a ranger station at Playa Grande to view leatherback turtles at night. **DAYS 2–3**

Follow the dirt coast road south past a string of surfing beaches to arrive at the wildlife preserve at Playa Ostional. You'll want to linger if the Ridley turtles are nesting. Otherwise, ford the Río Montaña to reach Nosara and relax on Playa Guiones. **DAY 4**

It's a fun drive south to Sámara, perhaps stopping en route at Flying Crocodile Lodge for an ultra-light flight. Surf, stroll along the beach, or hang loose in a hammock until it's time to check out the local nightlife. **DAY 5**

A challenging drive today to Islita. Linger at the Open-Air Contemporary Museum, then check out the ibis and pelicans at Puerto Bejuco. Visit the Jungle Butterfly Farm. Have fun fording rivers to arrive in Malpaís. (If the rivers are impassable, the mountain route will add several hours to your journey.) **DAYS 6–7**

Dos and Don'ts

- ✗ Don't disturb the newborn turtles you find on the beach. Let them crawl to the sea on their own.
- ✓ When fording rivers, drive slowly to avoid swamping the engine. Consider wading the river to see how deep it is. Don't forget to calculate for the height of the doorsills!
- ✗ Don't leave any belongings in your parked car. Theft from cars is a major problem at beaches.
- ✓ Use caution when swimming. Riptides are a danger on beaches where surf breaks ashore. If caught in a riptide, swim parallel to the shore.

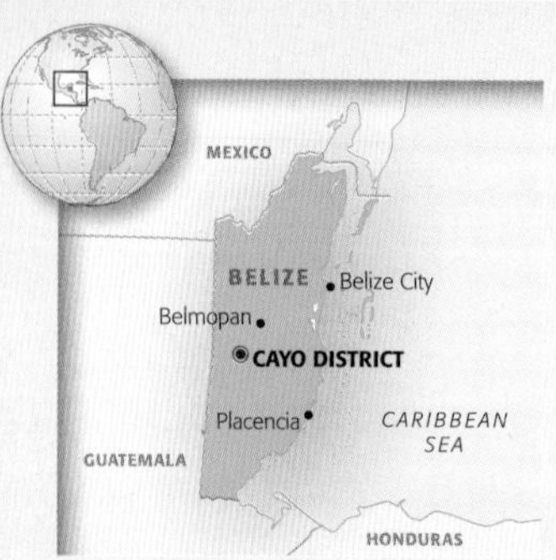

GETTING THERE **See map p324, C2**
Philip Goldson International Airport is 10.5 miles (17 km) northwest of Belize City.

GETTING AROUND
Regular buses travel between Belize City and Iganacio (1.5-hours); you can also hire a taxi or rent a car at the airport. In the Cayo District, it's best to have your own car or to explore with a tour operator.

WEATHER
Subtropical Belize receives year-round sun, but the ideal time to visit is from December to March, before the rainy season.

ACCOMMODATIONS
The Hi-Et Guest House, in San Ignacio, has basic but comfortable rooms; doubles from US$40; hietguesthouse.aguallos.com

Nature-lovers flock to Hidden Valley Inn, with easy access to Mountain Pine Ridge; doubles from US$190; www.hiddenvalleyinn.com

Blancaneaux Lodge is a luxury accommodation in the heart of Mountain Pine Ridge; doubles from US$359

EATING OUT
Belizean cuisine is a flavorful mix of Latin American and Creole-style Caribbean flavors, including rice and beans cooked in coconut oil, and fresh seafood. In the Cayo District, you'll also find an abundance of Guatemalan and Central American cuisine, including tasty empanadas from streetside shacks.

FURTHER INFORMATION
www.travelbelize.org

The First Eco-Lodge

The Cayo District has long been a pioneer when it comes to environmentally aware accommodations, and this is credited largely to the Lodge at Chaa Creek, one of country's first eco-lodges. Conceived in 1981 by Mick and Lucy Fleming, it sits on a large private reserve, and is a delightful mix of the sumptuous and sustainable. By day, you can embark on jungle treks, and by night, you can relax in the thoughtfully designed treetop suites. Many of the lodings here come with outdoor showers, and spacious sun decks for wildlife viewing.

Main: The Great Blue Hole, part of the World Heritage-listed Belize Barrier Reef System **Right panel (top to bottom):** The colorful keel-billed toucan; visitors at the Actun Tunichil Muknal cave; traditional textiles in San Ignacio; horseback riding in the Mountain Pine Ridge reserve

THE CAYO DISTRICT

THE CENTRAL AMERICAN NATION OF BELIZE MAY BE TINY, but it can lay claim to plenty of honors, including being home to the longest barrier reef in the Western Hemisphere. However, venture inland from the bright-blue waters of the country's east coast, and you'll encounter the Cayo District, a remarkable region that's rich in history and scenic beauty. Dubbed the "wild west" of the Belize, it offers an abundance of sights and outdoor activitities. Nature reigns supreme here, with rushing rivers and waterfalls, verdant pine forests, and ancient caves that extend deep underground. Its natural wonders all come together in the Mountain Pine Ridge, a massive forest reserve that's filled with feathery pines, sparkling pools, and dark caves. Here you'll find the mighty Macal River, and the awe-inspiring Thousand Foot Falls, one of the tallest waterfalls in Central America. If you're lucky, you may spot colorful toucans and parrots amid the forest vegetation.

Above: Impressive Mayan ruins at Caracol

WILD WEST DIARY

Blessed with fascinating history and captivating natural beauty, the Cayo District is also a hub for outdoor activities. Bring along your sense of adventure and choose from a range of activities, including hiking, horseback riding, river tubing, and caving.

Four Days of Nature

DAYS 1–2

Start your explorations in San Ignacio, a lively center with Belizean restaurants, tourist offices, and outdoor operators. From here you can explore Mountain Pine Ridge, visiting the Rio On pools, where you can take a dip in the cool waters. Then, trek to the crashing Thousand Foot Falls. For a dose of ancient history, hire a guide to visit Caracol, the largest Mayan site in Belize, which looms magnificently over the misty rain forest. Numerous jungle accommodations are dotted in the area, such as the lovely Blancaneaux Lodge, with spacious thatch cabañas overlooking a creek.

DAY 3

Venture to the Actun Tunichil Muknal cave and archeological site with an organized tour, the best way to access this subterranean wonder. On your adventure, you'll trek along jungle trails, traverse rivers, and descend deep into the cave system. Stay at the Caves Branch Lodge, which is set on the verdant banks of the Caves Branch River, and can arrange an array of river sports, including tubing.

DAY 4

Visit Mountain Equestrian Trails, the country's premiere horseback-riding center, which also arranges bird-watching tours. Nearby is Green Hills Butterfly Ranch, where you might spot up to 50 of Belize's magnificent butterfly species and learn about their life cycles. The botanical gardens and bird life are also well worth seeing.

The Cayo District also contains some of the earliest Mayan archeological sites in Central America. One of the standouts is Caracol, the largest site in Belize, dating back more than 1,200 years. Today, its ruins include weather-worn pyramids surrounded by lush jungle. Another highlight is the Actun Tunichil Muknal cave system, which runs some 3 miles (5 km) deep. Aside from the amazing limestone formations of the cave, it is an important archeological site, containing the calcified skeletons of sacrifice victims, plus stoneware and ceramics. Those in search of even more history can visit Cahal Pech, perched on a hill just south of town of San Ignacio. Settled between 1500 and 1000 BC, this fascinating site features well-preserved plazas and ballcourts.

While Belize's capital, Belmopan, is also in the Cayo District, the region's bustling hub is San Ignacio. This friendly town offers plenty in the way of budget lodging, Belizean restaurants, and outdoor bars. But no matter where you visit in the region, after a few days you'll soon agree with the locals: "West is best!"

Dos and Don'ts

- ✓ Be sure to taste Marie Sharp's pepper sauce, a proudly made-in-Belize hot sauce that appears on most restaurant tables. The powerful condiment adds a kick to every dish, and makes for a great gift to bring home.
- ✓ Though the official language of Belize is English, in the Cayo District, which nudges up against Guatemala, many locals also speak Spanish, so bring your Spanish phrasebook.
- ✓ Stay well hydrated, especially if you plan to spend entire days outdoors. The sun is especially strong in the non-rainy season, from December to April.
- ✗ Don't get confused by the prices: the Belize dollar is fixed to the rate of two to the US dollar (BZ\$2 = US\$1), but since they both use the same designation (\$), you'll often have to confirm which dollar is being referred to.

GETTING THERE See map p326, G4
The base camp for trips to Angel Falls is the settlement of Canaima, located inside Canaima National Park. Canaima can only be reached by air – daily flights from Caracas with Avior airlines (www.aviorair.com).

GETTING AROUND
The falls can be viewed by small plane or helicopter, but the best view is obtained by traveling up the Churun river by *curiaras* (canoes), then hiking to the base of the falls.

WEATHER
Daytime temperatures are hot – from 68 to 86°F (20 to 30°C). Although often sunny in December, there is always the possibility of rain and fog.

ACCOMMODATIONS
Angel Adventures offers 3-day/2-night expeditions to the falls, with accommodation in jungle camps and hammocks; US$220 per person; www.salto-angel.com

Jungle Rudy Campamento is located a short boat ride from Canaima, above Ucaima Falls; US$267 per person for two days, including a trip to Angel Falls and airport transfers; www.junglerudy.com.

EATING OUT
Meals are provided either by your lodge or your tour operator.

FURTHER INFORMATION
www.salto-angel.com

Above (left and right): A colorful keel-billed toucan; a *tepuy*, or flat-topped mountain, swathed in cloud

ANGEL FALLS

THE ROLLING HIGH SAVANNAH LAND OF SOUTHERN VENEZUELA is the natural home of the *tepuy*, a kind of rugged, eerie, flat-topped mountain, draped in rain-forest green. *Tepuys* are some of the last holdouts from the Cretaceous era, stubborn rock extrusions that held firm while the weaker stone around them wore away, leaving each *tepuy*-top an isolated little island in the clouds. Sherlock Holmes' creator, Sir Arthur Conan Doyle, postulated that the *tepuys* might provide a refuge to living creatures from that long-lost epoch. In his 1912 novel *The Lost World*, the shrouded *tepuy*-tops were a place where pterodactyls and brontosaurs still roamed...

Dinosaurs may no longer exist, but mysteries and unknowns around the falls persisted. Two decades after Conan Doyle, an American bush pilot named Jimmie Angel came back with an incredible tale of the world's highest waterfall – a ribbon of white water falling from a *tepuy* so tall that its peak was hidden in the clouds. It was not until 1949 that the National Geographic Society firmly fixed the newly christened Angel Falls' exact height at 3,212 ft (979 m) – 15 times the height of Niagara.

A visit to Angel Falls is still a journey into the unknown. Canaima, the small Pemon Indian village that serves as base camp, is a place of beauty set on the edge of a dark lagoon fringed by pink-sand beaches. The journey upriver by *curiara* (a dugout wooden canoe) passes several smaller falls and rapids on the way. Passing Orchid Island you pull in to the river landing and trek uphill through the jungle. As you climb, small glimpses of the misty white ribbon that is Angel Falls peek here and there through the rain forest canopy, and the air grows cool and damp, the rocks underfoot slick with moisture. The isolated environments of the *tepuys*' flat plateaus are home to species found nowhere else on earth, many of them as yet undescribed. At the base of the falls, you gaze up through a sheer fine mist, like an eternal spring rain. The sound is curiously calm, even muted. Unlike Niagara or Victoria, Angel Falls doesn't come roaring over its precipice, but spills relentlessly and gently into the ominously named Devil's Canyon below.

Jimmie Angel's Falls

Angel Falls are named not for their seraphic beauty, but for the American bush pilot, Jimmie Crawford Angel, who happened to fly over the falls in 1933 while on a search for gold. Angel returned in 1937, but crashed his plane while attempting to land on the flat-topped *tepuy* above the falls. He and his three companions were forced to descend the falls on foot – an 11-day journey through the trackless interior. News of their ordeal spread, and as a result the falls were named in his honor.

Main: The mighty cascade of Angel Falls
Below (left and right): A *curiara* (dugout canoe); Canaima Lagoon waterfall

Above: Canaima Lagoon and the waterfalls

CASCADE DIARY

Angel Falls is at its best in early December at the end of the rainy season, when clear skies offer the best visibility but the flow of water is still impressive, and the rivers leading to the falls can still be navigated by canoe. The journey from Canaima includes a night in a hammock at the foot of the falls.

Three Adventurous Days

DAY 1

Flights from Caracas arrive mid-morning. After a transfer to your lodge, take a guided trek to gushing Ara-Meru Falls where you can swim in the deep natural pools and wander over the natural jade formations. After an outdoor lunch, hike to Sapo Falls, with its fabulous white curtain of water. Keep an eye on the gallery forests by the river's edge for toucans and howler monkeys, particularly later in the day.

DAY 2

Set out early to travel up the Carrao river by *curiaras* (dugout canoes) to Isla Orquídea (Orchid Island), where most tours make a stop to admire the orchids and have some breakfast. Then it's back into the canoes, this time on the smaller Churun river, snaking up the Cañón del Diablo (Devil's Canyon) to a small island at the base of the falls called Isla Ratoncito (Little Mouse Island). From here it's another hour's hike uphill through the forest to the pools at the foot of Angel Falls. Time to relax and stare in awe, and then plunge in for a swim. Relax by the falls until late afternoon, then hike back down and return to the camp on Ratoncito for a meal and a night in a comfortable hammock.

DAY 3

After another early start, hike back up the forest in the early morning light for a last lingering gaze at the high clear stream of Angel Falls. For those brave enough to withstand the bracing waters, this is also the opportunity for another refreshing plunge in the pools at the foot of the falls. Then it's back through the rain forest to the landing point for the canoe ride back downstream to Canaima.

Dos and Don'ts

- ✓ Read the book before you go. *The Lost World*, written by Sir Arthur Conan Doyle, is a rollicking good adventure yarn (though alas with no Sherlock Holmes).
- ✓ Book tours well ahead of your trip: places in December are limited and highly sought-after.
- ✗ Don't forget that on flight-seeing tours, you pay full fare whether or not the falls are shrouded in mist and cloud.
- ✓ Bring some US dollars in cash, as there may be long lines at ATMs (which frequently run out of money).

MEXICO'S COLONIAL HEARTLAND

Roam Mexico's colonial heartland, and it's easy to see why this area has inspired such a rich tradition of arts and crafts. Amid the rugged peaks of the country's central highlands lie beautifully preserved cities such as San Miguel de Allende, Querétaro, Guanajuato, and Zacatecas. Designated UNESCO World Heritage Sites, these centers charm travelers with a vibrant mix of history, culture, and cuisine, and the welcoming, easygoing spirit of the locals.

The early wealth of these cities was rooted in the region's booming silver production during the 16th century. As the riches rolled in, the cities sprouted magnificent Baroque and Moorish architecture, from grand cathedrals to ornate fountains. In San Miguel de Allende, you can wander the cobblestone streets, gazing up at eye-catching buildings such as the Parroquia de San Miguel

GETTING THERE **See map p323, E5**
The nearest main airport to San Miguel de Allende is Guanajuato International Airport, which lies 59 miles (95 km) to the west.

GETTING AROUND
To fully explore a region, it's best to rent a car. Buses also travel the main routes between cities.

WEATHER
San Miguel de Allende enjoys beautiful year-round balmy weather. November to April is ideal, when the rain is minimal and the temperature pleasantly warm.

ACCOMMODATIONS
The relaxing Belmond Casa de Sierra Nevada is set in several historic buildings in the heart of San Miguel de Allende; doubles from US$230; www.belmond.com

Unwind in the elegant suites at Villa María Cristina in Guanajuato; doubles from US$190; www.villamariacristina.net

The lovely La Casa del Atrio is in a renovated 19th-century house in historic Querétaro; doubles from US$139; www.lacasadelatrio.com

EATING OUT
The Colonial Heartland features a superb array of local cuisine, including salsas, enchiladas, gorditas, and pozole. Don't miss Moxi, which features dishes such as beef with pickled *nopales,* and sweet-corn *tamales*.

FURTHER INFORMATION
www.visitmexico.com

Mexican Independence

The Mexican independence movement was launched in the Colonial Heartland. Catholic priest Miguel Hidalgo delivered his famous Grito de Dolores (Cry of Dolores) speech in 1810 in the region of Guanajuato, calling for the end of Spanish rule. Other revolutionary leaders included Ignacio Allende, a captain of the Spanish army who became one of the most ardent crusaders for independence. Executed by Spanish authorities in 1877, he is now lauded as a national hero, with many places named in his honor, such as San Miguel de Allende.

Main: The vibrant city center of Guanajuato

Left: The stately facade of Teatro Juárez in Guanajuato

Right (left and right): A plaza beside the San Francisco church in Querétaro; a performer in traditional dress

Arcángel, with detailed spires that were inspired by Gaudí's Sagrada Familia in Barcelona. The city has long been a magnet for US expats, who have enthusiastically continued its artistic legacy, opening art studios, galleries, and craft centers. The city's calendar is packed with year-round festivals, which include everything from musical performances to religious celebrations.

Elsewhere in the Colonial Heartland, you can visit the city of Querétaro to trace its history along wide, airy plazas, and inside the handsome 17th-century San Francisco church. Another city of historical note is Guanajuato. A feast for the eyes, its streets are lined with colorful houses and impressive buildings such as Teatro Juárez, while lively town squares are filled with al fresco restaurants. Zacatecas, the northernmost of Mexico's former silver-mining cities, is nestled in a ravine between two imposing hills. Its streets are teeming with gorgeous architecture, including the stately Plaza de Armas, which is presided over by an impressive pink-sandstone cathedral.

Above: The pink sandstone of Catedral de Zacatecas

Below: Colorful banners outside the Parroquia de San Miguel Arcángel in San Miguel de Allende

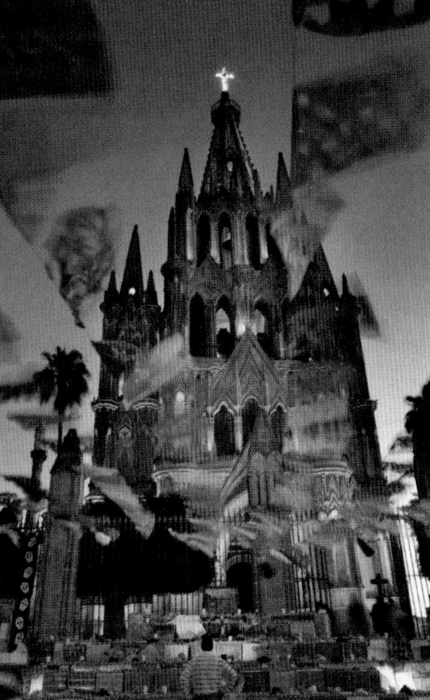

Above: A cable car making its way across Zacatecas

ART-LOVER'S DIARY

Trace Mexico's history in its colonial heartland, which lies north of Mexico City, and is dotted with beautifully preserved historic cities. Six days is the perfect amount of time to take in all the sights during the day, and soak up the best of the local nightlife.

Six Days of Colonial Splendor

DAYS 1–2

Stroll the cobblestone streets of San Miguel de Allende, taking in the sun in the central plaza and perusing the many shops. One of the most thriving art bases in the region, the city is dotted with galleries. Atenea Gallery exhibits both established and emerging artists. Come evening, head to the restaurants in the heart of town to dine on fresh tacos and margaritas.

DAY 3

Founded in 1531 by Franciscan monks, Querétaro is packed with history. Pay a visit to the Teatro de la República, where Mexico's constitution was signed in 1917. Stop in the Jardín Zenea, where a band performs classic tunes on the weekend, and is near to the stately San Francisco church. View the superb collection of colonial art at the Museo de Arte, in the former convent of San Agustín.

DAYS 4–5

When in Guanajuato, don't miss the 18th-century Templo Valenciana, a bold example of Churrigueresque architecture. Visit the splendid Teatro Juarez, with its looming columns and Moorish interior. Diego Rivera, one of Mexico's great artists, lived in Guanajuato, and his home has been turned in the fascinating Museo Diego Rivera. In the evenings, enjoy the array of excellent local and international restaurants.

DAY 6

Top off your tour of the region in Zacatecas. Hop on the *teleférico* (cable car) to the Cerro de la Bufa, a rocky outcrop over the city that affords sweeping views. Here you'll also find the Museo de la Toma de Zacatecas, which features historical photos and artifacts on the capture of Zacatecas by Pancho Villa and his revolutionary forces.

Dos and Don'ts

- ✗ Don't miss sampling the famous local Irapuato strawberries, either fresh with cream or as a strawberry liquor.
- ✓ Look for one-day art and painting workshops in San Miguel de Allende. These are a great way to interact with the local community of artists, and to bring back a handmade souvenir from your travels.
- ✓ Time your visit to coincide with the Festival Internacional Cervantino in Guanajuato. Named after famed Spanish writer Miguel de Cervantes, it features all manner of performing arts, including theater, classical music, and folk dances.

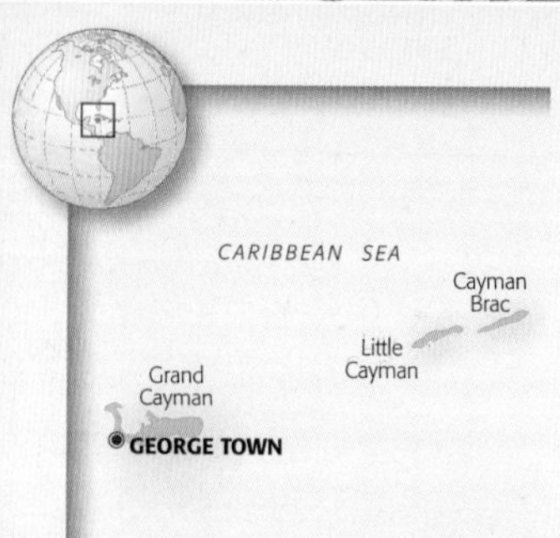

CAYMAN ISLANDS

THE COBALT-BLUE WATERS FRAMING THE CAYMAN ISLANDS in the western Caribbean conceal a breathtaking underwater world studded with flashing shoals of brightly colored fish, dazzling coral reef formations, and eerie shipwrecks. This is a scuba diver's paradise. Warm waters, crystal-clear visibility, stunning marine life, and the sheer number and diversity of sights draw dive enthusiasts back here year after year. The dramatic, submerged landscape around the islands hosts more than 150 superb dive spots, each with its own distinct character, and catering to all levels of ability. You can do night dives, day dives, wreck dives, or cave dives. The choice is dizzying.

Cayman Brac, the farthest east of the three main islands, is home to one of the Caribbean's most sensational dive spots. Here, the famed North Wall drops away to an astonishing 14,000 ft (4,250 m), while the steeper and more awesome South Wall drops away farther still, into the velvet blackness of the precipice below. The walls are alive with sponges, finger corals, sea fans, and an incredible diversity

Below (top to bottom): Brac Reef Beach Resort; offshore fishing; wreck diving in Grand Cayman

GETTING THERE See map p325, B4
The international airport on Grand Cayman is the main arrival point, but another serves Cayman Brac. Little Cayman has daily inter-island flights. Cruise ships call regularly.

GETTING AROUND
Rental cars, motorbikes, and bicycles are available on Grand Cayman and Cayman Brac; bicycles and 4WD vehicles on Little Cayman. Taxis are plentiful.

WEATHER
Highs average 83°F (28°C), nighttime lows around 75°F (24°C), with clear skies and little rain. December is not hurricane season.

ACCOMMODATIONS
Eldemire's Tropical island Inn is a family-run hotel near George Town and Seven Mile Beach; doubles from US$129; www.eldemire.com

Comfort Suites and Resort is smoke-free and has its own scuba center; suites with kitchenettes from US$200; www.caymancomfort.com

Grand Cayman Marriott Beach Resort offers a wide range of activities; doubles from US$219; www.marriott.com

EATING OUT
Food is typically Caribbean, with exotic fruits and vegetables, spicy seasonings, and plenty of seafood, especially conch.

FURTHER INFORMATION
www.caymanislands.ky

Cayman Homes

Traditional Cayman homes are built cabin-style, with a separate kitchen out back. Known as the "cook-rum" (cooking room), it is set a little way from the house. That way, if the open fire, over which food was traditionally cooked, should burn down the cook-rum, the main house at least would be safe. The houses themselves are built of wattle and daub (strips of wood and lime plaster). Many stand on ironwood posts, to provide ventilation beneath the building and protect the house from floods.

of marine life, which includes moray eels, parrotfish, stingrays, and green sea turtles. Less intrepid divers might prefer to opt for the excellent shallow dives nearby, which lead divers through caves and tunnels, and out across canyons and sublime towers of coral reef, where, on particularly clear days, the visibility can reach up to 150 ft (46 m).

Aside from the world-class diving, visitors come to the Cayman Islands to relax on the fabulous beaches, enjoy a wealth of other water- and land-based sports, and explore the sights. There are areas of strong swell for windsurfing and surfing, sheltered coves for swimming and snorkeling, and spectacular terrain perfect for golf, hiking, and horseback riding. Must-visit places include one of the region's finest stretches of beach, Seven Mile Beach on Grand Cayman, with its luxury resorts, galleries, and shopping malls; George Town, the islands' tiny, characterful capital; the village of Hell (if only to get your postcards stamped with the name at the post office); the spectacular ridge and caves of Cayman Brac; and the island of Little Cayman, which has more iguanas than people and is a paradise for bird-watching opportunities and, of course, first-rate diving.

Above: Embarking for a boat trip from George Town Harbor

Main: Divers swimming with stingrays at Stingray City Sandbar

Above (top and bottom): Queen Elizabeth Botanic Park; Devil's Hangout giftshop in Hell

Below: Iguana on a Little Cayman beach

TROPICAL DIARY

The Cayman Islands are simply the perfect Caribbean adventure playground. They offer world-class diving and sportfishing and a wealth of other water sports, as well as a wide range of dry-land activities. In five days you can pack in all manner of active adventures and still find time to do a little exploring and lazing in the sun.

Five Days in the Islands

DAY 1 Explore George Town and visit the Cayman Island National Museum in the Old Court House to learn about its colorful history. Check out some of the traditional cabin-style houses on the outskirts of town. Take a voyage in the *Atlantis* submarine which visits the Cayman Wall and the wreck of the *Kirk Pride*, that lies in 780 ft (238 m) of water.

DAY 2 Spend the whole day diving and/or snorkeling at the location of your choice. If you are in the mood for a leisurely afternoon, take the trip to Stingray City Sandbar where, in only a few feet of water, you'll be surrounded by dozens of gentle, inquisitive stingrays You can dive, snorkel, or simply stand among them.

DAY 3 Take an early morning flight to visit delightful Little Cayman. Hire a bicycle and spend the day exploring, snorkeling and swimming. Stop at one of the dive resorts for lunch but don't be late for your return flight.

DAY 4 If you are fit, explore the eastern end of Grand Cayman by bicycle (it is flat), or you could drive. Visit Bodden Town and the Queen Elizabeth Botanic Park to discover the wealth of flora and fauna on the island, and then enjoy lunch at one of the many lively beachside restaurants along the coast. Be back by late afternoon to get ready for a spectacular night dive.

DAY 5 Go to Hell and back. Visit this strangely-named village and then perhaps saddle up for a horseback ride along the beach before enjoying another magical sunset and a leisurely last night's dinner.

Dos and Don'ts

- ✓ Visit the reefs, whether you scuba, snorkel, or go by glass-bottomed boat. They are fabulous.
- ✓ Try to visit the islands – each is different in its own way – and do go to Hell!
- ✗ Don't forget that driving is on the left here – be extra careful when crossing the road, cycling, or driving.
- ✗ Don't leave unattended items on the beach or on open view in your car.

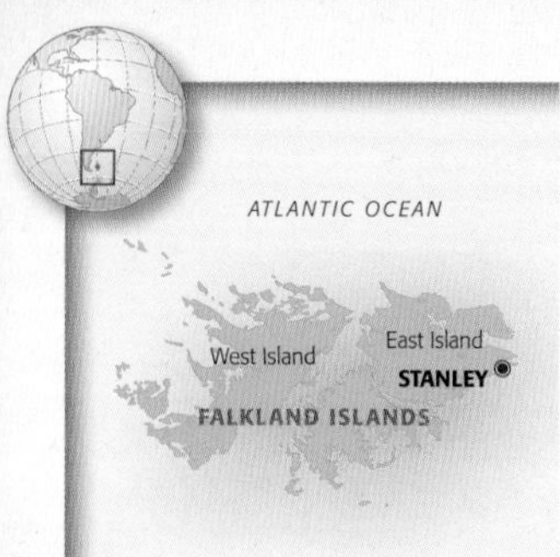

FALKLAND ISLANDS

Isolated at the bottom of the world and engulfed by the South Atlantic Ocean, the Falklands may appear an unforgiving destination. Yet, they make for one of the Americas' most breathtaking stops, edged by spectacular virgin coastline that draws wildlife enthusiasts for its rare marine fauna.

The experience begins in Stanley, the capital of an island archipelago comprising two main islands – the East and the West – and hundreds of smaller ones. With its colorful cottages and quaint pubs, Stanley reminds you of an English village. Off-road excursions nearby reveal dramatic shorelines of jagged cliffs and white-sand beaches teeming with marine life. Thousands upon thousands of penguins – the islands shelter five different species – waddle along the shore, looking irresistibly cute. Ocean-bashed rocks shelter sealions, and giant petrels and cormorants soar above in search of food.

Main: Stretching out to unwind – a king penguin on the Falkland Islands

GETTING THERE See map p331, F8

The Falklands lie off the southern tip of South America, 311 miles (500 km) from the mainland. Weekly flights to the islands depart from Santiago, Chile, stopping en route at Puerto Montt and Punta Arenas. The Falklands' Mount Pleasant Airport is 37 miles (60 km) from Stanley, an hour away by taxi.

GETTING AROUND

To visit places near Stanley, hire a driver-guide with an off-road vehicle. Light aircraft fly between airstrips around the islands.

WEATHER

The average nighttime temperature is 43°F (6°C), while the average daytime high is 59°F (15°C). Expect sunshine and long daylight hours but high winds in coastal areas.

ACCOMMODATIONS

Kay's B&B in Stanley offers harbor views; doubles from US$72; tel. (500) 21071

Stanley's Malvina House Hotel boasts spacious rooms and a sauna; doubles from US$185; www.malvinahousehotel.com

Stone House Cottage on Saunders Island is one of four self-catered cottages sleeping six to ten people; cottages from US$40 per person; www.saundersfalklands.com

EATING OUT

Mussels, oysters, scallops, and crabs are delicious options. Do also try upland goose pâté, a local delicacy.

FURTHER INFORMATION

www.falklandislands.com

Flying High in the Falklands

The black-browed albatross is the seabird highlight on most visits to the Falklands. Every October, some 80 percent of the world's population of this beautiful species migrates to the archipelago to form nesting colonies on precipitous cliffs. Come December, adults are observed with their young. The enormous adult seems ungainly on land, with its large, flat webbed feet, but in flight it is a magnificent sight, when its 8-ft (2-m) wingspan is silhouetted beautifully against the crystal-blue sky.

Left: Stanley, a quaint and colorful capital

Right (left to right): Time for a swim – pod of dolphins in a cove; hefty South American sealion bull; rockhopper penguins climbing the cliff face

Visits to the offshore islands reveal even wilder scenery. A gentle hike along the ocean-battered cliffs on Saunders Island ends at a colony of black-browed albatrosses, trusting birds that wander over as you sit silently nearby. Sea Lion Island comes alive with rockhopper penguins leaping out of the emerald sea to waddle up cliffs, while elephant seals laze on bleached-white sands and Commerson's dolphins bask in pounding surf. The magical scene is capped by the sight of killer whales patrolling the shoreline, hoping to surprise a sealion pup frolicking at the water's edge.

It's fascinating drama, and as you sit on the beach amid its cacophony of roars, barks, and cries, you suddenly realize that the wildlife here in the Falklands has little fear of humans. Each time an inquisitive gentoo penguin waddles up to you or – during a small-boat excursion – a sealion surfaces within touching distance, its inky-black eyes the size of saucers, the sensation is one of experiencing wildlife at its most uninhibited.

Above: Gentoo penguins riding the surf

Below: Magellanic penguin near its burrow

Above: A haven of natural beauty and exotic fauna

ATLANTIC DIARY

A trip to the Falklands is the journey of a lifetime, so allow yourself at least a week to explore the islands. December is midsummer here, so the days are long and the light is magnificent. Between nature trips, explore Stanley and the various haunting sites of the main battles fought during the 1982 Falklands War.

Eight Days of Rare Wildlife

DAY 1

Arrive in Stanley and hike the stretch of coast at Gypsy Cove, where Commerson's dolphins bask in the surf and millions of birds congregate.

DAYS 2–3

Fly to Saunders Island to observe large concentrations of gentoo and Magellanic penguins.

At sunrise, make the memorable hike to a nesting colony of black-browed albatrosses. Sit amid the birds and wait for them to approach you.

Later, take a hilltop walk for breathtaking vistas. Then head to the ruins of a historic garrison at Port Egmont.

DAYS 4–5

Fly to Sea Lion Island in the southeast of the archipelago for two days of wildlife-watching.

Observe rockhopper and rare macaroni penguins, colonies of giant petrels and cormorants, and killer whales. Watch the large harems of elephant seals and sealions and wait for the brutal territorial fights between the males of the two species.

DAY 6

Fly back to Stanley and visit the ruins of Goose Green, a site of fierce fighting in the Falklands War between Great Britain and Argentina.

DAY 7

Your final nature tour takes you to Volunteer Point for a close encounter with majestic king penguins, the archipelago's biggest penguin species.

DAY 8

Do some last-minute shopping in Stanley before you hop on your return flight.

Dos and Don'ts

- ✓ Bring good-quality sunglasses and high-factor sunblock; the hole in the ozone layer sits right above the Falklands.
- ✗ Don't go too close to elephant seals. These blubbery hulks are aggressive and surprisingly quick on land.
- ✓ Browse shops in Stanley for locally made soft woollens.
- ✓ Pack binoculars, waterproof clothing, and plenty of memory cards for your camera – the wildlife here is spectacular.
- ✓ Brush up on different species, so you can easily recognize a rockhopper from a macaroni or a sealion from a fur seal.

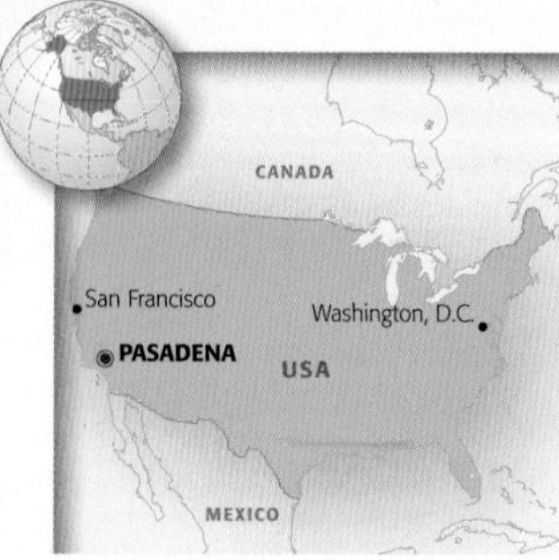

GETTING THERE **See map p321, C5**
Pasadena is a 40-minute drive northeast from Los Angeles International airport. Domestic carriers serve Bob Hope Airport in Burbank, which is a 20-minute drive from Pasadena.

GETTING AROUND
Rent a car at the airport or take the metro, which is a cheap, easy way to get around Pasadena. Taxis are widely available.

WEATHER
The average high in January is 68°F (20°C); the average low is 50°F (10°C). Rain is a rarity.

ACCOMMODATIONS
Holiday Inn Express has doubles from US$148; www.ihg.com

Set on 23 acres (9 ha), The Langham is a 1906 estate-like landmark; doubles from US$250; pasadena.langhamhotels.com

Stylish The Westin Pasadena is a block from the Rose Bowl parade route; doubles from US$280; www.starwoodhotels.com

EATING OUT
Pasadena offers everything from casual outdoor cafés to swanky restaurants serving innovative cuisine. The upscale Parkway Grill offers California cuisine in an elegant setting (US$70); or pop into one of the many local Mexican-American eateries for an inexpensive big-plate meal.

FURTHER INFORMATION
www.visitpasadena.com
www.tournamentofroses.com

The Birth of the Bungalow

Heavily influenced by the British-born Arts and Crafts movement that began in the 1860s, American Craftsman-style bungalows began to take shape in the early 1900s as part of a design-reform movement. Influential brother architects Charles Sumner Greene (1868–1957) and Henry Mather Greene (1870–1954) built a number of Pasadena's bungalows including the masterful 1908 Gamble House. With Japanese and Swiss-chalet influences on its exterior, this National Historic Landmark contains a treasure of fine cabinetry, carved woods, and stained glass.

Above (left to right): Huntington Botanical Gardens; Trojans player at the Rose Bowl Stadium; Pasadena at dusk
Main: A spectacular floral float at the Tournament of Roses

Above: A dazzling rider at Equestfest

PASADENA

FORGET THE GLITZY COUNTDOWNS AND LAVISH FIREWORKS that dominate most New Year's Eve celebrations: in Pasadena at New Year, the streets are literally coming up roses. The world-renowned Tournament of Roses Parade has grown from a simple display of flower-festooned horse-drawn carriages in the 1890s to a theme-driven extravaganza of elaborate floats covered in a riot of roses and other botanical bounties. Included in the mix is a lengthy roster of high-stepping equestrians, well-tuned marching bands, a Rose Queen and her court, and a celebrity Grand Marshal. Approximately 40 million viewers watch the spectacle on television, while an estimated one million visitors head to Pasadena to witness the dazzling sights that can only be truly appreciated in person.

Reserve a seat in the grandstand, or join the locals partying at the curbside overnight to claim the much-coveted space along the nearly 6-mile (10-km) route. Wherever you sit you will be treated to a lavish spectacle. Come early for a tour of the heavenly scented floats or to catch a football game at the Rose Bowl Stadium before the parade pageantry begins. If the festivities become overwhelming, take some time out to explore some of the city's other attractions.

Set at the base of the San Gabriel Mountains, Pasadena is luxuriously laid-back, low-key, and compact, with hip restaurants, boutiques, and Mediterranean-style piazzas. Don't miss the Norton Simon Museum, which holds one of the world's finest private art collections. Tour Gamble House, a perfectly preserved American Craftsman-style bungalow and one of the city's architectural gems, to get a close look at Greene and Greene artistry. Finally, make time to visit nearby San Marino, where an entire day can be spent at the Huntington Library, Art Collections, and Botanical Gardens to view one of the world's most important collections of 18th-century British and French art, the legacy of pioneer railroad tycoon Henry Huntington.

The Tournament of Roses Parade is a theme-driven extravaganza of floats covered in a riot of roses.

Inset: An ornate fountain at the Huntington Library
Below (left and right): The Rose Queen and her royal court; *Star Wars* stormtroopers parading at the Tournament of Roses

NEW-YEAR DIARY

For five magical days in late December and early January immerse yourself in the action at one of the world's most exciting and spectacular New Year's celebrations. Then spend two more days visiting the area's trove of world-famous art and architecture, and taking in a play at the city's theater.

A Week of Celebrations

DEC 29 Spend the afternoon at Equestfest, strolling the stables, chatting with the riders, and watching the show horses as they perform dances and other demonstrations.

DEC 30 Take in the early show of Bandfest and tap your toes to prize-winning bands. Then visit the Rose Bowl Stadium where volunteers busy themselves putting the finishing touches to the floral floats.

DEC 31 Get into the spirit of the festival at the high-energy Kickoff Luncheon, which features the Rose Bowl Hall of Fame induction ceremony, celebrity sportscasters, athletes, and university coaches. Come evening, Pasadena turns into one big party.

JAN 1 Be in your grandstand seat early for the parade kickoff at 8am. In the afternoon, make a beeline for the Rose Bowl Game to cheer for your favorite team and join the contagious excitement.

JAN 2 View the floats in all their elaborate detail at the Post Parade Showcase of Floats. Later, visit the Norton Simon Museum to view its superb art collections.

JAN 3 Join a tour of the landmark Gamble House, Pasadena's supreme Craftsman-style dwelling. In the evening, take in a play at intimate Pasadena Playhouse, the starting point for many top-name actors.

JAN 4 Spend the day in San Marino exploring The Huntington's expansive library, art collections, and botanical gardens, taking a break in the Rose Garden Tea Room.

Dos and Don'ts

- ✓ Consider booking a package that includes accommodations, reserved grandstand seats, Rose Bowl game tickets, some meals, motorcoach transportation, and other perks.
- ✗ Don't be shocked when hugged by strangers upon first meeting – it's a Californian custom.
- ✓ Research the city's many museums in advance so you won't miss the collections that are of the most interest to you. Don't try to see everything in one visit.
- ✓ Dress stylishly if you want to get beyond the velvet rope at Pasadena's swanky bars and nightclubs.

GETTING THERE See map p329, G4
A major transport hub in South America, Rio de Janeiro is connected by direct flights to cities in Europe, Canada, and the USA. Flights are costlier during Christmas and New Year.

GETTING AROUND
Rio has an excellent subway system, but it's not safe to use after 9pm. The best way to get from Ipanema to Copacabana is by cab.

WEATHER
In December, Rio's daytime temperature range is 77–104°F (25–40°C), which drops to a minimum of 60°F (16°C) at night.

ACCOMMODATIONS
During Réveillon, most hotels offer four-night packages at much higher rates than usual.

Arpoador Inn on Ipanema Beach has expansive views, and packages from US$800; www.arpoadorinn.com.br

Ipanema Beach House offers packages from US$880; www.ipanemahouse.com

At the luxurious Fasano a four-day package costs from US$6,000; www.fasano.com.br

EATING OUT
Restaurants such as Roberta Sudbrack are pioneers in Brazilian fusion cooking. There are plenty of cheap restaurants and juice bars, too, offering *prato feito* (dish of the day) or a tropical fruit drink and snack.

FURTHER INFORMATION
www.rio.com

Iemanjá's Day

For African Brazilians practicing the religion of Candomblé, New Year's Eve is significant as Dia de Iemanjá, or Iemanjá's Day, a day spent thanking the goddess of the sea for the goodness she has brought during the year. All day and night, and especially at dawn, gifts, offerings, and messages of gratitude are put in tiny wicker baskets, which are then floated out to sea. "Magic" circles drawn into the sand are lit with candles, and devotees chant and sing to Iemanjá and other *orixá* (goddesses).

RIO DE JANEIRO

If you thought the carnival was the biggest festival of the Brazilian year, think again. The title goes to the overwhelming spectacle known as Réveillon, the annual New Year's Eve celebrations in Rio. Days before the big occasion, convoys arrive on Avenida Atlântica – the broad highway running the full length of Copacabana – to unload the tubes and boards that are ultimately transformed into vast sound stages. Banners unfurl to announce star-studded shows, visitors rush in from all over, and the beach gets even more crowded with bikini-clad women, men with toned torsos, old ladies with poodles, toddlers, and teenagers. On the day itself, as the afternoon's sun rays turn the talcum-white sands of Copacabana to a deep golden honey, the crowds start to leave and, for a while, all is quiet. Then, as the sun sinks behind the glorious statue of Christ on Corcovado, Copacabana comes alive again – Rio returns, all dressed to party. Bands plug in and the rhythmic beats of the samba, *forró*, and *pagode* dances pound through the air. Steadily, the beach fills up with millions of partygoers until the crowds spill out on to the streets. By night, every inch of Copacabana's sandy 4-mile (6-km) crescent is carpeted by dancers, and the smell of the surf is overpowered by sweat, perfume, and the fragrance of corn on the cob, coconuts, and ice-cold beer sold at stalls.

As the party fever hots up, the bands get louder and the dancing more frenetic, and just as it appears to reach its climax, the fireworks erupt, shooting into the sky in a cacophony of violets, greens, and peacock blues.

As the party fever hots up, the bands get louder and the dancing more frenetic, and just as it appears to reach its climax, the fireworks erupt, shooting into the sky in a cacophony of violets, greens, and peacock blues. The crowd roars, the drumbeats rise, and then suddenly, it's midnight. All is quiet for a while, until hundreds of streaming Roman candles and Catherine wheels pour brilliantly crackling gunpowder, phosphorus, and magnesium off the precipitous sides of a towering skyscraper, showering it with an iridescent waterfall of flame.

When dawn breaks, the crowds begin to disperse and leave the sand to the Candomblé priestesses, clad in billowy white robes. As they chant to Iemanjá, the goddess of the sea, the sun drenches the beach in a golden light, warmly heralding the first day of a brand-new year.

Main: Kaleidoscopic shower in the sky – New Year's Eve in Rio
Below (left and right): Ipanema Beach and the mountains beyond; lively samba-club performers
Inset: Ritualistic Rio – "magic" circles of sand, aglow with candlelight

Above: Christ the Redeemer, watching over Rio

BEACH PARTY DIARY

For the biggest New Year party, Rio is the place to be. About two million people from all over the world meet up to join in the celebrations and witness a spectacular display of fireworks. Four days will give you time to see a little of the city itself as well as soak in Rio's exuberant, end-of-the-year party spirit *(see p307)*.

New Year's Eve in Rio

DEC 30

The best way to get straight into holiday mode is to hit the beach. Once you arrive, check into the hotel, head to the stylish shops on Rua Visconde de Pirajá in Ipanema, and buy some Brazilian-cut swimwear.

Following a light lunch, spend a few hours simply chilling out on the beach and then sipping some refreshing coconut water in one of the beachside kiosks. In the evening, eat out in a fashionable restaurant in Leblon or the Lagoa and follow this with drinks overlooking the beach.

At 11pm or later, head to one of Lapa's vibrant samba clubs and sip on a *caipirinha* – practically the national drink of Brazil – before returning to the hotel to sleep.

DEC 31

Wake up late and gorge on a hearty Rio breakfast of French bread rolls, strong coffee, and tropical fruit juice – Suco de Açai is the best for energy. Do little for the rest of the day other than take a tour to the Christ the Redeemer statue on Corcovado. Return to the hotel to shower and put on light casuals, put some notes in your pocket but leave your wallet in the safe, and head out to the festival.

JAN 1

This is rest and recuperation day, and there's no better place to spend it than on Ipanema Beach. If you have the energy, visit Tijuca National Park, a rain forest in the heart of Rio, or take a cruise on Guanabara Bay.

JAN 2

Spend your morning on the Sugar Loaf, arriving at 8am to catch the first cable car to the top and beat the crowds. Spend the afternoon in the Botanical Gardens. Then either catch an evening flight out of Rio or spend a few more days in the city before heading home.

Dos and Don'ts

- ✓ Book a hotel at least six months in advance for New Year.
- ✗ Don't expect to get by without any Portuguese.
- ✓ Stay in Ipanema or Copacabana, the hubs of the festival.
- ✗ Don't display your wallet and camera openly when you're walking around the city.

January – June: **Festivals**

JANUARY

JAMAICA Maroon people gathering under the "kindah tree," Accompong

CANADA

Daaquam River International Dog Sled Race
Saint-Just-de-Breteneires, Québec
Mid-January
The biggest dogsled race in the world with 1,700 dogs taking part.
www.daaquam.qc.ca

USA

Mummer's Parade
Philadelphia
January 1
Parade with string bands, comic groups, and costumed revelers. It is believed to be the oldest folk festival in the USA.
www.mummers.com

Tournament of Roses Parade
Pasadena, California
January 1
Parade with hundreds of elaborate floats, marching bands, and high-stepping horses.
www.tournamentofroses.com
(See pp300–1)

Sundance Film Festival
Park City, Salt Lake City, and Sundance, Utah
Late January
Renowned showcase for independent cinema with Q&As given by leading international film-makers. Around 200 films from all over the world are screened each year. The actor and director Robert Redford is the founder and president of the festival.
www.sundance.org

Miami Art Deco Weekend
Ocean Drive, South Beach, Miami, Florida
Mid-January
Event highlighting Miami's beautiful Art Deco buildings with big band jazz, vintage car parades, and classic cinema screenings.
www.mdpl.org

CARIBBEAN

Accompong Maroon Festival
Accompong, Jamaica
January 6
Traditional independence celebration of the Maroon people.
www.visitjamaica.com/accompong-maroon-festival

MEXICO AND CENTRAL AMERICA

San Sebastian
Chiapa de Corzo, Chiapas, Mexico
January
Religious festival with a dancing parade between churches.

SOUTH AMERICA

Festival de Doma y Folklore
Jesus Maria, Córdoba, Argentina
Early–mid-January
Horse fair with rodeo contests and displays of horsemanship.
www.festival.org.ar

La Procession de La Divina Pastora (The Procession of the Divine Shepherdess)
Barquisimeto, Venezuela
January 14
Religious and folkloric parade. Worshipers and musicians accompany the statue en route.
www.alboradavenezuela.com

Feria de Alasitas
La Paz, Bolivia
January 24
Stalls sell miniatures of consumer goods to honor Ekeko, the Aymara god of abundance.

Hay Literary Festival
Cartagena, Colombia
Late January
Tropical offshoot of the famous Hay-on-Wye literary festival in a beautiful walled city.
www.hayfestival.com/cartagena
(See pp16–7)

FEBRUARY

CANADA Snow sculpture being carved at Winterlude, Ottawa

CANADA

Winterlude
Ottawa, Ontario
Early February
Wintery fun. Huge skating park and snow playground.
www.canada.pch.gc.ca
(See pp34–5)

Québec City Winter Carnival
Québec City, Québec
February
Winter party with parades, dogsled races, and ice sculptures.
www.carnaval.qc.ca

Festival du Voyageur
Winnipeg, Manitoba
Mid–late February
Winter festival celebrating French-Canadian heritage.
www.festivalvoyageur.mb.ca

USA

Groundhog Day
Punxsutawney, Pennsylvania
February 2
Phil the groundhog informs visitors when spring will begin.
www.groundhog.org

National Toboggan Championships
Camden, Maine
Mid-February
Fun, games, and a thrilling 400-ft (122-m) toboggan chute.
www.camdensnowbowl.com

Mardi Gras
New Orleans, Louisiana
Movable date, week before Lent
Carnival with parades, live street music, and non-stop partying.
www.neworleansonline.com

CARIBBEAN

Feria Internacional del Libro
Havana, Cuba
February
Important Latin American literary affair.
www.cubaliteraria.com

Holders Season
St. James, Barbados
February–April
Glamorous arts festival held in the grounds of a 17th-century plantation house.
www.holders.net

Carnival
Port of Spain, Trinidad (and smaller towns in Trinidad and Tobago)
Moveable date, week before Lent
A frenzied few days of costumed parades, soca music, and dancing in the streets.
www.ncctt.org

MEXICO AND CENTRAL AMERICA

Día de la Candelaria (Candlemass)
Tlacotalpan, Veracruz, Mexico
February 2
Tlacotalpan marks the end of the Christmas season with bull fighting and parades.

Fiesta de Virgen de Suyapa
Tegucigalpa, Honduras
February 3
The tiny statue of Honduras' patron saint is venerated by worshipers who make their way to her grand Basilica home.

SOUTH AMERICA

Carnaval
Salvador (various sites), Brazil
Moveable date, week before Lent
Carnaval is celebrated in the city of Salvador with a spectacular street festival.
www.salvadorcentral.com
(See pp50–1)

Fiesta de la Pachamama
February 6
Purmamarca, Argentina
Folk concerts, ancient rituals and mass feasts are held as the indigenous and mestizo groups pay tribute to the fertility goddess Pachamama.

MARCH

GUATEMALA Colorful procession during Semana Santa

CANADA

Beauceron Maple Festival
Saint-Georges, Québec
March
Celebrating one of Canada's major exports – maple syrup. Stands selling pancakes are abundant.
www.festivalbeaucerondelerable.com

Snowking Festival
Yellowknife, Northwest Territories
March
An expression of local spirit. Arts take center stage along with some unusual events such as a short horror film competition.
www.snowking.ca

USA

Daytona Bike Week
Daytona Beach, Florida
March
Ten-day motorcycle event with speedway, dirt track racing, stunt bike shows, biker weddings, and a blessing of bikes ceremony.
www.officialbikeweek.com

South by Southwest
Austin, Texas
March
Indie music showcase. Emerging bands perform, with new media and film festivals alongside.
(See pp58–9)

Calle Ocho
Little Havana, Miami, Florida
Mid-March
Street party hosts the region's best performers on outdoor stages. Local food and drink stalls and a huge conga line as finale.
www.carnavalmiami.com/event-view/calle-ocho

St. Patrick's Day Parade
New York and cities all over the USA, particularly Boston and Chicago
March 17
Irish parade with bagpipes, marching bands, and ubiquitous green costumes and decorations.
www.nycstpatricksparade.org
(See pp62–3)

CARIBBEAN

Oistins Fish Festival
Oistins, Barbados
March/April
Fish-boning and net-throwing competitions, cook-offs, and local calypso and reggae music.
www.barbados.org/off.htm

British Virgin Islands Spring Regatta and Sailing Festival
Nanny Cay, Tortola, BVI
March/April
World-class sailing competition that offers daytime races and after-sundown partying.
www.bvispringregatta.org

MEXICO AND CENTRAL AMERICA

Semana Santa (Holy Week)
Antigua, Guatemala (and many other areas)
Moveable date, Easter
Statues of Christ and the Virgin Mary are taken through the streets accompanied by sacred music and clouds of incense.
www.aroundantigua.com

SOUTH AMERICA

Vendimia
Mendoza, Argentina
March
Grape harvest festival with Blessing of the Grapes ceremony, parades, and lots of red wine.
www.wander-argentina/vendimia-fesitval

Festival Iberoamericano de Teatro de Colombia
Bogotá, Colombia
March
Theater festival which takes place every two years. Theater premieres, fringe plays, street shows, puppetry, and much more.
en.festivaldeteatro.com.co

APRIL

LOUISIANA, USA Musicians at Festival International de Louisiane

CANADA

Toonik Tyme
Iqualuit, Nunavut
Mid-April
The beginning of spring in the Arctic is celebrated with fascinating Inuit folklore, throat singing, igloo building, and snowmobile racing.
www.tooniktyme.com

USA

Alaska Folk Festival
Juneau, Alaska
Early–mid April
Week-long folk music festival with accordian and fiddle music, square dancing, and open performance spots.
www.akfolkfest.org

French Quarter Festival
New Orleans, Louisiana
Mid-April
Jazz music flavors this musical street party. Cajun food, patio tours, and a world champion oyster-eating contest.
www.fqfi.org

Kentucky Derby Festival
Louisville, Kentucky
Mid–late April
Lead-up to the famous Kentucky Derby horse races. It kicks off with the huge "Thunder over Louisville" firework display over the Ohio river. The month is filled with basketball, volleyball and golf tournaments, a marathon, the Pegasus Parade, the Great Steamboat Race and open-air concerts. There are also hot-air balloon events, live bed racing and the grand Fillies Derby Ball.
www.kdf.org

Festival International de Louisiane
Lafayette, Louisiana
Late April
Celebration of French cultural heritage in southern Lousiana. Free outdoor music and dance events are highlights.
www.festivalinternational.com

CARIBBEAN

Trelawney Yam Festival
Albert Town, Jamaica
Moveable date, Easter Monday
Community festival with cooking competitions, best-dressed goat, and throbbing sound systems.
www.stea.net

Buccoo Goat Race
Buccoo, Tobago
Moveable date, Easter Tuesday
Hilarious annual goat race conducted with much pomp and ceremony. Prize steeds are trained for months in advance and at the event commentators pick out potential winners at a pre-match paddock parade. Often accompanied by crab racing.
www.visittobago.gov.tt

MEXICO AND CENTRAL AMERICA

Fiesta de Centro Historico
Mexico City, Mexico
Mid–late April
Diverse and long-established arts and cultural festival in the atmospheric old center of the capital. Profits go to restoring the crumbling buildings in the area.
www.festival.org.mx

Feria de San Marcos
Aguascalientes, Mexico
April–May
Three weeks of Mexican partying in the heartland of the country. Mariachi bands, cock fights, fortune telling, and some of the best bullfighting talent in the world.
www.feriadesanmarcos.com

SOUTH AMERICA

Rupunani Rodeo
Lethem, Guyana
Easter weekend
Popular rodeo festival with cultural activities. Traditional Guyanese cowboy culture includes the energetic *faha* dance, similar to Brazilian *forro*.
www.guyana-tourism.com

MAY

PERU Dancers in elaborate masks, Señor de Qoyllur Rit'i festival

CANADA

Festival Mutek
Montréal, Québec
May–June
Workshops, performances, and showcases of electronic music and digital creativity.
www.mutek.org

Bard on the Beach
Vancouver, British Columbia
May–September
Multi-month Shakespeare festival with open-air performances in the spectacular riverside setting of Vanier Park.
www.bardonthebeach.org

USA

Sweet Auburn Springfest
Auburn, Atlanta, Georgia
Mid-May
Street festival celebrating Afro-American culture with markets, workshops, and craft displays.
www.sweetauburn.com

Spoleto Festival
Charleston, South Carolina
May–June
Upscale arts festival with classical music concerts, opera, jazz, ballet, and theater.
www.spoletousa.org

Indianapolis 500 Festival
Indianapolis, Indiana
May
Historic car race with an adrenalin-fueled atmosphere as drivers compete for the top prize and glory.
www.indy500.com

Memphis in May
Memphis, Tennessee
May
This event includes a music festival, performances by the Memphis Symphony Orchestra, and the renowned World Barbecue Championships.
www.memphisinmay.org
(See pp104–5)

Portland Rose Festival
Portland, Oregon
May–June
Festival includes floral floats, tall ships, and a children's fair.
www.rosefestival.org

CARIBBEAN

St. Lucia Jazz Festival
Pigeon Island, St. Lucia
April/May
Jazz festival with an emphasis on Afro-Caribbean performers.
www.stluciajazz.org
(See pp122–3)

Calabash International Literary Festival
Treasure Beach, Jamaica
Late May
Free literary event. Readings, seminars, and discussions.
www.calabashfestival.org

Crop Over
Barbados
May–June
Celebrating the end of the sugar cane harvest. Don't miss the Pic-O-De-Crop contest.
www.barbados.org

SOUTH AMERICA

Día de las Glorias Navales
Valparaiso, Chile
May 21
Speeches and processions to celebrate Chile's naval success at the Battle of Iquique.

La Diablada
Puno, Peru
May
Drinking, dancing, and devilish costumes in a day of parades and water fighting.
www.peru-explorer.com

Señor de Qoyllur Rit'i
Cusco, Peru
Moveable date, begins a week before Corpus Christi
Traditional festival sees pilgrims heading up to an icy glacier to camp out under the stars.
www.cuscoperu.com

JUNE

PERU Locals dressed in warrior costume, Inti Raymi Festival of the Sun, Cusco

CANADA

Adäka Cultural Festival
Whitehorse, Yukon
Late June
The "coming into the light" festival celebrates and fosters Yukon's First Nations culture.
www.adakafestival.ca

Montréal Jazz Festival
Montréal, Québec
June–July
Largest jazz festival in the world with over 3,000 artists and 450 free concerts. Book tickets for headlining acts well in advance.
www.montrealjazzfest.com

USA

Chicago Blues Festival
Grant Park, Chicago
Early–mid-June
The largest free outdoors blues music event in the world with six stages and 90 performers.
www.cityofchicago.org
(See pp130–31)

Country Music Association Festival
Nashville, Tennessee
Early–mid-June
"Country music's biggest party" with hundreds of great performers and an emphasis on artist/fan interaction.
www.cmaworld.com

International Festival of Arts and Ideas
New Haven, Connecticut
June
Arts festival with thinkers and philosophers as well as stars of opera, dance, jazz, classical music, and experimental performances.
www.artidea.org

Telluride Bluegrass Festival
Telluride, Colorado
Mid-June
Accessible and intimate folk festival with songwriting contests and jamming sessions in a picturesque mountain town.
www.bluegrass.com/telluride

CARIBBEAN

Noche de San Juan
San Juan, Puerto Rico
June 23
Celebration of midsummer and St John the Baptist's feast day with beach parties, bonfires, and numerous superstitious activities – principally running backwards into the sea which is supposed to bring good luck.
www.discoveringpuertorico.com

Vincy Mas
Kingstown, St. Vincent
June–July
Summer carnival fun in St. Vincent and its smaller islands, the Grenadines, with colorful parades, soca music, and costumed revelers.
www.carnivalsvg.com

SOUTH AMERICA

Bumba Meu Boi
São Luis, Maranhão, Brazil
June
Bizarre festival where animal costumes are donned to recreate the folk story of an ox which dies and then comes back to life. Noisy percussion accompanies the dance-drama.
www.maria-brazil.org

Inti Raymi Festival of the Sun
Cusco, Peru
June 24
Important Inca festival of the Sun performed by costumed actors in Cusco in the Peruvian Andes.
www.cuscoperu.com

International Fishing Festival
Caceres, Mato Grosso, Brazil
September
Huge fishing competitions on the banks of the river Paraguay. Boat shows, folkloric dancing, local gastronomy, and music add color.
www.pantanalescapes.com

July – December: **Festivals**

JULY

MEXICO Young dancers in the Guelaguetza Festival procession, Oaxaca

CANADA

Calgary Stampede
Calgary, Alberta
Early–mid-July
Rodeo competition, chuckwagon races, and blacksmithing contests.
www.calgarystampede.com
(See pp168–9)

Just for Laughs Comedy Festival
Montréal, Québec
July
Festival of stand-up comedy with the best international humorists.
www.hahaha.com/en

Seafest
Yarmouth, Nova Scotia
July
Pageants, parades, races, cruises, storytelling sessions, a lobster boil and chowder cook-off.
www.seafest.ca

Great Northern Arts Festival
Inuvik, Northwest Territories
Mid-July
Festival with performing artists from the First Nation communities.
www.gnaf.org

Honda Celebration of Light
Vancouver, British Columbia
Late July
Fireworks contest. Displays of the latest techniques and materials.
www.hondacelebrationoflight.com

USA

Hopi Festival of Arts and Culture
Flagstaff, Arizona
Early July
Native American storytelling, music, dance, and crafts at the Museum of North Arizona.
www.musnaz.org

Cheyenne Frontier Days
Cheyenne, Wyoming
Late July
Rodeo competitions, music, and historical re-enactments.
www.cfdrodeo.com

Vectren Dayton Air Show
Vandalia, Ohio
July
America's largest air show with static planes and aerial stunts.
www.daytonairshow.com

Newport Folk Festival
Newport, Rhode Island
End of July
Folk music galore at this American institution.
www.newportfolk.org

Santa Fe Chamber Music Festival
Santa Fe, New Mexico
July–August
Performances from some of the finest orchestras and musicians.
www.sfcmf.org

CARIBBEAN

Reggae Sumfest
Montego Bay, Jamaica
Mid-July
Reggae festival with international acts and local performers.
www.reggaesumfest.com

Carriacou Regatta
Carriacou, Grenada
End of July
Yachting festival with locally built "workboats" and entertainment.
www.grenadaexplorer.com

MEXICO AND CENTRAL AMERICA

Guelaguetza
Oaxaca, Mexico
Last two Mondays of July
Prehispanic harvest festival of thanksgiving and prayers.
www.visitmexico.com/en/oaxaca

SOUTH AMERICA

Fiesta de la Virgen del Carmen
La Tirana, Chile
Mid-July
Festival honoring an indigenous woman converting to Catholicism.
www.chile.travel

AUGUST

CANADA Crowds at the Edmonton Folk Festival

CANADA

Edmonton Folk Festival
Edmonton, Alberta
2nd weekend in August
Variety of international folk music is performed in pretty parkland setting.
www.edmontonfolkfest.org

Opaskwayak Indian Days
Opaskwayak, Manitoba
Third Week in August
Vibrant festival held by and about the local Cree Indian community.
www.aboriginalmusic.ca

Winona Peach Festival
Winona, Ontario
Late August
Produce fair with children's entertainers, live music and craft stalls. Also includes the Grand Peach Ball.
www.winonapeach.com

USA

Wisconsin State Fair
West Allis, Wisconsin
Early August
Festival with pig racing, moo-ing contests, and fairground rides. Fun for all the family.
www.wistatefair.com
(See pp182–3)

Tennessee Walking Horse National Celebrations
Shelbyville, Tennessee
Late August
Comprehensive rodeo contest, blacksmith competition, and barn decorating contest.
www.twhnc.com

CARIBBEAN

Festival of Women Cooks
Pointe-á-Pitre, Guadeloupe
August
Women cooks parade through the streets with baskets of home-cooked food.
www.antilles-info-tourisme.com

Merengue Festival & Caribbean Rhythms
Santo Domingo, Dominican Republic
Last week of August
Merengue fans gather for a week of celebrations.
(See p176–7)

MEXICO AND CENTRAL AMERICA

Fiestas Agostinas
San Salvador, El Salvador
First week of August
Celebrating the country's patron saint, El Salvador del Mundo.
www.elsalvador.com

Crab Soup Festival
Corn Islands, Nicaragua
End of August
Marking the end of slavery with parades and sporting contests.
www.nicaragua.com

Fiesta de los Mariachis
Guadalajara, Jalisco, Mexico
August–September
Shows by some of the finest performers of mariachi music.
www.mariachi-jalisco.com.mx

SOUTH AMERICA

Anniversario de la Fundacion de Asunción
Asunción, Paraguay
August
Demonstrations of local cuisine and traditions.
www.senatur.gov.py

Festa do Peão Boiadeiro
Barretos, São Paulo, Brazil
Late August
Rodeo and cowboy festival in the south of the country.
www.independentes.com.br
(See pp202–3)

Tango Buenos Aires Festival & Mundial
Buenos Aires, Argentina
August
Skilled dancers compete. Free concerts and dance classes are also part of the festival.
festivales.buenosaires.gob.ar

SEPTEMBER

HAWAI'I, USA Parade during the Annual Floral Parade

CANADA

Vancouver Fringe Festival
Vancouver, British Columbia
September
Ten days of offbeat theater with over 500 different shows as well as workshops and talks.
www.vancouverfringe.com

Toronto International Film Festival
Toronto, Ontario
Mid-September
North America's premier film festival with industry showcases as well as public screenings.
www.tiff.net

Ottawa International Animation Festival
Ottawa, Ontario
September/October
Festival of animated film with top-notch guest animators, displays of the latest technology, and over 2,000 screenings.
www.animationfestival.ca

USA

Annual Floral Parade
Honolulu, Hawai'i
Late September
The procession, with marching bands, Hawaiian horseback riders and floats covered in native flowers, has been conducted for the past seven decades.
www.alohafestivals.com

Boardwalk Weekend/ Neptune Festival
Virginia Beach, Virginia
Late September
Weekend finale of summer festival. Sporting events, sand-sculpting competition, live music, and local produce stalls.
www.neptunefestival.com

Bumbershoot
Seattle, Washington
Labor Day weekend Arts festival with music, comedy, theater, film, dance performances, and visual arts.
www.bumbershoot.org

MEXICO AND CENTRAL AMERICA

Belize Independence Day
Belize City, Belize
September
Three weeks of all-night parties, carnival parades, and celebrations.
www.belize.com

Independence Day
Nationwide, Mexico
September 15 & 16
At 11pm each September 15, the Mexican president rings the Liberty Bell in Mexico City with a cry of "Mexicanos, viva Mexico." September 16 is a day of speeches, military parades, and general festivities.
www.visitmexico.com

SOUTH AMERICA

Yamor Fiesta
Otavalo, Ecuador
Early–mid-September
Highland harvest festival with music, processions, fireworks, carnival queens, and much drinking. Yamor is the name of a toxic drink made from seven kinds of corn.
www.ecuador.com

CARIBBEAN

Bonaire Day
Bonaire, Dutch Antilles
September 6
Independence Day starts with a drum and bugle corps performance, and evolves into a series of all-day block parties, with local foods, crafts and other perfomances.
www.infobonaire.com

SOUTH AMERICA

Eisteddfod
Gaiman, Argentina
Early September
Patagonia celebrates its immigrant heritage with this ancient festival of Welsh culture. Music, art, photography and literature feature.
(See pp72–3)

OCTOBER

NEW MEXICO, USA Balloons fill the sky, Albuquerque Balloon Fiesta

CANADA

Okanagan Wine Festival
Okanagan Valley, British Columbia
Early October
Sample over 60 different wines from across the valley, as well as enjoying live music and local food.
www.thewinefestivals.com

Oktoberfest
Kitchener-Waterloo, Ontario
October
The largest Bavarian festival outside of Germany. As well as 17 *festhallen* and 40 events, there is also a Thanksgiving Day parade.
www.oktoberfest.ca

USA

Albuquerque International Balloon Fiesta
Albuquerque, New Mexico
Early October
World's largest balloon event. Special shape competitions and serious balloon races.
www.balloonfiesta.com
(See pp242–3)

Big Pig Jig
Vienna, Georgia
October/November
Pork cooking contest. Live animals also with hog calling and piggy parades.
www.bigpigjig.com

Northeast Kingdom Fall Foliage Festival
Various towns, Northeast Kingdom, Vermont
End of September/early October
Festival celebrating spectacular leaf fall in seven Vermont towns.
www.nekchamber.com

Parke County Covered Bridge Festival
Rockville, Indiana
Mid-October
Daily bus tours over the weekend of nine local communities with covered bridges, arts and crafts vendors, and food stands.
www.coveredbridges.com

Fantasy Fest
Key West, Florida
Late October
Camp parades, outrageous fancy dress costumes, and rum cocktails characterize this festival. The theme of the event changes every year so be sure to wear an appropriate outfit.
www.fantasyfest.com

CARIBBEAN

National Warri Festival
St. Johns, Antigua
First week in October
Championships of Antiguan board game which involves shuffling beads around a hollowed out fish-shaped board.
www.antigua-barbuda.org

World Creole Music Festival
Roseau, Dominica
October
Three days of pulsating sounds with performers from the Creole-speaking world and beyond.
www.wcmfdominica.com

MEXICO AND CENTRAL AMERICA

Festival of the Black Christ
Portobelo, Panama
October 21
Worshipers from far and wide crawl along the route, some flagellating themselves, to the shrine of the dark-skinned Christ, patron saint of singers. Food and drink stalls line the way.
www.coloncity.com/blackchrist.html

SOUTH AMERICA

Círio de Nazaré
Belém, Brazil
Second half of October
Belém's Virgin Mary is carted around the town in a grave procession which is followed by a fortnight of drinking and general revelry.
www.ciriodenazare.com.br

NOVEMBER

GUATEMALA Traditional horseback race, Dia de Todos Santos

CANADA

Canadian Western Agribition
Regina, Saskatchewan
Late November
Huge livestock fair with thousands of animals, a rodeo, and country music.
www.agribition.com

Banff Lake Louise Winterstart Festival
Banff, Alberta
November–December
Several weeks of entertainment in the Canadian Rockies with emphasis on winter sports – snowboarding and skiing. Film screenings, parades, and gigs feature too.
www.banfflakelouise.com

USA

Lady of the Lakes Renaissance Fair
Tavares, Florida
Early November
The best of medieval fairs with costumed revelers, jugglers, jousters, and all manner of games.
www.medievalfest.com

Gatlinburg Winter Magic
Gatlinburg, Tennessee
November–February
The city is lit up with over three million fairy lights. Traditional hay rides and a spectacular parade are both highlights.
www.gatlinburgwintermagic.com

CARIBBEAN

Pirates' Week
George Town, Grand Cayman, Cayman Islands
Early–mid-November
Boat races, fancy dress competitions, a mock pirate invasion, and more make this week-long celebration of the Cayman Islands' heritage particularly popular with young children.
www.pirateweekfestival.com

Gimistory
Grand Cayman, Cayman Islands
November–December
Storytelling in island-wide venues with calypso accompaniment and free *swank* (lemonade) and fishcakes served up to both audience and performers alike.
www.cayman.com

MEXICO AND CENTRAL AMERICA

Dia de Todos Santos
Todos Santos de Cuchumatanes, Guatemala
November 1
All Saints' Day celebrated in the highlands with an anarchic horse race. Bareback jockeys get drunker and drunker as the day wears on and cling ever tighter to their mounts while they tear through the town. Firecrackers, firewater, and marimba music in abundance.

Day of the Dead
Pátzcuaro, Michoacan, Mexico
November 1 & 2
Celebrated all over Mexico, the candle-lit cemetery vigils when the dead are remembered with flowers, sweets, and singing are particularly moving on the lake island of Janitzio.
www.patzcuaromexico.com

Garifuna Settlement Day
Dangriga, Belize
November 19
A celebration of the arrival of the Garifuna, an escaped slave community from St. Vincent who have retained their African roots. The actual landing is re-enacted with small fishing boats, laden with banana leaves and palm fronds, riding the surf into the Belizean shore. Traditional *punta* rock music, drumming, dancing, and general merriment.
www.ngcbelize.org

DECEMBER

BRAZIL Spectacular New Year's fireworks, Copacabana beach, Rio

CARIBBEAN

Festival of New Latin American Cinema
Havana, Cuba
Early–mid-December
Major Latin American cinema showcase with world premieres.
www.cuba-culture.com/new-latin-american-cinema

Junkanoo
Nassau, New Providence, Bahamas
December 26
Carnivalesque parade commemorating slave hero John Canoe, lasting from 2am to 9am.
www.bahamasgateway.com/junkanoo.htm

MEXICO AND CENTRAL AMERICA

La Purísima
Countrywide, Nicaragua
December 8
The Virgin Mary is honored with a collective cry (La Griteria) on December 7 at 6pm.
www.vianica.com

Quema del Diablo (Burning of the Devil)
Guatemala City, Guatemala
December 7
The start of the Christmas season is marked by the burning of household junk on the streets.
www.guatemala.com

Día de la Virgen de Guadalupe
Mexico City, Mexico
December 12
Worshipers mark the day of the symbol of Mexico. Some shuffle on their knees to Tepeyac where she was first sighted.
www.virgendeguadalupe.org.mx

Fiesta de San Cristobal de las Casas
San Cristobal de las Casas, Chiapas
December
Town festival with processions by Tzotzil and Tzetzal Indians.
www.visitmexico.com

Fiesta de Santo Tomas
Chichicastenango, Guatemala
December 21
Festival in Guatemala's highlands. Parades, marimba music, indigenous clothing, fireworks, and lots of local firewater.
www.visitguatemala.com

Noche de los Rabanos (Night of the Radishes)
Oaxaca, Mexico
December 23
The central square in Oaxaca is set up with stalls displaying radishes carved in all manner of intricate shapes.
www.visitmexico.com/en/oaxaca

Fiesta de los Diablitos (Festival of the Devils)
San Isidro del General, Costa Rica
December/January
Festival which recreates a fight to the death between the Indians (the Diablitos) and the Spaniards, represented by a bull. Traditional music provides atmosphere.
www.costarica.com

SOUTH AMERICA

Feria de Cali
Cali, Colombia
December
Summer festival with an emphasis on salsa dancing. Concerts, parades, and high energy merriment.
www.feriadecali.com

Surifesta
Paramaribo, Suriname
December–January
Several weeks of street parties in December, including New Year's Eve.
www.surifesta.com

Réveillon/New Year's Eve
Rio de Janeiro, Brazil
December 31
Celebrations on Copacabana Beach with party-goers dressed head to toe in white, for purity and new beginnings.
www.brazilmax.com
(See pp302–3)

Travel and the Environment

GETTING THERE
The impact of air travel and tourism on the global environment has been well publicized but there are ways to limit the damaging effects of your own travels. Consider trains and ships as alternatives to flying. If flights are unavoidable, look at carbon offsetting or the trips offered by Better World Travel, and other ecologically aware operators.

CARBON OFFSETTING SCHEMES
These enable you to "offset" the effects of carbon emissions by planting sustainable forests or contributing to biodiversity schemes that notionally "match" the amount of CO2 you've generated. Organizations like Better World, Carbon Neutral, and Climate Care offer assistance on making an offset contribution.

HIGH- AND LOW-IMPACT TOURISM
Tourism also directly affects the ecology and local economy of the destination countries. Major resort complexes can damage the landscape and local infrastructure. Not all resorts are the same but don't be afraid to ask questions, such as: how is waste disposed of? Where does their energy come from?

Locally run hotels and tour operations often have a more positive impact, especially if they use zero-impact bathrooms and other environmentally friendly features. The best will work with local communities and guides so that locals have alternatives to harmful practices like deforestation and strip-farming.

Trips to see wildlife and into remote areas should be made in small groups, with local guides, not in big bus tours. It is not only the environment that gains by this – it will also give you a far more memorable experience.

Better World Club
www.betterworldclub.com
Carbon Neutral
www.carbonneutral.com
Climate Care
www.climatecare.org
Responsible Travel
www.responsibletravel.com

Think Global, Shop Local

Spread the financial benefits of tourism by shopping for souvenirs in local shops and markets, instead of hotel stores and large malls. A little research on the customs of the country you're visiting and a few courteous questions will reduce any language barriers. Do not assume that everything you buy should be very cheap because you're in a poor country: people have a right to be paid for their work. And – avoiding the cheapest, shabbiest places – eat in local restaurants rather than those set aside for tourists. The food will usually be more interesting.

Above (left to right): ATM machine in Orlando, Florida; taxis on a New York street; hiking a trail on O'ahu, Hawai'i

TRAVEL INFORMATION

WEBSITES, ONLINE BOOKING, and all the other developments in modern travel and communications, have made every part of the Americas more accessible than ever before. But, to make the most of your trip, you should attend to certain details before you set off – border formalities, insurance, how you're going to travel around, and so on. By doing a little planning you can save yourself money and minimize the chances of something going wrong.

TRAVEL SAFETY ADVICE

UK Foreign and Commonwealth Office
www.gov.uk/foreign-travel-advice
US Department of State
travel.state.gov/
Australia Department of Foreign Affairs and Trade
dfat.gov.au/
smartraveller.gov.au/

Visitors can get up-to-date travel safety information from the Foreign and Commonwealth Office in the UK, the State Department in the US and the Department of Foreign Affairs and Trade in Australia.

USA & CANADA

HEALTH AND MEDICAL INSURANCE

American Express www.americanexpress.com
MD Travel Health www.mdtravelhealth.com
Travel Guard www.travelguard.com

It is essential to have travel and medical insurance. Health facilities are extremely expensive. If you plan to do any sports, you should check that these are covered too.

PERSONAL SECURITY

Foreign & Commonwealth Office www.fco.gov.uk
US State Department www.travel.state.gov

Avoid dark or deserted streets and keep valuables hidden. Carry photocopies of important documents and lock away the originals. If you are a victim of crime, report it to the police and keep a copy of the statement for your insurance claim. Report missing passports to your country's consulate.

PASSPORTS AND VISAS

Canada Government www.canadainternational.gc.ca
US State Department www.travel.state.gov

Citizens of many Western countries can enter the USA without a visa under the Visa Waiver Program (VWP), with a machine-readable passport (with a biometric chip). Anyone else must obtain the correct visa in advance. VWP entry is for 90 days only – for longer trips a visa must be obtained in advance. Citizens of many countries can also enter Canada without a visa. Check government websites for details.

MONEY AND COMMUNICATIONS

Travelex www.travelex.com

A major credit or debit card is needed for big transactions. There's usually a fee for withdrawing cash from ATMs.

Internet cafés are common, and many hotels have internet access.

GETTING AROUND

There are hundreds of airports in North America, and many budget airlines serving the country.

Buses are the cheapest alternative to air travel. Greyhound has the largest long-distance network, and offers an unlimited-travel Discovery Pass.

Train travel, though extremely time consuming for long distances, is the best overland option in many cases. Trains are operated in the USA by Amtrak and by Via Rail in Canada. Unlimited passes are available from each, covering one or both countries.

In many parts of North America a car is indispensable. Rental rates are better if you book ahead. Many nations' driving licenses are valid in the USA, but for Canada an International Driving License, available from drivers' organizations, is recommended. To take a vehicle across the USA–Canadian border, you must show an insurance certificate. Vehicles rented in the USA may not be taken into Mexico.

THE WESTERN HEMISPHERE TRAVEL INITIATIVE (WHTI)

The WHTI is a system for regulating travel between the USA and its neighbors (except Haiti and Cuba). Under the WHTI, full passports are obligatory for air travel between the participant countries. For land or sea borders, a full passport or other WHTI-compliant document (such as the US Passport Card and the US-Canadian NEXUS card) are permitted. For the full list of acceptable documents, see government websites.

MEXICO, CENTRAL & SOUTH AMERICA

HEALTH AND MEDICAL INSURANCE

MD Travel Health www.mdtravelhealth.com

Full travel and medical insurance is essential, with additional cover for adventure sports. In most cities and tourist areas there are high-quality private clinics, nearly always with English-speaking staff. Elsewhere, facilities are scarce. Many countries have public health clinics which can provide basic emergency treatment, but your insurance should cover evacuation to a fully equipped hospital, or repatriation.

Check current health guidelines before you travel. You should at least be immunized again hepatitis A and B, typhoid, tetanus, and diphtheria. In tropical forest areas there may be a risk of yellow fever and/or malaria, and insect repellent is vital. In the High Andes, altitude sickness is a risk. The most common problems, though, are stomach ailments. Drink bottled water and pack anti-diarrhea medications, along with bite lotion, antiseptic cream and wipes, and dressings for cuts and scratches.

PERSONAL SECURITY

Foreign & Commonwealth Office www.fco.gov.uk
US State Department www.travel.state.gov

Apply the same rules as for North America, but be even more vigilant. There are high levels of crime in many cities, and bag-snatching is common. Extra caution is needed, especially on public transport. If you are a victim of crime, report it to the police straight away and keep a copy of the statement for your insurance. Report missing passports to your country's consulate.

PASSPORTS AND VISAS

Foreign & Commonwealth Office www.fco.gov.uk
US State Department www.travel.state.gov

North American citizens can enter Mexico by land or sea (including from cruise ships) with a birth certificate and photo ID, but to re-enter, a passport or other WHTI-compliant document is needed. A full passport is needed to travel by air. A Mexican Tourist Card (FMT), marked at immigration with the length of your permitted stay, is required by some North American visitors in some circumstances. Check government websites for details. Citizens of many countries do not need a visa to enter Mexico, but must have full passports and an FMT card.

For many travelers, a visa is not needed for stays of up to 90 days in most other Latin American countries, just a full passport valid for at least six months after the date of entry. Citizens of the USA, Canada, and Australia must get visas in advance to visit Brazil or Paraguay, and US citizens need visas to enter Bolivia. Americans must also have visas to visit Chile, obtained on arrival. For details of entry requirements, check the website of the embassy of the relevant country before traveling.

MONEY AND COMMUNICATIONS

Travelex www.travelex.com

A major credit or debit card is useful. ATMs are common in Latin America, even in small towns, but the efficiency of the network varies; and not all cards are accepted by all machines. Carry some dollars or euros and US travelers' checks as back-up. In remote areas you may need to take enough local currency for the whole trip, but keep it in a money belt, out of sight. Use cards only for payments to larger businesses, such as car rental agencies. It is essential to notify your card company that you are traveling to Latin America. Concerns about fraud and money-laundering mean that unauthorized use might result in your account being frozen.

Internet cafés are common, and pay-phone cards are usually sold at convenience stores. Phone offices, where the number is dialed for you, are cheaper for long-distance calls. Most cell (mobile) phones in Latin America work on similar frequencies to those used in North America.

DIRECTORY OF USEFUL CONTACTS

USA & CANADA

Adventure Finder
www.adventurefinder.com
Links to sites for every type of active sport, worldwide

Adventure Sports Online
www.adventuresportsonline.com
Directory of worldwide adventure travel options

Adventure Travel Trade Association
www.adventuretravel.biz
Adventure travel trade website

Amtrak
www.amtrak.com

Australian Department of Foreign Affairs and Trade
dfat.gov.au
www.smartraveller.gov.au
Information for travelers

Better World Club
www.betterworldclub.com
Environmentally friendly travel services, such as carbon offsetting

BootsnAll
www.bootsnall.com
A wide range of resources for independent travelers

Budget Airline Guide
www.budgetairlineguide.com
Guide to low-cost airlines in the USA and Canada

The Bus Station
www.busstation.net
A country-by-country guide to bus services worldwide

Canada Travel
www.canada.travel.
Official tourist information site

Canadian Department of Foreign Affairs and International Trade
www.dfait-maeci.gc.ca
Travel advice and consulate details

Centers for Disease Control & Prevention (CDC)
www.cdc.gov/travel
Health information for travelers including lists of travel health clinics throughout the USA

Coach USA; Coach Canada
www.coachusa.com
Bus routes in northeast and mid-west US, Ontario, and Québec

Dogtag Worldwide Assistance
www.dogtag.com
UK-based sports and adventure-travel insurance specialists

Greyhound Bus Company
www.greyhound.com

GSM World
www.gsma.com
Cell phone information and worldwide frequency guide

International Association for Medical Assistance to Travellers
www.iamat.org
Non-profit-making organization and a good information source

Magellan's Travel Supplies
www.magellans.com
Travel clothing and equipment

The Man in Seat 61
www.seat61.com
A worldwide guide to rail and other alternatives to air travel

MD Travel Health
www.mdtravelhealth.com
User-friendly worldwide travel health information and resources

Motor Coach Canada
www.motorcoachcanada.com.
Local bus routes across Canada

Nomad Travel
www.nomadtravel.co.uk
UK-based travel health advice and on-site vaccination clinics

Oanda Currency Converter
www.oanda.com/currency/converter
Quick currency converter

Official Airline Guide
www.oag.com
Worldwide flight and airport information

Responsible Travel
www.responsibletravel.com
One of the world's largest agents for eco- and socially aware travel

Scuba Spots Diving Directory
www.scubaspots.com
Diving operators, courses, and facilities worldwide

Travel Insurance Center
www.worldtravelcenter.com
Worldwide travel insurance

UK Foreign & Commonwealth Office
www.fco.gov.uk
Travel advice and warnings

US National Hurricane Center
www.nhc.noaa.gov

US State Department
www.travel.state.gov

Via Rail Canada
www.viarail.ca

Wi-fi Free Spot
www.wififreespot.com
Comprehensive guide to Wi-Fi and hotspots around the world

World Nomads
www.worldnomads.com
Insurance for independent and adventure travelers worldwide

Worldtravellers
www.worldtravellers.com
Directory of information on all kinds of travel worldwide

MEXICO, CENTRAL & SOUTH AMERICA

Adventure Mexican Insurance
www.mexadventure.com
Insurance for US and Canadian vehicles, and boats, in Mexico

Exito Travel
www.exitotravel.com
Latin American travel specialists

GOL Brazil/GOL South America
www.allairpass.com
Only available for travel in South America.

Latin American Travel Association
www.lata.org
Trade organization of UK-based Latin-America tour companies

Mexico Online
www.mexonline.com
Guide to traveling in Mexico

Planeta
www.planeta.com
Information on eco-tourism in Mexico and elsewhere

What Latin America
www.whatlatinamerica.com
Travel information for Latin America and the Caribbean

THE CARIBBEAN

Caribbean Travel
www.caribbeantravel.com
Official Caribbean tourism website

Leeward Airlines Air Transport
www.liat.com
Inter-island flights throughout the eastern Caribbean

Above (left to right): Train to Machu Picchu at Aguas Calientes, Peru; Internet café in Cancún, Mexico; cruise ship entering the harbor of Castries, St. Lucia

GETTING AROUND

Domestic and regional flights can be expensive. The GOL South America and GOL Brazil Airpass *(see p309)* are the most comprehensive discount tickets, but are for non-Americans only and must be purchased in advance.

Argentina, Bolivia, Peru, and Ecuador still have sizeable railroad networks, but elsewhere in Latin America services are scarce, and there are few long-distance trains. Buses are the main form of land transport, with services even to the smallest village. Check local infomation for details.

There are stringent restrictions on driving your own vehicle in Mexico, including import permits, a bond to prevent selling, and local insurance. Most other Latin American countries have their own temporary import procedures, so check carefully in every instance.

Cars rented in the USA or Canada cannot usually be taken into Mexico, but there are plenty of rental agencies in the country to choose from. Local agencies in Latin America often give better rates than the international franchises, so shop around. Due to chaotic traffic it's inadvisable (and slow) to drive in many cities, but a vehicle is often a must for exploring villages, beaches, and pre-Hispanic ruins. In remote and mountainous areas, it may be better to rent a car with a driver, or to take advantage of the many small-group tours offered by local agencies.

THE CARIBBEAN

HEALTH AND MEDICAL INSURANCE

MD Travel Health www.mdtravelhealth.com

Comprehensive travel and medical insurance is essential. Most Caribbean countries have good-standard public or private hospitals in main towns, but foreigners must pay for treatment. Few are equipped to deal with serious injuries, so your insurance must cover air evacuation to the USA or your home country. Foreigners using the Cuban health service must pay in hard currency, not Cuban pesos.

Check current inoculation and health advice for your destination. The only problems most travelers have to deal with are stomach upsets and insect bites.

PERSONAL SECURITY

Foreign & Commonwealth Office www.fco.gov.uk
US State Department www.travel.state.gov

Be on your guard against petty street and car crime. Tourist areas attract opportunist criminals who rob from villas and beaches, and some cities have high levels of crime.

If you are a victim of crime, report it to the police immediately and keep a copy of the police statement for an insurance claim. Report lost or stolen passports to your country's consulate.

PASSPORTS AND VISAS

Foreign & Commonwealth Office www.fco.gov.uk
US State Department www.travel.state.gov

For citizens of most Western countries, no visa is required for stays of up to 90 days in most Caribbean states. US and Canadian nationals need a passport to enter by air, but can travel to, and return from, many Caribbean countries by sea with any WHTI-compliant document. However, the State Department recommends a full passport to avoid confusion. Non-US citizens who travel via the USA must meet US entry requirements.

All visitors to Cuba must have a visa. This can usually be obtained for a small fee from the travel company arranging your trip. US citizens are currently not allowed to visit Cuba except under special circumstances, though this may change in the future.

MONEY AND COMMUNICATIONS

Travelex www.travelex.com

Local currencies are often linked to the US dollar, but French islands use the euro. A major credit or debit card is useful. ATMs are scarce on some islands, but you can withdraw cash against a card at bank counters. Bring some cash and travelers' checks as back-up, nearly always in US dollars.

For Cuba, avoid US-related cards, cash, and traveler's checks. There are currently few ATMs, and the street economy is cash-only. Many traders prefer to be paid in hard currency (sterling or euros) rather than pesos.

Internet cafés are common except in Cuba, where hotels are the likeliest place to find Internet access. Most countries, including Cuba, sell pay-phone cards; cell (mobile) phone coverage is extensive across the islands, and restrictions in Cuba have now been lifted.

GETTING AROUND

The Caribbean's main hub airports are in Jamaica, the Dominican Republic, Puerto Rico, Antigua, and Trinidad, from where local airlines link to other islands. Check for local discount deals before traveling. Cuba has direct flights from many countries; the quickest and cheapest route is from Cancún.

Ferry services link many islands, but there is no ferry guide for the whole region. Each island has bus services, and most have agencies offering rental transport, often with some restrictions. In former British territories, vehicles drive on the left.

HURRICANE SEASON

The North Atlantic hurricane season officially runs from June to November, and affects the whole of the Caribbean, Central America, the Gulf of Mexico, and the eastern seaboard of the United States. During the season the timing, strength, and route of storms cannot be predicted more than a few days in advance, but some major storms are likely each year. The best source of information on everything to do with hurricanes and tropical storms, including the progress of a storm if you think it is likely to threaten your trip or your destination, is the US National Hurricane Center.

Atlas of the Americas

The map references given for all entries in the book refer to the maps in this section.

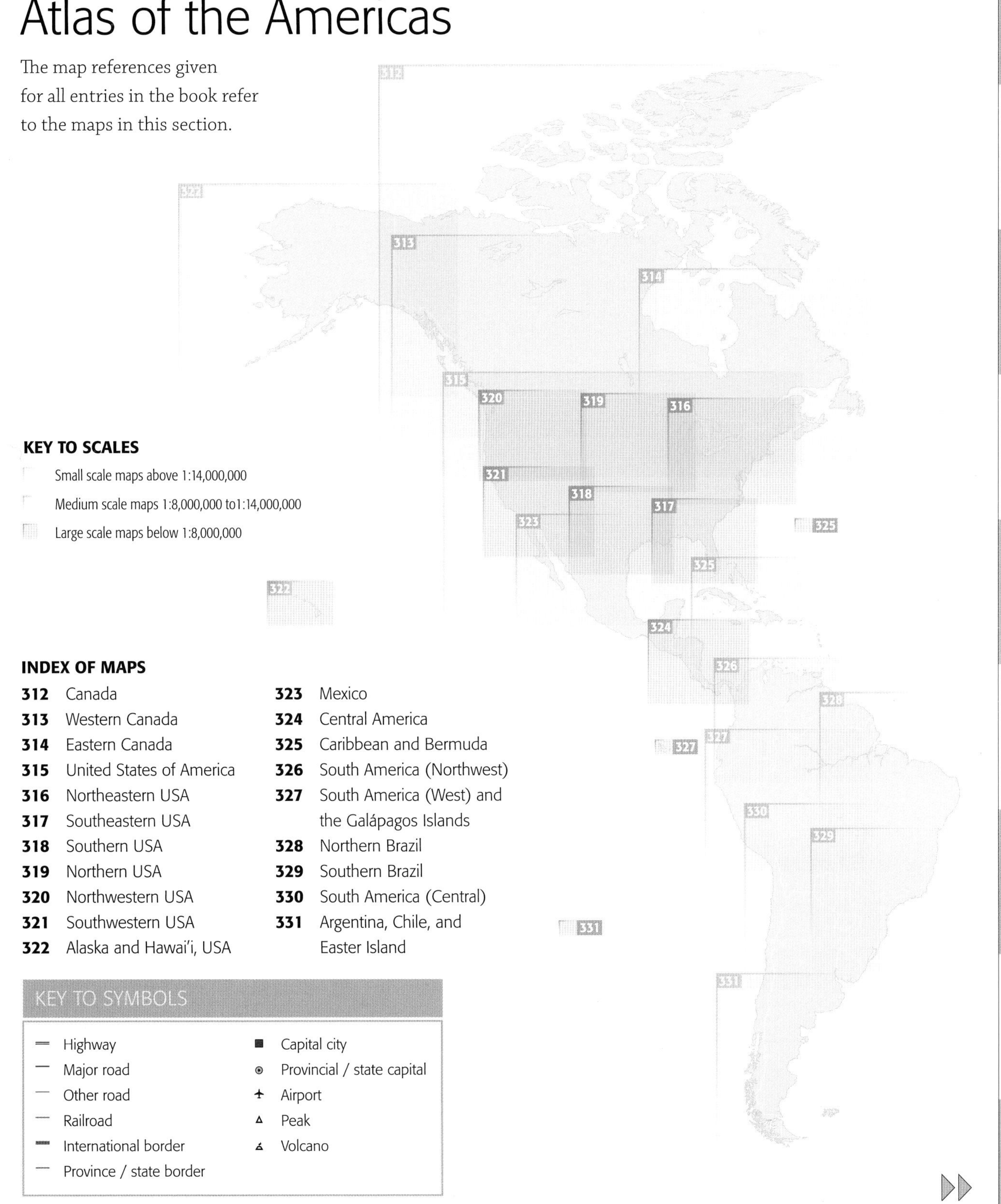

KEY TO SCALES

Small scale maps above 1:14,000,000

Medium scale maps 1:8,000,000 to1:14,000,000

Large scale maps below 1:8,000,000

INDEX OF MAPS

312 Canada
313 Western Canada
314 Eastern Canada
315 United States of America
316 Northeastern USA
317 Southeastern USA
318 Southern USA
319 Northern USA
320 Northwestern USA
321 Southwestern USA
322 Alaska and Hawai'i, USA
323 Mexico
324 Central America
325 Caribbean and Bermuda
326 South America (Northwest)
327 South America (West) and the Galápagos Islands
328 Northern Brazil
329 Southern Brazil
330 South America (Central)
331 Argentina, Chile, and Easter Island

KEY TO SYMBOLS

- Highway
- Major road
- Other road
- Railroad
- International border
- Province / state border
- Capital city
- Provincial / state capital
- Airport
- Peak
- Volcano

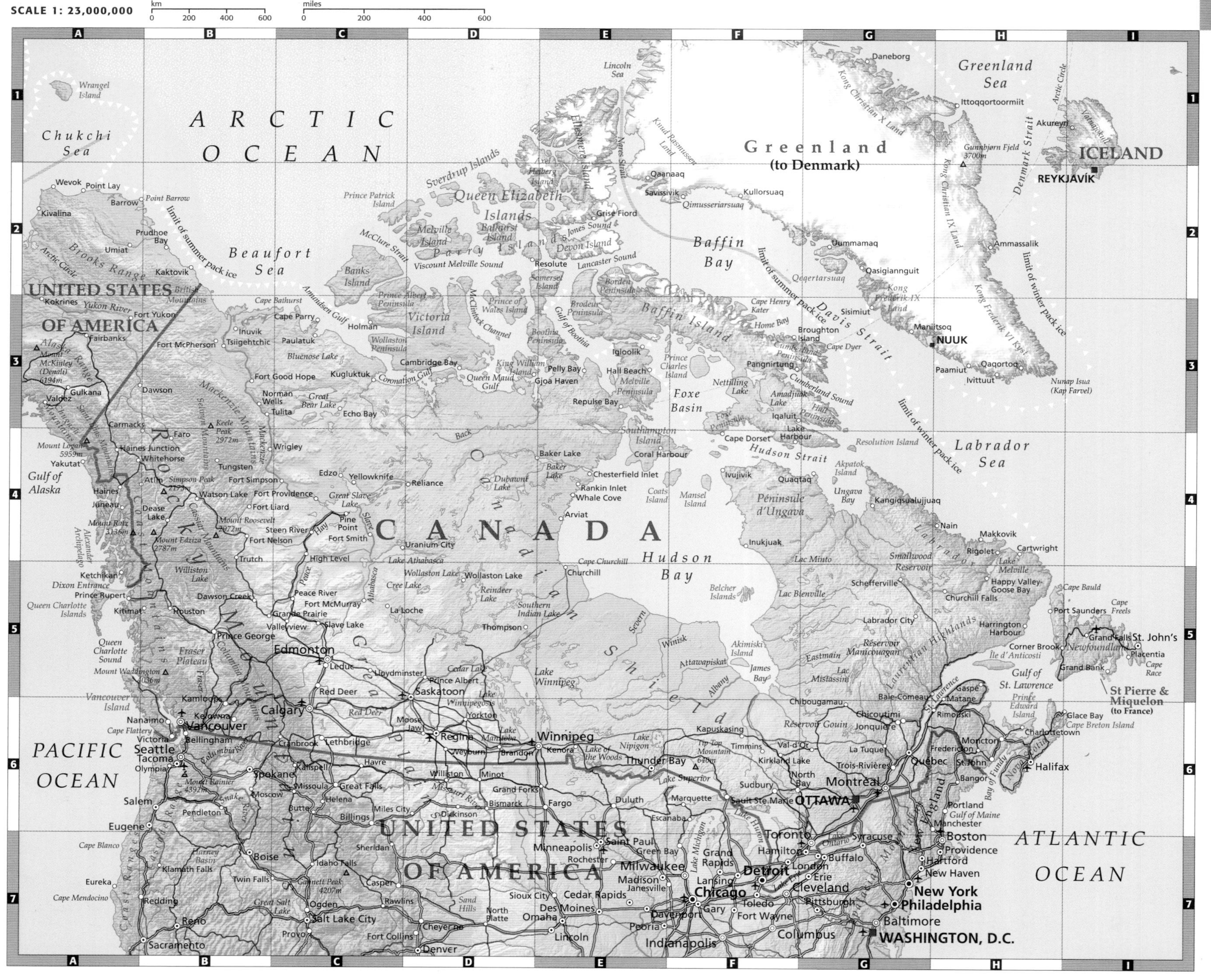
SCALE 1: 23,000,000
km 0 200 400 600
miles 0 200 400 600
ARCTIC OCEAN
ATLANTIC OCEAN
PACIFIC OCEAN
CANADA
UNITED STATES OF AMERICA
Greenland (to Denmark)
ICELAND
REYKJAVÍK
NUUK
OTTAWA
WASHINGTON, D.C.
Hudson Bay
Baffin Bay
Labrador Sea
Beaufort Sea
Greenland Sea
Chukchi Sea
Gulf of Alaska
Lincoln Sea
Davis Strait
Hudson Strait
Denmark Strait
Foxe Basin
Baffin Island
Victoria Island
Ellesmere Island
Queen Elizabeth Islands
Banks Island
Wrangel Island
Canadian Shield
Vancouver
Seattle
Calgary
Edmonton
Winnipeg
Saskatoon
Regina
Toronto
Montréal
Québec
Halifax
St. John's
Chicago
Detroit
New York
Philadelphia
Boston
limit of summer pack ice
limit of winter pack ice
St Pierre & Miquelon (to France)

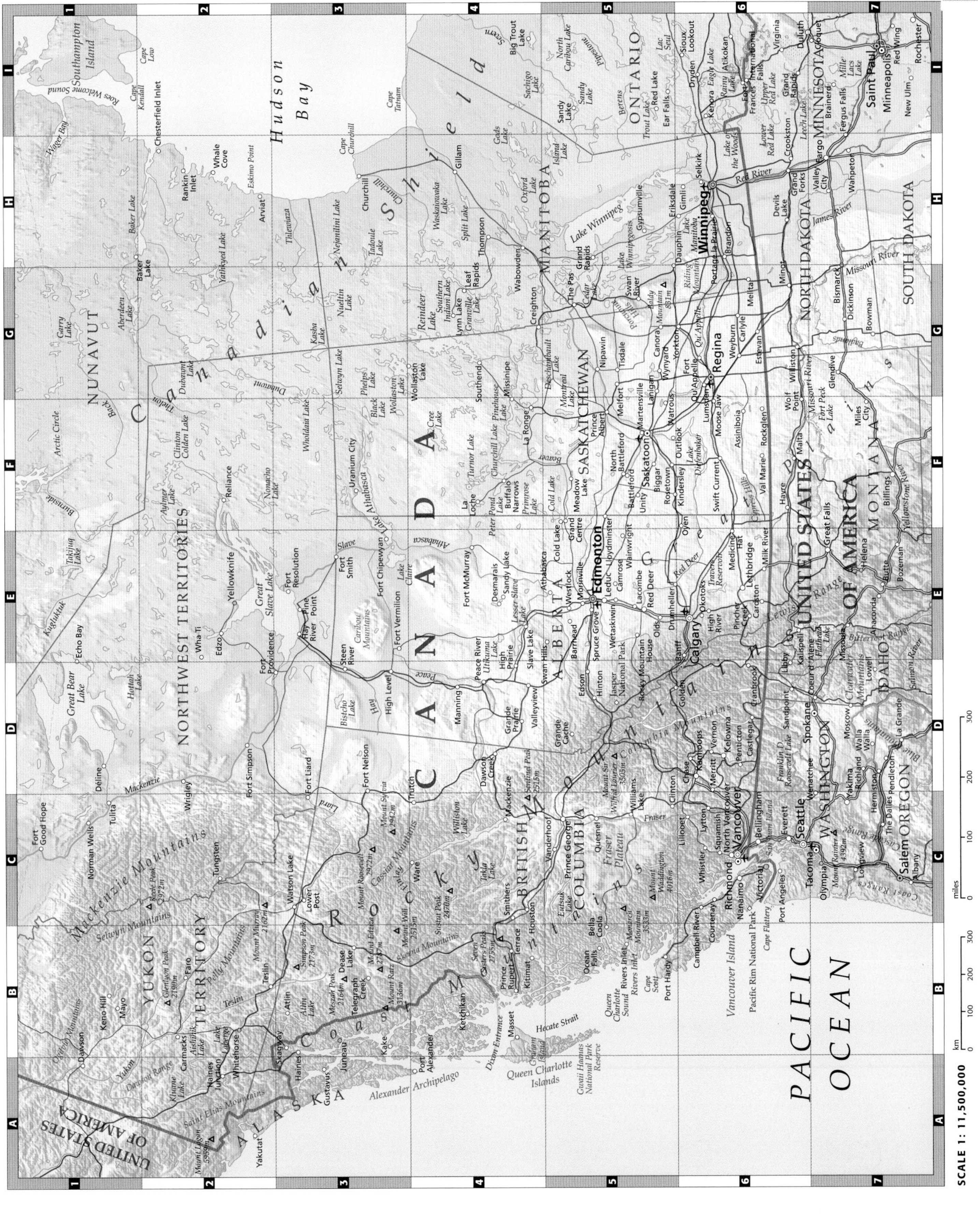

CANADA

UNITED STATES OF AMERICA

NUNAVUT

NORTHWEST TERRITORIES

YUKON TERRITORY

BRITISH COLUMBIA

ALBERTA

SASKATCHEWAN

MANITOBA

ONTARIO

ALASKA

WASHINGTON

OREGON

IDAHO

MONTANA

NORTH DAKOTA

SOUTH DAKOTA

MINNESOTA

PACIFIC OCEAN

Hudson Bay

Canadian Shield

Rocky Mountains

Coast Mountains

Great Plains

SCALE 1: 11,500,000

km 0 100 200 300

miles 0 100 200 300

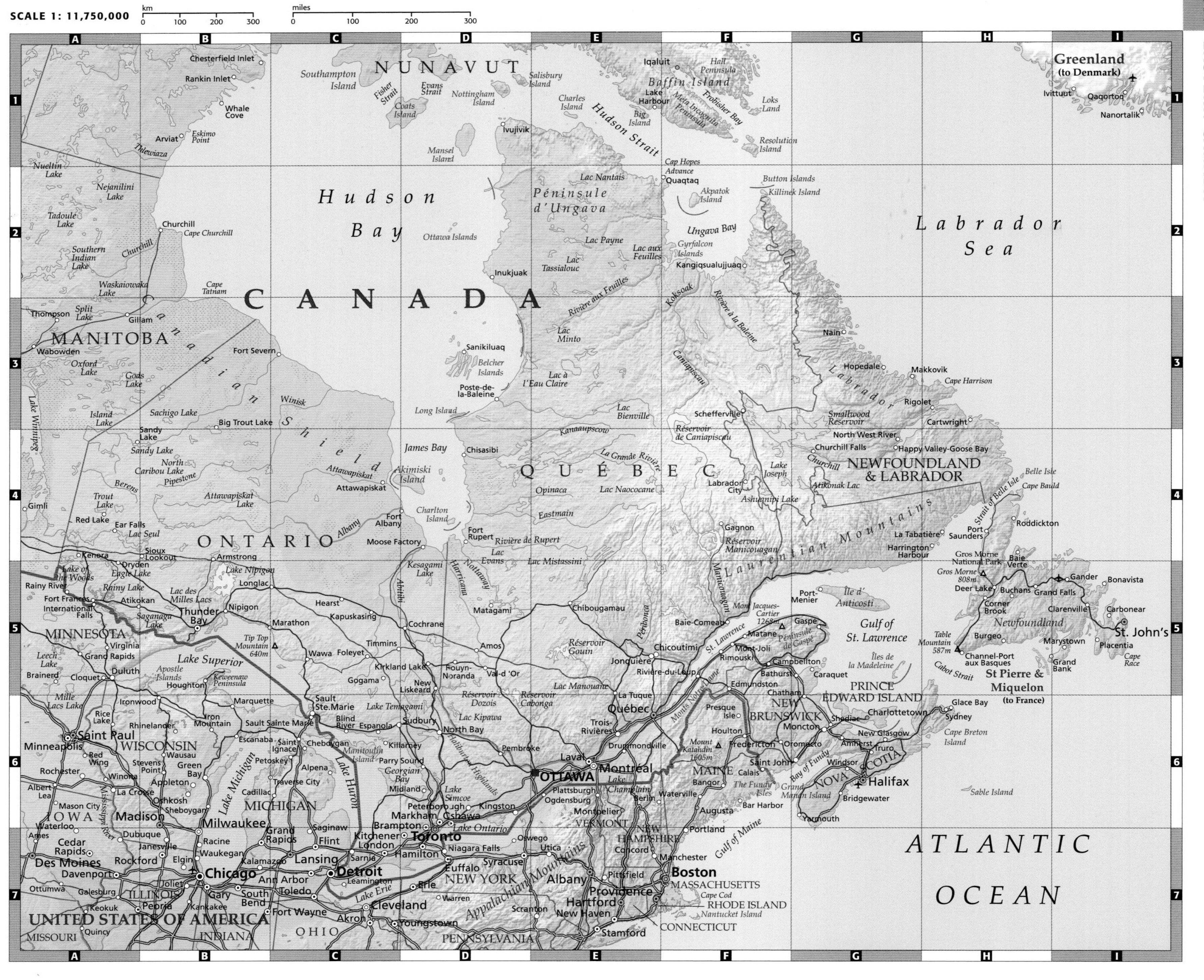
SCALE 1: 11,750,000
km 0 100 200 300
miles 0 100 200 300
CANADA
NUNAVUT
MANITOBA
ONTARIO
QUÉBEC
NEWFOUNDLAND & LABRADOR
NEW BRUNSWICK
NOVA SCOTIA
PRINCE EDWARD ISLAND
UNITED STATES OF AMERICA
Greenland (to Denmark)
St Pierre & Miquelon (to France)
Hudson Bay
Labrador Sea
ATLANTIC OCEAN
Hudson Strait
James Bay
Ungava Bay
Gulf of St. Lawrence
Baffin Island
Southampton Island
Coats Island
Mansel Island
Nottingham Island
Salisbury Island
Akimiski Island
Belcher Islands
Ottawa Islands
Resolution Island
Île d'Anticosti
Newfoundland
Cape Breton Island
Sable Island
Péninsule d'Ungava
Canadian Shield
Laurentian Mountains
Appalachian Mountains
Labrador
Lake Superior
Lake Michigan
Lake Huron
Lake Erie
Lake Ontario
Lake Winnipeg
Lake Nipigon
Lake of the Woods
Lac Mistassini
Smallwood Reservoir
Réservoir Manicouagan
Réservoir de Caniapiscau
Réservoir Gouin
Lac Minto
Lac Bienville
Lac à l'Eau Claire
Lake Joseph
Ashuanipi Lake
OTTAWA
Québec
Montreal
Toronto
Halifax
St. John's
Charlottetown
Fredericton
Moncton
Saint John
Sydney
Iqaluit
Churchill
Thunder Bay
Sudbury
Sault Ste.Marie
Timmins
Kingston
Hamilton
London
Chicoutimi
Trois-Rivières
Gaspé
Rimouski
Baie-Comeau
Schefferville
Labrador City
Happy Valley-Goose Bay
Nain
Hopedale
Corner Brook
Gander
Grand Falls
Chicago
Detroit
Cleveland
Milwaukee
Minneapolis
Saint Paul
Boston
Buffalo
Albany
Providence
Hartford
Des Moines
MINNESOTA
WISCONSIN
MICHIGAN
IOWA
ILLINOIS
INDIANA
OHIO
PENNSYLVANIA
NEW YORK
VERMONT
NEW HAMPSHIRE
MAINE
MASSACHUSETTS
RHODE ISLAND
CONNECTICUT
MISSOURI

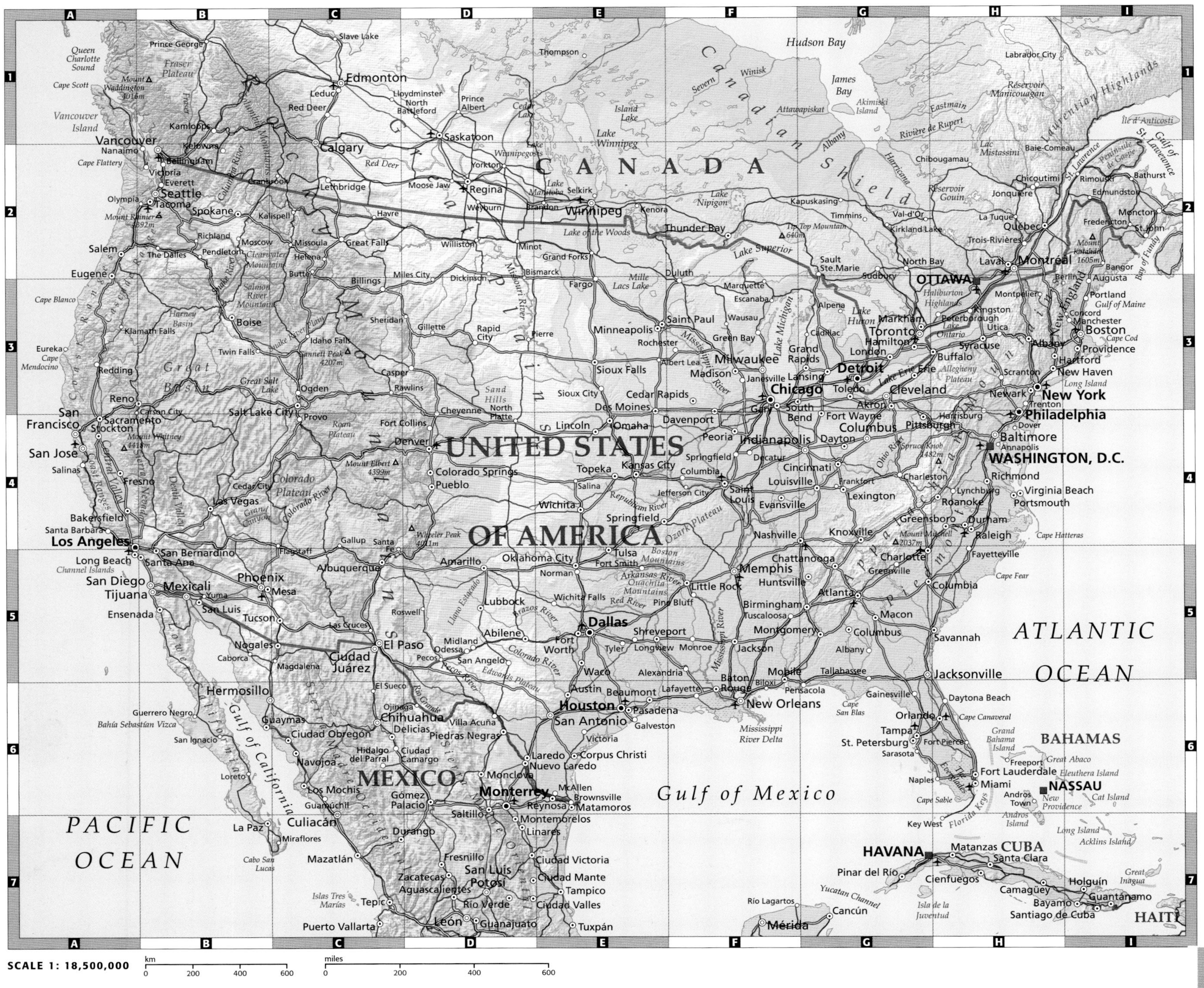

CANADA
UNITED STATES OF AMERICA
MEXICO
CUBA
BAHAMAS
HAITI
ATLANTIC OCEAN
PACIFIC OCEAN
Gulf of Mexico
Gulf of California
Hudson Bay
James Bay
Gulf of St Lawrence
Canadian Shield
Great Plains
Rocky Mountains
Great Basin
Appalachian Mountains
Coastal Plain
Sierra Madre Oriental
Sierra Madre Occidental
Lower California
OTTAWA
WASHINGTON, D.C.
HAVANA
NASSAU
New York
Philadelphia
Boston
Chicago
Detroit
Toronto
Montréal
Los Angeles
San Francisco
Seattle
Vancouver
Dallas
Houston
Miami
Monterrey
SCALE 1: 18,500,000
km
miles

SCALE 1: 7,200,000

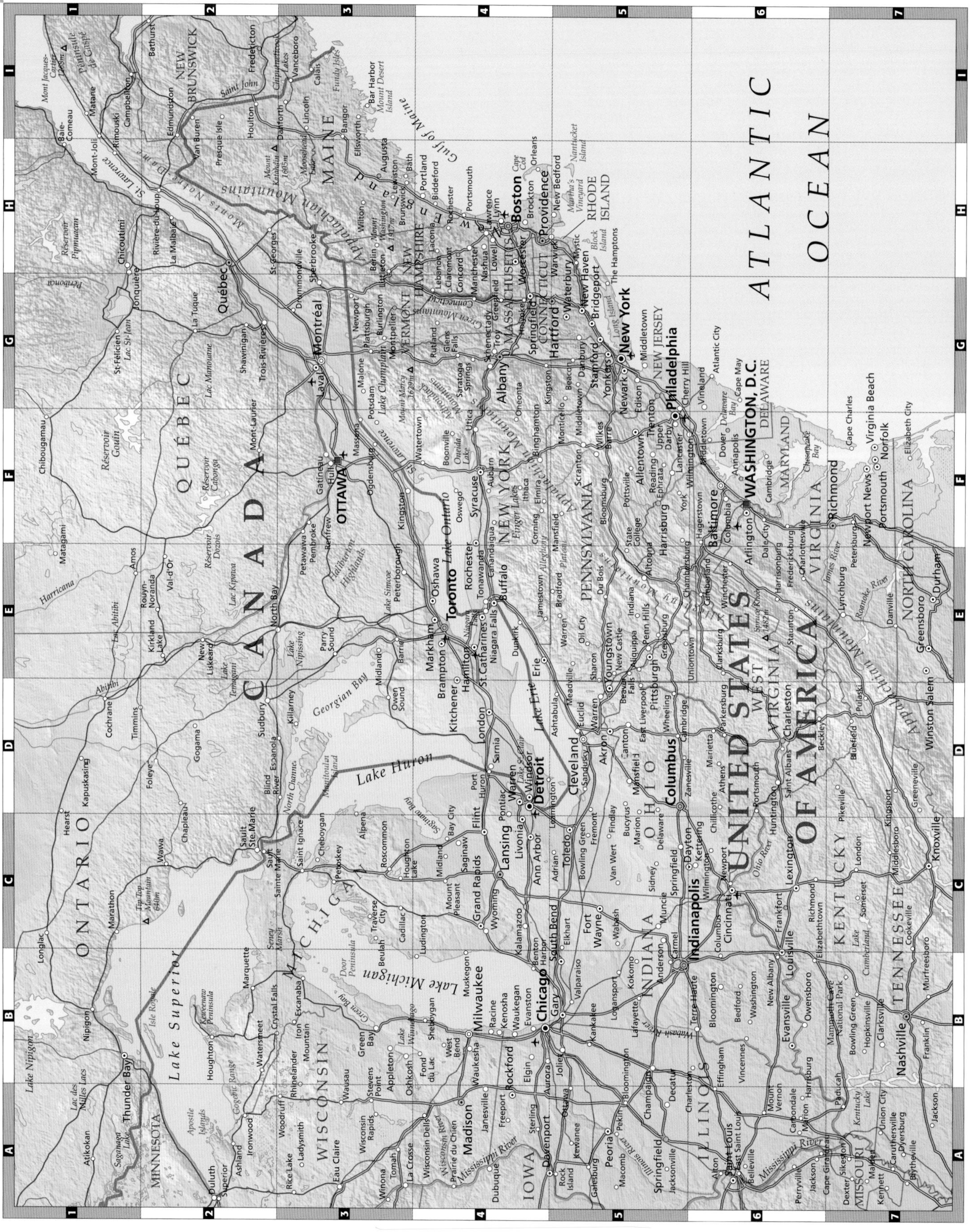

km 0 50 100 150 200

miles 0 50 100 150 200

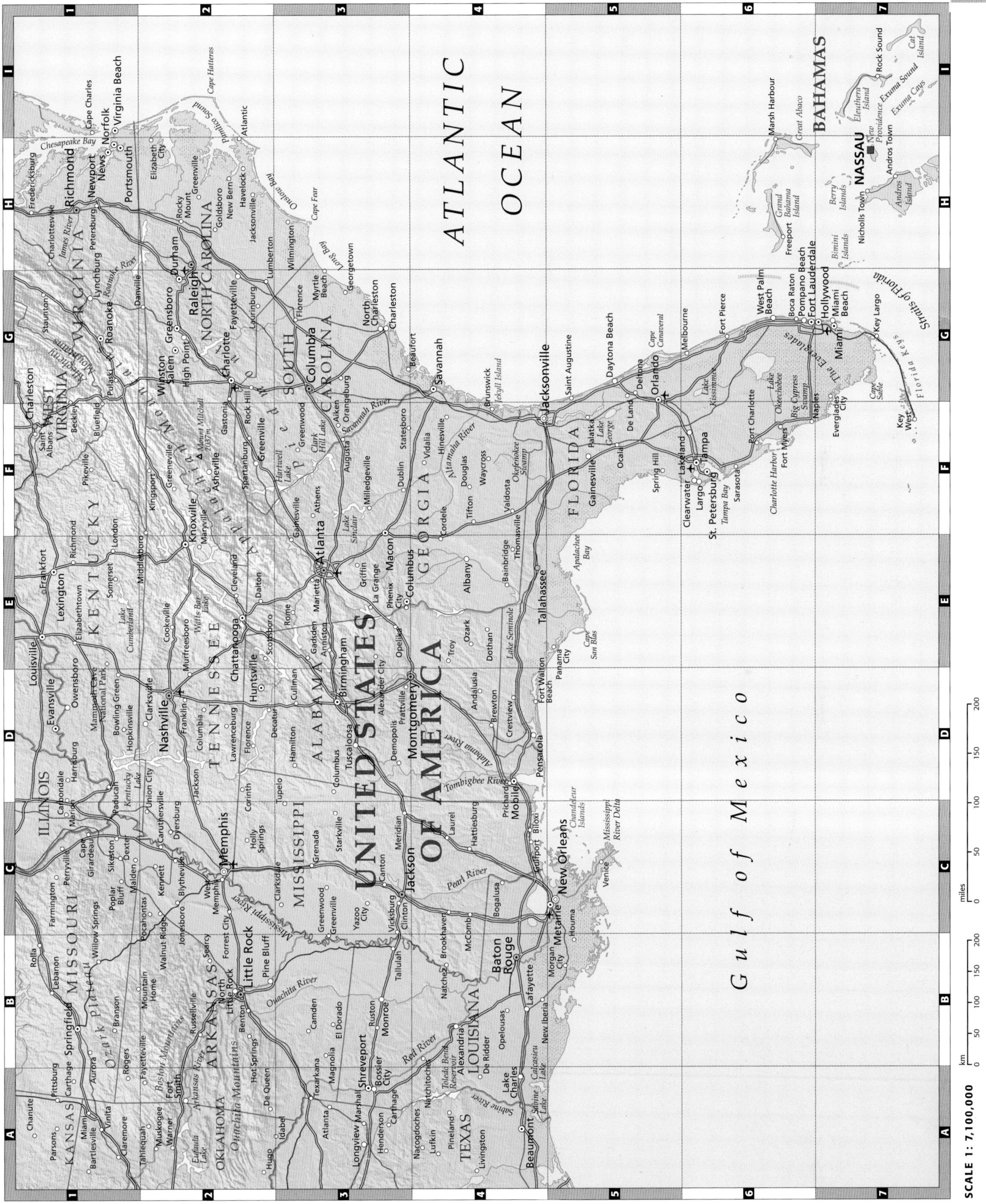

ATLANTIC OCEAN

Gulf of Mexico

UNITED STATES OF AMERICA

BAHAMAS

NASSAU

KANSAS
MISSOURI
ILLINOIS
KENTUCKY
WEST VIRGINIA
VIRGINIA
NORTH CAROLINA
SOUTH CAROLINA
TENNESSEE
ARKANSAS
OKLAHOMA
TEXAS
LOUISIANA
MISSISSIPPI
ALABAMA
GEORGIA
FLORIDA

Chanute
Parsons
Bartlesville
Miami
Vinita
Claremore
Pittsburg
Carthage
Aurora
Springfield
Rolla
Lebanon
Farmington
Perryville
Cape Girardeau
Carbondale
Marion
Harrisburg
Paducah
Poplar Bluff
Sikeston
Dexter
Malden
Kennett
Caruthersville
Dyersburg
Union City
Blytheville
West Memphis
Memphis
Jonesboro
Pocahontas
Walnut Ridge
Mountain Home
Willow Springs
Branson
Rogers
Fayetteville
Fort Smith
Tahlequah
Muskogee
Warner
Eufaula Lake
Hugo
Idabel
De Queen
Hot Springs
Benton
Russellville
North Little Rock
Little Rock
Searcy
Forrest City
Pine Bluff
Camden
El Dorado
Magnolia
Texarkana
Atlanta
Longview
Marshall
Henderson
Carthage
Shreveport
Bossier City
Ruston
Monroe
Natchitoches
Nacogdoches
Lufkin
Pineland
Livingston
De Ridder
Alexandria
Opelousas
Lake Charles
Calcasieu Lake
Sabine Lake
Beaumont
Lafayette
New Iberia
Morgan City
Baton Rouge
Houma
Metairie
New Orleans
Venice
Bogalusa
McComb
Brookhaven
Natchez
Tallulah
Vicksburg
Clinton
Jackson
Yazoo City
Greenwood
Greenville
Clarksdale
Canton
Grenada
Holly Springs
Corinth
Tupelo
Starkville
Columbus
Meridian
Laurel
Hattiesburg
Gulfport
Biloxi
Pascagoula
Prichard
Mobile
Pensacola
Crestview
Fort Walton Beach
Panama City
Brewton
Andalusia
Dothan
Troy
Ozark
Opelika
Montgomery
Prattville
Alexander City
Demopolis
Tuscaloosa
Hamilton
Birmingham
Cullman
Gadsden
Anniston
Huntsville
Decatur
Florence
Lawrenceburg
Columbia
Franklin
Nashville
Clarksville
Hopkinsville
Bowling Green
Mammoth Cave National Park
Owensboro
Evansville
Louisville
Elizabethtown
Lexington
Frankfort
Richmond
Somerset
London
Middlesboro
Cookeville
Murfreesboro
Jackson
Chattanooga
Cleveland
Scottsboro
Dalton
Rome
Marietta
Atlanta
Griffin
La Grange
Phenix City
Columbus
Macon
Albany
Bainbridge
Thomasville
Tallahassee
Valdosta
Tifton
Cordele
Waycross
Douglas
Dublin
Milledgeville
Athens
Gainesville
Augusta
Aiken
Orangeburg
Statesboro
Vidalia
Hinesville
Savannah
Beaufort
Brunswick
Jekyll Island
Jacksonville
Saint Augustine
Palatka
Gainesville
Ocala
De Land
Daytona Beach
Deltona
Orlando
Melbourne
Cape Canaveral
Lakeland
Tampa
Clearwater
Largo
St. Petersburg
Tampa Bay
Sarasota
Port Charlotte
Charlotte Harbor
Fort Myers
Naples
Everglades City
Cape Sable
Lake Okeechobee
Big Cypress Swamp
The Everglades
Fort Pierce
West Palm Beach
Boca Raton
Pompano Beach
Fort Lauderdale
Hollywood
Miami
Miami Beach
Key Largo
Key West
Florida Keys
Straits of Florida
Spring Hill
Lake Kissimmee
Lake George
Okefenokee Swamp
Apalachee Bay
Cape San Blas
Lake Seminole
Chandeleur Islands
Mississippi River Delta
Knoxville
Maryville
Kingsport
Greeneville
Asheville
Mount Mitchell 2037m
Pikeville
Bluefield
Beckley
Saint Albans
Charleston
Pulaski
Roanoke
Staunton
Lynchburg
Charlottesville
Fredericksburg
Richmond
Petersburg
Newport News
Norfolk
Portsmouth
Virginia Beach
Cape Charles
Chesapeake Bay
Elizabeth City
Pamlico Sound
Cape Hatteras
Atlantic
Greenville
Rocky Mount
Goldsboro
New Bern
Havelock
Jacksonville
Onslow Bay
Cape Fear
Wilmington
Lumberton
Laurinburg
Fayetteville
Raleigh
Durham
Greensboro
High Point
Winston Salem
Danville
Charlotte
Gastonia
Rock Hill
Spartanburg
Greenville
Greenwood
Columbia
Florence
Myrtle Beach
Long Bay
Georgetown
North Charleston
Charleston
Danville
Lake Sinclair
Clark Hill Lake
Hartwell Lake
Lake Cumberland
Kentucky Lake
Watts Bar Lake
Toledo Bend Reservoir
Appalachian Mountains
Allegheny Mountains
Ozark Plateau
Boston Mountains
Ouachita Mountains
Piedmont
Mississippi River
Arkansas River
Ouachita River
Red River
Sabine River
Pearl River
Tombigbee River
Alabama River
Altamaha River
Savannah River
Roanoke River
James River
Marsh Harbour
Great Abaco
Grand Bahama Island
Freeport
Bimini Islands
Berry Islands
Nicholls Town
Andros Island
Andros Town
New Providence
Eleuthera Island
Exuma Sound
Exuma Cays
Rock Sound
Cat Island

A B C D E F G H I
1 2 3 4 5 6 7

km 0 50 100 150 200
miles 0 50 100 150 200

SCALE 1: 7,100,000

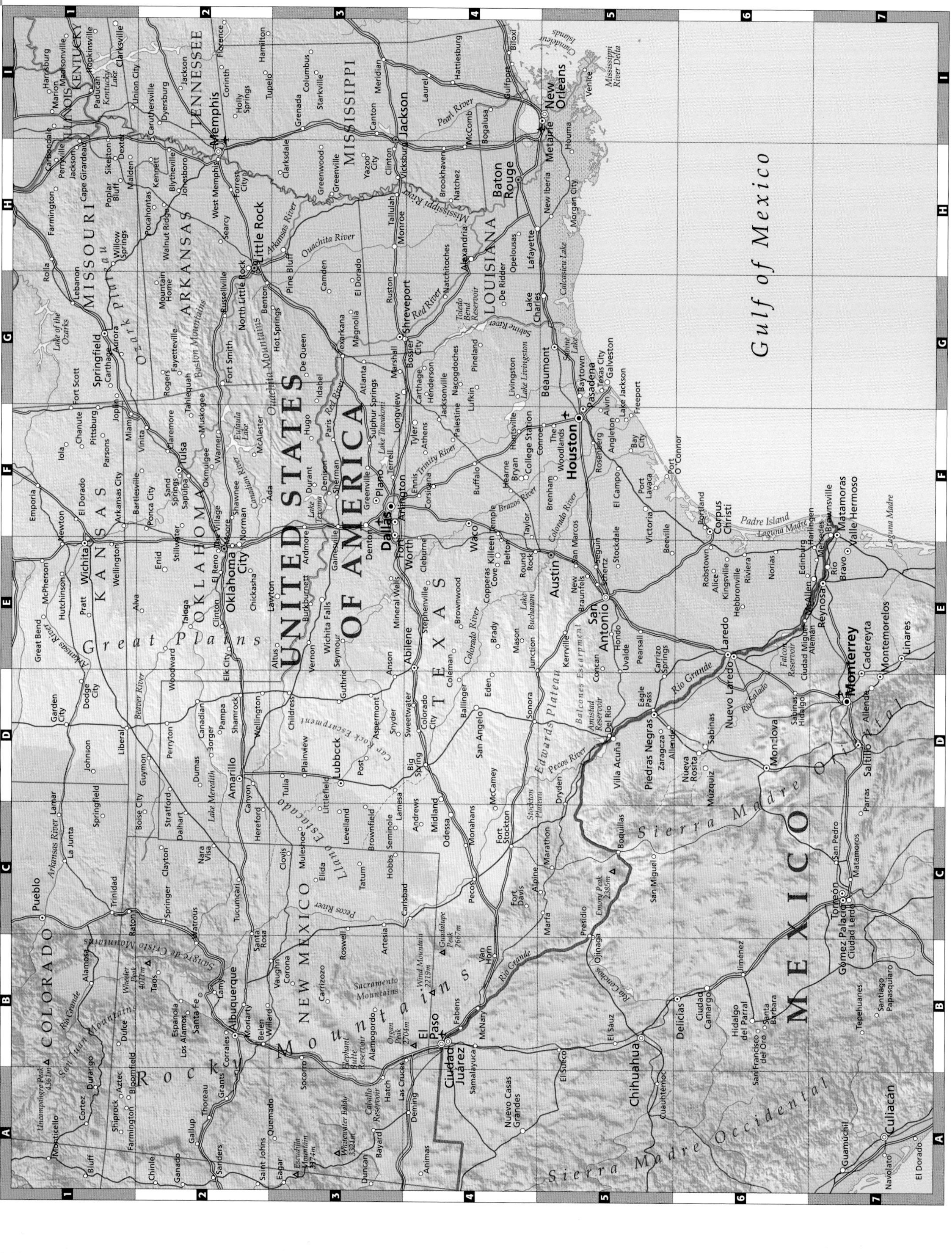

SCALE 1: 7,100,000

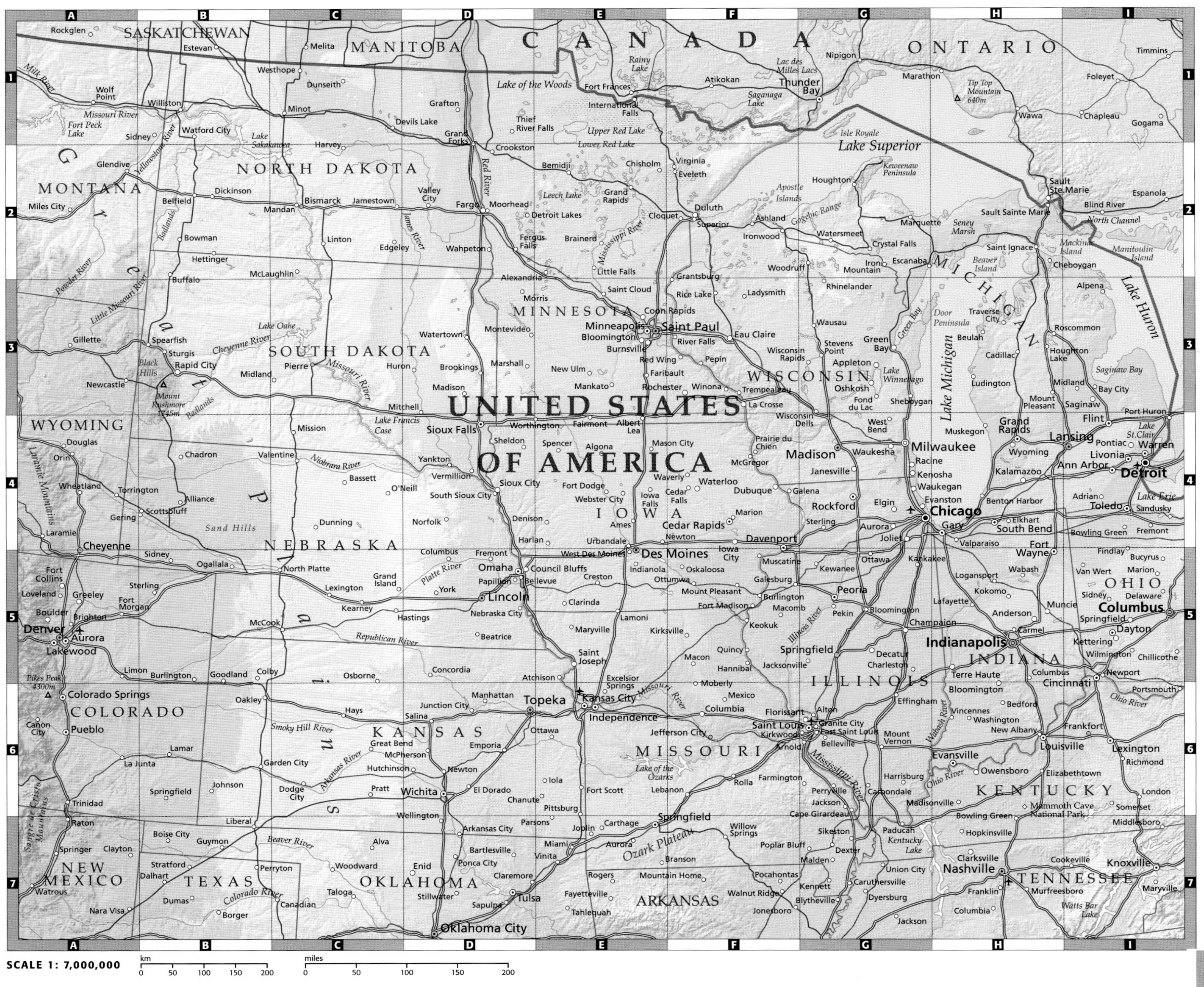

SCALE 1: 7,000,000

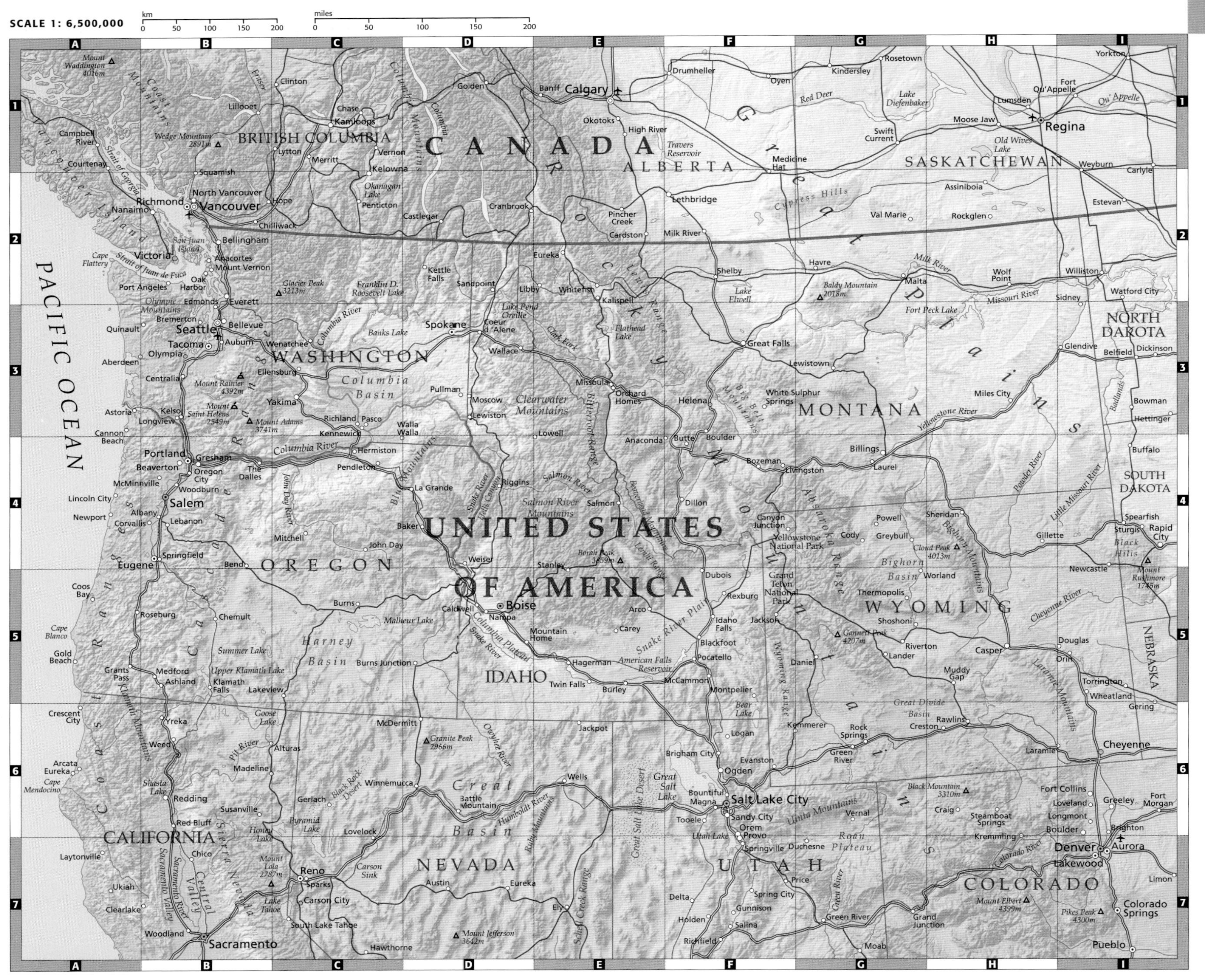
SCALE 1: 6,500,000
km
miles
PACIFIC OCEAN
CANADA
UNITED STATES OF AMERICA
BRITISH COLUMBIA
ALBERTA
SASKATCHEWAN
NORTH DAKOTA
SOUTH DAKOTA
NEBRASKA
MONTANA
WYOMING
COLORADO
IDAHO
UTAH
WASHINGTON
OREGON
NEVADA
CALIFORNIA
Great Plains
Rocky Mountains
Cascade Range
Coast Ranges
Great Basin
Columbia Basin
Columbia Plateau
Harney Basin
Bighorn Basin
Great Divide Basin
Coast Mountains
Columbia Mountains
Cypress Hills
Bitterroot Range
Lewis Range
Big Belt Mountains
Clearwater Mountains
Salmon River Mountains
Blue Mountains
Absaroka Range
Bighorn Mountains
Laramie Mountains
Wyoming Range
Uinta Mountains
Roan Plateau
Klamath Mountains
Sierra Nevada
Central Valley
Sacramento Valley
Great Salt Lake Desert
Black Rock Desert
Ruby Mountains
Schell Creek Range
Badlands
Black Hills
Vancouver Island
Strait of Georgia
Strait of Juan de Fuca
San Juan Island
Cape Flattery
Cape Blanco
Cape Mendocino
Columbia River
Snake River
Missouri River
Little Missouri River
Yellowstone River
Powder River
Cheyenne River
Milk River
Colorado River
Green River
Owyhee River
Humboldt River
Sacramento River
Pit River
Salmon River
Clark Fork
John Day River
Fraser
Qu'Appelle
Red Deer
Great Salt Lake
Utah Lake
Bear Lake
Lake Tahoe
Pyramid Lake
Honey Lake
Goose Lake
Shasta Lake
Upper Klamath Lake
Summer Lake
Malheur Lake
Banks Lake
Franklin D. Roosevelt Lake
Okanagan Lake
Lake Pend Oreille
Flathead Lake
Fort Peck Lake
Lake Elwell
Lake Diefenbaker
Old Wives Lake
Travers Reservoir
American Falls Reservoir
Carson Sink
Snake River Plain
Mount Waddington 4016m
Wedge Mountain 2891m
Glacier Peak 3213m
Mount Rainier 4392m
Mount Saint Helens 2549m
Mount Adams 3741m
Baldy Mountain 2018m
Cloud Peak 4013m
Gannett Peak 4207m
Borah Peak 3859m
Mount Rushmore 1745m
Black Mountain 3310m
Mount Elbert 4399m
Pikes Peak 4300m
Granite Peak 2966m
Mount Jefferson 3642m
Mount Lola 2787m
Calgary
Regina
Vancouver
Victoria
Seattle
Tacoma
Portland
Salem
Eugene
Spokane
Boise
Salt Lake City
Denver
Sacramento
Reno
Cheyenne
Yellowstone National Park
Grand Teton National Park

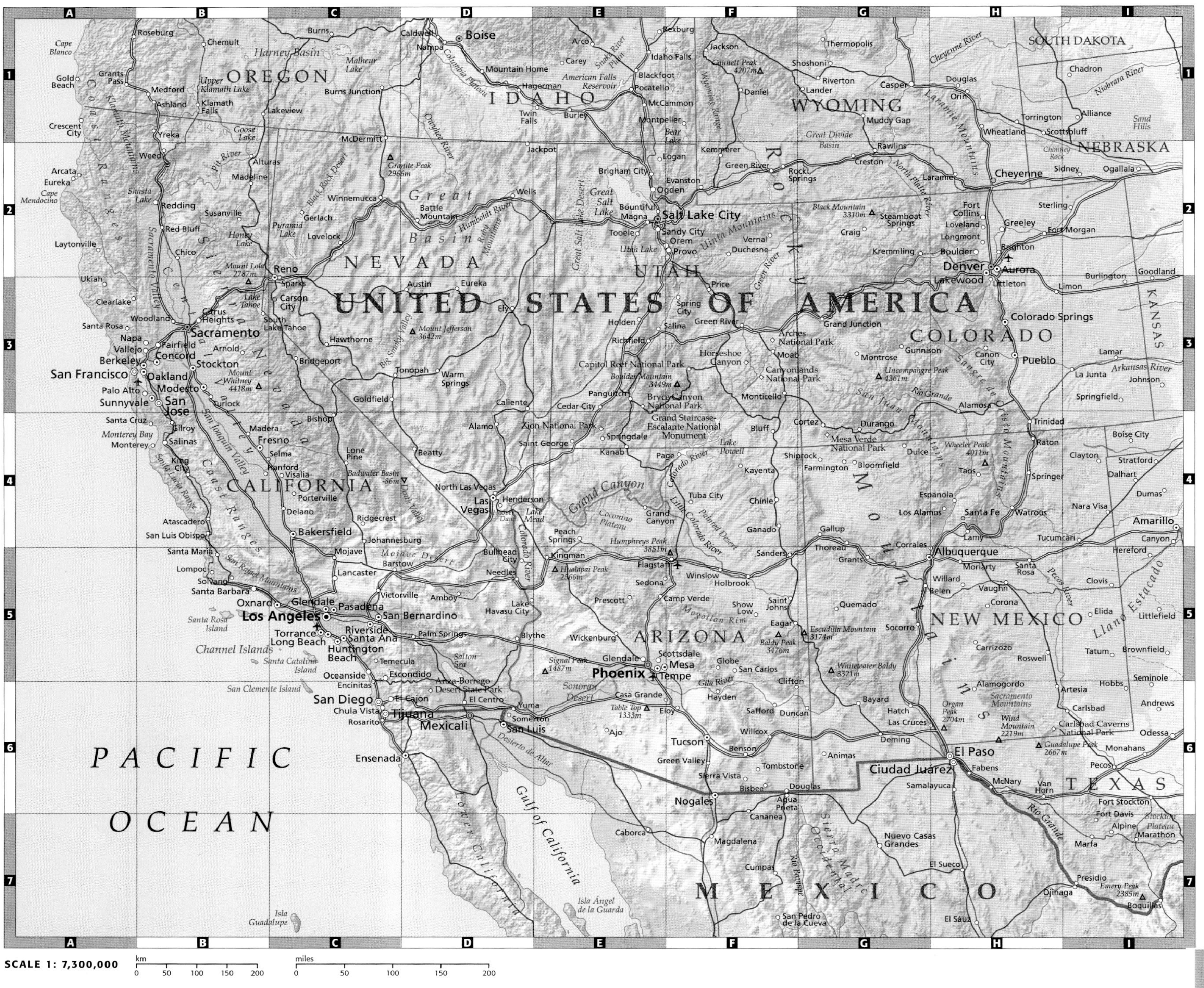

SCALE 1: 7,300,000

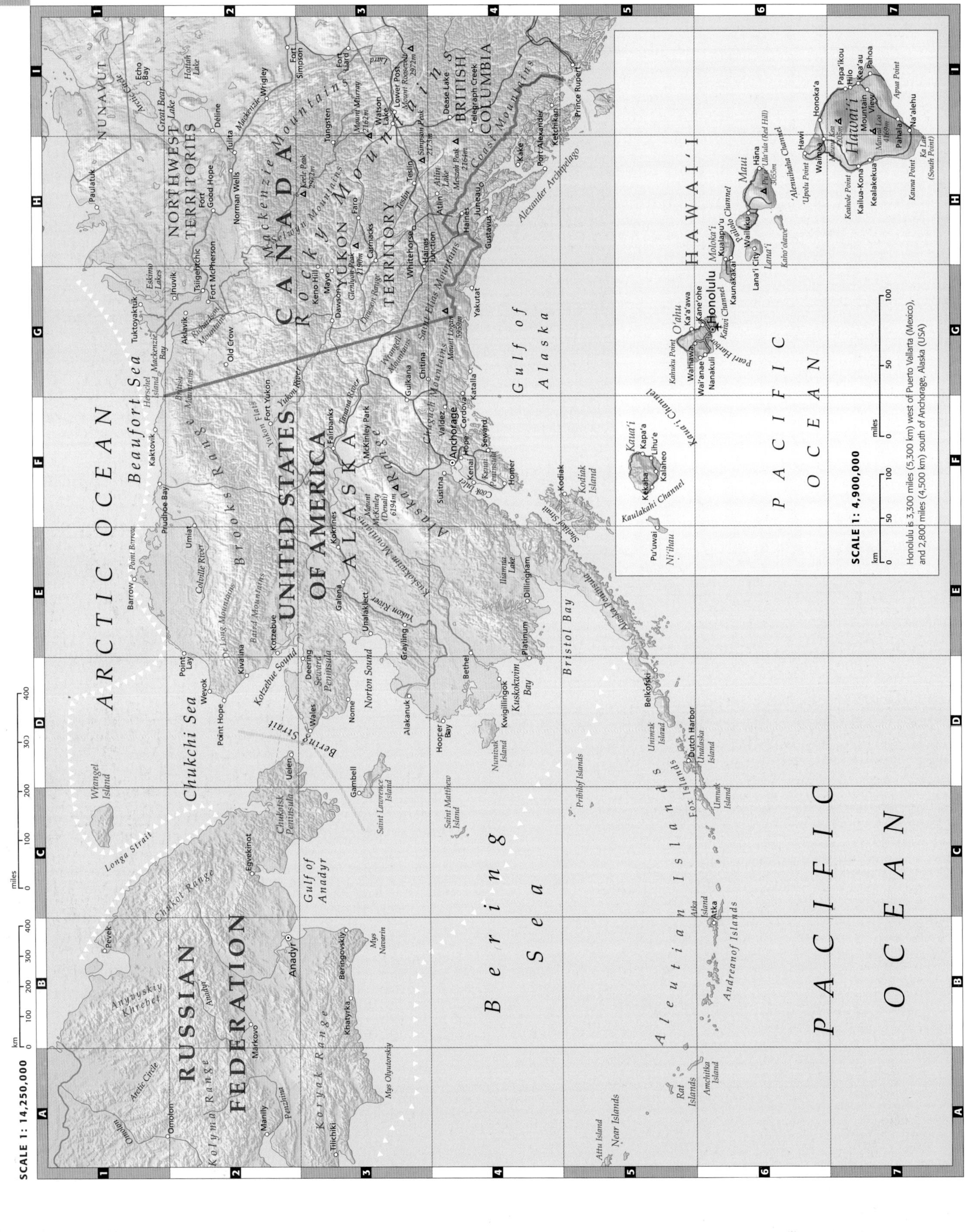
SCALE 1: 14,250,000
km 0 100 200 300 400
miles 0 100 200 300 400
ARCTIC OCEAN
Beaufort Sea
Chukchi Sea
Bering Sea
Gulf of Alaska
PACIFIC OCEAN
Bristol Bay
Norton Sound
Kotzebue Sound
Bering Strait
Longa Strait
Gulf of Anadyr
UNITED STATES OF AMERICA
ALASKA
CANADA
YUKON TERRITORY
NORTHWEST TERRITORIES
NUNAVUT
BRITISH COLUMBIA
RUSSIAN FEDERATION
Brooks Range
Alaska Range
Rocky Mountains
Mackenzie Mountains
Coast Mountains
Saint Elias Mountains
Chugach Mountains
Kuskokwim Mountains
Mount McKinley (Denali) 6194m
Mount Logan 5959m
Aleutian Islands
Andreanof Islands
Fox Islands
Rat Islands
Near Islands
Pribilof Islands
Kodiak Island
Nunivak Island
Saint Lawrence Island
Saint Matthew Island
Wrangel Island
Chukotsk Peninsula
Seward Peninsula
Alaska Peninsula
Kenai Peninsula
Alexander Archipelago
Anchorage
Fairbanks
Juneau
Nome
Barrow
Prudhoe Bay
Kotzebue
Bethel
Dillingham
Kodiak
Valdez
Homer
Dutch Harbor
Whitehorse
Dawson
Inuvik
Prince Rupert
Anadyr
Pevek
Arctic Circle
HAWAI'I
Ni'ihau
Kaua'i
O'ahu
Moloka'i
Lana'i
Maui
Kaho'olawe
Hawai'i
Honolulu
Lihu'e
Hilo
Kailua-Kona
Mauna Kea 4205m
Mauna Loa 4169m
Pu'u 'Ula'ula (Red Hill) 3055m
Ka Lae (South Point)
Kaua'i Channel
Kaulakahi Channel
'Alenuihaha Channel
SCALE 1: 4,900,000
km 0 50 100
miles 0 50 100
Honolulu is 3,300 miles (5,300 km) west of Puerto Vallarta (Mexico), and 2,800 miles (4,500 km) south of Anchorage, Alaska (USA)

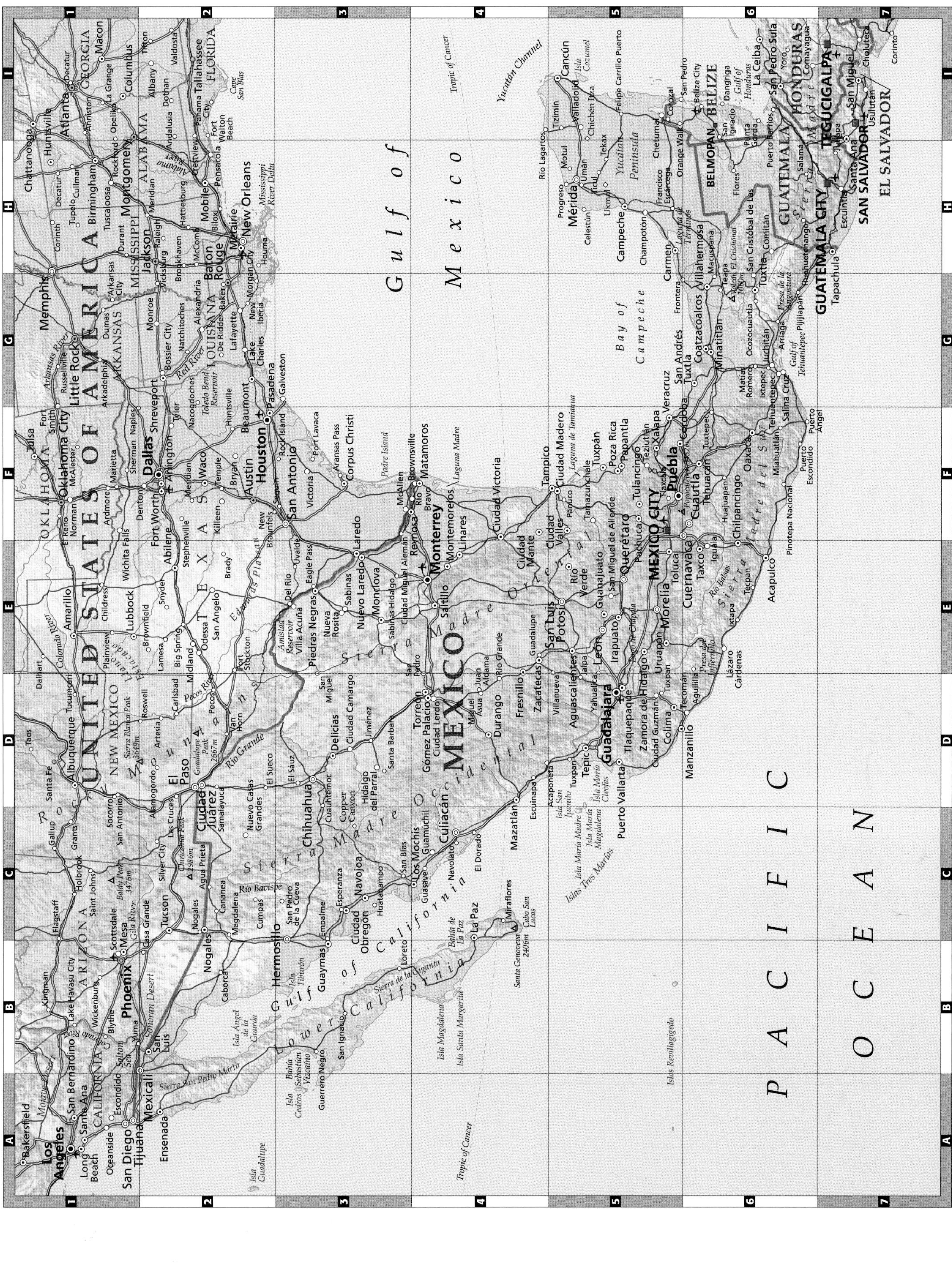

SCALE 1: 12,200,000

km 0 100 200 300

miles 0 100 200 300

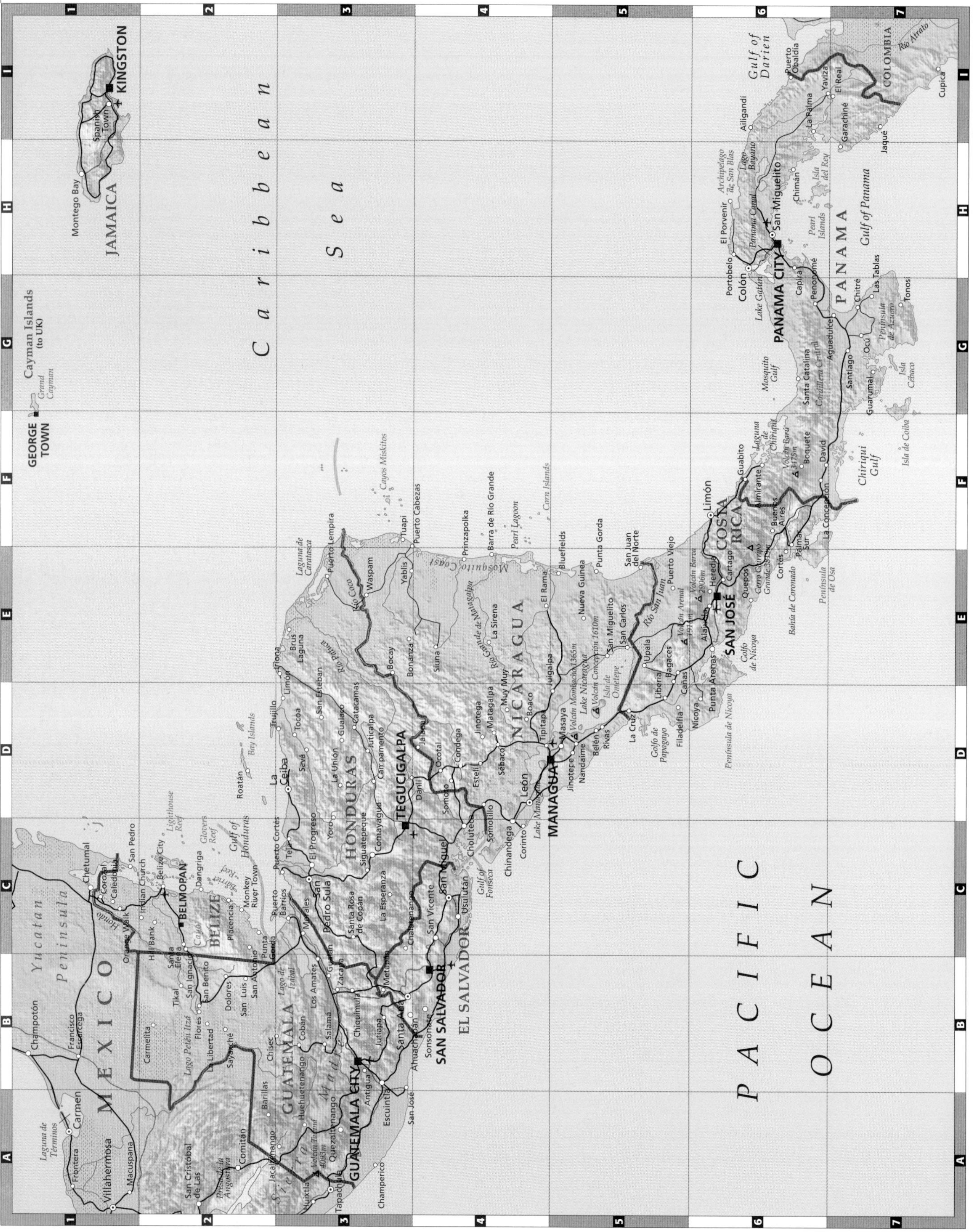

SCALE 1: 7,100,000

km 0 50 100 150 200
miles 0 50 100 150 200

Caribbean Sea
PACIFIC OCEAN
MEXICO
Yucatan Peninsula
BELIZE
GUATEMALA
HONDURAS
EL SALVADOR
NICARAGUA
COSTA RICA
PANAMA
COLOMBIA
JAMAICA
Cayman Islands (to UK)
Grand Cayman
GEORGE TOWN
KINGSTON
Spanish Town
Montego Bay
Laguna de Términos
Carmen
Champotón
Francisco Escárcega
Frontera
Villahermosa
Macuspana
San Cristobal de Las Casas
Comitán
Presa de la Angostura
Jacaltenango
Huixtla
Tapachula
Champerico
Carmelita
Lago Petén Itzá
Flores
La Libertad
Sayaxché
Tikal
Dolores
San Luis
San Antonio
Chetumal
Hondo
Orange Walk
Corozal
Caledonia
San Pedro
Indian Church
Belize City
BELMOPAN
Hill Bank
Santa Elena
San Ignacio
San Benito
Dangriga
Placencia
Monkey River Town
Punta Gorda
Lighthouse Reef
Glovers Reef
Barrier Reef
Gulf of Honduras
Roatán
Bay Islands
Puerto Barrios
Lago de Izabal
Los Amates
Chisec
Cobán
Salamá
Huehuetenango
Quezaltenango
Barillas
Volcán Tajumulco 4093m
GUATEMALA CITY
Antigua
Escuintla
San José
Chiquimula
Zacapa
Jutiapa
Metapán
Gualán
Santa Ana
Ahuachapán
Sonsonate
SAN SALVADOR
San Vicente
Usulután
San Miguel
Chalatenango
Gulf of Fonseca
Morales
San Pedro Sula
Santa Rosa de Copán
La Esperanza
Puerto Cortés
Tela
El Progreso
La Ceiba
Yoro
Siguatepeque
Comayagua
TEGUCIGALPA
Choluteca
Danlí
Trujillo
Limón
Tocoa
Sevá
La Unión
San Esteban
Gualaco
Catacamas
Juticalpa
Campamento
Iriona
Brus Laguna
Laguna de Caratasca
Puerto Lempira
Río Coco
Río Patuca
Waspam
Yablis
Tuapi
Puerto Cabezas
Cayos Miskitos
Mosquito Coast
Prinzapolka
Barra de Río Grande
Pearl Lagoon
Corn Islands
Bluefields
El Rama
Nueva Guinea
Punta Gorda
San Juan del Norte
Bonanza
Siuna
Bocay
Jalapa
Ocotal
Condega
Somoto
Estelí
Jinotega
Matagalpa
Muy Muy
Sébaco
Río Grande de Matagalpa
La Sirena
Boaco
Juigalpa
Tipitapa
Somotillo
Chinandega
Corinto
León
Lake Managua
MANAGUA
Masaya
Jinotepe
Nandaime
Volcán Mombacho 1365m
Volcán Concepción 1610m
Lake Nicaragua
Isla de Ometepe
Belén
Rivas
San Miguelito
San Carlos
Río San Juan
La Cruz
Golfo de Papagayo
Upala
Bagaces
Liberia
Cañas
Filadelfia
Nicoya
Península de Nicoya
Golfo de Nicoya
Punta Arenas
Volcán Arenal 1633m
Alajuela
Volcán Barva 2906m
Puerto Viejo
Heredia
SAN JOSÉ
Cartago
Quepos
Cerro Chirripó Grande 3820m
Limón
Cortés
Bahía de Coronado
Buenos Aires
Palmar Sur
Península de Osa
La Concepción
Almirante
Guabito
Laguna de Chiriquí
Volcán Barú 3475m
Boquete
David
Chiriquí Gulf
Isla de Coiba
Mosquito Gulf
Santa Catalina
Cordillera Central
Guarumal
Santiago
Aguadulce
Ocú
Isla Cébaco
Península de Azuero
Chitré
Las Tablas
Tonosí
Penonomé
Capira
Colón
Portobelo
Lake Gatún
Panama Canal
PANAMA CITY
San Miguelito
El Porvenir
Archipiélago de San Blas
Lago Bayano
Chimán
Pearl Islands
Isla del Rey
Gulf of Panama
Ailigandi
La Palma
Garachiné
Jaqué
Yaviza
El Real
Puerto Obaldia
Gulf of Darien
Río Atrato
Cupica

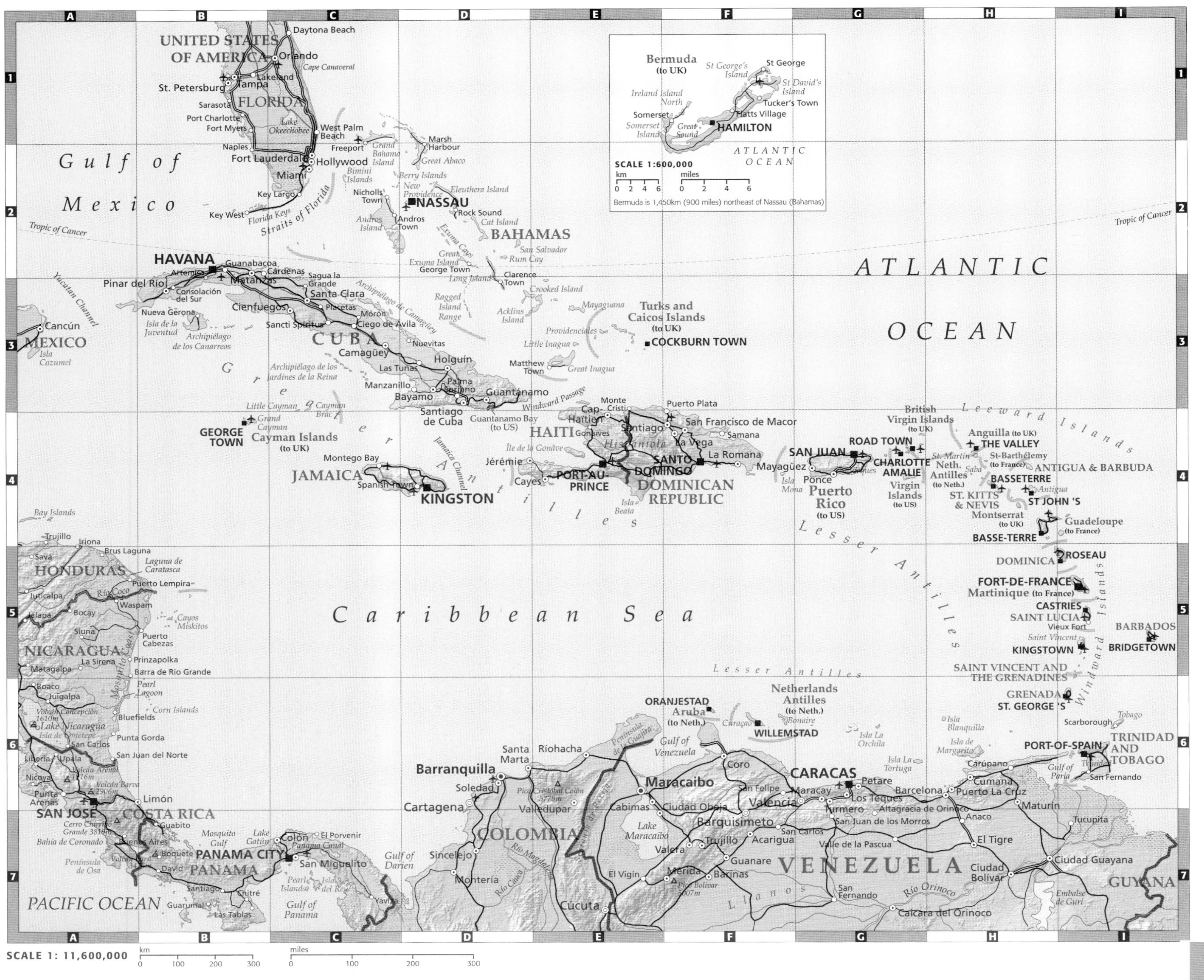
ATLANTIC OCEAN
Gulf of Mexico
Caribbean Sea
PACIFIC OCEAN
Bermuda (to UK)
HAMILTON
St George
St George's Island
St David's Island
Tucker's Town
Flatts Village
Ireland Island North
Somerset
Somerset Island
Great Sound
SCALE 1:600,000
Bermuda is 1,450km (900 miles) northeast of Nassau (Bahamas)
UNITED STATES OF AMERICA
FLORIDA
Orlando
Daytona Beach
Cape Canaveral
Tampa
Lakeland
St. Petersburg
Sarasota
Port Charlotte
Fort Myers
Naples
Fort Lauderdale
Hollywood
Miami
West Palm Beach
Lake Okeechobee
Key Largo
Key West
Florida Keys
Straits of Florida
Tropic of Cancer
BAHAMAS
NASSAU
Freeport
Marsh Harbour
Nicholls Town
Andros Town
Andros Island
Grand Bahama Island
Great Abaco
Bimini Islands
Berry Islands
New Providence
Eleuthera Island
Cat Island
Rock Sound
Long Island
Clarence Town
George Town
Great Exuma Island
Exuma Cays
San Salvador
Rum Cay
Crooked Island
Acklins Island
Ragged Island Range
Mayaguana
Great Inagua
Little Inagua
Matthew Town
Providenciales
Turks and Caicos Islands (to UK)
COCKBURN TOWN
CUBA
HAVANA
Pinar del Río
Artemisa
Consolación del Sur
Guanabacoa
Matanzas
Cárdenas
Sagua la Grande
Santa Clara
Placetas
Cienfuegos
Sancti Spíritus
Morón
Ciego de Avila
Nuevitas
Camagüey
Las Tunas
Holguín
Bayamo
Manzanillo
Palma Soriano
Santiago de Cuba
Guantánamo
Guantanamo Bay (to US)
Archipiélago de Camagüey
Archipiélago de los Jardines de la Reina
Archipiélago de los Canarreos
Isla de la Juventud
Nueva Gerona
Yucatan Channel
MEXICO
Cancún
Isla Cozumel
Cayman Islands (to UK)
GEORGE TOWN
Grand Cayman
Little Cayman
Cayman Brac
Greater Antilles
JAMAICA
KINGSTON
Montego Bay
Spanish Town
Jamaica Channel
Windward Passage
HAITI
PORT-AU-PRINCE
Cap-Haïtien
Monte Cristi
Gonaïves
Jérémie
Cayes
Île de la Gonâve
Hispaniola
DOMINICAN REPUBLIC
SANTO DOMINGO
Santiago
Puerto Plata
San Francisco de Macor
La Vega
Samana
La Romana
Isla Beata
Puerto Rico (to US)
SAN JUAN
Mayagüez
Ponce
Isla Mona
British Virgin Islands (to UK)
ROAD TOWN
CHARLOTTE AMALIE
Virgin Islands (to US)
Anguilla (to UK)
THE VALLEY
St-Martin
Saba
Neth. Antilles (to Neth.)
St-Barthélemy (to France)
ANTIGUA & BARBUDA
BASSETERRE
Antigua
ST. KITTS & NEVIS
ST JOHN 'S
Montserrat (to UK)
Guadeloupe (to France)
BASSE-TERRE
Leeward Islands
DOMINICA
ROSEAU
FORT-DE-FRANCE
Martinique (to France)
CASTRIES
SAINT LUCIA
Vieux Fort
Saint Vincent
KINGSTOWN
BARBADOS
BRIDGETOWN
SAINT VINCENT AND THE GRENADINES
GRENADA
ST. GEORGE 'S
Windward Islands
Lesser Antilles
Tobago
Scarborough
TRINIDAD AND TOBAGO
PORT-OF-SPAIN
Trinidad
San Fernando
Gulf of Paria
Netherlands Antilles (to Neth.)
ORANJESTAD
Aruba (to Neth.)
Curaçao
Bonaire
WILLEMSTAD
Isla La Orchila
Isla La Tortuga
Isla Blanquilla
Isla de Margarita
Península de la Guajira
Gulf of Venezuela
VENEZUELA
CARACAS
Maracaibo
Lake Maracaibo
Cabimas
Ciudad Ojeda
Coro
San Felipe
Valencia
Maracay
Los Teques
Petare
Turmero
Barquisimeto
San Carlos
Acarigua
Trujillo
Valera
Guanare
Mérida
Pico Bolívar 5007m
Barinas
El Vigín
Barcelona
Carúpano
Cumana
Puerto La Cruz
Altagracia de Orinoco
San Juan de los Morros
Valle de la Pascua
Anaco
El Tigre
Maturín
Tucupita
Ciudad Guayana
Ciudad Bolívar
Embalse de Guri
San Fernando
Caicara del Orinoco
Río Orinoco
Llanos
GUYANA
COLOMBIA
Barranquilla
Soledad
Cartagena
Santa Marta
Riohacha
Pico Cristóbal Colón 5775m
Valledupar
Sincelejo
Montería
Río Magdalena
Río Cauca
Cúcuta
PANAMA
PANAMA CITY
Colón
El Porvenir
Panama Canal
Lake Gatún
San Miguelito
Pearl Islands
Isla del Rey
Gulf of Panama
Gulf of Darien
Yaviza
Chitré
Las Tablas
Santiago
Guarumal
David
Boquete
Mosquito Gulf
COSTA RICA
SAN JOSÉ
Limón
Guabito
Puntarenas
Nicoya
Liberia
Upala
Bahía de Coronado
Península de Osa
NICARAGUA
Lake Nicaragua
Bluefields
Puerto Cabezas
Prinzapolka
Barra de Río Grande
La Sirena
Matagalpa
Boaco
Juigalpa
San Carlos
San Juan del Norte
Punta Gorda
Pearl Lagoon
Corn Islands
Mosquito Coast
Cayos Miskitos
HONDURAS
Trujillo
Iriona
Brus Laguna
Laguna de Caratasca
Puerto Lempira
Waspam
Bocay
Siuna
Jalapa
Juticalpa
Savá
Bay Islands
Río Coco
SCALE 1: 11,600,000

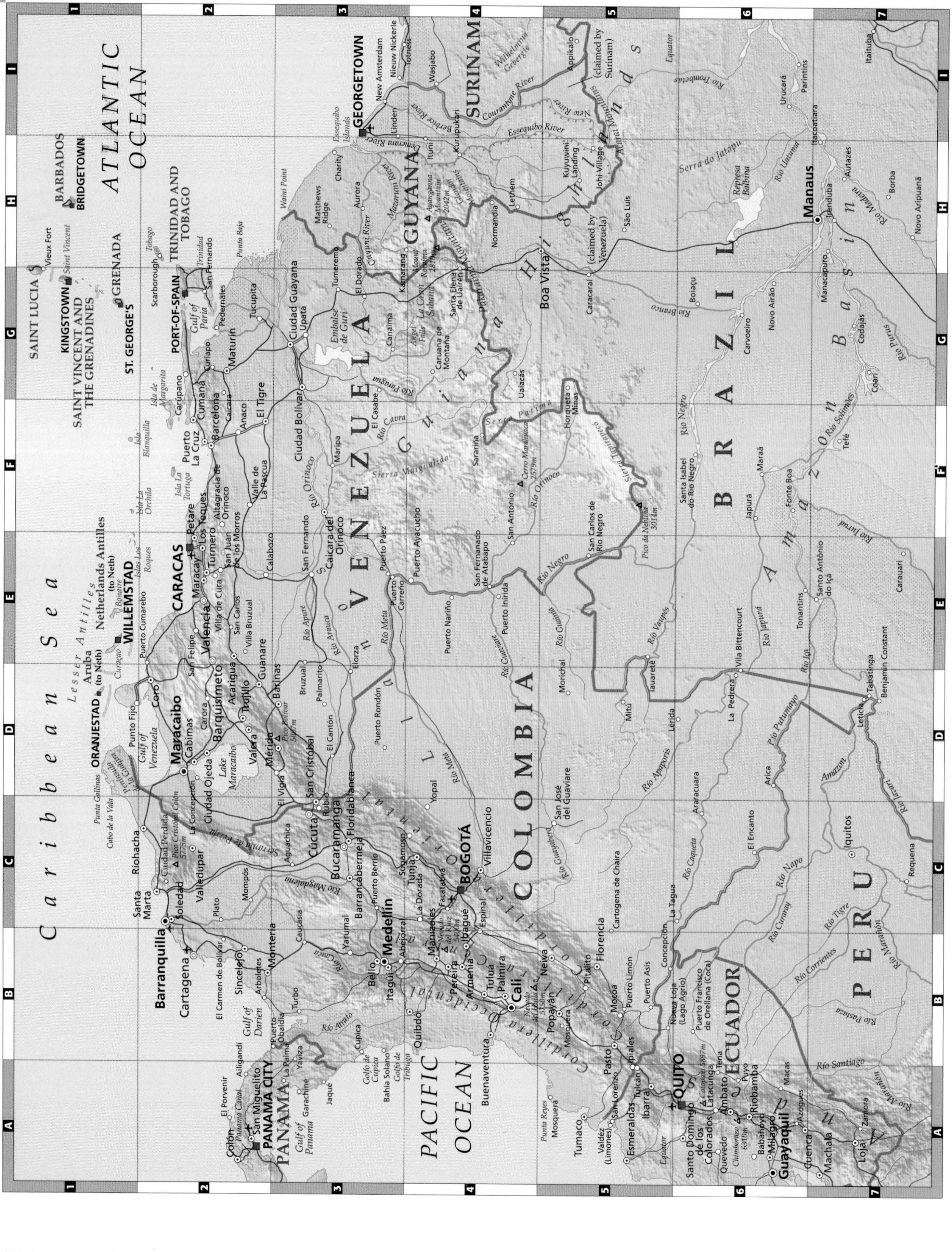

SCALE 1: 10,200,000

km 0 100 200 300
miles 0 100 200 300

Caribbean Sea
ATLANTIC OCEAN
PACIFIC OCEAN

SAINT LUCIA
Vieux Fort
KINGSTOWN
Saint Vincent
SAINT VINCENT AND THE GRENADINES
BARBADOS
BRIDGETOWN
GRENADA
ST. GEORGE'S
Lesser Antilles
Aruba (to Neth)
ORANJESTAD
Netherlands Antilles (to Neth)
Bonaire
Curaçao
WILLEMSTAD
Punta Gallinas
Cabo de la Vela
Península de la Guajira
Islas Los Roques
Isla La Orchila
Isla Blanquilla
Isla de Margarita
Isla La Tortuga
Scarborough
Tobago
PORT-OF-SPAIN
TRINIDAD AND TOBAGO
Trinidad
San Fernando
Gulf of Paria
Punta Baja
Waini Point

VENEZUELA
CARACAS
Maracaibo
Cabimas
Lake Maracaibo
Gulf of Venezuela
Punto Fijo
Coro
Puerto Cumarebo
San Felipe
Valencia
Maracay
Petare
Los Teques
Turmero
Villa de Cura
San Juan de los Morros
Altagracia de Orinoco
San Carlos
Villa Bruzual
Carora
Barquisimeto
Acarigua
Trujillo
Valera
Guanare
Mérida
Pico Bolívar 5007m
Barinas
El Vigía
San Cristóbal
Rubio
Ciudad Ojeda
La Concepción
Puerto La Cruz
Barcelona
Cumaná
Carúpano
Cariaco
Caicara
Maturín
Pedernales
Tucupita
Anaco
El Tigre
Valle de La Pascua
Calabozo
San Fernando
Río Apure
Río Orinoco
Río Arauca
Caicara del Orinoco
Bruzual
Palmarito
El Cantón
Elorza
Ciudad Bolívar
Ciudad Guayana
Upata
Embalse de Guri
Tumeremo
El Dorado
Maripa
El Casabe
Río Caura
Río Paragua
Sierra Maigualida
Canaima
Angel Falls
La Gran Sabana
Caruana de Montaña
Santa Elena de Uairén
Puerto Páez
Puerto Carreño
Río Meta
Puerto Ayacucho
Puerto Nariño
San Fernando de Atabapo
Puerto Inírida
Río Guaviare
San Antonio
Sarariña
Serra Parima
Cerro Marahuaca 2579m
Río Orinoco
Uaiacás
Horqueta Minas
San Carlos de Río Negro
Sierra Tapirapecó
Pico da Neblina 3014m
Guiana Highlands

GUYANA
GEORGETOWN
Essequibo Islands
Charity
Matthews Ridge
Aurora
Cuyuni River
Mazaruni River
Demerara River
Kamarang
Mount Roraima 2810m
Ayanganna Mountain 2042m
Pakaraima Mountains
Glendor Mountains
Ituni
Linden
New Amsterdam
Nieuw Nickerie
Totness
Wasjabo
Berbice River
Kurupukari
Normandia
Lethem
Essequibo River
Kuyuwini Landing
Johi Village
(claimed by Venezuela)
Acarai Mountains

SURINAM
Courantyne River
Wilhelmina Gebergte
New River
Appikalo
(claimed by Surinam)

COLOMBIA
BOGOTÁ
Ríohacha
Santa Marta
Barranquilla
Soledad
Cartagena
Ciudad Perdida
Pico Cristóbal Colón 5775m
Valledupar
Serranía de Perijá
Plato
El Carmen de Bolívar
Mompós
Sincelejo
Arboletes
Montería
Caucasia
Aguachica
Río Magdalena
Río Cauca
Río Atrato
Cúcuta
Bucaramanga
Floridablanca
Barrancabermeja
Puerto Berrío
Yarumal
Bello
Medellín
Itagüí
Abejorral
Sogamoso
Tunja
La Dorada
Manizales
Nevado del Ruiz 5400m
Facatativá
Pereira
Armenia
Ibagué
Espinal
Villavicencio
Tuluá
Palmira
Cali
Nevado del Huila 5750m
Neiva
Popayán
Mosquera
Pitalito
Florencia
Mocoa
Puerto Limón
Puerto Asís
Pasto
Ipiales
Tumaco
Punta Reyes
Buenaventura
Quibdó
Cupica
Golfo de Cupica
Bahía Solano
Golfo de Tribugá
Cordillera Occidental
Cordillera Central
Cordillera Oriental
Llanos
Puerto Rondón
Yopal
San José del Guaviare
Río Guayabero
Morichal
Río Guainía
Río Negro
Cartogena de Chaira
Mitú
Iauaretê
Río Vaupés
Río Apaporis
Lérida
Concepción
La Tagua
Río Caquetá
Araracuara
La Pedrera
El Encanto
Arica
Río Putumayo
Leticia
Tabatinga
Benjamin Constant

PANAMA
PANAMA CITY
Colón
Panama Canal
El Porvenir
Ailigandí
San Miguelito
Gulf of Darien
Puerto Obaldía
La Palma
Yaviza
Turbo
Gulf of Panama
Garachiné
Jaqué

ECUADOR
QUITO
Valdéz (Limones)
San Lorenzo
Esmeraldas
Tulcán
Ibarra
Equator
Nueva Loja (Lago Agrio)
Puerto Francisco de Orellana (Coca)
Santo Domingo de los Colorados
Cotopaxi 5897m
Latacunga
Tena
Quevedo
Ambato
Chimborazo 6310m
Puyo
Riobamba
Babahoyo
Milagro
Guayaquil
Macas
Azogues
Cuenca
Machala
Loja
Zamora
Andes

PERU
Iquitos
Requena
Río Curaray
Río Napo
Río Corrientes
Río Tigre
Río Pastaza
Río Santiago
Río Marañón
Amazon
Río Javari

BRAZIL
Amazon Basin
Boa Vista
Caracaraí
São Luís
Río Branco
Boiaçu
Serra do Jatapu
Río Trombetas
Santa Isabel do Rio Negro
Río Negro
Carvoeiro
Novo Airão
Represa Balbina
Río Uatumã
Urucará
Parintins
Itacoatiara
Manaus
Manacapuru
Iranduba
Autazes
Río Madeira
Borba
Novo Aripuanã
Itaituba
Japurá
Río Japurá
Maraã
Fonte Boa
Tonantins
Río Içá
Santo Antônio do Içá
Vila Bittencourt
Tefé
Río Solimões
Codajás
Coari
Río Purus
Río Juruá
Carauari

COLOMBIA
ECUADOR
PERU
BRAZIL
BOLIVIA
CHILE
VENEZUELA
GUYANA
PACIFIC OCEAN
Amazon Basin
Cordillera Occidental
Cordillera Oriental
Andes
Guiana Highlands
Altiplano
Pantanal
Chapada dos Parecis
Serra do Jatapu
Serra do Cachimbo
Sierra Tapirapecó
QUITO
LIMA
LA PAZ
SUCRE
Manaus
Porto Velho
Rio Branco
Iquitos
Guayaquil
Cuenca
Trujillo
Chiclayo
Piura
Arequipa
Cusco
Santa Cruz
Cochabamba
Oruro
Cuiabá
Callao
Huancayo
Ayacucho
Pucallpa
Tacna
Arica
Esmeraldas
Manta
Tumaco
Pasto
Florencia
Lake Titicaca
Lake Poopó
Río Napo
Río Putumayo
Río Marañón
Río Ucayali
Rio Purus
Rio Madeira
Rio Negro
Rio Juruá
Río Mamoré
Rio Guaporé
Río Beni
Rio Japurá
Rio Iça
Amazon
Pico da Neblina 3014m
Chimborazo 6310m
Cotopaxi 5897m
Nevado Huascarán 6768m
Manu National Park
Galápagos Islands (to Ecuador)
SCALE 1: 7,500,000
Isla Isabela
Isla Fernandina
Isla Santa Cruz
Isla San Cristóbal
Isla Santa María
Isla San Salvador
Isla Marchena
Isla Genovesa
Puerto Ayora
Puerto Baquerizo Moreno
Puerto Villamil
Volcán Wolf 1646m
Volcán Santo Tomás 1490m
Equator
Puerto Ayora is 1,900 miles (1,200 km) west of Guayaquil (Ecuador)
SCALE 1: 11,200,000

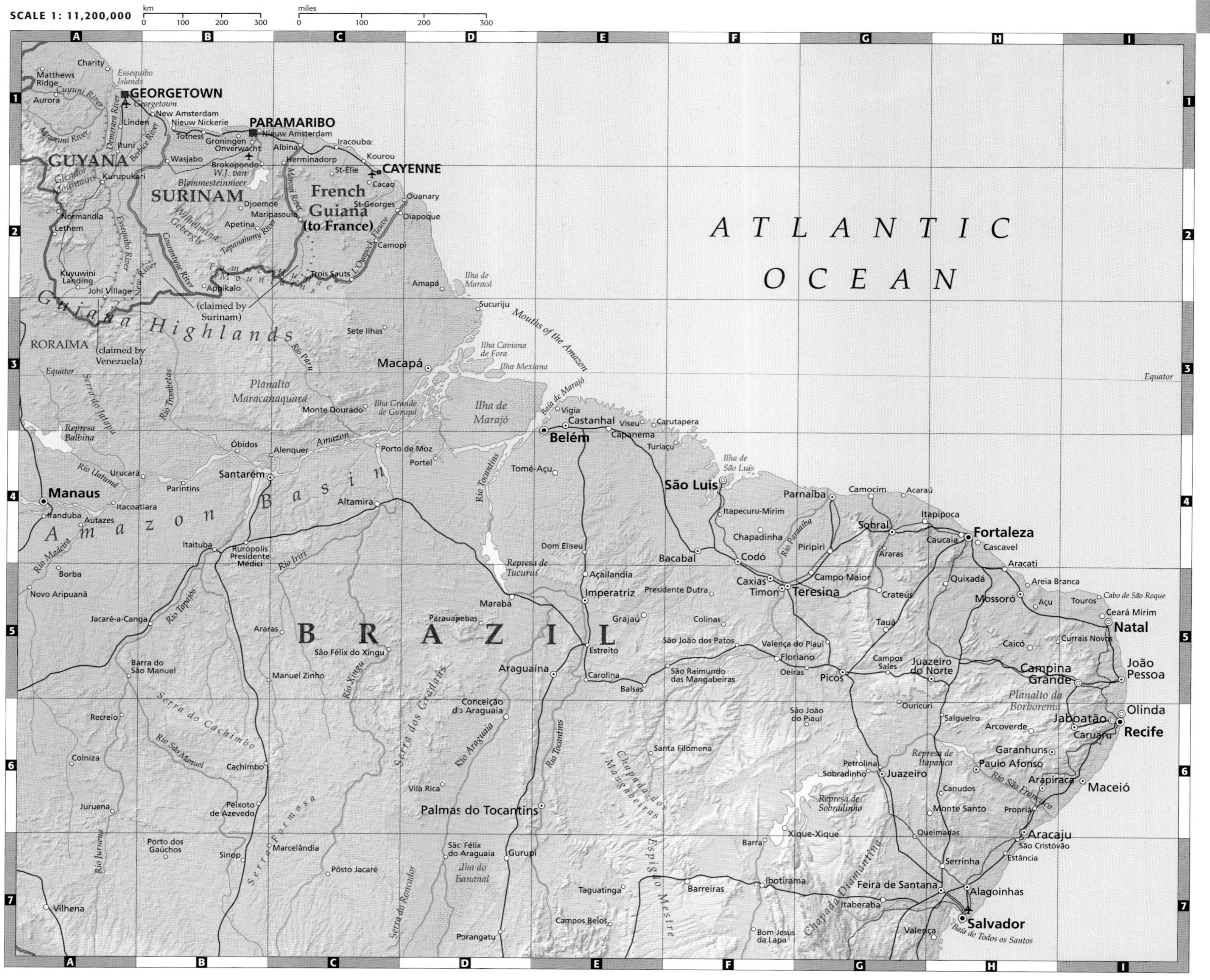
SCALE 1: 11,200,000
km 0 100 200 300
miles 0 100 200 300
ATLANTIC OCEAN
Equator
BRAZIL
Amazon Basin
Guiana Highlands
GUYANA
SURINAM
French Guiana (to France)
(claimed by Surinam)
(claimed by Venezuela)
RORAIMA
GEORGETOWN
PARAMARIBO
CAYENNE
Macapá
Belém
São Luís
Fortaleza
Natal
João Pessoa
Olinda
Recife
Jaboatão
Caruaru
Maceió
Aracaju
Salvador
Manaus
Santarém
Teresina
Timon
Caxias
Imperatriz
Marabá
Araguaína
Palmas do Tocantins
Campina Grande
Juazeiro do Norte
Juazeiro
Petrolina
Feira de Santana
Mossoró
Sobral
Parnaíba
Picos
Arapiraca
Garanhuns
Paulo Afonso
Altamira
Itaituba
Ilha de Marajó
Mouths of the Amazon
Rio Tocantins
Rio Xingu
Rio Tapajós
Rio Madeira
Rio São Francisco
Chapada Diamantina
Chapada das Mangabeiras
Espigão Mestre
Serra dos Gradaús
Serra do Cachimbo
Serra do Roncador
Serra Formosa
Planalto Maracanaquará
Planalto da Borborema
Baía de Todos os Santos

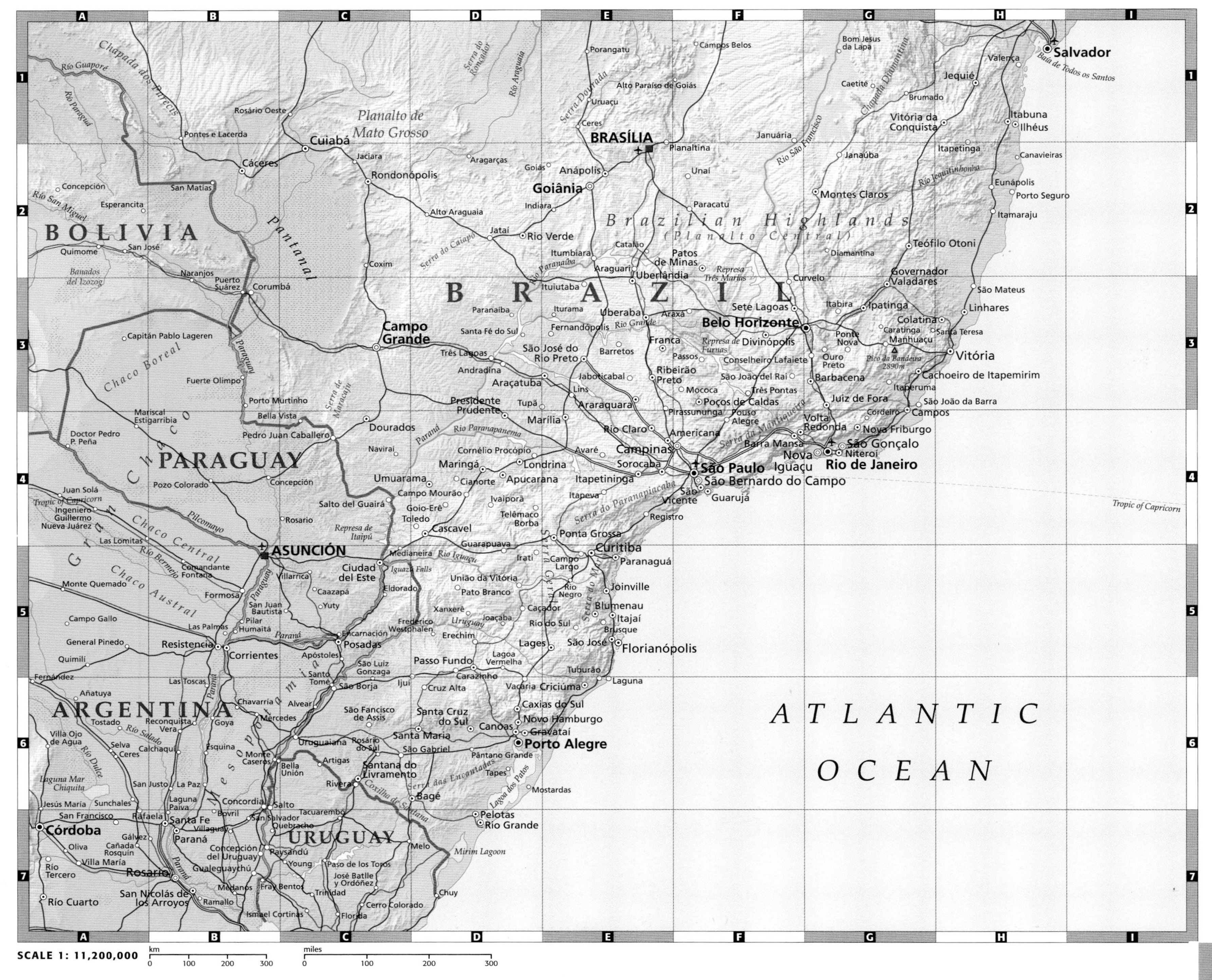
ATLANTIC
OCEAN
BRAZIL
BOLIVIA
PARAGUAY
ARGENTINA
URUGUAY
Brazilian Highlands
(Planalto Central)
Planalto de Mato Grosso
Pantanal
Chaco Boreal
Chaco Central
Chaco Austral
Gran Chaco
Mesopotamia
Chapada dos Parecis
Chapada Diamantina
Serra do Caiapó
Serra do Roncador
Serra Dourada
Serra Geral
Serra do Mar
Serra da Mantiqueira
Serra do Paranapiacaba
Serra de Maracaju
Serra das Encantadas
Coxilha de Santana
Tropic of Capricorn
Salvador
Baía de Todos os Santos
Valença
Jequié
Itabuna
Ilhéus
Vitória da Conquista
Brumado
Caetité
Bom Jesus da Lapa
Canavieiras
Eunápolis
Porto Seguro
Itamaraju
Itapetinga
Janaúba
Montes Claros
Januária
Diamantina
Teófilo Otoni
Governador Valadares
São Mateus
Linhares
Colatina
Vitória
Cachoeiro de Itapemirim
Pico da Bandeira 2890m
Belo Horizonte
Sete Lagoas
Curvelo
Ipatinga
Itabira
Divinópolis
Juiz de Fora
Barbacena
Campos
São João da Barra
Nova Friburgo
Volta Redonda
Barra Mansa
Rio de Janeiro
Niterói
São Gonçalo
Nova Iguaçu
São Paulo
São Bernardo do Campo
Guarujá
São Vicente
Campinas
Sorocaba
Americana
Rio Claro
Araraquara
Ribeirão Preto
Franca
Uberaba
Uberlândia
Araguari
Patos de Minas
Represa Três Marias
Represa de Furnas
BRASÍLIA
Planaltina
Unaí
Paracatu
Goiânia
Anápolis
Porangatu
Campos Belos
Alto Paraíso de Goiás
Uruaçu
Ceres
Goiás
Indiara
Rio Verde
Jataí
Itumbiara
Catalão
Ituiutaba
São José do Rio Preto
Araçatuba
Presidente Prudente
Marília
Londrina
Maringá
Apucarana
Cascavel
Ponta Grossa
Curitiba
Paranaguá
Joinville
Blumenau
Itajaí
Florianópolis
Lages
Criciúma
Tubarão
Laguna
Caxias do Sul
Novo Hamburgo
Canoas
Gravataí
Porto Alegre
Santa Maria
Passo Fundo
Santa Cruz do Sul
Pelotas
Rio Grande
Lagoa dos Patos
Mirim Lagoon
Bagé
Santana do Livramento
Uruguaiana
Chuy
Campo Grande
Cuiabá
Rondonópolis
Cáceres
Corumbá
Puerto Suárez
Dourados
Pedro Juan Caballero
Concepción
ASUNCIÓN
Ciudad del Este
Iguaçu Falls
Represa de Itaipu
Encarnación
Posadas
Corrientes
Resistencia
Formosa
Santa Fe
Paraná
Rosario
San Nicolás de los Arroyos
Córdoba
Río Cuarto
Villa María
Salto
Paysandú
Concordia
Tacuarembó
Rivera
Melo
Río Guaporé
Río Paraguá
Río San Miguel
Río Paraguay
Río Paraná
Río Uruguay
Rio São Francisco
Rio Jequitinhonha
Rio Araguaia
Rio Paranaíba
Rio Grande
Rio Paranapanema
Rio Iguaçu
Río Pilcomayo
Río Bermejo
Río Salado
Río Dulce
Laguna Mar Chiquita
Bañados del Izozog
SCALE 1: 11,200,000
km 0 100 200 300
miles 0 100 200 300

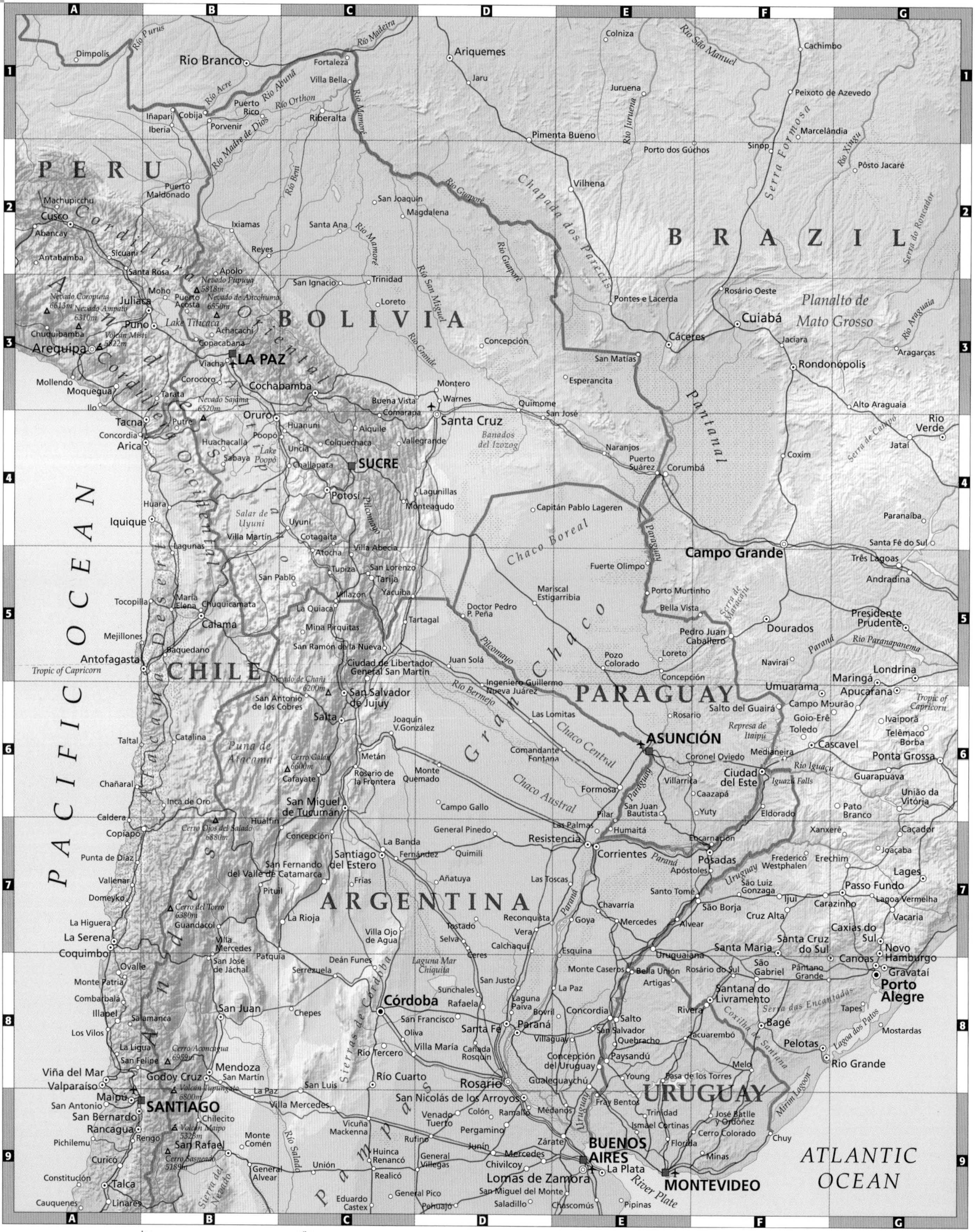

A B C D E F G

PERU
BOLIVIA
BRAZIL
CHILE
PARAGUAY
ARGENTINA
URUGUAY
PACIFIC OCEAN
ATLANTIC OCEAN

Dimpolis
Rio Purus
Rio Branco
Fortaleza
Rio Madeira
Ariquemes
Colniza
Rio São Manuel
Cachimbo
Jaru
Villa Bella
Rio Abunã
Rio Acre
Puerto Rico
Rio Orthon
Riberalta
Rio Mamoré
Juruena
Peixoto de Azevedo
Iñapari
Cobija
Porvenir
Iberia
Rio Madre de Dios
Pimenta Bueno
Rio Juruena
Porto dos Gúchos
Sinop
Marcelândia
Serra Formosa
Rio Xingu
Pôsto Jacaré
Puerto Maldonado
Rio Beni
Vilhena
Chapada dos Parecis
Rio Guaporé
Machupicchu
Cusco
Abancay
Antabamba
Cordillera Oriental
San Joaquín
Magdalena
Ixiamas
Santa Ana
Reyes
Sicuani
Santa Rosa
Apolo
Nevado Pupuya 5818m
Nevado Coropuna 6613m
Nevado Ampato 6310m
Moho
Juliaca
Puerto Acosta
Nevado de Ancohuma 6550m
San Ignacio
Trinidad
Loreto
Río San Miguel
Río Grande
Pontes e Lacerda
Rosário Oeste
Planalto de Mato Grosso
Serra do Roncador
Rio Araguaia
Cuiabá
Puno
Lake Titicaca
Achacachi
Chuquibamba
Volcán Misti 5822m
Arequipa
Copacabana
LA PAZ
Viacha
Concepción
Cáceres
Jaciara
Aragarças
San Matías
Rondonópolis
Mollendo
Moquegua
Corocoro
Cochabamba
Montero
Esperancita
Pantanal
Tarata
Nevado Sajama 6520m
Buena Vista
Warnes
Quimome
Alto Araguaia
Ilo
Tacna
Putre
Oruro
Huanuni
Comarapa
Santa Cruz
San José
Rio Verde
Concordia
Arica
Huachacalla
Poopó
Aiquile
Bañados del Izozog
Jataí
Serra de Caiapó
Sabaya
Lake Poopó
Uncía
Colquechaca
Vallegrande
Naranjos
Puerto Suárez
Corumbá
Coxim
Challapata
SUCRE
Potosí
Lagunillas
Monteagudo
Pilcomayo
Huara
Salar de Uyuni
Uyuni
Capitán Pablo Lageren
Chaco Boreal
Iquique
Villa Martín
Cotagaita
Villa Abecia
Paranaíba
Lagunas
Atocha
Campo Grande
Santa Fé do Sul
Três Lagoas
Fuerte Olimpo
Paraguay
Tupiza
San Lorenzo
Tarija
Andradina
San Pablo
Tocopilla
María Elena
Chuquicamata
Villazon
Yacuiba
Mariscal Estigarribia
Porto Murtinho
La Quiaca
Tartagal
Doctor Pedro P. Peña
Bella Vista
Serra de Maracaju
Presidente Prudente
Calama
Mina Pirquitas
Dourados
Pedro Juan Caballero
Mejillones
San Ramón de la Nueva
Baquedano
Atacama Desert
Cordillera Occidental
Antofagasta
Tropic of Capricorn
Ciudad de Libertador General San Martín
Juan Solá
Pozo Colorado
Loreto
Navirai
Paraná
Rio Paranapanema
Londrina
Nevado de Chañi 6200m
San Salvador de Jujuy
Ingeniero Guillermo Nueva Juárez
Concepción
Maringá
Apucarana
Umuarama
Campo Mourão
San Antonio de los Cobres
Salta
Río Bermejo
Gran Chaco
Las Lomitas
Rosario
Salto del Guairá
Goio-Erê
Toledo
Represa de Itaipú
Ivaiporã
Telêmaco Borba
Joaquín V.González
Chaco Central
ASUNCIÓN
Taltal
Catalina
Puna de Atacama
Cerro Galán 6600m
Metán
Comandante Fontana
Coronel Oviedo
Medianeira
Cascavel
Ponta Grossa
Rosario de la Frontera
Monte Quemado
Ciudad del Este
Rio Iguaçu
Iguazu Falls
Guarapuava
Chañaral
Cafayate
Villarrica
Caazapá
Chaco Austral
Formosa
União da Vitória
Inca de Oro
San Miguel de Tucumán
Campo Gallo
Pilar
San Juan Bautista
Yuty
Pato Branco
Eldorado
Caldera
Hualfín
Las Palmas
Humaitá
Copiapó
Cerro Ojos del Salado 6880m
Concepción
La Banda
General Pinedo
Resistencia
Encarnación
Xanxerê
Caçador
Corrientes
Posadas
Joaçaba
Punta de Díaz
Santiago del Estero
Fernández
Quimilí
Frederico Westphalen
Erechim
Vallenar
San Fernando del Valle de Catamarca
Añatuya
Las Toscas
Apóstoles
Lages
Frías
Uruguay
Passo Fundo
Pituil
Santo Tomé
Domeyko
Cerro del Toro 6380m
Chavarría
São Luiz Gonzaga
Ijuí
Carazinho
Lagoa Vermelha
Guandacol
La Rioja
Reconquista
São Borja
Cruz Alta
La Higuera
Tostado
Goya
Mercedes
Alvear
Vacaria
La Serena
Villa Ojo de Agua
Vera
Caxias do Sul
Coquimbo
Villa Mercedes
Selva
Calchaquí
Santa Cruz do Sul
Novo Hamburgo
Patquía
Deán Funes
Laguna Mar Chiquita
Ceres
Esquina
Uruguaiana
Santa Maria
São Gabriel
Canoas
Ovalle
San José de Jáchal
Serrezuela
Monte Caseros
Bella Unión
Rosário do Sul
Pântano Grande
Gravataí
Monte Patria
San Justo
Artigas
Porto Alegre
Combarbalá
Sunchales
La Paz
Santana do Livramento
Serra das Encantadas
Tapes
San Juan
Laguna Paiva
Illapel
Chepes
Córdoba
Rafaela
Bovril
Concordia
Salto
Rivera
Coxilha de Santana
Salamanca
San Francisco
Santa Fe
Paraná
Bagé
Mostardas
Los Vilos
Sierras de Córdoba
Oliva
San Salvador
Tacuarembó
Villaguay
Quebracho
La Ligua
Cerro Aconcagua 6959m
Villa María
Cañada Rosquín
Pelotas
Lagoa dos Patos
San Felipe
Río Tercero
Concepción del Uruguay
Paysandú
Melo
Rio Grande
Viña del Mar
Mendoza
San Martín
Valparaíso
Godoy Cruz
Río Cuarto
Rosario
Gualeguaychú
Young
Paso de los Torres
Mirim Lagoon
Volcán Tupungato 6800m
San Luis
La Paz
Maipú
SANTIAGO
San Nicolás de los Arroyos
San Antonio
Villa Mercedes
Venado Tuerto
Colón
Ramallo
Médanos
Fray Bentos
Trinidad
José Batlle y Ordóñez
San Bernardo
Chilecito
Rancagua
Volcán Maipo 5326m
Vicuña Mackenna
Pergamino
Ismael Cortinas
Cerro Colorado
Chuy
Rengo
Monte Comén
Río Salado
Pampas
Rufino
Zárate
Pichilemu
San Rafael
Cerro Sosneado 5189m
Huinca Renancó
General Villegas
Junín
Mercedes
BUENOS AIRES
Florida
Minas
Curicó
Unión
General Alvear
Chivilcoy
La Plata
Constitución
Sierra del Nevado
Realicó
Lomas de Zamora
MONTEVIDEO
Talca
General Pico
San Miguel del Monte
River Plate
Cauquenes
Linares
Eduardo Castex
Pehuajó
Saladillo
Chascomús
Pipinas

SCALE 1: 11,200,000
km 0 100 200 300
miles 0 100 200 300

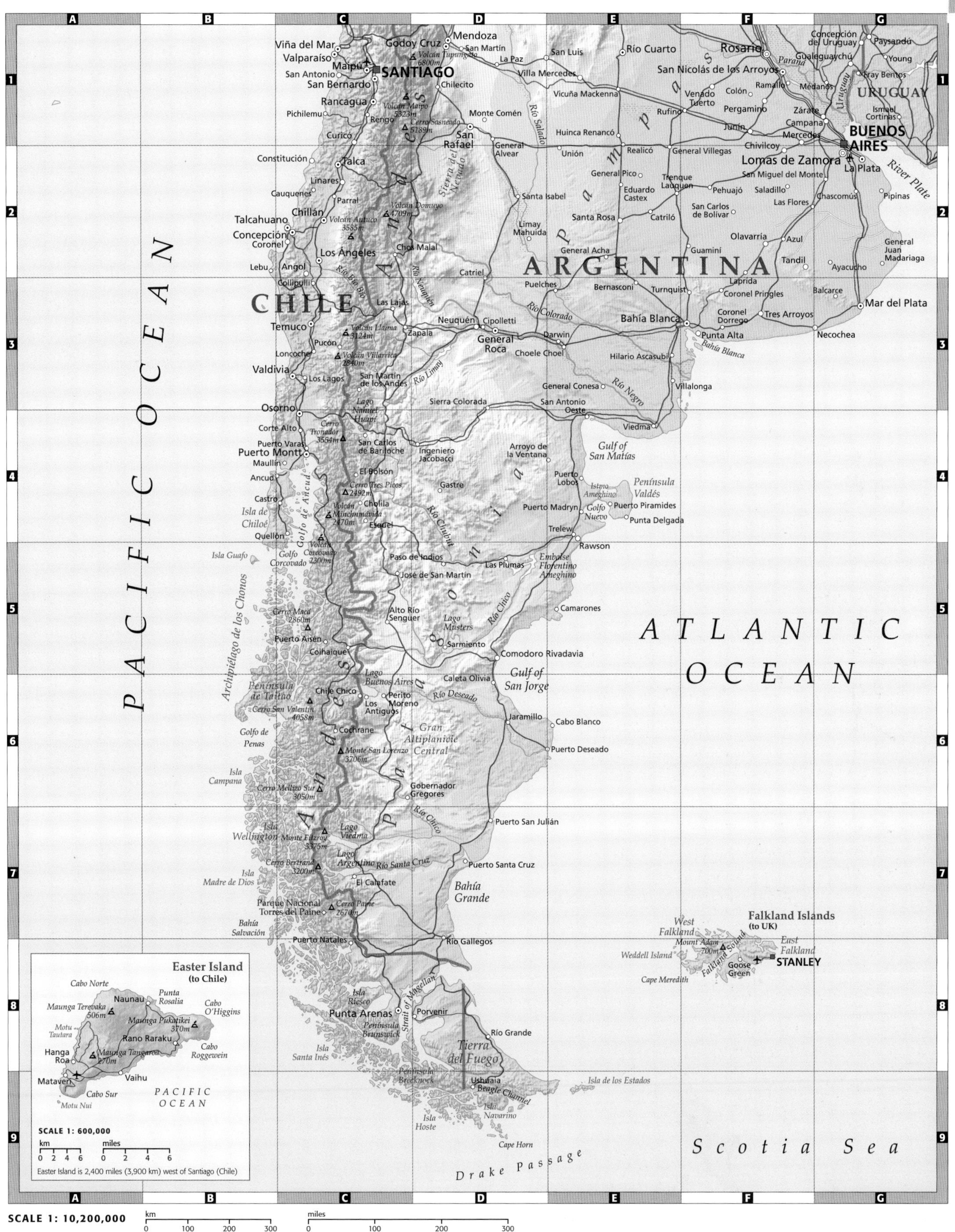

SCALE 1: 10,200,000 km 0 100 200 300 miles 0 100 200 300

Index

Page numbers in **bold** indicate main references

A

Acadia National Park (Maine, USA) 237
Acapulco (Mexico) 279
Active adventures 11, 33, 55, 77, 103, 129, 153, 181, 209, 233, 257, 279
Alabama (USA), Gulf Shores 33
The Alamo (Texas, USA) **280**, 281
Alaska (USA)
  Alcan Highway 152
  Dog Sledding 33
  Folk Festival (Juneau) 305
  Frozen Alaska 278
  Glacier Bay National Park 111, 180
  Inside Passage 102, **110–11**
  Kodiak Island 128
  Northern Lights 278
Albuquerque (New Mexico, USA)
  International Balloon Fiesta 232, **242–3**, 307
Alcan Highway (USA/Canada) 152
Algonquin Provincial Park (Canada) 208
Aloha Festivals (Hawai'i, USA) 208, 306
Altiplano (Peru) 32
Alto Puelo Lake (Patagonia) 72–3
Amazon River
  Brazil 102, **114–15**
  Ecuador 55
  Iquitos (Peru) 208
Ambergris Caye (Belize) 102, **106–7**
The Andes
  Altiplano Train (Peru) 32
  Avenue of the Volcanoes (Ecuador) 128
  Fitz Roy Massif (Argentina) 257
  La Paz (Bolivia) 103, **108–9**
  Laguna Verde (Chile) 278
  Manú National Park (Peru) 180, **200–201**
  Mendoza (Argentina) 209, **216–17**
  Quito (Ecuador) 208, **218–19**
  Salta and Jujuy (Argentina) 180, **190–91**
  Skiing in the Chilean Andes 153
  Teleférico, Santiago (Chile) 256
Andromeda Botanical Gardens (Barbados) 102
Angel Falls (Venezuela) 261, 278, **292–3**
Annapolis (Maryland, USA) 232
L'Anse-aux-Meadows (Canada) 192, 193
Antigua (Guatemala) 54, 263
Apostle Islands (Wisconsin, USA) 181
Appalachian Trail (USA) 76, 128
Aquário Natural (Brazil) 233
Arches National Park (Utah, USA) 215
Archipelago de San Blas (Panama) **88–9**
Argentina
  Buenos Aires 232, **238–9**
  Fitz Roy Massif 257
  Glacier Perito Moreno 10
  Iguazú Falls 76, **82–3**
  Los Glaciares National Park 76
  Mar del Plata 257
  Mendoza 209, **216–17**, 304
  Old Patagonian Express 278
  Patagonia 10, 55, **72–3**
  Salta and Jujuy 180, **190–91**
  South Patagonian Fjords 232, **244–5**
Arizona (USA)
  Scottsdale 77
  Sedona 209
  Tucson 257, **258–9**
Arkansas (USA)
  Hot Springs National Park Resort 33
Atitlán, Lago de (Guatemala) 256, 263
Atlanta (Georgia, USA) 11
Austin (Texas, USA) **58–9**
Avalon Peninsula (Canada) 152, **172–3**
Avenue of the Volcanoes (Ecuador) 128
Aztec civilization 54, **60–61**

B

Badlands National Park (South Dakota, USA) 229
Baffin Island (Canada) 103
The Bahamas (Caribbean) 257, **268–9**
  The Exumas 279
  Junkanoo 278, 307
Bahía Concepción (Mexico) 233
Baja California Sur (Mexico) 33, **36–7**
Baltimore (Maryland, USA) 278
Banff (Canada) 227, 256, 307
Banff National Park (Canada) 209
Bar Harbor (Maine, USA) 237
Barbados (Caribbean) 257, 304, 305
  Andromeda Botanical Gardens 102
  Holetown 33
  Island Cruise 272, 273
  Surfing at Bathsheba 103
Bard on the Beach (Vancouver, Canada) 157, 305
Barretos Rodeo Festival (Brazil) 180, **202–3**
Bathsheba (Barbados) 103
Beaches
  Acapulco (Mexico) 279
  The Bahamas (Caribbean) 257, **268–9**
  Bahía Concepción (Mexico) 233
  Baja California Sur (Mexico) 33, **36–7**
  Barbados (Caribbean) 257
  The Beaches, Toronto (Canada) 103
  Bermuda (North Atlantic) 129, **144–5**
  British Virgin Islands (Caribbean) 55, **64–5**
  Cape Cod (Massachusetts, USA) 153, **170–71**
  Cape May (New Jersey, USA) 77
  Cartagena (Colombia) 17
  Cayman Islands (Caribbean) 279, **296–7**
  Clearwater Beach (Florida, USA) 55
  Copacabana (Rio, Brazil) 233
  Dominican Republic 152, **176–7**
  Florida Keys (Florida, USA) 33
  Georgia (USA) 121
  Gulf Shores (Alabama, USA) 33
  The Hamptons (New York State, USA) 181, **194–5**
  Hawai'i (USA) 279, **284–5**
  Ilhabela (Brazil) 233
  Isla Margarita (Venezuela) 256, **260–61**
  Jamaica 11, 33, **282–3**
  Kaua'i (Hawai'i, USA) 232, **248–9**
  Kiawah Island (South Carolina, USA) 11
  Lowcountry (South Carolina, USA) 77, **78–9**
  Manzanillo (Mexico) 279
  Mar del Plata (Argentina) 257
  Maui (Hawai'i, USA) 27
  Mayan Riviera (Mexico) 14–15
  Miami (Florida, USA) 41
  Myrtle Beach (South Carolina, USA) 129
  Naples (Florida, USA) 233
  Nicoya Peninsula (Costa Rica) 279, **288–9**
  Oregon Coast (USA) 232, **246–7**
  Outer Banks (North Carolina, USA) 103, **124–5**
  Pawleys Island (South Carolina, USA) 181
  Private Islands (Caribbean) 55
  Puerto Escondido (Mexico) 55
  Puerto Vallarta (Mexico) 77
  St. Barts (Caribbean) **286–7**
  St. Kitts and Nevis (Caribbean) 77
  St. Lucia (Caribbean) 123
  Salvador (Brazil) 50–51
  Sanibel and the Captiva Islands (Florida, USA) 103
  Tortola (Caribbean) 64, 65, 279
  Turks and Caicos Islands (Caribbean) 77, **84–5**
  Uruguay 77, **96–7**
  US Virgin Islands (Caribbean) 33
  Vieques (Puerto Rico) 11, **22–3**
  Waikīkī (Hawai'i, USA) 129
Beaufort (South Carolina, USA) 79
Belize
  Ambergris Caye 102, **106–7**
  Cayo District 55, **290–91**
  Garifuna Settlement Day 307
  Independence Day 306
  Mountain Pine Forest Preserve 11
Bermuda (North Atlantic) 129, **144–5**
Big Bend National Park (Texas, USA) 10, 233
Big Sur (California, USA) 232
Birding
  Bosque del Apache (New Mexico, USA) 256
  Costa Rica 103
  Falkland Islands 298–9
  Kaua'i (Hawai'i, USA) 248
  Mackinac Island (Michigan, USA) 197
  Manú National Park (Peru) 200, 201
  Panama 32, **42–3**
  Witless Bay (Canada) 153
Black Hills (South Dakota, USA) 208, **228–9**
Blue Hole (Belize) 89, **106**, 107
Blue Mountains (Jamaica) 282–3
  Blue Mountain Peak 33
Blue Ridge Parkway (North Carolina, USA) 76, **92–3**
Bluegrass Country (Kentucky, USA) 128
Blues Festival, Chicago (Illinois, USA) 128, **130–31**, 305
Bocas del Toro (Panama) 77
Bolivia
  Cerro Rico Mines, Potosí 153
  Chiquitos 128, **148–9**
  Isla del Sol 208
  La Paz 103, **108–9**, 208, 304
  La Paz to Coroico 180
  Potosí 180
  Salar de Uyuni 152, **158–9**
  Tiwanaku, La Paz 208
  Trans-Apolobamba Trek 129
Bonito (Brazil) 233
Bosque del Apache (New Mexico, USA) 256
Boundary Waters (Minnesota, USA) 152
Branson (Missouri, USA) 77, **80–81**
Brazil
  Amazon River 102, **114–15**
  Aquário Natural 233
  Barretos Rodeo Festival 180, **202–3**
  Búzios 257
  Círio de Nazaré Festival 232, 307
  Copacabana Palace (Rio) 233
  Iguazú Falls 76, **82–3**
  Ilhabela 233
  Isla Fernando de Noronha 54
  Panatal 128
  Pedra Azul 54
  Rio de Janeiro 233, 278, **302–3**, 307
  Salvador 32, **50–51**, 304
British Virgin Islands (Caribbean) 55, **64–5**, 279, 304
Bryce Canyon (Utah, USA) 181, 214, 215
Buckskin Gulch (Utah, USA) 77
Buenos Aires (Argentina) 232, **238–9**
Bumbershoot (Seattle, USA) 208, 306
Búzios (Brazil) 257

C

Cabarete (Dominican Republic) 55
Cahuachi (Peru) 225
Calgary (Canada) 227, 304
  Calgary Stampede 153, **168–9**, 306
California (USA)
  Big Sur 232
  California Missions Trail 10
  Carmel Valley 153
  Death Valley National Park 278
  John Muir Trail (USA) 209
  Joshua Tree National Park 54
  Lake Tahoe 152
  Los Angeles 76, 181, 232
  Mammoth Mountain 11
  Mendocino 181
  Mount Whitney 209, 233
  Palm Springs **28–29**
  Pasadena 278, **300–301**
  Redwood National Park 256
  San Diego 11
  San Francisco 54, 209, **212–13**, 232
  Santa Ynez Valley 77
  Sequoia National Park 208
  Wine Country 233, **250–1**
  Yosemite National Park 102
Calle Ocho (Miami, USA) 54, 304
Campeche (Mexico) 71
Campobello Island (Canada) 210–11
Canada
  Alcan Highway 152
  Algonquin Provincial Park (Ontario) 208
  Avalon Peninsula (Newfoundland) 152, **172–3**
  Baffin Island (Nunavit) 103
  Banff (Alberta) 227, 256
  Banff National Park (Alberta) 209
  Cabot Trail (Nova Scotia) 76
  Calgary (Alberta) 153, **168–9**, 304, 306
  Cape Breton Island (Nova Scotia) 76, 209
  Cape Churchill (Manitoba) 233, **234–5**
  Charlevoix (Québec) 129
  Coast to Coast 208, **226–7**
  Fundy Isles (New Brunswick) 209, **210–11**
  Great Divide Trail (British Columbia) 180
  Gwaii Haanas National Park Reserve (British Columbia) 153, **160–61**
  Icefields Parkway (Alberta) 180, 227
  Iles de la Madeleine 32
  Jasper National Park (Alberta) 152, **162–3**
  Kluane National Park (Yukon) 152
  The Laurentians (Québec) 232, 279
  Montréal (Québec) 129, **142–3**, 152, 153, 227, 305, 306
  Mount Tremblant (Québec) 279
  Niagara Falls (Ontario) 128, **132–3**
  Northern Lights (Northern Canada) 278
  Ottawa (Ontario) 33, **34–5**, 306
  Pacific Rim National Park (British Columbia) **112–13**
  Prince Edward Island **24–5**, 181
  Québec City (Québec) 181, **186–7**, 279, 304
  Quttinirpaaq National Park (Nunavit) 152
  Tall Pine Lodges (Manitoba) 153
  Toonik Tyme, Iqalit (Nunavit) 76, 305
  Toronto (Ontario) 102, **118–19**, 227, 306
  Vancouver (British Columbia) 33, 111, 152, **156–7**, 227, 306
  Vancouver Island (British Columbia) 103, 208
  Viking Trail (Newfoundland) 180, **192–3**
  Waskesiu Lake (Saskatchewan) 153
  Whistler (Whistler) 55, **56–7**
  Whiteshell Provincial Park (Manitoba) 232
  Witless Bay (Newfoundland) 153
  Yukon 128
Canadaigua (New York State, USA) 147
Cancún (Mexico) 14–15, 70–71
Canoeing and kayaking
  Algonquin Provincial Park 208
  Angel Falls (Venezuela) 278, **292–3**
  Baffin Island (Canada) 103
  The Exumas (Bahamas) 279
  Gwaii Haanas National Park Reserve (Canada) 153, **160–61**
  Laguna San Rafael (Chile) 257
  The Laurentians (Canada) 232
  Mount Desert Island (Maine, USA) 237
  Parque Nacional Torres del Paine (Chile) 265
  San Juan Islands (Washington, USA) 167
Canyon de Chelly (Arizona, USA) 241
Canyonlands National Park (Utah, USA) 215
Cape Breton Island (Canada) 76, 209
Cape Churchill (Canada) 233, **234–5**
Cape Cod (Massachusetts, USA) 153, **170–71**
Cape Horn (Chile) 245
Cape Kiwanda State Park (Oregon, USA) 247
Cape May (New Jersey, USA) 77
Cape Meares (Oregon, USA) 247
Cape Perpetua (Oregon, USA) 247
Captiva Islands (Florida, USA) 103
Carbon offsetting schemes 308
Caribbean
  Island Cruise 257, **272–3**
  Pirates of the Caribbean **268**, 269
  Private Islands 55
  see also The Bahamas; Barbados; British Virgin Islands; Cayman Islands; Cuba; Curaçao; Dominica; Dominican Republic; Jamaica; Leeward Islands; Martinique; Nevis; Puerto Rico; St. Barts; St. Kitts; St. Lucia; Trinidad; Turks and Caicos Islands; US Virgin Islands; Windward Islands
Carmel Valley (California, USA) 153
Carnival
  Mardi Gras, New Orleans (Louisiana, USA) 32
  Salvador (Brazil) 32, **50–51**, 304
  Trinidad (Caribbean) 32, **48–9**, 304
Carretera Austral (Chile) 32
Cartagena (Colombia) 10, **16–17**, 304
Cascade Loop (Washington State, USA) 152
Castries (St. Lucia) 122–3
Catarata de Pulhapanzak (Honduras) **66**, 67
Cayman Islands (Caribbean) 279, **296–7**, 307
Cayo District (Belize) 55, **290–291**
Cenotes, Yucatán (Mexico) 256
Central America
  Inter-American Highway 32, **46–7**
  see also Belize; Costa Rica; El Salvador; Guatemala; Honduras; Mexico; Nicaragua; Panama
Cerro Rico Mines, Potosí (Bolivia) 153
Charleston (South Carolina, USA) **78–9**, 129, 305
Charlevoix (Canada) 129
Chauchilla (Peru) 225
Chavín people 164, 165
Chesapeake Bay (Maryland, USA) 103, 232
Chéticamp (Canada) 223
Chicago (Illinois, USA) 128, **130–31**, 305
Chichén Itza (Mexico) 70–71
Chichicastenango (Guatemala) 263, 278, 307
Chile
  Carretera Austral 32
  Chiloé 278
  Easter Island 76, **90–91**
  Laguna San Rafael 257
  Laguna Verde 278
  Lake District 11
  Parque Nacional Torres del Paine (Chile) 265
  Patagonia 55, **72–3**
  Skiing in the Chilean Andes 153
  South Patagonian Fjords 232, **244–5**
  Teleférico, Santiago 256
  Valle de la Luna 11
  Valparaíso 10, 305
Chiloé (Chile) 278
Chiquitos (Bolivia) 128, **148–9**
Círio de Nazaré Festival (Brazil) 232, 307
Ciudad Perdida (Columbia) **224–5**
Civil War (American)
  Gettysburg National Military Park (Pennsylvania, USA) 128, 221
  Lexington (Virginia, USA) 76
  Natchez Trace (Mississippi, USA) 68–9
Clearwater Beach (Florida, USA) 55
Climate 11, 33, 55, 77, 103, 129, 153, 181, 209, 233, 257, 279
Coatepeque, Lago de (El Salvador) 256
Colca Canyon (Peru) 76
Colombia
  Cartagena 10, **16–17**, 304
  Ciudad Perdida **224–5**
Colonia de Sacramento (Uruguay) 209
Colorado (USA)
  Denver 102
  Dude ranch 209
  Grand Canyon National Park 232, **240–41**
  Leadville 180
  Mesa Verde National Park 129, **136–7**
  Telluride 279, 305

Columbia River (USA) 102, 181, 247
Communications 308–10
Concepción (Bolivia) 149
Connecticut (USA)
New Haven 152
Copacabana (Bolivia) 109
Copacabana Palace (Rio, Brazil) 233
Cordillera Apolobamba (Bolivia) 129
Cordillera Blanca (Peru) 153, **164–5**
Coroico (Bolivia) 180
Costa Rica
Birding 103
Inter-American Highway 46–7
Manuel Antonio National Park 10
Nicoya Peninsula 279, **288–9**
Parque Nacional Tortuguero 54
Sports Fishing 33
Volcán Arenal 47, 76, **94–5**
Whitewater rafting 102
Craters of the Moon National Monument (Idaho, USA) 102
Crazy Horse Memorial (South Dakota, USA) 228, 229
Creel (Mexico) 295
Cruises
Amazon River (Brazil) 102, **114–15**
British Virgin Islands (Caribbean) 55, **64–5**
Caribbean Island Cruise 257, **272–3**
Columbia River (USA) 102
Galápagos Islands (Ecuador) 86–7
Inside Passage (Alaska, USA) 102, **110–11**
Isla de la Plata (Ecuador) 76
Mississippi Cruise 256
Panama Canal (Panama) 267
Patagonian Cruise (Argentina) 10
St. Lawrence River (Canada) 187
South Patagonian Fjords (Chile/Argentina) **244–5**
Cuba
Havana 33, **38–9**, 304, 307
Sierra Maestra 102
Cuenca (Ecuador) 128
Cumberland Island National Seashore (Georgia, USA) 121
Curaçao (Caribbean) 233
Cusco (Peru) 128, 129, 140, 141, 201, 305
Custer Country (Montana, USA) 129
Custer State Park (South Dakota, USA) 229
Cycling
The Andes (Ecuador) 257
Mount Cotopaxi (Ecuador) 181

D

Darién Gap (Panama) 46, 47
Day of the Dead (Mexico) 233, **252–3**, 307
Daytona Beach (Florida, USA) 129
Death Valley National Park (California, USA) 278
Deer Island (Canada) 210–11
Denver (Colorado, USA) 102
Devil's Tower National Monument (Wyoming, USA) 180
Dia de Iemanjá (Brazil) 302
La Diablada (Puno, Peru) 256, 305
Diving and snorkeling
Ambergris Caye (Belize) 102, **106–7**
Aquário Natural (Brazil) 233
The Bahamas (Caribbean) 257, **268–9**
Baja California Sur (Mexico) 33, **36–7**
Bocas del Toro (Panama) 77
British Virgin Islands (Caribbean) 55, **64–5**
Caribbean Island Cruise 272, 273
Cayman Islands (Caribbean) 279, **296–7**
Cenotes, Yucatán (Mexico) 256
Dominica (Caribbean) **98–9**, 279
Honduras 55, **66–7**
Isla Fernando de Noronha (Brazil) 54
Isla Margarita (Venezuela) 256, **260–61**
Mayan Riviera (Mexico) 15
Turks and Caicos Islands (Caribbean) 77, **84–5**
Vieques (Puerto Rico) 22–3
Dog sledding 304
Alaska (USA) 33
Daaquam River International Dog Sled Race (Canada) 304
Lakes Region (New Hampshire, USA) 44
Quttinirpaaq National Park (Canada) 152
Dominica (Caribbean) **98–9**, 279, 307
Dominican Republic (Caribbean) 33
Cabarete 55
Fiesta de Merengue 152, **176–7**, 306
Pico Duarte 54
Samaná Bay 11
Dubuque (Iowa, USA) 135
Duluth (Minnesota, USA) 232

E

Easter Island (Chile) 76, **90–91**
Ecola State Park (Oregon, USA) 247
Ecuador
The Amazon 55
Avenue of the Volcanoes 128
Biking, hiking and rafting 257
Cuenca 128
Ecuador (cont.)
Galápagos Islands 76, **86–7**
Isla de la Plata 76
Mount Cotopaxi 181
Quito 208, **218–19**
El Salvador
Inter-American Highway 46–7
Lago de Coatepeque 256
Empire State Building (New York City, USA) **116**, 117
Everglades National Park (Miami, USA) 10, **40**
The Exumas (Bahamas) 279

F

Falkland Islands (South Atlantic) 278, **298–9**
Family getaways 11, 33, 55, 77, 103, 129, 153, 181, 209, 233, 257, 279
Fantasy Fest (Key West, USA) 232, 307
Festival International de Louisiane (Lafayette, USA) 305
Festivals **304–7**
Festivals and culture 10, 32, 54, 76, 102, 128, 152, 180, 208, 232, 256, 278
Finger Lakes (New York State, USA) 128, **146–7**
Fishing
Costa Rica 33
Patagonia (Chile/Argentina) 55, **72–3**
Stanley (Idaho, USA) 129, **138–9**
Fitz Roy Massif (Argentina) 257
Florida (USA)
Clearwater Beach 55
Daytona Beach 129
Everglades National Park 10
Fantasy Fest (Key West) 232, 307
Florida Keys 33
Florida Panhandle 11
Miami 32, **40–41**, 54, 304
Naples 233
Orlando 18–19
Sanibel and the Captiva Islands 103
Fort Raleigh National Historic Park (North Carolina, USA) **124**, 125
Fossil Rim (Texas, USA) 55
Fredericksburg (Texas, USA) 77
Fundy Isles (Canada) 209, **210–11**

G

Galápagos Islands (Ecuador) 76, **86–7**
Galena (Illinois, USA) 134, 135
Garganta del Diablo (Devil's Throat) (Argentina) 83
Gauchos **96**, 97
Gauley River (West Virginia, USA) 233
George, Lake (New York State, USA) 209
George Town (Cayman Islands) 297, 307
Georgia (USA)
Atlanta 11
Savannah 103, **120–21**
Getting around 308–10
Gettysburg National Military Park (Pennsylvania, USA) 128, 221
Glacier Bay National Park (Alaska, USA) 111, 180
Glacier National Park (Montana, USA) 129
Glacier Perito Moreno (Argentina) 10
Golden Gate Bridge (San Francisco, USA) **212**, 213
Graceland (Memphis, USA) **104**, 105
Gran Sabana (Venezuela) 32
Grand Canyon National Park (Arizona, USA) 232, **240–41**
Grand Manan Island (Canada) 210–11
Grand Staircase-Escalante National Monument (Utah, USA) 215
Grand Teton National Park (Wyoming, USA) **20–21**
Grand Turk (Turks and Caicos Islands) 85
Great Divide Trail (Canada) 180
Great River Road (Midwest, USA) 128, **134–5**
Great Smoky Mountains National Park (North Carolina, USA) 54, 92–3
Gros Morne National Park (Canada) 193
Guadeloupe (Caribbean) 273, 306
Guanajuato (Mexico) 32, 294–5
Guatemala
Atigua 54, 304
Chichicastenango 263, **278**
Inter-American Highway 46–7
Lago de Atitlán **256**, 263
Tales of Tikal 256, **262–3**
Guyana
Iwokrama Rainforest 232
Kaieteur Falls 181
Gwaii Haanas National Park Reserve (Canada) 153, **160–61**

H

Haida people 160–61
Haleakalā volcano (Maui) 26, 27
Halifax (Canada) 227
Halloween (USA) 233
Hamilton (Bermuda) 145
The Hamptons (New York State, USA) 181, **194–5**
Hāna (Maui) 26–7
Harp seals (Iles de la Madeleine, Canada) 32
Hatteras Island (North Carolina, USA) 125
Havana (Cuba) 32, **38–9**, 304, 307
Hawai'i (USA)
Aloha Festivals 208
Hawai'i (Big Island) 279, **284–5**
Kaua'i 232, **248–9**
Maui 10, **26–7**
Waikīkī 129
Hay Literary Festival (Cartagena, Colombia) **17**, 304
Head Smashed-In Buffalo Jump (Canada) 168
Health 308–10
Hells Canyon (Idaho and Oregon, USA) 76
Highway 61 (USA) 232
Hiking and trekking
Angel Falls (Venezuela) 278, **292–3**
Appalachian Trail (USA) 76, 128
Black Hills (South Dakota, USA) 229
Blue Mountain Peak (Jamaica) 33
Buckskin Gulch (Utah, USA) 77
Cordillera Blanca (Peru) 153, **164–5**
Devil's Tower National Monument (Wyoming, USA) 180
Dominica (Caribbean) **98–9**, 279
Ecuador 257
Finger Lakes (New York State, USA) 147
Fitz Roy Massif (Argentina) 257
Glacier National Park (Montana, USA) 129
Grand Canyon National Park (Arizona, USA) 232, **240–41**
Great Divide Trail (Canada) 180
Inca Trail (Peru) 141
Inca trails (Bolivia) 108–9
Iwokrama Rainforest (Guyana) 232
Jefferson National Forest 128
John Muir Trail (California, USA) 209
Kaieteur Falls (Guyana) 181
Kaua'i (Hawai'i, USA) 232, **248–9**
Lago de Coatepeque (El Salvador) 256
Lakes Region (New Hampshire, USA) 45
The Laurentians (Canada) 232
Manu National Park (Peru) 201
Mesa Verde National Park (USA) 137
Mount Desert Island (Maine, USA) 237
Mount Whitney (California, USA) 209, 233
Mountain Pine Forest Reserve (Belize) 11
Olympic National Park (Washington State, USA) 209
Oregon Coast (USA) 247
Painted Canyon (North Dakota, USA) 32
Panama 43
Parque Nacional Torres del Paine (Chile) 265
Pico Duarte (Dominican Republic) 54
Quttinirpaaq National Park (Canada) 152
Sian Ka'an Biosphere Reserve (Mexico) 279
Sierra Maestra (Cuba) 102
Stanley (Idaho, USA) 139
Trans-Apolobamba Trek (Bolivia) 129
Utah's National Parklands (USA) 209, **214–15**
Valle de la Luna (Chile) 11
Yellowstone National Park (Wyoming, USA) 180, **188–9**
Hol Chan Marine Reserve (Belize) 107
Holetown (Barbados) 33
Honduras
Inter-American Highway 46–7
Rapids, Reefs, Rain Forests 55, **66–7**
Rio Plátano Biosphere Reserve 32
Horseback riding
Bluegrass Country (Kentucky, USA) 128
Colorado Dude Ranch (USA) 209
Dominica (Carribean) 279
Parque Nacional Torres del Paine (Chile) 265
Uruguay 77, **96–7**
see also Rodeos
Horseshoe Canyon (Utah, USA) 215
Hot Springs National Park Resort (Arkansas, USA) 33
HSBC Celebration of Light (Vancouver) 157, 306
Huaraz (Peru) 165
Huascarán National Park (Peru) 164
Huron, Lake (Canada/Michigan, USA) 196–7
Hurricane season 310

I

Ice skating see Winter sports
Icefields Parkway (Canada) 180, 227
Idaho (USA)
Craters of the Moon National Monument 102
Hells Canyon 76
Stanley 129, **138–9**
Iguazú Falls (Argentina/Brazil) 76, **82–3**
Iles de la Madeleine (Canada) 32
Ilhabela (Brazil) 233
Illinois (USA)
Chicago 128, **130–31**
Great River Road 134–5
Inca civilization 108–9, 129, 140–41, 208
Inside Passage (Alaska, USA) 102, **110–11**
Inter-American Highway 32, **46–7**
Inti Raymi Festival of the Sun (Cusco, Peru) 128, **140**, 305
Inuit culture 76, 235
Iowa (USA)
Great River Road 134–5
Iqaluit (Canada) 76, 305
Iquitos (Peru) 208
Irish heritage, Boston (USA) 54, **62–3**
Isla Fernando de Noronha (Brazil) 54
Isla Margarita (Venezuela) 256, **260–61**
Isla de la Plata (Ecuador) 76
Isla del Sol (Bolivia) 109, 208
Islas Ballestas (Peru) 54, **270–71**
Ithaca (New York State, USA) 147
Iwokrama Rainforest (Guyana) 232

J

Jackson Hole (Wyoming, USA) 11, 20–21
Jamaica (Caribbean) 11, **282–3**, 304, 305, 306
Blue Mountain Peak 33
Port Antonio 33
Jasper National Park (Canada) 152, **162–3**
Jazz Festival, Montréal (Canada) 143, 305
Jazz Festival, St. Lucia (Caribbean) 102, **122–3**, 305
Jefferson National Forest (Virginia, USA) 128
Jesuit missions (Chiquitos, Bolivia) 128, **148–9**
Jockey Ridge State Park (North Carolina, USA) 125
John Muir Trail (California, USA) 209
Joshua Tree National Park (California, USA) 54
Junkanoo (Bahamas) 278, 307
Just for Laughs Comedy Festival (Montréal, Canada) 152, 306

K

Kaieteur Falls (Guyana) 181
Kaua'i (Hawai'i, USA) 232, **248–9**
Kayaking see Canoeing and kayaking
Ke'anae Peninsula (Maui) 26–7
Kennedy Space Center (Florida) 19
Kentucky (USA)
Bluegrass Country 128
Derby Festival (Louisville) 305
Mammoth Cave National Park 180, **198–9**
Key West (Florida, USA) 232
Kiawah Island (South Carolina, USA) 11
King, Martin Luther 104, 105
Kite-boarding, Cabarete (Dominican Republic) 55
Klondike Gold Rush **110**, 111
Kluane National Park (Canada) 152
Kodiak Island (Alaska, USA) 128

L

La Paz (Bolivia) 103, **108–9**, 180, 208, 304
Lafayette (Louisiana, USA) 305
Laguna Challviri (Bolivia) 159
Laguna Colorada (Bolivia) 159
Laguna San Rafael (Chile) 257
Laguna Verde (Chile) 278
Lake District (Chile) 11
Lakes Region (New Hampshire, USA) 33, **44–5**
Lakeshore (Minnesota, USA) 103
Las Vegas (Nevada, USA) 10, **12–13**
Laurentian Mountains (Canada) 232, 279
Leadville (Colorado, USA) 180
Leeward Islands (Caribbean) 272–3
Lexington (Virginia, USA) 76
Lighthouse Reef Atoll (Belize) 106–7
Los Angeles (California, USA) 76, 181, 232
Los Cabos (Mexico) 33, **36–7**
Los Glaciares National Park (Argentina) 76
Los Roques (Venezuela) 260, 261
Louise, Lake (Canada) 275, 307
Louisiana (USA)
Lafayette 305
Mississippi Cruise 256
New Orleans 32, 304, 305
Low-impact tourism 308
Lowcountry (South Carolina, USA) 77, **78–9**
Luxury and romance 11, 33, 55, 77, 103, 129, 153, 181, 209, 233, 257, 279

M

Machu Picchu (Peru) 128, **140–41**
Mackinac Island (Michigan, USA) 181, **196–7**
Magellan, Straits of (Chile) 244–5
Magic Kingdom (Orlando) 18–19
Maine (USA)
Mount Desert Island 233, **236–7**
Maipu (Argentina) 217
Mammoth Cave National Park (Kentucky, USA) 180, **198–9**
Mammoth Mountain (California, USA) 11
Manú National Park (Peru) 180, **200–201**
Manuas (Brazil) 114–15
Manuel Antonio National Park (Costa Rica) 10
Manzanillo (Mexico) 279
Mar del Plata (Argentina) 257
Mardi Gras (New Orleans, USA) 32, 304
Martha's Vineyard (Massachusetts, USA) 171
Martinique (Caribbean) **274–5**
Marvel Cave (Missouri, USA) **80**, 81
Maryland (USA)
Annapolis 232
Baltimore 278
Chesapeake Bay 103

Massachusetts (USA)
Boston 54, **62–3**, 129
Cape Cod 153, **170–71**
Plymouth 257
Maui (Hawai'i, USA) 10, **26–7**
Mayan civilization **14–15**, **70–71**, 256, **262–3**, 279
Mayan Riviera (Mexico) 11, **14–15**
Medical insurance 308–9
Memphis (USA)
Memphis in May 102, **104–5**, 305
Mendocino (California, USA) 181
Mendoza (Argentina) 209, **216–17**, 304
Merengue Festival (Dominican Republic) 152, **176–7**, 306
Mérida (Mexico) 71
Merida (Venezuela) 11
Mesa Verde National Park (Colorado, USA) 129, **136–7**
Mexico
Acapulco 279
Bahía Concepción 233
Baja California Sur 33, **36–7**
Cenotes, Yucatán 256
Colonial Heartland **294–5**
Guanajuato 32, 294–5
Independence Day 306
Inter-American Highway 46–7
Lago Patzcuaro 10
Manzanillo 279
Mayan Riviera 11, **14–15**
Mexico City 54, **60–61**, 305
Oaxaca 233, **252–3**, 306, 307
Querétaro 294–5
Palenque 256
Puerto Escondido 55
Puerto Vallarta 77
San Miguel de Allende 10, 294–5
Sea of Cortez 32
Sian Ka'an Biosphere Reserve, Yucatán 279
Xochimilco, Mexico City 55
Yucatán 55, **70–71**
Zacatecas 294–5
Mexico City (Mexico) 54, **60–61**, 305
Miami (USA) 33, **40–41**
Art Deco Weekend 304
Calle Ocho 54
Michigan (USA)
Mackinac Island 181, **196–7**
Milwaukee (Wisconsin, USA) 183
Minnesota (USA)
Boundary Waters 152
Great River Road 134–5
Lakeshore 103
St. Paul Winter Carnival 10
Voyageurs National Park 129
Mississippi (USA)
Natchez Trace **68–9**
Mississippi River (USA)
Great River Road 128, **134–5**
Memphis **104–5**
Mississippi Cruise 256
Missouri (USA)
Branson 77, **80–81**
Ozark Mountains 80–81, 208
St. Louis 102
Moab (Utah, USA) 215
Moai 76, **90–91**
Money 308–10
Montana (USA)
Custer Country 129
Glacier National Park 129
Montevideo (Uruguay) 97
Montréal (Canada) 129, **142–3**, 153, 227
Comedy Festival 152, 306
Jazz Festival 305
Monument Valley (Utah, USA) 10, 241
Mount Cotopaxi (Ecuador) 181, 219
Mount Desert Island (Maine, USA) 233, **236–7**
Mount Licancabur (Bolivia) 159
Mount McKinley (Alaska, USA) 181, 199
Mount Rushmore (South Dakota, USA) **228**, 229
Mount St. Helens (Washington State, USA) 102
Mount Tremblant (Canada) 279
Mount Whitney (California, USA) 209, 233
Mountain Pine Forest Preserve (Belize) 11
Mystic Seaport (Connecticut, USA) 175

N

Nantucket (Massachusetts, USA) 171
Napa Valley (California, USA) 250, 251
Naples (Florida, USA) 233
Nassau (Bahamas) 268, 269
Natchez Trace (Mississippi, USA) 54, **68–9**
National Cherry Blossom Festival (Washington, D.C., USA) 77
Native American culture 58–9, 168–9, 208, 228–9, 256
Natural wonders 10, 32, 54, 76, 102, 128, 152, 180, 208, 232, 256, 278
Nebraska (USA)
Scotts Bluff 233
Negro, Rio 114, 115
Nevada (USA)
Lake Tahoe 152
Las Vegas 12–13
Nevis (Caribbean) 77, 273
New England (USA)
Fall 208, 232, **236–7**, 307
see also Connecticut; Maine; Massachusetts; New Hampshire; Rhode Island; Vermont
New Hampshire (USA)
Lakes Region 33, **44–5**
New Haven (Connecticut, USA) 152
New Jersey (USA)
Cape May 77
New Mexico (USA)
Albuquerque 232, **242–3**, 307
Bosque del Apache 256
High Road from Santa Fe to Taos 256
Santa Fe 181, **184–5**
Taos 209
New Orleans (Louisiana, USA) 32, 304, 305
New River Gorge (West Virginia, USA) 55
New York City (New York State, USA) 103, **116–17**, 233
New York State (USA)
Finger Lakes 128, **146–7**
The Hamptons 181, **194–5**
Lake George 209
New York City 103, **116–17**, 233
Niagara Falls 128, **132–3**
Thousand Islands 209
Newport (Rhode Island, USA) 152, **174–5**, 306
Niagara Falls (Canada/New York State, USA) 128, **132–3**
Nicaragua
Inter-American Highway 46–7
Lago de Nicaragua 32
Nicoya Peninsula (Costa Rica) 279, **288–9**
North America see Canada; United States
North Atlantic, Bermuda 129, **144–5**
North Carolina (USA)
Great Smoky Mountains National Park 54
Old Salem 256
Outer Banks 103, **124–5**
North Dakota (USA)
Painted Canyon 32
Northern Lights (Alaska/Northern Canada) 278

O

Oaxaca (Mexico) 233, **252–3**, 306, 307
Ocrakoke Island (North Carolina, USA) 125
O'Keefe, Georgia **184**, 185
Oklahoma (USA) 153
Old Salem (North Carolina, USA) 256
Olympic Games, Whistler (Canada) 56
Olympic National Park (Washington State, USA) 209
Oregon (USA)
Columbia River 102, 181
Hells Canyon 76
Oregon Coast 232, **246–7**
Pendleton Round Up 208
Portland **222–3**
Oregon Trail (Oregon, USA) 233
Orinoco Delta (Venezuela) 257
Orlando (Florida, USA) 11, **18–19**
Ottawa (Canada)
International Animation Festival 306
Winterlude 33, **34–5**, 304
Outer Banks (North Carolina, USA) 103, **124–5**
Ozark Mountains (Missouri, USA) 80–81, 208

P

Pacayá Volcano (Guatemala) 263
Pacific Rim National Park (Canada) **112–13**
Palenque (Mexico) 256
Palm Springs (California, USA) **28–9**
Panama
Archipelago de San Blas **88–9**
Birding 32, **42–3**
Bocas del Toro 77
Eco-lodges 55
Inter-American Highway 46–7
Panama City 256, **266–7**
San Blas Islands 278
Panama Canal (Panama) **266**, 267
Panatal (Brazil) 128
Paraguay 180, **204–5**
Paranaense rain forest (Argentina) 82
Pasadena (California, USA) 278, **300–301**, 304
Passports and visas 308–10
Patagonia (Chile/Argentina)
Fly-fishing 55, **72–3**
Old Patagonian Express 278
Patagonian Cruise 10
Península Valdés 257
South Patagonian Fjords 232, **244–5**
Patzcuaro, Lago (Mexico) 10
Pawleys Island (South Carolina, USA) 181
Pedra Azul (Brazil) 54
Pendleton Round Up (Oregon, USA) 208
Penguins
Falkland Islands (South Atlantic) 278
Laguna San Rafael (Chile) 257
Pennsylvania (USA)
Gettysburg National Military Park 128
Philadelphia 209, **220–21**
Pocono Mountains 153
Personal security 308–10
Peru
Colca Canyon 76
Cordillera Blanca 153, **164–5**
Cusco 128, 129, 140, 141, 201, 305
La Diablada (Puno) 256, 305
Inti Raymi (Cusco) 128, **140**, 305
Iquitos 208
Islas Ballestas 54, **270–71**
Machu Picchu 128, **140–41**
Manu National Park 180, **200–201**
Riding the Altiplano Train 32
Philadelphia (Pennsylvania, USA) 209, **220–21**, 304
Philipsburg (St. Maarten) 273, 291
Pico Duarte (Dominican Republic) 54
Pigeon Island (St. Lucia) 122–3
Pitons (St. Lucia) **122**, 123
Plymouth (Massachusetts, USA) 257
Pocono Mountains (Pennsylvania, USA) 153
Polar bears, Cape Churchill (Canada) 233
Portland (Oregon, USA) **222–3**
Port of Spain (Trinidad) 48–9
Potosí (Bolivia) 153, 180
Powell, Lake (Utah, USA) 214
Prairie du Chien (Wisconsin, USA) **134**, 135
Prince Edward Island (Canada) **24–5**, 181
Providenciales (Turks and Caicos Islands) 84–5
Provincetown (Massachusetts, USA) 171
Puebloan people **136–7**, **184–5**, 240, 241
Puerto Escondido (Mexico) 55
Puerto Iguazú (Argentina) 83
Puerto Rico, Vieques 11, **22–3**, 305
Puerto Vallarta (Mexico) 77
Puget Sound (Washington State, USA) 166
Puno (Peru) 256, 305
Punta Arenas (Chile) 244, 245

Q

Québec City (Canada) 181, **186–7**, 279, 304
Queen Charlotte Islands (Canada) 153, **160–61**
Querétaro (Mexico) 294–5
Quito (Ecuador) 208, **218–19**
Quttinirpaaq National Park (Canada) 152

R

Rail journeys
Coast to Coast (Canada) 208, **226–7**
Nariz del Diablo (Ecuador) 219
Old Patagonian Express (Argentina) 278
Riding the Altiplano Train (Peru) 32
Santa Fe Southern Railway (New Mexico, USA) 185
Vistadome train to Machu Picchu (Peru) 141
Ranches
Uruguay **96–7**
Rapanui people 90
Redwood National Park (California, USA) 256
Restinga National Park (Venezuela) 260, 261
Réveillon (Rio de Janeiro) 278, **302–3**, 307
Rhode Island (USA)
Newport 152, **174–5**, 306
Río Cangrejal (Honduras) 66–7
Rio de Janeiro (Brazil) 233, 278, **302–3**, 307
Rio Grande (Texas, USA) 10, 233, 257
Río Plátano Biosphere Reserve (Honduras) 32
Roanoke Island (North Carolina, USA) **124**, 125
Roatán (Honduras) 66–7
Rochester (New York State, USA) **146**, 147
Rocky Mountains
Banff (Canada) 256
Banff National Park (Canada) 209
Coast to Coast (Canada) 208, **226–7**
Jasper National Park (Canada) 152, **162–3**
Rodeos
Barretos Rodeo Festival (Brazil) 180, **202–3**
Calgary Stampede 153, **168–9**, 306
Pendleton Round Up (Oregon, USA) 208
Rupunani Rodeo (Lethem, Guyana) 305
Route 66 (USA) 54
Royal Alexandra Theatre (Toronto) **118**, 119

S

Sailing
British Virgin Islands (Caribbean) 55, **64–5**
Newport (Rhode Island, USA) 152, **174–5**
St. Barts (Caribbean) 273, **286–7**
St. George (Bermuda) 145
St. John's (Canada) 172–3
St. Kitts (Caribbean) 77, 272, 273
St. Lucia (Caribbean) 272, 273
Jazz Festival 102, **122–3**, 305
St. Maarten/St-Martin (Caribbean) **272**, 273
St. Patrick's Day Parade (Boston, USA) 54, **62–3**, 304
St. Paul (Minnesota, USA), Winter Carnival 10, 134, 135
Salar de Uyuni (Bolivia) 152, **158–9**
Salta (Argentina) 180, **190–91**
Salvador (Brazil) 32, **50–51**, 304
Samaná Bay (Dominican Republic) 11
San Antonio (Texas, USA) 279, **280–81**
San Blas Islands (Panama) 278
San Diego (California, USA) 11
San Francisco (California, USA) 54, 209, **212–13**, 232
San Juan Islands (Washington State, USA) 152, **166–7**
San Miguel de Allende (Mexico) 10, 294–5
San Salvador de Jujuy (Argentina) 180, **190–91**
Sanibel (Florida, USA) 103
Santa Barbara (California, USA) 251
Santa Catalina Mountains (Arizona, USA) 258, 259
Santa Cruz (Bolivia) 148, 149
Santa Fe (New Mexico, USA) 181, **184–5**, 243
Chamber Music Festival 306
High Road from Santa Fe to Taos 256
Santa Ynez Valley (California, USA) 77, 251
Santiago (Chile) 153, 256
Santo Domingo (Dominican Republic) 176–7
Savannah (Georgia, USA) 103, **120–21**
Sawtooth National Recreation Area (Idaho, USA) 139
Scotts Bluff (Nebraska, USA) 233
Scottsdale (Arizona, USA) 77
Sea of Cortez (Mexico) 32
Seattle (Washington State, USA) 208, 306
Sedona (Arizona, USA) 209
Semana Santa (Antigua, Guatemala) 54, 304
Sequoia National Park (California, USA) 208
Shenandoah National Park (Virginia, USA) 92–3
Sian Ka'an Biosphere Reserve, Yucatán (Mexico) 279
Skiing see Winter sports
Slagway (Alaska, USA) 110, 111
Smithsonian Folklife Festival (Washington D.C.) 154–5
Solimões, Rio 114, 115
Sonoma Valley (California, USA) 250, 251
Sonoran Desert (Arizona, USA) 258–9
South America see Argentina; Bolivia; Brazil; Chile; Colombia; Ecuador; Guyana; Paraguay; Peru; Uruguay; Venezuela
South Atlantic, Falkland Islands 278, **298–9**
South Carolina (USA)
Charleston 78–9, 129, 305
Kiawah Island 11
Lowcountry 77, **78–9**
Myrtle Beach 129
Pawleys Island 181
South Dakota (USA)
Black Hills 208, **228–9**
Squam, Lake (New Hampshire, USA) 45
Stanley (Falkland Islands) 298, 299
Stanley (Idaho, USA) 129, **138–9**
Superior, Lake (Canada/USA) 181
Surfing
Bathsheba (Barbados) 103
Cabarete (Dominican Republic) 55
Daytona Beach (Florida, USA) 129

T

Tahoe, Lake (California and Nevada, USA) 152
Tall Pine Lodges (Canada) 153
Taos (New Mexico, USA) 209, 256
Teatro Amazonas (Manuas) **114**, 115
Teleférico (Santiago, Chile) 256
Telluride (Colorado, USA) 279, 305
Temuco (Chile) 25
Tennessee (USA)
Great Smoky Mountains National Park 54
Memphis 102, **104–5**, 305
Tennessee (cont.)
Tennessee Walking Horse National Celebrations 306
Teotihuacán (Mexico) 61
Texas (USA)
Austin **58–9**
Big Bend National Park 10, 233
Fossil Rim 55
Hill Country 77
Rio Grande Valley 257
San Antonio 279, **280–81**
Thousand Islands (USA) 209
Tikal (Guatemala) 256, **262–3**
Titicaca, Lago (Bolivia/Peru) 108–9, 208, 256
Tiwanaku, La Paz (Bolivia) 208
Toonik Tyme, Iqaluit (Canada) 76, 305
Toronto (Canada) 102, 103, **118–19**, 227
International Film Festival 306
Torres del Paine, Parque Nacional (Chile) 265
Tortola (Caribbean) 64, 65, 279, 304
Tortuguero, Parque Nacional (Costa Rica) 54
Tournament of Roses Parade (Pasadena, USA) **301**, 304
Travel information 308–10
Trinidad (Caribbean) 32, **48–9**, 304
Tuaghannock State Park (New York State, USA) 147
Tucson (Arizona, USA) 257, **258–9**
Turks and Caicos Islands (Caribbean) 77, **84–5**
Turtles (Parque Nacional de Tortuguero, Costa Rica) 54

U

Unforgettable journeys 10, 32, 54, 76, 102, 128, 152, 180, 208, 232, 256, 278
United States of America
See also states by name
Albuquerque (New Mexico) 232, **242–3**, 306
Alcan Highway (Alaska) 152
Aloha Festivals (Hawai'i) 208, 306
Annapolis (Maryland) 232
Apostle Islands (Wisconsin) 181
Appalachian Trail (Eastern USA) 76
Atlanta (Georgia) 11
Austin (Texas) **58–9**
Baltimore (Maryland) 278
Big Bend National Park (Texas) 10, 233
Big Sur (California) 232
Black Hills (South Dakota) 208, **228–9**
Blue Ridge Parkway (Eastern USA) 76, **92–3**
Bluegrass Country (Kentucky) 128
Bosque del Apache (New Mexico) 256
Boston (Massachusetts) 54, **62–3**, 129
Boundary Waters (Minnesota) 152
Branson (Missouri) 77, **80–81**
Bryce Canyon (Utah) 181
Buckskin Gulch (Utah) 77
California Missions Trail 10
California Wine Country 233, **250–51**
Cape Cod (Massachusetts) 153, **170–71**
Cape May (New Jersey) 77
Carmel Valley (California) 153
Cascade Loop (Washington State) 152
Charleston (South Carolina) 78–9, 129, 305
Chesapeake Bay (Maryland) 103
Chicago (Illinois) 128, **130–31**, 305
Clearwater Beach (Florida) 55
Columbia River (Oregon) 102, 181
Craters of the Moon National Monument (Idaho) 102
Custer Country (Montana) 129
Daytona Beach (Florida) 129
Death Valley National Park (California) 278
Denver (Colorado) 102
Devil's Tower National Monument (Wyoming) 180
Dude Ranch (Colorado) 209
Everglades National Park (Florida) 10, **40**
Fantasy Fest (Key West, Florida) 232, 307
Finger Lakes (New York State) 128, **146–7**
Florida Keys 33
Florida Panhandle 11
Fossil Rim (Texas) 55
Gauley River (West Virginia) 233
Gettysburg National Military Park (Pennsylvania) 128
Glacier Bay National Park (Alaska) 111, 180
Glacier National Park (Montana) 129
Grand Canyon National Park (Colorado) 232, **240–41**
Grand Teton National Park (Wyoming, USA) **20–21**
Great River Road (Midwest) 128, **134–5**
Great Smoky Mountains National Park (North Carolina/ Tennessee) 54
Gulf Shores (Alabama) 33
The Hamptons (New York State) 181, **194–5**
Hawai'i (Big Island) (Hawai'i) 279, **284–5**
Hells Canyon (Idaho/Oregon) 76
High Road from Santa Fe to Taos (New Mexico) 256
Highway 61 232
Hill Country (Texas) 77
Hot Springs National Park Resort (Arkansaw) 33
Independence Day 155, 163
Inside Passage (Alaska) 102, **110–11**
Jackson Hole (Wyoming) 11, 20–21
Jefferson National Forest (Virginia) 128
John Muir Trail (California) 209
Joshua Tree National Park (California) 54
Kaua'i (Hawai'i) 232, **248–9**
Kiawah Island (South Carolina) 11
Kodiak Island (Alaska) 128
Lafayette (Louisiana) 305
Lake George (New York State) 209
Lake Tahoe (California/Nevada) 152
Lakes Region (New Hampshire) 33, **44–5**
Lakeshore (Minnesota) 103
Las Vegas (Nevada) 10, **12–13**
Leadville (Colorado) 180
Lexington (Virginia) 76
Los Angeles (California) 76, 181, 232
Lowcountry (South Carolina) 77, **78–9**
Mackinac Island (Michigan) 181, **196–7**
Mammoth Cave National Park (Kentucky) 180, **198–9**
Mammoth Mountain (California) 11
Maui (Hawai'i) 10, **26–7**
Memphis (Tennessee) 102, **104–5**, 305
Mendocino (California) 181
Mesa Verde National Park (Colorado) 129, **136–7**
Miami (Florida) 32, **40–41**, 54, 304
Mississippi Cruise (Louisiana) 256
Monument Valley (Utah) 10
Mount Desert Island (Maine) 233, **236–7**
Mount St. Helens (Washington State) 102
Mount Whitney (California) 209, 233
United States of America (cont.)
Myrtle Beach (South Carolina) 129
Naples (Florida) 233
Natchez Trace (Mississippi) 54, **68–9**
New Haven (Connecticut) 152
New Orleans (Louisiana) 32, 304, 305
New River Gorge (West Virginia) 55
New York City (New York State) 103, **116–17**, 233
Newport (Rhode Island) 152, **174–5**, 306
Niagara Falls (New York State) 128, **132–3**
Old Salem (North Carolina) 256
Olympic National Park (Washington State) 209
Oregon Coast 232, **246–7**
Orlando (Florida) 11, **18–19**
Outer Banks (North Carolina) 103, **124–5**
Ozark Mountains (Missouri) 80–81, 208
Painted Canyon (North Dakota) 32
Palm Springs (California) **28–9**
Pasadena (California) 278, **300–301**, 304
Pawleys Island (South Carolina) 181
Pendleton Round Up (Oregon) 208
Pennsylvania Dutch Country 153
Philadelphia (Pennsylvania) 209, **220–21**
Plymouth (Massachusetts) 257
Pocono Mountains (Pennsylvania) 153
Portland (Oregon) **222–3**
Redwood National Park (California) 256
Rio Grande Valley (Texas) 257
Route 66 54
St. Louis (Missouri) 102
St. Paul (Minnesota) 10
San Antonio (Texas) 279, **280–81**
San Diego (California) 11
San Francisco (California) 54, 209, **212–13**, 232
San Juan Islands (Washington State) 152, **166–7**
Sanibel and the Captiva Islands (Florida) 103
Santa Fe (New Mexico) 181, **184–5**, 243, 256, 306
Santa Ynez Valley (California) 77
Savannah (Georgia) 103, **120–21**
Scotts Bluff (Nebraska) 233
Scottsdale (Arizona) 77
Seattle (Washington State) 208
Sedona (Arizona) 209
Sequoia National Park (California) 208
Stanley (Idaho) 129, **138–9**
Taos (New Mexico) 209
Telluride (Colorado) 279
Thousand Islands (New York State) 209
Tucson (Arizona) 257, **258–9**
US Virgin Islands 33
Utah's National Parklands 209, **214–15**
Vermont in the Fall 208
Voyageurs National Park (Minnesota) 129
Waikīkī (Hawai'i) 129
Washington, D.C. 77, 153, **154–5**
Wisconsin State Fair 180, **182–3**, 306
Yellowstone National Park (Wyoming) 113, 180, **188–9**
Yosemite National Park (California) 102
Uruguay
Colonia de Sacramento 209
Playas and Pampas 77, **96–7**
US Virgin Islands (Caribbean) 33
Useful contacts 309
Utah (USA)
Bryce Canyon 181
Buckskin Gulch 77
Monument Valley 10
National Parklands 209, **214–15**

V

Valle de la Luna (Chile) 11
Valparaíso (Chile) 10, 305
Vancouver (Canada) 33, 111, 152, **156–7**, 227, 305, 306
Vancouver Fringe Festival 306
Vancouver Island (Canada) 103, 208
Venezuela
Angel Falls 261, 278, **292–3**
Gran Sabana 32
Isla Margarita 256, **260–61**
Merida 11
Orinoco Delta 257
Vermont (USA) 208, 307
Vieques (Puerto Rico) 11, **22–3**
Viking Trail (Canada) 180, **192–3**
Virginia (USA)
Jefferson National Forest 128
Lexington 76
Volcán Arenal (Costa Rica) 47, 76, **94–5**
Volcán Villarrica (Chile) 25
Volcanoes National Park (Hawai'i, USA) 285
Voyageurs National Park (Minnesota, USA) 129

W

Waikīkī (Hawai'i, USA) 129
Wapiti Valley (Wyoming, USA) 113
Wapusk National Park (Canada) 235
Washington, D.C. (USA) 77, 153, **154–5**
Washington State (USA)
Cascade Loop 152
Mount St. Helens 102
Olympic National Park 209
San Juan Islands 152, **166–7**
Seattle 208, 306
Waskesiu Lake (Canada) 153
Water sports
Apostle Islands (Wisconsin, USA) 181
Bathsheba (Barbados) 103
British Virgin Islands (Caribbean) 55, **64–5**
Cabarete (Dominican Republic) 55
Clearwater Beach (Florida, USA) 55
Columbia River (Oregon, USA) 181
Daytona Beach (Florida, USA) 129
Honduras 55, **66–7**
Isla Margarita (Venezuela) 261
see also Beaches; Diving and snorkeling; Fishing; Kite-boarding; Sailing; Surfing; Whitewater rafting; Windsurfing
Watkins Glen State Park (New York State, USA) 147
West Virginia (USA)
Gauley River 233
New River Gorge 55
Western Hemisphere Travel Initiative (WHTI) 308
Whale watching
Baja California Sur (Mexico) 33, **36–7**
Cape Cod (Massachusetts, USA) 171
Fundy Isles (Canada) 211
Hawai'i (USA) 284–5
Inside Passage (Alaska, USA) 102, **111**
Samaná Bay (Dominican Republic) 11
San Juan Islands (Washington State, USA) 152, **166–7**
Vancouver Island (Canada) 103
Whistler (Canada) 55, **56–7**, 306
White Mountains (New Hampshire, USA) 45
Whiteshell Provincial Park (Canada) 232
Whitewater rafting
Big Bend National Park (Texas, USA) 233
Costa Rica 102
Ecuador 257
Gauley River (West Virginia, USA) 233
Hells Canyon (Idaho and Oregon, USA) 76
Honduras 55, **66–7**
New River Gorge (West Virginia, USA) 55
Wildlife
Amazon River 115
Ambergris Caye (Belize) 102, **106–7**
Avalon Peninsula (Canada) 152, **172–3**
The Bahamas (Caribbean) 257, **268–9**
Baja California Sur (Mexico) 33, **36–7**
Cabot Trail (Canada) 76
Cape Churchill (Canada) 233, **234–5**
Cordillera Blanca (Peru) 165
Falkland Islands (South Atlantic) 278, **298–9**
Fossil Rim (Texas, USA) 55
Fundy Isles (Canada) 209, **210–11**
Galápagos Islands (Ecuador) 76, **86–7**
Gwaii Haanas National Park Reserve (Canada) 153, **160–61**
Iles de la Madeleine (Canada) 32
Inside Passage (Alaska, USA) 102, **110–11**
Isla de la Plata (Ecuador) 76
Isla Margarita (Venezuela) 256, **260–61**
Islas Ballestas (Peru) 54, **270–71**
Jasper National Park (Canada) 152, **162–3**
Kodiak Island (Alaska, USA) 128
Laguna San Rafael (Chile) 257
Manu National Park (Peru) 180, **200–201**
Montréal Biodôme (Canada) 142, 143
Nicoya Peninsula (Costa Rica) 279, **288–9**
Panatal (Brazil) 128
Parque Nacional Tortuguero (Costa Rica) 54
Pea Island National Wildlife Refuge (North Carolina, USA) 125
Penguins **244**, 245, **298–9**
Península Valdés (Argentina) 257
Rio Plátano Biosphere Reserve (Honduras) 32
San Blas Islands (Panama) 278
San Juan Islands (Washington State, USA) 152, **166–7**
Sea of Cortez (Mexico) 32
South Patagonian Fjords (Chile/Argentina) **244–5**
Vieques (Puerto Rico) 23
Viking Trail (Canada) 193
Voyageurs National Park (Minnesota, USA) 129
Yellowstone National Park (Wyoming, USA) 180, **188–9**
see also Birding; Whale watching
Wilmington (Delaware, USA) 163
Windsurfing, Columbia River (Oregon, USA) 181
Windward Islands (Caribbean) 272–3
Winnipesaukee, Lake (New Hampshire, USA) 45
Winnisquam, Lake (New Hampshire, USA) 45
Winter sports
Banff (Canada) 256
Grand Teton National Park (Wyoming, USA) **20–21**
Jackson Hole (Wyoming, USA) 11, 20–21
Lakes Region (New Hampshire, USA) 33, **44–5**
Mammoth Mountain (California, USA) 11
Winter sports (cont.)
Mount Tremblant (Canada) 279
Ottawa (Canada) 33, **34–5**
Québec and the Laurentians (Canada) 279
Skiing in the Chilean Andes 153
Telluride (Colorado, USA) 279
Whistler (Canada) 55, **56–7**
Winterlude (Ottawa, Canada) **35**, 304
Winterstart (Banff, Canada) 307
Wisconsin (USA)
Apostle Islands 181
Great River Road 134–5
State Fair 180, **182–3**, 306
Witless Bay (Canada) 153
Wyoming (USA)
Devil's Tower National Monument 180
Jackson Hole 11, 20–21, 113
Yellowstone National Park 113

X

Xochimilco, Mexico City (Mexico) 55

Y

Yale University (Connecticut, USA) 152
Yaquina Head Outstanding Natural Area (Oregon, USA) 247
Yellowstone National Park (Wyoming, USA) 113, 180, **188–9**
Yojoa, Lago de (Honduras) 67
Yosemite National Park (Caifornia, USA) 102, 209
Yucatán (Mexico) 14–15, 55, **70–71**, 253, 256, 279
Yukon (Canada) 128
Yungas region (Bolivia) 108–9

Z

Zacatecas (Mexico) 294–5
Zion Canyon (Utah, USA) 214, 215

Acknowledgments

The publisher would like to thank the following for their contributions and help (in alphabetical order): J.P. Anderson, Christopher Baker, Eleanor Berman, Tessa Bindloss, Shawn Blore, Emma Brady, Stephen Brewer, Louise Buckley, Samantha Cook, Kelsey Eliasson, Rebecca Flynn, Rachel Fox, Paul Franklin, Jennifer Greenhill-Taylor, Geoff Groesbeck, Eric Grossman, Andrew Hempstead, Marael Johnson, Claire Jones, Stephen Keeling, Rachel Laidler, Declan McGarvey, Nancy Mikula, Todd Obolsky, Laura Paquet, Susie Peachey, Don Philpott, Adrian Potts, Christopher Rice, Melanie Rice, Nick Rider, Alex Robinson, Polly Rodger Brown, AnneLise Sorensen, Deanna Swaney, Gavin Thomas, Greg Ward, Sarah Woods.

Picture Credits

The publisher would like to thank the following for their kind permission to reproduce their photographs:

Key: a–above; b–below/bottom; c–centre; f–far; l–left; r–right; t–top

123RF.com: Pablo Hidalgo 224fbl.
4Corners: Cozzi Guido 120bc; Cozzi Guido 171bl,171bc, 104-105, 228bc, 228br, 208tc; Borchi Massimo 155ca, 174bl, 164bl, 70-71, 109bl, 55tr; SIME / Ripani Massimo 266tc, 266ca, 267tl, 256tl, Reinhard Schmid 260bl; SIME / Reinhard Schmid 256crb, 260bc; SIME / Berhart Udo 130br, 128tl, 191ca, 221bl; SIME / Biscaro Alberto 142-143; SIME / Damm Fridmar 140c; SIME / Frances Stephane 70bl; SIME / Giampiccolo Angelo 106bc; SIME / Giovanni Simeone 12r, 106clb, 288r, 289br, 262clb, 263ca, 117tl, SIME / Gräfenhain Günter 50tc, 46tc, 96cla, 97br, 302bc, 122clb; SIME / Hans-Peter Huber 14-5, 227tr, 52-3, 18br, 116clb, 103tl; SIME / Johanna Huber 14br, 15fbr; SIME / Kaos02 148tc; SIME / Kaos03 121bc, 18-19; SIME / Pavan Aldo 299tr; SIME / Rinaldi Roberto 268r; SIME / Ripani Massimo 214ca, 189tr, 241cl, 232tr; SIME / Schmid Reinhard 289bl, 263tr, 19bl, 19br, 11tr, 256tc; Amantini Stefano 240cr, 136-137c, 136tl, 116r, 129tr.
Alamy Stock Photo: Chris A Crumley 124bl; aaron peterson.net 197tr; 196clb; Rubens Abboud 142cb; age fotostock 88ftr, 275tr; All Canada Images / Ron Erwin 193tc; All Canada Photos 25tl, 25tc, 25br, 112bc; All Canada Photos / Barrett & MacKay 211tr; All Canada Photos / Rolf Hicker 173cr; Alt-6 / David Babcock 142clb, 129crb; Arcaid / Mark Fiennes 300clb; Martin Arpon 96cl; The Art Archive 61tc; Aurora Photos 33crb; Mary Liz Austin 170bl; AWPhoto 148tr; 149tl; Ryan Ayre 161bl; Walter Bibikow 84bl, 85br, 171cl, 77tl, 153tl; blickwinkel 189tl; Steve Bloom Images 234cb; 234ca, 233tc; steve bly 214clb, 23bl, 139cl; Tibor Bognar 219ca; Ian Bottle 291c; Brandon Cole Marine Photography 107bc; brianlatino 224cra; Richard Broadwell 283bc; Bill Brooks 173tr, 211cb; Bryan & Cherry Alexander Photography 234-235; Buzzshotz 183bc; KIKE CALVO / VWPICS 88ca; Andrew Cawley 191bl; Charles O. Cecil 131br; Cephas Picture Library / Andy Christodolo 217bl, 217bc; Cephas Picture Library / Kevin Judd 216r; China Span / Keren Su 305tr; Loetscher Chlaus 149br; Jim Cole, Photographer 131bl; Gary Cook 17br, 87tc; Tony Craddock 19bc; Jan A. Csernoch 30-31; culliganphoto 62tr; Edward Curtis / Granger, NYC. 112clb; Ian Dagnall 21tc, 195bl; Danita Delimont / Walter Bibikow 105ca; Danita Delimont / Cindy Miller Hopkins 36bc; Danita Delimont / Doug Moler 17tc, 10tl; Danita Delimont / Greg Johnston 48br, 144ca; Danita Delimont / Joanne Wells 120bl; Danita Delimont / Kristin Piljay 165cb; Danita Delimont / Nik Wheeler 143cb; Danita Delimont / Russell Gordon 61br; Danita Delimont / Walter Bibikow 185tc; Carlos Davila 35br; Danita Delimont 135br; Daniel Dempster Photography 211tl; Douglas Peebles Photography 27bc; John Earnshaw 46tl; Chuck Eckert 183br; Chad Ehlers 307tl; John Elk III 229ca; Martin Florin Emmanuel 269tl; epa european pressphoto agency b.v. 59br; eStock Photo / Claudia Uribe Touri 244ca; Javier Etcheverry 190-191; Alissa Everett 285bc; Michele Falzone 51tc; FAN Stock / Katja Kreder 14bc; FAN travelstock / Rainer Grosskopf 69bc; Steven Folino 92bc; Lee Foster 90br; Tracey Foster 171ftl; Fisher Fotos 84cla; franzfoto.com 188tc; Dennis Frates 258tc, 257tl; S Friberg 1, Robert Fried 98clb; Robin Frowley 145br; Nick Gammon 222tc; Mark Goodreau 193ftr; Renato Granieri 224ca; Philippe Gras 130bl; Jeff Greenberg 85cra; Judith Haden 252clb; Dennis Hallinan 147bc; Blaine Harrington III 18c, 18bc, 90bc, 239bl; Vince Harris 158bc, Martin Harvey 285tl, Bill Heinsohn 105c, Bill Helsel 212br; Hemis 274br, 275ca, 287ca, 295tr; Hughes Hervé / Hemis.fr 61tr; Jon Hicks 238clb, 239br; Zach Holmes 125bc, 166-167; Cindy Miller Hopkins 234cr; Jeremy Horner 17cl; Chris Howarth 244c; Chris Howes / Wild Places Photography 137tr, D. Hurst 117cl; Image Source Aurora 215tr; Image Source Aurora 209tc; imageBROKER 274bc, 181tc; imagebroker / Oliver Gerhard 11clb; Arco Images / Therin-Weise 115br; INTERFOTO Pressebildagentur 172cr; Island Images 24c; Andy Jackson 284clb; Jacques Jangoux 47tl; Andre Jenny 45cl, 154clb, 146clb, 147bl, 194cb, 194bc, 195bc, 93br; Jerry and Marcy nkman / EcoPhotography.com 210-211; Jon Arnold Images Ltd / Walter Bibikow 45tl, 258clb; Jon Arnold Images Ltd / John Coletti 229bl; Norma Joseph 298bc; Wolfgang Kaehler 115c; Kim Karpeles 134cr, 135ca, 182clb, 183cl, 183bl, 180bc; Paul Kingsley 148clb; Terrance Klassen 162crb; Erich Kuchling 188tr, 180tr; Douglas Lander 160clb; LHB Photo 175bc, 170r; James Lipman 159bl; David Litschel 204ca; Lynne Siler Photography 92-93; David Lyons 69br, 68r; Manor Photography / Robert Slade 285c; Oyvind Martinsen 43ca; Gunter Marx 157cl; mediacolor's 282cr; Michael DeFreitas Underwater 15bc; Mira 106br; John Mitchell 70br; J.Enrique Molina 204cb; Gail Mooney-Kelly 244cr; Mountain Light / Galen Rowell 165bc; National Geographic Creative 99ca; Royalty Free / Ian Nellist 159ca; Ron Niebrugge 258c; Dale O'Dell 240ca; M. Timothy O'Keefe 196tc, 196ca, 196c, 102tl, 105bl; Sean O'Neill 193tl; Sean Pavone 117tr; PCL 187tc, 266tr, 301cl; Chuck Pefley 243cl; Mike Perry 63tc; Chuck Place 250cb; Porky Pies Photography 148tl, 128bc; Robert Fried 281tc, 306tl; Robert Harding Picture Library Ltd / Ken Gillham 245c, 244-245; Robert Harding Picture Library Ltd / R H Productions 289bc; Robert Harding Picture Library Ltd / Ruth Tomlinson 250c; robertharding 88tr; Emiliano Rodriguez 190br; rollie rodriguez 214cb; Crispin Rodwell 159bc; Pep Roig 141cl; Barrie Rokeach 212-213; Royalty Free / Darren Green Photography 237bl; Royalty Free / imagebroker / Florian Kopp 159c; Royalty Free / imagebroker / Oliver Gerhard 22br; Royalty Free / Steve Bly 22bc; Royalty Free / Steve Bly 23bc; Philip Scalia 147tc; Philip Scalia 210clb; James Schwabel 147tr; Andre Seale 114bc; Don Smetzer 134cl; Terry Sohl 229cb; Joe Sohm 154-5; SouthAmerica Photos 148-149, 149ca; Stephen Frink Collection 296bc, 279tc; Stephen Frink Collection / Bill Harrigan 66cl; Stockbyte 123tl; Sue Cunningham Photographic / Sue Cunningham 83tl; Frederic Sune 187cl; SuperStock 10tr, 25bl; Swerve 171tr; Timothy Swope 251cl; Jochen Tack 85cr; Angel Terry 239bc; Angel Terry 232clb; Weldon Thomson 284bc; David Tipling 42tr, 43cb, 200ca; travelstock44 15br, 82tc, 278tl, 302br; Tribaleye Images / J Marshall 141br; Genevieve Vallee 200tc; Greg Vaughn 23c, 259ca, 111bc; Visions of America, LLC 134-135t; Richard Wainscoat 285cb; John G. Walter 244clb; Brent Ward 133br, 128tr; H. Mark Weidman Photography 21bc; Nik Wheeler 78bc; Don White 162fcrb; A. T. Willett 259tc; Marek Zuk 258ca.
Alberta Tourism, Parks, Recreation & Culture: 168ca, 168bc.
Albuquerque International Balloon Fiesta, Inc.: 242clb.
AllCanadaPhotos.com: 156bl.
Ardea: John Cancalosi 240c; Bill Coster 248clb; Francois Gohier 261tr; Tom and Pat Leon 292tc; Duncan Usher 142ca; Adrian Warren 292tr; Adrian Warren 278tr.
Jon Arnold: Gavin Hellier 144-145, 144clb.
AWL Images: Peter Adams 294-295c; Danita Delimont Stock 295bl, 295bc; Hemis 88cb; Doug Pearson 283tl; Alex Robinson 290-291tc; Jane Sweeney 177cb, 177tr.
Axiom Photographic Agency: Jenny Acheson 61bc; Timothy Allen 118cb; Conor Caffrey 61bl; Chris Coe 157tl; Guy Marks 140cb; James Sparshatt 87br.
Tom Bean Photography: 69tr.
Branson CVB: 80bl.
BrazilPhotos: Delfim Martins 202br; Olhar / Catherine Krulik 203ca, 203bc, Pulsar / Mauricio Simonetti 203tr.
Bridgeman Images: 186clb; Private Collection, Peter Newark Historical Pictures 194bl.
Michel Burger: Michel Burger 164br, 165bl.
Calgary Stampede: 169tr.
Canada Press Images: Edmonton Sun / Brendon Dlouhy 306tc.
Pierre Carreau Photography: 287tc.
Coast Mountain Photography: Andrew Doran 57bl.
The Contemporary Austin-Jones Center, Austin, Texas, 2016: Brian Fitzsimmons 59bc.
Corbis: 87cl, 266clb, 110clb; James L. Amos 147tl; Gerry Angus / Icon Sportswire 119bl; Dave Bartruff 62clb; Bettmann 138clb; Walter Bibikow / JAI 197tc; John Conrad 87tl; Richard Cummins 301tr; Jad Davenport / National Geographic Creative 291ca; Reinhard Dirscherl 98cb; Norbert Eisele-Hein / JAI 269cl; EPA / Caetano Barreira 203bl, 180tl; Macduff Everton 72cr, 55tc, 123br; Sandy Felsenthal 281ca; Fotofeeling / Westend61 162clb; Philip Gould 305tl; Amy Harris 105bc; Lindsay Hebberd 13bc, 252-253; Hemis / Franck Guiziou 158-159; Jon Hicks 226-7tl; Bruno De Hogues / Ocean 274-275c; Dave G. Houser 122tc; William Henry Jackson 188clb; JAI / Peter Adams 159tr, 152tc; Wolfgang Kaehler 122tl; Catherine Karnow 176clb; Kelly-Mooney Photography 69cl; Layne Kennedy 118br; Bob Krist 85bc, 221cl; Lake County Museum 147cl; Robert Landau 246r; Frans Lanting 201tr, 178-9; Leemage 274bl; Danny Lehman 267tr; Michael Lewis 217tl, 209tl; Eduardo Longoni 216clb; Marilyn Angel Wynn / Nativestock Pictures 228-229; Dennis Marsico 68clb; Royalty Free / Perry Mastrovito 187bl; MedioImages 251tr; David Mercado / Reuters 149tc; Merritt 204clb; Momatiuk - Eastcot 254-5; Tom Myers 251c, 233cl; Kazuyoshi Nomachi 158bl, 150-151; Richard T. Nowitz 155tr, 304tc; Charles O'Rear 250ca, 250cr; Roberta Olenick / All Canada Photos 234clb; Douglas Peebles 285br; Neil Rabinowitz 236bl; Robert Harding World Imagery / Mark Chivers 159cb; Alex Robinson / JAI 291cb; San Francisco Chronicle / Kat Wade 36cr; San Francisco Chronicle / Kat Wade 36bl; San Francisco Chronicle / Kat Wade 33tc; Kevin Schafer 201tc, 260-1; Phil Schermeister 45tc, 45br; Â Chris Schwegler / Retna Ltd 130bc; Paul Seheult 260fbl; Scott T. Smith 206-7; Frédéric SOREAU / Photononstop 50clb; Paul Souders 297bc; Hubert Stadler 217tc; Keren Su 140clb; Rudy Sulgan 118ca; Steve Terril 247bl; Craig Tuttle 247ftr; Underwood & Underwood 228clb; Onne van der Wal 174-175, 174c; Patrick Ward 96-97; Stuart Westmorland 247cl, 296-297.; Jeremy Woodhouse / Masterfile 94clb; Inge Yspeert 51c; Zefa / Frank Krahmer 2-3; zefa / Fridmar Damm 245tr; zefa / Serge Kozak 6-7; Zefa / Svenja-Fotoefa 51br; Jeff Zelevansky / Icon SMI 221tc.
Corbis Malaysia: Atlantide Phototravel / Stefano Amantini 48bc, Atlantide Phototravel / Guido Cozzi 273tr, 90-91; Atlantide Phototravel / Massimo Borchi 71bl, 262-263; Tom Bean 240clb; Beateworks / Dency Kane 92br; Tibor Bognar 184-185; Brandon D. Cole 167cb; Richard Cummins 243tl, 269ftl, 184ca; Macduff Everton 268ftr; Stephen Frink 67cr; Raymond Gehman 161tl; Grand Tour / Massimo Ripani 91br; Gunter Marx Photography 240-241cb; Blaine Harrington III 184tc, 48tr, 48-49, 43tl, 32tr; Robert Holmes 249c; Jan Butchofsky-Houser 241cr; Gavriel Jecan 42tl, 32tr; Ann Johansson 161bc; Wolfgang Kaehler 289cl; Catherine Karnow 49br; Bob Krist 185tr, 181tr; Frans Lanting 249bc, 42-43c; Danny Lehman 243tr; Frank Lukasseck 264clb; Buddy Mays 93bc; Will & Deni McIntyre 93bl; MedioImages 272bl; Momatiuk - Eastcott 299bl; Amos Nachoum 106-107b; Richard T. Nowitz 35cr; O. Alamany & E. Vicens / Oriol Alamany 90clb; Carl & Ann Purcell 143tc; Neil Rabinowitz 161tr, 153c; Jose Fuste Raga 71c; Roger Ressmeyer 212bc; Andy Rouse 298clb; Galen Rowell 164-165, 153tc; San Francisco Chronicle / Paul Chinn 212cr; Kevin Schafer 47br, 42-43t; Carl Van Vechten 184clb; Ron Watts 35cla, 240-241t; Stuart Westmorland 67cl, 55cb; Michael S. Yamashita 132-133t; Zefa / Angelo Cavalli 71bc; Zefa / Kevin Schafer 47ca.
Courtesy Memphis Convention & Visitors Bureau: 104br.
Ron Dahlquist Photography: 26-7, 27cl.
Danita Delimont Stock Photography: Walter Bibikow 243tc; Gayle Harper 69bl, 54tc; Cindy Miller Hopkins 240cb; Greg Johnston 77cb.
Joeff Davis: 131ca.
DDB Stock Photography: Alex OCampo / Photoworks 72clb.
Dolly Parton's Dixie Stampede Dinner Attraction: 80br.
Dominican Republic Ministry of Tourism: 176crb.
Dorling Kindersley: 308tc; Demetrio Carassco 83br, 310tc, 82ca, 82-83; Eric Grossman 62tc, 62ca; Nigel Hicks 308tr, 310tr; Magnua Rew 308tl; Rough Guides / Angus Osborn 154br; Rough Guides / Enrique Uranga 118clb, 118bc; Scott Suchman 154bl; Linda Whitwam 308clb, 310tl.
Dreamstime.com: Adeliepenguin 117bc; Adnimh 163clb; Laurence Agron 28clb; Aiisha 162-163, 163tr; Alexmillos 17bc; Amilevin 95tc; Kushnirov Avraham 162ca; William Berry 94c; Claude Berthelot 275cb; Betty4240 20clb; Natalia Bratslavsky 222-223tc; Byelikova 270tl; Adrian Chelu 21bl; Alan Cole 58bc; Kobby Dagan 259tr, 13tl; David931 45tr; Demerzel21 117bl; Demerzel21 117br; Henrik Dolle 239ftl; Eautographhunter 45bl; Elena Elisseeva 113cb, 113br; F11photo 58-59c; Alexandre Fagundes De Fagundes 294bc; Fallsview 168clb; Ffennema 95bc; Steffen Foerster 95bl; Fabio Formaggio 12clb; Richard Goldberg 41cl; Scott Griessel 29bl; Gary Hartz 59c; Hugoht 95tl; Jeffrey Hutchinson 20c; Ingalin 98-99ca; Irishka777 283tc; Baker Jarvis 143ca; Jenny37 208tr, 224-225cb; Vladislav Jirousek 271ftr; Joannemcdonough 17bl; Jpldesigns 222-223c; Jacek Kadaj 270tc; Kalypsoworldphotography 218tc; Michal Knitl 204-205c; Knowledan 291tr; Jesse Kraft 224cla; Anna Krasnopeeva 41bc; Kwiktor 21cl, 54tr; Jesús Eloy Ramos Lara 295ca; Ryszard Laskowski 293tr; Chon Kit Leong 29tc, 300cr, 301bl; Loca4motion 304tr; Verena Matthew 25bc; Mellisandre 95br; Meunierd 270fclb; Muchak 199br; Noraluca 267ftr; Ollyfant 278tc; William Perry 294clb; Peterll 112br; Petthomas 11tl, 28cr; Philippehalle 275bl; Photogolfer 41bl, Prosiaczeq 25cl; Joshua Rainey 222tr; Replayall 131bc; Yelena Rodriguez 119br; Filippo Romeo 103tc, 108br; Sborisov 33tl, 41tl; Weldon Schloneger 199bl; Smandy 205bl; Stephenarcher179 89tl; Ignasi Such 88clb; Suebmtl 271tl; Tupungato 131c; Tusharkoley 21tl; Vitmark 271cra; Vladgalenko 17tl; Lawrence Weslowski Jr 111cl; Anne M. Fearon-wood 24clb; Antonio Lopez Zamorano 88-89; Paul Zizka 98tc; Zrfphoto 199tl.
Esther's Follies: Adam Schlender 58bl.
Michele Falzone: 13br, 61tl, 10bl, 54bl.
FLPA: Glenn Bartley / Minden Pictures 270tr; David Hosking 86bl; Imagebroker / Florian Kopp 82tr, 76tr; Donald M. Jones / Minden Pictures 162c; Gerard Lacz 271crb; Hugh Lansdown 95cl; Frans Lanting 200c, 200-201; Thomas Marent 291tc; Minden Pictures / GERRY ELLIS 106cb; Minden Pictures / Hiroya Minakuchi 298br; Minden Pictures / Tom Vezo 40clb; Minden Pictures / Yva Momatiuk / John Eastcott 193br; Mark Newman 229tr; Flip Nicklin / Minden Pictures 235tr, 115cb; Photo Researchers 199tc; Michael & Patricia Fogden / Minden Pictures 42clb.
Fotolia: Ostseefoto 267tc.
Fotoscopio Latin America Stock Photo Agency: 72c.
Fotostock Uruguay - Aguaclara: 97cl, 97cr.
Four Seasons Resorts: Michael Calderwood 289tl; Robb Gordon 289tr.
Frank Borges LLosa/Frankly.com: 22bl.
Paul Franklin: 280-281, 281cb, 78cl, 171ftr, 184c, 185c, 192clb, 193tr, 193cl.
Franz Marc Frei: 41tc, 61cl.
Getty Images: All Canada Photos / Chris Cheadle 157tr; altrendo nature 258-259; Nigel Atherton 144c; Gary Berdeaux / MCT 199ftr; Steve Bly 139bl; Julien Capmeil 96cr; Yvette Cardozo 103tr, 113bl; Cassio Vasconcellos 50c; Angelo Cavalli 50ca; Tom Cockrem 205br; Diane Cook and Len Jenshel 266cb; Richard Cummins 99cb, 99crb; De Agostini Picture Library 136-137tc; Discovery Channel Images / Jeff Foott 236ca; Grant Dixon 140ca; Stephen Dunn 301tc; Paul Edmondson 60r; Neil Emmerson 38br; Grant Faint 140cr; First Light / Peter Mintz 119bc; Xavier Font 98c; Robert Frerck 253tr; Stephen Frink 260br, 256tr; Mitchell Funk 195tr; Earl Gibson III 123ca; Tim Graham 77tc, 96bl; Hulton Archive 18bl; Jeff Hunter 284br; Image Bank / Jorg Greuel 100-1; Image Bank / Grant Faint 118-119; The Image Bank / IC Productions 174ca; The Image Bank / Micheal Melford 175tr, 174br; The Image Bank / Steve Dunwell 175bl; Frans Lemmens 115ca; Holger Leue 139tl; Alfredo Maiquez 88c; Yves Marcoux 172-3; Scott Markewitz 56clb; Will & Deni McIntyre 154bc; Michael Melford 214-5, 111tl; Michael Ochs Archives 282clb; National Geographic / Martin Gray 305tc; National Geographic / Steve Winter 124-125; David Nevala 77crb; New York Daily News Archive 198clb; Flip Nicklin 284-285; Michael Ochs Archives 38clb; Panoramic Images 281c, 279tr; Photodisc / Stuart Gregory 145c, 129tl; Photographer's Choice / Gerald French 250cl; Photographer's Choice / Darrell Gulin 8-9; Photographer's Choice / Darrell Gulin 230-231; Photographer's Choice / Jerry Kobalenko 192r; Photographer's Choice / Walter Bibikow 41tr; Anthony Pidgeon 283tr; Mike Powell 57tl, 57tr; Sankar Raman 222clb; Reportage / Christopher Pillitz 202clb; Lorne Resnick 39br; Roger Ressmeyer 188c; Vincent Ricardel 155c, Riser / Jason Todd 80tr; Norbert Rosing 172ca; Mario Ruiz / / Time Life Pictures 194ca; Nicolas Russell 191bc, 181bl; Evaristo Sa / AFP 114br; Sybil Sassoon 87bl; Scott S. Warren / Aurora 137c; Ron Sherman 134-135cb; Stephen Simpson 250-251; Jon Spaull 135c, 128tc; Stone / Donovan Reese 80tc; Stone / Gary Vestal 247tl; Stone / Stuart Westmorland 246clb, 232tc; Michael Taylor 191cb; The Image Bank 214tc; Michael Townsend 188ca; Greg Vaughn 285tr, 285ca; Aaron Black Veer 56r; Ron Watts 172c; Karl Weatherly 163cb; Stuart Westmorland 36br; Rich Wheater 214c; Darwin Wiggett 172clb; Tan Yilmaz 287cb; Jacobo Zanella 294br; Photographer's Choice / Solvin Zankl 276-277.
Getty Images/Visage Media Services: Aurora / Corey Rich 165tr; Aurora / David Nevala 79ca; Aurora / Kevin Moloney 298-299, Aurora / Peter Essick 160r; De Agostini Picture Library / DEA / M.SEEMULLER 70clb; Miles Ertman 133tc; Fred Felleman 166clb, 152tr; First Light / Ron Watts 161tc; First Light / Yves Marcoux 143br; Gallo Images / Martin Harvey 265tr; Hulton Archive / William England / Getty Images 132clb; Hans-Peter Merten / Getty Images 132-133c; National Geographic / Bill Curtsinger 288clb; National Geographic / Stephen St. John 239cl; Donald Nausbaum 82cb; Stone / David Hiser 71ca.
Glenbow Museum: 226clb.
Andrew Hempstead/Escapecentral: 173cl.
Houserstock: Ellen Barone 301ftr; Steve Bly 138r; Steve Bly 139tc, 139tr, 139br, 129tc; Jan Butchofsky-Houser 297tr, 297ca, 297cb; Dave G. Houser 272bc, 234c, 211tc.
Hue & Eye: Doug Hickok 78bl.
Fred Hurteau: 125bl.
Imagem Brasil: Gentil Barreira 203cb.
imagequestmarine.com: V&W / Mark Conlin 37br; V&W / T. Burnett-K.Palmer 74-75.
Insight Photography: 57cl, 57tc, 57bc.
iStockphoto.com: 217cl; Anna Bryukhanova 41br; Steve Dibblee 72cla.
JEAN-GUY LAVOIE: 187tr.
John Warburton-Lee Photography: Mark Hannaford 263tc.
jupiterimages: Howard Pyle IV 66cla.
Wolfgang Kaehler Photography: 197c.
Rusty Kennedy: 220r.
The Kobal Collection: New lIne Cinema 16clb.
Bob Krist: 221tl, 209tr.
Latitude: David Foreman 16r.
Laurence Parent Photography Inc: 68tl.
James Lemass: 62c.
Holger Leue Photography: Holger Leue 272br, 272-273, 188-189, 189tc.
Kyle Little: 66clb.
Lodge at Chaa Creek, Belize: 290clb.
Lonely Planet Images: Olivier Cirendini 39bc; Tom Cockrem 38bc, 32clb; Richard Cummins 13tc, 281tr; Mark Daffey 141c; Krzysztof Dydynski 96c; John Elk III 81br; Rhonda Gutenberg 39bl; Richard I'Anson 155bc; Lou Jones 62-3c; Ray Laskowitz 142tc; Witold Skrypczak 252bc, 233tr.
Lonely Planet Images Australia: Ann Cecil 249bl; Richard Cummins 46tr, Grant Dixon 165ca; Hanan Isachar 121br; Mark Newman 83tc.
Lucid Images: Mark Downey 247tc.
Magical Andes Photography: 191tr, 108bl, 108bc, 109bc, 109br, 109c, 149cb.
Maine Office of Tourism: 236c.
Marine Scenes: Steve Simonsen 64tl, 64tr, 64-65, 64bl, 64bc, 64br, 55tl.
Gunter Marx - Stock Photos: 57br.
Masterfile: J. David Andrews 171tl; Bill Brooks 210tl; Gloria H. Chomica 168-169; John Gertz 267ftl; Scott Gilchrist 60bl; Chris Hendrickson 235c; J. A. Kraulis 193bc; 157ftr, 211ca, 180tc; Peter Lavery 139bc; Mike Macri 235cl; Zoran Milich 115bl; Zoran Milich 102tc; Gail Mooney 104bc, 117tc; Roy Ooms 105br; Lloyd Sutton 76tc; Mark Tomalty 168c; Dale Wilson 173c; Jeremy Woodhouse 114-115.
Masterfile Deutschland: Daryl Benson 161cl; Garry Black 34-35t, 33tr, 34clb, 34-35c, 35cl, 248-249; Frank Krahmer 71br; J. A. Kraulis 243bc; Gail Mooney 34cr; Greg Stott 132t; Lloyd Sutton 92clb; Jeremy Woodhouse 46-47, 34cl, 262tl, 263cb.
Melvyn's Bar, Ingleside Inn: 29br.
Robert and Linda Mitchell: 280clb.
National Geographic Creative: Nicole Duplaix 106-107c; Raymond Gehman 212bl; Bobby Haas 262tr; Ralph Lee Hopkins 32tc, 47cb; Vlad Kharitonov 124clb; Tim Laman 262tc; Joe Scherschel 263tl; Steve Winter 242r.
naturepl.com: Onne van der Wal 286-287ca.
Newport Music Festival: 174cb.
NHPA / Photoshot: Trevor Mcdonald 260cr.
George Oze: 194br, 181tl.
Palm Springs Bureau of Tourism: 29bc.
Peter Langer/Associated Media Group: 190bc.
Photolibrary: 84cl; 183tr; AlaskaStock 110r, 111tc, 111tr, 111bl, 111br, 102bc; Animals Animals / Alan Fortune 45bc; Bill Bachman 126-7; Bill Beatty 125c; Walter Bibikow 196-197, 296bl; Ron Dahlquist 27bl; Perrine Doug 87bc; Neil Emmerson 39cb; Flirt Collection / Owaki-Kulla 236cb, 233tl; Flirt Collection / Susan G Drinker 237tr; Mickey Gibson 125br; Vaughn Greg 247bc; Robert Harding 144crb; Index Stock 182r; Index Stock Imagery / Barry Winiker 183tc; Index Stock Imagery / Bob Burch 4-5; Index Stock Imagery / Bruce Leighty 183tl; Jon Arnold Travel / Peter Adams 108-109; Mark Jones 86r; JTB Photo 13bl; Rafael Macia 194-195; Timothy OKeefe 296c; Oxford Scientific (OSF) 158br; Oxford Scientific / Berndt Fischer 244cb; Pacific Stock / David Fleetham 27br; Pacific Stock / William Waterfall 26br, 10tc; Robert Harding Travel / Ellen Rooney 26bc; Mike Rock 147br, 128cr; Royalty-Free / Index Stock Imagery / Everett Johnson 174bc; Roylty Free / Dennis Welsh 22-3; The Travel Library 122tr; Steve Vidler 104clb; Barry Winiker 124bc.
Photolibrary India: Animals Animals / FRANKLIN VIOLA 269tr, 257tr; Animals Animals / MICHAEL SACCA 167ca; Arcangel Images / Kobi Israel 239tr; Robert Armstrong 248br; Walter Bibikow 239tl; John Brown 43br; John Coletti 218clb; Chad Ehlers 243bl, 232tl; Robert Ginn 121c; Hemis / Hughes Hervé 239ftr; Iconotec / H.FougFre 265bc; Imagestate 269bl; Index Stock Imagery / Tim Brown 66c; Index Stock Imagery / Angelo Cavalli 106ca; Index Stock Imagery / Bibikow Walter 269bc; Index Stock Imagery / NR. Rowan 241tr; Jon Arnold Travel / Peter Adams 238r; JTB Photo 218-219, 132tr, 185ca; JTB Photo / Haga Library 48bl; Juniors Bildarchiv 82clb; Duncan Maxwell 78-79; Wendell Metzen 79c; Oxford Scientific / Carol Farneti Foster 107br; Oxford Scientific / Carol Farneti Foster 102tr; Oxford Scientific / Colin Monteath 265ftr; Oxford Scientific / Tui De Roy 46bl; Oxford Scientific / Tui De Roy 299bc; Pacific Stock / Allan Seiden 70bc; Pacific Stock / Dave Fleetham 248bl; Pacific Stock / Rosenberg Steve 66cr; Photodisc / Ernesto Rios Lanz / Sexto Sol 265cl; Photodisc / Jeremy Woodhouse 90t, 76tl; Robert Harding Travel / Marco Simoni 264r; Paul Thompson 65br; Jayme Thornton 79bc; Bibikow Walter 268clb.
Photoshot: NHPA / Laurie Campbell 265bl; NHPA / Kevin Schafer 164bc; World Pictures 292br.
Heinz Plenge: 200clb.
Portland Art Museum: 223tc.
Prairie du Chien Area Chamber of Commerce: 134clb.
Pulsar Imagens: Ricardo Azoury 302-303; Rogério Reis 302clb.
PunchStock: Photographer's Choice Getty Images 247tr; Royalty Free / CreatasImages 186r; Royalty Free / Radius Images 146r; Stockbyte 292-3.
Rainshadow Photographics: Mark Gardener 167tc, 167c, 167tr.
Rex by Shutterstock: Rob Crandall 153tr, 155bl.
Robert Harding Picture Library: 292bc; Bruno Barbier © StudioEIS 220clb; Angelo Cavalli 40r; Richard Cummins 144cb; Ian Dagnall 58br; Michael DeFreitas 29tl; Matthew Williams-Ellis 219tr; eye ubiquitous 283cl; Ken Gillham 279tl, 287tr; Godong 50-51ca; Alison Langley 286clb; Odyssey / Robert Frerck 219cb, 208tl; G Richardson 79br; Marco Simoni 265tl, 257tc; Thomas Vinke 204br.
Rocky Mountaineer Vacations: 226-7c, 227tc, 227cb, 208bc.
San Francisco Opera: San Francisco Opera 213tr.
Sanderling Inn: 124br.
Carlos Sastoque: 17tr.
SeaWorld Parks & Entertainment: 18ca.
Allen Blake Sheldon: 135cb.
Shutterstock: Sandra A. Dunlap 67br.
Silver Dollar City Attractions: 80bc, 80-1, 77tr.
South American Pictures: Ben Box 245cl; Robert Francis 252br; Kimball Morrison 217tr; Tony Morrison 252cr, 114clb.
South End Publishing: Francisco Bedeschi 72-73, 72bl, 73cl, 73cr, 73br.
St Lucia Tourist Board: 122-3; Chris Huxley 123cb.
SuperStock: 201tl; age fotostock 130-131, 259c, 283bl; Luis Castañeda / age fotostock 205ftr; Angelo Cavalli 84bc; Richard Cummins 300tl, 157ftl; Hemis.fr 296ca; George H.H. Huey / age fotostock 99tc; HUGHES Herv / Hemis.fr 89br; imageBROKER 204bc; Bruce Obee / All Canada Photos 113ca; George Ostertag 223tr; Prisma 226tc, 266-267; José Fuste Raga 289tc; Universal Images Group 11tc, 21br, Visual & Written 225tr; TJ Watt / All Canada Photos 112-113.
Terra Galleria Photography: 229bc, 136tr, 137tl, 136clb; Q T Luong 26br, 249tr, 120br, 120-121, 103clb, 121bl, 69tc.
The Art Archive: Dagli Orti 14clb.
Tourism New Brunswick: Dennis Minty 210tr.
The Travel Library: Stuart Black 38-39; John Carr 140-141; Rolf Richardson 39ca, 152bl.
Travel Pictures: Fotoconcept 145cl; Clive Sawyer 15bl, 11cr.
Tyba Photographic Agency: Ciro Mariano 303tr; Rogério Reis 302cr.
Vancouver Folk Music Festival: 156r, 157bl.
VIA Rail Canada: 226tr.
Visit Philadelphia: M. Edlow 221bc; R. Kennedy 221ftr; B. Krist 221tr.
Windstar Cruises & Majestic America Line: 272tl, 272tr, 257bc.
Jenny Woodruff: 66-67.
www.bardonthebeach.org: David Blue 157bc, 152tl.
Yves Tessier/Tessima: 187tl, 187bc.

Cover images: *Front:* **Alamy Stock Photo:** Dennis Frates c; *Back:* **Alamy Stock Photo:** Bill Bachmann fcr, Brian Jannsen cr; **AWL Images:** Hemis cl, Jane Sweeney c; *Spine:* **Alamy Stock Photo:** Dennis Frates tc